Shakespeare's Book

ALSO BY CHRIS LAOUTARIS

Shakespeare and the Countess: The Battle that Gave Birth to the Globe (Penguin)

Shakespearean Maternities: Crises of Conception in Early Modern England (Edinburgh)

Bleed and See – Poems (Broken Sleep Books)

Anne-thology: Poems Re-presenting Anne Shakespeare, edited with Paul Edmondson, Aaron Kent and Katherine Scheil (Broken Sleep Books)

The Devil and the Crown: Sir Robert Cecil, Queen's Statesman and Kingmaker (forthcoming, William Collins)

Women and Cultures of Portraiture in the British Literary Renaissance, edited with Yasmin Arshad (forthcoming, Arden Shakespeare)

CHRIS LAOUTARIS

Shakespeare's Book

The Intertwined
Lives Behind the
First Folio

WILLIAM
COLLINS

William Collins
An imprint of HarperCollins*Publishers*
1 London Bridge Street
London SE1 9GF

WilliamCollinsBooks.com

HarperCollins*Publishers*
Macken House, 39/40 Mayor Street Upper
Dublin 1, D01 C9W8

First published in Great Britain in 2023 by William Collins

1

A catalogue record for this book is
available from the British Library

ISBN 978-0-00-823838-4

Maps drawn by Martin Brown

Set in Adobe Caslon Pro
Printed and bound in the UK using 100%
renewable electricity at CPI Group (UK) Ltd

Dedicated to my parents, Thalia and John,
and to the memory of my brother, George

CONTENTS

Act Two – 1621
Negotiating the First Folio

Act Three – 1622
Printing the First Folio

Act Four – 1623
Making History Making Shakespeare: Finishing the First Folio

LIST OF ILLUSTRATIONS

The Preliminary Pages of the First Folio
All images are from the Folger Shakespeare Library

Integrated Images
Title page of *The Workes of Benjamin Jonson* (*Folger Shakespeare Library*)
Details from Claes Visscher's panorama of London (*Smithsonian Institution*)
'Pavier-Jaggard Quartos', *The Merchant of Venice* (*Folger Shakespeare Library*)
Final page of *Cymbeline* (*Folger Shakespeare Library*)
Detail of Agas Map, showing St Paul's and the surrounding area (*London Metropolitan Archives*)
Woodcut of St Paul's Cross (*Bridgeman*)
Detail of Agas Map, showing St Dunstan's in the West and the surrounding area (*London Metropolitan Archives*)
The bustling scene inside a printing shop (*Folger Shakespeare Library*)
A composing stick (*Smithsonian Institution*)
First Folio Diagram of a 'folio in sixes' (*Martin Brown*)
Pages from *Othello, Much Ado About Nothing, The Two Gentlemen of Verona* and *The Tempest* (*Folger Shakespeare Library*)
A seventeenth-century printing press (*Folger Shakespeare Library*)

Scenes from a seventeenth-century printing shop (*Folger Shakespeare Library*)

Labourers working in a paper-making shop (*Folger Shakespeare Library*)

Charlton Hinman Collator (*Folger Shakespeare Library*)

First page of *The Tempest* (*Folger Shakespeare Library*)

Title page of Ralph Brooke's *A Catalogue and Succession of the Kings* (*Folger Shakespeare Library*)

Francis Beaumont (*National Portrait Gallery*)

'The Actors Names' from *Henry IV, Part 2* (*Folger Shakespeare Library*)

A page from *Antony and Cleopatra* with errors (*Folger Shakespeare Library*) and without errors (*Folger Shakespeare Library*)

First Folio inscription to Augustine Vincent (*Folger Shakespeare Library*)

An engraver's shop (*Folger Shakespeare Library*)

Francisco de la Peña (*Biblioteca Nacional de España*)

Decorative woodblock border designs (*Folger Shakespeare Library*)

Thomas Coryate (*National Portrait Gallery*)

Sonnets by Hugh Holland and 'Cygnus' (*British Library*)

John Robinson's loan request (*Stationers' Company Archive*)

Drawing by Ralph Treswell (*Heritage Image Partnership Ltd/ Alamy*)

Title page of *The Mirror of Majesty* (*Huntington Library*)

'Names of the Principal Actors' annotated by a seventeenth-century hand (*Glasgow University Library*)

John Milton's own annotated First Folio (*Free Library of Philadelphia*)

First Folio 23 (*Folger Shakespeare Library*)

DRAMATIS PERSONAE

Key Characters in the Creation of the First Folio

The King's Men Playing Company's Representatives (sometimes referred to as the 'editors' of the First Folio):

John Heminges, actor, theatre manager, Shakespeare's former friend and colleague

Henry Condell, actor, theatre manager, Shakespeare's former friend and colleague

The Syndicate (publisher-booksellers who financed the First Folio):

William Jaggard, a senior member of the syndicate, owner of the shop in London's Barbican in which the First Folio was printed

Isaac Jaggard, William's son, a senior member of the syndicate, co-owner of the shop in which the First Folio was printed

Edward Blount, a senior member of the syndicate, based in St Paul's Cross Churchyard, London

William Aspley, based in St Paul's Cross Churchyard, London

John Smethwick, based in St Dunstan's Churchyard, London

The Patrons (members of the nobility to whom the First Folio was dedicated):

Sir William Herbert, 3rd Earl of Pembroke, also Lord Chamberlain; favourite of King James I and rival to courtier George Villiers, Marquess of Buckingham (later 1st Duke of Buckingham)

Sir Philip Herbert, 1st Earl of Montgomery, William's brother

The Commemorative Poets (who shaped William Shakespeare's posthumous identity by memorialising him in the First Folio):

Ben Jonson, poet and playwright, overseer of his own folio of collected *Works* in 1616; confessed to having been a Catholic; Shakespeare's former friend, colleague and rival

Hugh Holland, poet and scholar, so-called 'crypto-Catholic'

James Mabbe, poet, scholar, translator and hispanophile

Leonard Digges, poet, scholar, translator and hispanophile; stepson of Thomas Russell who was Shakespeare's close trusted friend and the overseer of his will

Engraver of Shakespeare's Iconic First Folio Portrait (the only likeness of the playwright independently authenticated by a living contemporary):

Martin Droeshout, engraver and artist, hispanophile who moved to Spain

The Rights Holders (mostly stationer-publishers who controlled the rights to plays included in the First Folio):

William Aspley

Edward Blount

Nathaniel Butter

Thomas Dewe

Lawrence Hayes

William Jaggard

Arthur Johnson
Matthew Law
Thomas Pavier
John Smethwick
Thomas Walkley
Henry Walley

The Royal Families of England, Spain and Bohemia:

King James I of England, patron of the King's Men

Prince Charles, James I's son, whose proposed marriage to the
Infanta Maria of Spain (known as the 'Spanish Match')
formed the dramatic political backdrop to the making of the
First Folio

Elizabeth, Electress Palatine (briefly Queen of Bohemia), James I's
daughter, married to Frederick V, Elector Palatine (briefly King
of Bohemia), whose political troubles formed another seismic
context for the creation of the First Folio

King Philip IV of Spain

Maria, the Infanta of Spain, sister of King Philip IV

Contributors to the Preparation and Printing of the First Folio:

Ralph Crane, scrivener, who produced 'fair copies' of some of the
plays printed in the First Folio

Edward Knight, the King's Men's Bookkeeper, who made changes
to the plays' performance texts

The Compositors who typeset the First Folio, particularly
Compositor B (who typeset the largest portion of the text) and
Compositor E (John Leason, the inexperienced apprentice
employed on the Folio project)

The pressworkers, inkers, paper-makers, annotating readers, editors
and other personnel involved in the production of the First
Folio

Industry Regulators:

Members of the Stationers' Company, responsible for regulating the
    publishing industry, licensing books, and managing the
    Stationers' Register

Sir John Astley, Master of the Revels, responsible for licensing plays

Sir George Buc, Master of the Revels, responsible for licensing
    plays

Sir Henry Herbert, Master of the Revels, responsible for licensing
    plays

Sir William Herbert, Lord Chamberlain, responsible for
    organising royal entertainments and the King's Men's court
    appearances; had influence over the Mastership of the Revels
    and Revels Office

Additional Contributors:

Richard Burbage, actor with the Chamberlain's/King's Men
    playing company, whose star status, talents and death shaped
    the theatre industry and influenced Shakespeare publishing

James Burbage, father of Richard Burbage and builder-impresario
    of the Theatre in Shoreditch and the Blackfriars playhouse (the
    Globe Theatre was funded by his sons, Richard and Cuthbert
    Burbage, and player-sharers in the playing company, including
    Shakespeare)

The Players, actors in the Chamberlain's/King's Men whose talents
    shaped the plays

Historical rights holders to Shakespeare's plays and poems, those
    formerly owning rights to Shakespeare's works, whose
    acquisitions and transfers of these assets determined the
    circulation and printing of the dramatist's output

Thomas Pavier, the stationer-bookseller whose collaboration with
    William and Isaac Jaggard on the 'Pavier-Jaggard Quartos' (a
    peculiar series of plays, not all authentically by Shakespeare)
    impacted on the creation of the First Folio

Shakespeare's friends and acquaintances in London, Stratford-upon-Avon and Oxford (including the powerful Combe family of Warwickshire, the friendship group of eccentric explorer Thomas Coryate, and scholars attached to Oxford University)

John Robinson, stationer, Shakespeare's London lodger at the Blackfriars Gatehouse?

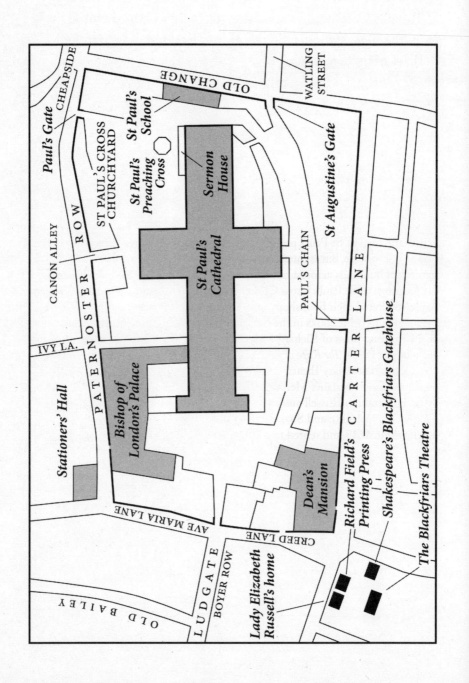

Paul's Gate

CHEAPSIDE

OLD CHANGE

WATLING STREET

St Paul's School

CANON ALLEY

ST PAUL'S CROSS CHURCHYARD

PATERNOSTER ROW

St Paul's Preaching Cross

Sermon House

St Augustine's Gate

PAUL'S CHAIN

IVY LA.

St Paul's Cathedral

Stationers' Hall

Bishop of London's Palace

CARTER LANE

Shakespeare's Blackfriars Gatehouse

AVE MARIA LANE

Dean's Mansion

Richard Field's Printing Press

CREED LANE

OLD BAILEY

LUDGATE

BOYER ROW

Lady Elizabeth Russell's home

The Blackfriars Theatre

MAPS

Schematic map of St Paul's precinct and the surrounding area. This cross-period map is not to scale, but is intended to convey a sense of the relative positions of significant buildings across a time-span covering c. 1593 to 1640. It indicates the locations of St Paul's Cross Churchyard, where Edward Blount and William Aspley operated their bookshops, and Stationers' Hall, where publishers logged their rights to print books in the Stationers' Register. It also shows the locations of the printing press of Richard Field, who printed William Shakespeare's *Venus and Adonis* (1593), *The Rape of Lucrece* (1594) and *The Phoenix and the Turtle* (1601); the Blackfriars Theatre (constructed in 1596 by James Burbage, from which the Chamberlain's Men were banned as a consequence of a petition led by Lady Elizabeth Russell and signed by Field, and which was reclaimed by the King's Men in 1608); and Shakespeare's Blackfriars Gatehouse, which he purchased in 1613 and rented to a lodger named John Robinson.

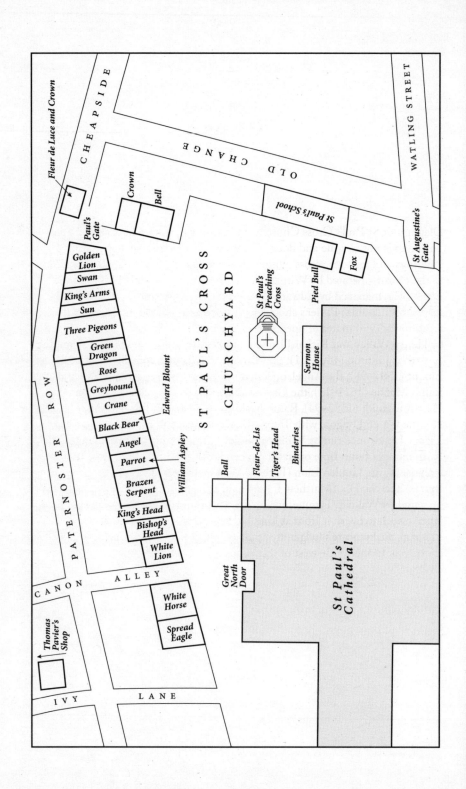

Diagram of St Paul's Cross Churchyard, London's primary bookselling hub. This map is not to scale and does not capture a single period, but records buildings and features across a time-span covering c. 1582 to 1640. In addition to the Parrot, operated by William Aspley between 1608 and 1640, and the Black Bear, managed by Edward Blount between 1609 and at least 1626, the map shows Thomas Pavier's shop, which stood in Ivy Lane. It also records the locations of (with dates of operation in brackets): the Spread Eagle, managed by Henry Walley and Richard Bonian (1609–10); the White Horse, belonging to Arthur Johnson (1604–21); the Bishop's Head, once controlled by Edward Blount (1597–98); the Angel, operated by Andrew Wise (1593–1602) and Ralph Mabbe (1611–13); the Greyhound, managed successively by John Harrison senior (1582–94), Ralph Mabbe (1614–16) and Robert Allot (1626–27); the Green Dragon, with Thomas Hayes in residence (1600–1); and the Tiger's Head, once run by William Aspley (1599–1600). Of interest are also (with names of one-time operators in brackets): the Three Pigeons (Humphrey Robinson), the Golden Lion (Richard Watkins), the Pied Bull (Thomas Butter) and the Fox (Matthew Law). The Fleur de Luce and Crown was operated by William Tymme, eventually with the aid of John Robinson, the latter associated with it from at least 1615. Could this Robinson have been William Shakespeare's lodger at the Blackfriars Gatehouse, which stood just a short walk to the south-west of this shop?

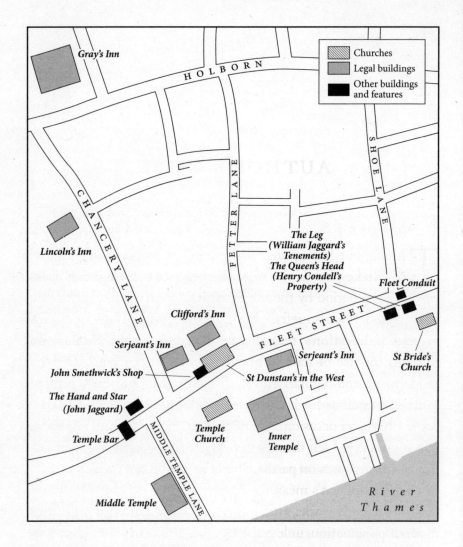

Map of St Dunstan's in the West, Fleet Street and the surrounding area. This diagrammatic rendering of an important bookselling centre in London is not to scale. It presents some of the area's most important legal buildings, alongside the bookshops of John Smethwick (which stood 'under the dial', that is, the clocktower of St Dunstan's Church) and his friend John Jaggard (the Hand and Star), as well as the properties of William Jaggard (the Leg) and Henry Condell (The Queen's Head), the latter two located in St Bride's parish.

AUTHOR'S NOTE

Throughout *Shakespeare's Book*, the 1623 first collected edition of Shakespeare's works is distinguished from other folio works of the period by the use of capital letters, as the First Folio or the Folio. It is also referred to as Shakespeare's Book (with this present publication's title distinguished from the First Folio through the use of italics). Spelling and punctuation have been modernised and regularised for all manuscript and early printed sources, as well as for later printed transcriptions of early source texts. I have, on occasion, retained original punctuation and capitalisation where I felt these better expressed the author's intentions or placed emphases on particular words in a manner which reflects or clarifies the text's meaning. I have modernised and regularised the titles of early works, attempting to present a uniform style with modern punctuation, unless the title is particularly well known in its original form (such as the original full title of Shakespeare's First Folio).

Until 1572 the new calendar year began in England on 25 March, which was Lady Day or the Feast of the Annunciation. I have converted all dates to our modern convention of beginning the new year on 1 January, often referred to as 'new-style' dating. Where I have provided an estimation of the value of a sum of money from the sixteenth or seventeenth century in today's pound sterling, I have used the National Archives' Currency Converter (https://www.nationalarchives.gov.uk/currency-converter/) and adjusted this calculation in line with more recent levels of inflation. This can only be a rough estimate and the sums listed in modern currency do not reflect the full extent of the purchasing power of the original early values to which they refer.

THE PRELIMINARY PAGES
OF THE FIRST FOLIO

To the Reader.

This Figure, that thou here ſeeſt put,
   It vvas for gentle Shakeſpeare cut;
Wherein the Grauer had a ſtrife
   with Nature, to out-doo the life :
O, could he but haue dravvne his vvit
   As well in braſſe, as he hath hit
His face ; the Print vvould then ſurpaſſe
   All, that vvas euer vvrit in braſſe.
But, ſince he cannot, Reader, looke
   Not on his Picture, but his Booke.

B. I.

Mr. WILLIAM
SHAKESPEARES

COMEDIES,
HISTORIES, &
TRAGEDIES.

Published according to the True Originall Copies.

Martin Droeshout sculpsit London.

LONDON
Printed by Isaac Iaggard, and Ed. Blount. 1623.

TO THE MOST NOBLE

AND
INCOMPARABLE PAIRE
OF BRETHREN.

WILLIAM
Earle of Pembroke, &c. Lord Chamberlaine to the
Kings most Excellent Maiesty.

AND

PHILIP
Earle of Montgomery, &c. Gentleman of his Maiesties
Bed-Chamber. Both Knights of the most Noble Order
of the Garter, and our singular good
LORDS.

Right Honourable,

*Hilst we studie to be thankful in our particular, for
the many fauors we haue receiued from your L.L
we are falne vpon the ill fortune, to mingle
two the most diuerse things that can bee, feare,
and rashnesse ; rashnesse in the enterprize, and
feare of the successe. For, when we valew the places your H.H.
sustaine, we cannot but know their dignity greater, then to descend to
the reading of these trifles: and, while we name them trifles, we haue
depriu'd our selues of the defence of our Dedication. But since your
L.L. haue beene plead to thinke these trifles some-thing, heereto-
fore; and haue prosequuted both them, and their Authour liuing,
with so much fauour: we hope, that (they out-liuing him, and he not
hauing the fate, common with some, to be exequutor to his owne writings) you will vse the like indulgence toward them, you haue done*

A 2   *vnto*

The Epistle Dedicatorie.

vnto their parent. There is a great difference, vvhether any Booke choose his Patrones, or finde them: This hath done both. For, so much were your L.L. likings of the seuerall parts, vvhen they were acted, as before they vvere published, the Volume ask'd to be yours. We haue but collected them, and done an office to the dead, to procure his Orphanes, Guardians; vvithout ambition either of selfe-profit, or fame: onely to keepe the memory of so worthy a Friend, & Fellow aliue, as was our SHAKESPEARE, by humble offer of his playes, to your most noble patronage. Wherein, as we haue iustly obserued, no man to come neere your L.L. but vvith a kind of religious addresse; it hath bin the height of our care, vvho are the Presenters, to make the present worthy of your H.H. by the perfection. But, there we must also craue our abilities to be considerd, my Lords. We cannot go beyond our owne powers. Country hands reach foorth milke, creame, fruites, or what they haue: and many Nations (we haue heard) that had not gummes & incense, obtained their requests with a leauened Cake. It vvas no fault to approch their Gods, by what meanes they could: And the most, though meanest, of things are made more precious, when they are dedicated to Temples. In that name therefore, we most humbly consecrate to your H.H. these remaines of your seruant Shakespeare; that what delight is in them, may be euer your L.L. the reputation his, & the faults ours, if any be committed, by a payre so carefull to shew their gratitude both to the liuing, and the dead, as is

Your Lordshippes most bounden,

IOHN HEMINGE.
HENRY CONDELL.

To the great Variety of Readers.

Rom the moſt able,to him that can but ſpell: There you are number'd.We had rather you were weighd. Eſpecially, when the fate of all Bookes depends vpon your capacities : and not of your heads alone, but of your purſes. Well !It is now publique, & you wil ſtand for your priuiledges wee know : to read, and cenſure. Do ſo,but buy it firſt. That doth beſt commend a Booke, the Stationer ſaies. Then,how odde ſoeuer your braines be, or your wiſedomes, make your licence the ſame,and ſpare not. Iudge your ſixe-pen'orth, your ſhillings worth, your ſiue ſhillings worth at a time, or higher, ſo you riſe to the iuſt rates, and welcome. But, what euer you do, Buy. Cenſure will not driue a Trade, or make the Iacke go. And though you be a Magiſtrate of wit, and ſit on the Stage at *Black-Friers*, or the *Cock-pit*, to arraigne Playes dailie, know, theſe Playes haue had their triall alreadie, and ſtood out all Appeales ; and do now come forth quitted rather by a Decree of Court, then any purchas'd Letters of commendation.

It had bene a thing, we confeſſe, worthie to haue bene wiſhed,that the Author himſelfe had liu'd to haue ſet forth, and ouerſeen his owne writings ; But ſince it hath bin ordain'd otherwiſe,and he by death departed from that right,we pray you do not enuie his Friends,the office of their care, and paine, to haue collected & publiſh'd them; and ſo to haue publiſh'd them, as where (before) you were abus'd with diuerſe ſtolne, and ſurreptitious copies, maimed,and deformed by the frauds and ſtealthes of iniurious impoſtors, that expos'd them : euen thoſe, are now offer'd to your view cur'd, and perfect of their limbes; and all the reſt, abſolute in their numbers, as he conceiued thē.Who,as he was a happie imitator of Nature,was a moſt gentle expreſſer of it.His mind and hand went together: And what he thought, he vttered with that eaſineſſe, that wee haue ſcarſe receiued from him a blot in his papers. But it is not our prouince,who ónely gather his works, and giue them you, to praiſe him.. It is yours that reade him. And there we hope,to your diuers capacities, you will finde enough, both to draw, and hold you : for his wit can no more lie hid, then it could be loſt. Reade him, therefore ; and againe, and againe : And if then you doe not like him, ſurely you are in ſome manifeſt danger, not to vnderſtand him. And ſo we leaue you to other of his Friends, whom if you need,can bee your guides : if you neede them not, you can leade your ſelues,and others. And ſuch Readers we wiſh him.

A 3   *Iohn Heminge.*
                       Henrie Condell.

To the memory of my beloued,
The AVTHOR
Mr. William Shakespeare:
And
what he hath left vs.

TO draw no enuy (Shakeſpeare) on thy name,
　Am I thus ample to thy Booke, and Fame :
While I confeſſe thy writings to be ſuch,
As neither Man, nor Muſe, can praiſe too much.
'Tis true, and all mens ſuffrage. But theſe wayes
　Were not the paths I meant vnto thy praiſe :
For ſeelieſt Ignorance on theſe may light,
　Which, when it ſounds at beſt, but eccho's right ;
Or blinde Affection, which doth ne're aduance
　The truth, but gropes, and vrgeth all by chance ;
Or crafty Malice, might pretend this praiſe,
　And thinke to ruine, where it ſeem'd to raiſe.
Theſe are, as ſome infamous Baud, or whore,
　Should praiſe a Matron. What could hurt her more ?
But thou art proofe againſt them, and indeed
　Aboue th'ill fortune of them, or the need.
I, therefore will begin. Soule of the Age !
　The applauſe ! delight ! the wonder of our Stage !
My Shakeſpeare, riſe ; I will not lodge thee by
　Chaucer, or Spenſer, or bid Beaumont lye
A little further, to make thee a roome :
　Thou art a Moniment, without a tombe,
And art aliue ſtill, while thy Booke doth liue,
　And we haue wits to read, and praiſe to giue.
That I not mixe thee ſo, my braine excuſes ;
　I meane with great, but diſproportion'd Muſes :
For, if I thought my iudgement were of yeeres,
　I ſhould commit thee ſurely with thy peeres,
And tell, how farre thou didſtſt our Lily out-ſhine,
　Or ſporting Kid, or Marlowes mighty line.
And though thou hadſt ſmall Latine, and leſſe Greeke,
　From thence to honour thee, I would not ſeeke
For names; but call forth thund'ring Æſchilus,
　Euripides, and Sophocles to vs,
Paccuuius, Accius, him of Cordoua dead,
　To life againe, to heare thy Buskin tread,
And ſhake a Stage : Or, when thy Sockes were on,
　Leaue thee alone, for the compariſon

of

Of all, that insolent Greece, or haughtie Rome
   sent forth, or since did from their ashes come.
Triumph, my Britaine, thou hast one to showe,
   To whom all Scenes of Europe homage owe.
He was not of an age, but for all time!
   And all the Muses still were in their prime,
when like Apollo he came forth to warme
   Our eares, or like a Mercury to charme!
Nature her selfe was proud of his designes,
   And ioy'd to weare the dressing of his lines!
which were so richly spun, and wouen so fit,
   As, since, she will vouchsafe no other Wit.
The merry Greeke, tart Aristophanes,
   Neat Terence, witty Plautus, now not please;
But antiquated, and deserted lye
   As they were not of Natures family.
Yet must I not giue Nature all: Thy Art,
   My gentle Shakespeare, must enioy a part.
For though the Poets matter, Nature be,
   His Art doth giue the fashion. And, that he,
Who casts to write a liuing line, must sweat,
   (such as thine are) and strike the second heat
Vpon the Muses anuile : turne the same,
   (And himselfe with it) that he thinkes to frame;
Or for the lawrell, he may gaine a scorne,
   For a good Poet's made, as well as borne.
And such wert thou. Looke how the fathers face
   Liues in his issue, euen so, the race
Of Shakespeares minde, and manners brightly shines
   In his well torned, and true filed lines :
In each of which, he seemes to shake a Lance,
   As brandish't at the eyes of Ignorance.
Sweet Swan of Auon! what a sight it were
   To see thee in our waters yet appeare,
And make those flights vpon the bankes of Thames,
   That so did take Eliza, and our Iames!
But stay, I see thee in the Hemisphere
   Aduanc'd, and made a Constellation there!
Shine forth, thou Starre of Poets, and with rage,
   Or influence, chide, or cheere the drooping Stage;
Which, since thy flight frō hence, hath mourn'd like night,
   And despaires day, but for thy Volumes light.

                    BEN: IONSON.

Vpon the Lines and Life of the Famous
Scenicke Poet, Maſter William
SHAKESPEARE.

THoſe hands, which you ſo clapt, go now, and wring
You *Britaines* braue; for done are *Shakeſpeares* dayes :
His dayes are done, that made the dainty Playes,
Which made the Globe of heau'n and earth to ring.
Dry'de is that veine, dry'd is the *Theſpian* Spring,
Turn'd all to teares, and *Phœbus* clouds his rayes :
That corp's, that coffin now beſticke thoſe bayes,
Which crown'd him *Poet* firſt, then *Poets* King.
If *Tragedies* might any *Prologue* haue,
All thoſe he made, would ſcarſe make one to this :
Where *Fame*, now that he gone is to the graue
(Deaths publique tyring houſe) the *Nuncius* is.
For though his line of life went ſoone about,
The life yet of his lines ſhall neuer out.

HVGH HOLLAND.

TO THE MEMORIE
of the deceased Authour Maister
W. SHAKESPEARE.

Shake-speare, at length thy pious fellowes giue
The world thy Workes : thy Workes, by which, out-liue
Thy Tombe, thy name must when that stone is rent,
And Time dissolues thy Stratford Moniment,
Here we aliue shall view thee still. This Booke,
When Brasse and Marble fade, shall make thee looke
Fresh to all Ages : when Posteritie
Shall loath what's new, thinke all is prodigie
That is not Shake-speares ; eu'ry Line, each Verse
Here shall reuiue, redeeme thee from thy Herse.
Nor Fire, nor cankring Age, as Naso said,
Of his, thy wit=fraught Booke shall once inuade.
Nor shall I e're beleeue, or thinke thee dead
(Though mist) vntill our bankrout Stage be sped
(Impossible) with some new straine t'out-do
Passions of Iuliet, and her Romeo ;
Or till I heare a Scene more nobly take,
Then when thy half=Sword parlying Romans spake.
Till these, till any of thy Volumes rest
Shall with more fire, more feeling be exprest,
Be sure, our Shake-speare, thou canst neuer dye,
But crown'd with Lawrell, liue eternally.

L. Digges.

To the memorie of M. W. Shake-speare.

WEE wondred (Shake-speare) that thou went'st so soone
From the Worlds=Stage, to the Graues-Tyring-roome.
Wee thought thee dead, but this thy printed worth,
Tels thy Spectators, that thou went'st but forth
To enter with applause. An Actors Art,
Can dye, and liue, to acte a second part.
That's but an Exit of Mortalitie ;
This, a Re-entrance to a Plaudite.

I. M.

A CATALOGVE

of the ſeuerall Comedies, Hiſtories, and Tragedies contained in this Volume.

The Workes of William Shakeſpeare,

containing all his Comedies, Hiſtories, and Tragedies: Truely ſet forth, according to their firſt *ORJGJNALL.*

The Names of the Principall Actors
in all theſe Playes.

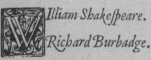

Illiam Shakeſpeare.

Richard Burbadge.

John Hemmings.

Auguſtine Phillips.

William Kempt.

Thomas Poope.

George Bryan.

Henry Condell.

William Slye.

Richard Cowly.

John Lowine.

Samuell Croſſe.

Alexander Cooke.

Samuel Gilburne.

Robert Armin.

William Oſtler.

Nathan Field.

John Vnderwood.

Nicholas Tooley.

William Eccleſtone.

Joſeph Taylor.

Robert Benfield.

Robert Goughe.

Richard Robinſon.

Iohn Shancke.

Iohn Rice.

Prologue

The Covenant?

Shakespeare's 'Fellows' and the First Folio

A book? O rare one,
Be not, as is our fangled world, a garment
Nobler than that it covers.

William Shakespeare, *Cymbeline*

Shakespeare's Book is the story of, arguably, the world's most influential secular book. *Mr William Shakespeares Comedies, Histories, & Tragedies* was published in 1623 and included thirty-six plays by the dramatist. Today this landmark in the history of publishing is more commonly known as the First Folio. Copies of this much-coveted volume have exchanged hands for millions of pounds, with one of the most recent complete examples selling at Christie's auction house in New York on 14 October 2020 for close to ten million dollars, roughly eight and a half million pounds sterling, making it the most expensive work of literature ever sold.

So why is the First Folio so important? It is difficult to imagine a world without *The Tempest*, *Twelfth Night*, *Antony and Cleopatra*, *Julius Caesar*, *The Winter's Tale* and *Macbeth*, but these are just some of the plays which were only preserved thanks to the astounding labour of love that was the first collected edition of Shakespeare's plays. When the First Folio hit the bookstalls, nearly eight years after the playwright's death in 1616, it provided eighteen previously unpublished plays, and significantly revised versions of close to a dozen other dramatic works, which may never have survived without the efforts of those who backed, financed, curated and crafted what is one of the most significant conservation projects in history.

Without the First Folio Shakespeare is unlikely to have acquired the towering international stature he now enjoys across the arts, the pedagogical arena and popular culture. Many of the familiar phrases that inform the texture of the English language would either simply not exist or would not have become so embedded in our lexical consciousness: 'sea change', 'brave new world', 'thereby hangs a tale', 'at one fell swoop', 'the be-all and the end-all', 'break the ice', 'what's done is done', 'rhyme nor reason', 'too much of a good thing', 'it's Greek to me', these constitute a mere fraction of the commonplaces that have taken root through the First Folio, alongside which we must place the many more Shakespeare coinages that have immeasurably enriched spoken and written discourse. Today a host of industries – universities, colleges and schools; theatre and film companies; actors' guilds; arts organisations and academic societies; publishers and online platforms; tourist sites and countless forms of merchandising – benefit from the legacy fashioned by the compilers, financiers, actors, publishers, printers, pressworkers, scribes, patrons and poets who, along with the engraver of Shakespeare's iconic portrait, collaborated in the making of the First Folio. Its lasting impact on English national heritage, and its circulation across cultures, languages and media, makes this one of the most noteworthy secular publishing events across the globe, in any historical period.

Aside from its precious hoard of dramatic works, the First Folio gathered together in one place the most that had ever been written *about* William Shakespeare up till that time, providing a point of origin for the posthumous identity of the man behind the works as we have come to know him today. It represents, therefore, the very beginnings of Shakespeare biography. Though its title page and prefatorial materials span a mere eleven pages of printed text, they have had an incalculable impact on the dramatist's reputation, global infiltration, and the narratives fashioned – and which continue to be told – about his life, character and achievements. These preliminary pages comprise five commemorative poems in the playwright's honour by four scholarly authors, Ben Jonson, Leonard Digges, James Mabbe and Hugh Holland; two epistles by his colleagues and friends John Heminges and Henry Condell, one addressed to the First Folio's patrons, Sir William Herbert, 3rd Earl of Pembroke, and his brother Philip Herbert, 1st Earl of Montgomery, and the other to 'the great Variety of Readers'; a list of 'Principal Actors' in the theatrical company that mounted Shakespeare's plays; a 'Catalogue' serving as a contents page dividing his oeuvre into Comedies, Histories and Tragedies; and his now-unmistakable portrait, by the engraver Martin Droeshout, which is still the only likeness of the dramatist in existence expressly authenticated by someone who knew him. It was Ben Jonson himself, Shakespeare's own colleague and comrade, who stated in a poem 'To the Reader' printed alongside the Folio's portrait, that the artist 'well ... hath hit/His face', that is, captured the sitter's resemblance. Droeshout could not, however, possibly 'have drawn his wit', that capacious and mysterious intelligence, undergirded by the feeling humanity of 'gentle Shakespeare', which defies definition or description but which, Jonson insists, readers can find by gazing 'Not on his Picture, but his Book'.

These preliminary pages have transmitted the physiognomy, mind and morality of the book's subject through the generations and across the furthest reaches of the planet, predicting the very universality their subject has acquired. In his memorial poem Hugh Holland declared that Shakespeare's 'dainty Plays' have 'made the Globe of heaven and earth to ring' and have crowned him 'Poets' King', while Leonard Digges, in his verse to the play-wright's memory, insisted that in years to come 'Posterity/Shall loathe what's new, think all is prodigy [that is, monstrous or new-fangled]/That is not Shakespeare's'. Ben Jonson confirmed the wide reach of the dramatist's influence, 'To whom all scenes of Europe homage owe' and through whose 'mind, and manners brightly shines' his 'Volume's light'. Those same pages have even shaped the ways we have defined the canon for centuries, deter-mining how we think about the genres in which Shakespeare wrote and which plays critics and arbiters of taste have stamped with that validating mark of authenticity that fixes them among the hallowed inventions of his unique genius. Those plays not included in the First Folio have acquired canonical status more slowly, like the collaboratively produced *Pericles* and *The Two Noble Kinsmen*, or have all but vanished without a trace, like *Cardenio*, which exists only in tantalising fragments, and the enigmatic *Love's Labour's Won*, which may be an entirely lost work. Not only has this volume moulded our appreciation of what is *Shakespearean*, its 'printed worth', to borrow a phrase from James Mabbe's short Folio poem, has also served as a barometer against which we measure the prod-ucts of culture. In short, for good or ill (and we must acknowledge that this has not been to the benefit of all cultures, all classes and all ethnicities at all times) Shakespeare's Book is the book *through* which we see so many of the literary and pedagogical artefacts that shape our understanding of the world and our place in it, often without our even realising it.

Around 235 complete or partially preserved copies of the First Folio are known to have survived to the present day, from an esti-mated original print run of 750. Known volumes are housed in libraries, public institutions, arts organisations, universities and private collections, while additional copies are hidden away, in vaults and bank safety-deposit boxes, secretly treasured or simply as yet undiscovered, beyond the reach of academics and Folio enthusiasts. The catalogued volumes are scattered across the United Kingdom, Ireland, the United States of America, Canada, Italy, Germany, France, Switzerland, Japan, South Africa, Australia and New Zealand. There is no doubt that this sought-after book has made its subject a global phenomenon. Countless countries, nationalities and local regions have not only made Shakespeare their own, but made their own 'Shakespeares', often as part of wider projects of cultural reclamation, self-actualisation and self-empowerment, sometimes with the intention of challenging the very regimes of social oppression and colonial subjugation that the playwright's works have historically been used to shore up. Indeed, a number of Folios, including those now in Texas, Australia, New Zealand and South Africa, among others, were originally owned by, or have made their way to their host countries with, influential figureheads and governors attached to colonising missions designed to impose the values of the British Empire on indigenous populations. These same volumes, which originally served as symbols of the supposed virtues of English and Western 'civilising' projects, have more recently become sites of resistance through post-colonial scholarship and a commitment to making them, and their complex transnational histories, more publicly accessible. It is sobering to think that after Nelson Mandela was arrested for his activist resistance to apartheid and incarcerated on Robben Island in South Africa, among the plays that he and other prisoners secretly read and annotated while imprisoned, in the copy of Shakespeare's complete works acquired by fellow inmate Sonny Venkatrathnam, were those preserved thanks to the First Folio. Thus old Shakespeares have been, and continue to be, replaced by new.

Intentionally or not, the financiers, enablers and makers of the First Folio created a monument to Shakespeare that more than lived up to Ben Jonson's prophetic utterance describing the play-wright as a creative wonder who 'was not of an age, but for all time!' But while this most mercurial of writers is endlessly re-constituted, endlessly reborn, what are the origins of his book, the volume that gave birth to the very idea of 'Shakespeare' not simply as author, but as man and cultural icon? Who put the First Folio together and under what circumstances? How was this project, which created a timeless masterpiece, shaped by the political crises and pressure points of its own time? Did William Shakespeare himself play a role in its inception beyond writing, or collaborating on, the works enshrined within it? *Shakespeare's Book* is an attempt to answer these questions, to provide a new way of looking at the creation of the 1623 First Folio; the book Shakespeare made, and the book that made Shakespeare.

On 25 March 1616, a frail and trembling William Shakespeare made a hasty addition to his will. He had been taken by surprise, not expecting the end to come so soon, for when he originally recorded the disposing of his estate he had confirmed that he was in 'perfect health and memory'. Now, at the age of fifty-two, his thoughts turned to the family and friends he would be leaving behind. Requesting the services of his solicitor Francis Collins, he made a new series of bequests that were more personal in nature. To his wife, Anne, he left 'my second best bed', probably the bed on which they slept, for the best bed tended to be reserved for guests. In addition to gifts for friends and neighbours in his native Stratford-upon-Avon, he gave legacies to the three intimates in London who, outside of his own family, probably knew him better than anyone else, bequeathing 'to my fellows John Heminges, Richard Burbage and Henry Condell' twenty-six shillings and eight pence 'a piece to buy them rings'.

The recipients were Shakespeare's friends, fellow actors and co-sharers in the playing company that was first known by the name of the Chamberlain's Men and then as the King's Men, all three becoming at various points in their careers part-owners of the troupe's two main playhouses: the Globe on London's Bankside and the Blackfriars Theatre in the well-to-do district of Blackfriars. These had been opened after the players vacated their original home venue, named the Theatre, in Shoreditch. Under the auspices of a noble patron, Sir Henry Carey, 1st Baron Hunsdon, who was Lord Chamberlain and cousin to Queen Elizabeth I, the players flourished. Commercial theatre companies were usually taken under the wing of a theatrical patron, who protected a troupe's interests, conferred their prestige on its members, and ensured that the company's plays were performed before royalty and visiting dignitaries at court, thereby providing players with an additional revenue stream. Henry was succeeded as patron by his son, Sir George Carey, in 1596, then by King James I himself in 1603, elevating the company's status further as the King's Men. By the time of his death in 1619, just three years after Shakespeare, Richard Burbage had become the age's most celebrated actor, the two having formed a partnership so productive that it contributed towards making the company one of the most successful in theatrical history up to that point.

Heminges and Condell would go on to become co-labourers in the project for which they too would acquire global renown: the creation of the First Folio. As we will see in the chapters that follow, the crisis of Burbage's death played a decisive role in the story of the Folio's production, and was of far more significance to that endeavour than has often been recognised by Shakespeare scholars. In particular, the loss of their beloved friend Burbage, coming so soon after that of the King's Men's star playwright, had a seismic effect on Shakespeare publishing and, in a more personal vein, on Heminges and Condell, serving as a catalyst for the scheme to commemorate the dramatist with a sumptuous edition of his collected plays. We do not know if Shakespeare's 'fellows' were working towards the creation of the First Folio in the first three or so years after his death. The earliest events with any relation to the making of the Folio took place in 1619, a pivotal year full of challenges and obstacles, both personal and professional, for the King's Men. *Shakespeare's Book*, therefore, will chart primarily the events from that important year to the Folio's publication in 1623.

Even before a single word was printed, the decision to publish 'Shakespeare' in folio was a grandiloquent statement in itself. A 'folio' is a book issued in a large format and was then considered a luxury item. Costing as much as forty times more than a single play printed in a smaller format known as a 'quarto', it was beyond the reach of most individuals in the period. Sizes of surviving First Folios vary considerably, because pages were often cropped with successive re-bindings over time, but they typically measure around 310–342 millimetres by 190–217 millimetres. Befitting the impressive size of such a publication, folio printing before Shakespeare's Book tended to be reserved for works of historiographical or national importance, or for religious treatises, legal tomes, grand heraldic volumes and genealogical tracts. A folio would have had that whiff of musty learnedness about it which signalled that its author was a revered and long-dead classical figure, university-trained scholar, cleric of note, or even a monarch. Despite the fact that Shakespeare's name had become a hugely marketable commodity during his lifetime, providing him with wealth, an impressive portfolio of properties in Warwickshire and London, and the confidence to secure a coat of arms which conferred the status of 'gentleman' upon him – reflected in the honorific title of 'Master' that is attached to his name in the First Folio – playwriting was not generally regarded in the sixteenth and seventeenth centuries as a prestigious occupation which produced elevated works of literature. Publishing commercial plays in folio was a bold, gutsy and daring initiative; one that says something about the value the creators and backers of the First Folio placed on the playwright's textual remains and, for those 'fellows' involved

Title page of Ben Jonson's *The Workes of Benjamin Jonson* (London: William Stansby, 1616). Jonson oversaw the collected edition of his own works, completed in 1616. His friend and rival William Shakespeare is likely to have known about this project, which may have inspired the creation of the First Folio.

in the project who had known him personally, his friendship. It
was also a highly risky venture, both in terms of financial burden
and potential reputational cost, to which John Heminges and
Henry Condell alluded in their dedicatory letter to the Herbert
brothers published with the Folio. There they confessed that the
project had taken an emotional toll, forcing them 'to mingle two
the most diverse things that can be: fear, and rashness; rashness in
the enterprize, and fear of the success'. Backing a folio of commercial plays, then, was an eccentric and even foolhardy act, and there
was every chance it would fail. To avert catastrophe the project
required careful planning; its initiators needing to muster a degree
of courage to embark on the 'enterprize' in the first place. And the
path towards its completion would be far from a smooth and
uneventful one.

It is tempting to speculate on whether Shakespeare, as he neared
his end, had meant his will to send a message to his beloved theatrical friends. Was an edition of collected plays something
Shakespeare had been preparing towards the end of his life? Was
his gift of money to his theatre colleagues for the purchase of
mourning rings intended to seal a special bond, a covenant? Did it
represent a promise that they would initiate such a publication
after his death? That year, in 1616, Ben Jonson, a dramatist like
Shakespeare, was in the final stages of overseeing the printing of
his own folio of collected *Works*, which would make history as the
first such book to include commercial plays, alongside more learned
works, including his poems and more genteel courtly entertainments. He and Shakespeare were friends – as well as rivals – and
had worked together on London's stages, so it is very likely
Shakespeare was aware of Jonson's ambitious project. Indeed, in
their address to the 'great Variety of Readers' in the Folio, Heminges
and Condell make an extraordinary claim:

It had been a thing, we confess, worthy to have been wished, that the author himself had lived to have set forth, and overseen his own writings; but since it hath been ordained otherwise, and he by death departed from that right, we pray you do not envy his friends, the office of their care and pain, to have collected and published them ... absolute in their numbers as he conceived them who, as he was a happy imitator of nature, was a most gentle expresser of it. His mind and hand went together, and what he thought, he uttered with that easiness, that we have scarce received from him a blot in his papers.

Shakespeare's friends imply that he would have 'overseen his own writings' and was only prevented from doing so by death. This, they insist, would have been his 'right'. Their own involvement in the making of the Folio was an intervention, necessitating an act of reclamation, conservation and collation that they were expecting the author himself to have undertaken. Had Richard Burbage lived longer and set his name to those letters in the Folio signed by Heminges and Condell, this would have been a suggestive gesture, possibly indicating that a pledge had been made by the three actors, sealed in response to Shakespeare's deathbed wish, to complete what the playwright had started or merely hoped to begin. Shakespeare's influence over his book, over and above his authoring of the plays contained within it, is an issue to which we shall return in the final chapters; but whatever the significance behind his bequest to his 'fellows', the playwright had advocates in John Heminges and Henry Condell who had the skills and experience needed to navigate such an uncertain adventure in the history of printing.

As well as being seasoned actors, Heminges and Condell were ambitious, forward-thinking and entrepreneurial, rising quickly up the playing company's ranks to become its principal theatre managers. Heminges was practical, skilled with numbers, good with money and had a logical business head. He could be unsentimental when it came to protecting his, and the theatrical company's, financial interests, even engaging in an acrimonious legal suit with his own daughter, Thomasina, in 1615 over control of shares in the Globe and Blackfriars playhouses after the death of her husband, William Ostler, an actor in the company who had initially secured those shares. Ostler's trace in the First Folio can be seen in its list of 'Principal Actors' in which his name appears sixteenth out of twenty-six members of the company. A surviving description of the theatre manager as 'old stuttering Heminges' with 'swollen eyes' may have been creative licence, as this lively portrait was penned in a sensationalised account of the burning down of the Globe Theatre in 1613. If it does record some difficulty or hesitation with speech from which Heminges genuinely suffered, this had not in any way impeded his career, and during the making of the First Folio he would prove himself more than robust enough to see this taxing project through to its conclusion. Neither did Condell permit any obstacles to prevent his own professional and social elevation. His desire to accumulate properties in the most fashionable parts of London and elsewhere, which he pursued with quite some tenacity, bordered on obsession, and he even acquired his own tavern, further augmenting his income.

Although Heminges' last recorded acting role would come in 1617, in a revival of Ben Jonson's play *Volpone*, he may have continued acting right up till 1621, thereafter focusing entirely on managing the King's Men's finances, court performances and day-to-day operations. In the surviving account books of the Treasurer of the Chamber, the holder of the office responsible for ensuring players received payment for royal entertainments, which record performances of plays by the King's Men at court, Heminges is normally listed as the man who received the players' payment in-hand. Described frequently as the company's 'presenter', his role would have been to oversee the practicalities of the King's Men's appearances at court, and to liaise with the Lord Chamberlain and Master of the Revels, the two most important figures for the players because their posts gave them responsibility for arranging royal performances and licensing plays. Condell's final known acting role would be in 1619 but he too may have continued performing beyond that, though he would increasingly take on a role as Heminges' supporter in the management of the troupe. On 27 March that year, when their royal patron reissued the King's Men's licence, Heminges would be logged first as company member, followed by Burbage and then Condell. The document would be ratified after Burbage's death but was drafted while he was still alive, meaning that Heminges and Condell were by that point the company's two most senior members; this management structure confirmed in the First Folio's two addresses by the King's Men colleagues four years later. Both Heminges and Condell had, therefore, acquired a degree of prestige and influence before that volume was even started, each boasting, like their friend Shakespeare, the status of 'gentleman'. Their word would have carried some weight and they would have been listened to by the other agents involved in the making of the book. By 1619 they were being described as of 'great living, wealth and power' with 'mighty and great friends', with both having amassed considerable estates.

What gives these two men added credentials as the facilitators of the First Folio's creation is that they had access to the papers of the King's Men. Their claim to have 'collected and published' Shakespeare's writings has led to their being commonly referred to as the 'editors' of the Folio. This is a misleading term because our modern understanding of editing does not quite fit the processes that underpinned the manufacture of this volume. Authority over the final texts that would appear in it was not concentrated in their hands alone. They did not simply gather together papers, directly from Shakespeare's hand, with scarce a 'blot' in them, as they boast in their epistle to the 'great Variety of Readers', and then arrange these untouched in the volume. The enticing picture they paint of the purity of the plays that they have 'received from him' is a fiction that has shaped the fantasy of Shakespeare's free-flowing and unfettered creativity for centuries. In reality the playwright's works had more complex textual histories, and did not stream from his pen in blissful isolation from the political and social pressures of his age; nor was the First Folio produced in a vacuum.

The King's Men's archive held an assortment of plays by the dramatist in varying formats, stretching back to the early 1590s, or even the late 1580s, when Shakespeare is likely to have begun writing plays, his first works probably being *Titus Andronicus*, *The Comedy of Errors* and the *Henry VI* plays. These documents would have included Shakespeare's own authorial manuscripts, sometimes known as 'foul papers'; 'fair copies' of the plays prepared by professional scribes, often using their own conventions for spelling, punctuation, act and scene divisions, stage directions and formatting, which may have been different to those favoured by Shakespeare himself; 'prompt books', which were the complete versions of the plays used for performance; and a stock of individual printed plays, each issued in a relatively cheap quarto format, sometimes marked up with changes or additions so that they could be used as prompt books for performance. The First Folio's plays each originated in one or more of these varied kinds of source text. Deciding on the 'final' version for a Folio play could be a messy and complicated business, one spread across several agents; a far cry from the 'easiness' of Shakespeare's textual production that Heminges and Condell imply was preserved in the works they had 'collected'. While Shakespeare's friends would have probably been involved in the herculean task of sorting through these manifold versions of the plays and deciding which – and sometimes in what combination – would be best for the collected edition, the play texts that made up the First Folio were filtered through a number of other hands before the book was finished. We shall meet some of the personalities behind those hands in *Shakespeare's Book*.

Posterity has assigned to Heminges and Condell an almost mythic status as the instigators of the First Folio. The magnificence of their achievement is recorded on a handsome memorial, erected in 1896 on the site of St Mary's Church in Aldermanbury, where they would be buried. Overlooked by an imposing portrait bust of Shakespeare, which lends authority to the monument's version of the story of the Folio's making, it boasts a plaque inscribed with a rousing summation of the theatre managers' accomplishment:

> To the memory of John Heminge and Henry Condell, Fellow actors and personal friends of Shakespeare. They lived in this parish and are buried here. To their disinterested affection the world owes all that it calls Shakespeare. They alone collected his dramatic writings regardless of pecuniary loss and without the hope of any profit gave them to the world. They thus merited the gratitude of mankind.

This enshrines Heminges and Condell's own affecting statement in their epistle to the First Folio's readers that they had undertaken the costly and laborious project 'without ambition either of self-profit, or fame'. *Shakespeare's Book* challenges the statement that 'They alone' were responsible for the Folio. We do not know if they were, in fact, the initiators of the volume. The creation of that book was not simply down to two 'editors', as is often popularly thought. It was brought to fruition by many hands, some less visible than others. This would include the syndicate who financed the project: father-and-son publishing and printing team William and Isaac Jaggard, in whose printing shop the First Folio would physically be put together, and the publisher-booksellers Edward Blount, William Aspley and John Smethwick, who between them represent the four bookselling businesses whose investment and expertise would underpin the whole scheme. The 'Shakespeare' bequeathed to posterity in the Folio's pages was also part of a collaborative enterprise between its patrons, the earls of Pembroke and Montgomery; its commemorative poets; the engraver of Shakespeare's timeless portrait; and the actors in the company who knew Shakespeare and performed his plays. In addition, the scribes who provided copies of some of the plays and the pressworkers who poured their labours into the book in the Jaggards' printing house shaped the text in fundamental ways. When we read, watch or listen to the plays we may not realise that those ever-hallowed words may bear the traces of interventions made by copyists, annotating readers, bookkeepers, censors, pressworkers and typesetters who touched and worked on those, to echo Ben Jonson's tribute to Shakespeare in the Folio, 'well turned, and true-filed lines', sometimes changing them in the process.

Larger institutions also played their part in the Folio's birth. Members of the Stationers' Company, the body that regulated the printing and book trades, were pivotal to its manufacture in an age when playwrights did not always own the rights to their own plays. Originally established as a guild for booksellers and manuscript illuminators in 1403, later incorporating printers after the invention of the printing press and granted a Royal Charter in 1557, the Stationers' Company was housed in Stationers' Hall, located near the hub of the bookselling industry in the precinct of St Paul's Cathedral during the making of the First Folio. This was where stationers and publishers would come to register their rights to issue books, pamphlets, ballads and other kinds of printed material. There was then no precise equivalent to copyright as we understand it today. Before a book could be published, stationer-publishers were obliged to seek a 'licence' or 'allowance' from an ecclesiastical authority, operating under the aegis of the Bishop of London, which testified to the fact that the work had been checked and was free of 'offence'. This power could, however, be transferred to other authorities. For plays, such a licence might instead be sought from the Master of the Revels, depending on the regulations in place at the time when permission was being requested. For an additional fee, a stationer could enter the title of their work in the Stationers' Register by demonstrating that they held a legitimate 'copy' of the text, which had been vetted and ratified in this way, securing through these means an independent record of the exclusive right to print it. This was an optional part of the process, but was an extra protection against competing publishers who might try to encroach on their privilege by issuing the same work. The surviving books of the register are among the most important historical records we have for piecing together the landscape of early theatrical culture and publishing more broadly, and the history of Shakespeare printing specifically.

As is the case with the King's Men, plays were normally the property of the playing company that staged them (though some playwrights in the period did appear to have kept hold of their own works to dispose of as they wished). Numerous Shakespeare plays, particularly those written in the earlier half of his career, were transferred to stationers and booksellers, mostly but not always through a legitimate transfer recorded in the Stationers' Register, some of whom issued these in single volumes, while others held on to the rights to these works without printing them. Those who secured licences to print plays that had slipped through the King's Men's fingers would have to be negotiated with if those works were to be legally incorporated into Shakespeare's Book, and so they are part of the cast of characters whose activities made the Folio possible.

But these interwoven lives are subject to a higher power. The King's Men were just that: the king's servants. As their royal patron, his policies, proclivities and concerns could not but guide the fortunes of the First Folio, which stood as a testament to a major portion of the theatrical troupe's historical achievements, as well as the fates of those involved in its creation. *Shakespeare's Book* will trace the sometimes troubled journeys of the individuals and communities whose labours, contributions, intercessions and interventions coalesced within this one volume, against a turbulent political backdrop that shaped the project in fundamental ways. This will reveal, more starkly than ever before, what was at stake for those who had put their hands to, and money and hearts into, this memorial to a Renaissance playwright. In the process, the chapters that follow will present a different slant on the impact of the crises of 1619 on the King's Men and the First Folio, suggesting that Richard Burbage's death was the trigger for a change to the broader culture of Shakespeare printing in ways that were bound up with the book's production; put forward a new theory about how the publishers and booksellers who financed the volume joined the syndicate that produced it; uncover the significance of a potentially rediscovered 'lost' Shakespeare sonnet in relation to the Folio; and find fresh answers to the question of the dramatist's involvement in its making by unveiling the personalities who formed, or intersected with, his social and scholarly networks – including a new candidate for the playwright's mysterious and still unidentified London lodger – and whose influence left a legible imprint of Shakespeare's will on his own book.

If we think of the First Folio as a fruit-bearing tree, its branches represent those who manifestly contributed towards its creation, those whose names are emblazoned on and enshrined within the volume. The roots are those invisible characters whose labours and contributions are not immediately apparent but without whom the tree could not survive or yield its bounty. *Shakespeare's Book* aims to restore the whole tree in all its living, multifarious and intertwining beauty.

Act One

1619

The Year of the 'False Folio'

Behold, my lords,
Although the print be little, the whole matter
And copy of the father …

William Shakespeare, *The Winter's Tale*

England's 'Delightful Proteus'

The Death of Richard Burbage

O n Friday 12 March 1619 the greatest actor of the age lay
dying. Richard Burbage, who had played such memorable
roles as Richard III, Hamlet, Othello and King Lear, who had
filled the stages and hearts of a generation with his – and through
him William Shakespeare's – words, had been deprived of that
once-enthralling voice, leaving little trace of his own thoughts as
he neared his end.

The fifty-one-year-old had not prepared a detailed last will and
testament. He could only muster the strength to nominate his
wife Winifrid, who was pregnant at the time, as his sole executrix
in a will dictated in haste from his deathbed. His brother,
Cuthbert, had not travelled far to be by his side, for he lived on
the same street, in what may have been an adjoining residence, in
Holywell Street in the parish of St Leonard's, Shoreditch, just a
stone's throw from where the Theatre had once stood: the playhouse their father, James Burbage, had built and which had been
the backdrop to Shakespeare's early career. The playwright may
have encountered or seen James when he was a boy, since the elder
Burbage had himself twice visited Stratford-upon-Avon with an

acting troupe in the 1570s. The precariousness of the itinerant performer's life, which James had experienced at first-hand, had convinced him that there was a better way to manage a theatre business; he wanted more for his son, Richard. Establishing the Theatre, serving as a permanent and fixed base for an acting troupe in London, meant laying the groundwork for a more organised and stable kind of playing company of which both Richard Burbage and Shakespeare had been the beneficiaries. Born in 1568, Richard was probably only around sixteen when he began in his acting vocation. He had become a versatile, hypnotic and robust performer, with a formidable presence both on and off stage. One of the earliest records which gives us a snapshot of his personality portrays him in a fittingly dramatic light, at around the age of nineteen, defending his family's business by seeing off disputants who were claiming, he felt unlawfully, a share of the Theatre's profits. Accosting one of these, Richard 'beat him with a broom staff, calling him "murdering knave"', while pulling the other by the nose and challenging him to a duel, having 'sent them packing' with his taunts and sonorous laughter booming in their ears. It was an early sign of Richard's fierce loyalty to his friends and colleagues, which had characterised his long and successful career.

Those friends would not forget him, right up to his very end. Another significant figure in the story of the First Folio is likely to have been at Richard Burbage's bedside. Ralph Crane was a scrivener who would produce fair copies of several of the plays that would be included in the volume, leaving his indelible stamp on the playwright's works in the process. Crane would be working for the King's Men that year and Burbage's surviving will is thought to be in his supremely elegant hand, indicating a particularly close personal bond. Also with Burbage during his final hours, and witnesses to his will, were fellow actors Nicholas Tooley and Richard Robinson. Both were likely to have been Burbage's protégés and may have lived with him during their apprenticeships while learning the ropes as actors.

Tooley had special reason to feel close to the Burbages. He was, in all likelihood, an orphan, having emigrated from Antwerp as an infant with his mother in the winter of 1583, within two and a half months of the death of his father, William Tooley, whose own family hailed from Shakespeare's native Warwickshire. With the Burbage family Nicholas Tooley had found a longed-for stability and continuity that had been lacking in his own life. He would not forget the kindness Richard and Winifrid had shown him, nor the trauma of growing up without his biological father, requesting in his will that his fellow actor Richard Robinson give the twenty-nine pounds and thirteen shillings that the latter owed him to Sara Burbage, Richard Burbage's daughter who would be born after the actor's death. Tooley himself would soon be dead, buried on 5 June 1623, just months before the publication of the First Folio in which he would be listed nineteenth out of the twenty-six recorded as being the 'Principal Actors' of the company.

Richard Robinson, whose name appears twenty-fourth on the Folio's roll-call of actors, had begun his career with the King's Men playing female roles. During Shakespeare's age women were not permitted to serve as professional actors on the commercial stages, though they did take on roles in lavish court entertainments known as masques and in exclusive private productions and readings in the homes of England's nobility. Female impersonation was a highly skilled and demanding discipline, and Robinson was clearly a noted talent. He had mastered the ample and challenging role of 'the Lady' in *The Second Maiden's Tragedy* in 1611 and Ben Jonson alluded to him in his play *The Devil Is an Ass* in 1616 as a 'very pretty fellow' and an 'ingenious youth', lauding his entertaining 'frolics' when 'Dressed like a lawyer's wife'. After he graduated to male roles, Robinson went on to play the part of the Cardinal in John Webster's *The Duchess of Malfi*, taking over from

Henry Condell, and his success is hinted at by the dramatist Abraham Cowley who described him as 'essential to a play'. So close was Robinson to the Burbage family that within a few years he would marry Richard Burbage's widow. He is listed as 'living at the upper end of Shoreditch' in the year of the First Folio's publication.

As the unrecorded disease which was ending Burbage's life tightened its grip, he would have heard the bells of the nearby St Leonard's Church tolling a mournful death-knell. Did he think, perhaps for a moment in his confusion, that they tolled for him? Or was he aware that they were ringing for the burial of his fellow actor and neighbour, Richard Cowley, who had lived on Holywell Street and whose funeral took place on the very day that Burbage's will was devised? This double tragedy for the King's Men may be the reason why there is no record of John Heminges and Henry Condell having been at Burbage's side during the dictating of the will. Heminges, along with Cuthbert Burbage and John Shank, another member of the King's Men, had been present when a dangerously ill Cowley mumbled his own will on 13 January 1618, an unusually long fifteen months before his death.

Cowley had been a senior member of the King's Men and was listed in 1601, when the company was the Chamberlain's Men, as joint payee for three performances at court in the presence of Queen Elizabeth I, his name appearing after that of John Heminges and thereby indicating his importance to the playing troupe. Cowley is likely to have begun acting with the company before that, in the mid- to late 1590s, and may have drawn the attention of the Burbages because he was a gifted comedic actor, for he would play the buffoonish constable Verges in *Much Ado About Nothing*. Cowley must have been very close to this theatrical family, since two of his children were named as tributes to the Burbage brothers: a son named Cuthbert baptised in May 1597 and another called Richard in April the following year, though the records of St Leonard's parish poignantly record the latter's burial on 26 February 1603.

While Burbage edged ever closer to death, Heminges and Condell were faced with an agonising choice. Should they remain at his bedside or attend Cowley's funeral, to comfort his grieving family in the knowledge that Burbage's life could end at any moment? As the church was only paces away, and Cowley's family were living in the same street, they may have moved restlessly between St Leonard's and these two homes on that terrible day. If Burbage had been aware of Cowley's death, those tolling funereal church bells could only have reminded him that he was soon to follow his friend to that 'undiscovered country, from whose bourn/ No traveller returns'; words he had himself spoken to great applause, Hamlet being one of his most oft-praised roles. The effect on Heminges and Condell in particular would have been to prompt a realisation: the theatrical company they knew and had devoted most of their lives to, and which had included both Shakespeare and Burbage as founder members, was itself dying.

For those who watched that huge and seemingly uncontainable life ebbing away, perhaps the setting of Richard Burbage's last scene would have struck them as being at odds with the sometimes grim realities from which that much-lauded career had taken root. In many ways the Burbages' meteoric rise had mirrored the progress of the Shoreditch neighbourhood that they had made both their home and the centre of their business operations. Pieces of the puzzle that contribute to the complete picture of the First Folio's story were laid down in this very area, largely because the Burbage family had established itself there.

James Burbage had been an out-of-pocket joiner turned theatrical impresario, who had borrowed money from his brother-in-law John Brayne, a citizen and freeman of the Grocers' Company, to build the Theatre in 1576. He chose to locate his new business on the site of what was once the Augustinian priory of Holywell, between lands owned by the earls of Rutland and the boundary wall of Finsbury Fields, near what is now Liverpool Street Station. The priory's old barn was still standing and so James had built his playhouse leaning against the fragile timbers of its north-eastern corner, probably providing it with some much-needed stability in the process. A fourteen-sided polygonal structure, the Theatre stood seventy-two feet in diameter adjacent to what was once the priory's orchard. Though James's son, Cuthbert, would later boast that his father was 'the first builder of playhouses', the Theatre was not strictly London's first playhouse, since James's brother-in-law had constructed the Red Lion in Stepney, in the Whitechapel area, in 1567. A second theatre in Newington Butts, in what is present-day Elephant and Castle, had just preceded the Theatre in 1576. These were short-lived, however, and probably designed within pre-existing repurposed buildings. As the Theatre was the first permanent structure created specifically *as* a playhouse from its first conception, and had operated successfully over a long period (between 1576 and 1597), Cuthbert's claim is not entirely without credibility.

Where the Burbages led, others would soon follow. The very next year the Curtain playhouse was completed, just a little further south, abutting but slightly outside the priory site's perimeter, located just east of what is now Curtain Road. The area would therefore become associated with less sacred pastimes, the influx of playgoers bringing with it an increased demand for brothels, drinking houses and other places of ill repute. James Burbage himself maintained a somewhat dubious establishment on his own street, a 'tippling house' to serve the thirsty pleasure-seekers who came to sample the district's delights. When James and his family moved into the neighbourhood they, like others who frequented the parish, may have been drawn there by its cock-fighting arenas and the array of entertainments on offer in Finsbury Fields, with tennis matches, wrestling contests and archery being fashionable pursuits. Over the years fields laid aside for common public use were enclosed by landlords hoping to make a quick profit by turning the land over to sheep-grazing pastures, and the 'daily exercises' and communal games became limited to special feasts like St Bartholomew's Day. The sports lovers and archers were left to 'creep into bowling-alleys and ordinary dicing houses nearer home', as John Stow lamented in his *Survey of London*, where they frittered away their inheritances in gambling rooms and wasted their wages on 'unlawful games'. The area's changing fortunes seemed to be symbolised by the building of a 'smith's forge' over the site on which there had once stood a huge cross, towering over the crossroads between the northern end of the field and St Leonard's Church. When Stow produced his *Survey* in 1598 there was a 'continual building of tenements ... for the most part lately erected' through Holywell across the High Street and into Shoreditch which, well into the seventeenth century, were accompanied by the more impressive homes of merchants and other middle-class professionals, putting to shame the older buildings, which included a 'row of proper small houses, with gardens for poor decayed people'.

When Richard Burbage came of age as an actor, therefore, he had a ready-made stage to showcase his talents. By 1590 he was performing in plays under the auspices of one of the age's most influential theatrical patrons, Ferdinando Stanley, Lord Strange. He also appeared at the Rose playhouse on Bankside in Southwark, whose theatre manager was Philip Henslowe, when Strange's Men formed a brief coalition with a theatrical troupe patronised by Queen Elizabeth I's Lord Admiral, Charles Howard, later to become Earl of Nottingham. It was around this time that Burbage may have crossed paths with John Heminges, who had himself become enamoured of the theatrical life and joined Lord Strange's playing company before the end of 1593. Most likely the son of a

George Heminges, John was baptised on 25 November 1566 at St Peter de Witton in Droitwich, Worcestershire. He had arrived in London in 1578 to begin a nine-year apprenticeship with the Grocers' Company, during which time he undoubtedly acquired the financial skills, entrepreneurial nous and numerical dexterity that would serve him well as a future theatre manager. Completing his apprenticeship in April 1587, he became a 'freeman' of the City of London, able to exploit the full privileges of his profession and ready to take up gainful employment in his own right. But the theatre had his heart, and when an outbreak of the plague closed the playhouses in London from February 1593 the players at the Rose toured the provinces. Heminges joined them and was working alongside Henry Condell and Augustine Phillips, though it is not known if Burbage was among them, for his name is not recorded in the list of those granted a licence to travel.

Condell was ten years Heminges' junior and hailed from East Anglia. He was the son of a fishmonger named Robert Condell of St Peter Mancroft in Norwich, where he was baptised on 5 September 1576. His mother was Joan Yeomans from the Norwich market town of New Buckenham. Like Heminges, Condell probably came to London to train for a solid profession protected by a guild, for his uncles William and Humphrey Yeomans were both blacksmiths and owned a property in the parish of St Bride's in Fleet Street. After William died it is likely that Condell came to live with Humphrey in the Fleet Street residence, devoting himself to acting after the latter's death in 1594. That very year, following the demise of Lord Strange, an extraordinary opportunity presented itself. A new theatrical troupe was formed by no less illustrious a personage than Queen Elizabeth's I's Lord Chamberlain, Henry Carey, 1st Baron Hunsdon. While the monarch insisted on referring to him as her 'cousin', he was rumoured to have in fact been her half-brother, the product of an affair between her father Henry VIII and Mary Boleyn. The new playing company, formed under the patronage of one so close to the royal bloodline, was called the Chamberlain's Men and Burbage, Heminges, Condell, Shakespeare and Phillips, among other actors, rushed to become members. At this company's inception Burbage was one of eight equal sharers, which included Heminges and Shakespeare, taking a portion of the profits while shouldering some of the burden for the costs of managing the business. Condell acquired his shares some time later, probably in or not long after 1602.

Just two years into the Chamberlain's Men's operation, the company faced a crisis. The Theatre had been built on rented land and James Burbage had failed to agree a renewal of the lease with the puritanical landlord Giles Allen. With the lease due to expire in 1597, James took a huge gamble, sinking £1,000 – then a considerable sum – into the construction of a modern new indoor playhouse in the upmarket Blackfriars district of London. This would come to be known as the Blackfriars Theatre. But before the playhouse had even opened for its first performance the residents, led by the influential and indomitable noblewoman Lady Elizabeth Russell, mounted a campaign to ban the Chamberlain's Men from the site. Their anti-theatrical crusade was successful and from November 1596 the players were forbidden from using the Blackfriars Theatre. For Shakespeare that year was particularly catastrophic; he had lost his only son, Hamnet, in August at the age of eleven. This had occurred just two weeks after the death of the company's patron, Henry Carey. James Burbage died the following year. A story persists that the strain of losing his beloved new business enterprise was the cause of his swift demise.

By the end of 1597, therefore, Richard and Cuthbert Burbage had lost their father, the company's powerful patron, and two theatres, in the process inheriting crippling debts from the expense of building the Blackfriars Theatre. What happened next saw a radical shift in the playing company's workings and structure. The

Chamberlain's Men began to collaborate with an up-and-coming talent named Ben Jonson. Born on 11 June 1572, Jonson hailed from a Scottish family once based in Carlisle, his biological father having been a minister. He was 'posthumous born, a month after his father's decease' and 'brought up poorly', as he later confessed to the poet William Drummond. Yet Jonson's gifts were recognised at a young age and he was supported in his education by a family friend, possibly John Hoskins, who would become attached to the Middle Temple, or the renowned pedagogue and antiquary William Camden, who arranged for him to attend Westminster School, where Camden was himself an instructor. Jonson's mother's second husband was probably one Robert Brett who would become Master of the Tylers' and Bricklayers' Company. For Jonson, however, bricklaying was a profession, as he told Drummond, 'which he could not endure', though he had become an apprentice in the craft. He gravitated instead towards the Pembroke's Men at the Swan Theatre, which had opened in Southwark in 1595. Philip Henslowe, meanwhile, had embarked on something of an aggressive head-hunting mission to entice Jonson to the Lord Admiral's Men at the Rose playhouse, for the theatre proprietor's records show a payment to Jonson at the end of July 1597, and evidence of a play commissioned on 3 December of that year, for which 'he showed the plot unto the company'.

Jonson was not an easy man to get along with. Drummond recorded his somewhat narcissistic nature as 'a great lover and praiser of himself, a contemner and scorner of others, given rather to lose a friend than a jest'. He was a complex character, therefore, who could be by turns 'vindictive', intensely jealous, 'passionately kind and angry'. He was also given to overindulge in drink, 'which is one of the elements in which he liveth', noted Drummond, which enflamed his more negative traits. Hardly surprisingly, not long after he came to Henslowe's attention, Jonson entered into a feud with Gabriel Spencer, an actor at the Rose, and this may have caused tensions with the company's manager, for by the end of the next year Jonson had offered his play *Every Man In His Humour* to the Chamberlain's Men. Premiering in September 1598, it proved to be a hit and featured Shakespeare, Burbage, Heminges, Condell and Phillips among its 'principal comedians'. That was the very month in which Jonson had fatally stabbed Spencer, drawing a complaint from Henslowe that 'it is for me hard and heavy ... I have lost one of my company which hurteth me greatly, that is Gabriel, for he is slain ... by the hands of Benjamin Jonson', adding perhaps in spite, for Jonson was sensitive about his less than illustrious beginnings, a 'Bricklayer'.

Jonson escaped the death penalty, but his experience resulted in his conversion to Catholicism, having taken 'his religion by trust, of a priest who visited him in prison'. Though he formally returned to the Church of England, possibly around 1610, which he celebrated at his first communion as a restored Protestant by draining 'all the full cup of wine', William Drummond was cynical about the extent to which Jonson had left behind his Catholic proclivities, for he was 'For any religion, as being versed in both'. Jonson's religious sympathies would thrust him into a sometimes clandestine world of Catholic ministers, preachers, academics and authors; contacts he would maintain for most of his life and which would see him becoming part of a literary network whose traces are evident in the First Folio, determining, at least in part, the character of its preliminary matter in ways that contoured the public image of its subject, William Shakespeare.

In the winter following the Chamberlain's Men's mounting of Jonson's play, the Burbages and the players took the momentous decision to dismantle the beams of the Theatre and transport them from Shoreditch to Bankside, in what was then the County of Surrey, to create a larger open-air playhouse which they would name the Globe. Even before it opened, the company was planning its next partnership with Jonson, with whom its members were

keen to work again. Capitalising on the success of his ingenious and ribald brand of 'humours' comedy, they quickly staged a sequel, *Every Man Out of His Humour*, which was first performed in 1599, though this time without Shakespeare in the cast list. This would begin a long and fruitful collaboration between the one-time apprentice bricklayer and the playing company. That was the year in which the Chamberlain's Men's new home venue, the Globe Theatre, opened. By this point the company was operating under a new patron, George Carey, 2nd Baron Hunsdon, who had succeeded his father, Henry, as the company's protector after the

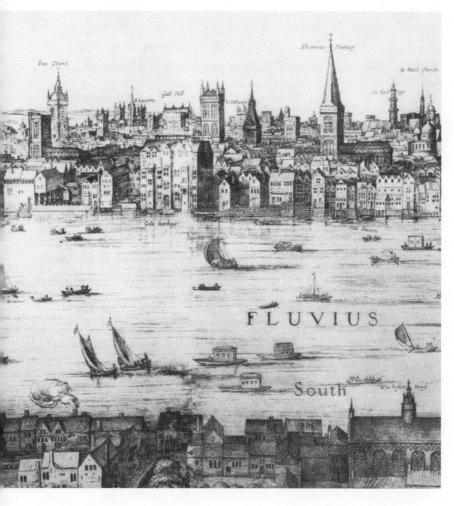

Detail from Claes Visscher's panorama of London from 1616, showing St Paul's Cathedral and two London theatres, including the Globe, which was opened in 1599.

latter's death. Richard Burbage and his brother Cuthbert became majority stakeholders in the Globe venture, establishing an unprecedented business model in which they secured a joint 50 per cent ownership of the playhouse, while five other sharers, including Shakespeare, Heminges and Phillips, held a 10 per cent portion each, becoming part-owners of the theatre. This rose to 12.5 per cent when one of the sharers, the actor William Kemp, sold his share and left the company in 1599. Cuthbert, three years older than his brother, remained a silent partner. Not for him the actor's life.

By the time the players passed to the patronage of James I on his accession in 1603, the formal licence granted on 19 May of that year to the newly dubbed King's Men enshrined the hierarchical structure of the troupe: William Shakespeare's name appeared first, followed by Richard Burbage, Augustine Phillips, John Heminges and Henry Condell. Richard Cowley was also included among the company's eight leading members. It was the beneficence of the king that ensured that the players were able, finally, to reacquire the Blackfriars Theatre in 1608, which had been leased from 1600 to the Children of the Chapel Royal, the monarch's choristers, who used the playhouse as their training space but who also functioned as a troupe of child actors for whom Ben Jonson had written successful plays. A string of ill-judged productions between 1605 and 1608, which satirised James I's court, including one by Jonson, so infuriated the king that he cancelled their licence. The Burbage brothers, Shakespeare, Heminges and Condell became members of the lucrative new Blackfriars syndicate.

For Burbage this meant his control of a significant portion of the theatrical landscape was consolidated by his continuing, and highly fruitful, collaboration with Shakespeare which provided him with a stream of show-stopping meaty roles. Long before his death he had become a household name, lauded on public stages and among England's nobility. Ben Jonson had praised him as the 'best actor' in his play *Bartholomew Fair*, and in his *Masque of Christmas* in 1616 had presented the goddess of love, Venus, as a tire-woman (someone who attended to the hair-dressing and wigs of wealthy women) who boasted suggestively 'Master Burbage has been about and about with me, and so has old Master Heminges too'. When the court gossip John Chamberlain related an argument between Sir

Edward Coke and his wife Elizabeth in May 1617, he commented jocularly that she 'declaimed bitterly against him, and so carried herself that divers said Burbage could not have acted better'. One of the most evocative contemporary portraits, published in 1614, offered a thinly veiled tribute to Burbage through the itemisation of the characteristics fittingly belonging to 'An Excellent Actor':

> Whatsoever is commendable in the grave Orator, is most exquisitely perfect in him; for by a full and significant action of body, he charms our attention: sit in a full Theatre, and you will think you see so many lines drawn from the circumference of so many ears, whiles the actor is the centre ... for what we see him personate, we think truly done before us ... He adds grace to the poet's labours: for what in the poet is but ditty, in him is both ditty and music ... I observe, of all men living, a worthy actor in one kind is the strongest motive of affection that can be: for when he dies, we cannot be persuaded any man can do his parts like him.

This would prove prescient. Burbage was now dying indeed, that sweet music that had so graced the 'poet's labours' fading and soon to be silenced for ever. As he looked around him, at the accoutrements of wealth and status he had accumulated, he must have reflected on how far he had come. His home had certainly contained wonders enough to catch a thief's eye, for a few years before it had been broken into and such items stolen as a sumptuous carpet worth six shillings and eight pence, forty pieces of pewter valued at twenty shillings, 'holland aprons', laced cuffs, laced handkerchiefs and several parcels of linen estimated to have cost twenty shillings, among other prized possessions. By the time death approached, he had acquired over £300 worth of land; a sizeable estate.

Burbage's life formed a familiar pattern for many of the age's theatrical luminaries; from relatively humble beginnings to considerable wealth. Before his death Shakespeare had, like Heminges and Condell, acquired 'gentleman' status, which he augmented with a grand house named New Place in his native Stratford-upon-Avon, a property in London's Blackfriars, just paces from the Blackfriars Theatre, and vast tracts of land in Stratford and the Welcombe fields, among other properties. Heminges had built a splendid 'fair house' on the grounds of the Globe Theatre and managed a 'tap-house' or drinking tavern attached to the playhouse. Condell had also made some smart decisions, one of them being to marry one Elizabeth Smart, daughter of the wealthy John Smart who had acquired gentry status. In addition to the enviable dowry brought by this match, Condell inherited a share of his uncle Humphrey's home in Fleet Street when his son, Humphrey Yeomans junior, died in 1603. Thereafter Condell would doggedly pursue the shares that were divided between other Yeomans kinfolk until he acquired most, if not all, of the property, to which was attached a popular local tavern named the Queen's Head. He soon became something of a property magnate, acquiring 'freehold messuages, lands, tenements, and hereditaments' on the Strand 'and elsewhere in the County of Middlesex'; more than one property in St Bride's in Fleet Street, where his tavern was located, close to the upmarket hub of the legal profession, the Inns of Court; 'messuages, houses and places' situated in the Blackfriars district, next to the Blackfriars Theatre, and close to the Globe Theatre; and a pleasant country residence in the parish of Fulham in Middlesex.

Aside from Shoreditch, Heminges and Condell were connected by their acquisition of property in St Mary's, Aldermanbury, London, where they both lived for much of their careers. Both were invested in the area, becoming community leaders of note as administrators and churchwardens in the parish. Condell had probably looked to put down roots there because Heminges had moved to the neighbourhood, having married Rebecca Knell in St

Mary's Church in 1588. Both actors would baptise sons named William in the same church, possibly in honour of Shakespeare, though it was a common name in Condell's family. The two Williams would survive into adulthood. Most of their siblings, however, would not be so blessed. Of the Heminges' fourteen known children, only half survived infancy, while the Condells would see only three of their nine children living into their adult years.

Shakespeare may have witnessed much of the drama of his fellow actors' lives – their joys and their heartaches – unfolding in St Mary's, for in the early 1600s he moved to the neighbouring parish of St Olave's, taking up residence in a property among a row of 'diverse fair houses' in Silver Street belonging to the French Huguenots Christopher and Marie Mountjoy, who operated a shop below his lodgings that specialised in the making of head-dresses. In 1612 Shakespeare would state that he had known the couple for 'the space of ten years or thereabouts', indicating his long-standing association with the district. St Mary's and Silver Street were part of the administrative area of London designated as Cripplegate Ward, and Shakespeare had only to step out of his rooms, on the corner of Silver Street and Muggle Street (present-day Monkwell Square), and walk east through Silver Street and into Adle Street to find himself at the intersection of Aldermanbury, at the back of St Mary's Church, its tall crenellated cross-capped clock tower looming above him.

While it is known that Shakespeare probably moved to Silver Street from the parish of St Helen's Bishopsgate, where he was living in the late 1590s, it is less certain where he was lodging when he was building his career in its – literally – earliest stages. If we are to believe John Aubrey, who compiled a series of manuscript accounts recording *Brief Lives* of notable figures in the early 1680s, he was living in Shoreditch, perhaps with or close to the Burbages. The area's two theatres in the early 1590s, and its placement at the social crux between the illicit and the up-and-coming, made it a popular base for actors. The playwright Christopher Marlowe had resided in nearby Norton Folgate, just south of Shoreditch, and round the corner from Holywell Street was Hog Lane, the street on which the actor Gabriel Spencer lived before he was killed in a duel by Ben Jonson in nearby Hoxton Fields in 1598. This may have therefore seemed an attractive base for Shakespeare, offering an opportunity to mix with other up-and-coming actors and playwrights, while forging deeper bonds with the Burbage family. Aubrey's source for the playwright's residency was the Shoreditch-born William Beeston, whom he interviewed around August 1681 when Beeston was in his seventies and living in Hog Lane. Beeston's father, from whom he had inherited his Shoreditch property, was Christopher Beeston, who had acted with the Chamberlain's Men in the later 1590s, though he is not listed in the First Folio's list of 'Principal Actors'. He was, however, included, alongside Shakespeare and his fellows in the cast list for Jonson's *Every Man in His Humour*. Before moving to the Earl of Worcester's Men around 1600, Beeston had been apprenticed to Augustine Phillips who had left him the generous sum of 'thirty shillings in gold' in his will, the very amount he left to Shakespeare and Condell. According to William Beeston, Shakespeare resisted the seductions of the area, for though he 'lived in Shoreditch', he explained, 'he was not a company keeper' and 'wouldn't be debauched'. Not everyone was so convinced that Shakespeare's lifestyle was without adventures of a more 'debauched' nature. According to the diarist John Manningham, in a racy anecdote recorded on 13 March 1602:

Upon a time when Burbage played Richard 3rd, there was a citizen grew so far in liking with him, that before she went from the play she appointed him to come that night unto her by the name of Richard the 3rd. Shakespeare overhearing their conclusion went

before, was entertained, and at his fame ere Burbage came. Then
message being brought that Richard the 3rd was at the door,
Shakespeare caused return to be made that William the Conqueror
was before Richard the 3rd.

Whether or not this tale of the exploits of a somewhat rakish pair
of actors is true, it points to a wider perception of the camaraderie
between Shakespeare and Burbage. We can only speculate on the
significance of Burbage's decision to name one of his daughters
Juliet, but it is likely that he called his son William, baptised in St
Leonard's in November 1616, as a memorial to his friend
Shakespeare just over six months after the playwright's death; a
legible mark of affection left in an official record of a parish
community that may have been the stage for the flowering of the
relationship between these two men.

Another kind of collaboration between Burbage and Shakespeare
may also have been the result of an early Shoreditch connection.
The land adjacent to that on which the Theatre had been
constructed was in the possession of Edward Manners, 3rd Earl of
Rutland, at the time of its building. It had been leased to his grandfather Thomas Manners, the 1st Earl, by the Crown. Eventually
the Rutland inheritance came into the possession of Francis
Manners, the 6th Earl, who commissioned the two actors to fashion an impresa – an armorial emblem with a motto used in
tournaments – for the Accession Day tilt of March 1613.
Shakespeare appears to have designed it and devised the motto,
while Burbage, famed for being a talented artist, was paid 'for
painting and making it'. Francis Manners would almost certainly
have encountered Shakespeare's plays, and Burbage's stellar roles,
at the nearby Curtain Theatre, as well as at the Globe playhouse on
Bankside. He and Henry Wriothesley, the Earl of Southampton, to
whom Shakespeare would dedicate his bestselling narrative poems
Venus and Adonis (1593) and *The Rape of Lucrece* (1594), often

frequented plays together, as witnessed by Rowland Whyte, servant to Sir Robert Sidney, who reported on 11 October 1599 that
'My Lord Southampton and Lord Rutland come not to the court
… they pass away the time in London merely in going to plays
every day'.

These may all have been happy memories for Burbage, one of
the three King's Men to whom Shakespeare had bequeathed twenty-six shillings and eight pence in his will for the purpose of buying
mourning rings, as he was dying. If he had cemented a pledge with
Heminges, Condell and Shakespeare over the publication of the
latter's plays in one grand volume, we will never know if his final
moments were plagued by guilt over his not having fulfilled this
covenant with his friends. But the bond between the players was
not itself dead. As he neared his end, it would have been some
comfort to have his wife, brother, the King's Men's copyist Ralph
Crane, and his actor comrades Nicholas Tooley and Richard
Robinson beside him, and Heminges and Condell looking in on
him whenever they could. He must also have known that he would
soon be buried in a parish church whose graves and monuments
were a material witness to the theatrical community that had gathered around the Burbage family in Shoreditch, a testament to their
intertwined lives as actors. There he would join his father, James
Burbage, his dear friend and colleague Richard Cowley, and the
great Richard Tarlton, one of the most celebrated comic actors of
the Tudor era, who was buried there in 1588. Tarlton may have
been a kind of mentor to Richard Burbage, for he had acted in the
Shoreditch Theatre and lived in Holywell Street. Lodged eternally
in the same sacred space was the ill-fated Gabriel Spencer, as well
as Burbage's fellow actor in the King's Men William Sly, the latter
one of the earlier members of the Chamberlain's Men and an original King's Men sharer in the Blackfriars syndicate, having possibly
joined the playing company as far back as 1594. Buried in 1608,
Sly had left Cuthbert Burbage the personal gifts of his sword and

his hat in his will and was an executor of Augustine Phillips' estate. St Leonard's would come to be known as 'the actors' church'.

Richard Burbage died on 13 March 1619 and was buried three days later. When his demise became public knowledge the reaction was quite unlike the relative silence that had followed news of William Shakespeare's death. It was as if a pall of black mourning-cloth had been thrown over the entire city of London. An outpouring of grief followed, so unprecedented for an actor that it even threatened to overshadow the funeral rites of Queen Anne, who had died eleven days before Burbage, on 2 March. One elegist remarked that 'in London is not one eye dry:/The deaths of men who act our Queens and Kings/Are now more mourned than are the real things', adding that 'The Queen is dead! … Queens of the Theatre are much more worth'. For this elegist the extremity of national sorrow had reached proportions that were absurd:

Dick Burbage was their mortal God on earth.
When he expires, lo! all lament the man,
But where's the grief should follow good Queen Anne?

Not even Edward Alleyn, Burbage's theatrical rival at the Admiral's Men who would die in 1626, would be lauded with such an intensity of elegiac pathos on his own account as Burbage, though both were sometimes remembered together. Richard Baker, in his *Chronicle of the Kings of England*, for example, described them as 'two such actors, as no age must ever look to see the like', and in a later work, the *Theatrum Redivivum*, called them 'the best actors of our time'. The public display of grief following Burbage's death, however, was in a league of its own. It seemed as if every actor, playwright, historian or poet of note was vying to out-elegise his competitors. Fellow playwright Thomas Middleton painted an apocalyptic picture of Burbage's death as 'a visible eclipse of playing'. The historian Edmund Camden's epitaph read poignantly and simply 'Exit Burbage'. Thomas Bancroft, a contemporary of Burbage who may have seen him perform, emphasised his ability to embody the emotional states of his characters, marvelling at how he 'sent each passion to his heart' to 'languish in a scene of love, then look/Pallid for fear'; or, when taking on the role of a blood-thirsty revenger, 'Recall his blood' to his undying grudge; or, when accosted by enemies, 'Grow big with wrath, and make his buttons fly'. Richard Flecknoe, in his *Treatise of the English Stage*, referred to him as a kind of early method actor, 'a delightful Proteus, so wholly transforming himself into his part, and putting off himself with his clothes, as he never (not so much as in the tiring-house) assumed himself again until the play was done'. Perhaps in recollection of Burbage's close association with Shakespeare, Flecknoe, in a later work, called the great actor 'the soul of the stage', possibly echoing Ben Jonson's description of Shakespeare in the First Folio as the 'Soul of the Age!' One of the most arresting tributes to have survived is probably by dramatist John Fletcher and captures the power of Burbage's collaboration with Shakespeare in a heart-thumping allusion to his role as Hamlet:

> Oft have I seen him leap into the grave
> Suiting the person which he seemed to have
> Of a sad lover with so true an eye
> That there (I would have sworn) he meant to die.
> Oft have I seen him play this part in jest,
> So lively, that spectators and the rest
> Of his sad crew, whilst he but seemed to bleed,
> Amazed, thought he then had died indeed …
> How did his speech become him, and his pace,
> Suit with his speech, and every action grace
> Them both alike, whilst not a word did fall,
> Without just weight, to ballast it with all.

From far and wide the plaudits and elegies came pouring in, recall-
ing Burbage's oratorical skills, the emotive punchiness of his roles
and, above all, his ability to embody dramatic characters as if he
had lived a lifetime in their shoes. Just as he had moved audiences
to tears during his stellar career, his last leave-taking from the stage
of life prompted the affections of London's populace. No other
actor was so mourned, so loved, so missed.

When John Heminges and Henry Condell stood before the
freshly dug graves of two senior King's Men actors in Shoreditch,
they would have felt a more personal coalescence of loss. In
Burbage and Cowley they had not just buried colleagues, but
friends. What did they see when they surveyed the living
members of the company? Or rather, who did they not see? Since
they knew the make-up of the company and its history, it is very
likely that they supplied the twenty-six 'names of the Principal
Actors in all these Plays' that would be included in the First
Folio's preliminaries. The first nine names on this list – William
Shakespeare, Richard Burbage, John Heminges, Augustine
Phillips, William Kemp, Thomas Pope, George Bryan, Henry
Condell and William Sly – represent, near enough, the original
sharers at the inception of the Chamberlain's Men in 1594, save
that Condell graduated from his apprenticeship in 1595 and did
not become a sharer until later. The first six names represent the
first group of investors in the Globe venture in 1598–9. From
this founding group none but Heminges and Condell were still
alive.

With so many of their fellow actors gone, how could Heminges
and Condell not reflect on their own mortality and their status as
the last living link to the younger Shakespeare, to the totality of
all the playwright had been from the earliest years of his career to
his final days? They knew his works better than anyone. They
understood something of the conditions in which his plays were
originally conceived, and would have recalled when and why parts

of his dramatic works were censored. They would have remembered the bitter lash of discovering that his plays had been printed piratically or in less than satisfactory editions, and had a sense of when and how Shakespeare may have revised parts of his oeuvre for revivals or royal command performances. They would also have appreciated his personal preferences with regards to the expression of his characters on stage, and recollected something of his plays' intricate publishing histories, including at least some of the identities of those to whom rights to print selected early works were sold or leased. Heminges and Condell must have been aware that without them a collected volume of Shakespeare's plays would not have been all that it could be, may not even have been possible. Who else could they trust to oversee such an important project? They were the last hope for Shakespeare's Book; the breathing, feeling archives of the dramatist's working practice, of the circumstances that shaped his writing, of the humanity in his words and, most crucially, of his hopes for his own legacy. It was now or never.

But there were more practical issues they had to deal with in the immediate future. No matter how deep the loss with which they were dealing, and regardless of any plans they may have been making to alleviate this with some commemorative tribute to Shakespeare, they would have to put their personal feelings aside for the good of the company. By this point Heminges and Condell were devoting themselves increasingly to the management of the King's Men. They had to ensure the troupe's archive of authorial papers, prompt books and individual quarto editions of previously printed plays was well kept; liaise with the Lord Chamberlain to schedule performances at court; submit new plays to the Master of the Revels for approval; oversee the company's finances; receive payments from the Treasurer of the Chamber for court productions; and distribute profits to their fellow co-sharers. They would also have been aware that they had to find a way to steer their troupe through this present crisis and into its next phase, without its star actor, even as the rest of London's theatre-going populace and, as it would turn out, the publishing community seemed unwilling to let him go.

'The loss of my old acquaintance'

The First Folio's Patrons and the Courtiers' War

In the tumultuous aftermath of the loss of Richard Burbage, the King's Men were facing a new challenge. Their livelihood was now being put at risk due to a ban on public playing enforced as a consequence of Queen Anne's death. On 19 March John Chamberlain, who loved to collect the kind of racy and scandalous gossip that was plentiful around the bustling public meeting places of St Paul's Cathedral, close to his own home, wrote to Sir Dudley Carleton, King James I's ambassador to the Netherlands, to explain that the 'queen's funeral is put off till the 29th of the next month, to the great hinderance of our players, which are forbidden to play so long as her body is above ground; one special man among them, Burbage, is lately dead'.

The next day Carleton heard that Anne's funeral would cost £24,000, which was £6,000 more than Queen Elizabeth I's ceremony and considerably greater than the cost of Prince Henry's obsequies, completed with a still immodestly colossal cost of £15,600. But before the appointed date of the funeral Carleton received word that it would be postponed 'perhaps longer, unless they can find out money faster, for the Master of the Wardrobe is loath to wear his own credit threadbare', referring to the spiralling costs of decking out the entire funeral entourage in mourning attire. The late queen's female courtiers had grown 'weary of watching' her body, which lay in state in Denmark House on the Strand, as was the custom, while a constant stream of mourners filed past to pay their respects 'all day long', bringing 'more concourse than when she was living'. There was talk of melting down her golden plate, and an inventory was made of her jewels 'and other movables' – with four carts of valuables conveyed from Denmark House to Greenwich for the purpose – to 'sell or pawn diverse of them to good value' in hopes that turning her possessions into ready cash would hasten preparations for the funeral, which had grown 'beyond proportion' in expense.

April came and went, but the funeral was 'still deferred', since there was 'no money to put the king and prince's servants in mourning [attire], as intended'. A further cause of delay was the king's failing health. Languishing from kidney stones, he was now so 'weak and faint' that John Chamberlain was already imagining 'what a loss we should have if God should take him from us'. James I used this as an opportunity to examine his courtiers and hangers-on closely, appointing his spies to determine who 'during the king's sickness ... carried their heads high' and who indulged in 'all manner of feasting and jollity' when they should have been praying for his recovery. This proved to be a pivotal moment. Step forward the rising star of the royal court: George Villiers, Marquess of Buckingham. The political culture into which the First Folio was born was, in very tangible ways, shaped by the tensions between this up-and-coming courtier and Sir William Herbert, 3rd Earl of Pembroke.

William's birth is recorded as being on 8 April 1580, four years before that of his brother, Philip, who was born on 10 October 1584. They were descended from a powerful and much-celebrated Protestant dynasty. Their father was Henry Herbert, 2nd Earl of

Pembroke, and their mother was the authoress Mary Sidney, sister of the poet and soldier Sir Philip Sidney, who had become the stuff of legend following his death defending the Netherlands against Spanish forces at the Battle of Zutphen in 1586. Philip Herbert had been named after his famous uncle and had inherited a proclivity towards the active life, nurturing a love of the outdoors and hunting. It had been said of him that he 'pretended to no other qualifications than to understand horses and dogs very well', and this endeared him to James I who, sharing with him a passion for hunting, was willing to accommodate Philip's bouts of explosive violence towards, and ill-judged railings against, other courtiers. In 1605 the king had elevated him to 1st Earl of Montgomery and awarded him a post of significant trust, appointing him his Gentleman of the Bedchamber. By the end of 1617 Philip had been made Keeper of Westminster Palace and St James's Park.

Philip was less politically minded than his brother, and avoided the factionalism that would mark William's more turbulent career. Becoming one of the age's most prolific patrons of literature, the arts and drama, William Herbert may have been responsible for convincing King James, after his accession to the English throne in 1603, to take over the patronage of the Chamberlain's Men. James was instantly drawn to the handsome, highly educated and accomplished Herbert, shocking witnesses by allowing the courtier to kiss him publicly on his face. That very year the king had appointed both brothers Gentlemen of the Privy Chamber and made William Keeper of Clarendon Forest. From October to December the newly enthroned monarch moved the royal court to William's home, Wilton House in Wiltshire, where the theatrical troupe, the newly dubbed King's Men, including Shakespeare, performed for the king, the entertainments overseen by William Herbert himself. Further performances followed at Hampton Court Palace on 30 December and 1 January 1604, six in all, with John Heminges receiving payment for 'his pains and expenses of himself and the rest of his Company'. Additional payments were made to the players in their capacities as Grooms of the Chamber, 'waiting and attending on his Majesty's service by commandment', a benefit of royal patronage which made them insiders in court circles.

Thereafter William Herbert's rise to prominence had been swift. In September 1611 he was granted a place on the Privy Council, the body of royal advisers and politicians who helped steer England's ship of state, and was appointed Lord Chamberlain on 23 December 1615, a position he had long coveted. The latter was one of three principal posts in King James I's court. The Lord Steward oversaw the running of the royal household and court; the Master of the Horse supervised the royal stable; and the Lord Chamberlain had a range of responsibilities which included administration of the Royal Wardrobe, supervision of the Officers of the King's Armoury, the appointment of the king's servants and private retinue, the management of the Royal Chapel, the reception of ambassadors and visiting dignitaries, and the charge of the Office of the Works, which regulated construction and renovation projects funded by the Crown. The Lord Chamberlain also managed royal progresses, court entertainments and masques, including the King's Men's own appearances at court during holiday seasons, feast days and command performances for royal, civic and ambassadorial events. With a direct line of influence extending to the Office of the Revels, which controlled the licensing of plays, he was a tremendously important figure for those involved in the theatre industry.

It was originally Sir William Herbert who had backed the out-of-pocket would-be courtier George Villiers as an attempt to challenge the supremacy of his rival at court, Robert Carr, the Earl of Somerset. Pembroke believed Carr had thwarted his own promotion, having initially beaten him to the office of Lord Chamberlain in 1614. Herbert had responded by using his growing friendship with Queen Anne to push Villiers forward. Born on

28 August 1592 in Leicestershire, Villiers had been struggling to integrate into high society following the death of his father Sir George Villiers in 1606, and was only twenty-three when Pembroke lent him some fine clothing so that he could draw the eyes of the nobility at court. The intention had been to create a pro-Herbert faction by ensuring that the king's attraction to the handsome Villiers' mesmeric charms would wean him from his reliance on Carr. While not a particularly adept scholar, the young courtier was confident, sometimes to the point of brashness, a dextrous fencer and accomplished horseman. James I was putty in his hands.

By the end of April 1615 Pembroke had succeeded in convincing James to appoint Villiers Groom of the Royal Bedchamber. Thereafter the latter became a favourite of the king and a succession of honours followed. His appointment as Master of the Horse, a coveted induction into the venerable Order of the Garter, and the Lord Lieutenancy of Buckingham augmented his natural graces in 1616. Early the following year, he was elevated to Earl of Buckingham, which he celebrated in high style in lavish court entertainments devised by Ben Jonson. Thereafter his athletic physique and his skills as a graceful dancer would ensure that he became an ever more regular participant in royal entertainments and masques created by, among other authors and artists commissioned by the Crown, Jonson and his collaborator Inigo Jones, the celebrated architect and designer of dramatic sets and costumes for the court's most spectacular theatrical projects.

By the start of 1618 Villiers had been made Marquess of Buckingham, effectively becoming the Herbert brothers' social superior. During the turbulent early months of 1619, following Queen Anne's death and the king's sickness, Villiers had so endeared himself to James that he was given 'a portion' of the revenues from the sale of the late queen's treasures, along with the Keepership of Denmark House on the Strand and an annual stipend of £1,200, 'for his good service and tender care of the king in his last sickness'. The new marquess's magnetic charisma was also having an effect on other members of the royal family, including the king's son, Charles. '[The] prince and Buckingham grow very friendly', one gossip-monger noticed; a fact that would have a decisive impact on the political arena in a manner which would come to leave a clear trace on the First Folio.

All this while, the Earl of Pembroke, himself suffering ailing health, could only look on as he and his brother, Philip, were displaced by the Marquess of Buckingham in the king's affections. That year the cracks began to show in the relationship between Pembroke and Villiers. When the latter attempted to install one of his own clients in the post of Groom Porter to the king, Pembroke was furious. This office, he believed, was 'in his gift' as Lord Chamberlain, and he felt Villiers' attempt to grant it 'to a follower of his' was an encroachment on his own privilege. Buckingham bit back, accusing Herbert of 'malice' and insisted he had the right to dispose of the position as he saw fit, in consultation with the king, taking this opposition to his will 'unkindly'. James tried to appease Herbert, protesting that he meant to do him 'no wrong'. For Pembroke, however, this seemed like an attempt to dilute the authority of the Lord Chamberlainship, which had cost him much labour in the acquisition and was a role he could ill afford to lose.

Both in the run-up to and during the printing of the First Folio numerous attempts would be made to divest Herbert of this important post. If a rumour circulating in 1617, that he would be granted the office of Lord Admiral with the understanding that he relinquish the role of Lord Chamberlain, was based on fact, he had rejected the offer. Between 1618 and 1619 Herbert was touted as a potential candidate for the lucrative office of Lord Treasurer. He again made no motion to secure the post, stating that he was 'nothing fond of it unless he might leave his place [of Lord Chamberlain] to his brother [the Earl of] Montgomery'. Indeed, so insistent was he that his brother succeed him in the office that he continued to refuse the Treasurer's post even when the Mastership of the Horse, another of the pre-eminent offices in the royal household, was thrown in as an added incentive early the following year. When it was suggested that his friend James Hay, Viscount Doncaster, should take over the Chamberlainship in his place, giving him some measure of influence over the appointment, Pembroke still resisted. As John Chamberlain noted, 'It is said the Earl of Pembroke is loath to remove unless his brother Montgomery may succeed him.'

This would all have been good news for the King's Men who had cultivated strong ties with the Earl of Pembroke and who would have been thrown into turmoil with the induction of a new Lord Chamberlain. At a time of uncertainty and jostling over the Chamberlainship, John Heminges must have been reminded of the theatrical troupe's reliance on Pembroke when, no doubt with some relief, he was able to claim on 'behalf of himself and the rest of his Fellows, the King's Majesty's players upon the Lord Chamberlain's warrant' seventy-three pounds, six shillings and eight pence owed to them for eight plays performed before the king during the Christmas season the previous year. This would have been a welcome cash injection during the closure of the theatres.

The players' agony came to an end on 13 May as Anne was finally led to her burial. Some of the onlookers, however, did not judge the ceremony worth the wait. 'The procession at the Queen's funeral was very dull,' wrote John Chamberlain to Dudley Carleton. This was despite the fact that the queen's effigy had been laid out on a fabulous octagonal catafalque, festooned with flags and banners bearing vividly coloured armorial crests, boasting a huge pyramid supported by eight Corinthian columns, topped with a glistening crown finial. The hearse was drawn on a chariot by six horses, Prince Charles riding in state before it and Aletheia Howard,

Countess of Arundel, following behind as chief mourner, with 280 poor women trailing along in their wake. The procession, with its languid entourage, was a 'drawling, tedious sight', the mourners 'apparelled all alike', shuffling and 'laggering [that is, lagging] all along, even tired with the length of the way and weight of their clothes'. The ladies of the court struggled to keep up the pace, heaving along the twelve yards of broadcloth that the College of Heralds – the institution responsible for managing the funerals of the elite of Renaissance society – demanded they wear. The countesses fared worse. Their elevated station meant they had to drag sixteen yards of mourning cloth. As if the whole affair was not depressing enough, one poor spectator was killed by a large stone, which had dropped onto his head after breaking off the gargantuan crest and motto adorning Northampton House.

The dullness and despondency that attended Anne's funeral served only to highlight the contrasting strength of emotion ignited by Richard Burbage's death. How strange it must have felt to the King's Men to return to their profession without their principal player and friend; and no less strange for his admiring audiences. When the ban on playing was lifted, one of the first productions the King's Men mounted was a revival of *Pericles*, which many scholars believe Shakespeare co-authored with George Wilkins. First performed around 1607–8, it had quickly become a popular play thanks largely to the magnetic performance of Burbage. Just how popular can be seen in the pamphlet *Pimlico, or Run Redcap*, issued in 1609, in which the sight of a large crowd is compared to those who 'swarm' to 'a new play' as if 'all these/ Came to see … *Pericles*'. It was still highly regarded in 1613, when it was mentioned in the prologue to Robert Tailor's play *The Hog Hath Lost His Pearl*, in which the players, hoping to avoid being 'pelted … /With apples, eggs, or stones' by a dissatisfied audience, craved their 'gentle sufferance', voicing their hopes that 'if it prove so happy as to please,/We'll say 'tis fortunate like *Pericles*'. Wilkins himself cashed in on the play's success by releasing a narrative account called *The Painful Adventures of Pericles Prince of Tyre* in 1608, in which he boasted that it was 'by the King's Majesty's Players excellently presented'.

Originally, the character of Pericles had been penned as a vehicle for Burbage's talents. The role itself has 570 lines, about 260 lines more than the next longest part in the play. In the new production Burbage's role – along with his shares in the King's Men and many of his other leading parts, including Hamlet – was taken over by Joseph Taylor. His first royal command performance, which would see him step into the part of Pericles, took place on 20 May 1619, during a sumptuous feast and entertainments at court, which began in the queen's bedchamber, where the guests were treated to a musical interlude with an Irish harp and viol. The poetess Aemilia Lanyer delighted the audience by 'excellently singing and playing on her lute'. The proceedings continued in the king's Great Chamber where 'they went to see the play of *Pericles King of Tyre* which lasted till 2 o'clock'. The performance must have dragged on somewhat, for after two acts the production was paused so that the noble guests and diplomats in attendance could refresh themselves with sweetmeats, wine and ale, after which 'the play did begin anew'. The courtiers that day were still wearing black mourning garments, in memory of the queen. They had nevertheless been content to throw themselves into the festivities. The Earl of Pembroke, however, was mourning another. He excused himself and left the revel-makers while, in a dark and pensive mood, he sat down to write a letter to Viscount Doncaster, the ambassador to Germany, in which he confessed that 'even now all the company are at the play, which I being tender-hearted, could not endure to see so soon after the loss of my old acquaintance Burbage'.

Homage to Richard Burbage may also have been the motivation for the plays included on a shortlist of potential royal performances ahead of the Christmas season of 1619–20. The Master of the

Revels, Sir George Buc, almost certainly compiled this list in consultation with the King's Men, and among those under consideration were Thomas Kyd's perennially popular tale of bloody revenge *The Spanish Tragedy*; Ben Jonson's comedy of greed and hubris *Volpone*; a dramatic work by John Fletcher and Francis Beaumont, entitled *Philaster*; and Shakespeare's *Hamlet*, *The Two Noble Kinsmen*, *The Winter's Tale* and the second part of *Henry IV*, which was listed under the alternative title 'Second part of Falstaff'. While this latter title drew attention to the crowd-pleasingly anarchic character Falstaff, who helped make *Henry IV, Part 1* arguably Shakespeare's most popular dramatic work during his lifetime, *Henry IV, Part 2* was less popular, and Buc noted that it had not been 'played these 7 years'; its last performance probably being during the 1612–13 court season.

Hamlet, the *Henry IV* plays, *The Spanish Tragedy* and *Volpone* were referred to frequently, both during Burbage's lifetime and posthumously in elegies and other kinds of writing, as containing roles in which he particularly excelled or which had captured the public imagination. The *Henry IV* plays, in which he played the roguish Prince Hal, were alluded to in numerous letters and other documents of the period, with Falstaff having become something of a household name among court wits thanks to his humorous antics. Taken together with the decision to stage *Pericles*, which featured one of Burbage's most celebrated parts, just weeks after his death, it might plausibly be argued that the tear in the cultural fabric caused by the loss of this powerful theatrical personality led to a resurgence of interest both in the plays he had raised to the status of classics as well as in the authors – such as Shakespeare, Jonson, Beaumont, Fletcher and Kyd – whose words in his mouth created that unique stage magic that had so impressed itself on tens of thousands of spectators during his spectacular career.

At the forefront of these we must place Shakespeare. Indeed, when the prolific poet John Davies of Hereford had declared rapturously in a published poem of 1603 'Players, I love ye', he added the initials of Shakespeare and Burbage together beside this statement, repeating this specific identification in a later poem of 1611 in which he praised players for being 'mirrors' of the times 'by their acting Arts'. Shakespeare and Burbage were seen as a powerful team both during and after their lifetimes. As one scholar eloquently expressed it, 'In the characters Shakespeare wrote for him Richard Burbage attained his greatest glory. Men did not realise that Shakespeare was dead while Burbage lived.'

The King's Men had experienced two kinds of shock in 1619, which circulated, as life's grandest events always do, around the polarities of death and love. They had attended the funerals of two senior fellow actors within five days in the parish of St Leonard's, and Heminges would lose his wife Rebecca in September of that year. They had also witnessed the unprecedented outpouring of grief and affection that attended Richard Burbage's death, an event that seemed to envelop the whole of London and resonated even further afield. The national nostalgia that this prompted could only have put back in the spotlight the creative source behind Burbage's own magnificence: Shakespeare's genius as a playwright.

While it is not possible to disentangle a clear sequence of events leading directly to the printing of the First Folio, if a volume commemorating Shakespeare was being planned in the years following the playwright's death, these incidents would almost certainly have delayed it. They may, however, also have spurred on its creation thereafter, through the emotional impact the crises of 1619 had on Heminges and Condell. If Burbage's death was at the centre of a renewed commitment to celebrating Shakespeare in print on the part of the King's Men's theatre managers, then they may not have been the only ones to be so inspired.

The 'Pavier-Jaggard Quartos'

A Shakespearean Printing Mystery

Imagine you are a book browser in 1619. An avid theatregoer, reader and collector of plays, you are drawn to a particularly intriguing volume of eleven bound dramas in the shop identified by the sign of the Half-Eagle and Key in London's Barbican. At first you think this is much like any other *sammelband* or 'nonce' collection, a gathering of individually printed miscellaneous plays bound together in one volume. But you have a discerning eye and notice something strange.

All but one of these plays appear to be by William Shakespeare, with one by his contemporary Thomas Heywood, but you are sure that at least a couple of the plays identified as being by Shakespeare were in fact written by other playwrights. You notice too that despite the fact that most of these playbooks bear different dates, all bar one of their title pages look alike, boasting the same printer's device: an emblematic rose and gillyflower within an elaborate flower-and-scroll bestrewn ornamental border, engraved with the Welsh motto 'HEB DDIEV HEB DDIM', 'Without God, Without Anything'. You are sure you have seen the device before, because it belongs to other books printed by the owner-managers of the shop in which you are standing: the outlet attached to the printing house of father and son entrepreneurial team William and Isaac Jaggard. Isaac watches you with suspicion as you leaf through the collection. There is something unsettling about his stare. His father, fifty-two-year-old William, who has been losing his sight for the last seven years and relies ever more on his son's support with managing the printing business, listens intently as you ask Isaac about the collection. They both seem relieved when, after a brief exchange of pleasantries, you simply pay for the volume and leave the shop without further comment. But you cannot quite shake off the feeling that something is amiss.

What you have purchased would come to be known collectively as the 'Pavier Quartos', or more sensationally as the 'False Folio'; both rather misleading labels, and so they will be referred to here as the 'Pavier-Jaggard Quartos' in acknowledgement of the involvement of the two businesses that collaborated in their creation. When this group of plays was initially rediscovered it was thought that it consisted of nine individual editions published in quarto, a quarto being a small single volume containing one or only a few works (so not, in fact, a Folio of any kind), with one of these containing two plays. These were *The Whole Contention between the Two Famous Houses, Lancaster and York*, with no date on its title page; *Pericles*, dated 1619; *A Yorkshire Tragedy*, dated 1619; *The Merchant of Venice*, dated 1600; *The Merry Wives of Windsor*, dated 1619; *King Lear*, dated 1608; *Henry V*, dated 1608; *The Life of Sir John Oldcastle*, dated 1600; and *A Midsummer Night's Dream*, dated 1600. *The Whole Contention* is in fact two plays printed together continuously, what came to be called *Henry VI*, Parts 2 and 3 in the First Folio. *A Yorkshire Tragedy* and *The Life of Sir John Oldcastle* are attributed to Shakespeare in this collection but are now believed not to have been written by him. As more recent scholarship has shown, Thomas Heywood's play, *A Woman Killed with Kindness*, was also included in some bindings of this collection when it originally went on sale. Five of the playbooks attributed to Shakespeare indicated on their title pages that they were 'printed for T.P.', the initials of the stationer Thomas Pavier who would become known among Shakespeare scholars as a 'notorious piratical publisher'.

In 1908 the bibliographer and early First Folio scholar W.W. Greg made a startling announcement. Having examined the watermarks and the provenance of the paper stocks used in the printing of this peculiar series of playbooks, originally discovered by fellow bibliographer Alfred W. Pollard in two *sammelbands*, he concluded that they had all been issued in the same year, 1619, and by the same press: that of William and Isaac Jaggard. Furthermore, some of these plays had false imprints, with *The Merchant of Venice*, *A Midsummer Night's Dream*, *King Lear*, *Henry V* and *The Life of Sir John Oldcastle* all deceptively dated. He also drew attention to the fact that *The Whole Contention* and *Pericles* had continuous signatures – the letters and numbers that appeared at the bottom of the pages in many early printed books, primarily as guides to press-workers, but which functioned much as page numbers. This indicated that this set of dramatic works had originally been intended to form one large volume of consecutively paginated plays, but that the publisher or printer had, for some unknown reason, changed his mind during the printing process and instead devised a devilish scheme that would make them look as if they were individual playbooks that had been printed at different times. Since Pavier's initials were emblazoned on most of these works, Greg blamed the stationer for instigating this 'rather shady bit of business', for 'falsifying the dates' on the plays with the intention of hoodwinking the King's Men who, he imagined, must have 'conceived their rights to have been invaded'. Because these plays had been hiding their collective printing by a single press – since William Jaggard's name was not actually included on any of the works' imprints – the 'Pavier-Jaggard Quartos' became an infamous part of Shakespeare's legacy. Subsequently they were related directly to the printing history of the First Folio because they looked like the very first, but aborted, attempt to create a 'Shakespeare collection' in one volume. Early scholars were quick to associate Heminges and Condell's complaint, in their epistle to the reader that they printed with the Folio in 1623, with the 'Pavier-Jaggard Quartos':

> [W]e pray you, do not envy his [Shakespeare's] Friends, the office of their care, and pain, to have collected and published them; and so to have published them, as where (before) you were abused with diverse stolen, and surreptitious copies, maimed, and deformed by the frauds and stealths of injurious imposters, that exposed them: even those, are now offered to your view cured, and perfect of their limbs, and all the rest, absolute in their numbers as he [Shakespeare] conceived them.

Heminges and Condell claim that the world had been 'abused' with fraudulent copies of the plays that had been issued in unauthorised piratical editions. This turns the First Folio into a rescue operation, restoring Shakespeare's works to some kind of original, pure state. As will become clear, their insistence that the Folio offers perfected works 'absolute' as Shakespeare 'conceived them' is straining the truth. But what is significant here is the suggestion that the First Folio was, somehow, righting an earlier wrong that had 'abused' both Shakespeare's works and reputation through the illicit printing of 'stolen' plays in inadequate, 'maimed, and deformed' versions.

But if this was the case, then why and how did William and Isaac Jaggard become two of the primary syndicate members of the First Folio shortly after the printing of the 'Pavier-Jaggard Quartos'? Were the plays issued collaboratively by Pavier and the Jaggards really illegal in the first place and was Pavier the mastermind behind the 'False Folio' and the unscrupulous, piratical publisher that early bibliographers and historians of the First Folio made him out to be?

Born around 1570 to John Pavier, a yeoman hailing from Shropshire, Thomas originally trained as a draper but would be admitted to the Stationers' Company in 1600. It is true that his career had begun somewhat shakily, with his being convicted on numerous occasions by the Court of Stationers (the body that regulated the printing of books and the activities of booksellers, publishers and printers) of various misdemeanours and punished with prison sentences or heavy fines. This included a conviction 'for printing certain books and ballads without a licence' or 'without authority or entrance' in the Stationers' Register, which would have asserted his rights to these disputed works, as well as for the employment of unregistered apprentices; the latter in fact a trans-gression for which he would continue to be fined up until 1620. On another occasion he was accused, along with his brother Roger, his former master William Barley to whom he had been appren-ticed as a draper, and the printer Simon Stafford, who had also been a draper, of illegally printing a book on Latin grammar. Members of the Stationers' Company broke into and searched Stafford's house in St Peter's parish, Cornhill, but turned up noth-ing suspicious. They then decided to raid Roger's home next door, discovering there four thousand copies of the book, which they confiscated.

In June 1598 Stafford issued a bill of complaint in an attempt to prosecute Cuthbert Burby and five others, who had been acting on the orders of the Stationers' Company, for riot. Burby was a book-seller who clearly had an interest in Shakespeare, for in the year of his feud with Stafford he published the dramatist's *Love's Labour's Lost* and owned the rights to *Romeo and Juliet*, which he would publish the following year. Stafford claimed that Burby and his henchmen had 'very riotously' entered his home 'being armed and arrayed with several weapons as well invasive as defensive' and 'did forcibly and riotously take and carry away' printing equipment, 'tools and instruments' valued at twenty pounds. Thomas Pavier, aged twenty-eight at the time, backed the thirty-seven-year-old Stafford, denying that they or Barley, then aged thirty-three, had in any way been involved in the printing of the grammar manual. Instead he blamed his brother Roger who, he insisted, had contrived it all and who had encouraged him to 'bind, stitch and sell' the printed copies of the book. Furthermore, he deposed that the printing 'instruments' that the Stationers had confiscated from Stafford's premises had 'never [been] employed ... in the printing' of the book 'or other thing unlawfully'. This was a striking act of loyalty to Stafford, and a surprising betrayal of his brother. Stafford owed him, and this may be important, as we will see.

The Stationers were far from impressed with Simon Stafford's legal action and Thomas Pavier's defence of him. They asserted the legality of Burby's licence to search these properties and convicted the draper-printers for having 'unlawfully and without licence ... printed and sold great store' of these books, after setting up their own illicit printing press without permission from the Stationers' Company. As to the 'supposed riot', the Stationers' Court found that Stafford's case was mounted solely to indulge his own 'malice and revenge' and was therefore instantly 'dismissed'. The escapade earned Thomas Pavier and his accomplices a spell in the Fleet prison.

Despite this, Pavier would later become a successful publisher, with close to two hundred works to his name. His early output disclosed a penchant for producing news books, pamphlets and ballads which fed the public hunger for sensational stories. The shop he opened in 1600 was identified by the jaunty sign of the Cat and Parrots and was located adjacent to Popeshead Alley, at the southern end of Cornhill Street, close to, and probably sharing an entryway into, the Royal Exchange and within a stone's throw of the premises of his former cell-mate Simon Stafford. The Exchange's upmarket retail arcade, with its shop-lined covered walkways, which brought the trade and wares of the world to London, was the perfect spot to sell political gossip and tales of wonders beyond imagining: of voyages to strange lands, and the chimerical beasts and monsters encountered there, of witches and their devilish acts of infanticide, of brutal and bloody murders, of death-boding calamities, and of continental wars and the stratagems of foreign spies and agents. Pavier would later become best known for publishing religious works, with only a fraction of his output consisting of plays, sixteen in all excluding the 'Pavier-Jaggard Quartos'. He had, for example, the foresight to secure the rights to Thomas Kyd's tremendously popular *The Spanish Tragedy*, in which Richard Burbage had made his name playing the revenger Hieronimo.

While Pavier had experienced a somewhat uncertain beginning as a stationer, he earned the trust of his colleagues and quickly rose up the ranks of the Stationers' Company, becoming a 'Stock Keeper' in 1608, which meant he was granted membership to the committee of shareholders who managed the Company's 'English Stock' – indicating the investment in English books in what was, in effect, a joint-stock business venture established by the Stationers to secure lucrative publishing patents – directly under its Master and Wardens. The key to the warehouse of the Stock which Pavier was granted was more than a practical tool: it was a talisman of his new-found status within the company. Before the end of the following year, he was granted responsibility for the Treasurer's Stock accounts. On 14 June 1619, he was elected to sit on the governing board of the Stationers' Company and within three years would become a Junior Warden, with the authority to ratify entries in the Stationers' Register and to collect payments and fines. By this point Pavier had relocated his business to Ivy Lane, close to Paternoster Row. Gone was the copious creeping ivy that had clung to the prebend houses comprising the area's ecclesiastical estates, and from which the street took its name; now replaced with the neat rows of 'fair houses' that belonged to the wealthy middle classes, overlooked by the Prerogative Court of the Archbishop of Canterbury and the offices of the Exchequer. This was a location fitting for Pavier's turn to a more serious and weighty kind of publishing output.

By the time of Richard Burbage's death, Pavier had become a respected member of the profession, highly regarded by his peers in the Stationers' Company and unlikely to embark on a project with the intention of breaking laws against piracy; laws he was himself partly responsible for enforcing. But what of William Jaggard and his son Isaac?

The elder Jaggard in particular has acquired an equally dubious reputation among Shakespeare scholars and biographers which, to many, made him the natural accomplice of the 'piratical' Pavier. Since William and Isaac Jaggard would become involved with the First Folio project as its co-financial backers and printers just four years later, if there was something illicit about this 'Pavier-Jaggard' collection then their role in the Folio's printing needs explaining. How could Heminges and Condell entrust Shakespeare's collected plays to the Jaggards if the printer-stationers had 'abused' the dramatist's name with illegal publications in the past?

History has bequeathed to the present a portrait of William Jaggard as the nemesis of William Shakespeare, the perennial thorn in his side. And no wonder, for in 1599 the printer issued a text that would become notorious for igniting the playwright's fury. *The Passionate Pilgrim* was Jaggard's first foray into Shakespeare publishing and was a miscellany of poems, of which five are by the dramatist and fifteen others are by a selection of contemporary authors. Despite the variety of voices represented by the work, the earliest extant version of the title page (not in fact the first edition) asserts the authorship of the entire book as being 'By W. Shakespeare'. In 1612 Jaggard reissued the publication with additional content: poems by Thomas Heywood from his work entitled *Troia Britanica*, which Jaggard had previously published. This led Heywood to exclaim bitterly against the 'manifest injury' done to him by Jaggard in his *Apology for Actors* that same year, in which he accused the printer of 'taking' some of his works without his permission and 'printing them … under the name of another [that is, Shakespeare], which may put the world in opinion I might steal them from him'. Heywood also made a point of highlighting Shakespeare's own feelings on the matter: 'The Author [Shakespeare] I know [is] much offended with M[aster] Jaggard (that altogether unknown to him) presumed to make so bold with his name.'

According to Heywood these were brazen 'dishonesties' which Jaggard, unlike Nicholas Okes, the printer of his *Apology*, would never be 'clear of'. In contrast to Jaggard, whose 'negligence' ensured works issued from his press were full of 'misquotations, mistaking of syllables, misplacing half-lines, coining of strange and never heard of words', Okes was 'so careful, and industrious, so serious and laborious to do the author all the rights of the press', deserving of congratulation for his 'honest endeavours'. While this would not be the last time that Jaggard would be publicly condemned for poor printing practices, he may have felt entitled to print Heywood's poems because he had legitimately obtained the rights to the work from which they derived. It was not unusual, in fact, for publishers to claim such privilege in an age in which the licence to print work was not governed by a sense of authorial 'originality' and ownership of creative or intellectual property, as it is today, but could be secured through permission from a church authority and the Stationers' Company, under the name of the stationer into whose hands the sole rights to the work were being transferred. Nor was it unusual for plays to be misattributed in this period. Between 1595 and 1622, ten editions, encompassing seven plays, have title pages that attribute non-Shakespeare works to the playwright. Nevertheless, Jaggard's assigning of *The Passionate Pilgrim* to Shakespeare on its title page was an attempt to cash in on the reputation of a dramatist who had gained significant plaudits as the author of two tremendously successful narrative poems, *Venus and Adonis* (1593) and *The Rape of Lucrece* (1594), the former of which was Shakespeare's single most reprinted work during his lifetime, going through ten known editions to 1616. It is easy to infer guilt on Jaggard's part because of the fact that some of the impressions of the 1612 edition of *The Passionate Pilgrim* were issued with the attribution to Shakespeare removed, possibly in response to Heywood's complaint.

This all cemented William Jaggard's tarnished reputation. To a generation of early Shakespeare scholars, therefore, he and Pavier seemed like two piratical peas in a pod. Apart from small fines, however, which included the payment of ten shillings in 'damages' for encroaching on another printer's rights to the 'printing [of] apprentices' indentures, contrary to order', there is little sign that Jaggard was anything other than a much-decorated publisher (three-quarters of whose output consisted of works he himself had secured the rights to publish) and trade printer (whose printing on behalf of other publishers made up close to a third of his known outputs). Ambitious and business-savvy, he had, since his admission to the Stationers' Company in 1591, kept his eye firmly on the acquisition of lucrative printing monopolies. In May 1604 he had sought the right to supply 'every parish church and chapel' with English versions of the Ten Commandments 'at the charges of the parish'. He was probably not successful, however, since Sir Robert Cecil, then secretary of state, appears to have 'staid', that is stopped, Jaggard's bid, which was noted as 'not sealed'.

Jaggard was more fortunate – eventually – in securing the desirable monopoly on the printing of playbills 'for the company of

stage players', which were used to advertise plays. He had peti-
tioned strenuously for the monopoly since 1593, only to see the
licence pass to the stationer James Roberts in 1594. Roberts
evidently felt working with Jaggard would be wise, granting him,
by way of concession, the right to print a limited number of playbills appertaining only to the Earl of Worcester's Men and 'to
meddle with the printing of no other bills for players but these
only of the said Earl's company of players'; rights transferred to the
printing of playbills for Queen Anne's players in the early April of
the following year. With the Chamberlain's Men only just having
then been established, the troupe's members, including Shakespeare
and Heminges, would have followed these developments keenly,
keeping their curious eyes on Jaggard in the knowledge that a
stationer who had been working his way so rapidly into the business of theatre advertising may soon become someone of
significance to their own company.

They would not have been wrong to do so. For Jaggard, a few
theatrical patents from Roberts' hands were not enough. He set his
sights on the latter's entire printing business, somehow acquiring
it, along with his premises in the Barbican, in 1606, and the infamous printers' devices that would appear on the title pages of the
'Pavier-Jaggard Quartos'. His appointment as 'Printer to the City
of London' followed, by 17 December 1610, which meant he was
tasked with printing royal proclamations and civic announcements.
More important than the annual stipend of forty shillings as basic
pay for this role, was the fact that it meant his name and printer's
device appeared next to the royal arms in thousands of notices
pinned in public spaces – on buildings, on posts, on shopfronts, in
markets and squares, outside gathering places of all kinds – across
the city. He had, therefore, the visible endorsement of the Crown.
By 1615 he had also scored the licence that granted him the full
monopoly over the printing of playbills, gaining thereby an annual
profit of somewhere close to three pounds, which was not far off

the annual wage of many artisans. This turn of events did indeed make Jaggard a very important figure for the King's Men.

The collaborative practices of Pavier and Jaggard equally shows them in a different light to their popular posthumous reputations. The two had regularly worked together on publication projects, including a total of twelve plays, two of which they co-produced in 1605, and several non-dramatic works. They had also laboured to secure their infiltration into the ranks of the Stationers, often in tandem. Both had served on the committee that governed the English Stock, requesting between 1605 and 1607 that they be made shareholders in the company, a joint goal they eventually achieved. Shares in the Stock were not given away easily. A petition by John Jaggard, William's brother, who was also a stationer, which sought to protect the Company of Stationers' exclusive printing rights, indicated that this privilege depended on a 'special regard' to 'the ancient honesty and good behaviour' of the individual considered for such an honour. So coveted were these shares that the company had to take measures to prevent 'divers wealthy persons of different professions' from encroaching on the prerogatives of booksellers, bookbinders and printers 'to the great prejudice and future undoing' of those trained in the profession. The move was intended to block members of other guilds and companies, such as those trained as grocers and goldsmiths, who were buying their way into the Stock and the hallowed committees of the Stationers' Company. The fact that William Jaggard and Pavier were among those highly regarded few accorded these honours suggests they were trusted by their colleagues. But Jaggard and Pavier were more than simply professional co-workers. They would remain intimates their entire lives, with Jaggard referring to his fellow stationer as one of his 'very good friends'. It is probable that Heminges and Condell would soon discover that being on good terms with Jaggard would help facilitate business relations with Pavier when it came to setting in motion the creation of the First Folio.

The syndicate members behind the 'Pavier-Jaggard Quartos' do not in reality quite fit the dubious reputation they have since acquired. If they did not enter into the venture of printing the first collected edition of Shakespeare plays with the intention to deceive, why did they undertake this entirely new project? An edition of Shakespeare's plays would, on the surface, have appeared as a challenging sell. No matter how we interpret the evidence, there is no doubt that the dramatist's popularity in print had begun to wane markedly from 1613, when he stopped writing plays for the professional theatre. Two works attributed to him were published that year (only one of those genuinely by him), and thereafter just one new edition appeared per year, excluding 1614 and 1618 when there were no editions at all. Those Shakespeare works reissued in 1616 and 1617 were not plays, but the perennially popular narrative poems *The Rape of Lucrece* and *Venus and Adonis* respectively. This means that not a single Shakespeare play had been published since 1615, when *Richard II* was reprinted. This is a far cry from the state of play at the high point in Shakespeare's career in 1600 – just two years after his name first begins appearing on the title pages of his plays, turning the author into a vendable commodity – when his published works represented a staggering 4 per cent of the total number of all the printed books issued that year, making the playwright a publishing phenomenon, a giant on the bookselling scene. While Shakespeare plays represented an impressive 17 per cent of the total playbook market between 1594 and 1616, there was a downturn in Shakespeare publications after the midpoint in his career, partly due to what appears to have been a decision by the King's Men to limit the release of newly authored Shakespeare plays onto the book market. But this still left the rights to approximately half the Shakespeare canon in the hands of stationers who could have issued or reissued those plays at any time during the final years of the dramatist's life and within the first three or so years after his death. They simply chose not to. Then suddenly, from 1619, there was an explosion of plays attributed to Shakespeare in print, ten in total (with eight of these authentically by him), apparently intended for the same 'Pavier-Jaggard' volume.

The mystery is compounded by the fact that the plays printed in 1619 were not Shakespeare's most popular during his lifetime. Of far more interest to the buyers of playbooks had been *Henry IV, Part 1* which went through six editions, *Richard III* which saw five, *Richard II* with at least four, and a few plays which were issued in three editions, such as *Hamlet*. Apart from *Pericles*, which had been printed in three editions between 1609 and 1611, the genuine Shakespeare plays to be represented by the 'Pavier-Jaggard Quartos' had previously been released in either one or two editions and none would be recent plays in 1619. Various plausible explanations for this particular choice of dramatic works include the proposal that they were meant to tap into 'older, somewhat forgotten' works in order to remind would-be purchasers of these 'rediscovered masterpieces', the theory that they were intended to cash in on a vogue for historical cycles and serials, and the hypothesis that they functioned as a 'pre-publicity stunt' for the First Folio itself, designed 'to whet' readers' appetites for a larger volume of collected plays.

An alternative answer is that Pavier and the Jaggards had taken the temperature of the theatre-going and book-buying public and realised that a valuable business opportunity had presented itself; that they had resolved to capitalise on the recent wide-scale inter-est in Burbage and Shakespeare, the theatre industry's most successful – and now lamentably lost – double-act. In other words, it was Burbage's death which changed the landscape of Shakespeare publishing from 1619.

'Forged invention former times defaced'

Negotiating and Printing the 'False Folio'

W ho first suggested the bold scheme to create an edition of selected Shakespeare plays in quarto format is not known. But the decision was taken and a collaborative partnership or syndicate was formed. Thomas Pavier and the Jaggards, William and Isaac, would have anticipated that such a volume would require some effort to pull together. Authoritative copies of the plays would need to be sourced and negotiations entered into with those who owned rights to some of the works they wished to include in the project. Time was of the essence. A venture like this could only be successful if it captured the upswell of public emotion following the death of Richard Burbage: and that could wane rapidly.

As Pavier embarked on this project with the Jaggards, he must have looked over his own back catalogue of plays. He would have found that he owned the rights to five works that he could tie to Shakespeare: *The Whole Contention* (that is, *Henry VI*, Parts 2 and 3); *A Yorkshire Tragedy*, which he had originally published in 1608 and incorrectly attributed to Shakespeare; *Henry V*, issued in 1602; and *The Life of Sir John Oldcastle*, initially released in 1600, also not a genuine Shakespeare play. This was a good start if he was looking for plays that may have had, for prospective buyers, associations with crowd-pleasing Burbage roles. The second and third part of the *Henry VI* series of plays introduced the character of 'Crookback Richard', who would become Richard III. Frequently recalled in elegiac responses to Burbage's death, the actor had made this role so popular that his interpretation was referred to in other plays nearly a decade after its debut showing. Another witty story recounts how a tour guide at Bosworth Field, where the historical Richard III was believed to have been killed, was so affected by a performance he had seen that 'he mistook a player for a King,/For when he would have said, King Richard died,/And called "a Horse, a Horse", he "Burbage" cried'. In the absence of the *Richard III* play itself, kept tightly in the clutches of the stationer Matthew Law, who clearly had no intention of parting with such a prized commodity, *The Whole Contention* would serve as an alternative with a close association with one of Burbage's most admired roles. Book buyers would have got their fix of the deliciously devious villain Richard.

When the Jaggards began working on the quartos in their printing house, they started by typesetting these very plays. As they held a licence to operate two printing presses, they probably began working on *Pericles* at much the same time, adding another role strongly associated with Burbage. How they acquired the rights to this play which, according to the Stationers' Register, was in publisher Edward Blount's possession since 1608, is not known. While stationers were obliged to acquire a 'licence' to print a work from a church authority, a representative of the Stationers' Company or, in some periods, the Master of the Revels – the 'allowance' for which would be recorded on the physical manuscript or 'copy' text itself – entry in the register was an *additional* form of protection available to stationers, for which an extra fee was demanded, and was not a legal requirement at that time.

Blount may have transferred the rights to another stationer without a corresponding entry in the register. It was Henry Gosson who published it one year after Blount's acquisition. It has been suggested that Pavier secured the licence to print the play from Gosson, with whom he would later collaborate on the establishing of a syndicate for the printing of ballads. It is possible, however, that it was Pavier's association with Stafford, who had been the most recent publisher of *Pericles* in 1611, which gave him access to the play. Stafford was still an active presence in the Stationers' Company till at least 9 March 1619, just four days before Richard Burbage's death, when he was granted an annual pension of four pounds. He may have been in the process of offloading some of his assets and came to an agreement with Pavier, if he had obtained the rights to this play. It should be recalled that this is the very same Stafford who had, like Pavier, been apprenticed as a draper and who had been supported by the latter in a legal case in 1598 when Pavier was willing to betray his own brother in an attempt to extricate Stafford from charges of illegal printing. Pavier must have secured rights to *Pericles* unequivocally because his widow entered her transfer of the licence to publish it, along with 'Master Pavier's right in Shakespeare's plays', in the Stationers' Register in 1626 in a manner which looks entirely legal. Either way, Pavier had strong connections with two stationers who could have provided him with legitimate printing rights to *Pericles*.

When the printing began in earnest *The Whole Contention* was produced alongside *Pericles* because these plays were paginated consecutively. The Jaggards had every intention of rendering the other plays in a continuously paginated sequence at this stage. Before completing *Pericles* they turned their attentions to an anonymous work called *Troubles in Bohemia*, which they added to their printing schedule. They did have other books that needed to be seen through their presses after all. Then, with *Pericles* still unfinished, they began work on *A Yorkshire Tragedy*. But why publish this non-Shakespearean play as part of a Shakespeare collection? This may have been an attempt to profit from Burbage's association with *The Spanish Tragedy*, which had prompted one contemporary to write of the actor's accomplishments in that part: 'I have seen the knave paint grief/In such a lively colour, that for false/And acted passion he has drawn true tears/From the spectators.' The role of the 'Husband' in *A Yorkshire Tragedy*, as one Renaissance theatre scholar has confirmed, has 'all the hallmarks' of a prime Burbage part. The pitching for *A Yorkshire Tragedy* on its title page refers to the story as 'Not so New, as Lamentable and True'. This echoes the advertising for *The Spanish Tragedy*, reprinted in 1615 and 1618 with its original tagline drawing attention to 'the lamentable end of Don Horatio, and Belimperia, with the pitiful death of Hieronimo'. When first published in 1592, the play had appeared on bookstalls beside another, a sensational true-life crime story called *Arden of Faversham*, billed as 'The Lamentable and True Tragedy'. A further play that tapped into this vogue was Shakespeare's *Titus Andronicus*, described on its 1594 title page as a 'most lamentable Roman tragedy', completing a run of works that exploited public tastes by recycling the same evocative advertising styles.

This canny pitching – referring to plays as 'Lamentable' or 'Lamentable and True' – seems to have originated with the bookseller Edward White who had issued two editions of *The Spanish Tragedy*, two of *Arden of Faversham* and no fewer than three of *Titus Andronicus*. Pavier would have understood the importance of such strategic billing, because he himself had secured the rights to both *The Spanish Tragedy* and *Titus Andronicus* in 1602, printing three editions of the former play up to 1610. He appears to have made a connection between these and *A Yorkshire Tragedy*, for his edition borrowed White's marketing strategy. Though *The Spanish Tragedy* and *Titus Andronicus* are not thought of as domestic tragedies, as *Arden of Faversham* and *A Yorkshire Tragedy* are, they all capitalised on a fad for racy scandal and bloody gore. That *The Spanish Tragedy*, with its 'Lamentable' tag, was re-published the year before the 'Pavier-Jaggard Quartos' may have inspired Pavier and the Jaggards to reissue *A Yorkshire Tragedy* as a way of reminding audiences of one of Burbage's greatest roles, that of Hieronimo the revenger, promising their book buyers the kind of blood-soaked play that had made *The Spanish Tragedy* such a hit.

As the Jaggards neared the completion of *A Yorkshire Tragedy*, they continued working across plays simultaneously at breakneck speed. In this period, the typesetting and printing of works did not always proceed in a linear manner. It is likely, as revealed by recent extraordinary scholarship conducted on the paper stocks and watermarks of these quartos, that the typesetting for a portion of *The Merchant of Venice* intersected with the final sheets of *A Yorkshire Tragedy*, with the latter succeeded by the possibly concurrent printing of part of *A Midsummer Night's Dream* (which did not include its title page) and a gathering of initial leaves of *The Merry Wives of Windsor* (which did include the title page). All those plays that had been printed in full or started up to this point, apart from *The Merchant of Venice* and *A Midsummer Night's Dream*, survive in copies bearing the correct date of 1619.

At this point something happened; something that stopped the Jaggards dead in their tracks and forced them to change course.

On 3 May 1619 a man made his way to Stationers' Hall on the north-western corner of St Paul's Cathedral's outer perimeter. The hall was the base of the Company of Stationers, the destination for publishers wishing to register plays or other works in their names, or for those hoping to make interventions in the publishing industry through the operations of the Court of Stationers. He had been dispatched by the King's Men on an important mission: the delivery of a letter which would change the course of Shakespeare printing.

The carrier of this missive may have come from the Globe Theatre, after crossing the Thames, or walked directly from the Blackfriars Theatre, heading north with the lapping Thames at his back, and crossing Carter Lane into the narrow winding alley of Creed Lane. On the way he would have seen the crenellated towers of Ludgate rising to his left as he traversed the western flank of the mansion and gardens reserved for successive deans of St Paul's, before entering Stationers' Hall at the intersection of Ave Maria Lane and Paternoster Row; the latter a long street that ran parallel with a line of bookshops just within the cathedral's precinct. Once inside he presented the letter to the Court of Stationers. Those appointed to oversee the court's sessions that day would have instantly grasped the importance of the document, for it had been penned by the Lord Chamberlain, Sir William Herbert. The original missive has not survived but its contents were later summarised by William's brother Philip who explained that:

> ... complaint was heretofore presented to my dear brother and predecessor by his Majesty's servants the players, that some of the Company of Printers and Stationers had procured, published and printed diverse of their books of Comedies, Tragedies, Chronicle Histories, and the like, which they had (for the special service of his Majesty and for their own use) bought and provided at very dear and high rates, by means whereof not only they themselves had much prejudice, but the books much corruption to the injury and disgrace of the authors ...

The King's Men, it seems, had sought the aid of the Earl of Pembroke, claiming that plays in the company repertory were being 'procured' and published by stationers who had been issuing corrupted versions of these dramatic works without their authorisation. The earl had heeded their pleas and provided them with a letter, which was presented to the court, so the records of the Stationers inform us, by one 'Henry Hemminges'. After deliberating its contents the court returned the verdict that 'It is thought fit and so ordered that no plays that his Majesty's Players do play shall be printed without consent of some of them.' We can be fairly certain that among those meant by 'some of them' were John Heminges and Henry Condell, since they were the principal managers of the King's Men. The outcome of William Herbert's intervention is confirmed by Philip, who reflected that 'the Masters and Wardens of the Company of Printers and Stationers were advised by my brother to take notice thereof and to take order for the stay [that is, stopping or prevention] of any further impression of any of the plays or interludes of his Majesty's servants without their consents', which was, he insisted, 'a caution given with such respect and grounded on such weighty reasons, both for his Majesty's service and the particular interest of the players'. The order meant that henceforth no stationer could publish any work associated with the King's Men's playing company without its members' express permission. It is not clear if Henry Hemminges was a relation of John Heminges, or if the record-keeper had confused Henry Condell with John Heminges – one of whom had in fact delivered the letter – and conflated their names, but the ease with which the protection of the players' 'interest' resulted in decisive action by the Lord Chamberlain indicates the special closeness of their relationship.

Among those overseeing proceedings at the Court of Stationers that day was John Jaggard, William Jaggard's brother, who had received his 'freedom' with the Stationers' Company in 1593 and thereafter set up a bookshop in Fleet Street, close to St Dunstan's Church, called the Hand and Star. He was now a regular presence at court sessions and may have told his brother about the Earl of Pembroke's order. If William did not hear of these events from John, he may have been informed by Pavier, who was there at the

Stationers' Hall that very day, having presented himself before the court in order to tender payment for the right to publish three works under licences granted by the Company of Stationers. However the syndicate behind the 'Pavier-Jaggard Quartos' found out about the ban on printing Shakespeare's plays, news did reach them.

Pavier and the Jaggards were now plunged into a crisis. They had already invested in the printing of numerous plays, as well as in the securing of the rights to issue some of them. Do they abandon the scheme or try to salvage it in some way? The Jaggards, perhaps in consultation with Pavier, took a decision that would determine their posthumous reputation for centuries to come, and in ways they could not have imagined. They abandoned the idea of a cohesive collection of Shakespeare plays and stopped paginating these works consecutively. But they would push on with the printing nevertheless. Having already printed the first pages of *The Merry Wives of Windsor* with the 1619 title page, they did not go back and reprint these. Instead they resumed work on the play and completed *The Merchant of Venice*, to which they added a false date of 1600 on its title page, along with a fake publisher, James Roberts. Concurrently, alternating plays between their two presses, they proceeded with *A Midsummer Night's Dream*, to which they also added a misleading date of 1600, along with a different printer's device from those featured on the title pages of the other plays in the sequence: a Half-Eagle and Key emblem that had once belonged to Roberts, and which William Jaggard had inherited when he took over Roberts' shop in 1606. As recent scholarship has shown, the Jaggards had only used this device six times on their books, and only on works they printed for others. It was, therefore, sufficiently distanced from their public brand and meant that they could complete the deception by adding below it the words 'Printed by James Roberts', making it look like yet another play from Roberts' old stock.

THE
EXCELLENT
Hiſtory of the Mer-
chant of Venice.

With the extreme cruelty of *Shylocke*
the Iew towards the ſaide Merchant, in cut-
ting a iuſt pound of his fleſh. And the obtaining
of *Portia*, by the choyſe of
three Caskets.

Written by W. SHAKESPEARE.

Printed by *J. Roberts*, 1600.

This edition of William Shakespeare's *The Merchant of Venice* was one of the
'Pavier-Jaggard Quartos', also known as the 'False Folio', issued by Thomas
Pavier and the printing house of William and Isaac Jaggard with misleading
imprints and false dates. The printing of the 'False Folio' was a first attempt at
creating an edition of selected Shakespeare plays. The Jaggards went on to
become part of the consortium of financial backers who helped create the First
Folio, which was printed in their printing house.

But were these comedies acquired illegally? James Roberts had logged his rights to *The Merchant of Venice* in the Stationers' Register on 22 July 1598. It was an entirely legal entry. A bookseller and printer since 1593, Roberts clearly had good taste, for he had acquired the rights to the works of such literary greats as Samuel Daniel, Michael Drayton and Sir Philip Sidney, alongside plays by Shakespeare, including *Hamlet*, which he had entered in the Stationers' Register in 1602 (before John Smethwick had acquired the licence to publish it), and *Troilus and Cressida*, entered in the register in February 1603. Roberts did not himself act as publisher for any of the Shakespeare plays for which he owned the rights. He did, though, print *The Merchant of Venice* for Thomas Hayes, to whom publishing rights had been transferred in October 1600. It is not known if Pavier or the Jaggards reached an agreement for *The Merchant of Venice* with Hayes, who appears to have held on to the rights, since he passed them to his son Lawrence Hayes in July 1619. If a business arrangement was entered into, it would probably have been a one-time deal. While Lawrence Hayes may have been spurred on to confirm his rights to the play (asserting his ownership as an inheritance from his father in the Stationers' Register that year) because he perceived it to be an illegal printing by Pavier and the Jaggards, it is equally possible that William Jaggard, who had taken over Roberts' printing business along with the use of his printers' devices, simply felt he had an entitlement to print the work.

A Midsummer Night's Dream was originally published legitimately in 1600 by the stationer Thomas Fisher, who had entered his rights to the play in the Stationers' Register in October that year. There is no record of a formal transfer to Roberts, Pavier or Jaggard. Many bibliographers believe that the rights to this play became 'derelict' – that is, they were not owned by anyone and therefore could be claimed by any stationer – due to Fisher's death. Fisher was a draper who had entered the Stationers' Company at the same time as Pavier. It is possible therefore that Pavier had been closely associated with him through both his draper and stationer links. This could explain why he knew about the derelict rights and how he was able to claim them.

While the imprints to *The Merchant of Venice* and *A Midsummer Night's Dream* are clearly illicit, the Pavier-Jaggard syndicate's right to these plays is ambiguous and cannot be confirmed as piratical. We cannot know if Burbage was particularly lauded for roles he played in these comedies but *The Merry Wives of Windsor*, as we will see, does have a logical link to other plays that were associated with one of his most celebrated parts and may have been included for this reason. This play was recorded in the Stationers' Register in January 1602 by Arthur Johnson, who went on to publish it that year. The book was originally sold at 'a little bookseller's shop' identified by the sign of the Fleur-de-lis and Crown in St Paul's Churchyard, built against the north-eastern corner of the cathedral's Great North Door, opposite Cannon Alley. Since the 'Pavier-Jaggard' issue of the play bears the correct date on its title page, while also indicating that it was 'Printed for Arthur Johnson', the rights to print must have been legitimately acquired from him.

The Jaggards turned next to a play that is much easier to tie to a prominent Burbage part: *King Lear*. Shortly after the actor's death the dramatist John Fletcher lamented that there would be 'no more young Hamlet, old Hieronimo,/King Lear, the grieved Moor [Othello]', placing Lear as one of his stellar roles. Since they did not reach an agreement for the rights to *Hamlet* with Smethwick, Pavier and the Jaggards may have turned to Nathaniel Butter, who had secured the rights to *King Lear* in November 1607. His father, the bookseller Thomas Butter, had bequeathed to him the shop known by the sign of the Pied Bull, which stood a short stroll to the east of Arthur Johnson's shop, still within St Paul's Churchyard. So if Pavier had entered into a legitimate agreement with Johnson over *The Merry Wives of Windsor*, he did not have far to go to negotiate with Butter over *King Lear*. The latter was very possessive about his rights to the newsbooks, pamphlets and plays that he published in a very large number of reprints. He was not one, therefore, to allow his licence to a text to lapse or to pass easily into another's hands without putting up a fight. Pavier had worked with Butter on publications three times between 1605 and 1610, so they already had a professional relationship. Butter also owned the rights to *The London Prodigal*, which he had published in 1605 as a play he erroneously attributed to Shakespeare, indicating his interest in the selling power of the playwright's name. This play was not a Burbage vehicle, according to recent scholarship, but saw Henry Condell take the lead role. This may explain why Pavier and the Jaggards did not include it in their collection, despite its attribution to Shakespeare.

Before completing *King Lear* the printing team picked up *Henry V*. This was the play which, at its debut in 1599, signalled a change in the way Shakespeare wrote parts for Burbage. According to calculations made by one theatre scholar, this dramatic work saw the actor speaking at least 30 per cent of the lines, and thereafter Burbage's roles became larger showpieces for his genius. Pavier owned the rights to this and *The Life of Sir John Oldcastle*, the final play to be printed in the sequence, which was produced from leftover paper stocks kept in the printing room from previous print work. Paper was an expensive commodity and not to be wasted. It may be significant that these two plays were printed together last. The 'Pavier-Jaggard' syndicate could not secure the more popular *Henry IV, Part 1*, with its rogue Prince Hal (played by Burbage) and raucous cowardly knight Sir John Falstaff. This was also owned by Matthew Law, along with the popular *Richard II* which formed part of the same tetralogy of history plays. The 'Pavier-Jaggard' syndicate did have *Henry V*, the title role belonging to the character into which Prince Hal would grow. What of the spuriously attributed *Oldcastle* play? This is fairly easy to explain. When

Shakespeare initially wrote *Henry IV, Part 1*, and part of *Henry IV, Part 2*, Falstaff trod the boards by another name: that of Sir John Oldcastle. The historical Oldcastle, the first Lord Cobham, was the figurehead of a religious sect known as the Lollards. He had been tried for heresy and executed on a charge of treason in 1417. By Shakespeare's day he was viewed as a forerunner of the early Church reformers, due to the Lollards' challenging of some doctrines of the Catholic Church. Thanks to objections, probably from Oldcastle's living descendant, Sir William Brooke, the Lord Cobham, or another member of the illustrious Cobham family, Shakespeare was forced to expunge his name from the *Henry IV* plays. He chose to replace it with Falstaff. Originally produced by the Chamberlain's Men's rivals the Lord Admiral's Men, *The Life of Sir John Oldcastle* began with a prologue that presented the drama as a strenuous rebuttal of Shakespeare's own *Henry IV* plays:

> It is no pampered glutton we present,
> Nor aged counsellor to youthful sin,
> But one, whose virtue shone above the rest,
> A valiant Martyr, and a virtuous peer,
> In whose true faith and loyalty expressed
> Unto his sovereign, and his country's weal:
> We strive to pay that tribute of our love,
> Your favours merit, let fair Truth be graced,
> Since forged invention former time defaced.

The 'pampered glutton' and 'aged counsellor to youthful sin' are unmistakable references to Shakespeare's Oldcastle/Falstaff, a creation defined as a 'forged invention' that has 'defaced' the real Oldcastle's heroic status. Shakespeare had taken too many liberties with the character, to the detriment of Oldcastle's reputation. But this intricate backstory is not something prospective book buyers would necessarily have known, though they may well have been aware of the scandal that accompanied Shakespeare's changing of Oldcastle's name to Falstaff; for the dramatist had been made to issue a humiliating public apology at the end of his *Henry IV, Part 2* for abusing Oldcastle's memory. Court gossips continued to refer to the controversial Oldcastle/Falstaff character long after the first showing of Shakespeare's plays. Placing *Henry V* alongside this Oldcastle play in the 'Pavier-Jaggard Quartos' could have been an ingenious way of fooling readers into believing they were getting a 'set' of Shakespeare's Oldcastle/Falstaff plays, conjuring Burbage's association with the *Henry IV* and *Henry V* sequence. To purchasers of playbooks in this period the distinction between the original Oldcastle plays and the Admiral's Men's production may not have been instantly apparent. The fact that Pavier did not initially attribute the *Oldcastle* play to Shakespeare in 1600, but did so in 1619, may be due to this strategy. This also explains the inclusion of *The Merry Wives of Windsor*, a spin-off to the tremendously popular *Henry IV, Part 1*, featuring more of the misadventures of the larger-than-life Falstaff.

The printing of the 'Pavier-Jaggard Quartos' was a swift and efficient operation. For the most part these plays seem to have been secured through legitimate channels and were not piratical works as such; and where there are question marks over the acquisition of rights, there are also plausible routes to permissible ownership or at the very least signs of the exploitation of a legal grey area. The real deception lay elsewhere. When they finished the printing the Jaggards must have looked around their printing shop as their assistants gathered up the individual printed sheets and started ordering them in preparation for stitching into complete books. What had they ended up with? An apparently anomalous group of plays, three of which were consecutively paginated (if we view *The Whole Contention* as two plays printed together), with three displaying the correct date of 1619, and four with false dates. What next? This is when they embarked on one of their most dishonest acts.

Recent stunning forensic work on the 'Pavier-Jaggard Quartos' has revealed that they, or booksellers they instructed, began vandalising the title pages dated 1619, scraping out, tearing or punching through the true dates and possibly repairing them with erroneous dates. They also very likely sent instructions to booksellers to separate *The Whole Contention* from *Pericles* in any bound volumes of the series, to obfuscate the project's origins as a cohesive collection and make the plays appear like unsold remainders that happened to be gathered together, just like the *sammelbands* with which booksellers enticed eager playbook-hunters. To complete the ruse they inserted copies of Thomas Heywood's *A Woman Killed with Kindness*, for which the Jaggards held the rights and which they had printed in 1617, further disrupting the unity of this 'Shakespeare' series. Some booksellers sold these as individual works, while others had them bound together. It seems that Pavier and the Jaggards would, in a manner of speaking, have their way after all, with many purchasers acquiring this so-called 'False Folio' as a collection.

But who were Pavier and the Jaggards trying to fool? It is unlikely that other experienced stationers would have been taken in by such a homogeneous-looking group of plays, so the Company of Stationers was probably not the target of this deception. The King's Men would also not have been duped. They would have recognised that these works, with all but one bearing the same printer's device, were spurious and would have known that two were misattributed to Shakespeare. The ploy must have been intended to hoodwink the book-buying public. This would only make sense if Pavier and the Jaggards had reached an agreement with the King's Men, specifically with Heminges and Condell, permitting them to complete and sell their newly minted plays on the understanding that they were made to look like older editions that would be superseded by superior versions in the soon-to-be-printed First Folio. In return, the Jaggards may have been offered a stake in the more ambitious Folio venture. This would explain why the King's Men did not challenge the issuing of the genuine Shakespeare plays of 1619 through the formal mechanisms of the Court of Stationers, despite the Lord Chamberlain's edict giving them the power to do so.

It is commonly thought that Heminges and Condell heard about the 'Pavier-Jaggard' endeavour and *then* responded aggressively by initiating the Lord Chamberlain's edict, enforced by the Court of Stationers, that brought the printing to a standstill. But it is also possible that the players had approached William Herbert in response not to any specific publishing scheme but to the death of Richard Burbage: that Heminges and Condell realised that the overwhelming public reaction to the actor's demise would result in a rush of King's Men plays to press by stationers wanting to capitalise on this nostalgic outpouring of love both for Burbage and the dramatists who showcased his talents, not just through legitimately acquired plays but through works illicitly procured, copied or memorially reconstructed. The Stationers' ban, after all, forbade the printing of *any* plays from the King's Men's repertory, not just Shakespeare's. Indeed, that year saw the beginning of a series of King's Men plays by Francis Beaumont and John Fletcher – including *Philaster*, the work that made their reputations – hit the bookstalls, which some scholars believe were illegally acquired.

Heminges and Condell would have understood that such a turn of events would have jeopardised any project to commemorate their beloved friend Shakespeare, had this been on their minds at this time. They would also have wanted to protect the troupe's entire repertory at this pivotal period in the company's history. It is possible therefore that Pavier and the Jaggards received news of the Court of Stationers' regulation prohibiting the printing of works attached to the King's Men *before* Heminges and Condell had even heard of their publishing scheme. If so, they would have had no choice but to *make themselves* and their activities known to the theatre managers, as the edict commanded, seeking permission to continue with the printing of their play collection. In any ensuing negotiation Pavier and the Jaggards would have had a strong bargaining chip: their collaboration represented rights to a significant group of Shakespeare's plays. Whenever plans for the First Folio finally got underway, Heminges and Condell would have known – and so would the Jaggards – that they could not bring their project to fruition without the support of the syndicate behind the 'False Folio'.

If the 'Pavier-Jaggard Quartos' did pose a threat to any plans the King's Men had for a larger volume of Shakespeare plays, the problem seems to have been resolved quickly and in a manner that would benefit all the parties involved. The Jaggards' association with the 'False Folio', and their relationship with Pavier, ironically aided the progress of the First Folio project. With the Jaggards on board, an important group of much-loved plays could be secured for a grand edition of Shakespeare's works in folio. Into the bargain, the Folio syndicate would gain members with the reputation, resources and experience to help make a success of this ambitious project.

'Of great living, wealth and power'

The King's Men's Public and Private Enemies

In January 1619 the Lord Mayor of London, Sir Sebastian Harvey, received two documents that would cause a great deal of trouble for John Heminges, Henry Condell and their fellow players in the King's Men. Addressed to the mayor and his aldermen, these parchments crackled with the rancour of London's anti-theatricalists, whose hands had been set to them and whose avowed mission was to close down the Blackfriars Theatre once and for all.

Located just south of Ludgate and south-west of St Paul's Cathedral, the Blackfriars Theatre stood a mere few strides away from Carter Lane where the Stratford-born stationer and printer Richard Field had first typeset Shakespeare's words, issuing his incredibly popular narrative poem *Venus and Adonis* in 1593. Field's printing press stood at the edge of the boundary of an upmarket district that had once been the site of the Dominican priory of the Black Friars and which was now a labyrinth of tenements and winding alleyways. The local Church of St Anne was practically next door to, and shared an entryway with, the Blackfriars Theatre. Harvey knew all too well how the district's layout contributed to the tensions between the players and their neighbours, particularly those of a more radical religious outlook who frequented the primarily Puritan-controlled St Anne's. The players had been sitting on a powder keg since James Burbage had made the fateful decision to purchase rooms in the area in 1595, with the intention of converting them into a new theatre, completing the sale in February of the following year.

Picking up the first document, the mayor noticed that it was a collaborative petition between the precinct's officers, local workers and professionals, and the wardens of the church. He realised this was a complaint against the Blackfriars Theatre and that it drew attention to a notable precedent: a petition of November 1596, led by the formidable Lady Elizabeth Russell, the grandiloquently self-styled Dowager Countess of Bedford. This had successfully prevented the players from occupying the playhouse even while it was still under construction; when they were known, for a brief period between July 1596 and March 1597, as the Lord Hunsdon's Men. This earlier petition had been addressed to Queen Elizabeth I's Privy Council and recorded the grievances of 'divers both honorable persons and others then inhabiting the said precinct' who enumerated 'what inconveniences were likely to fall upon them by a common playhouse'. Foremost among those 'honorable persons' was Lady Russell, who held court as one of the chief patrons of St Anne's Church and its then minister Stephen Egerton.

After the players were banned from the playhouse, the company of boy actors that took over the space from 1600 began performing a string of successful public plays there, despite the fact that the theatre was operating under the pretence that it was a 'private' training ground for the child choristers who entertained the royal household. The signatories of the 1619 petition emphasised how much worse conditions in Blackfriars had become since the King's Men had regained possession of the playhouse in 1608 and accused them of continuing to run a public theatre under the guise of its former private status:

> The owner of the said playhouse doth, under the name of a private house (respecting indeed private commodity only) convert the said house to a public playhouse, unto which there is daily such resort of people, and such multitudes of coaches (whereof many are hackney coaches, bringing people of all sorts) that sometimes all our streets cannot contain them, but that they clog up Ludgate also, in such sort that both they endanger the one the other, break down stalls, throw down men's goods from their shops, and the inhabitants there cannot come to their houses ... nor the tradesmen or shop-keepers utter their wares, nor the passenger go to the common water stairs, without danger of their lives and limbs, whereby also many times quarrels and effusion of blood hath followed.

These 'inconveniences', the 1619 petitioners claimed, continued almost every day, even during Lent, blocking the route to the church, 'being close by the playhouse door', and disrupting sacred services. The petition was signed first by the minister of St Anne's, William Gouge, followed by two churchwardens and two sides-men or assistant churchwardens. Then two constables added their names to the list, with a note that they believed the playhouse to be 'a great occasion for the breach of the peace'. Two collectors of alms signed too, explaining that the continuation of a theatre in the district was a 'hindrance to our poor'; their names succeeded by those of two 'scavengers' or street cleaners, who indicated that the Blackfriars Theatre was 'a great annoyance for the cleansing of the streets'. They had mounted a robust case, but these objections were not deemed to be sufficient.

The inhabitants of the precinct started to galvanise, mounting their own crusade, which they coordinated with the area's ecclesiastical and civic officials. Before long they had pulled together their own petition. This, as the Lord Mayor would have understood, was closer to the model established by the 1596 action, and contained their pleas for 'some remedy ... that we may go to our houses in safety and enjoy the benefit of the streets without apparent danger', presenting their collective raised voices against the 'unruliness of some of the resorters to that house'. The document was signed by twenty-four residents, including seven women. Some of the signatories may have used the petition to settle old scores with the playing company, for one of the signers was none other than Sir Thomas Posthumous Hoby, son of the Lady Elizabeth Russell, who had inherited his mother's house in Blackfriars which was located right next door to the premises that had once housed the printing press of Richard Field. Field had, remarkably, acted against his own professional interests by signing Lady Russell's petition in 1596, along with the then Chamberlain's Men's own patron, Sir George Carey, the Lord Hunsdon. Just three years before Field betrayed Shakespeare, he had acquired a new landlord, one William de Lawne (also known as De Laune), minister of London's French Church, who had been a member of Lady Russell's circle of intimates and who also signed her anti-theatrical petition. It is not surprising then that the new 1619 petition was signed by William's son, Paul Delane or De Laune, a physician and anatomy lecturer, educated in the famed medical schools of Padua and Bologna in Italy, who would become professor of physic at Gresham College. The reversal of the 1596 petition therefore met with strong objections from those with personal ties to the earlier generation of protestors, as well as from their neighbours in this affluent parish of St Anne's. Together they formed an intimidating alliance with the district's legal and spiritual governing bodies.

For a while it looked as if history would repeat itself. The 1619 petitions were initially successful. On 21 January a swift order was duly issued from the Corporation of the City of London commanding that 'the said playhouse be suppressed, and that the players shall from henceforth forbear and desist from playing in that house, in respect of the manifold abuses and disorders complained of'. Heminges and Condell, and indeed Richard Burbage who was still alive at this point, would have remembered the devastating effect that the 1596 petition had on the company and in particular on James Burbage who, according to his son Cuthbert, had purchased the property 'at extreme rates' and with 'infinite cost and pains'. The eviction of the Chamberlain's Men from the precinct had nearly crushed the Burbages' business, plunging them into an abyss of debt from which they almost never recovered.

It is true that the King's Men's situation was not as bad as it was in 1596. For one thing they still had the Globe Theatre which meant they could rely on a reasonable revenue stream during the summer season. However, the uncertainty over the fate of the Blackfriars Theatre dragged on for a further two months, during which time they lost both their star actor Richard Burbage and a beloved senior member of the company, Richard Cowley. In this disorienting and uncertain period, the grief-stricken Heminges and Condell turned to their patron, James I, for succour. Their prayers would soon be answered. On 27 March 1619, from his palace in Westminster, the king issued a licence 'under our Great Seal of England', addressed to Edward Somerset, Earl of Worcester, Keeper of the Privy Seal, and commanding by 'our special grace' that his 'well-beloved servants' be permitted 'freely to use and exercise the art and faculty of playing comedies, tragedies, histories, interludes, morals, pastorals, stage plays, and such other like as they have already studied or hereafter shall use or study, as well for the recreation of our loving subjects as for our solace and pleasure'. The edict left no doubt that they could perform, 'show and exercise publicly' within 'their now usual houses called the Globe within our County of Surrey, and their private house situate in the precincts of the Blackfriars within our City of London'. James I, it seems, was willing to play along with the deception that the Blackfriars Theatre was still a 'private' playhouse. For further assurance the licence forbade any 'lets, hindrances, or molestations' that might aggravate the players, insisting rather that there must be 'aiding and assisting to them if any wrong be to them offered', and emphasising their honoured 'place and quality' as the King's Men. The king had spoken. The Blackfriars Theatre was now safe and the players had fought off the angry residents of the district; a welcome relief following the funerals of Burbage and Cowley just two weeks or so before.

Their jubilation would be short-lived.

No sooner had the clouds started to lift when John Heminges and Henry Condell faced another setback. The shadow that now spread across their lives came in the form of John Witter of Mortlake in Surrey. Witter had married Anne, the widow of Augustine Phillips, in 1606. In his will Phillips, an original sharer in the Globe Theatre in 1599, had nominated his wife as sole executrix of his estate. In order to pre-empt any mismanagement of his legacy and protect his children's interests, he added a clause which specified that if Anne 'do at any time marry after my decease, that then and from thenceforth she shall cease to be any more or longer executrix of this my last will'. Instead, the management of any properties, 'goods, [and] chattels' that formed part of his estate would instantly revert to fellow King's Men John Heminges, Richard Burbage and William Sly, along with one Timothy Whithorne. This included any shares in, and profits deriving from, Phillips' interest in the Globe Theatre. On the transfer of the estate back into the hands of Heminges and his fellow overseers, Witter had been granted the lease for Phillips' share in the Globe. It was not long before Witter started causing trouble for Heminges. Not only did he fail to pay the required portion of the ground rent for his share, but he refused to contribute towards the cost of rebuilding and refurbishing the playhouse after it had burned down during a performance of Shakespeare's *Henry VIII*, also known as *All Is True*, in 1613. Heminges cancelled Witter's lease and granted half of the interest to Condell. Witter was outraged but bided his time.

Heminges had regarded Anne with great affection and at her death in 1618 Witter began to sense that his last link with the King's Men had been severed. He therefore acted swiftly to initiate a legal suit against Heminges and Condell, issuing a bill of complaint against them in April 1619. In this he claimed that Heminges and Condell had 'wrongfully and without any just title' seized the shares of the 'sixth part' of the Globe, its 'galleries and gardens', and were withholding 'rents, issues and profits' that were his by legal right. To conceal their crime, he maintained, they were secreting vital evidence, including Augustine Phillips' original will and the lease agreement for the playhouse, which they could, he argued, be guarding 'in any chest, cupboard, or trunk locked, or any bag or box sealed'. He then painted a pitiable picture of himself as a victim of two ruthless oppressors who had taken advantage of a vulnerable man who was 'not of ability and power to contend in law with the said John Heminges and Henry Condell who are of great living, wealth and power, and have many more mighty and great friends than your said subject [Witter], whereby he is and shall be destitute of all help, remedy and hope'.

Heminges and Condell were ordered to appear in court on 23 April. Five days later, they delivered their formal riposte to Witter's accusations. With all the theatrical flair of a seasoned actor revealing a canny plot twist, Heminges informed the court that he would undermine Witter's entire case by presenting 'diverse writings', which included the documents Witter claimed (it turns out accurately) were being withheld. After reasserting the terms of Augustine Phillips' will, Heminges set about turning the tables on his accuser with some elegantly delineated character assassination, accusing Witter of contriving to 'be secretly married' with Anne in order to circumvent Phillips' iron-clad clause. Furthermore, he claimed Witter had an extravagant and wasteful lifestyle and, without any regard for his wife and her children, had 'lavishly and riotously spent, wasted and consumed almost all the rest of the said goods and chattels which were of the said Augustine Phillips'. Heminges had, he insisted, done everything he could to restore their fortunes, giving in 'charity' to Witter, Anne and her children 'diverse sums of money amounting in the whole to a great sum'. Poor Anne lived in dire poverty and had no choice but to beg for her children's food, since 'diverse years before the said Anne died [Witter] did suffer her to make shift for herself to live [that is, she had to fend for herself] and at her death', Heminges lamented, 'this defendant [Heminges] out of charity was at charges of [that is, paid for] the burying of her'.

The case continued through the end of April and into the next month when, on 10 May, Witter returned his 'replication' or answer to Heminges' and Condell's bruising testimony. Perhaps their legal opponent had married Augustine Phillips' widow because he was himself smitten with the theatre, for it was a bravura performance. The defendants' answers were, he averred, 'stuffed full of idle, imperfect and frivolous matters'. He even denied they had 'any manner of right' to the disputed shares in the Globe, but had converted these 'unduly and wrongfully to their own proper use', depriving him, and in the process his wife and her children, of their living. As to the supposed colossal amounts that Heminges had given him and his family in 'charity', his opponent had merely used his 'cunning and craft' in 'alleging it to be a great sum'. It had, he continued, been rather a trifling amount and, in any case, Heminges should 'be ashamed or abashed (if any shame at all he had) to express any sum at all', for he had made a 'great profit' from the money he owed to Witter, having had 'far more money … out of the rents and profits' of these Globe shares than he had ever paid out to the Witters in supposed handouts. In short, Heminges' gains were 'more than sufficient' to recompense the King's Men for Witter's share in the renovation costs for the Globe. He urged the court to see through Heminges' 'dissimulation and hypocrisy' to the hidden man who 'mightily (although in vain) raketh and stretcheth his wits for very poor and simple shifts, quirks, and galls' to excuse himself of his crimes.

Heminges must have been left reeling from the strength of these accusations; but Witter was just warming up. In a further shocking twist, he accused the King's Men of being responsible for the destruction of the Globe Theatre, since 'the said defendants and some other of their partners and fellow players did in their default suffer [the playhouse] to be burnt and consumed wilfully or at the least very negligently'. He did not, however, provide any evidence for this or explain why they would have wanted to burn their own playhouse to the ground. Instead he declared, with a streak of lashing bitter envy, that Heminges was growing wealthier by the day by taking advantage of a large and 'fair house' which he had newly built 'to his own use' on lands included in Phillips' Globe shares, and for which he only paid twenty shillings a year, without releasing profits now legally owed to Witter, 'which house will in a few years yield a greater sum in rent than the new building of the said playhouse and galleries did cost'. He concluded his venting by declaring 'Heminges showeth how liberal he could be of another man's goods and lease, and what large thongs he can cut out of another man's hide'. Heminges was, he quipped, industriously employed, 'as the proverb sayeth' in a 'kind of robbing, to rob Peter to pay Paul'.

Witter had made some potentially damaging claims. Heminges and Condell were at worst arsonists and thieves, at best negligent thugs who had dishonestly exploited legal grey areas in order to consume another's rightful inheritance. There was much at stake. If the King's Men failed to shake off this interloper they could find themselves locked in a permanently uneasy partnership with a difficult man who owned a significant share in the business. They had to act and began looking for further support. The case seemed to crawl along, continuing well into 1620. In the interim, Heminges and Condell managed to track down witnesses to corroborate their case. These came in the form of Thomas Woodford, a 'salter' of London, and James Knasborough, a gentleman, who had become entangled with Witter before, having brought a suit against him after suffering a 'wounding' at his hands. Their testimonies are now lost, but they must have been effective, since they forced Witter into retreat. Heminges and Condell were victorious. The case would eventually be 'clearly and absolutely dismissed forever' in November 1620 with Witter ordered to pay damages of twenty shillings 'for their costs herein most wrongfully sustained'.

Some years afterwards Cuthbert Burbage, his nephew William Burbage and Richard Burbage's widow Winifrid Robinson would complain that the Burbages had 'built the Globe, with more sums of money taken up at interest, which lay heavy on us many years; and to ourselves we joined those deserving men, Shakespeare, Heminges, Condell, Phillips, and others'. They had, they remembered, been too generous with the terms under which this had been agreed, and they may have been thinking of the Witter conflict when they lamented that 'making the leases for twenty-one years hath been the destruction of ourselves and others; for they dying at the expiration of three or four years of their lease, the subsequent years became dissolved to strangers, as by marrying with their widows, and the like by their children'. Lesson learned.

But was Witter responsible for more than just trying to seize a portion of the King's Men's shares in the Globe? Did he also try to steal something else from them, something just as precious? It has been argued that between 1618 and 1620 plays in the King's Men's repertory were stolen, with some sold on to publishers illegally. The company's vital manuscripts and prompt books were, some believe, covertly slipped out of their covers by a light-fingered pilferer, particularly hits by Beaumont and Fletcher, and possibly even by Shakespeare, including *Othello* and *The Winter's Tale*. Witter has been suggested as the culprit, with an axe to grind and access to the troupe's papers. This remains unproven; but it is suggestive perhaps that most of these plays – almost all of which were produced with either bookseller-stationers Thomas Walkley or Nicholas Okes, or both working together – were reprinted in better editions shortly after they first hit the bookstalls, suggesting that the first impressions may not have had the King's Men's seal of approval.

Whether or not Heminges and Condell were dealing with the theft of the playing company's performance texts, their conflict with their Blackfriars neighbours and their protracted legal battle with the headstrong and recalcitrant Witter would have delayed any plans for a collected volume of Shakespeare plays if, that is, they had started working on or were preparing for such a venture before the end of 1620. In any case, with their anti-theatrical antagonists kept at bay by royal command and their legal opponent defeated, the way was open for Heminges and Condell to devote more of their time to the commemoration of their late friend, Will.

Act Two

1621

Negotiating the First Folio

Kind gentlemen, your pains
Are registered where every day I turn
The leaf to read them.

William Shakespeare, *Macbeth*

'Care and pains'

Hunting the King's Men's
Lost Shakespeare Plays

In 1621 John Heminges and Henry Condell were emerging from a challenging couple of years. They had witnessed the death of the playing company's star actor Richard Burbage and the loss of another senior member of their troupe, Richard Cowley, within days of each other, and Heminges buried his beloved wife Rebecca. They were almost certainly taxed with the problem of the 'Pavier-Jaggard Quartos', which could have been unwelcome competition for an expensive volume of William Shakespeare's plays in a handsome folio format, and may have entered into negotiations with the backers of the 'False Folio' in an attempt to preserve the saleability of the grander project.

It is not known in fact whether Heminges and Condell instigated the First Folio – possibly acting in accordance with Shakespeare's own wishes – or whether one of the stationers who would become attached to the venture was inspired to create it and approached the theatre managers with a business proposal. It is also possible that plans for the volume emerged organically from the aborted 'Pavier-Jaggard' collection. Either way, the project could not have been completed without the support and express approval of the two senior actors, since they, as representatives of the King's Men, controlled a stock of fourteen plays outright (and suspected, erroneously, that they held in their possession a further two) which would be included in Shakespeare's Book. A project like this, however, was a symbiotic effort. Even if Hemings and Condell were the Folio's prime movers, they themselves could do nothing without a dedicated team of sponsors and stationers, with the resources to bring the project to fruition. They would have no doubt been daunted by the fact that in order to complete a publishing endeavour of this scale, the ownership of up to twenty-two plays previously licensed or belonging by inheritance to up to twelve booksellers, stationers or rights holders had to be determined (inclusive of those plays registered to the four chief financier-businesses of the Folio).

A syndicate was formed to help manage and fund this ambitious project. This would have spread the financial risk while portioning out some of the labour involved in tracking down, and negotiating with, those who owned the rights to the plays that the King's Men no longer governed. Those works that had never been printed or transferred to a publisher through an entry in the Stationers' Register remained the property of the playing company and could easily be placed under the auspices of a newly assembled Folio syndicate. It is not known, however, if Heminges and Condell paid some kind of fee to the other sharers in the King's Men for divesting them of what were, in effect, their collectively owned assets, with funds derived from the syndicate itself, or if some other form of payment structure was agreed with the Folio's investors. It is likely that the troupe, and probably Heminges and Condell themselves, were promised copies of the volume upon publication as a form of remuneration for their own diligent labours.

The King's Men did not retain the rights to all of the eighteen plays which were printed in the Folio for the first time. Four of these had long been in the possession of other stationers. Even with the transfer of the fourteen as yet unpublished plays the company did own to the syndicate, as part of what was essentially a collaboration between the players and the volume's financiers, the rights to only eight belonged collectively to the group of bookseller-stationers who became involved in its financing and creation. This still left eight individual rights holders with whom the Folio's backers and stationers had to negotiate over a possible fourteen already-registered plays. Because the syndicate members were probably unaware that they held the rights to two of the eight plays which they did in fact own when they embarked on this bibliographical adventure, they would have assumed the total number of works for which negotiations were required was sixteen. No easy task.

Printing the First Folio was a pricey endeavour and would have required some canny business nous to bring to fruition. One calculation for the cost of producing each individual Folio is six shillings, eight pence. With an estimated print run of 750 copies, that would have meant a total outlay of £250, well over £33,000 today; though this is not an accurate reflection of the purchasing power of that sum in 1621. The scale of the venture is brought into perspective when we recall that many artisanal professions, like goldsmithing or shoe-making, brought in an annual salary of just four to five pounds, though the cost of the Folio project would have been the equivalent of over five thousand days of waged labour for even a skilled artisan or tradesperson. One of the first obstacles faced by the syndicate was financing the paper stocks required to complete such a project. Requiring around 229 sheets per book, the First Folio needed a total of 180,000 sheets across its print run, including about 5 per cent extra to cover mishaps or losses during the printing process. Despite this, the syndicate would not opt for the cheapest form of paper. Indeed, in 1633 William Prynne would complain that 'Some playbooks ... are grown from Quarto to Folio' and that 'Shakespeare's plays are printed on the best Crown paper, far better than most Bibles'. Though he was probably referring to the 1632 Second Folio of Shakespeare's works, the same applied to its predecessor. Imported from France and bearing a watermark of a crown, this kind of paper, from which most of Shakespeare's Book was produced, was in fact of medium quality. The Folio required just over 360 reams of this paper, costing about four shillings, six pence per ream. With 500 sheets per ream, this was a significant investment on paper alone: over £81, more than £11,000 today. The cost of the physical labour needed to complete the task would also have included a portion of pressworkers' wages paid for in kind, with copies of this sumptuous volume, which reduced the syndicate's projected profit.

These costs do not include the sums that must have been paid to secure the rights to print plays previously registered with the Stationers' Company. When a publisher-stationer was approached by one of the First Folio's financiers, he could accept an upfront sum in exchange for his 'copy' of a play – either selling or leasing the right to print it from a manuscript in his possession or from a previously issued quarto edition he had funded – or broker a deal that meant he became part of the syndicate in exchange for a share of the eventual profits from the volume's publication. Payment would have included a portion of the stock of Folios printed in proportion to the level of investment in the project. But how much did the business of securing rights to plays cost?

Recording a work in the Stationers' Register normally commanded a fee of around six pence per work, though this was an additional, and optional, part of the process. The stationer was obliged to obtain a ratified 'copy' of a work to be printed – in manuscript form if it had not been printed before, with the approval of an ecclesiastical or other authority affirming that it was fit for publication – and this also cost money. It is not easy to fix on a price for this because it could vary, depending on the type of work registered, its size and projected print run. For books of differing genres, the licence secured direct from the Stationers'

Company (which also sold 'licences' for books) could come with a charge of anywhere from a few shillings to three pounds or more, with one survey of the process indicating that a standard charge of forty shillings, or two pounds, per edition of a work, was frequent. But negotiating pre-assigned rights with publisher-stationers who understood the value of their assets was a somewhat different ball-game. A guide to the challenges and costs involved survives in the prefatorial matter to the folio of the works of Francis Beaumont and John Fletcher, which would be published in 1647 with a dedication to one of the First Folio's patrons, Sir Philip Herbert, drawing attention to the labours involved in printing the 'flowing compositions of then expired sweet Swan of Avon SHAKESPEARE', which provided a model for the later work. This was financed by two stationers, both operating from St Paul's Cross Churchyard: Humphrey Moseley and Humphrey Robinson. In a somewhat tetchy epistle from the 'Stationer to the Readers', Moseley complained:

> 'Twere vain to mention the chargeableness [that is, cost] of this work; for those who owned the manuscripts too well knew their value to make a cheap estimate of any of these pieces, and though another joined with me in the purchase and printing, yet the care and pains was wholly mine, which I found to be more than you'll easily imagine, unless you knew into how many hands the originals were dispersed. They are all happily met in this book, having escaped these public troubles, free and unmangled.

This indicates that, in terms of the First Folio negotiations, every play commanded a different price which, for a previously published work, depended on its popularity, print run and the number of editions it commanded. Shakespeare's works had ended up in many hands, so the Folio syndicate could expect problems and obstacles similar to those described by Moseley.

We do not know the order in which each syndicate member joined the team responsible for producing Shakespeare's Book. The First Folio's 'colophon', a statement that provides details of the printing and publication of a book, simply indicates the names of those who met the considerable costs of producing the first edition of Shakespeare's collected plays in folio format. It reads: 'Printed at the Charges of W. Jaggard, Ed. Blount, J. Smithweeke, and W. Aspley, 1623'. With William Jaggard we might also infer his son, Isaac Jaggard, who co-ran the family printing business, since his name appears along with Blount's on the Folio's title page, where both are identified as having 'printed' the book; though at that time this could also mean 'published' or financed. Despite the inclusion of Blount's name, the entire project was executed in the Jaggards' printing house in the Barbican. In both cases – in the Folio's colophon and its imprint – a Jaggard name appears first, perhaps indicating that the Jaggards had seniority in the project or shelled out the greatest portion of the investment. Their 'charges' may have included payment in kind through the material resources and labour they could bring to this highly risky venture.

The Jaggards were, in so many ways, ideal helmsmen for the Folio scheme. Probably born around 1568, William had entered the service of the printer Henry Denham as an apprentice in 1584 and became a 'freeman' of the Stationers' Company in December 1591. Isaac was baptised on 19 April 1595 and acquired his freedom with the Stationers' Company 'by patrimony' in 1613, skipping the customary apprenticeship because he was the son of an established stationer. By that point William Jaggard had started to lose his sight, with syphilis, or mercury poisoning due to concoctions used to treat it, suspected as the cause. Despite the additional support William needed from Isaac to manage the business, the pair formed a dynamic and productive team. Their licence to operate two printing presses in their printing house meant they could run an efficient operation – William is known to have taken on at

Make no Collection of it. Let him shew
His skill in the conſtruction.

Luc. *Philarmonus* .

Sooth. Heere,my good Lord.

Luc. Read,and declare the meaning.

Reades.

WHen as a Lyons whelpe,ſhall to himſelfe vnknown,with-
out ſeeking finde, and bee embrac'd by a peece of tender
Ayre: And when from a ſtately Cedar ſhall be lopt branches,
which being dead many yeares,ſhall after renine, bee ioynted to
the old Stocke , and freſhly grow, then ſhall Poſthumus end his
miſeries, Britaine be fortunate, and flouriſh in Peace and Plentie.

Thou *Leonatus* art the Lyons Whelpe,
The fit and apt Conſtruction of thy name
Being *Leonatus*, doth import ſo much:
The peece of tender Ayre,thy vertuous Daughter,
Which we call *Mollis Aer*, and *Mollis Aer*
We terme it *Mulier*; which *Mulier* I diuine
Is this moſt conſtant Wife,who euen now
Anſwering the Letter of the Oracle,
Vnknowne to you vnſought,were clipt about
With this moſt tender Aire.

Cym. This hath ſome ſeeming.

Sooth. The loſty Cedar,Royall *Cymbeline*
Perſonates thee : And thy lopt Branches,point
Thy two Sonnes forth : who by *Belarius* ſtolne
For many yeares thought dead,are now reuiu'd
To the Maieſticke Cedar ioyn'd; whoſe Iſſue

Promiſes Britaine, Peace and Plenty.

Cym. Well,
My Peace we will begin: And *Caius Lucius,*
Although the Victor,we ſubmit to *Cæſar,*
And to the Romaine Empire ; promiſing
To pay our wonted Tribute, from the which
We were diſſwaded by our wicked Queene,
Whom heauens in Iuſtice both on her,and hers,
Haue laid moſt heauy hand.

Sooth. The fingers of the Powres aboue, do tune
The harmony ot this Peace : the Viſion
Which I made knowne to *Lucius* ere the ſtroke
Of yet this ſcarſe-cold-Battaile, at this inſtant
Is full accompliſh'd. For the Romaine Eagle
From South to Weſt,on wing ſoaring aloft
Leſſen'd her ſelfe, and in the Beames o'th Sun
So vaniſh'd ; which fore-ſhew'd our Princely Eagle
Th'Imperiall *Cæſar*, ſhould againe vnite
His Fauour,with the Radiant *Cymbeline,*
Which ſhines heere in the Weſt.

Cym. Laud we the Gods,
And let our crooked Smoakes climbe to their Noſtrils
From our bleſt Altars. Publiſh we this Peace
To all our Subiects. Set we forward : Let
A Roman,and a Brittiſh Enſigne waue
Friendly together : ſo through *Luds-Towne* match,
And in the Temple of great Iupiter
Our Peace wee'l ratifie: Seale it with Feaſts.
Set on there: Neuer was a Warre did ceaſe
(Ere bloodie hands were waſh'd) with ſuch a Peace.

Exeunt.

FINIS.

Printed at the Charges of W. Jaggard, Ed. Blount, I. Smithweeke,
and W. Aſpley, 1623.

The final page of *Cymbeline*, showing the 'colophon' which provides the
printing information for the First Folio, indicating that William Jaggard,
Edward Blount, John Smethwick and William Aspley financed its creation.

least nine apprentices between 1597 and 1622 – and they were already experienced producers of folios, having issued works which emanated that aura of the epic, nationally significant or encyclopaedic that was most associated with books in this large format, such as Edward Topsell's richly illustrated encyclopaedia *The History of Four-Footed Beasts* in 1607, Thomas Heywood's grand nationalistic tome *Troia Britanica* in 1609, and Helkiah Crooke's intimidatingly dense anatomical treatise *Mikrokosmographia* in 1615. They also held the monopoly for the printing of playbills, making them regular collaborators with the King's Men. Blount equally had a great deal to recommend him as a bankable professional with the ability to add value to a demanding book project, and he had worked with the Jaggards before in 1614, joining forces to produce an edition of the works of the cleric Edward Dering. When Edward Blount and Isaac Jaggard came to record their rights to the unpublished Shakespeare plays controlled by the King's Men in the Stationers' Register, the name 'Mr Blount' appeared in the senior position, written above that of his fellow syndicate member. This all suggests that Aspley and Smethwick had a less prominent role in the syndicate's financial and managerial scheme than the Jaggards and Blount, and were probably brought into the project in exchange for the rights to the plays they held. However, their involvement would be crucial to the volume's success.

Before embarking on this ambitious undertaking neither the King's Men nor any members of the First Folio syndicate had paid for a thorough search of the Stationers' Register as a means of tracking down the stationers who owned rights to previously registered Shakespeare plays. If they had, they would have discovered that the Jaggards owned the rights to *As You Like It* and that Blount was in possession of *Antony and Cleopatra* long before Isaac and Edward registered their rights to the King's Men's unpublished Shakespeare works just days or weeks before the Folio's publication.

This is confirmed by the fact that they paid a fee of seven shillings to record their rights, the price for fourteen plays, rather than for all sixteen listed in the register. How did they locate so many stationers without a prior search of the Stationers' archives, particularly when they were dealing with rights that had been claimed as early as the early-to-mid 1590s? Even if the company owned and used numerous quarto versions of the plays as performance books, could they have kept up to date with when and to whom rights had been transferred across a span of, in some cases, nearly three decades? It seems unlikely. So when the players, probably led by Heminges and Condell, approached Sir William Herbert in 1619 and asked him to issue a command to the Court of Stationers, in his capacity as Lord Chamberlain, to block the further printing of plays in the King's Men's repertory, this may have not simply been in anticipation of an increased demand for published plays associated with their company sparked by the death of Richard Burbage. It may also have been a cunning ploy to flush out the stationers who held rights to Shakespeare plays and bring them to the negotiating table. This would have forced those rights holders, who had discovered their Shakespeare assets were potentially worthless just at the point when Burbage's death had brought the playwright's work back into the spotlight, into negotiation initially with Heminges and Condell and ultimately with the Folio syndicate. One thing is certain: putting together Shakespeare's Book would have been far more difficult without this edict, so helpfully penned by Herbert and enforced by the Company of Stationers.

Even if the Lord Chamberlain's assistance did help draw rights holders out of the woodwork, thereby saving the syndicate much labour in tracking them down, the volume's backers would still have to locate those who did not respond to the edict, or had no intention of publishing the plays in their possession. They would also have to convince stationers, perhaps disgruntled by the way in which the King's Men were holding their rights to ransom, to part with plays the value of which they were well aware and which they would not be willing to give up cheaply. As will become clear, this did present the syndicate with problems, causing delays to the typesetting of some of the plays, and indicating that negotiations over the rights to these works were ongoing throughout the printing of the First Folio. Since the printing of the Folio is estimated to have started early in 1622, possibly around February, the syndicate would have needed some of the rights to previously published comedies in hand some time in 1621, so we will proceed on the assumption that negotiations were fully underway in that year. This does not mean that deals over the plays were not struck or discussed with rights-holders much earlier, even during the printing of the 'Pavier-Jaggard Quartos'.

Crucial to the whole enterprise was the fact that the Folio's syndicate members were based across long-established London hotspots for bookselling and printing which stretched from St Paul's Cross Churchyard to the Barbican near Smithfield in the north and Fleet Street in St Dunstan's parish to the west. Together they formed a network that helped them track down and secure these rogue plays. This may have determined the composition of the syndicate in ways we will better understand if we map their locations across the city, as well as their connections both to the stationers with whom they had to agree terms and to each other: these being just some of the individual branches which form the magnificent tree that is Shakespeare's Book.

Bears, Parrots and Angels

St Paul's Cross Churchyard, London's Publishing Powerhouse

B y the time the First Folio syndicate was formed, St Paul's Cross Churchyard had long been the hub of England's book-selling industry. Around twenty-eight booksellers had set up shop within its boundary by the turn of the century. An irregularly shaped communal space skirting the north-eastern perimeter of St Paul's Cathedral, St Paul's Cross Churchyard spanned over 310 feet from east to west and 250 feet north to south at its longest points. Among the wider precinct's jutting angles and smaller winding alleys were radiating paths that connected St Paul's to its neighbouring parishes.

A stroll north-east from the cathedral grounds, through Paul's Gate, took the traveller to Paternoster Row and then either to Cheapside in the east or, in the opposite direction, to Ivy Lane where one could browse in the bookshop of the Jaggards' recent collaborator Thomas Pavier, who owned the rights to four Shakespeare plays outright, and possibly controlled the rights to a fifth. If a visitor chose to pass through Paul's western Great Gate they would find themselves crossing Bower Row into Ludgate. This pathway bisected Ave Maria Lane and Creed Lane which, along with Paternoster Row, took their names from the Latin prayers included in the religious books that scribes and early printers in the area had been renowned for producing during the district's medieval history. Walking east from the churchyard, one could cross Augustine's Gate to the Old Change and Watling Street, which led towards Bow Church and Bread Street, a favourite address for wealthy merchants. Taking the narrow passage of Paul's Chain south, the wanderer would find themselves on Carter Lane where William Shakespeare's publisher and fellow Stratfordian Richard Field once operated a printing house abutting onto Ludgate; the very business that had first brought Shakespeare's words to press through his narrative poem *Venus and Adonis* in 1593.

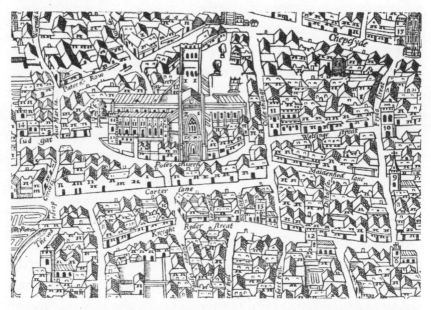

Detail from the 'Agas Map', first produced in 1561 but slightly revised in 1633, showing St Paul's and the surrounding area, including Paternoster Row and Cheapside to the north and Carter Lane to the south. The bookshops of Edward Blount, William Aspley and other publishers who owned the rights to plays by William Shakespeare were located within the St Paul's precinct. Stationers' Hall stood at the intersection of Paternoster Row and Ave Maria Lane.

Visitors to St Paul's Cross Churchyard in 1621 would not have seen very much evidence of the renovations to the crumbling cathedral, which James I authorised that year, for these were slow to take shape. But when they were done gazing in wonder at the impressive three- and four-storey houses that lined the outer edge of the yard, with their beamed frontages and high-pitched gabled roofs, onlookers would have noted the rows of busy bookstalls and shops competing for business, particularly in the north-eastern and eastern quarters of the precinct. They may have stopped to read the individual title pages of books, extra copies of which would have been produced by printers as advertisements for the booksellers' wares, pinned to the posts and side-boards of the stalls which projected from the shopfronts into the yard. If they were not there to book-browse, visitors could attend a religious service or hear a sermon at Paul's Cross: an elaborate platform designed as a stage for preaching, which stood around forty feet from St Paul's Choir at the cathedral's northern façade, with St Paul's School just a hundred feet to the east. This was a wooden octagonal structure, around seventeen feet in diameter, standing on a huge stone base thirty-four feet in length, the whole construction topped with a lead roof featuring a large cross at its apex. The preaching stand was so high that it could only be reached via a flight of steps leading up from an earth-and-dirt ground packed hard from decades of visitor footfalls. On occasions when nobility and even royalty came to hear sermons, they could view the scene from the comfort of purpose-built boxes that protruded from the front of Sermon House, attached to the northern wall of the choir, complete with an elaborate polygonal royal box for James I.

Overlooked by the cathedral's gargoyles, shimmering stained-glass windows and flying buttresses, this was a vibrant, heady and noisy place to be. Fire-and-brimstone preachers reminded the masses of their sins from the Cross. Strains of song and sacred chant emanated from the choir, when these were not, that is, being drowned out by the din coming from Paul's Walk, the cathedral's long and echoing nave, which was alike an attraction for locals and visitors to London, whose sounds were said to spill out into the churchyard in thrumming waves of human chatter and bustle. Boisterous schoolboys shouted, fought and played on their way to and from St Paul's School. The clatter of horses' hooves and carriages signalled the arrival of worshippers, shoppers, workers or deliveries of books, paper stocks, leathers and other materials to the shops and binders which lined the perimeter of the yard. Booksellers touted their wares to the area's bibliophiles or called out tantalising nuggets of gossip to sell ballads and pamphlets to a news-hungry public. And this was all punctuated by the bells of St Paul's calling parishioners to service and the chiming of the cathedral's great clock, which sounded every quarter hour.

View of S.t Paul's Cross as it appeared in the Year 1621.

Woodcut of St Paul's Cross and its surrounding churchyard in the year 1621, showing a preacher addressing a large audience. Attending public sermons and lectures at St Paul's preaching cross was a popular pastime for city dwellers in the period. These, sometimes controversial, events would have taken place just opposite the shops of Edward Blount and William Aspley.

Around 145 feet north of Paul's Cross stood a line of bookshops running parallel with Paternoster Row just behind the churchyard's wall. These ranged in size between 225 and 750 square feet. Each would have been arranged in a similar way, with the main retail outlet on the ground floor from which projected a wooden stall, for the display of the newest or most popular books, which could be niftily folded away in the evenings. Behind this there was usually a front room densely packed with books piled onto shelves, tables or counters, with some shops having a storeroom at the back. The upper levels could be used for storage or as lodgings for the owners and renters of, or workers in, the shops below. Here stood the bookshop identified by the sign of the Black Bear, located opposite the cathedral's Great North Door and just six shops away from Canon Alley, the path that led into Paternoster Row and Stationers' Hall. Since at least 1609, this shop had belonged to the publisher-stationer Edward Blount, who had in his possession the rights to *Antony and Cleopatra*, and had certainly once owned *Pericles*, though he himself had published neither play, and *Pericles* would not be included in the First Folio, possibly because the King's Men knew it to be a collaborative work. A four-storey building, the Black Bear comprised Blount's own home in its upper floors, as well as boarding rooms for paying lodgers. It would have been a busy shop, with a regular stream of visitors, shoppers, newsmongers and tradespeople bringing a variety of goods and provisions. Blount, like other booksellers, acted as a courier and provided storage-and-collection services, taking deliveries of letters, seeds, fruit and even sweet delights like treacle, and supplying the latest books and almanacs to influential patrons, as well as offering financial services, which included transferring funds to agents in other countries. He also conveyed gossip of a more sensitive nature, both to and from the continent, and from other parts of England, on behalf of agents on ambassadorial missions to other countries, and procured the most recent news gazettes for James I's

well-informed courtiers. He is known to have worked in this
capacity for court gossip John Chamberlain, who lived nearby and
had served on the committee overseeing the renovations to St
Paul's; for Sir Dudley Carleton, ambassador to Venice and then to
the Netherlands; Sir William Trumbull, ambassador to Brussels;
and, later on, possibly Sir Isaac Wake, ambassador to Paris, among
others. He was, therefore, more than just a publisher. He had his
finger on the pulse of London's thriving political culture, at the
crossroads of its international news networks.

Baptised in St Lawrence's Church, Pountney, in London on 31
January 1562, and attending the Merchant Taylors' School where
he was probably taught by the celebrated humanist scholar and
pedagogue Richard Mulcaster, Edward Blount had gained his
freedom with the Stationers' Company in June 1588. On 10 May
1611 he underwent the elaborate and solemn ceremony of investi-
ture in which he was 'sworn and admitted into the livery' of the
company. Thereafter he continued his rise up the Stationers' ranks,
acquiring shares in the English Stock, brandishing the coveted
Stock Keeper's key both to the company's reserve of Latin and
English books, and eventually becoming an Under Warden.

Blount was not just a respected member of the Stationers'
Company. He would become, in the words of his biographer, 'the
most important publisher of the early seventeenth century', going
on to acquire a towering reputation as one of the leading literary
figures of his generation, with an unrivalled instinct for identifying
authors whose works would stand the test of time. Like the
Jaggards, he had financed other folios, including John Florio's
translation of Michel de Montaigne's *Essays* in editions of 1603
and 1613; Samuel Daniel's *Panegyricke Congratulatory Delivered to
the King's Most Excellent Majesty*, which was produced in celebration of James I's accession to the English throne in 1603; and
Lucan's epic poem *Pharsalia* in 1614. His fondness for folios was
probably inspired by William Ponsonby, to whom he had been

apprenticed between 1578 and 1588, who had brought to the world the works of literary giants like Sir Philip Sidney and Edmund Spenser. Blount would surpass even his master in one significant way, becoming a pioneer of the dramatic series. He published the first English collection of plays, William Alexander's *The Monarchic Tragedies*, in 1604, and in an expanded edition of 1607, and would go on to issue John Lyly's *Six Court Comedies* in 1632. He also flirted with Shakespeare's works. In addition to his rights to *Antony and Cleopatra* and *Pericles*, which he registered in May 1608, Blount's pre-Folio acquaintance with the playwright extended to his publication of *Love's Martyr* in 1601, in which Shakespeare's strange and mystical poem *The Phoenix and Turtle* appeared. For this latter text Blount selected Shakespeare's former Stratford neighbour Richard Field as his printer. Though the publisher had apparently forgotten he owned the rights to *Antony and Cleopatra*, and it is unclear if he was directly involved with Henry Gosson's 1609 edition of *Pericles*, Blount was close to Thomas Thorpe, who published Shakespeare's *Sonnets* in 1609, referring to him as 'his kind and true friend'. Shakespeare had, in many respects, through Blount already received the stamp of approval of a noted arbiter of taste and literary quality, who was instrumental in popularising the play series.

Despite Blount's somewhat patchy history with the publishing of Shakespeare's plays, he was intimately associated with numerous key figures attached to the publication of the First Folio. He was close to the Herbert brothers, to whom Blount also dedicated numerous works, including his translation of a book about the arts of courtiership that he issued in 1607, testifying that 'my particular duty ... bind[s] me the most humbly devoted to your honours'. Significantly, just a year before the Folio's publication, he published an edition of Gonzalo de Céspedes y Meneses' *Gerardo the Unfortunate Spaniard*, which was dedicated to both brothers as an act of 'public good'. This was translated from the Spanish by

Leonard Digges, the scholarly hispanophile who would commemorate Shakespeare in the Folio's prefatorial poem 'To the memory of the deceased author Master W. Shakespeare'. The work was part of a larger literary programme initiated by Blount. As the publisher of Thomas Shelton's translation of Cervantes' *Don Quixote* in two volumes in 1612 and 1620 respectively, and other works from Spanish authors, Blount popularised Spanish literature and letters in England and it is not, therefore, surprising that he should have been drawn to a collaboration with Digges. This was no less true of his association with James Mabbe, almost certainly the 'I.M.' or 'J.M.' identified as the author of the Folio's commemorative poem 'To the memorie of M[aster] W. Shake-speare'.

Late in the very year in which Blount published Digges's translation, he issued Mabbe's English rendering of Mateo Alemán's *The Rogue*, which was originally published in Spanish. Blount had known Mabbe for over a decade by this time, the two becoming firm friends and drinking companions, with the academic staying at the stationer's home above his bookshop when he visited him, the pair downing toasts of sweet wine with other acquaintances, including Thomas Thorpe. Blount's own epistle to the reader in *The Rogue* faces verses penned by Digges and Ben Jonson, bringing together a fourth personality associated with the Folio. Blount had previously published a poem by Mabbe in a book he issued in 1611, John Florio's *Queen Anna's New World of Words*, and would go on to work on Mabbe's translation of a Spanish text entitled *Christian Policy* in English in 1632.

Blount also held the rights to Jonson's *Sejanus*, which has a connection to another of the poets who would commemorate Shakespeare in the Folio. In the printed version of this play Hugh Holland, author of the First Folio's elegy 'Upon the Lines and Life of the Famous Scenic Poet, Master William Shakespeare', produced a commendatory verse to Jonson in which he called him his 'worthy Friend'. Holland, whose family hailed from Wales, was born in 1563, just a year before Shakespeare, and had studied at Westminster School under Ben Jonson's own one-time tutor, William Camden, who referred to him as 'one of the most pregnant wits of these our times', assessing his achievements as equal to those of Jonson and Shakespeare, and the authors of epic romances Sir Philip Sidney and Edmund Spenser. Holland was noted by his seventeenth-century biographer Anthony à Wood as an 'excellent Latin poet, and by some thought worthy to be mentioned by Spenser, Sidney and others, the chiefest of our English poets'. Wood also believed that he had 'always been *in animo Catholicus*', that is, a crypto-Catholic. He was widely travelled, having spent time in Rome, Jerusalem and Constantinople (present-day Istanbul), 'where he received a reprimand from the English ambassador, for the former freedom of his tongue'. He was clearly someone who spoke his mind and was not afraid to enter into disputes when he felt this was necessary. Indeed, he had an interest in, and fought a long legal battle over, a property that spanned the intersection of Paternoster Row and Ivy Lane, just behind Blount's Black Bear. Such close-knit associations with the memorialisers of Shakespeare's Book has led some to believe that Blount was responsible for gathering these scholarly poets together for that project.

Blount had an uncanny knack not only of spotting but setting the latest trends in publishing. His name attached to the Folio project would have lent the entire venture a sense of exclusivity, good taste and grandeur. Whether or not he was the conduit for the participation of Jonson, Digges, Mabbe and Holland, his location in St Paul's Cross Churchyard could have been the soil from which some of these friendships flourished. His shop, the Black Bear, was located right next door to the outlet known by the sign of the Angel, which the stationer Ralph Mabbe had occupied between 1611 and 1613, before moving into a shop on the opposite side of Blount, the Greyhound, which he operated for close to three years. Ralph Mabbe had also collaborated with Nathaniel Butter, who owned the rights to Shakespeare's *King Lear*, whose shop was identified by the sign of the Pied Bull and was located near St Augustine's Gate on the eastern edge of St Paul's Cross Churchyard. Ralph would remain a stationer for the rest of his life, though he struggled financially after moving out of the Greyhound, taking at least three substantial loans from the Stationers' Company between 1619 and 1623. He and Blount may have commiserated about their money woes together, for they were both serial loan-seekers from the Stationers. Significantly, Ralph may have been a kinsman or even the brother of the Folio's James Mabbe, providing Blount with a close connection to the Mabbe family.

Blount's address is noteworthy in other ways; it was located in the immediate vicinity where Shakespeare play publishing arguably began, and where the dramatist's collected *Sonnets* would first be sold. The shop directly next door to his, the Angel, was located within a building that was divided into two shops on its ground floor, its neighbouring premises on the other side being a shop identified by the sign of the Parrot. Before Ralph Mabbe had come to occupy the Angel, it had been the business premises of Andrew Wise, who managed it between 1593 and 1602. Wise was probably the stationer with the canniest eye for a Shakespeare play, for he had acquired the rights to five of the dramatist's works, becoming the first stationer to enter non-collaborative Shakespeare plays in the Stationers' Register in 1597–8. At the time Blount was based at the shop identified by the sign of the Bishop's Head, just five doors from the Black Bear. Three of Wise's Shakespeare assets were probably the playwright's most popular plays – *Richard II*, *Henry IV, Part 1* and *Richard III* – and, after his death in 1603, these were transferred to the stationer Matthew Law. Law's shop was known by the sign of the Fox and stood adjacent to the south-eastern edge of St Paul's Choir, near St Augustine's Gate, next to what had been Nathaniel Butter's own shop at the Pied Bull. Despite their proximity and the fact that Law had worked with Blount on James I's *Basilikon Doron*, a book of national importance about kingly governance issued in collaboration with fourteen stationers, this would not stop him from causing some trouble to the Folio syndicate because of his unwillingness to give up the rights to these works easily when the time came to print them in Shakespeare's Book.

The other two works which made up Wise's stash of Shakespeare plays were secured in partnership with the man who would become one of the First Folio's syndicate members: William Aspley. These were *Much Ado About Nothing* and *Henry IV, Part 2*, jointly licensed in August 1600, the rights for which passed entirely to Aspley, probably after Wise's death, and were still in his possession when the negotiations over the Folio's plays began. Aspley clearly had a good instinct when it came to spotting a talented playwright on his own account, issuing works by some of the finest of his generation, including Ben Jonson, John Marston and George Chapman, by 1607. In addition Aspley, like Blount, was close to Thomas Thorpe, with whom he had collaborated on several projects. In 1605 he had published the controversial play *Eastward Ho!*, co-authored by Jonson, Chapman and Marston, and jointly entered in the Stationers' Register with Thorpe. The reaction to the play from the state censors proved devastating for Aspley, but even worse for the authors who earned a spell in prison due to its satirical mockery of James I's Scottish court. So dire were the circumstances that Jonson's mother procured a 'lusty strong poison', which, according to the playwright's own testimony, she planned to convey secretly into the prison for her son to mix into his drink should the death sentence be pronounced. '[S]he was no churl,' Jonson claimed she had said, for 'she minded first to have drunk of it herself.'

Perhaps a more positive experience for Aspley was his association with Thorpe over the latter's publication of Shakespeare's *Sonnets*; they reached an agreement that the text would be sold from Aspley's own shop, none other than the Parrot, which he had moved into in 1608, just a year before Blount occupied the Black Bear; the latter settled into his new premises just in time to see the work displayed on his neighbouring bookseller's shelves. Aspley had also worked with Nathaniel Butter, jointly entering rights to a work with him in the Stationers' Register in July 1613 and co-publishing it the following year. While Butter had used the Jaggards as his printers numerous times between 1605 and 1616 – they had previously issued *King Lear* in the 'False Folio', meaning that they could have been the conduits for that play into the First Folio – the web of connections we have traced, governed by physical proximity, makes it likely that St Paul's Cross Churchyard was the centre of negotiations over the rights to plays held by Law, if not by Butter too.

Aspley had been no less ambitious than Jaggard and Blount when it came to his career in the Stationers' Company. Born in Hertfordshire some time during or before 1573, Aspley had been apprenticed to the bookseller George Bishop in February 1588. By April 1597 he had become a freeman of the Stationers' Company. Thereafter his career trajectory ran in parallel to that of others involved with the Folio project, leading to his own ceremonial induction into the Company's livery just two months after Blount in 1611, and on the same day as William Jaggard and John Smethwick, along with one of the copyright holders to Shakespeare's plays, Arthur Johnson. Clearly a spirited and strong-willed individual, Aspley was just the kind of person who could be relied upon to doggedly go after the rights to Shakespeare's plays on behalf of the Folio syndicate. He would later cause 'a tumult or combustion amongst the whole corporation' after insulting members of the Stationers' Company with 'disgraceful and scan-dalous speeches' in a 'jeering and scornful manner', for which he was temporarily suspended from enjoying the profits arising from his shares in the English Stock until he apologised before the

Court of Stationers. He proved stubborn and was slow to do so. This did not impact his long-term progression in his chosen vocation, however, since he acquired numerous positions among the Stationers' managerial ranks and would become a Warden in 1632, just in time for the publication of Shakespeare's Second Folio for which he and John Smethwick would be syndicate members.

While Aspley may have consulted with William Jaggard for the latter's *Catalogue of Such English Books*, a survey of the publishing industry, which included some of Aspley's greatest hits to date, his closest connections appear to have been with Blount, for they had collaborated on numerous occasions on publishing projects. These included English translations of a Spanish work about the East and West Indies by José de Acosta in 1604, an Italian book by Thommaso Buoni evocatively Englished as *Problems of Beauty and All Human Affections* in 1606, and three editions of Pierre Charron's philosophical treatise *Of Wisdom*, with the last appearing in 1620. Aspley, like Blount, had an interest in continental books, including those associated with Spain, and he and Blount were part of a syndicate that backed versions of Richard Perceval's *A Dictionary of Spanish and English* in 1623. By 1619 Aspley had become interested in printing impressive folios, but had not published a single book in 1621. Recent research has indicated that it is possible that this cessation in activities was due to his conserving money not just for a large folio of the *Works* of the theologian and Doctor of Divinity John Boys, which he would publish the following year, but for the First Folio project, which may suggest that he was brought into the venture for the making of Shakespeare's Book fairly early in the negotiations.

When Aspley stood outside the door of the Parrot and looked directly ahead, towards the eastern edge of the cathedral's north transept, the old church's monumental Great North Door and its glittering stained-glass windows towering over him, he saw a shop he had once managed for at least a year from 1599, identified by the sign of the Tiger's Head. Just behind that were at least two binderies where books could be professionally bound. On Aspley's own row of shops, six doors down from his premises, and eight doors from Blount's, stood the shop once known as the Spread Eagle during 1609–10 when Henry Walley occupied it, in partnership with Richard Bonian. Though Blount and Aspley did not know it in 1621, Walley would cause them a great deal of trouble over the rights to *Troilus and Cressida* during the printing of the First Folio. Next to the Spread Eagle, the stationer Arthur Johnson had maintained the shop with the sign of the White Horse since at least 1604. It stood against Canon Alley, which led into Paternoster Row, and was prominently located directly opposite the cathedral's Great North Door. Johnson had owned the rights to *The Merry Wives of Windsor* since 1602, when he was at the shop identified by the sign of the Fleur-de-lis and Crown, next door to the Tiger's Head.

While we cannot know when all the negotiations for the Folio's previously registered plays took place, it is reasonable to assume that the syndicate would have needed to secure the rights to print what they considered a 'safe' number of comedies (the first plays to be printed in the Folio) to ensure the whole enterprise was viable and to justify beginning the printing process, ahead of which a considerable investment in paper stocks and other materials was required. It is likely, therefore, that the first batch of comedies for which negotiations were needed were tied up fairly early in the process. So Johnson would have been one of the very first stationers with whom the Folio syndicate would have had to come to some kind of agreement, since *The Merry Wives of Windsor* was the third play to be printed and the first of those for which the syndicate held no licence.

Johnson would vacate the White Horse by the end of 1621, the last year in which he published books, so the negotiations for this play were probably tied up in or before that year. He may have decided to pack up his shop and move to Dublin, where in 1624 he would become involved with the management of the Stationers' Company's Irish Stock. Although it is by no means certain that Johnson had given his full permission for the publication of *The Merry Wives of Windsor* by Pavier and Jaggard in 1619 (the name of his shop is not identified on the play's title page; the only one of his published works not to include it), Johnson's other traceable connections are with Blount, with whom he owned a share in a publication in 1611. A year before, he and Blount had been jointly appointed as officers responsible for managing part of the Stationers' Company's English Stock, which would have meant working closely together that year. Their precious shares in the company may not have been so easy to keep hold of, for both were listed as 'behind' in their payments and informed that failure to 'pay the sums of money they owe' would result in the confiscation of their shares, indicating their joint presence in hearings of the Stationers' Court. These close associations increase the likelihood of a transfer of rights to print *The Merry Wives of Windsor* from Johnson to Blount.

The second comedy that the King's Men did not own the rights to print belonged to Aspley himself. This was *Much Ado About Nothing*, which was the sixth Folio play to be printed. It is interesting to note that the negotiations for the first two plays for which the King's Men did not own the rights – *The Merry Wives of Windsor* and *Much Ado About Nothing* – would have taken place with stationers who were in close physical proximity to Blount, with both Johnson and Aspley located just paces away in the same row of shops. It seems logical to assume, given the fact that the order of the printing of these plays in the First Folio matches the proximity of these stationers, that in addition to securing the rights from Johnson for *The Merry Wives of Windsor*, Blount brought Aspley into the First Folio scheme as a sharer, in the process netting *Much Ado About Nothing* and *Henry IV, Part 2*.

This meant that, probably fairly early on in the negotiating process, the syndicate had firmly clinched the first six plays that would be printed through the network of connections around Blount in St Paul's Cross Churchyard, since the King's Men had at their disposal the rights to *The Tempest*, *The Two Gentlemen of Verona*, *Measure for Measure* and the *Comedy of Errors*. Though the backers of the First Folio may have been uncertain about the ownership of *As You Like It* (probably believing that it belonged to the King's Men when in fact the rights were William Jaggard's property), as we will see, if John Smethwick was included in the syndicate at an early stage too, the financiers could in fact have procured the rights to print all the comedies before a single word was typeset.

8

Dials, Legs and Harts

In St Dunstan's Churchyard and Fleet Street

L ess than a mile west of St Paul's Cross Churchyard was another of London's bookselling hubs: the churchyard of St Dunstan's in the West. Built against the church's tower, underneath its impressive clock and intersecting with Fleet Street, stood the shop belonging to John Smethwick. This could be reached from St Paul's by traversing its western gate and passing through Ludgate into Fleet Street, walking over the Fleet Bridge above a bubbling tributary of the Thames that once flowed around Bridewell Prison but which had, by Smethwick's time, been largely paved over. The traveller would then stroll past St Bride's Church and the Fleet's water conduit, before crossing Fetter Lane on the corner of St Dunstan's Churchyard.

This was the heart of what was then, and still is, London's legal district, overlooked by the Inns of Court, and on a path leading directly to the district's looming gateway at Temple Bar. St Dunstan's shared a boundary with Clifford's Inn at its northern end, which was itself just paces from Serjeant's Inn, abutting onto Chancery Lane which, when followed to its northern-most point, would take the walker past Lincoln's Inn to Gray's Inn on Holborn.

The Temple Church stood directly opposite, just to the south, of St Dunstan's Churchyard, and behind that was the Inner Temple. An upmarket district, with well-heeled and educated residents, it was a good place to maintain a bookshop, and there were at least six in the area, which serviced legal professionals and over a thousand law students across Fleet Street and Holborn. It made sense to have a foothold in this precinct, and bringing Smethwick into the First Folio enterprise was a canny move, which would have increased the customer base as well as potential contacts through which to sell a volume of plays to students wanting a break from their legal training to immerse themselves in the high drama of Shakespeare's characters, or to other wealthy professionals who could afford an expensive luxury commodity like a folio. Shakespeare's plays had been staged in the vicinity, and printed versions of his works issued from there, so it carried a kind of residual memory of the dramatist's presence.

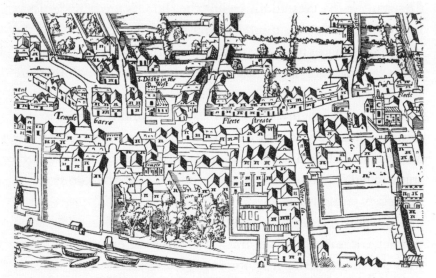

Detail from the 'Agas Map', showing St Dunstan's in the West and the surrounding area, including Fleet Street, Temple Bar, the Inns of Court and Holborn to the north. John Smethwick's bookshop was located 'under the dial' of the clock attached to the church of St Dunstan's in the West. William Jaggard and Henry Condell owned properties in nearby Fleet Street.

To the south-west of St Dunstan's stood the Middle Temple, a temple to the law indeed, completed in 1572 and boasting London's finest hammerbeam roof, under which *Twelfth Night* had been staged in February 1602. From this area too were released editions of Shakespeare's *Romeo and Juliet* in 1609 and *Hamlet* in 1611, both issued by Smethwick, and acquired by him as part of a job lot, which included *Love's Labour's Lost* and *The Taming of the Shrew*, in November 1607 from fellow St Dunstan's stationer Nicholas Ling after his death. This claim to the latter play actually came about tangentially from Ling's ownership of a different, but related dramatic work, *The Taming of a Shrew*. Ling had published *Hamlet* from St Dunstan's in 1603, after moving from St Paul's Churchyard (where he had been based at the shop identified by the sign of the Crane, neighbouring the Black Bear), having relocated right next door to Smethwick the previous year. Smethwick's fortuitous association with Ling therefore meant that, as well as these two important and incredibly popular tragedies, the First Folio project secured two of the four remaining comedies for which rights needed to be negotiated, leaving *A Midsummer Night's Dream* and *The Merchant of Venice*. To boot, the Folio's backers were gaining an ally who already had experience of backing large folio projects, since Smethwick had worked on a folio edition of the works of Michael Drayton in 1619 and been involved in the pioneering 1616 folio of the *Works* of Ben Jonson, having been approached initially for his ownership of the rights to Jonson's incredibly popular play *Every Man Out of His Humour*. Apparently pleased with the return on his investment in Jonson's works, Smethwick seems to have made the same decision when faced with the choice between selling the licences to his four significant Shakespeare plays or becoming a sharer in the First Folio.

Smethwick's closest connections at this time were with the Jaggards, and these appeared to have been rooted in the parish of St Dunstan's, where both William Jaggard and his brother John had been apprenticed to stationers in the vicinity, and where they had originally established a shop in the churchyard. Smethwick was born in the area, his parents, Richard (a draper by profession) and Johan, having married in St Dunstan's Church in 1560. In this parish too, Smethwick had been apprenticed to Thomas Newman for seven years from 1590, before his admission to the Stationers' Company in 1597, and went on to serve as a churchwarden of St Dunstan's. His career in the company would flourish, and he too would eventually reach the upper echelons of the corporation, becoming a Stock Keeper and then a Warden.

That the Jaggards were primarily responsible for the introduction of Smethwick to the First Folio syndicate, or at least were a persuasive force in the matter, is made more likely by their geographical reach. While William Jaggard had moved to his Barbican printing house from 1606, taking over the Half-Eagle and Key from James Roberts, for many years he maintained a business relationship with his brother John, who continued operating the shop in St Dunstan's known by the sign of the Hand and Star, a little further along from the church into Fleet Street. The Half-Eagle and Key, which was north of the St Paul's precinct, on the corner of Aldersgate Street and the Barbican, in between Smithfield and Moorfields, was by no means far from Smethwick and St Dunstan's. Smethwick and John Jaggard became particularly close, participating together in several administrative and civic posts in the parish, including the role of 'scavengers' in 1613, tasked with overseeing the cleaning of the streets, serving on the ecclesiastical jury for St Dunstan's in 1616, and becoming constables of the parish between 1619 and 1620, among other posts. They both baptised children and buried loved ones in the church, so the two families were closely affiliated.

William Jaggard did in fact have a foothold closer to St Dunstan's, in Fleet Street, in between it and St Paul's Cross Churchyard. Here, significantly or not, close to the properties owned by Henry Condell, which included the Queen's Head Tavern, he maintained not just a home but a complex of tenements, houses and shops, identified by the sign of the Leg. The inheritance was part of a legacy claimed by William's wife Jane and her sister Agnes, daughters to one Robert Lee, and revolved around a disputed will alleged to have been written by the latter but which Jane deposed was 'a thing invented to give colour [that is, lend credence to a deception] whereby to defeat and debar her of her child's part' in her father's estate. The Bishop of London, then George Abbot, had intervened directly and reassigned the disputed legacy to a team that included William Jaggard. Perhaps the stationer had come to regret his interest in the property, for it was 'in great decay' by the time he successfully secured control of his wife's share of the lease. The condition for his ownership was that he and those who inherited the lease after him replace the 'old houses' with 'good, strong and sufficient new tenements or dwelling houses' at least three stories in height. In addition, his lease agreement specified that he and his legatees undertake for the next fifty years to 'sufficiently repair, sustain, uphold, maintain and mend' every part of the property, including the pavements around it, its privies (toilets) and windows.

The lease was dated 20 June 1618 and specified that the rebuilding had to be completed within seven years. By 1621 William Jaggard would have been nearly halfway through his allotted schedule and would almost certainly have started this extensive renovation project, with the help of his son Isaac upon whose support he relied, incurring huge costs. All this would have added to the Jaggards' financial burdens just as the negotiations for the First Folio were likely to be starting. An investor like Smethwick, who owned the rights to four plays, would have been a useful addition to the team. He would also have provided a list of contacts in the St Dunstan's vicinity which may have proved helpful in the negotiations for the Folio's plays.

The appeal of the Shakespeare brand around St Dunstan's and Fleet Street – something of which Henry Condell and the Jaggards would have seen in evidence in the bookshops closest to their properties – is also hinted at by the fact that in the very same year that Smethwick's *Hamlet* first graced his shop's bookshelves, another neighbouring stationer, John Helme, issued *The Troublesome Reign of John, King of England*, which on its title page he had erroneously boasted was 'Written by W. Sh[akespeare]'. The intention was probably to make the book look like Shakespeare's as yet unpublished *The Life and Death of King John*, which would be printed for the first time in the First Folio. *The Troublesome Reign* was also printed in 1622 by stationer Thomas Dewe, described on its title page as being 'sold at his shop in St Dunstan's Churchyard in Fleet Street'. Dewe's control of this play may also have allowed him to claim the rights to Shakespeare's own version – though he did not print it – which may have put him on the Jaggards' radar during negotiations for the Folio's plays. Dewe and William Jaggard were acquaintances, for that same year Dewe had selected William as the printer for a work by Daniel Tuvill, entitled *Christian Purposes and Resolutions*, increasing the likelihood that the Jaggards were involved in the negotiations over Shakespeare's *King John*.

One of the two remaining comedies for which the Folio syndicate may have needed to enter into some kind of negotiation was originally financed from a shop located a short distance from St Dunstan's. Thomas Fisher had published Shakespeare's *A Midsummer Night's Dream* in 1600 from the sign of the White Hart, which stood in Fleet Street close to the Jaggards' tenements. While Thomas Pavier may have acquired the text for the 'Pavier-Jaggard Quartos' because Fisher's death left the rights 'derelict' (unclaimed), it is possible that it became part of discussions between the Jaggards and Pavier over works needed for the First Folio simply because Pavier was its most recent publisher.

Interestingly, this would be the very next comedy printed after one of the Smethwick-owned plays, *Love's Labour's Lost*; indeed the latter would be the first of Smethwick's plays to be printed in the Folio. This may indicate that, if there is some correlation between the order of the printing of the comedies and the order in which negotiations may have been conducted for previously printed plays, the Folio syndicate secured *A Midsummer Night's Dream* shortly after Smethwick was brought into the project. Since Pavier may have, as we have seen, snapped up the latter play through his draper links to Fisher, what may lie behind its acquisition for the Folio is the Jaggards' placement at the heart of the St Dunstan's community as well as their close association with Pavier.

If the Jaggards, therefore, had brought Smethwick into the Folio syndicate, they may have secured the rights to print *A Midsummer Night's Dream* from Pavier around the same time or shortly thereafter. Pavier also held the rights to *Titus Andronicus*, along with three of the plays that had been included in the 'False Folio', *Henry V*, *Henry VI, Part 2* and *Henry VI, Part 3*. A prolific collaborator, he had worked on projects with John Smethwick and William Aspley, as well as with other rights holders with whom the Folio syndicate were negotiating, including Arthur Johnson and Nathaniel Butter, making it possible that other members of the Folio syndicate had brought in Pavier's own plays. After all, his shop in Ivy Lane was just a short walk to the north – across a narrow path and the crossing of one street – from Blount's Black Bear. Yet Pavier's known personal connections, along with his history of Shakespeare printing, link him most strongly with the Jaggards.

The Folio syndicate also had to enter into negotiations for *The Merchant of Venice*. This would be printed in Shakespeare's Book straight after *A Midsummer Night's Dream*, both plays having previously appeared together as part of the 'Pavier-Jaggard Quartos'. Perhaps it is no coincidence that these, the two plays with the murkiest histories with regards to their ownership and inclusion in the 'False Folio', were printed close together in the First Folio. The rights to *The Merchant of Venice* were, as we have seen, owned by Lawrence Hayes, who had inherited the play from his father Thomas. Not a publisher in his own right, Lawrence may have sought to make a quick profit by leasing the rights. The Jaggards could have been the means through which the Folio syndicate acquired the play due to their involvement in the 'Pavier-Jaggard' project, particularly if Thomas Hayes had come to a friendly agreement with them over its publication in 1619. Alternatively, it could have come down to a longer-standing connection between the Hayes family and Blount since the elder Hayes had operated the shop known by the sign of the Green Dragon in St Paul's Cross Churchyard in 1600–1. At the time Blount had been based at the Bishop's Head, just nine doors away.

In 1621 William Jaggard was not aware that he held the licence to print Shakespeare's *As You Like It*, which would be the Folio's next printed play. He is likely to have inherited the title from James Roberts when he took over the latter's shop. The syndicate would not find out, until after 8 November 1623, that Roberts had entered his 'copy' of the play in the Stationers' Register in 1600. But the King's Men may initially have believed the rights belonged to their playing company and felt confident about printing it. This would mean that, with Smethwick's rights at least, and *A Midsummer Night's Dream* and *The Merchant of Venice* secured, they could proceed with the printing safe in the knowledge that they had gained the rights for most, if not all, of the comedies.

So what does this complex network of intertwined lives tell us? When William and Isaac Jaggard and Edward Blount became leading members of the First Folio syndicate, it was not because they held the rights to a significant number of Shakespeare plays. While between them they could claim the rights to two works, they appeared to be unaware that they were in possession of these until relatively late in the printing of the volume. Aside from the prestige, experience and financial resources they brought, they were the ideal partnership because they had footholds in two key centres of the book trade: St Paul's Cross Churchyard to the east and St Dunstan's Churchyard and Fleet Street to the west. Most of the stationers and rights holders with whom negotiations were needed were based in, or had strong historical ties to, either one of these areas. The First Folio syndicate members had long-established connections primarily to either one of these locations and their involvement in the creation of Shakespeare's Book enshrines a strategic division of London's publishing industry. While the bookselling world was relatively small, meaning there were notable overlaps between some of the plays' rights holders and the Folio's financiers across both areas, Blount is likely to have brought Aspley, based just two doors from his own shop, into the syndicate, while the Jaggards were responsible for including Smethwick, whose shop was in the very same street in which their major renovation project was underway. Here physical proximity matched the closest personal and professional ties we have been able to trace between these syndicate members.

We can look at this another way. Of the up to twenty-two plays for which rights had to be secured for the First Folio project to succeed, St Paul's Cross Churchyard and its environs represented a potential ten plays, and St Dunstan's Churchyard and Fleet Street represented five dramatic works, excluding the four (possibly five if we include *A Midsummer Night's Dream*) controlled by Pavier, based just behind the St Paul's precinct. Of the rights holders from whom licences had to be sought, only the stationer Thomas Walkley, who held the rights to *Othello*, is not known to have been directly associated with either of these areas. Walkley may, however, have been connected to the Folio syndicate through Blount, since the latter owned the rights to a non-Shakespearean King's Men play which Walkley printed in 1619.

The First Folio syndicate was perfectly placed, geographically and professionally, to divide between them the rights holders with whom they needed to negotiate. And they succeeded, completing what was, from its very inception, a highly ambitious and challenging project. As with most books published during this period, they also had to negotiate the complicating factor of the age's tense political atmosphere. In 1621, even while they were engaged in negotiations over the rights to plays that had escaped the King's Men's grasp, the royal court was being overshadowed by Anglo-Spanish politics. The ever-oscillating relations between these two nations throughout the Folio's creation would leave an indelible mark on its printed pages. Those involved in preserving the playwright's legacy would be left in no doubt about the significance of the strategic manoeuvres taking place on the world stage. They too, like all those close to the centres of power, would have to navigate tempestuous diplomatic waters in a factious age where the alliances and sympathies of influential patrons could turn an unassuming-looking volume into an incendiary document. The makers of Shakespeare's Book would need their wits about them if they wanted to produce a textual monument fit for a former King's Man while staying on the safer side of an ever more entrenched political divide.

'Sister of a star'

Staging the Spanish Match

In 1621 the playwright and poet Ben Jonson, at least two of the King's Men, and the First Folio's patrons, the Herbert brothers, were present at, and participated in, a series of performances of Jonson's *The Masque of the Gypsies Metamorphosed*. A masque was a courtly form of entertainment, performed in royal palaces or the households of gentry and the nobility, in which non-professional performers often took part alongside more seasoned actors. Jonson had gained notoriety as an accomplished author of masques and this one had a politically important function. Commissioned by the king's favourite George Villiers, the Marquess of Buckingham, and performed on 3 August at his home in Burley-on-the-Hill in Leicestershire, it was intended to align him and his coterie with James I's foreign policy. Apparently a hit, the masque was performed two days later at Belvoir Castle, the estate of Francis Manners, 6th Earl of Rutland, and again in September at Windsor Castle, at the king's own behest.

This entertainment was daring, risky even, and featured a bold innovation. Up to this point, the more demanding roles in masques had been taken on by professional actors, while members of the nobility showed off their dancing abilities or helped display some of the symbolic elements of the production through elaborate costumes and emblematic props. Villiers, however, had been given a meaty and attention-grabbing role as the captain of a ribald gypsy band, performing alongside members of the King's Men. Jonson had selected the masque's theme carefully – as a witty riposte to those courtiers who were scandalised by Villiers' rapid rise to prominence. By 1621 the marquess's influence with James I rivalled that of Sir William Herbert, the Earl of Pembroke. Having taken full advantage of his role as Master of the Horse, which gave him ready access to the royal household, Villiers was intent on becoming a persuasive voice in the political arena. Accorded a seat on the Privy Council, he became one of an elite group of personal advisers to the Crown. In 1620 James I himself had facilitated Villiers' marriage to Katherine Manners, daughter of the Earl of Rutland, further expanding Buckingham's sphere of influence among the nobility. Along with this ever-flowing fountain of royal favours came the opportunity to secure peerages for members of his family and profit from the sale of prestigious titles to his grow-ing clique of supporters. To those who watched Villiers' apotheosis from outside his charmed circle, he seemed like an interloper whose groping hands were snatching the Crown's most glittering estates and titles, like those of the Herberts, from more established and entrenched noble families. It was Jonson's genius to confront this head on. Since gypsies were, in the statutes of the period as well as in the popular imagination, connected with masterlessness, vagrancy and theft, the masque's satirical slant exploited Villiers' reputation and sought to laugh away – or laugh down – the criti-cisms of James's disgruntled courtiers.

After an entertaining preamble featuring members of the King's Men, it was time for Villiers to enter the scene. This he did with his accustomed bravura, bringing with him six additional actors who joined him and the King's Men actors in a rousing song-and-dance act. Then, with a boldness few could have pulled off without insult, he marched up to the king and took his hand, planting thereon a kiss. A round of comic understatements followed. Casting his dazzling eyes over James's figure, Villiers declared him to be 'a man of good means', blessed with 'Some book-craft' and 'pretty well spoken'. Perhaps he paused and turned to the audience with a mischievous smile while praising the king for being 'no great wencher', potentially raising a half-concealed chuckle or two behind gloved and ringed fingers, since James's interest in his male courtiers, sometimes bordering on obsessive, was a constant talking-point at court. Though it was common for men to share a bed during this period, with no sexual connotation, Villiers' own fond recollection of a night he and the king spent together, when 'the bed's head could not be found between your Master and his Dog', is suggestive.

But behind the flatteries and flirtatious insinuations, there was the more serious business of the king's foreign policy. Tensions between England and Spain had been evident since Henry VIII formally declared himself Head of the Church of England in the 1530s, severing national and administrative ties with the Catholic Church, which was governed by the Pope of Rome. The Anglo-Spanish wars had intensified from the mid-1580s, reaching a crescendo when the Spanish Armada made a failed attempt to invade England in 1588. A landmark peace treaty with Spain was signed in 1604, just one year into James I's reign, but this did not eradicate Catholic conspiracies or prevent Spanish-backed attempts to assassinate him and return England to Catholicism. To manage this threat, those found practising and preaching publicly in defence of the Catholic faith remained subject to heavy fines and imprisonment, though the king continued to look for ways to create a more harmonious settlement between Protestant England and Catholic Spain. In his guise as 'Captain' of the gypsies in Jonson's masque, Villiers lauded his sovereign as 'the prince of your peace' who desired 'to make/All Christian differences cease', a deliberate allusion to James's conciliatory strategy. Before long the entertainment proceeded to the subject on the minds of all of his subjects at this time: the so-called 'Spanish Match'. This referred to the king's scheme to marry his son to a Spanish princess. To this end Viscount Fielding, Villiers' brother-in-law, was next to flatter the monarch in his role as 'Second Gypsy':

> Of your fortune be secure,
> Love and she are both at your
> > Command, sir.

> See what states are here at strife
> Who shall tender you a wife,
> > A brave one ...

> She is sister of a star;
> One the noblest now that are,
> > Bright Hesper ...

The 'Bright Hesper' refers to Philip IV of Spain, who had acceded to the throne on 31 March 1621 at just sixteen years of age, after the death of his father, Philip III; the 'she' glances at his sister, the Infanta Maria, mooted future bride of Prince Charles. Jonson, in his scripting of the piece, even went so far as to use this speech to kindle in James's fantasy the fruits of the young couple's 'marriage night'. It seems Villiers' attempts to ingratiate himself with James, through his outspoken support of the Spanish Match during the king's summer progress, met with royal approval. John Chamberlain wrote to Sir Dudley Carleton on 18 August that year, informing him that 'The king was so pleased and taken with his entertainment at the Lord Marquess's [Villiers'], that he could not forbear to express his contentment', being enthralled by its suggestion 'that there was hope of a smiling boy within a while', which inspired the Bishop of London there and then 'to give them a benediction' by way of a resounding 'Amen'. This may have prompted Jonson to add a new segment to the masque for its performance in Windsor the following month, featuring an endearing vignette of 'a little James at play' between 'his grandsire's knees', a child endowed with his grandfather's charms and able to 'move/All the pretty ways of love/And laughter'.

Another member of Villiers' inner circle, who would soon play a central role in the Spanish Match, was Endymion Porter, who took on the part of 'Third Gypsy' in Jonson's masque. Porter was a poet and Buckingham's confidant, whose appointment as a Groom of the Bedchamber formed part of James's strategy for carefully guiding Prince Charles's outlook, sympathies and politics through the influence of a hand-picked entourage of trusted courtiers who could be counted on to promote the monarch's optimistic vision for an Anglo-Spanish union. Porter's grandmother was Spanish and he had spent his formative years in Spain. He was therefore fluent in Spanish and had a good relationship with Gaspar de Guzmán y Pimentel, 3rd Count of Olivares, one of King Philip's closest advisers. Charles was only twenty-one years of age in 1621 and still impressionable. He was self-conscious about his physique, for he was small in stature, and swung from intense shyness to bouts of explosive fury, fuelled by the attention his father lavished on his male courtiers at the expense of their own relationship. Through the Spanish Match he had finally found a way to draw the king's focus onto himself, and through Villiers, who was eight years his senior, acquired a mentor and mediator who appeared solicitous to bring father and son together. Jonson's masque had cleverly pushed Villiers into the limelight as the head of a pro-Spanish faction at court, one working assiduously to guide the young prince into the arms of the Infanta, and in the process bring the English people into a hoped-for perpetual accord with Spain. But Jonson would have been aware that this grand project was not quite so simple as his idealistic entertainment made it seem. One person in the audience at the Windsor performance of the masque would have been less than content with the direction in which James's foreign policy was moving: Jonson's own – and soon to be the First Folio's – patron William Herbert, the 3rd Earl of Pembroke.

The cataclysmic events which concerned parts of the Bohemian estates, in which the king's family were enmeshed, were alarming to Pembroke and those who were in sympathy with his anti-Catholic outlook. James's daughter Elizabeth Stuart was wife to Frederick V, Elector Palatine, who had been offered the crown of Bohemia in 1619 following the ousting of the Catholic King Ferdinand II. Elizabeth became queen of Bohemia, her husband a noted Calvinist, ruling a state that had long been governed by the Holy Roman Empire under Catholic Habsburg rulers. This triggered a new wave of persecutions of Protestants in the Palatinate – an area which stretched from the upper Rhine in present-day Germany to Alsace and Lorraine in France – and a tussle for power in the region, with Ferdinand launching an aggressive military campaign with the aid of Spanish forces to reclaim what he saw as his right to rule. Upon hearing of Frederick's accession, Edward Blount's associate, John Chamberlain, predicted gloomily that 'there is now no place left for deliberation, nor for mediation of peace till one side be utterly ruined', fearing it would start a European conflict which would 'set all Christendom by the ears'. And so it did, with these events bound up with the triggering of the bloody conflict which came to be known as the Thirty Years' War, which had begun in 1618. For James this was a disastrous turn of events, which put him under pressure to stage a more robust military intervention in the Palatinate, declaring war on Spain if necessary; something he was reluctant to do.

For his part, Pembroke never forgot that his uncle, Sir Philip Sidney, after whom his brother, the Earl of Montgomery, had been named, had died at the hands of Spanish soldiers while defending England's Protestant allies in the Netherlands. His mother, Mary Sidney Herbert, had created textual memorials to her brother by overseeing and revising his grand fantasy narrative the *Arcadia*, published in editions of 1593 and 1598 by Edward Blount's former mentor William Ponsonby, and translating, writing, enabling and patronising countless other works that furthered the Protestant cause. Pembroke was therefore staunchly opposed to the conciliatory approach James was taking in his dealings with Spain and wanted England to adopt a stronger martial stance, hoping he would come to the aid of his Protestant neighbours. In 1619 Pembroke wrote:

> I believe the king will be very unwilling to be engaged in a war, if by any means with his honour he may avoid it. And yet, I am confident, when the necessity of the cause of religion ... and his own honour calls upon him, that he will perform whatsoever belongs to the defender of the faith, a kind father-in-law, and one careful of the preservation of that honour which I must confess by a kind of misfortune hath long lain in a kind of suspense ...

It was James's solemn duty, Pembroke believed, to oppose those who, like Villiers, 'are nourished too much with Spanish milk', and he had put his efforts into ensuring his fellow Privy Councillors would 'prevail' in challenging the monarch's placatory approach. It had seemed initially that Pembroke's hopes would soon be realised when, in January 1621, James recalled Parliament. The earl believed he could bring the matter to a satisfactory conclusion due to his influence because he was a suasive force in Westminster. That year his powerbase was expanding in the west of England, for he would be appointed Lord Lieutenant of Somerset and Wiltshire, increasing his control of seats in the Commons, either directly or through his own clients and supporters, which included those representing

Cardiff, Wilton, Cornwall, Portsmouth and Oxford, among others. That year Pembroke controlled at least twenty-six seats in the Commons, giving him considerable leverage against the pro-Spanish faction led by Villiers. An indication of Pembroke's thinking comes in a later assessment of his belief in the potency of the constitutional structure when it came to opposing the king's will, stating that his 'chief object' was 'leaving to parliament the dissolution of the treaty with Spain'.

On the surface at least the king appeared to be playing along with the wishes of Pembroke and the anti-Spanish faction. It was clear to James that he could not afford to ignore the increasingly desperate situation in the Palatinate; but he also knew he could not afford, financially, to act. He had always displayed extravagant tastes, indulging his love of hunting and entertaining, and his ungovernable impulse to shower his male favourites with lavish gifts and opulent estates. He had therefore been less careful with the Crown's coffers than his frugal predecessor, Elizabeth I. Top of the agenda in the 1621 Parliament was the securing of a subsidy to bankroll a military campaign, with the aim of restoring Frederick V to his estates. The MP Sir Simonds D'Ewes remembered how James I 'promised, with the people's assistance and consent, to aid the king of Bohemia, his son-in-law, and not to enforce the Spanish Match without their consent'. A subsidy was agreed to, but it fell far short of the sum James had been hoping to receive. He quickly realised that the Commons were unwilling to grant more without further assurance of his intentions regarding his son's marriage and a clarification of his attitude to a rapprochement with Spain in the present circumstances. He had no intention, however, of laying aside his plans. In desperation, he complained to Parliament that Elizabeth I had received far more generous amounts in subsidies during less desperate times, and promised that they were assured victory, and at a reasonable cost no less, with the backing of the Commons, because of Villiers' newly invested military powers, extending from his recent election as Lord High Admiral of England: 'I made not choice of an old beaten soldier for my admiral, but rather chose a young man, whose honesty and integrity I knew, whose care hath been to appoint under him sufficient men to lessen my charges.' But the Commons were not fooled. It was clear to them that the monarch was banking on the match being the bargaining chip that would secure Spanish aid in the Palatinate or at least a withdrawal of King Philip's forces from the region. The king's plan was to sell England to Spain instead of opposing its might. D'Ewes put a rather more negative spin on the fantasy that the proposed union would result in grandchildren for James I. After the prince 'should once have two or three children by the Spanish lady', he lamented, she 'would be sure to train up her offspring in the Romish [that is, Catholic] religion, to the utter ruin of this flourishing Church and Kingdom'.

As Jonson's masque unfolded in Windsor, he would have been aware that he was in a challenging position: caught between James I's desire to promote Villiers as the champion of the Anglo-Spanish union and his loyalty to his patron, the Earl of Pembroke. His solution was simple but effective. He composed an encomium in praise of the earl, which he directed to be delivered by one of the gypsy band, a character named Jackman, in all likelihood played by a King's Men actor:

> You know how to use your sword and your pen,
> And you love not alone the arts, but the men;
> The graces and muses everywhere follow
> You, as you were their second Apollo ...

Apollo was the god of arts and poetry, a fitting emblem for William Herbert, one of the most prolific patrons of arts in the period, who had nurtured countless talents. He was the patron of playwrights, poets, painters, architects, composers, actors and radical Protestant churchmen, including the architect and stage-set designer Inigo Jones, the supremely gifted painters Nicholas Hilliard, Marcus Gheeraerts the Younger and Daniel Mytens, and the most celebrated musicians of the day, with composer John Dowland among this blessed circle. His support of Ben Jonson was never-ending. Pembroke had been the dedicatee of Jonson's play *Catiline* and his collection of *Epigrams* and, in July 1619, in his capacity as chancellor of the University of Oxford, the earl had arranged for an honorary Master of the Arts to be conferred upon the author. He also gave him a generous annual stipend of twenty pounds to purchase books. After Jonson's imprisonment for his involvement in the scandalous play *Eastward Ho!*, the playwright appealed to Pembroke, reminding him that '[n]either am I or my cause so much unknown to your lordship' and fondly recalled that 'you have ever been free and noble to me'. Lamenting that 'the king's anger hath buried me', he had nevertheless no doubt that he would receive 'the same proportion of your bounties' in this time of crisis. It is very likely that Pembroke's intercession was responsible for Jonson's release. If we are to believe Heminges and Condell's own words, enshrined in the First Folio's dedication to William and his brother Philip Herbert, Shakespeare received equal 'bounties' from their hands. Both Herbert brothers had, they insisted, showered the playwright when 'living, with so much favour'. They also thanked their noble patrons 'in our particular, for the many favours we have received from your Lordships', with Shakespeare's Book, in part, standing as a testament to the players' 'gratitude'.

Just a year before Jonson's masque, Heminges and Condell were reminded of the importance of the Earl of Pembroke's support when he intervened to protect the King's Men from the incursions of competing theatre companies. On 29 September 1620 James I had written to the earl after granting a 'Licence ... to build an Amphitheatre' to one John Cotton and others. Probably responding to complaints from the King's Men, either directly to their royal patron or to Pembroke, James acknowledged that this licence meant Cotton and his business partners could exploit 'greater liberty both in the point of building, and using of exercises, than is any way to be permitted', and conferred on Pembroke the 'authority … to cause that already passed to be cancelled' and for new 'directions and reservations' to be drawn up. Pembroke was working behind the scenes to secure the King's Men's future in other ways. It is likely he was responsible for the honours Jonson received shortly after the final performance of *The Masque of the Gypsies Metamorphosed*, the king being so taken with it that there was talk of knighting him. This did not transpire, but in October 1621 Jonson was granted the 'reversion' of the Mastership of the Revels. This formally enshrined an order of proceeding which meant that should the current Master of the Revels, Sir John Astley, die in office or vacate the post, it would immediately pass to Jonson. This was part of Pembroke's own scheme for seizing control of an influential position which granted its holder authority over the licensing of plays; and for the King's Men, the reversion meant that the future of their craft could one day be in the hands of Jonson, a frequent collaborator.

While Jonson would not, in fact, acquire this post, Pembroke's strategic manoeuvres, in a bid to expand his power over the theatre industry, may have determined the choice of the Herbert brothers as patrons of the First Folio. Indeed, William Herbert continued to resist pressure to give up the Lord Chamberlainship. Two further attempts were made in 1621 to convince him to exchange the post for other offices, including offering him that of Lord Treasurer for a second time. Sensing that Pembroke would not vacate his office without a promise that his brother would inherit it after him, James I turned his attention to the bribing of Philip, dangling before him a place on the Privy Council and the gift of a handsome estate in Yorkshire. Both Herbert brothers refused the king's generous offer. Next a proposal was made to ennoble Pembroke with the office of Lord Privy Seal, a talismanic ceremonial role that would have made him responsible for the king's private seal ratifying all business within the royal household. For Pembroke this was not a patch on securing the transition of the Lord Chamberlainship to Philip. For Heminges and Condell, and their fellow King's Men, the Herbert brothers' stubbornness over the issue would have been welcome assurance of the steadfast patronage of the Herbert family.

On 14 April 1621 Frederick V and Elizabeth arrived at the Hague in Holland, having taken their children and fled for their lives as the armies of the Catholic League – an alliance of Catholic German states under the auspices of the Holy Roman Empire formed in 1609 – closed in. Ferdinand II, dubbed in England the 'Bloody Emperor', cut a lethal swathe through upper Germany and Prague, executing the chief members of the Protestant nobility who had failed to escape in time. The Palatinate had fallen and the royal couple were now exiles, Frederick's short-lived reign forever remembered through his own moniker, 'The Winter King'. Sir Simonds D'Ewes despaired that 'the Bohemian cause [was] utterly overthrown, which the king might in all human reason easily have supported had he but appeared for his son-in-law in time'. For this D'Ewes blamed the Spanish ambassador, Diego Sarmiento de Acuña, 1st Count of Gondomar, whose 'subtle contrivements' and 'wicked instruments' had been responsible for leading James I on with false hopes of a solution to his son-in-law's troubles through the Spanish Match, and who had succeeded in coaxing Villiers over to the pro-Spanish faction.

Gondomar had arrived in England enveloped in a gilded cloud of splendour in March 1620, bringing with him new articles for the match. In Dover he had been met by a caravan of royal coaches, including a particularly magnificent one James reserved for only the most important dignitaries, before being escorted to Gravesend by 'the king's best barges'. At Ely House in Holborn, the residence of the Bishop of Ely, a grand room was prepared 'extraordinarily furnished for him, with a rich cloth of estate', wrote John Chamberlain, 'a thing more than I remember ever afforded before to any other ambassador'. A chapel had been 'trimmed up with an altar' so that he could practise his Catholic rites. This proved too much for some.

The treatment of James I's daughter and the Protestant Bohemian royal family, and the English Crown's continuing flirtation with Spain, led to a public outcry. On 10 March 1621 Chamberlain had reported that a preacher of London's St Martin's-in-the-Fields, Dr John Everard, 'was sent to the Gatehouse for glancing … at the Spanish match, and deciphering the craft and cruelty of the Spaniards in all places where they come'. He would be imprisoned for the same offence again the following year, prompting a furious James I to comment 'What is this Dr Ever-out? his name shall be Dr Never-out.' Helping to stoke these flames was the publication the previous year of a lurid and sensational pamphlet by an anonymous author, entitled *Vox Populi, Or News from Spain*. Timed to coincide with Ambassador Gondomar's arrival in England, it had purported to be a leaked secret report written by him documenting his attempts to bring England under Spanish rule. Part of the plan involved fermenting 'such a dislike betwixt the king and Lower House' in order to encourage James to dismantle Parliament entirely and 'furnish himself by marrying with us', without further need of subsidies from the Commons. In reality the pamphlet was a cunning anti-Spanish propagandist plot, authored by the Reverend Thomas Scott, rector of St Saviour's in Norwich, who was also the personal chaplain of Sir William Herbert, the Earl of Pembroke.

When Gondomar discovered the ruse he did not hide his rage from James. The Venetian ambassador, Girolamo Lando, recorded with relish how Gondomar 'foams with wrath in every direction and it is said that he has sent it to the king to make complaint'. When it became clear that Gondomar was now the target of attacks by anti-Catholic protestors, James had no choice but to take action. By 8 April 1621 a royal proclamation was issued for the suppressing of apprentices and the 'inferior and baser sort of people' from their 'rude and savage barbarism ... towards ambassadors and public ministers of foreign princes and states, whose persons ought to be sacred and privileged'; an edict prompted by the rebellion of three young apprentices who were whipped at a cart's tail for 'abuse offered to the Spanish ambassador and his litter as he passed through the streets'. The proclamation was printed by a team of two royal printers which included Edward Blount's friend, the stationer John Bill.

Before long Sir Simonds D'Ewes was reporting 'a general sadness in all men's faces (except papists or popishly addicted)' because, it was rumoured, the king had 'concluded the Spanish Match for the Infanta Maria'. With James I pursuing an ever more aggressive stance against anyone who dared to speak out against the match, this became a hot-button issue. As more preachers were arrested for their anti-Spanish sermonising, as more anti-Catholic propagandist works were thrown onto the state censors' bonfires, paranoia gripped the royal court, with Protestant courtiers fearing the spread of the Popish faith at every level of society. It was even rumoured that the Bishop of London, John King, had mustered the strength to convert to the Popish faith just before his death on 30 March that year. One member of the First Folio syndicate was keeping a close watch on these developments.

Edward Blount had been spying out those who had been supporting Catholic converts and sent news of the 'scandal raised of that Bishop', John King, to Sir William Trumbull, James I's agent in Brussels. During his last sickness the bishop had, Blount discovered through the clergyman's physician, heard about the unfortunate fate of a Catholic monk and controversialist who had 'long endured imprisonment' and was forced to take the oath designed to ensure allegiance to James I. Because of this 'his best Catholic friends and relieving benefactors gave him over and withdrew their supplies from him', leaving him destitute. This had apparently 'moved the Bishop to send him some relief' in the form of a generous five-pound donation, conveyed on his behalf by his doctor. This was not the only scandal which drew Blount's attention in his role as Trumbull's informant on the unfolding state of Catholic politics.

In April 1621 he had attended a 'private conference between our English divines and ministers and that dangerous Champion Musket'. The Catholic priest George Fisher, alias Musket, had twice escaped prison only to be recaptured in 1620, and would soon be accused of authoring an account of the Bishop of London's conversion, issued from a secret press abroad, in which it was claimed 'That he altered his Religion before his death, and died Catholic is most certain'. The disputation was one of a series in which Musket pitted his wits against the Protestant clerics Daniel Featley and Thomas Goad. Two of their meetings took place at the home of Blount's close friend, John Bill, who had only recently, on 2 October 1620, been raised into the governing ranks of the Stationer's Company and who had served jointly with Blount as one of the officers overseeing the English Stock. Thanks to Blount's 'nearness of friendship' with Bill, he scored entry into this exclusive event, and was allowed to bring a select group with him, among whom was the author Sir Robert Dallington, whose works Blount had twice published. It was a lively occasion attended, according to Blount, by 'Catholic gentlemen and learneder priests than Musket', who had failed miserably in defending his position:

I never heard nor knew a more simple, ignorant, audacious, shameless fool than Musket, such an one as I dare undertake to find in every College of Oxford and Cambridge that have not yet taken degree of Master of Arts and that shall make an ass of him. For he had nothing in him but mere sophistry and would never abide to follow or conclude an argument. In a word, it was (as Master Dallington saith) the unequalest match of cockfight that ever he was at.

So embarrassed were the other priests in Musket's retinue that they made excuses not to attend the next day's debates being 'ashamed of their disputant'. Not even Goad and Dallington, being sent to plead with them, could persuade them to come, for 'they durst not abide the test any longer', wrote Blount gleefully, gloating over 'the great Musket's conquest'.

Featley may well have seen *Pericles*, authored by Shakespeare and George Wilkins, which was revived in 1619, and had it in mind when he began his book, which included an account of the conference, in which he described Catholic disputants in colourful terms: 'though their [the Catholics'] redoubted wrestlers, in grappling with our Divines, are put to the worst, yet (like *Pericles* in the theatre) be they indeed never so much foiled, they will go about, by their eloquence, to persuade the spectator, that they received not, but gave the foil'. Featley's text was sold near Blount's shop, from premises abutting onto the Great South Door of St Paul's, published by one Robert Milbourne, who had made Blount's own shop his centre of operations in 1617–18. One wonders if Blount had ever spoken directly with Featley about the conference, as they were both hosted in Bill's home, for it was Blount who had once acquired the rights to *Pericles*.

A different play in the King's Men's repertory became the focus of attention on 5 November, when the players were back at court performing Philip Massinger's *The Woman's Plot* before the king at Whitehall. Since lost, and possibly intended to commemorate the Gunpowder Plot, it was one of six performances that earned

Heminges and the players a retrospective payment of £60 in the Chamberlain's accounts the following year. Another of this group of plays continued the misogynistic theme. The text of *The Woman is Too Hard for Him*, staged three weeks later, has not survived but it may have been, much like Shakespeare's *The Taming of the Shrew*, a tale of an unruly woman ultimately brought under the control of her husband or other male authority figure. The King's Men could have been pandering to an interest, bordering on obsession, of James at the time. John Chamberlain had written to Sir Dudley Carleton in January 1620, informing him that the Bishop of London, then still living, 'called together all his clergy about this town, and told them he had express commandment from the king to will them to inveigh vehemently and bitterly in their sermons against the insolency of our women'. The focus of James's ire was a recent trend in feminine attire, particularly 'their wearing of broad-brimmed hats, pointed doublets, [and] their hair cut short or shorn'. Chamberlain wrote again on 12 February to point out how obediently not only the ministers and priests, but also the playing companies, had put James's request into practice:

> Our pulpits ring continually of the insolence and impudence of women; and to help the matter forward, the players have likewise taken them to task, and so do the ballads and ballad singers, so that they can come nowhere but their ears tingle. And if all this will not serve, the King threatens to fall upon their husbands, parents, or friends that have or should have power over them and make them pay for it.

One of the texts to spin off the press that year was called *A Caveat or Warning for all sorts of men both young and old to avoid the company of lewd and wicked women*; but most sensational was the pamphlet *Hic Mulier: or the Man-Woman*, which condemned all 'masculine-feminines' who were 'most monstrous' and worthy of 'Goblins themselves [to] stare at' because their sartorial statements were made through items of clothing which were 'short, base and French'. This attention to the pernicious influence of French manners and dress on England's female population may have had a political purpose, a misogynistic moralising of women's bodies that was in step with James I's own brand of international relations; a leaning away from alignments with France and towards conciliation of Spain. This was precisely what the court's anti-Spanish faction, led by men like Sir William Herbert, had focused on undermining, preferring instead the forging of alliances with the Netherlands and France. The earl's outspokenness in this regard may have caused tensions with James, or at least may have been rumoured to have done so, for on 5 November 1621, the very day the King's Men staged *The Woman's Plot* for the king, news was circulating around the Barbican area that Pembroke was about to lose his most jealously guarded office, with one gossip stating 'there is a report in the town that the Earl of Pembroke's staff [of the office of Lord Chamberlain] is taken from him and so confidently is it spoken that the preacher in St Mary's … in his prayer forbore to give him the title of Chamberlain'. The story proved unfounded, but may have reflected Pembroke's increasingly public opposition to James's foreign policy.

Misogynistic texts continued to be published through the year. The King's Men may well have been following this trend over an even longer period, given the suggestive titles of plays they performed since James I's proclamation to the Church of England's clergy: *Women Pleased*; *The Woman's Plot*; *The Woman is Too Hard for Him*; *Women, Beware Women*; and *More Dissemblers Besides Women*. Perhaps the King's Men had something to do with the First Folio's choice of headline play, *The Tempest*, which tells the story of a patriarchal figure, Prospero, guiding the marriage of his chaste and demure daughter Miranda in a manner that consolidates his dynastic line. *The Merry Wives of Windsor*, the third play in the

Folio, is a witty reversal of the 'taming' theme, in which two 'Merry Wives' prove their fidelity to their husbands by shaming the unruly and lascivious Falstaff who has designs on their chastity and their purses, while the sixth play, *Much Ado About Nothing*, presents the popular scalding and rebellious character Beatrice who subversively embraces the stereotype of the 'shrewish' woman but who is eventually brought under the 'yoke' of marriage. Could the King's Men's own performance of a run of women-focused plays, which pandered to James I's prejudices even as the Folio was being planned, have influenced the decision to place these works towards the beginning of Shakespeare's Book?

If the King's Men plays performed at Whitehall in 1621 fed some kind of fantasy James I had nurtured of the 'taming' of unruly women, the monarch would find the taming of his rebellious MPs was not a script he could author or commission as easily as a royal command performance. It is possible he had wanted *The Woman's Plot* performed on the anniversary of the Gunpowder Plot to remind his courtiers and parliamentarians of the price to be paid for treason as he geared up to recall Parliament for another gruelling session. On 21 November, any fears he may have had in this regard proved well-founded. As the first session proceeded, he found himself facing a hostile, and very vocal, group of MPs who not only refused to be diverted from the issue of the Spanish Match but proposed that James declare a full-scale war against Spain and the Holy Roman Empire if Philip IV refused to support England's bid to restore Frederick and Elizabeth to the Bohemian throne. In addition, they demanded tighter laws against Catholics and an assurance that Prince Charles would be married to a Protestant. The king was furious and the Spanish ambassador Gondomar retaliated with a threat of war against England.

On 3 December, James laid down the law, stating that 'some fiery and popular spirits' had been 'emboldened' to encroach on his 'prerogative royal' and warned the Commons not 'to meddle with anything concerning our Government or deep matters of State, and namely, not to deal with our dearest son's match with the daughter of Spain'. The House of Commons produced a searing response in the form of a 'Protestation' on 18 December, arguing that the 'liberties, franchises, privileges, and jurisdictions of Parliament are the ancient and undoubted birthright and inheritance of the subjects of England', and that this gave them every right to intervene in 'urgent affairs concerning king, state, and defence of the realm, and of the Church of England, and the maintenance and making of laws'. They demanded 'freedom of speech' and the opportunity to pursue the 'redress of mischiefs and grievances'. On reading this the king, in a fit of blind rage, tore the Protestation out of the House of Commons' journal.

James's status as supreme master in matters of state, religion and defence was profoundly shaken and he wanted to chasten the unrepentant members of the House of Commons. The privileges they were claiming, he declared defiantly in a letter to his secretary, Sir George Calvert, which was clearly intended to be circulated among the offending MPs, 'were derived from the grace and permission of our ancestors', adding 'we cannot with patience endure our subjects to use such Antimonarchical words to us concerning their liberties'. Then a warning: 'Let them go on carefully in their business, rejecting the curious wrangling upon words and syllables.' The king now threatened to dissolve Parliament. Sir William Herbert was bitterly opposed to the idea, and unlikely to have endeared himself to his monarch, during the period in which those parliamentary hearings were in session, when he advocated for a harder line against Catholic rebels and a more decisive military response against the Holy Roman Empire. But the king was in an impossible position, aware that public opinion coincided with that of a growing faction among his own courtiers and MPs who were displeased with his overtures to Spain. This pushed him further into a reliance on the Spanish Match, believing that with the military might of England's former enemy behind him he could stabilise his increasingly precarious state and acquire a degree of financial and national security.

For those involved in creating the First Folio, who were on the brink of beginning the printing of the volume, this tension between demonstrating support for the Crown – the monarch, after all, was the King's Men's own theatrical patron – and heeding the pull of popular opinion among the book-buying public must have been palpable. The situation strung a tightrope beneath the project on which the backers of Shakespeare's Book had to balance in an increasingly volatile and uncertain atmosphere.

Act Three

1622

Printing the First Folio

I have been
The book of his good acts, whence men have read
His name unparalleled, happily amplified ...

William Shakespeare, *Coriolanus*

'The author's genius'

Inside the Half-Eagle and Key

Had you walked into the printing shop of William and Isaac Jaggard at the sign of the Half-Eagle and Key in London's Barbican when the First Folio was being printed, you would first have been struck by the din: the clatter of thousands of individual lead pieces of movable type arranged at speed by dextrous fingers into Shakespeare's sentences and iambic verse lines; the smack of ink balls dabbed over the surface of print-ready metal type; the cranking of levers pushing paper-loaded carriages through printing presses; the slurp and rip of papers being peeled from the sticky inked surfaces of type-filled frames; and the rattle of used slivers of type being emptied from their frames for cleaning or placed back into their storage compartments ready for re-use.

You would have noticed the smell too. The blood-and-iron-like waft of ink from freshly printed pages having been hung to dry, like so much linen strung out on clothes lines, pushing with their slow undulations particles of paper, dust motes and the odour of the workmen's sweat into the air and around the busy printing house. The whole space would have pulsed with its own rhythm, as printers, compositors, inkers and pressworkers performed a kind of choreographed ballet around their assigned sections of the workshop or in specially designated rooms devoted to specific tasks: the strange cacophonous song of Shakespeare's words translated into the symbiotic dance of human and machine.

Printing was highly skilled, physically demanding and eye-straining work. The Jaggards were often working on two, three or more books simultaneously, and this did not include the almost constant run of 'job work' which saw them producing playbills, official proclamations emblazoned with the Royal Arms, and other smaller publications. The press was therefore a hot hive of activity as dedicated workmen set about their allotted responsibilities with razor-sharp focus. Before a book could be printed a process known as 'casting off' had to be completed. This was the work of experienced professionals who had to judge how much of the copy text

IMPRESSIO LIBRORVM.

Potest vt vna vox capi aure plurima :   Linunt ita vna scripta mille paginas.

The bustling scene inside a printing shop, represented in a print based on an image by Jan van der Straet, dated c. 1580–1605.

A composing stick, used by a 'compositor' to set type for a printed page, from volume two of Joseph Moxon's *Mechanick Exercises: or, The doctrine of handyworks* (London: Printed for Joseph Moxon, 1683).

(the manuscript or older printed work that formed the basis of the new book) would fit into each printed page. After the copy text was marked up into portions that corresponded to what would become printed pages, it was passed to the 'compositors' whose job was to assemble the individual pieces of lead type carved with letters, punctuation marks, special characters, or blank spaces used to separate out words or whole lines, into a print-ready 'forme'. For a folio-sized work, a forme corresponded to one side of a printed sheet of paper split into two pages. In other words, if you turned a folio sheet to its landscape rotation and then folded it in half, you would get two pages of space for text on each side, making a total of four pages that could be filled with printed matter.

To set a forme each compositor stood in front of a sloping case that was subdivided into individual compartments or trays containing lead type of differing fonts and styles, including punctuation, special characters and blank type designed to introduce spaces of varying widths in between the text. The cases in the upper compartments usually contained the capital letters, while those in the lower boxes included the smaller characters. This is where we derive the terms 'upper case' for capital letters and 'lower case' for non-capitals. The First Folio was set primarily in roman type, with stage directions, speech prefixes and names often rendered in italic type. In order for the printed page to appear the right way round, the character on each piece of type was engraved in reverse, and the compositors had the fiendishly intricate task of picking the correct pieces of type from over 150 compartments, and placing them in long handheld trays called 'composing sticks' backwards and upside down, working left to right. In effect this meant that they had to become adept at reading the text the *wrong* way round, in reverse and as a mirror image, as they slotted the pieces of type into each composing stick, each of which held a few lines of text. Once the composing stick was filled with type, up to around six lines, its contents would be transferred to a larger tray known as a 'galley', which was gradually filled until a full page of type had been laid, including any metal dividers introduced into the forme to preserve the correct spacings between characters and lines. When both pages corresponding to a forme had been completed, they were transferred to a metal frame known as a 'chase', into which wedges of wood were hammered to ensure the pieces of type were packed tightly together and unable to move during the printing process.

Part of the skill inhered in ensuring that the lines of text were all perfectly aligned, with the blocks or dividers inserted in the right places to space out the lines evenly and create cleanly justified margins. It was fiddly and sometimes frustrating work, which required speed and precision. Selecting the wrong piece of type, or inserting type in a composing stick the wrong way round or wrong side up, would be time wasted in 'stop-press corrections'; when a page would be checked for errors hot off the press, with subsequent pages corrected during the printing.

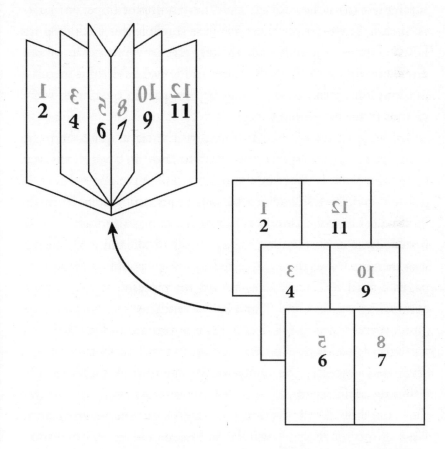

The First Folio is a book often referred to as a 'folio in sixes'. This means it consists of batches of three large sheets which, when folded and sewn together, provide six individual leaves, making up twelve sides on which to print text.

To add to the complexity of the process, formes were not set in the order in which one would read the text. A type of book known as a 'folio in sixes', the First Folio would be constructed from sections comprising three sheets of paper each, which, when stacked and folded, create six individual leaves. These were sewn together to form 'quires', each of which provided a total of twelve sides of paper for printed material. While the Folio was mostly made up of these 'sixes', corresponding to around eighty quires in all, there were also sections of irregularly grouped sheets. Some surviving First Folios, for example, have quires of three, or four, or even eight leaves, while there are four single leaves, including the Folio's famous engraving of Shakespeare by Martin Droeshout. There are nine such irregular quires in the Folio. Most of the plays in the volume required an average of two quires, equating to twenty-four pages of printed text.

To help visualise this, imagine you took a quire of pages numbered 1–12 and spread them flat, so that the three sheets were open. The bottom sheet of the quire would have pages 1 and 12 printed on its reverse, and pages 2 and 11 printed face up. Normally the two centre pages would be set by the compositors and printed first, a forme corresponding to pages 6 and 7 of a quire. While this was being printed, the next forme to be set would correspond to pages 5 and 8. The process would be repeated for the forme comprising pages 4 and 9, and so on until the final forme of the quire, representing pages 1 and 12, was typeset and printed. This method of working relied on accurate casting off. If this was not estimated correctly the compositors would find that they had either too much space left to fill or an over-abundance of text that they somehow had to fit into the page or section assigned for it. Having too much space was fairly easy to address. Compositors could expand the width of the dividers that separated lines of type, thereby spreading the text more evenly to fill up the sheet. They could add ornamental woodblock decorations at the foot of the

Caf. This did I feare, but thought he had no weapon:
For he was great of heart.
Iod. Oh Sparton Dogge:
More fell then Anguifh, Hunger, or the Sea:
Looke on the Tragicke Loading of this bed:
This is thy worke:
The Obiect poyfons Sight,

Let it be hid. *Gratiano,* keepe the houfe,
And feize vpon the Fortunes of the Moore,
For they fucceede on you. To you, Lord Gouernor,
Remaines the Cenfure of this hellifh villaine:
The Time, the Place, the Torture, oh inforce it:
My felfe will ftraight aboord, and to the State,
This heauie Act, with heauie heart relate. *Exeunt.*

FINIS.

The Names of the Actors.
(:*₊*:)

Thello, *the Moore.*
Brabantio, *Father to Defdemona.*
Caffio, *an Honourable Lieutenant.*
Iago, *a Villaine.*
Rodorigo, *a gull'd Gentleman.*
Duke *of Venice.*

Senators.
Montano, *Gouernour of Cyprus.*
Gentlemen of Cyprus.
Lodouico, *and* Gratiano, *two Noble Venetians.*
Saylors.
Clowne.

Defdemona, *wife to Othello.*
Æmilia, *wife to Iago.*
Bianca, *a Curtezan.*

When the compositors found they had too much space left at the end of the First Folio's *Othello*, they added a character list, an elaborate ornamental device and spaced out line dividers to fill the page.

page, which, for example, they would do at the end of *The Comedy of Errors*, *As You Like It* and *All's Well That Ends Well*. They might introduce more spaced out indicators of characters' entrances or exits, or even add a list of characters. The latter recourse was followed for the last page of *Othello*, where 'FINIS' was added after the end of the final scene, with generous spaces and line dividers on either side, followed by a list of 'The Names of the Actors', recording character names rather than the actors' real names. This was followed by further page-dividing lines around an elaborate decorative woodblock. A similar format was followed for *The Winter's Tale*, though there was not quite enough space for the customary 'FINIS' to be inserted in between line dividers, so it was added in a smaller font in between the list of characters and an ornamental woodblock. When the compositors came to work on *Henry IV, Part 2*, they found that the casting-off process had resulted in an overestimation of the space needed for the play by a whole page. To deal with this they decided to include a longer and more widely spaced roll-call of characters, topped and tailed with intricate ornamental borders.

Far more difficult to deal with was a lack of space. This meant the compositors had some difficult decisions to make about the level of interference, and the number of changes, they were prepared to introduce into the text. They could incorporate more abbreviations or contractions for individual words or phrases – with *on it* becoming *on't*, for instance – or turn lines of verse into continuous prose. More radically, they could remove stage directions, eliminate or contract speech prefixes, change or cut words, or even remove whole lines, along with other space-saving tricks. What we do not often realise, when reading what we think are Shakespeare's words, the emanations of his own unique genius, is that the compositors may actually have – quite literally – had a hand in the composition of those lines. As the compositor neared the end of *Much Ado About Nothing*, for example, he realised that he was seriously short of space. He decided to remove the whole line 'Here comes the Prince and Claudio' that had appeared in the earlier quarto version of the play that served as a copy text for the Folio printing, recognising that this simply repeated the information given in the stage direction, which read 'Enter Prince, And Claudio, And Two Or Three Other'. He also abbreviated speech prefixes and stage directions, omitted the customary 'Exeunt', which indicated that the characters were to leave the stage at the end of the play, and squashed the closing 'FINIS' without dividing lines onto the base of the main play text.

Changes to words, phrases, speech prefixes and other features could also occur as a result of the compositor wanting to ensure lines were neatly and consistently 'justified', particularly when typesetting prose that was rendered with a clean right-hand margin. The compositor was, therefore, more than just a manual labourer. Joseph Moxon, author of the first detailed guide to printing, accords to this skilled worker a form of agency over the text:

> A good compositor is ambitious as well to make the meaning of his author intelligent to the reader, as to make his work show graceful to the eye, and pleasant in reading. Therefore if his copy be written in a language he understands, he reads his copy with consideration; that so he may get himself into the meaning of the author, and consequently considers how to order his work the better … the better to sympathize with the author's genius, and also with the capacity of the reader.

The compositors have left their marks on the Folio's plays in other ways too: through their unique spelling habits, preferred use of italics, manner of rendering speech prefixes and characters' entrances and exits, idiosyncratic uses of contractions and ways in which they interpreted individual words in accordance with the 'genius' of the playwright. Compositors therefore varied in the

Then this for whom we rendred vp this woe.   *Exeunt.*

Enter Leonato, Bene. Marg. Vrsula, oldman, Frier, Hero.

Frier. Did I not tell you she was innocent?

Leo. So are the *Prince* and *Claudio* who accu'd her,
Vpon the errour that you heard debated:
But *Margaret* was in some fault for this,
Although against her will as it appeares,
In the true course of all the question.

Old. Well, I am glad that all things sort so well.

Bene. And so am I, being else by faith enforc'd
To call young *Claudio* to a reckoning for it.

Leo. Well daughter, and you gentlewomen all,
Withdraw into a chamber by your selues,
And when I send for you, come hither mask'd:
The *Prince* and *Claudio* promis'd by this howre
To visit me, you know your office Brother,
You must be father to your brothers daughter,
And giue her to young *Claudio*.   *Exeunt Ladies.*

Old. Which I will doe with confirm'd countenance.

Bene. Frier, I must intreat your paines, I thinke.

Frier. To doe what Signior?

Bene. To binde me, or vndoe me, one of them:
Signior *Leonato*, truth it is good Signior,
Your neece regards me with an eye of fauour.

Leo. That eye my daughter lent her, 'tis most true.

Bene. And I doe with an eye of loue requite her.

Leo. The sight whereof I thinke you had from me,
From *Claudio*, and the *Prince*, but what's your will?

Bened. Your answer sir is Enigmaticall,
But for my will, my will is, your good will
May stand with ours, this day to be conioyn'd,
In the state of honourable marriage,
In which (good Frier) I shall desire your helpe.

Leon. My heart is with your liking.

Frier. And my helpe.

Enter Prince and Claudio, with attendants.

Prin. Good morrow to this faire assembly.

Leo. Good morrow Prince, good morrow *Claudio*:
We heere attend you, are you yet determin'd,
To day to marry with my brothers daughter?

Claud. Ile hold my minde were she an Ethiope.

Leo. Call her forth brother, heres the Frier ready.

Prin. Good morrow *Benedike*, why what's the matter?
That you haue such a Februarie face,
So full of frost, of storme, and clowdinesse.

Claud. I thinke he thinkes vpon the sauage bull:
Tush, feare not man, wee'll tip thy hornes with gold,
And all *Europa* shall reioyce at thee,
As once *Europa* did at lusty *Ioue*,
When he would play the noble beast in loue.

Ben. Bull *Ioue* sir, had an amiable low,
And some such strange bull leapt your fathers Cow,
A got a Calfe in that same noble feat,
Much like to you, for you haue iust his bleat.

Enter brother, Hero, Beatrice, Margaret, Vrsula.

Cla. For this I owe you: here comes other reckning.
Which is the Lady I must seize vpon?

Leo. This same is she, and I doe giue you her.

Cla. Why then she's mine, sweet let me see your face.

Leon. No that you shal not, till you take her hand,
Before this Frier, and sweare to marry her.

Clau. Giue me your hand before this holy Frier,
I am your husband if you like of me.

Hero. And when I liu'd I was your other wife,
And when you lou'd, you were my other husband.

Clau. Another *Hero*?

Hero. Nothing certainer.
One *Hero* died, but I doe liue,
And surely as I liue, I am a maid.

Prin. The former *Hero*, *Hero* that is dead.

Leon. Shee died my Lord, but whiles her slander liu'd.

Frier. All this amazement can I qualifie,
When after that the holy rites are ended,
Ile tell you largely of faire *Heroes* death:
Meane time let wonder seeme familiar,
And to the chappell let vs presently.

Ben. Soft and faire Frier, which is *Beatrice*?

Beat. I answer to that name, what is your will?

Bene. Doe not you loue me?

Beat. Why no, no more then reason.

Bene. Why then your Vncle, and the Prince, & *Claudio*, haue beene deceiued, they swore you did.

Beat. Doe not you loue mee?

Bene. Troth no, no more then reason.

Beat. Why then my Cosin *Margaret* and *Vrsula*
Are much deceiu'd, for they did sweare you did.

Bene. They swore you were almost sicke for me.

Beat. They swore you were wel-nye dead for me.

Bene. Tis no matter, then you doe not loue me?

Beat. No truly, but in friendly recompence.

Leon. Come Cosin, I am sure you loue the gentlemā.

Clau. And Ile be sworne vpon't, that he loues her,
For heeres a paper written in his hand,
A halting sonnet of his owne pure braine,
Fashioned to *Beatrice*.

Hero. And heeres another,
Writ in my cosins hand, stolne from her pocket,
Containing her affection vnto *Benedicke*.

Bene. A miracle, here's our owne hands against our
hearts: come I will haue thee, but by this light I take
thee for pittie.

Beat. I would not denie you, but by this good day, I
yeeld vpon great perswasion, & partly to saue your life,
for I was told, you were in a consumption.

Leon. Peace I will stop your mouth.

Prin. How dost thou *Benedicke* the married man?

Bene. Ile tell thee what Prince: a Colledge of witte-
crackers cannot flout mee out of my humour, dost thou
thinke I care for a Satyre or an Epigram? no, if a man will
be beaten with braines, a shall weare nothing handsome
about him: in briefe, since I do purpose to marry, I will
thinke nothing to any purpose that the world can say a-
gainst it, and therefore neuer flout at me, for I haue said
against it: for man is a giddy thing, and this is my conclusion: for thy part *Claudio*, I did thinke to haue beaten
thee, but in that thou art like to be my kinsman, liue vn-
bruis'd, and loue my cousin.

Cla. I had well hop'd ȳ wouldst haue denied *Beatrice*, ȳ
I might haue cudgel'd thee out of thy single life, to make
thee a double dealer, which out of questiō thou wilt be,
if my Cousin do not looke exceeding narrowly to thee.

Bene. Come, come, we are friends, let's haue a dance
ere we are married, that we may lighten our own hearts,
and our wiues heeles.

Leon. Wee'll haue dancing afterward.

Bene. First, of my vvord, therefore play musick. *Prince*,
thou art sad, get thee a vvife, get thee a vvife, there is no
staff more reuerend then one tipt with horn. *Enter Mes.*

Messen. My Lord, your brother *Iohn* is tane in flight,
And brought with armed men backe to *Messina*.

Bene. Thinke not on him till to morrow, ile deuise
thee braue punishments for him: strike vp Pipers. *Dance.*

L   *FINIS.*

degree to which they followed the spelling, punctuation and formatting of any given copy text which formed the basis of a printed page.

At some point before the casting-off process began, the professional scribe Ralph Crane was employed to produce fair copies of at least the first four plays in the Folio: *The Tempest*, *The Two Gentlemen of Verona*, *The Merry Wives of Windsor* and *Measure for Measure*. It is also thought that he may have prepared the last of the comedies, *The Winter's Tale*, and other plays have been suggested as contenders for having received the Crane treatment, including *The Comedy of Errors*, *Cymbeline*, *Henry IV, Part 2*, and *Othello*, among others. Crane's most intense period of work serving the theatre industry came between 1618 and 1625. In 1621, just a year before his Shakespeare transcriptions were used as the basis for the First Folio, he boasted of his association with the King's Men in a poem printed in his *The Works of Mercy, both Corporal and Spiritual*, claiming 'some employment hath my useful pen/Had amongst those civil, well-deserving men,/That grace the stage with honour and delight/ ... Under the kingly service they do hold'. Crane had also worked for the King's Men in 1619, producing a copy of Philip Massinger's *The Tragedy of Sir John Van Olden Barnavelt*, and there are surviving Crane transcripts for Ben Jonson's masque *Pleasure Reconciled to Virtue*, which was performed in January 1618, John Fletcher's *Demetrius and Enanthe* and Thomas Middleton's *The Witch*, parts of which were incorporated into Shakespeare's *Macbeth* for revivals of the play.

Crane's influence can be traced through some of his working practices, which have shaped the plays he touched in significant ways: the division of dramatic works into acts and scenes; a prefer-

Opposite: the final page of the First Folio's *Much Ado About Nothing*, showing that the compositors had run out of space when typesetting this play and decided to remove stage directions and squeeze the closing 'FINIS' between the scene's final words and the surrounding border.

ence for 'massed entries', in which he groups together all the characters appearing in a given scene at the start, regardless of when they enter; copious use of italics and other forms of punctuation, such as parentheses and apostrophes; a tendency towards elisions; a revelling in inventive hyphenated compound words or phrases, like 'heaven-sake' or 'bemockt-at-Stabs'; and the itemising of elaborate stage directions which are evaluative, descriptive, add emotive drama to a scene beyond the purely functional, or which interpret characters' demeanour and reactions to the unfolding events around them. One such stage direction of Crane's own devising may be *The Tempest*'s description of an on-stage masque in which 'Reapers' appear and 'join with Nymphs, in a graceful dance', in response to which 'Prospero starts suddenly and speaks, after which to a strange hollow and confused noise' the dancers 'heavily vanish'. In such instances, how we envisage Crane-touched plays has been shaped, without our realising it, by the scribe's proclivities and may not reflect Shakespeare's initial aims.

It would appear that the Folio syndicate had planned to commission Crane to produce fair copies of all the plays, but changed their minds. It is not clear if the costs of the project had already begun to spiral, forcing them to look for ways of shaving off some of their expenses. Since Crane would go on to provide transcription services for the King's Men, producing a copy of Thomas Middleton's controversial anti-Spanish play *A Game at Chess* in 1624, an unamicable disintegration of the scribe's working relationship with them and the Folio syndicate is unlikely to have been the cause. During the first stages of the Folio project, the

Right: a page from the First Folio's *The Two Gentlemen of Verona* (Act 3, Scene 1), showing an example of Ralph Crane's favoured method of inserting a 'massed entry' at the start of scenes. The Duke, Thurio, Proteus, Valentine, Launce and Speed are presented here as entering together, when in fact some of these characters have their entrances staggered across the scene. Valentine does not appear until fifty lines into the scene, while Proteus and Launce enter at around line 187, followed by Speed at line 276.

Scena Septima.

Enter Julia and Lucetta.

Iul. Counfel, *Lucetta,* gentle girl affift me,
And even in kind love, I doe conjure thee,
Who art the Table wherein all my thoughts
Are vifibly Charaſter'd, and Engrav'd,
To leſſon me, and tell me fome good mean.
How with my honour I may undertake
A journey to my loving *Protheus.*
  Luc. Alaſs, the way is wearifome and long.
  Iul. A true devoted Pilgrim is not weary
To meafure Kingdomes with his feeble fteps,
Much leſſe ſhall ſhe that hath loves wings to flie,
And when the flight is made to one fo dear,
Of ſuch divine perfeſtions as Sir *Protheus.*
  Luc. Better forbear till *Protheus* make return.
  Iul. Oh, know'ſt thou not, his looks are my fouls food?
Pity the dearth that I have pined in,
By longing for that food fo long a time.
Didſt thou but know the inchly touch of Love,
Thou would'ſt as foon go kindle fire with fnow
As feek to quench the fire of Love with words.
  Luc. I doe not feek to quench your Loves hot fire,
But qualifie the fires extream rage,
Leaſt it ſhould burn above the bounds of reafon.
  Iul. The more thou dam'ſt it up, the more it burns:
The Current that with gentle murmur glides
(Thou know'ſt) being ſtop'd, impatiently doth rage:
But when his fair courfe is not hindered,
He makes fweet muſick with th'enameld ſtones,
Giving a gentle kiſſe to every fedge
He overtaketh in his pilgrimage.
And fo by many winding nooks he ſtrayes
With willing ſport to the wild Ocean.
Then let me go, and hinder not my courfe:
I'le be as patient as a gentle ſtream,
And make a paftime of each weary ſtep,
Till the laſt ſtep have brought me to my Love,
And there I'le reſt, as after much turmoil
A bleſſed foul doth in *Elizium.*
  Luc. But in what habit will you go along?
  Iul. Not like a woman, for I would prevent
The loofe encounters of lafcivious men:
Gentle *Lucetta,* fit me with fuch weeds
As may befeem fome well reputed Page.
  Luc. Why then your Ladiſhip muſt cut your hair.
  Iul. No girl, i'le knit it up in ſilken ſtrings,
With twenty od-conceited true-love knots:
To be fantaſtick, may become a youth
Of greater time then I ſhall ſhow to be.   (ches?
  Luc. What faſhion (Madam) ſhall I make your bree-
  Iul. That fits as well, as tell me (good my Lord)
What compaſſe will you wear your Farthingale?
Why even what faſhion thou beſt likes (*Lucetta.*)
  Luc. You muſt needs have them with a cod-piece (Ma-
Iul. Out, out, (*Lucetta*) that will be ill-favord.   (dam
  Luc. A round hofe (Madam) now's not worth a pin
Unleſſe you have a cod-piece to ſtick pins on.
  Iul. Lucetta, as thou lov'ſt me let me have.
What thou think'ſt meet, and is moſt mannerly,
But tell me (wench) how will the world repute me
For undertaking fo unſtaid a journey?

I fear me it will make me ſcandaliz'd.
  Luc. If you think fo, then ſtay at home and go not.
  Iul. Nay, that I will not.
  Luc. Then never dream on Infamy, but go:
If *Protheus* like your journey when you come,
No matter who's difpleas'd when you are gone:
I fear me he will ſcarce be pleas'd withall.
  Iul. That is the leaſt (*Lucetta*) of my fear:
A thoufand oathes, an Ocean of his tears
And inftances as infinite of Love,
Warrant me welcome to my *Protheus.*
  Luc. All thefe are fervants to deceitfull men.
  Iul. Bafe men, that ufe them to fo bafe effeſt;
But truer ſtars did govern *Protheus* birth,
His words are bonds, his oathes are oracles,
His love fincere, his thoughts immaculate,
His tears pure meſſengers, fent from his heart,
His heart as far from fraud, as heaven from earth.
  Luc. Pray heaven he prove fo when you come to him.
  Iul. Now, as thou lov'ſt me, do him not that wrong,
To bear a hard opinion of his truth:
Onely deferve my love, by loving him,
And prefently go with me to my chamber
To take a note of what I ſtand in need of,
To furniſh me upon my longing journey:
All that is mine I leave at thy difpofe,
My goods, my Lands, my reputation,
Onely in lieu thereof, difpatch me hence:
Come; anfwer not: but to it prefently,
I am impatient of my tarriance.

Exeunt.

Actus Tertius. Scena Prima.

Enter Duke, Thurio, Protheus, Valentine,
Launce, Speed.

  Duk. Sir *Thurio,* give us leave (I pray) awhile,
We have fome fecrets to confer about.
Now tell me *Protheus,* whats your will with me?
  Pro. My gracious Lord, that which I would difcover,
The law of friendſhip bids me to conceal,
But when I call to mind your gracious favours
Done to me (undeferving as I am)
My duty pricks me on to utter that
Which elfe no worldly good ſhould draw from me:
Know (worthy Prince) Sir *Valentine* my friend
This night intends to ſteal away your daughter:
My felf am one made privy to the plot.
I know you have determin'd to beſtow her
On *Thurio,* whom your gentle daughter hates;
And ſhould ſhe thus be ſtoln away from you,
It would be much vexation to your age.
Thus (for my duties fake) I rather chofe
To croſſe my friend in his intended drift,
Then (by concealing it) heap on your head
A pack of forrows, which would preſſe you down
(Being unprepared) to your timeleſſe grave.
  Duk. Protheus, I thank thee for thine honeſt care,
Which to requite, command me while I live.
This love of theirs, my felf have often feen,
Happily when they have judg'd me faſt afleep,
And oftentimes have purpos'd to forbid

Sir

Iuno sings her blessings on you.

Earths increase, foyzon plentie,
Barnes, and Garners, neuer empty,
Vines, with clustring bunches growing,
Plants, with goodly burthen bowing:
Spring come to you at the farthest,
In the very end of Haruest.
Scarcity and want shall shun you,
Ceres blessing so is on you.

Fer. This is a most maiesticke vision, and
Harmonious charmingly : may I be bold
To thinke these spirits?

Pro. Spirits, which by mine Art
I haue from their confines call'd to enact
My present fancies.

Fer. Let me liue here euer,
So rare a wondred Father, and a wife
Makes this place Paradise.

Pro. Sweet now, silence :
Iuno and *Ceres* whisper seriously,
There's something else to doe : hush, and be mute
Or else our spell is mar'd.

Iuno and Ceres whisper, and send Iris on employment.
Iris. You Nimphs cold *Nayades* of y̆ windring brooks,
With your sedg'd crownes, and euer-harmelesse lookes,
Leaue your crispe channels, and on this greene-Land
Answere your summons, *Iuno* do's command.
Come temperate *Nimphes,* and helpe to celebrate
A Contract of true Loue : be not too late.

Enter Certaine Nimphes.
You Sun-burn'd Sicklemen of August weary,
Come hether from the furrow, and be merry,
Make holly day : your Rye-straw hats put on,
And these fresh Nimphes encounter euery one
In Country footing.

Enter certaine Reapers (properly habited:) they ioyne with the Nimphes in a gracefull dance, towards the end whereof, Prospero starts sodainly and speakes, after which to a strange hollow and confused noyse, they heauily vanish.

Pro. I had forgot that foule conspiracy
Of the beast *Callibon,* and his confederates
Against my life : the minute of their plot
Is almost come : Well done, auoid : no more.

Fer. This is strange : your fathers in some passion
That workes him strongly.

Mir. Neuer till this day
Saw I him touch'd with anger, so distemper'd.

Pro. You doe looke (my son) in a mou'd sort,
As if you were dismaid : be cheerefull Sir,
Our Reuels now are ended : These our actors,
(As I foretold you) were all Spirits, and
Are melted into Ayre, into thin Ayre,
And like the baselesse fabricke of this vision
The Clowd-capt Towres, the gorgeous Pallaces,
The solemne Temples, the great Globe it selfe,
Yea, all which it inherit, shall dissolue,
And like this insubstantiall Pageant faded
Leaue not a racke behinde : we are such stuffe
As dreames are made on ; and our little life
Is rounded with a sleepe : Sir, I am vext,
Beare with my weakenesse, my old braine is troubled:
Be not disturb'd with my infirmitie,
If you be pleas'd, retire into my Cell,
And there repose, a turne or two, Ile walke
To still my beating minde.

Fer. Mir. We wish your peace. *Exit.*

Pro. Come with a thought; I thank thee *Ariel* : come.
Enter Ariell.
Ar. Thy thoughts I cleaue to, what's thy pleasure?
Pro. Spirit : We must prepare to meet with *Caliban.*
Ar. I my Commander, when I presented *Ceres*
I thought to haue told thee of it, but I fear'd
Least I might anger thee.

Pro. Say again, where didst thou leaue these varlots?
Ar. I told you Sir, they were red-hot with drinking,
So full of valour, that they smote the ayre
For breathing in their faces : beate the ground
For kissing of their feete ; yet alwaies bending
Towards their proiect : then I beate my Tabor,
At which like ynback't colts they prickt their eares,
Aduanc'd their eye-lids, lifted vp their noses
As they smelt musicke, so I charm'd their eares
That Calfe-like, they my lowing follow'd, through
Tooth'd briars, sharpe firzes, pricking gosse, & thorns,
Which entred their fraile shins : at last I left them
I'th' filthy mantled poole beyond your Cell,
There dancing vp to th'chins, that the fowle Lake
Ore-stunck their feet.

Pro. This was well done (my bird)
Thy shape inuisible retaine thou still :
The trumpery in my house, goe bring it hither
For stale to catch these theeues. *Ar.* I go, I goe. *Exit.*

Pro. A Deuill, a borne-Deuill, on whose nature
Nurture can neuer sticke : on whom my paines
Humanely taken, all, all lost, quite lost,
And, as with age, his body ouglier growes,
So his minde cankers : I will plague them all,
Euen to roaring : Come, hang on them this line.

Enter Ariell, loaden with glistering apparell, &c. Enter
Caliban, Stephano, and Trinculo, all wet.
Cal. Pray you tread softly, that the blinde Mole may
not heare a foot fall : we now are neere his Cell.

St. Monster, your Fairy, w̆ you say is a harmles Fairy,
Has done little better then plaid the Iacke with vs.

Trin. Monster, I do smell all horse-pisse, at which
My nose is in great indignation.

Ste. So is mine. Do you heare Monster : If I should
Take a displeasure against you : Looke you.

Trin. Thou wert but a lost Monster.

Cal. Good my Lord, giue me thy fauour stil,
Be patient, for the prize Ile bring thee too
Shall hudwinke this mischance : therefore speake softly,
All's husht as midnight yet.

Trin. I, but to loose our bottles in the Poole.

Ste. There is not onely disgrace and dishonor in that
Monster, but an infinite losse.

Tr. That's more to me then my wetting :
Yet this is your harmlesse Fairy, Monster.

Ste. I will fetch off my bottle,
Though I be o're eares for my labour.

Cal. Pre-thee (my King) be quiet. Seest thou heere
This is the mouth o'th Cell : no noise, and enter :
Do that good mischeefe, which may make this Island
Thine owne for euer, and I thy *Caliban*
For aye thy foot-licker.

Ste. Giue me thy hand,
I do begin to haue bloody thoughts.

Trin. O King *Stephano,* O Peere : O worthy *Stephano,*
Looke what a wardrobe heere is for thee.

Cal. Let it alone thou foole, it is but trash.

Tri. Oh, ho, Monster : wee know what belongs to a
frippery, O King *Stephano.*

Left: this page from the First Folio's *The Tempest*, shows an example of what may be Ralph Crane's imaginative and descriptive stage directions. In this instance, the mood, movement and emotional textures of the scene are indicated, including Prospero's startled reaction 'to a strange hollow and confused noise'.

compositors in the Half-Eagle and Key would have been grateful for Crane's neat copy texts. There was nothing more frustrating than an illegible handwritten manuscript, especially if it had been overworked with editorial comments, corrections or interpolations. As Moxon states, such texts represented 'bad, heavy, hard work'. Crane's manuscripts, offering predictable conventions, were accounted 'good copy, light, easy work'. When setting his transcripts, however, the compositors did not always slavishly follow his texts, but occasionally used their own spelling and punctuation conventions, blending their own tendencies with Crane's, thereby embedding these in the transmission and preservation of Shakespeare's words.

Compositors, like everyone else, are subject to human error. Misinterpretation of poorly rendered manuscripts, accidental repetitions of words or phrases, the misplacing of words or even whole lines and sections across wrong portions of a given page, and the inevitable eye skip resulting in missing words or the splicing together of different parts of the forme during typesetting, conspired to alter the text or introduce errors that have either been 'fixed' as an eternal part of the Shakespeare canon, or altered (through sometimes conjectural emendations) by subsequent editors. When it came to mistakes unwittingly introduced by the compositors, some of these might be picked up through the stop-press corrections process, where initial printed pages would be checked for errors, which would be marked up, even while the printing was on the go, and corrected in subsequent printed formes. The erroneous sheets were often incorporated into finished Folios because paper was too valuable a commodity to waste. This process ensured that no two surviving First Folios are completely alike across their total of 898 pages of printed text. Add to this the fact that there are both small and extensive differences between surviving individual quarto printed plays and their Folio counterparts, and the whole notion of a 'stable' Shakespeare text becomes a shaky one indeed.

Even if John Heminges and Henry Condell had consciously worked towards providing posterity with plays which, in their estimation, reflected Shakespeare's 'original' – a word used more than once in the First Folio's pitching – intentions, the process of deciding between existing copies of some of the plays would have meant making tough decisions. Do they stick with Shakespeare's authorial papers for a given play, or base the copy text on a previously published quarto edition, with or without marked-up changes and 'improvements'? Do they use a professional scribe to regularise conventions within and across play texts or use one of the company's prompt books as the basis of a print-ready copy text? If the latter, then which prompt book: a text based on the play as performed during Shakespeare's lifetime or a later revival, with interpolations by other dramatists, such as Thomas Middleton? Or should they use a combination of sources to arrive at what, in their opinion, would be the 'best' version? Do they restore scenes previously deleted from plays by censors because they were too topical when first performed or leave them out because their political contexts are no longer relevant? And how were any decisions shared between Heminges and Condell and the Folio's syndicate members?

Which texts formed the basis of the Folio's plays are hotly contested by Shakespeare editors. Some believe that *Henry V*, *Coriolanus* and *Antony and Cleopatra*, for example, were based on Shakespeare's own authorial manuscripts or transcripts of them, while *Julius Caesar* was typeset using a performance text of some kind. It has been argued that the Folio's *Much Ado About Nothing* reproduced a previously printed single edition with annotations and editorial changes, while *A Midsummer Night's Dream* was largely grounded on the second printed edition with interpolations and corrections. *Richard II* may have had an even more complex history, possibly derived from a conflation of the third and fifth editions of the play, compared with a performance text or prompt book. This work also provides us with an illuminating example of the kinds of decisions that had to be made during the printing of the Folio, since the 1608 and 1615 editions, published by Matthew Law, included a previously deleted Parliament scene which, dramatising the deposition of King Richard, proved too politically incendiary for the censors and had been removed from all earlier printings of the play since its first appearance in 1597. Should the controversial scene be retained in the Folio or removed? It was kept. It is not possible to be certain about who guided such decisions; whether it was Heminges and Condell or the Folio syndicate. It has been argued, however, that *Romeo and Juliet* and *Love's Labour's Lost* may have been edited by John Smethwick or an annotating reader assigned by him, with an eye towards improving the reading experience. These texts' changes in the Folio indicate that Smethwick 'valued the progressive improvement' of the plays, rather than attempting to reconstruct some lost Shakespeare 'original'. Indeed, in one work of the period that he published he took the blame for any errors, stating that he was 'sometimes mis-led by doubt and difficulty of the copy', suggesting that he was responsible for changes to the copy text. In reality, therefore, the composition of the plays' source texts and the kinds of interventions to which they were subject might reflect the tastes and preferences of the King's Men, of the Folio's chief financiers, of scribes or annotators, or of the conventions of the period, rather than serve to recreate Shakespeare's own purpose. After all, what 'landed' with audiences and readers in 1596 might not stir the passions in the same way in the early 1620s.

This distance from Shakespeare's 'original' conception is compounded by other kinds of external intervention. In 1606, for example, an Act to Restrain Abuses of Players was enforced in an attempt to clean up the profanities used on the English stage. Actors were commanded not to 'jestingly or profanely speak or use the Holy Name of God, or of Christ Jesus, or of the Holy Ghost or of the Trinity'. Infringements would be punished with an instant fine of ten pounds. While this applied formally to performance, not print, many plays in the Folio show signs that those written before this date (perhaps, at least in some cases, due to the copy texts used to print them deriving from performance-based texts or texts prepared by scribes sensitive to more uncouth forms of speech) were shorn of swearing, cursing, cussing and blasphemous oaths before they were published. Some of Shakespeare's most engaging and vivid characters, such as Iago and Falstaff, revelled in profanities like 'Zounds!', a contraction for 'God's wounds', and ''Sblood', short for 'God's blood', and 'Fore God', meaning 'Before God', the latter of which was uttered by Falstaff in an earlier quarto version of *Henry IV, Part 2* and replaced with 'Trust me, a likely Fellow' in the Folio. The Folio version of *Othello*, for instance, has had over fifty profanities removed, comparing it with the 1622 quarto issue. In redacting these from the Folio, the speech patterns, attributes and personal quirks of these characters have been changed from the personalities Shakespeare conjured in his imagination when writing them. Hamlet's impassioned protest to Rosencrantz and Guildenstern ''sblood do you think I am easier to be played on than a pipe?' becomes in the Folio 'Why do you think, that I am easier to be played on, than a pipe?', a change that alters the emotional intensity of the moment.

Some of the alterations may have been down to the King's Men's bookkeeper. He was responsible for the company's performance texts and prompt books, ensuring that these both conformed to the state of current productions and that performances followed the contents of these texts. He would also implement changes demanded by the censors. It is possible that from 1619 the King's

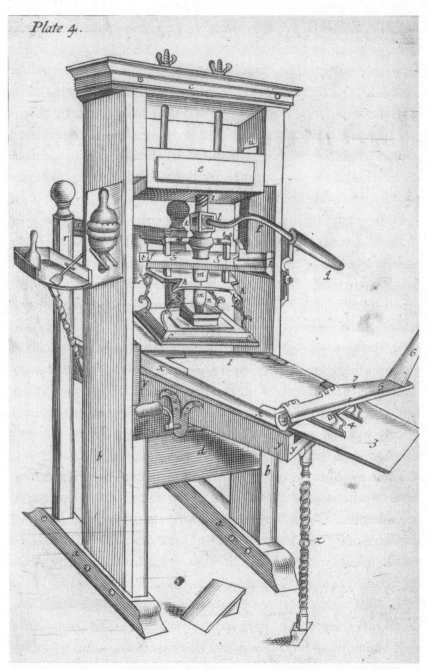

A seventeenth-century printing press, from volume two of Joseph Moxon's *Mechanick Exercises: or, The doctrine of handy-works* (London: Printed for Joseph Moxon, 1683).

Men's bookkeeper was Edward Knight, but he could have joined the company any time up till 20 December 1624 when he is first listed as one of the 'necessary attendants' of the King's Men. Few samples of Knight's emendations to performance-based texts survive, none dating from before the Folio's publication, but recent research has indicated that Knight could cut roles, reassign speeches to different characters or splice different parts of speeches together, change stage directions and speech prefixes, misalign verse and even change the author's original words.

Shakespeare's plays, therefore, as they have come down to us through the First Folio are, in many ways, the result of a silent collaboration which includes the scribes who created fair copies of the works, those responsible for the casting-off process, the compositors, the bookkeepers, annotating editors of pre-printed copy texts, revisers of plays for new performances, and those who selected the sources that made up the copy texts from which the plays would be printed. The mechanisms of censorship and changes in literary and theatrical taste also shaped the Folio's plays in fundamental ways. These were organic, fluid processes; chaotic, intersecting, the hidden roots of the tree that made Shakespeare's Book grow in the unique way it did.

Once a forme was typeset from a copy text it was time to print. Enter the inkers, tasked with coating the type with an even layer of ink. They did this using ink balls, stuffed leather bundles, which they grasped from a wooden handle attached to each ball. To ensure maximum efficiency a dextrous inker could dip two balls in ink at a time and apply these simultaneously over the surface of the type. This required careful judgement and a sensitive touch: too much ink would cause blotting, while not enough would result in faded or only partially legible text. That this could be messy work is attested to by the fact that some of the surviving Folios' pages still preserve the inky fingerprints of the Jaggards' pressworkers; ghostly traces of the invisible hands that helped make Shakespeare's Book.

Inking complete, the 'chase' of type was then secured onto the printing press on a slidable frame or carriage while the paper, dampened with water so that it could absorb the ink more readily, was pinned to an adjacent hinged frame called a 'tympan', which was lowered onto the inked type. These were then slid under a heavy suspended block known as a 'platen'. Turning a lever attached to the platen pushed the block down onto the paper, forcing it onto the inked type and creating the ink impression of the text the right way round. Pulling the lever back released the platen, allowing the carriage to be guided back out. The tympan was then lifted back on its hinge and the paper peeled off and hung on lines or wooden frames to dry. The process was repeated until the desired number of printed copies had been completed. Some estimates for the quantity of 'impressions' or printed sheets these pressworkers could produce in an hour place the figure up to an optimistic 250, though

Scenes from a seventeenth-century printing shop, showing freshly printed pages being hung to dry and the operation of a lever and platen, from volume two of Joseph Moxon's *Mechanick Exercises: or, The doctrine of handy-works* (London: Printed for Joseph Moxon, 1683).

this may have depended on a range of factors, including the quantity of stop-press corrections required and the number of pressworkers assigned to each task. In reality the output could have been of a more modest nature.

The Jaggards clearly cared about how the First Folio 'felt' as well as how it looked. The process of paper-making meant that each side of a Folio sheet would have created a different sensation as a reader ran their fingers across it. The paper that made up Shakespeare's Book did not begin life as tree wood but as mulched up wet linen rags, pressed into a ribbed mould against a wire frame and then laid on felt cloth. Each piece of paper was stacked with felt in alternate layers, taking the impression of the felt. The bundle was then squeezed of its remaining water and each sheet scrubbed clean and hung to dry. The result would be a much more tactile form of paper than we are used to today, with a smoother 'felt side' and the ghostly impressions of 'chain-lines' and the ribs of the mould detectable both visibly and through the less even texture of the other side of the sheet. Most of the title pages for the Folio's plays are printed on the more pristine 'felt side'. When the earliest readers of the First Folio leafed through the first nine title pages they would have *felt* the opulence of Shakespeare's words before even reading these plays' opening scenes, with perhaps a drama of anticipation thrumming through their fingers.

Maintaining such attention to detail in the organised chaos of the printing house was no easy task, and not every title page was printed on the felt side. This desire to build the reader experience into the printing process, however, demonstrates the great care with which the project was conducted. No part of the procedure could be performed without a nuance-detecting eye. After the pressworkers had finished with each 'chase', the individual pieces of type were removed and cleaned, every single one restored to the compartment from which it had been taken. Placing type in the wrong compartments could result in errors to ensuing formes, so accuracy and focus were paramount. After the sheets were fully dried, they were collected together and sent to a binder whose job was to sew them, in linear order, into individual books. As a steer they followed the 'signatures' (the series of letters and numbers printed at the base of some of the Folio's pages) and the 'catch words' (the first word of the next page printed in the bottom-right-hand margin of its predecessor), which indicated the sequence in which the sheets should be assembled, making up what amounted to a giant textual puzzle.

Labourers working in a paper-making shop, showing the manufacture of paper from linen rags. The worker on the left is the 'vatman' who dips a mould into a vat of waterlogged linen fragments, draining out the water until the fibres form the basis of the paper in the mould. The figure in the middle is the 'coucher', who empties the moulds and lays the newly created sheets on a 'couch board'. The resulting sheets are laid on felt and pressed, after which the labourer on the right, known as the 'layer', separates them out into a print-ready stock of paper.

Type was a very expensive commodity and had to be treated with care. It was to be cherished and passed down from generation to generation or from printer to printer. William Jaggard had inherited much of the type used in the First Folio from James Roberts when he acquired his printing business, along with decorative woodblocks which added fetching embellishments to some of the head lettering and borders of pages, augmenting the volume's aura of luxury. Type was kept as long as it was useable and sometimes would become chipped or develop distinctive scratches, each as unique as a fingerprint. It is thanks to painstaking work by the bibliographer Charlton Hinman, who scrutinised thousands of pieces of Folio type for these marks, chasing them across the volume's pages, and even through other books produced in the Jaggards' printing house at the time, that we have a good sense of the order in which the plays were printed and when delays are likely to have intervened in the process. He was inspired to do this after serving as a cryptographer during the Second World War, using his skills as a code-breaker to invent an ingenious device now known as the 'Hinman Collator', which allowed him to compare individual pieces of type across First Folios owned by those obsessive Shakespeare enthusiasts and collectors Henry and Emily Folger. He added to this an attention to the idiosyncrasies in spelling, punctuation and other quirks demonstrated by individual compositors, allowing him to begin piecing together a conjectural inventory of the personnel who had worked on the Folio. Over time dedicated bibliographers and scholars, along with experts on paper stocks and their watermarks, added to Hinman's findings, building up a more precise picture of the compositors who typeset each forme and their pattern of working.

These pressworkers, hidden characters in the story of the First Folio, would have been ready to begin printing the volume as soon as the syndicate had supplied them with a fair number of copy texts acquired from Heminges and Condell, as well as from

The Hinman Collator is the machine developed by the dedicated bibliographer Charlton Hinman to help him examine thousands of characters from the First Folio's printed pages. He used his expertise as a cryptographer during the Second World War to construct it. This enabled him to build up a picture of the printing of Shakespeare's Book and the personnel (the compositors) who worked on it in the printing house of William and Isaac Jaggard.

stationers who had agreed to sell or lease their rights to plays, with some of these valuable assets delivered straight from Ralph Crane's industrious hands. But as the process was getting underway, there was something in the air; a tangible sense that James I's subjects were living through a time of great change, both culturally and politically. A change was coming indeed, and it would unfold like a dramatic theatrical backdrop to the creation of Shakespeare's Book, shaping it in lasting and legible ways.

11

'Our Will Shakespeare'

Comedies, Pilgrims and Spain's Golden Age

The printing of the First Folio probably began early in 1622, most likely placed in the hands of the Half-Eagle and Key's pressworkers in the month of February. The order in which the plays were printed largely matches the Folio's contents page, starting with the comedies, then the histories, followed by the tragedies, leaving the preliminary pages to last. The Jaggards kept largely to this schedule but there were exceptions, hiccups along the way that forced the printing team to make changes to the order in which the plays were prepared. One play, *Troilus and Cressida*, would prove to be such a source of exasperation that it was initially removed from the Folio, with some of the first copies sold without it. But this was not the only problem the Jaggards encountered during the nearly two years that it would take to complete the whole project.

As we know, the licences to print at least the first few plays, possibly most if not all of the comedies, for which the King's Men no longer held the rights, had very likely been negotiated by the Folio syndicate before printing began. Yet the first phase of printing, focusing on *The Tempest*, *The Two Gentlemen of Verona* and *The*

Merry Wives of Windsor, initially proceeded rather slowly. This was not because of the state of the copy texts being used by the compositors, for these were among the plays known to have been produced by the scribe Ralph Crane in highly legible copies. The printers used the same limited stock of type across consecutively produced formes, with each comprising two pages of the Folio, indicating that the compositors were proceeding in a linear fashion, forme by forme, quire by quire, roughly in sequential order. This was a less efficient way to proceed than printing formes concurrently across plays or parts of a play.

Estimates as to how many compositors worked on the whole project vary, with some bibliographers placing the figure at five and others detecting as many as nine different pairs of hands in the finished text. When work commenced on the comedies it is likely that the Jaggards had appointed three compositors to execute the typesetting. We do not know their identities or if a John Shakespeare, 'son of a Warwickshire butcher', who was apprenticed to William Jaggard in 1610, was among them. The prospect of a potential kinsman of William Shakespeare working on the playwright's book fires the imagination but we know only the identity of one of these compositors for certain (we will meet him later in the Folio's story). The rest are identified only by letters. Three compositors worked on the Folio during this period, known today as Compositor B, Compositor C and Compositor F, each dipping a hand into a different case of type. Throughout, Compositor B appears to have undertaken the lion's share of the typesetting, preparing over half its pages for printing, and may have been among the most experienced of the Jaggards' pressworkers. It has been speculated that this could have been John Shakespeare, but there is no evidence for the attribution.

If we were to take two photographs of the scene unfolding around the compositors' cases from the start of work on *The Tempest*, the first showing the typesetting of the initial eight or so pages and the second capturing progress on pages nine to twelve, in the former we would see Compositor B standing beside his favourite case, working with his habitual practice of spelling 'heere' instead of 'here' and 'griefe' for 'grief', aided occasionally by Compositor F, using type from a different case. In the latter image we would see Compositor C, with his fondness for spelling 'do' as 'doe' and 'go' as 'goe', having taken over from Compositor B, working from a third case, again supported by Compositor F from his own case. Since it took about half a day to print off one forme, excluding the time required for the typesetting, this method of working would have been a ponderous way to begin.

There were other reasons for this relative slowness of production. The compositors and pressworkers clearly cared about the quality of the text, wanting to ensure that the reader would be left with the best possible impression of the work from the start. *The Tempest*'s very first page was checked for errors and corrected at least four times. Additional care may have been taken over this play because it had special significance for the King's Men. Prospero was, in all likelihood, the last role Shakespeare acted before retiring as a performer; his farewell to the stage. Heminges and Condell may have felt presenting this as the lead work would have been a fitting tribute to their friend. They may also have calculated that this play, with its evocation of the wonders of the New World, would have appealed to the Herbert brothers who were investors in the Virginia Company, which financed expeditions to the Americas and Bermuda. Shakespeare was probably inspired to write it through his association with William Strachey, who had been the owner of a one-sixth share in the Blackfriars Theatre from 1606, which he had acquired during the period when the playhouse was leased to the child players. Strachey, a close friend of Ben Jonson, was an investor in the Virginia Company and had produced an account of a disastrous voyage to the New World in 1609, during which he and other colonists bound for Jamestown had been shipwrecked on the coast of Bermuda. Shakespeare may have read the manuscript, since elements of it were incorporated into *The Tempest*, including a dazzling account of a 'sea-fire' that appeared as 'an apparition of a little round light, like a faint star', which had 'stricken amazement' in the mariners. Shakespeare's Prospero orders Ariel to transform into a similar ball of fire, which 'flamed amazement' among the soon-to-be shipwrecked crew. Leonard Digges's brother, Dudley, was heavily involved in the Virginia Company and it has been argued by some that he may have supplied Shakespeare with Strachey's text. In fact either Strachey directly or one of the Digges brothers could have been the conduit. Representing what were potentially once personal associations for Shakespeare, Heminges and Condell, and a newly charged relevance for the Herbert brothers who were enticed by opportunities

Uncorrected first page of *The Tempest*, from Folger Shakespeare Library First Folio 24, showing that the first elaborately carved initial letter 'B' was set backwards and upside down. As this is the headline play, the Jaggards' pressworkers checked its opening pages many times because they wanted to leave the reader with the best possible impression. The error was duly corrected in subsequent printed pages.

in the New World, *The Tempest* was a play the backers of the First Folio would have been determined to get right.

At the same time, the Jaggards were working on another ambitious book, Thomas Wilson's *Christian Dictionary*. This may have led Compositor B, for example, largely to set aside work on the First Folio during the printing of *The Two Gentlemen of Verona*, because more experienced hands were needed to speed up work on the *Dictionary*. Towards the end of its printing schedule, Wilson's text shared the same stock of type as the first three Folio plays, so we can be fairly certain that typesetting was underway on both texts at once. With the Jaggards' compositors divided between the Shakespeare and Wilson projects, sometimes working alternately across them, they inevitably picked out some of the same pieces of type, using them to set formes for both works. For example, damage to two pieces of type – those for the letters 'n' and 'd' – can be seen in both books, strongly suggesting that they were printed from the same stock. Wilson's text was completed fairly early in 1622, probably around March, giving us a good basis on which to estimate the start of the Folio's printing. The final sheet of the *Christian Dictionary* was finished at some point between the end of the print run for *The Merry Wives of Windsor* and the start of *Measure for Measure*. In all, the printing of the first three plays would have required roughly two months, taking the press team up till the end of March or beginning of April.

Meanwhile, with the eye of every English citizen on the issue of James I's next move in his diplomatic dance with Spain, the King's Men were being swept up in the change to the cultural landscape which was being prompted by recent political events. They are likely to have been busy with performances of a couple of plays recently added to their repertoire: Philip Massinger's *The Duke of Milan* and Thomas Middleton's *More Dissemblers Besides Women*, which was licensed for performance by the then Master of the

Revels Sir George Buc some time before the end of March 1622. The latter play continued the trend for dramatisations of misogynistic themes and may well have been influenced by the success of *The Masque of the Gypsies Metamorphosed*, Ben Jonson's propagandist endorsement of the Spanish Match, since Middleton had also incorporated a gypsy band into the action. But the king's players would make a bolder statement that year with a run of court performances which tapped into the topical interest in Spain and which allied them closely with the endeavours of Edward Blount.

On the first day of 1622 the court celebrated the new year at Whitehall Palace with John Fletcher's *The Pilgrim*. The play's sources included works by authors whose notoriety in England had been expanding at this time, partly thanks to the publishing efforts of Blount, and who are still today regarded as masters in the Spanish 'Golden Age' of literary accomplishment. One of these was the second part of Thomas Shelton's English translation of Miguel de Cervantes' *Don Quixote*, published by Blount in 1620 with a dedication to the head of the Spanish faction at court, George Villiers, the Marquess of Buckingham, composed by Blount himself and expressing his hope that the marquess's intercession would allow the work to be received with 'courtesy in the Court of Great Britain'. The other piece of textual inspiration behind the play was William Dutton's English translation of a work by Félix Lope de Vega published in 1621 as *The Pilgrim of Castile*. Considered to have been surpassed only by Cervantes, this Spanish poet and playwright was another towering figure in Spanish literary circles and has an interesting connection to the First Folio, for he was known to at least two of the commemorative poets attached to it.

When Lope de Vega's *Rimas*, a collection of poems, was published in Madrid in 1613, Leonard Digges wrote enthusiastically to a friend, informing him that 'Mr Mabbe was to send you this book of sonnets, which with Spaniards here is accounted their

Lope de Vega as in England we should of our Will Shakespeare.'
Mr Mabbe is none other than James Mabbe, and both Folio poets
were probably in Spain together when this was written, as part of
an embassy to Madrid in the entourage of Sir John Digby. It is
thought that Mabbe, born around 1571–2 in Surrey in the Diocese
of Winchester, was 'of gentle Parents', and descended from a
dynasty of goldsmiths. His mother was Martha Denham, his father
the goldsmith John Mabbe. His grandfather, also named John
Mabbe, was likewise a member of the Goldsmiths' Company and
had been afforded the honour of being appointed Chamberlain of
London in 1577. Aside from his closeness to Blount, it is possible
that James Mabbe had a connection to the Folio syndicate in
another way. William Jaggard was brother-in-law to one Elizabeth
Mabb, who married his brother John in St Dunstan's Church on 5
June 1597. James Mabbe had an uncle and possibly brother both
named Edward. We cannot be sure if either is the Edward Mabbe
who is listed as guarantor for a loan from the Stationers' Company
to John Jaggard in 1622, but the fact that he is identified in that
record as a 'Goldsmith of London, dwelling in the Parish of St
Dunstan in the West', strongly suggests the possibility that he is
one of these. The loan was for fifty pounds, but the custom was for
the bond for which guarantors would be liable to be double the
loan amount. Edward's willingness to risk £100 suggests a closeness between the Jaggards and this Mabbe family, indicating that
Elizabeth Mabb may indeed have been a kinswoman of the
Mabbes associated with the Folio's James Mabbe.

A well-travelled and highly skilled linguist, James Mabbe,
according to his earliest biographer, Anthony à Wood, 'was
esteemed a learned man, good orator, and facetious conceited wit',
and around 1611 joined John Digby as his secretary in Spain,
'where remaining with him several years, [he] improved himself in
various sorts of learning, and in the customs and manners of that
and other countries'. We can glean something of Mabbe's flamboy-

ant personality through his dedicatory epistle to Sir Thomas Richardson in his later translation of Fernando de Rojas' play *La Celestina* as *The Spanish Bawd*, in which he praises the beauty and vitality of the work in its original Spanish:

> Howsoever therefore these rigid reprehenders will not stick to say of *Celestina*, that she is like a crow amongst so many swans; like a grasshopper amongst so many nightingales; or like a paper-blurrer amongst so many famous writers; yet they that are learned in her language, have esteemed it (in comparison of others) as gold amongst metals; as the carbuncle amongst stones; as the rose amongst flowers; as the palm amongst trees; as the eagle amongst birds; and as the sun amongst inferior lights; in a word, as the choisest and chiefest.

There is here an earnest desire to elevate works of Spanish literature as worthy of the attention of the English intelligentsia; a project to which the poet Leonard Digges was also committed. Born in 1588, the latter's mother was Anne, daughter of Sir Warham St Leger, and his father was the famous mathematician Thomas Digges, whose celebrated works on warfare some believe were plundered by Shakespeare when he wrote *Henry V* and *Coriolanus*. Leonard's elder brother was the diplomat and courtier Sir Dudley Digges. After their father's death in 1595, Anne married Thomas Russell, Shakespeare's trusted friend and the overseer of his will. As a result Leonard became the stepson of a close confidant of Shakespeare, both of whom may have been pleased to be affiliated to a scholar deemed accomplished and well-heeled by his peers, having, like Mabbe, travelled into several countries. Leonard Digges would have been useful to Digby for he was, wrote Wood, 'a perfect understander of the French and Spanish, a good poet and no mean orator'. Although Digges had mixed with many Catholics in his lifetime, he appears to have been a committed Protestant, for he would even edit out anything he deemed too 'Catholic' from his translations. In his *Gerardo the Unfortunate Spaniard*, he confessed that he had 'left wholly out' part of the text 'as superstitiously smelling of Papistical miracles; in which I have no belief'.

Digby would go on to play a central role in the Spanish Match during the very period in which the First Folio was being printed. Shortly after his elevation to Earl of Bristol by James I, he was sent to Spain on another mission, this time with the express aim of tying up the Anglo-Spanish marriage negotiations before the end of 1622. What Digges's appraisal of Lope de Vega's work reveals is that he and Mabbe were, like Edward Blount, living barometers of literary taste and, like him, were working to popularise Spanish letters and intellectual culture in England. The incident also indicates that the two hispanophiles who would go on to celebrate Shakespeare in the First Folio had a deep and shared appreciation of the playwright's work, and were labouring to augment his reputation as a national poet: 'our Shakespeare'. We will return to Digges's intriguing letter later on; but it may not be incorrect to surmise here that both Digges and Mabbe had every reason to follow the drama of the Spanish Match closely, given that the fortunes of their former master, Sir John Digby, were bound up with the enterprise.

Nine years after Digges and Mabbe declared what they felt were the equivalent merits of Shakespeare and Lope de Vega, the King's Men were reflecting the national interest in Spanish literary culture through their own repertory, acknowledging in the process the profound shift in tastes. Around the very period in which John Fletcher was engaged with *The Pilgrim*, his reading may well have included James Mabbe's translation of another work eventually published in late 1622 by Blount: Mateo Alemán's *The Rogue*. This includes two dedicatory verses by an 'I.F.' or 'J.F.', who has been plausibly identified as John Fletcher, in which Mabbe's 'gentler spirit' and the quality of his 'worthy lines' are lauded. Strikingly, this book brings together two more personalities attached to the First Folio, making four in total, including Blount himself. On the very next page, after the potential offerings by Fletcher, there are two further dedications. The first is by Leonard Digges, in which he gives 'thanks and praise to this translator's pain'. The second, placed directly below it, is by Ben Jonson, in which he refers to Mabbe as a 'Friend' whose gifts make him 'wish myself, the man/ That would have done, that which you only can'. Blount's own dedicatory note is presented on the page facing the poems by Digges and Jonson and confirms that the book's flattering verses are 'uttered in their just commendation'.

It is hardly surprising then that Fletcher's *The Pilgrim*, with its Spanish context and sources, which showcased a shared interest in James I's foreign policy by the King's Men (and whose sources implicitly confirmed the efforts of Blount and his coterie of English hispanophiles to promote Spanish letters), would be one of the six court performances for which John Heminges received a retrospective payment of sixty pounds at the end of March 1622. This production was perfectly timed to capture the excitement, and trepidation, fuelled by rumours that the Spanish marriage had been concluded, with Blount's associate John Chamberlain reporting on 4 January, rather over-optimistically, that this would see 'the Palatinate … restored out of hand' with the aid of Spanish forces. He was more accurate in his pessimistic prediction that it would be 'enough to break off the Parliament, which I make no question will be dissolved'.

The prospect of Spain wading in to drive out Ferdinand II's forces from Bohemia and offer an attractive dowry with the Infanta Maria, which would solve James I's financial problems into the bargain, were still fantasies when Ben Jonson's *The Masque of Augurs* was performed at Whitehall on 6 January as part of the Twelfth Night festivities, just five days after the King's Men's showing of *The Pilgrim*. The two productions may have been intended to deliver a grand interrelated message, for Jonson's entertainment contained an 'antimasque of Pilgrims' and included among its cast members Villiers and Prince Charles himself, who took a leading role as 'President of the Augurs', decked out in a fabulous taffeta-lined satin suit, slashed in the fashionable style, sporting white taffeta sarsenet hose, white silk stockings with finely embroidered garters, satin-trimmed gloves, a cap topped with bobbing white feathers and a perfumed mask. It was a lavish affair, with nearly £300 spent on costumes, over £27 of which was used to purchase the 'rich white satin' alone. The 'augurs' prophesied the success of James I's conciliatory agenda, but sought to allay the anxieties of the court's anti-Spanish contingent, promising that through his 'peace' with Spain he 'shalt control/ The course of things' and his subjects 'live free/From hatred, faction, or … fear'.

The masque ended with the prediction that Charles would lead in James's wake, 'triumphing over all/Both foes, and vices; and your young, and tall/Nephews, his sons, grow up in your embraces,/ To give this island princes, in long races'. At this time 'nephews' could mean grandchildren. Charles may not have been pleased to hear of the hoped-for tallness of his offspring, which could only glance at his own smallness of stature. In other ways, however, Jonson's *Masque of Augurs* was carefully crafted to elevate Prince Charles as the hope of England's future. As with his *Masque of the Gypsies Metamorphosed*, it aligned Villiers with the king and his son as the leaders of a pro-Spanish faction. Soon the court wits were spreading suggestive stories of the growing affection between the prince and the king's favourite: how, while waiting to perform, Charles and Villiers were tarrying in the cold in their flimsy costumes, and how the prince took off his own cloak and wrapped it around the Marquess of Buckingham's shoulders to shield him from the chill.

Jonson's masque provided an opportunity to reassure one audience member in particular of the English court's commitment to the match. When the Spanish ambassador, Diego Sarmiento de Acuña, 1st Count of Gondomar, surveyed his fellow attendees he would have noted, approvingly, that there was one obvious absentee. The French ambassador, Tanneguy le Veneur, 3rd Count of Tillières, had not been invited. Members of the court's anti-Spanish faction were dismayed and, just three days later, on 9 January, Sir Simonds D'Ewes observed that a formal proclamation declaring the 'abortive dissolving of Parliament' had been issued. This, he lamented, 'gave a tincture of sadness to most men's countenances, their hope of the delivery of God's Church in Germany being thereby quite dashed, and the poor distressed Protestants of France left to the execution of their merciless enemies'.

The absence of the French ambassador only confirmed the direction of the king's foreign policy. It particularly troubled William Herbert, the Earl of Pembroke, who had strenuously 'interceded with the king' against the dissolution of Parliament and, according to one purveyor of gossip who was writing the very next day, 'so hoped his majesty will be pacified' and appeal instead to the Commons for support to stage a more robust intervention in the Palatinate. He was mistaken. While Pembroke 'spoke vehemently at the Council table' against an ignominious dissolution, he was powerless to prevent what he furiously argued would be an 'error' that would come to be 'imputed' to the honourable members of the Privy Council 'and not the king'. James I's actions were, according to the earl, bringing shame to the entire court and Parliament in the eyes of the populace. But the king was resolved and nothing would divert him from his longed-for match. Charles began to learn Spanish, taking his first lesson on 19 January, while Villiers pulled strings with Ambassador Gondomar, writing that month:

[I]t only rests now that, as we have put the ball to your foot, you take a good and speedy resolution to hasten a happy conclusion of this match. The Prince is now … more than full ripe for such a business. The King our master longs to see an issue proceed from his loins, and I am sure you have reason to expect more friendship from the posterity that shall proceed from him and that little angel your Infanta than from his majesty's daughter's children.

Gondomar's fantasy was now filled with the promise that, with the sidestepping of Elizabeth and Frederick's lineage, a Protestant succession would be avoided. With Charles surrounded by hispanophiles, the stage was set for James to choreograph his own departure. As March drew to its close, during a meeting of the Privy Council, he made a poignant speech in which he declared that he was ageing and not long for this world. From now on, Charles would take an increasingly prominent role in affairs of state. Councillors wept as the king spoke. For James there had been at least one positive outcome of that humiliating Parliament. Charles had begun to assert himself and had delivered, via the king, a message to the Commons, informing them 'how unkindly he took it, that they should busy themselves and intermeddle so much in his marriage'. The prince would choose his own bride. And his heart was set on the Infanta. No one, henceforth, was to speak ill of the Spanish Match. John Chamberlain wrote to Sir Dudley Carleton on 16 February, brooding that 'the times are dangerous, and the world grows tender and jealous of free speech'.

James had been so taken with the kaleidoscopic fiction that Jonson's *Masque of Augurs* had paraded before his eyes, so awed by the image of his son, resplendent in glistening white silk and taffeta, that it was as if he were seeing him for the first time. Hoping to hold on to that spectral image, he demanded that the performance be reprised on 5 March. A bout of ill health waylaid him, so the entertainment could not proceed until the evening of 5

May when it played a dual function, serving as a grand farewell to Ambassador Gondomar, who had been recalled to Madrid by King Philip IV and whose departure would take place on 16 May, and a welcoming feast for his successor, Ambassador Don Carlos Coloma. 'I have never treated with another prince's ambassador with greater love,' wrote James to the Spanish king, complaining of Gondomar's departure. Shortly after these events, as a goodwill gesture, James began releasing Catholics from prison. Villiers, who kept up a correspondence with Gondomar after his return to Spain, wrote to tell him what he knew would be welcome news, that 'priests and recusants [are] all at liberty, all Roman Catholics well satisfied, and, which will seem a wonder unto you, our prisons emptied of priests and recusants and filled with jealous ministers for preaching against the Match'.

Whatever their own personal feelings about the Spanish Match, the King's Men, as the monarch's servants, had no more choice in the matter of falling in line with foreign policy than either Ben Jonson or Edward Blount. As the anti-Spanish preachers persisted, in defiance of the king's edicts, in the raising of their voices against the match, the players continued to serve their royal patron's interests. With Parliament disastrously dissolved, the king now firmly pinned his hopes on his son's union with the Infanta, believing this would help him restore his lost authority with the Commons, save the Palatinate and clear him of the crippling debts he had amassed. England could only hold its breath and watch as the next move in this strategic diplomatic game was played.

12

'Like an old Fencer upon the stage'

William Jaggard's War and the Bard's Comeback

I n the Jaggards' printing house in April 1622, with Thomas Wilson's *Christian Dictionary* out of the way, the typesetting for *Measure for Measure* could begin in earnest. Despite a change in personnel when Compositor F was replaced by Compositor D, who in turn was briefly replaced by Compositor F, the pattern of consecutive Folio formes continued. But, from the printing of the next play, *The Comedy of Errors*, the pulse of work changed.

There seemed to be a determination to push on with the project, which received a boost when the Jaggards instructed compositors to begin setting formes concurrently across plays. While working on this play, therefore, compositors B, C and D also turned their attention to pages of *Much Ado About Nothing*. Now they were getting into a productive rhythm, with a three-compositor pattern of typesetting.

This did not last long. With other projects placing a demand on resources, the compositors returned to setting consecutive formes about halfway through *Much Ado About Nothing*. As they progressed through the next comedies they were only able to switch to simultaneous typesetting across plays in fits and starts, whenever there was a lull in the intensity of the press's other projects. Despite this they moved at a steady pace through *Love's Labour's Lost*, *A Midsummer Night's Dream* and *The Merchant of Venice*. When they reached *As You Like It*, however, one case of type was put to some other use – probably for another book or 'job work' projects – and two compositors, standing at two different cases, worked largely simultaneously without any major disruptions through most of that play, aside from a brief period during the printing of this and the start of *The Taming of the Shrew*, when our experienced Compositor B took over sole responsibility for the Folio for the equivalent of nearly a quire and a half while his colleagues turned to the Jaggards' other printing needs. In short order, compositors C and D returned to help Compositor B complete the latter play and some of *All's Well That Ends Well*. Then they hit a problem. After the setting of the first eleven pages of that play printing seems to have all but ground to a halt.

From the point at which work had begun on *Measure for Measure* around two and a half months had passed, bringing the printing up to roughly the middle of July when the break occurred, but how long this interruption lasted is not known for certain. It has been estimated that it probably continued, completely or intermittently, until October and was due to a particularly pressurised period for the Jaggard press. As well as their regular run of ongoing 'job work', which included royal proclamations, playbills and other smaller publications, they were working on other books concurrently. They published William Burton's *The Description of Leicestershire*, a lavish folio, in 1622. To this Burton attached a preface dated 20 October, indicating that the book was probably completed shortly after this date. As the compositors were using type that had also been applied to the Folio, it is likely that work on Shakespeare's Book was suspended to concentrate on the completion of this text. The press at the Half-Eagle and Key was also working on another major

Elaborate title page of Ralph Brooke's *A Catalogue and Succession of the Kings* (London: William Stansby, 1622). Brooke entered into a public dispute with William Jaggard, blaming him for errors in an earlier version of this book, which Jaggard had printed. Jaggard retaliated with a blistering attack on Brooke in another publication, *A Discovery of Errors*, which he produced during the period in which his printing house was working on Shakespeare's First Folio.

publication at this time, one which was to prove particularly taxing for William Jaggard. This was Augustine Vincent's monumental work of genealogy and heraldry *A Discovery of Errors*. It is fitting that the compositors had just finished with *The Comedy of Errors*, for this text would itself prove to be a comedy of errors indeed. The Jaggards had the tricky task of keeping the work on this volume ticking over while attempting to finish Burton's book.

Vincent's tome was personally very important to William Jaggard. In 1619 he had printed *A Catalogue and Succession of the Kings*, an ambitious genealogical work by the historiographer Ralph Brooke who held a senior position as York Herald in the College of Arms (also known as the College of Heralds), the body that governed heraldic and genealogical order, the issuing of coats of arms, and the christenings, marriages and burials of the nobility; an institution still active today in a handsome crest-festooned building just across the road from St Paul's Cathedral. Brooke adorned the work with a letter to King James I, in which he boasted, with a pomposity characteristic of his flamboyant personality, that his self-proclaimed mission was to 'discover and reform many things heretofore grossly mistaken, and abused by ignorant persons; who venturing beyond their own element and skill to write of this subject, have showed themselves more bold and busy, than skilful in heraldry'. These talentless genealogists were mere 'upstarts and Mountebanks within this our profession' and had, he claimed, 'greatly blemished and obscured' the true lineages of the nobility and even of James himself. The work was dedicated to an unusually large number of noblemen and members of the king's Privy Council, including the rivals George Villiers and William Herbert. Seeking their 'noble protection and patronage', Brooke could not help but brag that he had 'acquainted' the king with his project and received his royal approval to correct the heretofore 'misshapen, ill wrought, and deformed' pedigrees of England's nobility.

It was not long before the book's dedicatees had cause to repent their support, for Brooke's volume was recalled by the Privy Council due to its many genealogical inaccuracies. This was no trivial matter, for such infelicities could cause confusion and even legal difficulties over competing inheritance claims for the families entangled in the work's web of errors. Seeking to save face, the humiliated author took the book to William Stansby who issued a revised and corrected edition in 1622, complete with a blistering attack on Jaggard whom Brooke blamed for the mistakes in the first edition. Accusing the printer of taking advantage of his ill health, which meant he was unable to oversee the printing of the book himself, Brooke insisted that its many 'mistakings' were 'committed by the printer, whilst my sickness absented me from the press, at the first publication'. As a consequence Jaggard had produced a '*Catalogue* of untruths', full of embarrassing slips, which Brooke foregrounded with a list of faults committed in the printing.

William Jaggard's reputation was at stake. He had spent years cultivating a public persona as a careful, precise and learned printer, an arbiter of taste whose career depended on his integrity. That same year, while working on the Folio, he set about printing a new and more authoritative genealogical work, engaging another among the ranks of the heralds of the College of Arms: Augustine Vincent. Jaggard was not going to let the opportunity pass to add his own spirited rebuttal to his nemesis's accusations. Brooke was not, he declared, up to the task of writing such a book and should have realised his own 'weakness' and 'unfitness to undertake a work of that strength'. He had thought too well of himself when he decided foolishly to 'enter the lists with men, in all men's opinion, infinitely above his sphere' and was, Jaggard quipped, 'like the frog in the meadow, that swelled up herself, till she burst, in envy of the heifer's bigness'. It could only be 'evident to common understanding, that such material faults' as Brooke had alleged were due to

Jaggard and his workmen 'cannot slip through the fingers of a compositor, or fall upon the printer's score'.

But how on earth could these mistakes have crept into the book? How else, Jaggard wrote, now giving vent to his sarcasm, but during 'Master York's absence from the press, occasioned by his unfortunate sickness' of course, 'who all the time before, while he stood sentinel at the press, kept such strict and diligent guard there, as a letter could not pass out of his due rank, but was instantly checked and reduced into order'. How unfortunate that he had been forced to confine himself to his chamber, giving occasion to the printer 'to bring in that "Trojan horse of Barbarisms", and literal errors, which over-run the whole volume of his *Catalogue*'. Far from it, Jaggard stated, since Brooke had been sent the proofs to review 'and he perused them', or so they assumed; 'yet what is all this to the presence of an old Herald at a press?' 'I must confess,' he added sardonically, enjoying the absurdity of the image, 'that the sight alone of such a reverend man in a printing-house, like an old Fencer upon a stage, would do more good for keeping the press in order, than the view, and review of twenty proofs by himself with all his Latin, and other learning.' Rather than introducing errors into Brooke's text, his compositors had corrected many mistakes that would otherwise have been printed to the author's further shame. Had they instead, Jaggard averred, building to yet another theatrical metaphor, and alluding to one of the most accomplished comic actors in recent theatrical memory, 'given him leave to print his own English (which they now repent they did not) he would (they say) have made his reader as good sport in his *Catalogue* as ever Tarleton did his audience in a clown's part'. One might venture that these theatrical metaphors flowed so easily from Jaggard's venom-dipped pen because he was at that very moment at work on Shakespeare's own collected plays.

Now, thanks to Brooke's stung ego, a revised edition of the unfortunate genealogical work was in print before the first had been sold. This meant that Jaggard had some two hundred worthless copies of the book left 'rotting by the walls' in his printing house. And since Brooke could not admit 'how false he hath played with his own conscience' or care 'how grossly abused both the printer and his reader' had been by his actions, he should excuse the wronged printer for issuing his own superior work of heraldry through the travails of a more competent scholar. Jaggard ended with a curse on those printers who dared take on a publishing project with Brooke in the future, his invective rendered with an almost Shakespearean pathos:

> And thus I hope I have, in the opinion of Master York's 'Judicious Reader', washed my hands clean of that aspersion which he casts upon me, concerning the errors of his book; the main error excepted, of defiling my fingers at all with his pitch, which cleaves so fast to my hands, as I shall never shake them off, but with loss, wherein if ever again I be taken faulty, let that curse light upon me, which I prophesy will befall any printer that hath to do with him: that he work by day in fear, and like a thief in the night, that he bring forth his works like bastard fruits by stealth, and vend them in corners like stolen wares, and that in recompense of his pains, his reward be no other but loss and repentance by the work, and detraction and disgrace from the author.

Jaggard's strength of character, his wit, charisma and resilience emerge vividly from his writing, suggesting his ability to lead his team despite his blindness. His schooling is also evident, for his writing discloses a mastery of a full arsenal of rhetorical devices, which he uses to take down his enemy with an adroitness that is utterly breathtaking. The intensity of his feeling might give us a rare glimpse of the emotional miasma that permeated the Barbican printing press in the run-up to this break in the work on the First Folio, as William Jaggard was composing this defence, which was typeset during that hiatus. One can only imagine the detractions and oaths, the rancorous slurs pronounced against his enemy, which rose from his lips and echoed through his shop and the pressworkers' stations, and which formed the soundscape for part of the printing of the First Folio. This must, for a time, have made for a tense working environment.

There may have been other reasons, above and beyond the Jaggards' busy printing schedule, however, which occasioned this pause during the typesetting of *All's Well That Ends Well*. This play, originally composed by Shakespeare around 1605, was probably revived in 1622, perhaps with revisions by Thomas Middleton. It had not been printed before in a smaller quarto version, and it is possible that the King's Men needed their copy text back as they worked on the revival, or may have replaced a text based solely on Shakespeare's authorial papers with one containing newer, more current, interpolations in Middleton's hand, since the First Folio's version of the play does appear to enshrine Middletonian contributions. But the syndicate had to deal with something else which may explain why the printing had to be halted for such an extended period: a sudden resurgence of Shakespeare play-printing by other stationers that year, something of a comeback for the Bard.

On London's Strand, among the emporia nestled along the elegant colonnades of the upmarket three-storey shopping arcade called Britain's Burse, also known as the New Exchange, stood the bookshop bearing the sign of the Eagle and Child. In 1622 book addicts could purchase from here a freshly printed first edition of William Shakespeare's *Othello*. This play's appearance in print broke a trend for the King's Men, who had kept a tight grip on previously unpublished Shakespeare works since 1609. No fledgling editions of his plays had been issued after the quarto version of *Troilus and Cressida* hit the bookstalls that year. *Othello* had not been published for close to twenty years after its first known staging. Now here it was, on sale, making its debut even as work on the collected plays of Shakespeare was underway in the Jaggards' printing house.

The Eagle and Child belonged to Thomas Walkley, a bookseller and stationer from 1618, who had entered the play in the Stationers' Register on 6 October 1621. When he came to publish it he selected Nicholas Okes as his printer; the same Okes who was praised to the skies by Thomas Heywood for the quality of his printing work, in contrast to his appraisal of William Jaggard's, in his estimation, less than adequate skills. In his dedicatory epistle to *Othello* Walkley had stated that 'the Author [Shakespeare] being dead, I thought good to take the piece of work upon me' and that he had been made 'bolder, because the author's name is sufficient to vend his work'. Walkley clearly believed that, by this point, Shakespeare was a potent brand again and this may well have been due to the sudden presence of his plays in print from 1619 as a result of the efforts of Thomas Pavier and the Jaggards. Could Walkley have also heard about the Folio project and resolved to exploit his property before it was issued in a more sumptuous version, stamped with the authority of the King's Men? If so, how did he get around the Lord Chamberlain's edict forbidding the publication of plays from the troupe's repertory? He did not divulge how he came by the manuscript of the play, nor whether the rights to publishing it were granted by the King's Men or other legitimate agents or intermediaries.

Walkley and Okes were among the stationer-printers involved in the publication of that peculiar group of King's Men plays which included offerings by Francis Beaumont and John Fletcher, and

Opposite: a 1792 line engraving of the playwright Francis Beaumont by George Vertue, based on a portrait by an unknown earlier artist. Beaumont had been a frequent collaborator with John Fletcher. Some scholars think the stationers Thomas Walkley and Nicholas Okes were involved in the unauthorised publication of works by this duo, works craftily stolen from the King's Men's archives, alongside plays by Shakespeare.

Iudicis argutum qui n̄ [...] Formidat [...]men[...]

FRANCIS
BEAVMONT. E.
[...]A Xtat Circā XX AD:16[...]

Geo: Vertue Sculp. 172[...]

Celsissimæ Principi LEONELLO Duci de DORSET &c

which some scholars believe were stolen from the playing company. Both had been accused of piratical practices, and Okes may have been alluded to by Ben Jonson as a 'ragged rascal'. There are hints that Walkley oversaw a 'counterfeit' edition of the works of the poet George Wither, who claimed that manuscripts of his poems 'were stolen from the author' by the stationer and 'impertinently imprinted ... without the said author's knowledge'. It is, though, far from certain that Walkley was to blame for this. He may have been guilty only of incorporating three or four unauthorised poems into a largely legitimate text. Walkley was, however, engaged in a heated legal battle over his mishandling of another publication, *Bellona's Embrion* by Sir Michael Everard, whose death before the end of 1622 saw the publication of his book taken over by his cousin Dr John Everard – the very same who recurrently endured prison sentences for speaking out against the Spanish Match. In that case we learn that Walkley had been arrested over his dubious financial dealings, that he was 'indebted to several persons' and that he 'meant nothing but fraud and deceit, to cozen [that is, trick] Everard', resorting to a show of 'weeping tears' and telling 'him that unless he [Everard] would be bound to him he [Walkley] would be utterly undone'. The bill of complaint against him states that 'Walkley, for all his labour and expenses, is in continual fear of danger of arrest.'

Walkley was certainly present at a riot involving two hundred apprentices who marched up to Whitehall, armed with clubs, staves and swords, and threatened to hang the bishops and 'Popish Lords', pelting those who tried to stop them with 'clods of dry dirt', though he minimised his own role in the fracas, claiming he was a mere witness. He was accused, on a separate occasion, of uttering 'indecent speeches' against a nobleman, and later a warrant would be issued for his arrest on charges of having distributed 'scandalous declarations' against the royal family in print. Time and again, Walkley's name crops up in less than wholesome circumstances. But a dubious reputation does not necessarily mean he engaged in foul play with the King's Men's precious stock of dramatic works. It is possible that Walkley simply exploited the situation when the First Folio syndicate engaged him over the leasing of the rights to *Othello*, refusing to release the play unless he was permitted to publish his asset as a single volume first.

This scenario is made all the more likely by the fact that this was not the only Shakespeare play published in 1622. Matthew Law reissued fresh quarto versions of *Richard III* and *Henry IV, Part 1* that year, though it is possible that any agreements with regards to these were not resolved until later in the printing schedule for the First Folio, and Thomas Dewe published the anonymously authored *The Troublesome Reign of John, King of England*. As the latter was not technically the version by Shakespeare once performed by the King's Men, Dewe may have been able to circumvent the Lord Chamberlain's ban against the printing of plays in their repertory. However, its erroneous attribution to the dramatist, and Dewe's claim to a theatricalised version of the life of King John in the Stationers' Register, may have forced the Folio syndicate to approach him for permission to print the play. Since, as we have seen, Dewe was working with William Jaggard on another project in 1622, it is likely that they reached an amicable agreement. Any discussions and bargaining which took place over these plays would have taken time to complete and may have resulted in some uncertainty about the inclusion of these plays in the First Folio as long as issues over licensing remained unsettled.

Meanwhile, not long after the King's Men had acquired permission from the Revels Office to mount *The Prophetess*, a play by Philip Massinger and John Fletcher that bears the ghostly traces of Shakespeare's *Julius Caesar* as a work which had influenced some of its rhetorical flourishes, the theatrical troupe undertook something of a pilgrimage; perhaps in search of their own ghosts of Shakespeare.

In the summer of 1622 they visited Stratford-upon-Avon, the home town of their one-time colleague and comrade, as part of a tour of the provinces. They would, in all likelihood, have paid their respects at the playwright's grave, poignant at any time but more significant still during the period in which the First Folio was being printed. Did John Heminges and Henry Condell look at Shakespeare's monument and *see* what could become the title page of the Folio? Was it this experience that influenced the decision to grace the volume with a striking, plain bust-like portrait that Jonson himself, in his shorter Folio poem about the image, described as 'cut' by a 'Graver [that is, engraver] … in brass' like a hewn monument?

Perhaps the King's Men also went to see Shakespeare's widow, Anne, who was nearing the end of her life, giving Heminges and Condell an opportunity to tell the dramatist's family about their project to commemorate him through an opulent folio-sized book that would preserve his plays for posterity. Did Anne and her family volunteer their own thoughts on the endeavour? While the King's Men were in Stratford they offered to perform at the Guildhall, just paces away from the Shakespeares' grand family home New Place, but due to a long-standing prohibition of play-ing established by the Stratford Corporation, which was responsible for civic governance in the area, the actors were told they were forbidden from doing so and paid six shillings 'for not playing in the Hall'.

It is tempting to speculate, as some have done, on whether Heminges and Condell had wanted to visit Stratford because they were searching for Shakespeare's papers to use as copy texts for plays printed in the First Folio. Had his wife, Anne, been holding on to versions of his plays? Had the senior members of the King's Men sought access to the playwright's stash of documents, still preserved perhaps in his desk, in a casket or chest of drawers? The feminist scholar and activist Germaine Greer has pointed out that 'Scholars have never given any consideration to the possibility that the Bard's wife might have been involved in the Folio project', asking whether 'she might be entitled to some credit for the preservation of her husband's work'. Just over four months into the Folio's printing, there were still plenty of plays for which good-quality copy was needed, and part of Heminges and Condell's role was to ensure that the Folio syndicate had these in versions approved by them, as far as possible, as the genuine work of the dramatist. It is tempting to speculate on whether their appearance in Stratford, around the start of the long break in the Folio's printing, is an indication that the pause in the project was also partly due to the need for authoritative copy texts, which the players were seeking from Shakespeare's family. But this cannot be proved. Their visit may, however, have imprinted in their imaginations the vision of Shakespeare's grave and prompted them to ponder on the life within his words, for in their dedicatory epistle to the Herbert brothers in the Folio's preliminary matter, they insisted that they had 'collected them', those plays as hallowed and 'precious' as their friend's 'remains', which they had 'humbly consecrate[d]' by enshrining them in Shakespeare's Book.

The King's Men may have relished their escape from the pressures that came with serving the monarch, breathing in the fresher air on the banks of the River Avon or being entertained by Anne Shakespeare, and reminiscing about the exploits and achievements of their dear friend Will, in one of the most impressive houses in Stratford. But this proved all too brief. Shortly after their return to the bustle and chaos of London they continued their collaboration with Massinger and Fletcher, premiering another play by them entitled *The Sea Voyage*. Perhaps Heminges and Condell were keen on mounting this play, with its protagonists cast onto an island after a violent storm, because it was heavily influenced by *The*

Tempest. It also shared a source with the earlier play, William Strachey's account of the ill-fated Virginia voyage which had so inspired Shakespeare. They would have felt the genius of the dead dramatist flowing through the very veins of this new production. All this made *The Tempest* a more relevant play in 1622, when the Folio's comedies were being printed; another reason to place a work on a fashionable theme as the first dramatic work in the volume.

It is not possible to determine what Heminges and Condell, and their fellow players, made of the rush of Shakespeare plays (and in the case of *The Troublesome Reign of John, King of England*, a play attributed to the playwright) being printed in quarto editions in 1622. Were they happy that the memory of their one-time star author was still being revived after the release of the 'Pavier-Jaggard Quartos' – that England had not forgotten him – or were they dismayed, fearing that this would reduce the public appetite for the soon-to-be-released, and far more expensive, collected edition of Shakespeare's works? They would have had little time to worry about this, however, because once back on the political scene in London things were hotting up – in more ways than one.

13

Calves, Cows and Cyphers

Edward Blount's Secrets and the Comedies' Completion

In the summer of 1622 a stifling heat wave began to set in over London. On 5 August the Spanish ambassador, Don Carlos Coloma, had been entertained with a grand feast, during which Prince Charles drank copious healths to King Philip of Spain and the Infanta Maria 'with much ceremony'. The court gossips noted how much closer he and the Marquess of Buckingham had become. They were spied on as they sought relief from the soaring temperatures and the din of the court, discarding their heavy clothing to cool off every evening by swimming in the waters near Eton.

Even as the courtiers caroused with the Spanish ambassador and his entourage, liberties continued to be granted to Jesuits and priests, who were delivered from prisons in increasing numbers and, as John Chamberlain reported to Sir Dudley Carleton on 10 August, 'not henceforward to be troubled for … praying of mass, or refusing the oath of allegiance, supremacy, or the like'. Dr John Everard was once more committed to the Marshalsea Prison 'for saying somewhat he should not have done' about the Spanish Match, only for the preacher appointed as his substitute during his

imprisonment to be thrown into the Gatehouse Prison for following his example. On 25 August a preacher named Clayton, a
minister of Hackney, earned a prison sentence for delivering an
inflammatory sermon at St Paul's Cross, right across the way from
the shops of Edward Blount and William Aspley. His theme was a
crafty tale of 'a Spanish sheep, brought into England in Edward
the First's time, which infected most of the sheep of England with
a murrain, and prayed God no more such sheep might be brought
over from thence hither'. It did not require much imagination to
deduce that the disease-ridden sheep represented the Infanta
Maria. Blount and Aspley, had they been at their shops, would
have noticed the commotion, for the cheers and roars of approval
rose up, like flocks of agitated seagulls, from the crowds packed
into St Paul's Cross Churchyard, for 'many of his hearers cried out
"Amen"'. In this increasingly heated atmosphere, rumours were
circulating that George Villiers' mother, Mary, Countess of
Buckingham, had 'relapsed into Popery' and converted to
Catholicism; this amid intelligence that the Pope of Rome had
prepared a dispensation for the Spanish Match which he would
only be willing to ratify 'on condition that the king carry a good
respect to the Roman Catholics, which, no doubt,' added
Chamberlain ruefully when he reported the news in September,
'will be done in good measure'.

With the Spanish Match looking like a certainty and an ever
more robust clampdown on freedom of speech, the King's Men
continued to respond to these political pressures with more overtly
Spanish-themed scene-setting, mounting *The Spanish Curate* by
their popular playwrighting double act John Fletcher and Philip
Massinger. This play, which tapped topically into anxieties about
the competition between siblings over lineage, succession and
inheritance, was made starkly relevant through its allusions to
recent wars between Spain and the Low Countries, part of what
would become the Netherlands. Performed during the late autumn

and early winter of 1622 at the Blackfriars Theatre, it had one very notable Spanish source text: Gonzalo de Céspedes y Meneses' *Gerardo the Unfortunate Spaniard*, translated by Leonard Digges. This was hot off the press and, as we have noted, published by Edward Blount and contained a dedicatory epistle by Digges to both the Herbert brothers, whose own dual dedication in the First Folio the Jaggard press would be printing the following year. In this Digges presented himself as their 'devoted servant' and stated that he had undertaken the translation 'to do a public good, by publishing the moral examples contained' within, and hoped that he would 'be esteemed' because the entire 'world ... takes notice of your noble goodness'. In mounting this play, the King's Men were building on the increasing public curiosity over Spanish letters and culture in England, fuelled by the endeavours of hispanophiles like Digges, whose translation had also been a source for Thomas Middleton and William Rowley's play *The Changeling*, which was part-set in Spain and performed by the Lady Elizabeth's Men at the Cockpit Theatre 'with great applause' from around May 1622.

The King's Men's continuing dependence on one of the two men who would soon become patrons of the First Folio was also apparent at this time. They had approached the Master of the Revels, Sir John Astley, with a play by Lodowick Carlell called *Osmond, the Great Turk*, hoping to secure his approval for its performance. Astley, however, had taken some exception to the work and 'refused to allow [a licence] at first'. John Heminges and the King's Men's actor John Rice appealed to Sir William Herbert in his office as Lord Chamberlain, who leaned on Astley to change his mind, which he did on 6 September. On 20 November Pembroke intervened again to protect the King's Men's privileges, sending an edict to mayors and justices of the peace commanding them to restrain the 'abuses, daily committed by divers and sundry companies of Stage Players', who had managed to procure illegal licences giving them 'licentious freedom to travel, as well to show, play and exercise in eminent cities … without the knowledge and approbation of his Majesty's Office of the Revels'. Their plays, he insisted, 'for the most part are full of scandal and offence, both against the Church and State', and were performed by those who 'greatly abuse their authority, in lending … and selling … licences to others'. This move limited the King's Men's competition, since only licences granted 'under the hand and seal' of the Master of the Revels, or his deputy, would be valid, with local justices of the peace being commanded to seize and take away all suspect licences and 'forbid and suppress' all unauthorised plays. The players had another reason to feel grateful to Pembroke. During this period news had spread of a scheme to push Herbert out of his office of Lord Chamberlain, installing one of Villiers' own intimates in his stead. William Fielding, Buckingham's brother-in-law, had been created 1st Earl of Denbigh that year, a new honour devised by James to assist in the expansion of Villiers' powerbase. An attempt was again made to entice Herbert with the office of the king's Lord Privy Seal on condition that he agree to transfer the Chamberlainship to Denbigh. He resisted, even in the face of the combined pressure from his monarch and Villiers' increasingly powerful family.

Meanwhile Blount was cementing ties with another of the Folio's commemorative poets whose feats of Spanish-to-English translation he was publishing that year: James Mabbe. Blount was still acting as the agent of Sir William Trumbull (James I's ambassador to Brussels) when, on 8 November, the publisher wrote to him about his son's education:

> I must needs come in with a Postscript too and tell that your son is well and a great proficient in the Spanish tongue, by the means of Master James Mabbe of Magdalen College, who takes as much delight in reading to him and other gentlemen of that house as they take in that their desire.

Title page of *Mr. William Shakespeares Comedies, Histories, & Tragedies*, also known as the First Folio, published in 1623. Preserving around half of William Shakespeare's plays, this book was financed by a consortium or syndicate of publisher-booksellers which included William Jaggard and his son Isaac, Edward Blount, William Aspley and John Smethwick.

Portrait believed to be of William Shakespeare, associated with John Taylor, *c.*1610.

Portrait believed to be of Richard Burbage, British School, early seventeenth century. Burbage, an actor with the Chamberlain's Men, later the King's Men, played some of the most memorable roles created by William Shakespeare, including *Richard III*, *Hamlet*, *Othello* and *King Lear*. He became the greatest performer of the age and his death sparked an unprecedented outpouring of national mourning for an actor.

Portrait of Ben Jonson by Abraham van Blyenberch, *c*.1617. Jonson, a playwright and poet, was occasionally William Shakespeare's colleague, as well as his friend and rival. He contributed two commemorative poems to the First Folio and may have been involved with the process of commissioning the poets who added verses in memory of Shakespeare to the volume's preliminary pages (although Edward Blount has also been identified as the potential overseer of the Folio's preliminaries). Jonson oversaw an edition of his own collected works as an opulent folio-sized book, which he published in 1616; a project that may have inspired the First Folio.

The monument to John Heminges and Henry Condell, erected on the site of their burial in St Mary's, Aldermanbury, London, in 1896. Heminges and Condell were William Shakespeare's colleagues and close friends. They oversaw the gathering of the dramatist's plays for the First Folio, and contributed two epistles to its preliminary pages: a dedication to Sir William Herbert, 3rd Earl of Pembroke, and his brother Sir Philip Herbert, 1st Earl of Montgomery, and an address to the reader.

Portrait of the dramatist John Fletcher, by an unknown artist, c.1620. Fletcher wrote plays for the King's Men, including works inspired by topical events relating to England's political relations with Spain. He was a collaborator with William Shakespeare and may have worked with him on the lost play *Cardenio* in 1613, itself based on Spanish sources.

Detail from an engraving by Claes Visscher, showing a theatre labelled 'The Globe', beside 'The Bear Garden', 1616. The Globe was opened on Bankside in 1599 and was partially constructed from the timbers of the playhouse known as the Theatre, located in Shoreditch, from which the Chamberlain's Men were evicted in 1597.

The interior of the Sam Wanamaker Playhouse, inspired by the Blackfriars Theatre, which was originally built in 1596, but which William Shakespeare and the King's Men did not occupy until 1608 because the local residents, led by the formidable noblewoman Lady Elizabeth Russell, got up a petition to ban them from playing in the district.

Sir William Herbert, 3rd Earl of Pembroke, after Daniel Mytens, c.1625. He was one of the dedicatees or patrons of the First Folio. A favourite courtier of King James I, Herbert was one of the most influential patrons of the arts, literature, drama and music in the period.

Sir Philip Herbert, 1st Earl of Montgomery, later 4th Earl of Pembroke, by an unknown artist, c.1615. He was a dedicatee or patron of the First Folio, along with his brother Sir William Herbert.

A portrait of the flamboyant, athletic and charismatic George Villiers, 1st Duke of Buckingham, attributed to William Larkin (or the studio of William Larkin), *c.*1616. Villiers' competition and intense rivalry with Sir William Herbert formed the backdrop to the First Folio's creation.

King James I of England and VI of Scotland, by Daniel Mytens, 1621. He became the patron of the playing company to which William Shakespeare, Richard Burbage, John Heminges and Henry Condell belonged in 1603, making them the King's Men.

Anne of Denmark, by Isaac Oliver, c.1612.

The splendid funerary catafalque of Queen Anne of Denmark, displayed at her funeral in 1619, recorded in a manuscript preserved at the College of Arms, London. The outpouring of public grief after Richard Burbage's death, which occurred just a few days after Anne's, was said to have eclipsed the mourning over the loss of the queen.

The Prince of Wales (Prince Charles), by an unknown artist, *c.*1616. Charles's proposed marriage to the Spanish princess, the Infanta Maria, sister of King Philip IV of Spain, was one of the most controversial political issues of the period. Known popularly as the 'Spanish Match', this project for an Anglo-Spanish union, so favoured by King James I, may have influenced the choice of commemorative poets for the First Folio's preliminary pages, as well as the selection of the engraver who created the now-famous title-page portrait of William Shakespeare.

Elizabeth, Queen of Bohemia and Electress Palatine, by Robert Peake the Elder, *c.*1610. The political crisis in which Elizabeth and her husband Frederick, Elector Palatine, had become embroiled formed another significant context for the making of the First Folio.

It may have been through Blount's intercession that his friend
James Mabbe, a graduate and scholar of Magdalen College,
Oxford, had been appointed as the young man's Spanish tutor,
demonstrating the fact that to James I's senior courtiers the
publisher's name had become synonymous with the cultivation of
Spanish letters. The main substance of the missive may also have
concerned a sensitive, and hence clandestine, project with which
Blount, Trumbull and possibly Thomas Thorpe were engaged at
this time, and which may have concerned Spanish politics. The
majority of the letter is written in encrypted form, and refers to
two manuscripts, given the code-names 'calf' and 'cow', which
Blount had expected Trumbull to send him. In fact, Blount had
received the 'calf' and not the 'cow'. Trumbull too, it seems, had
been writing in code, because Blount informed him that parts of
his previous letter were a 'riddle' he could not easily decipher, since
'neither lame Thomas nor I can understand you, though it cost us
3 quarts of Canary to drink your health trebble'. 'Lame Thomas'
may refer to Thorpe, who had been acting as an agent between
Trumbull and Blount since at least July of the previous year. Blount
and Thorpe were close, the latter referring to 'Ned' Blount as 'his
kind, and true friend', and both having been part of a syndicate
which funded the translation and printing of Dutch works on
matters of religion which were sold at the Black Bear. It is, therefore, possible that the manuscripts referred to by Blount and
Trumbull in code related to a translation project.

Continuing their shared cypher, Blount promised to 'cure' the
calf, since 'a calf is but a creature and may be taught either to drink
or endure any water or light', and asked 'whether it may get free
course and be naturalised here with us or not'. The reference to
'curing' or the mending of a text is a fairly common one in this
period. Heminges and Condell boasted in the Folio that they were
offering the world the plays of Shakespeare 'cured, and perfect of
their limbs', in improved versions, and Thomas Walkley claimed

that his revised edition of Beaumont and Fletcher's *Philaster* corrected the errors in all previous copies, thereby 'bind[ing] up their wounds ... so maimed and deformed, as they at the first were'. To 'cure' a work meant to perfect or correct a potentially corrupted text or to produce an improved version or reprint. The term 'naturalised' could indicate to 'translate' the text, since 'naturalisation' was the process that ratified an immigrant's licence to remain in England. With regards to the 'calf' he had been sent, Blount promised that 'it shall be carried and cured with what discretion is fitting a creature of that nature', suggesting the need for secrecy and the potential danger in the mishandling of the situation. Could this indicate texts to be translated from the Spanish, about affairs relating to Spain? Or did this correspondence simply refer to Mabbe's translation of *The Rogue*, probably published towards the end of 1622? But if the latter, why the need for discretion?

What of the other text, the 'cow'? Of this Blount adds cryptically: 'I have known a cow hath been taught to speak to a king.' Could this refer to a text published – or soon to be published – which would offer some kind of advice to James I? If so, the most pressing and sensitive topic at this time was England's relation to Spain, and more specifically the Spanish Match. Indeed, Blount confirms that this is a matter of utmost secrecy and that 'but one pair eyes may survey it, till it be exposed in public view'. Significantly perhaps, he goes on to express a concern that Trumbull's agent might have 'mistaken himself, and delivered the cow to Master Secretary and brought the calf to me'. At this time the secretary of state was George Calvert, who had been in regular correspondence with both Trumbull and Sir John Digby, the Earl of Bristol, working collectively to bring about a speedy resolution to the business of the match by making concessions to demands from the Pope and King Philip IV on the sticking point of England's treatment of Catholics.

Through encrypted missives to Calvert, Trumbull had been conveying highly sensitive information about the secret conditions that were being drawn up for the restoration of the Palatinate and the security of James I's children, as part of negotiations for the match. In one surviving letter cyphers consisting of numbered codes have been partially decrypted by a contemporary hand, possibly that of Calvert, and indicate '619 (the King of Spain's) well intentions to gratify 653 (his Majesty [King James I])' in the matter 'of 300 (the Palatinate)' and 'of 88 (the Infanta's) sincerity, and good offices', of which 'there was no doubt to be made'. Sir John Digby had been kept informed of these developments and, sensing that the pro-Spanish faction abroad was on the brink of securing a final agreement, informed Calvert that 'unless his Majesty would be pleased to take away the persecution of Catholics … neither would the Pope dispense [a licence for the match], neither would the Infanta live but with much discomfort to see people persecuted merely for being of the religion she professed'. Without first seeking James I's permission, Digby agreed that both the king and Prince Charles would confirm in writing their commitment to ensuring that 'the Catholics shall not be molested or persecuted for their religion'.

If Trumbull and Blount had felt the 'cow' was too sensitive even to fall into Calvert's hands, there is a good chance the document had some relation to that which was, for the king's secretary, the issue at the forefront of his attention: England's relation to Spain, particularly as it concerned the Spanish Match and the matter of religious toleration for Catholics. This also correlates with Blount's intense interest in Spanish literature and affairs at this time. Whatever the truth of the 'calf' and the 'cow', the incident demonstrates Blount's close relationship with Mabbe, Digby's one-time secretary, and with another Shakespeare publisher, Thomas Thorpe, as well as with key figures at the heart of Spanish politics at a fraught period in England's history, even as he was working on bringing the First Folio to fruition.

At the Half-Eagle and Key, after a break in the printing of the Folio due to William Jaggard's quarrel with Ralph Brooke and the press's heavy workload, production of Shakespeare's plays got back on an uneven and somewhat unsteady track from around October 1622. Vincent's heraldic tome was not far from completion and it was now possible to return to *All's Well That Ends Well*, which had been left in limbo since July. Once again the long-suffering Compositor B shouldered the burden of the Folio's ample pages, working on this play entirely alone from his normally assigned case. This would have slowed down production considerably. Despite this, in the run-up to the resumption of the typesetting, the syndicate felt reasonably confident that they would be completing the First Folio in short order, for they had added a piece of advance advertising to the catalogue for the Frankfurt Book Fair, which informed book buyers and browsers attending this literary exhibition in October 1622 that they could soon expect to be able to purchase 'Plays, written by M[aster] William Shakespeare, all in one volume, printed by Isaac Jaggard, in fol[io].'

It is not known if William Jaggard was ailing significantly around the time of the fair, or whether this had necessitated the inclusion of Isaac's name as the head printer for the project, yet Jaggard the elder would die within a year. Before the Folio, Isaac had been explicitly identified on the title pages of only three works, one of which was a play, but this did not reflect the extent of his experience as a publisher-printer, given that he and his father had operated increasingly as a unit following William's blindness around 1612–13. Shakespeare's Book may have been seen as an opportunity for the twenty-seven-year-old Isaac to make his mark on the publishing scene by showcasing his leadership role in an opulent folio-sized work at Europe's largest and most influential book fair.

While printing on the Folio had recommenced, it would not be long before the Jaggards encountered another problem. The next play on the list was *Twelfth Night*, but instead Compositor B turned to the first history play, *King John*, and Compositor C was assigned to help him. Negotiations over the latter play were likely to have been wrapped up by this point because, as we have seen, the syndicate probably reached an agreement with Thomas Dewe which may have involved his printing of a non-Shakespearean version of the story of King John's life, so it was safe to proceed with its typesetting. This change of plan may have been necessitated by a problem with the copy text for the volume's penultimate comedy. *Twelfth Night* had not been issued as a quarto text before, and so difficulty with securing rights to print it could not have been the reason for the delay. This was, though, merely a brief hiatus, since the comedy was tied up shortly after *King John*, its final ten and a half pages typeset by the end of November, at the same time as the compositors were adding a list of 'errata' or errors to the back of Vincent's volume, the two works sharing the same type-stock.

For this run of typesetting for Shakespeare's plays, Compositor B continued to take a leading role, setting all of *Twelfth Night* by himself. The reason for the rerouting of personnel away from the Folio at this time may have been the addition of a further work to the Jaggards' schedule. André Favyn's *The Theatre of Honour and Knighthood*, another intricate and weighty work of heraldry, was logged in the Stationers' Register that October and started around the time that *King John* was being printed, even as the Jaggards were rushing to finish Vincent's text. William Jaggard needed to release the latter work as soon as possible in order to draw sales away from Brooke's own revised text, given that William had already suffered a financial hit through his much-regretted collaboration with the herald. This was, therefore, a brief period in which the Jaggards were working on three labour-intensive folios at once, with Favyn's tome occupying the syndicate throughout the printing of the First Folio's histories and tragedies.

After completing *Twelfth Night* the compositors did not proceed directly to the final comedy, *The Winter's Tale*. Rather they switched to the second history play on the list, *Richard II*, with Compositor C replaced by Compositor A as Compositor B's co-worker. Once again a problem with securing a good copy text for this first-time-printed comedy may have been responsible. The prompt book for *The Winter's Tale* would be reported 'missing' in 1623, but a record of a search of the company archives between 1619 and 1620 indicated that the play was still where it should have been. Was it stolen some time shortly afterwards, part of the cache of plays some scholars believe were taken from the King's Men from 1618–19 onwards? Whether or not this was the case, it is possible that Heminges and Condell needed to source an alternative copy before the typesetting and printing of that play could commence, turning perhaps to Shakespeare's own authorial manuscript. Since Ralph Crane has been suggested as the scribe who produced a fair copy of this play for the Folio, it is possible that a version of the work was turned over to him for copying, the resulting manuscript passed on to the Jaggards by the King's Men's theatre managers.

Within a short time the compositors had in their hands a suitable copy text of *The Winter's Tale*. Resuming the two-compositor pattern of simultaneous typesetting from two separate cases, compositors A and B abandoned *Richard II* twelve pages in, so that they could complete the comedy, finishing this in its entirety some time before the end of December. It was probably during the typesetting of *Richard II* that Vincent's *Discovery of Errors* was finally published, around late November or early December, much to William Jaggard's relief. The fact that the compositors were prepared to continue with the plays out of sequence, when potential problems arose with the copy texts of the last two Folio comedies and through the completion of the Vincent tome, meant they were keen to move on with the project, perhaps feeling pressured by the advertisement for Shakespeare's Book in the Frankfurt Book Fair's catalogue.

As the Jaggards were printing off the last of the comedies, the King's Men were reviving at least two plays that had premiered earlier that year, this time for the Christmas season at court. They put on *The Spanish Curate* again at Whitehall Palace on 26 December, with James I in the audience, and *The Pilgrim* on 29 December, these among nine plays performed by royal command for which John Heminges would be paid ninety pounds in arrears in March 1623. The bibliophile Sir Edward Dering was so taken by the performance of *The Spanish Curate* that he requested a copy of the play for a domestic recital in his estate in Surrenden, Kent, before the end of February 1623, demonstrating his potential closeness to Heminges and Condell. Dering would take on a role in the production and it may be for this event that he hired wigs and artificial beards, which he logged in his expenses book on 18 February 1623. It is possible that his interest in the King's Men's repertory gave him access to individuals who had informed him that the First Folio was in production, for as soon as it was ready for sale he would rush to acquire it, making him the first recorded purchaser of Shakespeare's Book. In fact his accounts bear testimony to the fact that he became the proud owner of two volumes.

As the year drew to its close the Jaggards could take stock of where they were with the printing of the First Folio. They were aware they had reached a milestone, having completed a full third of the volume's generic groupings, all fourteen comedies, in addition to one and a half of the history plays. Starting on the sixteenth play, they believed they had nineteen more left to print, in the event that they would be able to tie up the outstanding rights to all the plays the syndicate wanted to include. In fact, they would go on to print twenty more plays before the final version of the Folio was completed. Thanks to delays caused by problems with copy texts, a busy printing schedule, William Jaggard's personal squabbles, and possibly negotiations over Shakespeare plays issued in quarto versions, they had already taken nearly a full year to print fewer than half the total number of the Folio's plays. They had a lot of work to do in order to make up for this lost time.

Act Four

1623

Making History
Making Shakespeare:
Finishing the First Folio

[T]hese trees shall be my books,
And in their barks my thoughts I'll character,
That every eye which in this forest looks
Shall see thy virtue witnessed everywhere.

William Shakespeare, *As You Like It*

14

A 'hazardous experiment'

Playing Lovers and Printing Histories

Perhaps it was their exaggerated beards that gave them away; or their over-large riding coats into which they half-buried their faces; or maybe their bland generic names – Jack and Tom Smith – had that whiff of the incognito about them, too ordinary to be trusted *as* ordinary. The two men were apprehended in Canterbury, not long after they had set out from Tibolts in Hertfordshire on 17 February 1623, passing through Tilbury the next day, then crossing the Thames to Gravesend. There one of the travellers had to navigate an awkward moment when his beard fell off, necessitating an unseemly scramble to re-attach it, which only drew further attention to their peculiar behaviour and 'gave suspicions they were no such manner of men' as they appeared.

The officer who spied them sent an agent ahead to Rochester to accost the pair, but he arrived too late 'to have them stayed'. When they reached Canterbury, the mayor questioned them himself, indicating that he had detained them on the orders of Sir Henry Mainwaring, the Lieutenant of Dover Castle. How they 'untwined themselves' is like something out of a scarcely believable situation comedy. Sensing their cover was about to be blown, one of the apprehended men stepped forward and with a theatrical flourish removed his beard, revealing himself to be the king's favourite George Villiers, the Marquess of Buckingham. He had undertaken this mission in disguise, he claimed, in order to carry out a secret inspection of the king's fleet. If the young servant who had witnessed these unfolding events had recognised the other bearded man as Prince Charles, he would never have the opportunity to divulge what he knew. The records do not tell us by what means his silence was secured, merely that 'his mouth was easily shut'. The ruse worked. Donning their disguises again, the prince and Buckingham continued on their way to Dover, arriving at six that evening, just as the weather worsened. There they were detained again but were quickly able to give 'some secret satisfaction' to the port officers who allowed them to depart. After a stormy night, which prevented them from crossing the channel, they set sail for Boulogne the next morning at first light.

Their mission was so clandestine that not even the venerable members of the Privy Council were aware of it until the news had been leaked and was, according to John Chamberlain, who reported it on 22 February, 'in every man's mouth'. The whole affair had been prompted by the return of Endymion Porter from a diplomatic mission to Spain on 2 January, bearing news of the goodwill of King Philip IV and the draft treaty for the Anglo-Spanish marriage which had been engineered through the intercessions of the recently created Earl of Bristol, Sir John Digby (one-time mentor to Leonard Digges and James Mabbe, the latter having been his servant), and the king's secretary, Sir George Calvert. This apparent encouragement made James I 'very merry and jocund', and he allowed himself to believe 'the match is fully concluded on their parts'. Consequently, the end of the Christmas season had not put a stop to the atmosphere of celebration in the royal court. '[H]ere was nothing to write of but dancing and feasting,' wrote Chamberlain on 25 January, 'which was more frequent all this

Christmas than ever I knew or remember, and continues ever since, even till now.'

Before their departure, Prince Charles and George Villiers had caroused into the early hours, crashing parties to which they 'came unlooked for', as if they had been commissioned to tour the nation's great houses, as Chamberlain quipped, 'somewhat like fiddlers'. The two took centre-stage at yet another Ben Jonson offering, *Time Vindicated to Himself and His Honours*, which was performed on 13 January at the Banqueting House at Whitehall, with the post-performance revelry continuing till dawn the next day. Jonson had the canny idea of staging a harmonious reconciliation between Venus, goddess of love, and Saturn, god of war, with the latter declaring 'Between us it shall be no strife:/For now 'tis Love, gives Time his life'. The masque ended with an affirmation of James I's desire for 'soft peace' and a recognition that 'Man should not hunt Mankind to death' but, instead, follow the king's 'just example', who 'studies only ways of good', glancing implicitly at the anticipated union that would end all aggression between England and Spain. It had taken six days to prepare the masque, and extensive rehearsals in the palace's Great Hall had been attended by the Spanish ambassador, Don Carlos Coloma. The pro-Spanish courtiers, keen to assure their opposers that union with Spain would not be a threat to the Protestant Church, made much of the prince's dismissal of several musicians 'for assisting and helping to sing a mass at the Spanish ambassador's on Christmas Day'; but Chamberlain was cynical, adding 'though some say (how truly I know not) that they are received again at the ambassador's request'.

The court began to buzz with news that the Infanta would arrive in May. But even that seemed too late for some. It would soon be rumoured that Buckingham had filled the mind of his impressionable prince with romantic flights of fancy, assuring him 'how gallant and how brave a thing it would be, for his Highness to make a journey into Spain, and to fetch home his mistress'. Charles took little convincing, becoming 'transported with the thought of it, and most impatiently solicitous to bring it to pass'. For the prince, 'whose nature was inclined to adventures', this undertaking would be a great quest, a chance to prove to his father and the nation that he was master of his own destiny and could bend even King Philip IV to his will. All he had to do was arrive in Spain and the Infanta would fall into his arms. She would be his for the taking. There was even talk of dispatching Buckingham with a great English fleet of ten ships to escort the couple home.

The Privy Councillors were far from carried away by the romance of a venture about which they should have been informed before a decision was made. They demanded answers from the king. He explained that 'the cause why he imparted it not to them was that secrecy was the life of the business', and defended Buckingham by insisting 'that it was the Prince's own desire, that the Marquess had no hand in it'. He would, he promised, find a way 'to stay the amazement of the people' who were already calling this rash enterprise a 'very costly and hazardous experiment', one full of 'dangers enough every way'. For those opposed to the match there was the fear that James was ready to issue a proclamation 'imposing silence', to stop tongues wagging at home so the happy couple 'might be married at a mass'. What James was not telling his Privy Councillors was how reluctant he had been to send Charles on such a foolhardy mission; how he wept and pleaded with him not to go; and how Charles prevailed by entreating him on bended knees.

Within days of their departure, even as the 'very weary' travellers made their way from Boulogne to Paris, the entire Privy Council marched into St Paul's Churchyard and convened around the preaching cross. Had Edward Blount and William Aspley been there, and there is a very good chance they were, it would have been a strange sight to see so many senior courtiers descending on the area in their court finery. Anticipation hung thickly in the atmosphere as the crowds gathered, expecting to hear a sermon condemning the Spanish Match and the prince's unexpected departure, which even the Venetian ambassador, Girolamo Lando, had called 'a monster among decisions ... remote from all imagination ... to say nothing of reason'; a stirring speech around which they could all rally. When the preacher appeared, however, it became clear that he 'had his lesson' beforehand. The then Bishop of London, George Montaigne, had already warned him 'only to pray for the prince's prosperous journey and safe return'. Other priests who witnessed these events would not be so easily silenced. The very next day some refused to stick to the officially sanctioned script and 'proceeded further', with one preacher stating that he 'desired God to be merciful unto him now that he was going into the House of Rimmon', that is, now that he was being forced to betray his personal beliefs for the sake of conforming to royal edict.

Serial silence-breaker Dr John Everard could not resist adding his voice to the chorus of objection, earning himself yet another spell in prison. Since Blount, Aspley and the other syndicate members had probably only recently been in negotiations with Thomas Walkley over the rights to print *Othello*, it is tantalising to speculate about whether they talked about Walkley's enemy, Everard, whose imprisonments were becoming something of a habit. While the wayward preacher had at least managed to have his say, another parson in the parish church close to John Chamberlain's own home was not accorded that honour. When he began an oration in which he questioned the king's stance towards Spain he was drowned out thanks to his own clerk who ordered the choir to 'sing him down with a psalm before he had half done'. As Chamberlain observed, 'Many of our churchmen are hardly held in, and their tongues itch to be talking.'

The Folio syndicate, like practically everyone else in the country, could not have resisted debating the rapidly unfolding events around the Spanish Match. Perhaps discussions also took place in the Jaggards' printing house, the compositors, inkers and other pressworkers gossiping about the marriage, and the latest libels against it that began appearing with increasing frequency across the city, during their breaks in between working on the Shakespeare volume or André Favyn's *The Theatre of Honour and Knighthood*, which had been ongoing since the commencement of the history plays. Some of these libels were authored by Thomas Scott, chaplain to Sir William Herbert – and persistent thorn-in-the-side of James I and George Villiers – who had followed his incendiary anti-Spanish pamphlet *Vox Populi* with a series of diatribes pleading for the nation to unite in support of the king's daughter Elizabeth, ousted queen of Bohemia, and her husband Frederick, the Elector Palatine. No doubt Scott escaped severe punishment thanks to the protection of his patron, Pembroke. Just as the Folio syndicate and the Jaggards' pressworkers were turning back to the printing of the history plays, it must have seemed to them as if history was not just being made but rewritten, Spain soon to become England's closest ally. Even after the Anglo-Spanish peace treaty of 1604, the enmity between the two nations had remained entrenched along a religious fault line that seemed too wide to bridge. Now all that was changing. No mere libel was going to divert James from his mission of unification through his son's marriage.

The decision to present the history plays in chronological sequence in order of royal reign had already been made by this point since, towards the end of the previous year, *King John* and just over half of *Richard II* had been typeset and printed before the final comedy, *The Winter's Tale*, was largely completed. This was part of a deliberate and conscious design to make works that had, in reality, been composed out of sequence and in different periods appear like a cohesive group, a grand historiographical project worthy of the folio format which had transmitted some of the most celebrated genealogical, sacred and historical works to posterity, including Raphael Holinshed's *Chronicles of England, Scotland and Ireland*, Edward Hall's *Chronicle*, John Foxe's *Acts and Monuments*, and the King James Bible. When some of these plays had first been composed they were marketed in ways that cashed in on other popular genres. The *Henry VI* plays had been written between 1590 and 1592, possibly with *Henry VI, Part 1* having been produced last. *Henry VI, Part 2* was originally entitled *The First part of the Contention betwixt the two famous Houses of York and Lancaster* and advertised the 'Tragical end of the proud Cardinal of Winchester' on the title page of its 1594 quarto edition. *Henry VI, Part 3* was *The True Tragedy of Richard Duke of York* when first issued as a single volume the following year. Written around 1592–3, *Richard III* was initially entitled *The Tragedy of King Richard the Third*, and *Richard II*, authored around 1595, was similarly entitled *The Tragedy of King Richard the Second* when it was first published in quarto in 1597. This was succeeded by *King John* the following year, and the *Henry IV* plays, thought to have been written between 1596 and 1597 (though some date *Part 2* to 1598, being produced before *Henry V* in 1599), with *Henry IV, Part 1* tantalising the reader with the 'humorous conceits of Sir John Falstaff' on its title page. *Henry VIII* was the last of the history plays to have been composed, written by Shakespeare in collaboration with John Fletcher in 1613. In its earliest performances the latter play was known by a quite different title, *All Is True*, echoing the throwaway titles of comedies like *As You Like It* or *All's Well That Ends Well*.

The Folio syndicate resolved to smooth out the generic ambiguities of these plays and presented them as a sequence. Their titles were also regularised, conforming to a model that announced each reign with 'The Life of …' or 'The Life and Death of …', emphasising the biographical contours of a central royal personality as the unified structural principle for each play. By separating out the histories from the comedies and tragedies, and imposing a chronological order on them, the effect of the Folio's 'Catalogue' of plays was to present Shakespeare as a chronicler of the making of a nation, tracing a providential arc that culminated in England's present greatness. The Jaggard print-shop had issued grandiose works before that identified themselves as 'Catalogues'. In addition to Ralph Brooke's fated *Catalogue and Succession of the Kings* (1619), William Jaggard had produced his own *Catalogue of such English Books* (1618) and *A Catalogue of the Kings of Scotland* (1610), as well as numerous works which structured their contents internally through a 'Catalogue'. This might indicate that Jaggard had something to do with the division of the plays in the Folio's own 'Catalogue', though this could simply have been borrowed from Ben Jonson's collected *Works*, which heads its list of works as 'The Catalogue', though it does not divide its contents into genres.

Come the new year of 1623, following a disjointed start to the printing of the history plays, the Jaggards had every intention of recommencing the typesetting in sequence, *Richard II* having been left unfinished so that the comedies could be wrapped up. But this did not happen. A new problem presented itself, which forced them to skip the next two works in the sequence (*Henry IV, Part 1* and *Henry IV, Part 2*), with compositors A and B moving straight on to *Henry V*. Two of the deferred plays – *Richard II* and *Henry IV, Part 1* – were, along with *Richard III*, owned by Matthew Law and were, collectively, Shakespeare's most popular dramatic works in print. It is likely that the syndicate had instructed the Jaggards' pressworkers to begin the printing of Law's plays before they had formally secured the rights from him, or that the latter had changed his mind after they had reached a nominal agreement, perhaps realising the value of his Shakespeare assets and taking the decision to drive a harder bargain. The fact that he had, just weeks or months before, in 1622, published new quarto editions of *Richard III* and *Henry IV, Part 1*, indicates that perhaps he had been only recently, or was still, in negotiations with the Folio syndicate, possibly agreeing to release rights to his treasured plays in exchange for being permitted to profit from selling quarto versions of two of his prime Shakespeare assets. If this is the case, then he may have reneged on an earlier, but yet to be formalised, agreement during the printing of the history plays early in 1623.

But there may have been another reason behind this turn of events. What has not been noted by Folio scholars before is that at this time Law was in some financial trouble, and Edward Blount was aware of this because both were summoned before the Court of Stationers on 2 December 1622, having failed to pay back money they had jointly borrowed 'to pay their debts to the English Stock'. Among those presiding that day over the court were John Jaggard, Thomas Pavier and Richard Field. It must have been a challenging session because they, along with their Stationer colleagues, had to inform Blount and Law 'that they shall have no benefit of any stock in the Company till the debts and use be discharged'. Blount owed a colossal £166, while Law had to pay a not inconsiderable sum of £34. Between October 1619 and October 1624, Law had also been fined four times by the court for unruly speech and other misdemeanours. If he was requesting a higher fee for the inclusion of his plays in the Folio, his debts may have been the reason. The Folio syndicate's decision to allow him to print two of those plays in 1622 may not have simply been arrived at for business ends. There could have been a genuine sympathy for him, particularly from Blount whose own mounting debts were frequently attested to in the Stationers' archives. Earlier that year, on 20 May 1622, John Jaggard, Thomas Pavier and Richard Field had had to inform him that he was 'indebted to the English Stock £120', which he had to pay at interest with his own shares as surety.

This must have been a frustrating and difficult time, therefore; not just for Blount personally but for the Folio syndicate, who had recently seen a group of Shakespeare plays hit the bookstalls, including the two Law plays, along with *Othello* (losing the marketing benefit of having this previously unpublished play debut in the Folio) and the anonymous *The Troublesome Reign of John, King of England*, which could easily be confused with Shakespeare's own *King John* and which had been published with an attribution to the dramatist. This may all have been allowed – or endured – in exchange for the rights to print the plays the Folio's backers wanted for their own collected works. It is harder to explain why John Smethwick decided to publish an edition of *Romeo and Juliet* in 1623. The date was judiciously left off the imprint, perhaps to make the book look like an older remainder and prevent it from becoming competition for the First Folio. Was Smethwick, having seen the sudden release of competition for their volume in cheaper formats, becoming worried that the Folio might not provide a reasonable return on his investment? Did he reach an agreement with the other members of the syndicate, allowing him to profit from his asset with the understanding that he remove the publishing date?

While William Aspley held the rights to *Henry IV, Part 2*, the syndicate felt it was unwise to begin work on the play without knowing for sure if they could seal the deal with Law for *Part 1*. It was not until the Jaggards' compositors were at work on the next play, *Henry VI, Part 3*, that they finalised an agreement with Law, leaving the latter work unfinished – having printed just six pages – so that they could conclude *Richard II*. They then completed both parts of *Henry IV* in short order, but they miscalculated, leaving too much space at the end of *Henry IV, Part 2*, which they had to fill with a list of principal characters. Finally they were ready to tie up *Henry VI, Part 3*, before setting *Richard III*, with Compositor B still aided by Compositor A throughout the rest of the typesetting for this problematic sequence of plays.

Opposite: the compositors of the First Folio found they had too much space left when they reached the end of *Henry IV, Part 2*, overestimating by one whole page. They filled this with a generously spaced-out list of character names, topped and tailed with decorative ornamental borders.

THE
ACTORS
NAMES.

RVMOVR the Presentor.
King *Henry* the Fourth.
Prince *Henry*, afterwards Crowned King *Henrie* the Fift.

Prince *Iohn* of Lancaster.
Humphrey of Gloucester. } Sonnes to *Henry* the Fourth, & brethren to *Henry* 5.
Thomas of Clarence.

Northumberland.
The Arch Byshop of Yorke.
Mowbray.
Hastings. } Opposites against King *Henrie* the
Lord Bardolfe. } Fourth.
Trauers.
Morton.
Coleuile.

Warwicke.
Westmerland.
Surrey. } Of the Kings
Gowre. } Partie.
Harecourt.
Lord Chiefe Iustice.

Pointz.
Falstaffe.
Bardolphe. } Irregular
Pistoll. } Humorists.
Peto.
Page.

Shallow, } Both Country
Silence. } Iustices.
Dauie, Seruant to Shallow.
Phang, and Snare, 2. Serieants
Mouldie.
Shadow.
Wart. } Country Soldiers
Feeble.
Bullcalfe.

Drawers
Beadles.
Groomes

Northumberlands Wife.
Percies Widdow.
Hostesse Quickly.
Doll Teare-sheete.
Epilogue.

The compositors had almost completed *Richard III*, with just three and a half pages left, when they encountered another obstacle which affected the final history play, *Henry VIII*. This they left out entirely, and would not return to it, nor complete *Richard III*, until much later when they were printing the tragedies. *Henry VIII* was not one of the plays that the King's Men had released for publication in a previous smaller quarto format, so there could not have been rights problems to overcome. We now know that the play was co-authored with John Fletcher and this may have caused some uncertainty about its inclusion in the Folio. Other co-authored plays, such as *Pericles* and *The Two Noble Kinsmen*, were not incorporated into the volume. While this appears to accord with Heminges and Condell's insistence that they were giving the world Shakespeare's 'original' and 'perfect' plays 'as he conceived them', this claim, as we have seen, misrepresented the processes that underpinned the metamorphosis of the dramatist's words into the Folio's print-ready copy texts. What we know today complicates this picture considerably in other ways. Folio-enshrined plays such as *Titus Andronicus*, the *Henry VI* plays, *Macbeth* and *All's Well That Ends Well*, for example, were either potentially originally co-authored with other playwrights or, as is likely the case with the latter two, incorporated later additions, editing or interpolations by Thomas Middleton. *Henry VIII* would have completed the sequence of history plays nicely, bringing it nearly up to date with the tail end of the Tudor line and the birth of Elizabeth I, whose kinsman James I had inherited the English throne after her. As such the entire sequence of history plays would have built cumulatively towards ratifying the divinely preordained inevitability of the king's reign; a grand compliment to the monarch.

No matter what the cause of this change in printing sequence, the Jaggards were determined not to waste any more time. The typesetting and printing of the bulk of the histories had probably taken around two and a half to three months at most, from January till the middle or end of March 1623. The Jaggards had no choice but to lay *Henry VIII* aside for the time being and start preparing the tragedies. In doing so they were responding to, or were the prime instigators of, the re-pitching of some of these plays in a manner that mirrored editorial decisions made in relation to the rebranding of the histories. Here too the focus was on the plays' central tragic personalities, with some of the works' generic ambiguities artfully elided. The 1594 quarto's *The Most Lamentable Roman Tragedy of Titus Andronicus* became simply the snappier *Titus Andronicus*, shorn of its explicitly 'Roman' generic connection; the 1603 version of *The Tragical History of Hamlet, Prince of Denmark*, became *The Tragedy of Hamlet*, its blurring of the genres of tragedy and history resolved; and the 1608 quarto of the *True Chronicle History of the Life and Death of King Lear* was similarly divested of its association with the history play genre and starkly rebranded as *King Lear*.

These changes brought the plays closer to a classical and learnedly literary model of tragedy, in which the focus was on the downfall, according to Aristotle in his treatise on *Poetics*, of 'elevated' individuals and their families, the 'magnitude' of which prompted 'through pity and fear' the 'catharsis of such emotions'. In doing so, on the surface at least, the plays' pitching seemed to conform to a classical purity approved by Sir Philip Sidney, who had condemned modern dramatists of his generation whose 'plays be neither right Tragedies, nor right Comedies: mingling Kings and Clowns, not because the matter so carrieth it: but thrust in Clowns by head and shoulders, to play a part in majestical matters, with neither decency, nor discretion'. These he called purveyors of 'mongrel tragi-comedy'. Just as with Heminges and Condell's claim to present the works as Shakespeare 'conceived them', potential buyers of the Folio were fed another untruth, obfuscating the generic messiness and emotional complexities of these plays in order to present the dramatist as the heir of the great classical tragedians.

While the Jaggards had been busy trying to avert tragedies closer to home, those concerned with the seemingly endless obstacles placed in their path during the printing of the Folio's histories, the King's Men may have been aware of, and been watching very keenly, a controversy surrounding the Mastership of the Revels, the office which, next to that of Lord Chamberlain, governed their fortunes and careers. While William Herbert had arranged for Ben Jonson to claim the reversion of the Mastership of the Revels in 1620, early in 1623 one William Painter was mooted as a candidate for the reversion after Jonson. Pembroke did everything in his power to prevent Painter's succession, submitting a 'Bill' to the king conferring 'a grant in reversion of the place of Master of the Revels to Master Thorrowgoode', one of his own clients, in February 1623. The idea was to ensure that a member of Pembroke's faction would claim the post in the event that Jonson would either be unable to step into it when it next became vacant or would abandon the office or die while still in possession of it. Shortly after, on 2 March, Pembroke wrote to Edward Conway, who had been made secretary of state in January of that year (one of two secretaries serving James I), protesting what he felt to be the disposing of a post entirely under his own authority. He wanted Conway to convey 'to his Majesty's judgement, what the world may think when they shall find his Majesty hath denied me, for a place in mine own gift', giving the reversion to Painter 'whose face he never saw, nor ever received one hour's service from him'. Despite Herbert's extolling of Thorrowgoode's virtues, stating 'the man I have recommended I will answer for with my reputation', his 'Bill' was rejected by the king.

This was an alarming turn of events for the King's Men. Should Astley vacate the post and Jonson be unable to replace him for any reason, Painter would inherit the Mastership of the Revels. There was no telling how that would change the working practices of the King's Men or if, as has been suggested, Painter was a client of the Marquess of Buckingham who would use England's stages to push James's pro-Spanish agenda more vigorously. To make matters worse, Pembroke was again being pressured to relinquish his office of Lord Chamberlain. James Hay had been elevated to Earl of Carlisle and, emboldened by an obscenely generous pension of £2,000 per annum, was now looking to augment his influence in the king's household. To Pembroke's dismay, Carlisle and Villiers were becoming closer, both serving as joint godparents to the child of prominent courtiers in January of 1623. Hay was proposed as the next Lord Chamberlain, with the Privy Seal once more offered to Herbert as bait to lure him away from his long-held office. Pembroke clearly put up a fight, in a quite literal way, for shortly afterwards he had a falling out with Hay, the man to whom he had poured out his heart's grief over the death of Richard Burbage, for the warring pair entered into an argument and 'proceeded so far as to cross language, and some say further'. Nothing came of this scheme to promote Hay to Lord Chamberlain at this time.

But could Pembroke keep rebuffing such attempts to divest him of the Lord Chamberlainship? His health was failing and, at this point in the printing of the First Folio, it was not clear how long the Herberts would remain in control of the Chamberlainship and the Revels office. With the future so uncertain, Heminges and Condell could not afford to cross the king's will by appearing not to endorse his foreign policy. That could mean worrying repercussions later.

'Pursue the stars'

An Apprentice, a Widow's Funeral and other Tragedies

Not long after the Jaggards had finished printing Shakespeare's history plays, minus *Henry VIII*, Sir John Digby, the king's ambassador in Spain, wrote to Sir Dudley Carleton informing him of a peculiar occurrence. 'Nothing could have happened more strange and unexpected unto me,' he wrote, as the 'sudden and unthought of arrival' of Prince Charles and the Marquess of Buckingham. Turning up at the door of his ambassadorial residence in Madrid, known as the House of the Seven Chimneys, at eight o'clock in the evening of Friday 7 March 1623, Buckingham had presented himself to Digby's servants as Thomas Smith, requesting a conference with the ambassador. When the way was secured, the prince was able to enter 'with all privacy'. Digby was left to organise the adventuring pair's introduction to Philip IV and his senior courtiers, who were 'ravished with the rareness' of the prince's escapade, enough to make them 'forget for a while their Spanish gravity'. Following behind Charles and Buckingham was a small retinue, which included Endymion Porter who reported that they had been 'the braveliest received that ever men were'. When the former ambassador to England Gondomar set eyes on the prince he fell down before him, spreading himself flat on the floor, and refused to be raised, crying out *'nunc dimittis'*, the words St Simeon uttered upon first seeing the infant Jesus, as if he had 'attained the top of his desire'.

Two days after the royal party's arrival, a grand public procession was staged. Its purpose, to give Charles a tantalising glimpse of the Infanta. The prince was not permitted to talk to or sit with her, but was seated behind drawn curtains in a coach with Buckingham so that they could see the Spanish royal family gliding by in their own coaches. The throngs of people pressing in to see the prince were so great they had to be beaten back by the king's guards, but Charles's attention was not on the commotion outside his coach. He was too entranced by the vision that had materialised before him as he peered through a gap in the curtains; an apparition that made his young heart leap. '[T]he prince hath taken such a liking to his mistress, that now he loves her as much for her beauty, as he can for being sister to so great a king. She deserves it,' added Porter, 'for there was never seen a fairer creature.' Charles was satisfied. Within days, news reached England that the Marquess of Buckingham was to be made a duke.

On 1 April the skies of London were lit up by bonfires, the heavens re-echoing to the peel of a thousand church bells; all by order of the king in celebration of his son's safe arrival in Madrid. Many were less jubilant. Sir Simonds D'Ewes saw the match as a 'vast and unnecessary expense at a time when the king's wants pressed him much', while John Chamberlain felt 'this marriage one way or other is like to cost the king and realm as much as she brings', and was alarmed to see so many noblemen turning to Catholicism, predicting the number of converts would rise further 'at the Infanta's coming', which would cause many more to 'fall away as fast as withered leaves in autumn'. Unaware that Digby had already agreed, on behalf of James and Charles, a measure of freedom for all English Catholics, Chamberlain reported rumours that the Pope would only grant a full dispensation for the marriage in exchange for unreasonable demands regarding 'toleration in religion' and access to England's key ports for the king of Spain's naval fleet.

By early May James I was suffering another bout of ill health, which meant he had to be carried by servants in a chair. But this did not stop him from making preparations for the Infanta's arrival, which were overseen by Sir William Herbert, somewhat reluctantly, in his capacity as Lord Chamberlain. The Spanish ambassador, Don Carlos Coloma, inspected St James's Palace and Denmark House to oversee the appointing of her lodgings, and Inigo Jones was commissioned to produce designs for a new chapel of 'great state and costliness'. Within days the ambassador himself would be laying the foundation stone. The existing Savoy Chapel was to be 'converted to the use of her household' under the governorship of a Catholic bishop or 'superintendent over her priests and chaplains'. The naval fleet was elaborately decked out to receive her with all due ceremony, the prince's own ship 'so richly furnished with all manner of bedding, hangings and the like, as hath not been seen at sea'. An astonished John Chamberlain remarked that the preparations for her arrival were 'so carried as if we were to receive some goddess'.

On the evening of 29 May Edward Blount was enjoying a drink with the Spanish scholar and translator James Mabbe. They were joined by the author Sir Robert Dallington, whose works Blount had published, and a 'Doctor Fox', who may have been the physician Thomas Foxe, a fellow of Magdalen College like Mabbe, or Thomas's uncle Simeon, who was a fellow of the College of Physicians, located on Paternoster Row. This convivial group of bibliophiles may have discussed the hot topic of the time, the Spanish Match and the imminent arrival of the Infanta, while remembering, and drinking a toast to the health of, their absent friend Sir William Trumbull in Brussels.

That night Mabbe stayed with Blount in the rooms above his bookshop, the Black Bear, leaving for Oxford the next morning, after which Blount sat down to write a letter to Trumbull, assuring him that he and his drinking companions 'did remember your health in a glass of Canary', a sweet wine from the Canary Islands. The publisher also informed Trumbull that he and Mabbe had discussed an upcoming adventure together, since the latter had 'made half a promise to see Brussels this summer if his gout will give him leave; and hath prevailed with me to keep him company in that journey'. Blount also enclosed a letter 'by my good friend Master Mabbe', a further sign of the closeness between the Spanish scholar, Blount and Trumbull, and of the fact that Mabbe was visiting the very shop in which deals over the rights to the printing of plays in the First Folio may have been struck even as that volume was being printed.

Trumbull's involvement with the intricacies of the political situation undoubtedly influenced the selection of texts Blount sent to him for his perusal. Even John Chamberlain suspected that James's agent in Brussels was employed on a sensitive mission, 'but upon what errand ... I know not', entirely oblivious to the fact that Trumbull had been sending encrypted messages about the highly clandestine conditions for the Spanish Match and the restoration of the Palatinate to the king's secretary, Sir George Calvert. Among the new works Blount couriered to Trumbull, which he felt 'worthy your view', were *The Catholic Moderator*, a topical book by Henry Constable which was published by Nathaniel Butter, a former collaborator with the stationer Ralph Mabbe, and *The History of Xenophon*, translated by John Bingham and financed by the same Mabbe. The latter work included a 'comparison of the Roman manner of wars with this of our time', concealing its interest in Europe's current volatile political situation beneath its apparent focus on ancient history.

Could both these works have been recommended by James Mabbe during his visit to Blount? It has not yet been considered whether the two became acquainted through Ralph Mabbe (who for five years operated shops steps away from the premises of Blount and Aspley). The likelihood of this, and of a close familial association between the two Mabbes, possibly brothers or kinsmen, is reinforced by the Stationers' Register, which preserves Ralph's later logging of the rights to the play *The Spanish Bawd*, as well as a series of texts by Cervantes; works translated by James Mabbe under his pseudonym Don Diego Puede-Ser. Blount and both Mabbes clearly had in common their desire to popularise Cervantes in England and, significantly, the rights to *The Spanish Bawd* were originally owned by William Aspley, who published the work in a now lost edition, indicating that Aspley had a prior working relationship with James Mabbe. What is evident here is the impact of the physical proximity of these stationers' businesses on the evolution of these relationships and the publications which flowed from them, including the First Folio.

Not long after the merry meeting between Blount, Mabbe and their friends, Sir William Herbert set out towards Southampton to oversee the arrival of the Infanta. Under his guidance the local highways were mended, lodging for her ample entourage arranged and preparations made for a series of lavish 'shows and pageants'. For the better effecting of the latter, Inigo Jones and perhaps the greatest living actor of the age, Edward Alleyn, then described as an 'old player', accompanied the train. Meanwhile, plans were made to meet the Spanish ambassador at Gravesend and to escort him to lodgings festooned with elaborate canopies draped with cloths of estate, which signified the elevated rank of the dignitaries who reposed beneath them, that, remarked John Chamberlain, was 'a thing which I do not remember to have seen afforded to any ambassador in Queen Elizabeth's time'.

Ben Jonson was not part of the convoy entrusted with the task of preparing for the Infanta's arrival. This was a slight, given his closeness to the king's propagandist machine up to this point.

Though he had his doubts about the extent of the concessions made to Spain, Jonson had been a devoted Catholic and had enjoyed the limelight his role as a spokesperson for the pro-Spanish faction had given him. In a poem composed shortly after these events he bitterly declared his indifference to the foreign policy he had supported with his masques, but affirmed his willingness to go to war to rescue the Palatinate if necessary. 'What is't to me,' he wrote, 'Whether the dispensation yet be sent,/Or that the match from Spain was ever meant?' More important than the Pope's 'dispensation' agreeing to the Anglo-Spanish marriage was England's security and he, for one, would be willing to 'draw the sword' to 'force back that, which will not be restored', including the Bohemian crown, even if it meant 'To live, or fall, a carcass in the cause'. Despite this, Jonson, like Blount, continued publicly to endorse the Spanish Match and before long the playwright would be commissioned to produce a new masque, *Neptune's Triumph for the Return of Albion*, intended to celebrate Charles's glorious return with his radiant new bride, the Infanta Maria of Spain.

Back in the Jaggards' printing house, work on the Folio's tragedies progressed hot on the heels of the histories (apart from the still-to-be-printed final pages of *Richard III* and all of *Henry VIII*) from around April. The team were keen to press ahead, and so decided a change of strategy was in order. To speed up the process the compositors began to work on groups of quires concurrently, rather than progressing in a more linear fashion quire by quire; a process they had not followed since a spell in the printing of the comedies when three compositors were working on the Folio at once. While a two-compositor pattern of typesetting was maintained as a minimum, the intention was to pick up momentum through the addition of a new apprentice, the so-called Compositor E. This is the only compositor we can name with some certainty: a John Leason, son of a yeoman from Hampshire, who was apprenticed, probably as a teenager, to William Jaggard in November 1622. Tackling Shakespeare's First Folio around five months later, as one of his first major projects, turned out to be something of a baptism of fire for young Leason.

As a novice, Leason was assigned to a senior compositor whose role was to mentor and train him for this demanding job. This was Compositor B, the Folio's primary typesetter, who started Leason off with a test of skill. While the older compositor worked with Compositor A on *Coriolanus*, he would leave his case to oversee the apprentice's work and occasionally allocate tasks designed to induct him into some of the secrets of the trade and foster those finer skills required of a successful compositor. Near the commencement of Leason's work on the Folio he was assigned his own case to which Compositor B pinned the cast-off copy text for *Titus Andronicus* and drew his attention to the banquet scene in Act 3, which he asked him to begin setting. The scene was not one included in previous printed quarto versions of the play and is therefore likely to have been a handwritten manuscript. When Leason was finished, his handiwork was printed off and proofread carefully. It had clearly been a challenging task because the result did not satisfy his mentor. Drawing attention to the errors in the printed sheet, Compositor B explained to Leason that he was not yet ready to take on manuscript copy and assigned him instead to sections of the plays for which previous printed quartos served as the copy texts.

Compositor B took another precaution. He was careful initially to prevent Leason from typesetting the first pages of plays, because errors in these would be all the more noticeable and the layout had to be as sharp and neat as possible. Leason was permitted to work on sections of *Titus Andronicus* based on printed copy and began typesetting *Romeo and Juliet* while, to speed up the process, the more experienced compositors worked on other plays concurrently, completing *Coriolanus*, *Julius Caesar*, *Macbeth* and starting on

Hamlet. Compositor B needed all the patience he could muster, for Leason proved to be a less than skilled workman. Every time the older compositor or another pressworker left their posts to oversee the progress of the apprentice's formes through the press, they noticed that his typesetting revealed a high volume of errors that had to be corrected during the printing process. An analysis of the number of changes that were made to the texts as part of stop-press corrections indicates that Leason made forty times as many errors as Compositor B. More precisely, across fifty altered pages of the Folio text he made some three hundred mistakes, while Compositor B made only thirty-nine, most of these of a smaller, less significant, nature, across just seventeen corrected pages.

Despite this, the compositors were powering through more formes than they otherwise would have been able to manage without Leason's help. At this point the Jaggards intended to include *Troilus and Cressida* as the next play after *Romeo and Juliet*. Leason was briefly diverted from his work on the latter play and Compositor B turned his attention from *Hamlet*, so that apprentice and mentor could pair up for the typesetting of *Troilus and Cressida*. Then something unexpected happened. Work on this play was dropped. It may have been because the Folio syndicate had not yet secured the rights to print it from Henry Walley, or they had come only to a preliminary agreement and banked on his not offering any resistance. Whatever the cause, Walley called a halt to the printing of his play, throwing the press team into confusion.

At least the Folio syndicate had resolved whatever problems they had with *Henry VIII*, for around this time, in the middle of the typesetting of *Hamlet* to be more precise, they were able to instruct the compositors to complete that long-deferred history play, as well as the final three and a half pages of *Richard III*, with a new compositor assigned to help the ever-efficient Compositor B with the former play. That done, there was still no sign of Walley agreeing terms with the Folio's backers, so the Jaggards needed to

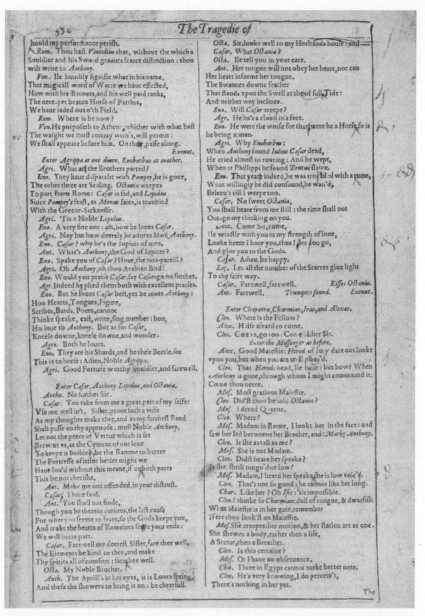

A page from *Antony and Cleopatra* showing the numerous errors that had been identified and marked as needing to be rectified during the printing. Many more such errors were incorporated into the initial printing of pages from the First Folio due to the lack of experience of an apprentice compositor named John Leason, also known as Compositor E, who had joined the team working on Shakespeare's Book during the printing of the tragedies.

Should my performance perish.

　Rom. Thou haſt *Ventidius* that, without the which a
Souldier and his Sword graunts ſcarce diſtinction : thou
wilt write to *Anthony.*

　Ven. Ile humbly ſignifie what in his name,
That magicall word of Warre we haue effected,
How with his Banners,and his well paid ranks,
The nere-yet beaten Horſe of Parthia,
We haue iaded out o'th Field.

　Rom. Where is he now ?

　Ven. He purpoſeth to Athens,whither with what haſt
The waight we muſt conuay with's,will permit :
We ſhall appeare before him. On there,paſſe along.

Exeunt.

Enter Agrippa at one doore, Enobarbus at another.

　Agri. What are the Brethers parted?

　Eno. They haue diſpatcht with *Pompey*,he is gone,
The other three are Sealing. *Octauia* weepes
To part from Rome: *Cæſar* is ſad,and *Lepidus*
Since *Pompey's* feaſt, as *Menas* ſaies,is troubled
With the Greene-Sickneſſe.

　Agri. 'Tis a Noble *Lepidus.*

　Eno. A very fine one: oh,how he loues *Cæſar.*

　Agri. Nay but how deerely he adores *Mark Anthony.*

　Eno. *Cæſar* ? why he's the Iupiter of men.

　Ant. What's *Anthony,*the God of Iupiter ?

　Eno. Spake you of *Cæſar* ? How,the non-pareill ?

　Agri. Oh *Anthony,*oh thou Arabian Bird!

　Eno. Would you praiſe *Cæſar,*ſay *Cæſango* no further.

　Agr. Indeed he plied them both with excellent praiſes.

　Eno. But he loues *Cæſar* beſt,yet he loues *Anthony* :
Hoo,Hearts,Tongues,Figure,
Scribes,Bards,Poets,cannot
Thinke ſpeake, caſt,write,ſing,number: hoo,
His loue to *Anthony.* But as for *Cæſar,*
Kneele downe,kneele downe,and wonder.

　Agri. Both he loues.

　Eno. They are his Shards,and he their Beetle,ſo:
This is to horſe : Adieu,Noble *Agrippa.*

　Agri. Good Fortune worthy Souldier,and farewell.

Enter Cæſar,Anthony,Lepidus,and Octauia.

　Antho. No further Sir.

　Cæſar. You take from me a great part of my ſelfe:
Vſe me well in't. Siſter,proue ſuch a wife
As my thoughts make thee,and as my fartheſt Band
Shall paſſe on thy approoſe : moſt Noble *Anthony,*
Let not the peece of Vertue which is ſet
Betwixt vs,as the Cyment of our loue
To keepe it builded,be the Ramme to batter
The Fortreſſe of it:for better might we
Haue lou'd without this meane,if onboth parts
This be not cheriſht.

　Ant. Make me not offended,in your diſtruſt.

　Cæſar. I haue ſaid.

　Ant. You ſhall not finde,
Though you be therein curious,the leſt cauſe
For what you ſeeme to feare,ſo the Gods keepe you,
And make the hearts of Romaines ſerue your ends :
We will heere part.

　Cæſar. Farewell my deereſt Siſter,fare thee well,
The Elements be kind to thee,and make
Thy ſpirits all of comfort : fare thee well.

　Octa. My Noble Brother.

　Anth. The Aprill's in her eyes, it is Loues ſpring,
And theſe the ſhowers to bring it on : be cheerfull.

　Octa. Sir,looke well to my Husbands houſe : and
　Cæſar. What *Octauia* ?

　Octa. Ile tell you in your eare.

　Ant. Her tongue will not obey her heart,nor can
Her heart informe her tougue.
The Swannes downe feather
That ſtands vpon the Swell at the full of Tide:
And neither way inclines.

　Eno. Will *Cæſar* weepe?

　Agr. He ha's a cloud in's face.

　Eno. He were the worſe for that were he a Horſe,ſo is
he being a man.

　Agri. Why *Enobarbus* :
When *Anthony* found *Iulius Cæſar* dead,
He cried almoſt to roaring : And he wept,
When at Phillippi he found *Brutus* ſlaine.

　Eno. That yeare indeed,he was trobled with a rheume,
What willingly he did confound,he wail'd,
Beleeu't till I weepe too.

　Cæſar. No ſweet *Octauia,*
You ſhall heare from me ſtill : the time ſhall not
Out-go my thinking on you.

　Ant. Come Sir,come,
Ile wraſtle with you in my ſtrength of loue,
Looke heere I haue you,thus I let you go,
And giue you to the Gods.

　Cæſar. Adieu,be happy.

　Lep. Let all the number of the Starres giue light
To thy faire way.

　Cæſar. Farewell,farewell.　*Kiſſes Octauia.*

　Ant. Farewell.　*Trumpets ſound.*　*Exeunt.*

Enter Cleopatra,Charmian,Iras,and Alexas.

　Cleo. Where is the Fellow ?

　Alex. Halfe afeard to come.

　Cleo. Go too,go too : Come hither Sir.

Enter the Meſſenger as before.

　Alex. Good Maieſtie : *Herod* of Iury dare not looke
vpon you,but when you are well-pleaſ'd.

　Cleo. That *Herods* head,Ile haue : but how? When
Anthony is gone,through whom I might commaund it:
Come thou neere.

　Meſ. Moſt gracious Maieſtie.

　Cleo. Did'ſt thou behold *Octauia* ?

　Meſ. I dread Queene.

　Cleo. Where?

　Meſ. Madam in Rome, I lookt her in the face : and
ſaw her led betweene her Brother, and *Marke Anthony.*

　Cleo. Is ſhe as tall as me ?

　Meſ. She is not Madam.

　Cleo. Didſt heare her ſpeake ?
Is ſhe ſhrill tongu'd or low ?

　Meſ. Madam,I heard her ſpeake,ſhe is low voic'd.

　Cleo. That's not ſo good : he cannot like her long.

　Char. Like her ? Oh *Iſis* : 'tis impoſſible.

　Cleo. I thinke ſo *Charmian:* dull of tongue, & dwarfiſh
What Maieſtie is in her gate,remember
If ere thou look'ſt on Maieſtie.

　Meſ. She creepes:her motion,& her ſtation are as one :
She ſhewes a body,rather then a life,
A Statue,then a Breather.

　Cleo. Is this certaine ?

　Meſ. Or I haue no obſeruance.

　Cha. Three in Egypt cannot make better note.

　Cleo. He's very knowing,I do perceiu't,
There's nothing in her yet.

The

buy more time. In the interim, Leason was told to complete *Romeo and Juliet* and then asked to help with the typesetting of *Hamlet* and *King Lear*. As they progressed, however, hopes of resolving the stalemate with Walley began to fade. The Folio syndicate came up with an alternative plan. They would fill the space left by *Troilus and Cressida* with another play, cancelling out the first pages of *Troilus* already printed. This also meant reprinting the final page of *Romeo and Juliet*, which had the first page of *Troilus* printed on its reverse side. But what to fill the space with?

It is possible that *Timon of Athens*, which was printed for the first time in the First Folio, may not have survived had this problem not occurred. The play had probably been co-authored with Thomas Middleton and so may have been less favoured by the King's Men for inclusion in the collection. But since the syndicate could not print *Troilus and Cressida* they almost certainly asked the King's Men to give them another Shakespeare play in their possession. The path of least resistance was for Heminges and Condell to dig out a work from the King's Men's archive that had not been issued in quarto before, meaning they could print it quickly without having to negotiate over rights with another stationer. The whole affair took about three weeks to resolve, and when the compositors did finally get a copy of *Timon of Athens*, Leason may well have looked at the manuscript in dismay and been relieved when Compositor B informed him that he would not be permitted to go near it. Instead, while the senior compositor took on *Timon of Athens*, padding out the final page with a widely spaced list of characters because the play was shorter than the work it was replacing, the apprentice was assigned the task of completing *King Lear*. Leason's lack of experience meant he made numerous errors that others in the pressroom had to root out and correct, and his mentor is likely to have regretted entrusting him with the last page of *Lear*, for he omitted to add a decorative woodblock-printed tailpiece to it, an elaborate carving of a mythical satyr, which Compositor B more consistently added to the final pages of plays when there was space to fill. What else could Leason's supervisor do but remain good-natured in the face of the apprentice's youthful mishaps as he learned the ropes? He too was once a novice like his student.

Meanwhile, on 17 July William Jaggard's nephew, John Jaggard junior, visited Stationers' Hall to request the transfer to himself of the fifty-pound loan his father, John Jaggard senior, had secured the previous year with the aid of Edward Mabbe, the St Dunstan's-based goldsmith. This was a sad moment for young John, who had only recently received his freedom of the Stationers' Company in 1620, because he was requesting the loan 'from three years from the day his father had it' as a consequence of the elder John's recent death. The management of the latter's shop, the Hand and Star near St Dunstan's Church, would be taken over by his wife Elizabeth Jaggard, née Mabb. William Jaggard, who had frequently collaborated with this business, would no longer see his beloved brother there, adding personal grief to the pressures of his printing work. After John senior's passing, John junior and Edward Mabbe became joint guarantors for Elizabeth's other sons. While a direct connection between Elizabeth Mabb and James Mabbe of the First Folio cannot be proved, some kind of kinship is a strong possibility, given that Ralph Mabbe was a stationer and Elizabeth married into something of a publishing dynasty. Interestingly, in the Stationers' Loan book, on the same page as the record for John senior's original loan, backed by Edward Mabbe, is a sum for the same amount paid to Ralph Mabbe 'Citizen and Stationer of London'.

Despite the Jaggards' private struggles at this time, the printing of the First Folio had to continue. At least the syndicate had averted a crisis of a more business-oriented nature by resolving to do without *Troilus and Cressida*. The Jaggards pushed on with the next play, *Othello*, with the help of Leason who was allowed to typeset a first page at long last, closely supervised by the heroic

Compositor B. It has been argued that at this point Leason's interventions proved too taxing and costly for the Folio's devisers and he was thenceforth removed from the project. This has been challenged by more recent scholarship which maintains that the rest of the typesetting of Shakespeare's Book was a two-hander: with *Othello*, *Antony and Cleopatra* and *Cymbeline* primarily the work of Compositor B, using young Leason as his helper, who was even allowed to try his hand at setting from manuscript copy again, with a trial from *Antony and Cleopatra*. If this is true, he failed the test a second time, because his hand is less in evidence on this tragedy and *Cymbeline*.

Othello took the press team to around the middle of August, when the printing of the next play, *Antony and Cleopatra*, was interrupted. In fact work on the Folio seems to have stopped altogether for a short period, perhaps for two reasons. The syndicate were unsure about the ownership of the rights to this latter play. As it had not been printed in a quarto edition before, the King's Men may have assumed they were in possession of the rights, either unaware or simply having forgotten that it was in fact Edward Blount who had secured a licence to print the play in 1608. Blount himself seems not to have remembered he had done this and the true status of the play would not be determined until November. The Jaggards also had some pressing 'job work' at this time, including a 'Heralds' Visitation Summons', which ordered named individuals claiming to be titled members of the gentry to appear before representatives of the College of Heralds with evidence confirming their nobility. This was dated 5 August, and because it shared type from a case used in the setting of *Othello*, it is clear that this play was being worked on at roughly this time.

During this period the King's Men lost a vital living link to Shakespeare. Just a day after the 'Visitation Summons' was formally declared, on 6 August, Anne Hathaway Shakespeare died at the age of sixty-seven. She was interred two days later in a freshly renovated chancel, close to her husband, in Holy Trinity Church. Her epitaph, ventriloquised by her daughter Susanna, is a testament to her nurturing role, but elides the importance of her labours as the manager of a large and productive household and the overseer of the family's financial interests and malt-making business while her husband was away building his career in London, as well as subsequently after his death:

> You, mother, gave me milk and life with your breasts,
>> Woe is me, for such great gifts will I give stones?
> How I would prefer the good angel remove this seal-stone from
>> the tomb-mouth!
>> So that your shade may escape, like Christ's body!
> But prayers do not prevail – come soon, Christ! That rising,
>> Though locked in the sepulchre, my mother may ascend and
>> pursue the stars.

Some scholars have challenged John Heminges' descent from George Heminges of Droitwich, arguing that the Heminges family may have hailed from Anne's native Shottery, and that the theatre manager was in fact born in that Warwickshire village around 1556. A John Hemynge witnessed the will of Anne's father, Richard Hathaway, in 1581. We may never know if the John Heminges of Shottery, who christened seven children in Stratford-upon-Avon's Holy Trinity Church between 1563 and 1582, including a John Heminges junior, is connected to the John Heminges of the King's Men. But it is notable that the troupe mounted *The Winter's Tale* during the first winter season at court after Anne's death, performing it at Whitehall on 18 January 1624. The play presents a striking image of monumentalised motherhood, with the apparent death and resurrection of Hermione, who is disguised as a memorial statue only to be wondrously reanimated at the close of the play. Hermione and her husband Leontes lose an infant son, Mamillius, who is not revived at the end. The heart-breakingly unresolved nature of his passing may have recalled the death of Anne and Shakespeare's own son Hamnet at the age of just eleven.

It is possible that Anne's death had caused the King's Men to report the prompt book of the play as missing in 1623, though there is no knowing how long it had been lost. On 19 August, it was relicensed on condition that Heminges confirm that there would be no changes made to it that would introduce profanities or blasphemies of any kind. Was the court performance of this play a tribute to the wife of a close friend, William Shakespeare, by his former colleagues and collaborators, or was it for Heminges a testament to an even more personal connection, a kinship with the Hathaways of Shottery?

The Winter's Tale was relicensed by a new Master of the Revels. 'It pleased the King at my Lord Chamberlain's motion to send for me unto his bedchamber,' wrote a jubilant Sir Henry Herbert on 7 August 1623, the day after Anne Shakespeare's death, 'and to knight me [at Wilton House] … and to receive me as Master of his Revels.' While repeated attempts had been made since 1617, possibly by agents of Villiers, to remove Sir William Herbert from his Lord Chamberlainship and to wrest the Revels Office from his control, he had been working behind the scenes to thwart these schemes. This included pulling the necessary strings to ensure that Henry Herbert could buy out the office of Master of the Revels from his predecessor Sir John Astley. It was a triumph for Pembroke and the King's Men, for Henry was not only brother to the famed poets George Herbert and Lord Herbert of Cherbury, he was William Herbert's kinsman. There was also still the possibility that, should all else fail, Ben Jonson could become Master of the Revels. He remained next in line should Henry Herbert die or be expelled from office. Little over three and a half months or so ahead of the publication of the First Folio, the future of the Revels Office seemed to be assured under the benevolent jurisdiction of a family that had long favoured Shakespeare and the King's Men.

This would have been a bittersweet time for Heminges and Condell. The death of Anne Shakespeare, the raking up of the earth around her husband's own grave when she was interred beside him, could only have stirred up recollections of the relationships that formed the backdrops to the high points in the actor-managers' careers. At the same time, the King's Men could look forward, with some relief, to a stable future association with the offices which mattered most to their profession: those of the Revels and the Lord Chamberlain. If this did influence the decision to dedicate the volume to the 'Incomparable pair of brethren', William and Philip Herbert, this is only part of the story; for there were, as we will see, other valid reasons for the choice of patrons for Shakespeare's Book.

16

'The Graver had a strife'

Portraying Shakespeare Through National Crisis

In the summer of 1623 the Spanish ambassador, Don Carlos Coloma, was being entertained in London by King James's ministers. He could have his choice of amusements. The city's theatres were once again cashing in on the interest in all things Spanish. Some time on or after 9 July at the Cockpit Theatre, the Lady Elizabeth's Men were playing *The Spanish Gypsy*, by a power-house collaborative writing team consisting of Thomas Dekker, John Ford, Thomas Middleton and William Rowley. It may have seemed topical given its Spanish-framed dramatisation of Don Roderigo's dastardly scheme to raid the family home of Don Pedro des Cortes and carry away his daughter Clara; regaling audiences even as Prince Charles was on his own mission to bring home his not-so-willing bride. The King's Men, not to be outdone, may have been playing *A Very Woman*, later retitled *A Spanish Lady*, which, somewhat relevantly, was set in Spanish-ruled Sicily.

The ambassador was not interested in these plays. He was 'much delighted in bear baiting' and preferred to visit Paris Garden, in St Saviour's parish in Southwark, instead, 'where they showed him all the pleasure they could both with bull, bear and horse, besides jackanapes'. They even threw a poor white bear into the Thames and cast savage dogs in after it, which 'baited him swimming'. The English king's ministers may well have regarded their Spanish guest with lumps in their throats. As the hounds bit and tore the drowning bear the ambassador cheered; for him, this 'was the best sport of all'.

To Londoners, awaiting the arrival of their new princess from a faraway nation, it must have seemed as if the Spanish Match had cast a strange spell over the land. That July a caravan of camels and an elephant were seen parading through the city; gifts from the king of Spain. An attempt was made to convey them through the town after midnight but they 'could not yet pass unseen', their bulky forms casting monstrous shadows against the walls and beamed frontages of the city's buildings, and drawing the wonder of the inhabitants who had never before seen such chimerical-seeming creatures. When a severe thunderstorm wrecked one of the ships carrying victuals for the king's fleet, tearing down its mast and causing the deaths of a man and two women who were 'struck dead' by lightning, it must have seemed as if God had cursed the union. Indeed, news had reached England that Prince Charles was still prevented from speaking to or even seeing the Infanta and was beginning to tire of waiting for permission from the Pope and Philip IV to escort her to England. As John Chamberlain commented, 'the Spanish delays are like to wear out his patience as well as ours', and there was always the danger that he could be prevailed upon by King Philip's 'cunning' priests and theologians to convert. Even the Pope had written to Charles in hopes of winning him over to the Catholic faith.

The anti-Spanish gossips of the English court revelled in the image of a despairing prince who 'wishes to be at home'. Endymion Porter, on the other hand, had better news for James I, writing to tell him the deal was as good as done, since 'the prince concluded the business himself with the king, so that it is now finished'. The

Infanta was expected 'to be delivered' the following March. Within days it was announced that 'the match was to be published' and the Infanta 'proclaimed Princes of Great Britain'. In Spain there was 'great applause and rejoicing', for it was thought Prince Charles's conversion was imminent. In England, on 20 July, James I took centre-stage in an elaborate ceremony in which he swore to the articles of the Anglo-Spanish marriage treaty. The Earl of Pembroke did not attend, sending his brother Philip, the Earl of Montgomery, in his place and claiming he was being kept away by ill health. By the end of August there was a general sense that the king was moving forward with a more 'public toleration' of Catholics.

The King's Men were taking the temperature of the court and knew what they had to do. They began preparing another strongly Spanish-inspired play, *The Maid of the Mill*, licensed for performance at the end of August and initially to be performed at the Globe. For this William Rowley, who had been part of the writing team for *The Spanish Gypsy* (performed by rival company the Lady Elizabeth's Men) that had premiered the month before, collaborated with John Fletcher. The story was palpably topical, a tale of young love set in Spain, in which the concluding wedding of the enamoured pair ended the feuding between two rival families. The production was clearly a hit with the English royal family, for it would be performed in the evening of Monday 29 September at Hampton Court, and again at St James's Palace on 1 November, All Hallows' Night. This play, like *The Spanish Curate*, another King's Men play performed the previous year, was based in part on Leonard Digges's translation of *Gerardo the Unfortunate Spaniard*. The underpinning presence of this work, part of Edward Blount's programme of bringing lesser-known Spanish texts to the attention of England's literati, demonstrated once again the King's Men's engagement with trends fuelled by their royal patron's foreign policy.

The King's Men and the First Folio syndicate were, at least on the surface, moving in the antithetical direction to Sir William Herbert. One gossip stated that the earl's fortunes were rapidly declining for he was 'not settled in the king's good opinion, as he was against the Spanish Match, and divers times it was reported that he was put forth of his place [as Lord Chamberlain] and that [Sir John Digby, the Earl of] Bristol should be his successor'. Pembroke continued to pursue the Protestant cause, keeping up a correspondence with James's daughter, Elizabeth, queen of Bohemia, expressing 'my zeal to her service and love to her' and his hopes for the restoration of the Palatinate, but urging her not to attempt to come to England. 'Nothing under heaven can be so dangerous unto her,' he wrote, for the country was now, in his estimation, too hospitable to Catholics.

Meanwhile, after a break in the printing of the First Folio, Compositor B, probably with the help of his apprentice Leason, resumed work on *Antony and Cleopatra* and *Cymbeline*, believing that they had left the unrest caused by the abandoned typesetting of *Troilus and Cressida* behind them. They returned to a slower, more linear, way of working through most of the quires of these plays, possibly finishing some time by the end of October.

In positioning *Cymbeline* at the end of the volume they were not only realising what must have been a deliberate marketing strategy by the First Folio syndicate: starting and ending each of the book's three main play sections with works that had never before been printed. They were also, in all likelihood, conforming to a design intended to imprint, quite literally, within its pages support for James I's treasured Spanish project. *The Tempest* may have been placed as the headline work because, as one scholar aptly put it, the play exemplified 'conflict resolution through dynastic marriage', which was highly pertinent to the Spanish Match. Closing the sequence of tragedies with *Cymbeline* created a potent narrative arc across the whole volume, resolving on a play which staged an accord between two ancient powers, Britain and Rome, in a manner that must have recalled James I's vision for a grand Anglo-Spanish union. For its earliest audiences, Rome was the very seat – the throne – of Catholic authority. The Folio could therefore have deliberately been book-ended with plays whose arrangement conveyed an ostentatious political message, one in step with the king's ambitions, the drama of which was unfolding around the players and the syndicate even as Shakespeare's Book was in production.

At the end of *Cymbeline* William Jaggard is named as one of the chief backers of the operation, so he must have been alive when the final page of that play was printed. By 4 November he was dead, having been succeeded by his son as official printer to the City of London, and recorded as Isaac's 'late father deceased'. His will was proved on 16 November. He was probably around fifty-six years old at his death. This tragedy probably necessitated at least a brief pause in the printing, so that his son Isaac, Edward Blount, William Aspley, John Smethwick and possibly the pressworkers who were working on the First Folio, could attend the funeral.

It seems fitting that one of the earliest Shakespeare Folios to be gifted was sent from William Jaggard to Augustine Vincent, whose *Discovery of Errors* had, in 1622, provided the platform from which William had defended himself against Ralph Brooke. For the

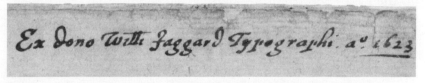

The Folio catalogued as Folger Shakespeare Library First Folio 1 bears a poignant inscription which indicates that William Jaggard had intended this book to be a gift for Augustine Vincent, possibly to thank him for his role in helping Jaggard defend himself during his acrimonious feud with Ralph Brooke while the First Folio was being printed. It was sent to Vincent after Jaggard's death.

publisher, the matter was a very personal one. This Folio survives in the Folger Shakespeare Library in Washington and contains an inscription by Vincent that reads 'Ex dono Willi Jaggard Typographi, an[no] 1623' ('A gift from William Jaggard, printer, in the year 1623'). It adds a note of poignancy to the history of Shakespeare's Book that one of the first printed copies was gifted from beyond the grave by one of its chief backers.

On 8 November, just a few days after William's death, Isaac Jaggard and Edward Blount walked to Stationers' Hall on Paternoster Row to log their rights to print sixteen of 'Master William Shakespeare's Comedies, Histories, and Tragedies', claiming a licence for 'so many of the said Copies as are not formerly entered to other men'. It was during a search of the Stationers' archives as part of this request that they discovered that Blount already owned the rights to *Antony and Cleopatra* and that Isaac had inherited from his father the licence to print *As You Like It*, which William Jaggard had probably acquired when he took over James Roberts' shop in 1606. Blount and Jaggard therefore paid seven shillings, the price for registering fourteen of the plays for the Folio.

With *Cymbeline* finished, and Isaac adjusting to life as the sole owner and head operator of the Half-Eagle and Key, it was time to print the preliminary pages. These form an initial quire of three sheets, two of which are numbered with signatures, a fourth unpaginated sheet and a single title-page leaf, featuring Shakespeare's portrait. The three paginated sheets comprise Ben Jonson's address 'To the Reader' and the 'Catalogue' which serves as a contents page; Heminges and Condell's dedication to the Herbert brothers and Hugh Holland's memorial poem; and Heminges and Condell's epistle to the 'great Variety of Readers' and Ben Jonson's poem commemorating Shakespeare. The additional unpaginated sheet includes the memorial verses of Leonard Digges and James Mabbe on the same page and the list of 'Principal Actors in all the Plays'. The lack of clear pagination for all the preliminaries' pages meant that they could be bound together in different ways, and so the order in which they appear in surviving Folios varies.

The title page of the First Folio was most likely completed after William Jaggard's death, as its imprint records that the volume was 'Printed by Isaac Jaggard, and Ed. Blount'. Today this page has an iconic status as the transmitter of the most authoritative portrait of Shakespeare in existence. Incorporating the portrait of an author on the title page of their book was a relatively new and bold thing to do at the time, so the backers wanted to emphasise the personality behind the works. The Ben Jonson folio of his *Works* had been published in 1616 with a title page that presented its textual matter within an elaborate architectural surround, adorned with allegorical figures. This same format was used for James I's *Works* that year. The First Folio's title page is starker, dispensing with symbolic intricacies and heavy decoration. It makes a bold statement by placing the book's textual material above and below an attention-grabbing, eye-pulling central portrait of Shakespeare who stares fearlessly back at the reader.

A costly and time-consuming hybrid method was employed in the creation of the title page. Shakespeare's portrait was printed from a copper plate engraving, which allowed for more detail and precision than a cheaper woodblock carving and was a marker of refinement and sophistication. In order to produce the title page, two techniques and two different kinds of press were needed. First the lettering had to be printed on the more common letter-press, the same kind used for the Folio's plays, with space left for the inclusion of the portrait, while a commissioned engraver set to work producing Shakespeare's portrait on copper, perhaps copied from an existing painted portrait. This was probably done in the workshop of the artist Martin Droeshout. After the portrait had been etched into a copper plate using a method known as *intaglio*, from the Italian meaning 'to cut in', it was heated to make the markings more yielding to the ink with which it was then coated

Painting of a sermon preached at St Paul's Cross, by John Gipkyn, 1616. Inflammatory lectures were sometimes delivered from the Cross, providing commentary on topical issues and political crises. The bookshops of Edward Blount and William Aspley (two investors in the First Folio project) stood just paces away from this preaching stand, which formed a kind of public theatre at the heart of London's bookselling hub.

A virtual recreation of St Paul's Cross Churchyard, constructed by Joshua Stephens and rendered by Jordan Gray, showing the Paul's Cross preaching stand and surrounding buildings. The churchyard was one of the primary centres of London's book trade, and was home to many bookshops, including numerous businesses owned by stationer-publishers who held the rights to works by William Shakespeare.

Another view of St Paul's Cross Churchyard, constructed by Joshua Stephens and rendered by Jordan Gray. This would not have been unlike the scene that Edward Blount and William Aspley saw from their neighbouring shopfronts. St Paul's Cathedral and its surrounding precinct was also a hotspot for gossip, and Edward Blount used his shop there as a centre of operations from which to trade in other goods (such as seeds, nuts, fruit and even treacle), as well as in news and political information that he sent to his international ambassadorial networks.

Engraving of St Dunstan's in the West in 1737, by Robert West. It was here that John Smethwick, one of the members of the First Folio syndicate, operated a shop located beneath the church's clocktower. William Jaggard, who printed the First Folio with his son Isaac from a printing shop in London's Barbican, was trained as a stationer in the St Dunstan's area and had collaborated with his brother John Jaggard who ran a bookshop and printing house in Fleet Street, close to St Dunstan's.

Coloured engraving of St Dunstan's in the West in 1811. William Jaggard and Henry Condell both owned properties in Fleet Street, close to John Smethwick's own business.

Replica of the first printing press by Gutenberg, held at the Printing Museum in California, USA.

Engraving of a printing press from the sixteenth century, showing 'compositors' at their cases in the background, engaged in the process of typesetting 'formes', and an 'inker' in the foreground coating print-ready 'formes' with an even layer of ink.

Page from the Stationers' Company Archive, London, SCA Liber D, f. 69. Edward Blount and Isaac Jaggard visited the Stationers' Hall at the intersection of Ave Maria Lane and Paternoster Row, just behind the bookshops of Blount and William Aspley in St Paul's Cross Churchyard, to enter sixteen previously unpublished Shakespeare plays in the Stationers' Register on 8 November 1623. This secured the rights of the syndicate to publish these works in the First Folio.

A wonderful example of seventeenth-century brown calf-skin binding. This is the cover and spine of Shakespeare Folger Library First Folio 16; a volume once owned by an early editor of William Shakespeare's works named Sir Thomas Hanmer, in whose possession it had been from about 1700.

Folger Shakespeare Library First Folio 10 still has its original seventeenth-century cover, and is bound in dark brown calf-skin, though it has a nineteenth-century re-backed spine. It once belonged to the antiquarian Ralph Sheldon, who may have purchased it in 1623 or shortly after. Sheldon's Coat of Arms is emblazoned in glistening gold leaf on the cover. The Sheldon family lived close to William Shakespeare's native Stratford-upon-Avon.

The First Folio's iconic title-page portrait of William Shakespeare was produced in at least three known versions. The makers of the First Folio clearly cared about the way Shakespeare was presented and wanted to get his likeness right. The portrait on the left is from the first version of the title page, while that on the right is from the third. In the original image Shakespeare's head seems to float above the collar, rather like a mask. In subsequent versions, more shading was added to the chin and around the jawline, anchoring the head to the body in a more natural way.

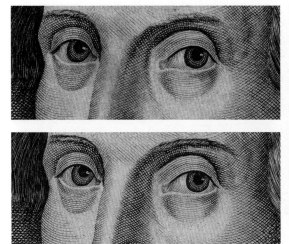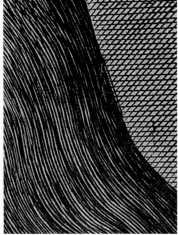

Streaks were also added to the eyes (in the bottom left image) to give them a livelier sparkle, while a single strand of protruding hair was engraved in the third version of the portrait, perhaps to make Shakespeare's head feel less static.

William Shakespeare's wall monument in Holy Trinity Church, Stratford-upon-Avon.

in an even layer. Once enough ink had collected in the cuts and grooves of the plate, the surface was wiped repeatedly until only the carved lines remained dyed. With the pre-printed paper (containing the Folio's title and imprint) having been sent to a specialist press, perhaps attached to Droeshout's workshop or a press with which he had a close working relationship, each page was moistened and placed atop the inked-over plate, covered with soft blankets and then run through a 'rolling press' of two heavy cylinders, controlled through a lever system. The pressure of the cylinders compressed the inked recessed grooves of the engraved image onto the paper. Once the required number of title pages had been printed, the batch was sent back to Isaac Jaggard's printing house for incorporation into the Folio. The whole process was labour-intensive and expensive, but the effect was worth it.

An engraver's shop, showing the use of a rolling press to print an engraved image, derived from an image by Jan van der Straet, dated 1580–1605. This was the kind of press which created the iconic portrait of William Shakespeare on the title page of the First Folio.

It is not clear who commissioned the First Folio's portrait of Shakespeare. Was Ben Jonson entrusted with the task of finding a suitable engraver? He has been identified by some Shakespeare scholars as the mastermind behind the preliminaries, responsible for bringing the commemorative poets together, partly because there are striking similarities between some of his writings and Heminges and Condell's letter to the 'great Variety of Readers'. The senior King's Men members give licence to the volume's readers to 'censure' it as they see fit, but with the proviso that they 'buy first' and 'Judge your six-pence worth, your shillings worth, your five shillings worth at a time, or higher, so you rise to the just rates, and welcome. But, whatever you do, Buy.' In his own preface to *Bartholomew Fair*, Jonson had similarly accorded all spectators of the play 'their freewill of censure', each having the right 'to judge his six pence worth, his twelve pence worth, so to his eighteen pence, two shillings, half a crown, to the value of his place'. Some believe, therefore, that Jonson penned the Folio's epistles signed by Heminges and Condell. Coincidentally or not, Jonson was at exactly this time engaged with the official processes of legal 'censure', for on 20 October 1623 he was called as a witness in a legal case over disputed parts of the estate of the late Sir Walter Ralegh, so if he was the Folio epistles' author, he may have recalled his earlier impressions of public judgement in print. However, such conceits were fairly commonplace in the period or might simply indicate Heminges and Condell's knowledge and emulation of Jonson's work. What we do know is that Jonson was seen as the best authority to confirm the authenticity of the playwright's likeness, for his own poem (one of two he contributed to the Folio's preliminary matter) sits opposite Shakespeare's face and provides its own 'censure' of the portrait:

This Figure, that thou here seest put,
   It was for gentle Shakespeare cut:
Wherein the Graver had a strife
   With Nature, to outdo the life:
O, could he but have drawn his wit
   As well in brass, as he hath hit
His face, the Print would then surpass
   All, that was ever writ in brass,
But, since he cannot, Reader, look
   Not on his Picture, but his Book.

Jonson's poem confirms the stately gravitas of the portrait; its evocation of monumental brass or tomb-sculpture engraving. Not for the backers of the Folio the heavily adorned style of title page that Jonson chose for his own *Works*, dripping with ornament and allegorical flourishes. Shakespeare's face, in contrast, is presented without adornment, his eyes staring almost confrontationally at the viewer: the man whose works were watched by thousands watching the watchers. The simplicity of the portrait recalls the monumental bust of the dramatist, close to his grave in the chancel of Stratford-upon-Avon's Holy Trinity Church. But that simplicity belies the fact that the portrait's sitter is wearing the attire of a gentleman, a doublet embellished with 'metal braid decoration' and 'flat band' collar. While this was more fashionable earlier in the seventeenth century than it was in 1623, a sign perhaps that Martin Droeshout had been copying from a portrait produced during Shakespeare's lifetime, the gentility the portrait exudes mirrors the work's title, 'M[aste]r William Shakespeare's Comedies, Histories and Tragedies', with its emphasis on the playwright's gentleman status designated by the word 'Master'.

Some critics have complained that the portrait 'has little technical merit' and that its deviser had 'much to learn about engraving'. However, Droeshout clearly cared about the quality of

Shakespeare's likeness. The portrait had, in fact, undergone more than one revision during the Folio's printing and exists in at least three versions or 'states'. When it was first printed the head was not satisfactorily connected to the body, but seemed to float spectrally above it like a death mask. To resolve this the engraver added shading under and around the chin, to give the sitter's head more weight. But then something else caught the attention, either of Droeshout, one of the Folio syndicate members, or of Heminges and Condell: where was the life, the sparkle, the waggish mischievousness that should have darted from Shakespeare's eyes? The engraver had certainly, as Jonson indicated, failed to capture the playwright's living 'wit'. The eyes looked dull and soulless. Highlights were duly added to the pupils, giving them the shimmering alertness they had lacked. Some further tinkering with the portrait added a single escaping strand of hair, perhaps because it was felt the image looked a little too static.

But who was this engraver and was he an inexperienced artist? The portrait is signed 'Martinus Droeshout: Sculpsit London', indicating that he executed the work in London. There are in fact two contenders for the hand behind the famous head. One is Martin Droeshout the younger. Born in London in 1601, he was aged around twenty-two when the Folio was completed, so he could not have known Shakespeare as an adult. The other is his uncle, Martin Droeshout the elder. Son of the painter John Droeshout, he was born in Brussels and is identified in some records as having worked as a limner or painter, who became a freeman of the Painter-Stainers' Company. There has been some disagreement as to which of the two was responsible for the portrait. A recent discovery of engravings and prints signed by a Martin Droeshout in the Biblioteca Nacional in Madrid, however, indicates that the artist behind these is more likely to have been the engraver behind the Folio's portrait, for they disclose some notable affinities. Among them is the portrait engraving of the priest and author Francisco de la Peña, poised quill in hand at his writing desk, which has been identified as being rendered with 'the same crude hand of the engraver [of the First Folio's portrait] who was never to master the representation of halftones'. This was one of a series of Spanish commissions for the younger Droeshout, which included some unmistakable 'Catholic' works such as the portrait of Don Gaspar de Guzmán, a leading figure in the Spanish Counter-Reformation. The elder Martin was a committed Protestant, and a member of the strongly reformist Dutch Church in Austin Friars, London. The younger Martin, however, emigrated to Spain some time between 1632 and 1635 and must have been Catholic. The last of the London-based works bearing his name was produced on the earlier date, while the latter represents the year in which the first Madrid engravings were executed. He may have continued working in Spain till at least 1644. Could he have been one of Jonson's friends, acquired through his Catholic networks? A 'returns of strangers', that is immigrants, living in Aldgate, ordered on 15 October and completed by 12 November 1635, indicates that 'Martin Drussett [Droeshout] Limner, born in Brussels ... hath lived here 30 years'. This refers to the elder Martin and makes it less likely that he was responsible for the Spanish engravings that share some uncanny similarities with the First Folio's title page.

This tallies with the First Folio's strong Spanish connotations. It is reasonable to assume that the Shakespeare portrait engraving and commemorative poems were commissioned some time ahead of the printing of the preliminaries, probably during the very period in which the Infanta Maria's arrival in England, as bride to Prince Charles, was believed to be imminent, with an unprecedented toleration for Catholics expected. So it is no surprise to find in the Folio's opening pages the work of an engraver who would soon emigrate to Spain, standing as a metaphorical window into a hallowed circle of hispanophile scholar-poets, mediated by

Engraved portrait of Francisco de la Peña by Martin Droeshout the younger, in the Biblioteca Nacional de España. This Martin Droeshout is likely to have been the engraver of William Shakespeare's title-page portrait in the First Folio. The similarities between this image and Shakespeare's portrait are striking.

Ben Jonson who, like Hugh Holland, had been a Catholic. Together with Blount as a chief backer, this group represented the flourishing of Spanish literature and letters in England. What better way for the king's players and the Folio's publisher-printers to show their sovereign that they were in support of his foreign policy?

But something stands out as an incongruous entity in the First Folio's opening pages: the dedication to the unwaveringly anti-Spanish Herbert brothers as the patrons of Shakespeare's Book. How do we explain this?

There is something missing from the First Folio's preliminary leaves. King James I is the King's Men's patron, yet he is not the volume's dedicatee. More puzzling still, nowhere in Shakespeare's Book is there any mention that the King's Men *are* the King's Men. Surely being the players to his majesty would be something to shout about, to record for posterity? Shakespeare himself, and Heminges and Condell, and many of the players represented in the Folio's list of 'Principal Actors' had, after all, achieved the distinct honour of being servants to the monarch. Why did the authors of the Folio's two dedicatory epistles not think to mention it? You might say this is like being awarded a royal warrant for a shop and deciding not to emblazon the fact on the shopfront or include it in the business's advertising materials.

There are two potential explanations for this lack of mention of the players' official status as the King's Men in the First Folio. It is possible that the king's ill health, which had been evident during the printing, had filled Heminges and Condell with trepidation about the uncertainty of the playing company's future under royal patronage. They might have, instead, identified the Herbert brothers as future patrons, emboldened by William Herbert's dogged insistence on the passing of the Lord Chamberlain's post to his brother, Philip, and on securing his family's control of the Revels

Office they decided to use the Folio as a prelude to a formal transfer of patronage. In under a year and a half, on 27 March 1625, the king would be dead. Another explanation is that Heminges and Condell had every intention of dedicating the volume to King James. In this scenario, they planned to include a dedicatory epistle, addressed to the monarch in high style, in which they identified themselves proudly as servants to his majesty, but then something happened during the printing of the preliminaries to make them change their minds. It is the latter possibility to which we will now turn.

On 5 October, just as the printing of the First Folio's plays (minus *Troilus and Cressida*) was about to enter its final phase, and almost certainly before work on the setting of the preliminary materials began, Prince Charles returned to England on 'a very foul and rainy day'. He and the Duke of Buckingham were met by the king, who threw his arms about their necks as they buckled to their knees. There the three remained awhile, weeping passionately; out of relief, out of frustration, out of grief for the absence of the Spanish bride on whom they had staked so much. Everything she had represented – Charles's newfound authority, the restoration of James's standing with the Commons, the prospect of national security and the restoration of the Palatinate – had slipped through their grasp. Immediately the Spanish ambassador requested to see the prince, but he was brusquely dismissed due to his 'unseasonable demand of audience'. It was a sign of things to come.

News of Charles's return began to spread through London the following day. It triggered an unprecedented national outpouring of ecstatic jubilation. 'I have not heard of more demonstrations of public joy than were here and everywhere from the highest to the lowest,' wrote John Chamberlain to Dudley Carleton. Tables were laid across the streets, decked with 'all manner of provisions' and 'whole hogsheads of wine', healths drunk from barrels of beer, as bonfires were lit in such numbers 'as is almost incredible'. The populace was 'so mad with excess of joy', he continued, 'that if they met with any cart laden with wood they would take out the horse and set cart and all on fire'. The prince further endeared himself to the populace when he made a public appearance just as a group of condemned prisoners were being led to their executions at Tyburn's gallows, and was moved to grant them a royal pardon 'in the very nick' of time.

Pamphlets and ballads soon began to spill from the presses, celebrating the prince's – and the nation's – escape from calamity. One of these, entitled *Prince Charles his Welcome from Spain*, described Charles's absence as 'a tedious torture to millions of loving and well-wishing hearts', recounting in nerve-tingling detail how the smoke and flames of the bonfires 'in all places, streets, lanes, courts, and corners ... ascended upwards in show of thankfulness' for his return and how 'the vast, empty, and subtle air was filled with the shouts and acclamations of people, with the rejoicing noises of instruments, ordnance, muskets, bells, drums, and trumpets'. A public holiday was declared and the Jaggards and their pressworkers – frail as William Jaggard may have been at this time – were able to stop work on the First Folio to participate in the festivities. The official line was that the celebrations were only intended to mark the safe return of Charles and did not imply the failure of the Spanish Match; that was still in prospect, or so James I wanted his subjects to believe. But few were fooled.

Like most entrepreneurs, Blount, Smethwick and Aspley also had to close their businesses to observe the holiday. They too would have been struck by the almost unearthly scenes of euphoria, when 'no shops were opened, no manner of work was done from morning till night, but carrying and re-carrying wood to make bonfires ... that all seemed as if the world was newly preserved from some second flood'. Isaac Jaggard and Henry Condell may have been concerned about their properties in one of the noted hotspots for these revelries, with the latter's investments including the Queen's

Head Tavern, since the 'very Vintners burnt their bushes in Fleet Street and other places, and their wine was burnt … into all colours of the rainbow', and 'whole pints, quarts, bottles, and gallons, were made into bonfires of sack [a type of wine from Spain or the Canary Islands] and claret, whilst good fellows like loving Salamanders swallowed those liquid fires most sweetly and affectionately'. There must have been carousing a-plenty in the Queen's Head, with barrel after barrel of alcohol carried from thence to fuel the conflagrations which set the very skies ablaze above Fleet Street. Soon songs printed in ballad form, setting these popular sentiments to familiar scores, could be purchased cheaply and sung on the streets, in public squares, in alehouses and inns. One such painted the Spanish Match as a cunning plot to 'overthrow' the nation:

> No more let Brittany [that is, Britain] lament with cares …
> Let not the fear of treason stir your thought:
> Treason, in treason's net will soon be caught;
> Danger is fled, and all your hopes stand fast …
> Long time the churlish winds did falsely blow,
> Long did they strive our fortunes to overthrow:
> While the southwest, blew such a prosperous gale,
> That caused a princely mind to hoist up sail …
> While princely Charles did happily return …

Though the king and his council did everything in their power to keep the collapse of negotiations over the Spanish Match secret, there was a general sense among the people that Charles's return without the Infanta spelled the end of the affair. Then, on 26 October, it seemed as if God himself had passed judgement on the matter of England's union with Catholic Spain. The events of that fateful day would have resonated with Heminges, Condell and the King's Men, for the troupe were performing at the Blackfriars

Theatre in that winter season. Just paces away, in an upper room in the Blackfriars district, the largest gathering of Catholics under one roof in England in over sixty years had taken place; a measure of their growing confidence following the height of the negotiations over the Spanish Match and the relaxing of the laws against those of their faith. Around four that afternoon, as they were listening to a sermon by a Jesuit priest, the beams and floor joists were 'not able to bear the weight' and collapsed 'with such violence' that they crashed through two floors. At least ninety-five people were killed. Many died from the impact of the fall, while others were 'smothered' under the mass of the debris that had buried them. Those who survived were maimed and injured, some with severed limbs. Writhing among the wreckage, they begged for help but their pleas were met with disdain by the district's largely Puritan population; 'Our people being grown so savage and barbarous that they refused to assist them with drink, aqua vitae or any other cordials,' commented a shocked Chamberlain, 'but rather insulted upon them with taunts and gibes in their affliction.' Those who attempted to get to their lodgings or to seek the aid of surgeons were held back and even torn from their coaches.

The dead were buried in two deep pits in the gardens behind the collapsed building; two large temporary black crosses placed above their makeshift graves. Soon news had spread that a diligent investigation had been made of the beams and floorboards, which were 'otherwise found upon search and view no way faulty or rotten but strong and sound'. The tragedy solidified public opposition to the match. Chamberlain sat down at his desk to pen this account on 8 November as more bonfires were being lit through the streets and especially around the Strand, where the Spanish ambassador and his entourage were sojourning, the smoking pyres laid 'thick ... even to their gates' so that 'they may easily perceive how welcome they are to our people'. This was written on the very day in which Isaac Jaggard and Edward Blount were making their way to the

Stationers' Hall to register their rights to the Shakespeare plays still in the King's Men's possession; even while columns of smoke could be seen throwing up smothering ash clouds across the city's darkening skies.

'[S]peech of the Spanish Match grows daily more cool,' wrote Chamberlain, who reported that a new bride for the prince was to be sought in Vienna. Before long, an enticing marriage prospect would be found in France, with Sir Simonds D'Ewes writing 'The English generally so detested the Spanish Match; as they were glad of any other [marriage] which freed them from the fear of that.' The political tectonic plates were shifting, with members of the court's anti-Spanish faction elated by signs of James's firmer commitment to dealing with the crisis in the Palatinate and to strengthening the alliance with the Netherlands, certain that now 'the king is resolved not to forsake his old friends the Hollanders'. Even Villiers sensed the way the wind was blowing and commissioned a new masque at his residence, York House, on 18 November, spending three pounds and six shillings on Spanish ruffs, no doubt for the impersonation of members of Philip IV's court. It was devised by John Maynard and offered a fulsome 'congratulation for the prince's return'. The entertainment's congratulatory tone may have been a little overenthusiastic for it enraged the Spanish ambassador and two other Spanish dignitaries in his entourage.

Meanwhile, a sense of how the collapse of the Spanish Match and the weight of public opinion was affecting the theatrical personnel involved in the making of the First Folio is evident from the next major projects they undertook. Ben Jonson quickly realised that his masque, *Neptune's Triumph for the Return of Albion*, which had been commissioned to commemorate the impending Anglo-Spanish marriage, would have to be altered to celebrate Charles's return without his Spanish bride. The revised entertainment, which was due to be performed on 6 January 1624, now presented a dramatic re-enactment of the prince's perilous voyage to Spain, and of his escape from the deadly 'sirens' who 'wooed him, by the way', of the 'monsters he encountered on the coast' and of 'How near our general joy was to be lost'. Jonson had also incorporated an anti-masque featuring numerous insulting japes at the expense of the Spanish. He was asked to censor the offending scenes, but at length fear of causing diplomatic offence led the king to drop the masque entirely from the season's programme of entertainments. Showing even less tact were the King's Men, who threw their weight behind a new venture: a comedy by Thomas Middleton entitled *A Game at Chess*. The play premiered in August 1624, satirising Anglo-Spanish political intrigues and flaunting far from subtle allusions to the Spanish Match. Its virulently anti-Spanish message proved popular with English theatregoers and it became a smash hit. The play was licensed by Sir Henry Herbert, Master of the Revels, kinsman to the Lord Chamberlain, the Earl of Pembroke, who almost certainly shielded the players from more serious repercussions after it was banned, when Middleton and the King's Men faced the prospect of prosecution for their seditious production.

Poised uneasily between the return of a still unmarried Prince Charles from Spain and the intensely anti-Spanish ethos which erupted in public spaces and stages shortly afterwards, was the printing of the First Folio's preliminaries. During the transition in mood that accompanied this seismic phase in England's history it must have seemed as if the world had flipped on its head. It is possible, therefore, that the King's Men and the Folio syndicate had realised that adding a dedication to James I at this time would reinforce the pro-Spanish outlook of Shakespeare's Book, for the king was still trying to hide the dissolution of the match, in hopes that he could somehow get the marriage negotiations back on track. But there was no turning the tide of public opinion. The collapse of the Anglo-Spanish union proved a winning strike for the court's anti-Spanish faction, at whose head was the Earl of Pembroke. In the war between James's chief courtiers, Herbert was, in this regard, the victor, and the Folio's backers knew it. Perhaps worried that the strength of the populace's feeling would reduce sales of the volume and put their investment at risk, Heminges and Condell, in consultation with the Folio syndicate, may have resolved to cancel a planned dedication to their royal patron and hastily incorporate in its place an epistle to the Herbert brothers, widely known for their family's commitment to the forward Protestant movement, for their opposition to the Spanish Match and their outspoken criticism of James's foreign policy. If this is true, the Folio has, almost as if preserved in aspic, enshrined within its pages an ink-and-linen microcosm of one of the most turbulent episodes in England's early modern history.

'Thy Stratford Monument'

The Grave, the Folio and Selling Shakespeare's 'Works'

William Jaggard did not live to see the completion of the First Folio. In the aftermath of his loss, his son Isaac Jaggard and his fellow syndicate members would finish it without him, having failed to come to an agreement with Henry Walley over the rights to *Troilus and Cressida*. By the end of November 1623 the backers had initially walked away from any further negotiations and turned their attentions to the sale and marketing of the volume.

As all the financiers of Shakespeare's Book were entitled to a share of the completed work as part of the return on their investment in the project, Isaac Jaggard kept a quantity of Folios to display in the shop attached to his printing house in the Barbican. Over in St Paul's Cross Churchyard, Edward Blount and William Aspley began stocking their neighbouring bookshops, ensuring that their first-rate new commodity would catch the eyes of would-be purchasers passing the stalls which protruded out from their shopfronts. Similarly, John Smethwick arranged copies on his own shelves under the shadow of the clocktower attached to St Dunstan's Church, where they could attract the legal set who worked or studied at the nearby Inns of Court and the area's other legal institutions. Between them, the syndicate had most of London's bookselling hotspots covered. In these, and any other retail outlets which stocked it, the First Folio originally appeared without *Troilus and Cressida*.

Shortly after the Folio's release, a book buyer named Thomas Longe would acquire a newly minted unbound copy for fifteen shillings; around £120 in today's money. Despite Heminges and Condell writing optimistically in their address to the 'great Variety of Readers' that they wanted their tribute to Shakespeare to appeal widely, 'From the most able, to him that can but spell', this was roughly a year's wages for the average labourer and would, therefore, have been beyond the reach of most. The high charge reflected the volume's wholesale price, which was around ten shillings, roughly eighty pounds today, and about two-thirds of a year's wages for a labourer. The basic cost of production per book was around six shillings and eight pence for the publishers, about half of which was used to pay for the acquisition of printing rights, copy texts, paper stocks and other physical materials, and the remainder allocated to the compositors and other pressworkers who manufactured it; a steep unit price and equivalent to around fifty-five pounds today. This made the First Folio the most expensive book of plays in English history up till that point.

Adding to the cost for the purchaser was the charge for binding. Books were often sold unbound in the first instance, with owners either paying to have them bound at a bindery or meeting an additional fee set by a bookseller to have the volume dressed in a binding of their choosing. Some booksellers used binderies with which they had a close working relationship. If a bookseller's shop was large enough it might incorporate its own binding services, with a seller charging a mark-up equal to that demanded by professional binders to maximise profits. If they wanted to, Edward Blount and William Aspley, for instance, could use book-binders

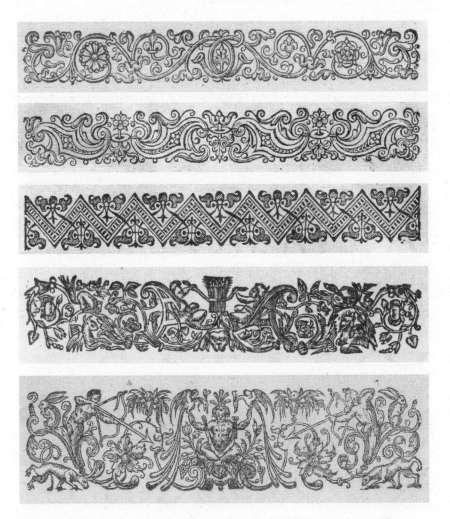

These intricate and intertwining decorative woodblock border designs from the First Folio are a testament to the care and attention its makers lavished on Shakespeare's Book. This was a luxurious and costly product, within the reach of only the most privileged members of society. When it was published the First Folio was the most expensive book of plays ever made up to that point.

just opposite their shops, a short stroll down the eastern edge of St Paul's Cathedral's north transept in St Paul's Cross Churchyard. Blount himself offered his own binding services, either in collaboration with other binders with whom he had entered into a business arrangement or as an independent service on his own premises, for in one piece of advertising in 1620 he encourages customers, having purchased a title, 'if the book please you, come home to my shop, you shall have it bound'. The whole process, acquiring the book with new binding, could cost anywhere between sixteen shillings and a pound, depending on the quality of the binding and the kind of embellishments requested by the purchaser. Unadorned 'forel' binding, which was made from sheepskin or goatskin, or an untanned calf skin sometimes called 'limp vellum', was the cheapest, at around one shilling per book, with the cover sewn onto soft leather supports. This flexible form of binding tended not to be used for large folios except as temporary protection, because it was flimsy, subject to cracking and flaking, though for an extra shilling it could be sewn onto harder, more durable boards. Calf skin was the most expensive, with the basic cost charged by a binder usually around three or four shillings, and a potential mark-up to around six shillings if commissioned by a dealer or bookseller. These covers could be embossed with elaborate decorative borders and adornments made using a heated brass incising tool called a 'fillet'. Varying the heat of the fillet and moistening the leather could change the colour and texture of the embossing, enriching the cover's designs with depth and contrast. Calf-skin binding could be gilded in gold leaf, pressed into the leather using a heated tool, thereby binding the leaf onto pre-incised patterns on the cover's surface through an adhesive called 'glair'. The more elaborate the designs, the higher the price. This was skilled work, requiring precision, artistry and the ability to judge the tolerance of the manipulated materials. Too much heat could burn the cover or damage the gold leaf. Too much moisture applied to the leather could result in scarring of the surface. Any mistakes would be costly.

The First Folio was a luxurious item by anyone's standards and that would have limited the market for such a book. It has long been believed that this risky venture effectively ended Edward

Blount's business, his publishing output virtually grinding to a halt after 1623. However, Blount had been severely in debt in the years leading up to the publication of the Folio and, as recent research has revealed, he was locked in an expensive legal case over potential debts of £2,000 owed to him by his brother-in-law, Roger Roydon, which led to a climactic series of legal hearings between October and November of 1623, just as the Folio was being completed. That he lost the case, and what would have been a small fortune at the time, is poignantly attested to by a later record that shows a payment to Blount from the Stationers' Company's poor relief fund. The downturn in Blount's fortunes was probably not caused by his commitment to Shakespeare's Book which, according to some estimates, did tolerably well enough on the market, given that it was reprinted in 1632. Ben Jonson's *Works*, initially published in 1616, would not see a reprint till 1640. The first folio of Francis Beaumont and John Fletcher's *Comedies and Tragedies* would be published in 1647, while the second folio would not be released until 1679. With the Folio syndicate taking about a third of the volume's wholesale price as profit, they would have needed to shift over half their printed stock to break even. That the Second Shakespeare Folio would be printed relatively quickly after the First, and include both Aspley and Smethwick as financiers, along with Robert Allot, who in 1630, some two years before Blount's death, took over the publisher's shop, buying out his share of the Shakespeare plays included in the Folio, indicates that the First Folio was a profitable undertaking. It also carried a prestige value that could not simply be quantified in monetary terms.

At some point, not long after the First Folio made its debut, Henry Walley realised that it was already on sale. Apparently he had decided he did not want to lose the opportunity to profit from such a high-status publication and finally agreed to lease his rights to *Troilus and Cressida* for a reasonable price. He may have gleaned that the Folio's form meant that its content would be marketed as literary in nature, appropriate for an elite and learned readership, and this may have appealed to him. When he had originally published *Troilus and Cressida* in 1609, he did so in two versions, one of which advertised on its title page that 'it was acted by the King's Majesty's servants at the Globe', while the other completely falsified this pitching, claiming in an epistle to the reader that it was 'a new play, never stalled with the stage, never clapper-clawed with the palms of the vulgar'. Stressing that the work was 'born in that sea that brought forth Venus', meaning that this play was alike in quality to Shakespeare's celebrated narrative poem *Venus and Adonis*, the epistle flaunted the work's literary credentials, which were to be favourably compared to the products of the much-revered classical authors Terence and Plautus.

It is possible that Blount and Jaggard gained some further leverage over Walley in another way. After requesting a search of the Stationers' Register, when logging their rights to the plays still in the ownership of the King's Men in early November 1623, they may have been informed of an anomaly in Walley's registering of *Troilus and Cressida*, leading to an ambiguity over his ownership of the play. This had previously been registered by James Roberts in February 1603 and listed as having been 'acted by my Lord Chamberlain's Men', indicating that it was a direct transfer of rights from the players to Roberts. There was no formal conveyance of a licence to print the play from Roberts to Walley and his co-financier Richard Bonian, perhaps because they had assumed the rights had become 'derelict'. Since William Jaggard had taken over Roberts' shop three years after his original registration of the play, and some time before Walley and Bonian's own logging of the rights in January 1609, Isaac had a potential claim to it. It is possible that Walley preferred not to take the risk of the matter being passed to the Court of Stationers and came to a swift bargain with them.

With an agreement in hand, Isaac Jaggard's pressworkers leaped into action, the ever-valiant Compositor B teaming up with at least one other to typeset *Troilus and Cressida* in consecutive quires. Copies were printed off in short order and rushed to the bookstalls, the play squeezed in after the histories and at the start of the tragedies without a mention in the Folio's 'Catalogue'. But even as this version was being sold, the syndicate decided it was not finished with the Folio or with this play. Now they added a prologue which introduced the action with a grandiloquent poetical flourish, setting before the reader's imagination a lively scene 'Fraught with the ministers and instruments/Of cruel war'. Early in its history, therefore, the First Folio went on sale in three primary states. The fact that the book's backers were willing to go to the trouble, and extra expense, of doing this indicates how much they cared about the project.

Selling the First Folio to Londoners in the winter of 1623 was just the beginning. The syndicate now wanted to introduce their volume to the world. By the spring of the following year, Shakespeare's Book was making its debut at the Frankfurt Book Fair. Then, as now, this busy, thriving, kaleidoscopic literary festival was the place to be if you were a bookseller, and the event you had your eye on if you were an author, financier, stationer, printer or anyone with an interest in the sale of a published text. Here agents and spies gathered news of the latest political intrigues, or returned intelligence about recent explosive propagandist texts to their respective royal courts, while pickpockets assessed the crowds, seeking out their next victims among the finely dressed and well-heeled book browsers as they were distracted by the wares on offer on row after labyrinthine row of bustling bookstalls.

It may have been Edward Blount himself who ensured the textual memorial to Shakespeare was advertised in the Frankfurt catalogue. The announcement itemised the sale of 'Master Shakespeare's works, printed for Edward Blount, in fol[io]'. This pitching for the First Folio shows a marked difference to that enshrined in the somewhat optimistic piece of advance advertising that had been included in the catalogue around October 1622, possibly by William Jaggard's son, long before the project was completed, heralding the anticipated publication of 'Plays, written by M[aster] William Shakespeare, all in one volume, printed by Isaac Jaggard, in fol[io]'. By 1624 'Plays' had become 'works'. This may not sound significant today, since we use these terms interchangeably when describing Shakespeare's output, but was controversial at the time.

When Blount proudly showcased his new volume at the Black Bear, he would have hoped that this luxurious product would appeal to a certain kind of buyer. That is, a buyer attracted to books freighted with a degree of intellectual gravitas, such as theological tomes, fiendishly detailed legal treatises, volumes recording heraldic pedigrees, or ambitious historiographical studies; books then identified as 'works'. Such a label suggested the grand achievement of the author – often an elite intellectual or university-trained scholar with a towering reputation – or indicated the text's national or religious importance. It may have been the marketing-savvy Blount who insisted on adding a headline that acted almost as a second title to the First Folio above 'The Names of the Principal Actors in all these Plays', which, in larger lettering, proclaimed the volume would be giving the reader access to 'The Works of William Shakespeare, containing all his Comedies, Histories, and Tragedies: Truly set forth, according to their first ORIGINAL'. This promise of the firstlings of Shakespeare's mind raised the products of his imagination to the status of 'Works'. It was a bolder move than may at first appear, since this was a transitional period in history, during which the craft of playwrighting was becoming professionalised but had not quite shaken off its association with less regarded artisanal occupations. In 1612 Sir Thomas Bodley had written to Thomas James, keeper of what would become better known as the Bodleian Library, objecting to the preservation of playbooks at Oxford University because of 'the harm that the scandal will bring to the Library, when it shall be given out, that we stuff it full of baggage books'. Such throwaway and ephemeral reading materials, as he regarded them, would be to the 'disgrace of the Library'.

Changes had since been afoot in the literary landscape. The drawing of attention to Shakespeare's 'works', in the promotion of the book at the Frankfurt Book Fair, indicates a strategy that had evolved at least towards the end of its production, when the preliminaries were being printed, and would have been in step with recent trends. The publication of the First Folio coincided with the reprinting of a sumptuous folio edition of the poet and playwright Samuel Daniel's *Works*, which included non-commercial plays read or performed as exclusive coterie productions among members of the nobility. Such select dramatic works, as original compositions or translations, had been published in compilations before. The bookish Daniel's collection first appeared in 1601 and some fourteen years before that plays in translation had been issued in George Gascoigne's *Whole Works*. But it was Ben Jonson who really made a splash with his folio edition of *The Works of Benjamin Jonson* in 1616, the very same year that saw the publication of King James I's grand folio edition of *The Works of the Most High and Mighty Prince James*. Jonson, with quite some audacity, had dared to oversee the production of his own *Works*, in which he included commercial plays, earning the scorn of critics who marvelled at his temerity, with one anonymous epigrammist writing: 'Pray tell me Ben, where doth the mystery lurk,/What others call a play you call a work?' The famous preacher and theologian John Boys did not hold back when expressing his own contempt for such posturing, writing: 'the very plays of a modern poet, are called in print his

works'. Such sentiments are hardly surprising, given that Boys' own
Works were published by First Folio syndicate member William
Aspley and sold at the sign of the Parrot, just two doors away from
Blount's shop, taking its place as one of a number of weighty theological *Works* competing for business in 1622–3. In Aspley's shop,
therefore, Shakespeare's plays would have sat beside John Boys'
hefty theological magnum opus. One wonders what Boys would
have made of that!

It paints an evocative picture to think about how the crowds
pouring out of St Paul's Cathedral's Great North Door would have,
had they turned west towards the precinct's preaching cross, walked
past at least two shops – first the Parrot, then the Black Bear,
standing practically side by side – from whose projecting stalls
printed clones of Shakespeare's face would have stared back at
them, peeping out from the title pages of unbound First Folios. For
some potential purchasers this would have been something of a
shock. The Folio went one step further than even Jonson's *Works*,
being entirely devoted to commercial plays, while elevating them
to the ranks of more learned 'works'. The fact that Shakespeare's
narrative poems and sonnets were omitted from its pages amplifies
the possibility that Heminges and Condell had exerted some kind
of guiding hand over the project. But the transformation of
commercial plays to 'works' is unlikely to have been their doing,
and was a pitching strategy which reflected the fact that this
volume was entirely unique at the time of its publication, a new
kind of folio product. This was further solidified through Leonard
Digges's contribution to the book's commemorative programme in
his poem 'To the memory of the deceased author Master W.
Shakespeare':

Shakespeare, at length thy pious fellows give
The world thy Works: thy Works, by which, out-live
Thy tomb, thy name must when that stone is rent,
And Time dissolves thy Stratford Monument,
Here we alive shall view thee still. This Book,
When brass and marble fade, shall make thee look
Fresh to all ages ...

Shakespeare's plays are twice referred to using the ennobling term 'Works', which would be echoed in the Frankfurt Book Fair's catalogue in 1624, possibly under Blount's own instruction. Digges also attributes the gathering of the collection to the labours of Shakespeare's 'pious fellows', giving these 'Works' a certain aura, veering on the sacred, as if they had been cultivated by an exclusive coterie of devout men; the kind who might oversee the literary legacy of a theologian or learned minister.

It is possible that Leonard Digges had seen Shakespeare's 'Stratford Monument'. He certainly had a compelling connection to Shakespeare, for his mother had married Thomas Russell, Esquire, of Alderminster on 26 August 1603. Russell, we may recall, was the overseer of Shakespeare's will and so the playwright clearly saw him as an intimate, a trusted individual. Since the Russell family's seat lay just outside Stratford-upon-Avon, Digges may have paid a visit to Shakespeare's grave when calling on his stepfather at his Warwickshire home. The affecting sight could have burned itself onto his imagination, only to spill onto the page when he sat down to write his elegiac poem for the First Folio. He was not, however, the only memorialiser of Shakespeare in the Folio to recall the playwright's Stratford monument. Ben Jonson implicitly alludes to Shakespeare's burial when he reflects on the most fitting place to inter his body:

My Shakespeare, rise; I will not lodge thee by
    Chaucer, or Spenser, or bid Beaumont lie
A little further, to make thee a room:
    Thou art a monument, without a tomb,
And art alive still, while thy book doth live,
    And we have wits to read, and praise to give.
That I not mix thee so, my brain excuses;
    I mean with great, but disproportioned muses …

The 'great' literary figureheads Geoffrey Chaucer, Edmund Spenser and Francis Beaumont were buried in England's grandest mausoleum: Westminster Abbey. Jonson rejects the idea that Shakespeare too should be laid beside them, being unwilling to 'mix' him in a shared grave with 'muses' whose art, he implies, is very different in character. It is, however, not generally known that Ben Jonson, in finding a Westminster monument inadequate to the task of commemorating the dramatist, is responding to what may in fact have been a controversial subject in the period, one debated among a select few: where Shakespeare should be buried. A poem, commonly attributed to William Basse, asserted the desirability of placing Shakespeare's remains in Westminster Abbey, and is entitled, in one version, 'On Mr William Shakespeare who died in April 1616':

Renowned Spenser, lie a thought more nye
To learned Chaucer, and rare Beaumont lie
A little nearer Spenser, to make room
For Shakespeare in your threefold fourfold tomb.
To lodge all four in one bed make a shift
Until Doomsday; for hardly will a fifth
Betwixt this day and that, by fate be slain
For whom your curtains may be drawn again.
If your precedency in Death doth bar

A fourth place in your sacred sepulchre
Under this carved marble of thine own
Sleep rare Tragedian, Shakespeare sleep alone,
Thy unmolested Peace, unshared cave
Possess as Lord, not Tennant of thy grave.
That unto us and others it may be
Honour hereafter to be laid by thee.

This seems to be a poem that Ben Jonson had in mind when writing his verse in memory of Shakespeare for the First Folio. It is therefore an important and often overlooked text which is in dialogue with Shakespeare's Book. Here the poet imagines Chaucer, Spenser and Beaumont making room for Shakespeare in their 'sacred sepulchre', presenting this as a fitting way to mark his greatness. Basse ends, however, resigned to the fact that the 'rare Tragedian' will lie perpetually 'under this carved marble of thine own' in his native Stratford. Ben Jonson's poem is thus a riposte, which confirms the need for Shakespeare's body to remain in Stratford, even while it presents the First Folio as superseding his stone monument.

Not everyone believes the poem to which Jonson was responding was written by William Basse. It was in fact first published in a book of poems by John Donne, to whom it has been attributed. Whether or not Donne actually wrote this verse, his name somehow became intertwined with it, possibly because he was part of those literary coteries that copied and exchanged it through the numerous manuscript versions that survive, indicating that he had an interest in the commemoration of Shakespeare. Perhaps, significantly, for reasons we shall see, Basse may have become acquainted with Donne through mutual Oxford connections; for the latter had studied at the university there and Basse most likely lived in Thame in Oxfordshire, producing works for noble patrons in that county, as well as issuing publications through Oxford University's

official printing press. When Jonson read the poem in manuscript
– brought to his attention possibly by Basse himself, or by Donne
– he must have felt the controversy about the fate of Shakespeare's
remains to which it referred would have been known to at least
some of the Folio's readers and therefore merited a mention within
its introductory pages.

While we tend to think of the First Folio as a London-centred
affair, produced by a group of city-based backers and financiers,
this is challenged by its preliminary materials, from which
Stratford-upon-Avon emerges as a location of significance. Indeed,
the link between Shakespeare's Book and the town of the playwright's birth and retirement is intuitively grasped when we
compare the Folio's iconic title-page portrait with the dramatist's
monumental bust in Holy Trinity Church, which share a strikingly
stark, direct and plain form of composition. If the decision to cultivate such a similarity was a deliberate one on the part of Heminges
and Condell or the Folio syndicate, or collectively of all the
volume's backers, then the book itself rejects the idea that the sole
right to commemorate the dramatist belongs to a London-based
community of literati. Even while the Folio's preliminaries demonstrate the primacy of the text over the physical monument,
Shakespeare's *local* identity is not severed from his 'works'.
However, as we will see, Stratford and London are not the only
localities on which the Folio's construction of 'Shakespeare' for
posterity depends. The other is Oxford, the centre of learning
which connects many of the men who supported the creation of
Shakespeare's Book, and almost all of those who contributed to its
preliminaries.

Uncovering the hidden role of Oxford in the intertwined lives
behind the First Folio will allow us to consider one important, yet
unanswered, question: aside from authoring the plays contained
within it, did William Shakespeare himself influence the creation
of his own book? Did he, in some way, determine the way in which

he would come to be commemorated in it? Following this line of enquiry will reveal something startling: that the makers of the volume may have been fulfilling Shakespeare's own wishes in their choice of memorialisers for its preliminary pages, that they were portraying the playwright as *he* wanted to be seen. If these scholar-poets were selected because they best fitted the Spain-centred political climate of the period, the wider group from which they were picked may have belonged to an Oxford network favoured by Shakespeare. In other words, the processes which ennobled his plays as 'Works' in the Folio had their origin in – or at least evolved within an ethos consciously cultivated by – the dramatist himself. Consequently, albeit subtly, Shakespeare's Book incorporates something of his own design, not simply from beyond the grave but *through* his grave.

Act Five

William Shakespeare's Will in His Book

Orpheus with his lute made trees,
And the mountain tops that freeze,
Bow themselves when he did sing.
To his music plants and flowers
Ever sprung, as sun and showers
There had made a lasting spring.

William Shakespeare, *Henry VIII*

18

The 'Sireniacal' Fraternity

Shakespeare and Oxford

In Stratford-upon-Avon's Holy Trinity Church William Shakespeare's effigy stares enigmatically from its wall-mounted monumental surround, engaging the viewer as unflinchingly as the First Folio's portrait. But it is sculpted with one significantly different feature: slightly parted lips through which you can see Shakespeare's teeth! One wonders if the intention is to present a speaking image. If so, what is the dramatist saying?

It was John Aubrey who first noticed that Shakespeare, as he is depicted in his funereal effigy, is dressed in 'a black gown like an undergraduate's at Oxford'. Pioneering research by the Renaissance scholar Lena Cowen Orlin has revealed that the style of the playwright's monument was indeed based on a model 'popular for scholars and divines' attached to that learned institution. She uncovered numerous monuments that enshrine postures similar to that adopted by Shakespeare in his memorial bust, presenting the deceased as if alive, leaning on a cushion, then used as a rest for books or papers during the delivery of lectures, which 'transformed the architectural niche into a *mise en scène* of preaching or lecturing'. When Shakespeare's memorial was erected, 'the epicentre of the cushioned funerary monuments was Oxford University', and by the time Leonard Digges alluded to the Stratford monument in the Folio 'all cushioned monuments in existence still had Oxford connections'. Such monuments were made to memorialise 'the most learned men of the age' and did sometimes present their subjects in their Oxford gowns. Shakespeare, Orlin revealed, may in fact have designed his effigy himself, while still alive, and that it was commissioned when the monument designer Nicholas Johnson came to Stratford to install the tomb of the dramatist's friend John Combe, who died two years before Shakespeare, in July 1614.

It has previously been thought that the monuments of Combe and Shakespeare were designed by Nicholas's brother Gerard who specialised mostly in garden design. The Johnson workshop was in London, in the immediate vicinity of the Globe Theatre, so Shakespeare may have known this family of sculptors and designers from his acting days. Such research offers us the tantalising possibility that Johnson had seen Shakespeare in the flesh and incorporated his living likeness into the effigy. The fact that the dramatist's lips are parted on his monument, while he leans on a preaching cushion, may indicate that he wanted to be preserved eternally in the act of speaking: in the mould of the Oxford lecturer or preacher.

The men Shakespeare was emulating were exactly the kind of revered individuals who published great 'Works'. It is not fanciful, therefore, to make a logical connection between the design of Shakespeare's monumental bust and the way in which the playwright's *image* is communicated through the First Folio's engraving by Martin Droeshout, as well as through the 'textual portraits' authored by the memorialisers in its preliminary pages: they speak the same language. They tell us Shakespeare is not just part of theatrical and publishing communities in London, or of familial or socially elevated networks in Stratford, but is an associate of scholars and poets who attended Oxford University. And like the

'Masters', divines, preachers and academics attached to that institution, 'Master William Shakespeare' is the purveyor not simply of plays and poems but of 'Works'. Whether or not Shakespeare designed his own monument, we have a new way of looking at the construction of the First Folio: as a continuation of the monumental programme installed in Holy Trinity Church, arising from the playwright's own network of personal and professional affiliations, and the sense of selfhood he wanted to bequeath to posterity. Shakespeare's Book therefore carries traces of its subject's own will, and of the intertwined and living relationships that fashioned his social identity.

There is some apocryphal evidence to demonstrate Shakespeare's connection to Oxford. John Aubrey stated that the dramatist, during his years as an actor and playwright in London, 'was wont to go into Warwickshire once a year', and that on the way he would stop off at a 'house in Oxford, where he was exceedingly respected'. This house was the Crown Tavern in Cornmarket Street, and belonged to the vintner John Davenant and his wife Jennet, 'a very beautiful woman, and a very good wit and of conversation extremely agreeable'. It was rumoured that their son, William Davenant, was sired by Shakespeare himself. It may not be a coincidence that he became an 'unofficial poet laureate' in 1638, succeeding Ben Jonson in the role. The Davenants had once operated their business from London and Jennet's brothers were glovemakers, just as Shakespeare's father had been, and were connected to Marie Mountjoy, the playwright's landlady during the years in which he lived in Silver Street.

While Shakespeare and his colleagues occasionally took their plays to Oxford University, the dramatist need not have visited Oxford regularly, or even attended lectures and sermons there, to be in touch with scholars, poets and intellectuals attached to that bastion of learning. We do not have to look far to glean the more immediate sources for Shakespeare's aspirations. His closeness to

the wealthy Combe family brought him into contact with William
Combe junior, a property magnate who had attended New College,
Oxford. William junior inherited vast tracts of land in Welcombe
in Warwickshire, where Shakespeare had also been busy accumu-
lating acres. He was an executor, with his uncle John Combe, of the
will of William Combe senior, the former high sheriff of
Warwickshire, who with John had sold to Shakespeare 107 acres of
land in Old Stratford. John, who developed a reputation as a notorious money-lender and, as one account put it, 'a covetous rich
man', left Shakespeare five pounds in his will, and numerous
(though unverifiable) accounts survive which state that the playwright composed a comic epitaph for him in which he wittily
presented the devil as laying claim to the damned soul of 'my John
a Combe'. John's nephew, Thomas Combe, was particularly close to
Shakespeare, for the latter left him an intensely personal gift in his
will: his own sword. This was the kind of bequest that would
normally be given to one's son, godson or son-in-law. Shakespeare's
decision to bestow this honour not on his own son-in-law John
Hall but on Thomas evidences their intimacy.

The fact that Shakespeare wanted his memorial to be produced
by the very same workshop that created the monument to a prominent member of the Combe family, indicates that he wanted to
cultivate a public identity in a very similar reputational vein. Some
of the personalities attached to the First Folio not only overlapped
with this Stratford coterie, they were embedded in communities
with which Shakespeare was connected and which were rooted in
the literary and intellectual cultures of Oxford University.

Ben Jonson, who may have taken a leading role in the compilation
of the First Folio's preliminary materials (though some scholars
accord this honour to Edward Blount), was described by one of his
earliest biographers, Anthony à Wood, as having been part of what
amounted to a kind of Oxford 'set' of authors:

His own proper industry and addiction to books, especially to ancient Poets and Classical authors, made him a person of curious learning and judgment, and of singular excellence in the art of Poetry. Which, with his accurate judgment and performance, known only to those few, who are truly able to judge of his works, have gained from the most eminent Scholars of his time ... an increasing admiration. Dr Richard Corbet of Christ Church [College, Oxford] and other Poets of this University, did in reverence to his parts, invite him to Oxon [Oxford], where continuing for some time in Christ Church in writing and composing plays, he was, as a member thereof, actually created Master of Arts in 1619, and therefore upon that account I put him among the Oxford writers ...

An air of exclusivity lingers over this revered group of 'Oxford writers', into whose ranks Jonson has been admitted. We will never know if Shakespeare, had he lived till 1619, would have been, like Jonson, accorded the honour of being awarded an honorary MA from Oxford University. It seems likely, since Jonson's degree was almost certainly conferred on him thanks to the intercessions of Sir William Herbert, Earl of Pembroke, in his capacity as chancellor of Oxford University. Pembroke himself had entered New College, Oxford, in March 1593, on the very same day as his brother Philip, but by the end of 1595 had left without taking a degree. Philip would only remain at the college for a few months. Pembroke was, though, awarded an MA in 1605, while Montgomery became high steward of Oxford University in 1615. There is no reason to suppose that Shakespeare who, according to Heminges and Condell, had received 'so much favour' at the hands of the Herbert brothers, would not have been awarded an honorary MA like his friend Jonson.

One wonders how Jonson managed to maintain these friendships, for he had a biting sense of humour and was notoriously competitive, leading sometimes to uneasy relations with his intimates. His relationship with Shakespeare was probably far from smooth. Just over two years after the latter's death, Jonson had sniped that 'Shakespeare wanted [that is, lacked] art' and accused him of taking a shoddy approach to researching his plays. Most notoriously, in a stunningly back-handed compliment, which he incorporated into his Folio elegy, he claimed the playwright had 'small Latin and less Greek', implying that he had fallen short of Jonson's own superior classical education.

Jonson's somewhat testing personality had caused friction in or around 1613, when he was working on a draft of his play *Bartholomew Fair*. In this work he gave vent to his mischievous streak by satirising his collaborator and rival Inigo Jones through the figure of a puppeteer he originally named 'Inigo Lantern'. Carried away with the ingenuity of his caricature, Jonson read it to 'diverse' individuals among his circle of intimates. Hugh Holland was one such unwilling ear, and was none too pleased about the public shaming of someone he clearly regarded as a friend. Holland appealed to John Donne, who conferred with his and Jonson's mutual friend Sir Henry Goodere, agreeing at length that Donne would urge Jonson to rethink his less-than-subtle mockery of Jones. The stung playwright protested 'that no hearer but Mr Holland apprehended it so' and that he could not see 'how Mr Holland will be excused' for accusing him of setting about to deliberately injure Jones. He did, though, relent, altering the name to 'Lantern Leatherhead'. Having carried out Goodere's 'commandment' to the letter, Donne agreed that it was a minor spat and that Holland had overreacted since 'There was nothing obnoxious but the very name, and he [Jonson] hath changed that'.

Despite his somewhat abrasive character, Jonson clearly cared about what his friends Donne and Holland thought, enough to change his plans for his comedy in hopes of allaying their anxieties. There is evidence to suggest that these three were part of a larger group of associates that included others involved with the First

Folio, as well as individuals closely affiliated with that volume's backers. We know this thanks to the traces in the historical record left by a peculiar man named Thomas Coryate. Jonson, Donne and Holland had appeared alongside Jones and Leonard Digges's

An 1801 line engraving of Thomas Coryate, based on an earlier portrait by an unknown artist. Coryate was an eccentric explorer who may have been part of a network of Oxford scholars and authors, which intersected with individuals known to William Shakespeare, and who were associated with the making of the First Folio.

brother Dudley in an eccentric work called *Coryat's Crudities*, published in a handsome folio edition in 1611. Coryate was an explorer whose accounts of his peripatetic adventures in other countries were prefaced with an embarrassingly copious quantity of dedicatory epistles, poems and panegyrics by some of the choicest literary flowers of the age, including offerings by these men. Ben Jonson oversaw the gathering of these verses, much as he may have done with the First Folio, but with the aim of producing the largest set of comically inflated preliminaries ever produced. He succeeded admirably, stuffing the book with well over a hundred pages of sometimes wittily deflating fluff, and sending up Coryate's colossal ego in the process.

Some of these eulogisers are related to Coryate through a university connection. He had entered Oxford's Gloucester Hall at the age of nineteen in 1596 to begin a three-year course of study, attaining 'by help of a great memory, to some competency in logic, but more by far in the Greek tongue'. John Donne also received some of his learning at the same university, having attended Hart Hall, present-day Hertford College, from 1584. Both Leonard Digges and his brother Dudley had been attached to University College, Oxford. Leonard matriculated in July 1603, aged fifteen, to pursue a Bachelor of Arts, graduating in 1606, but did not receive his MA till 1626. His brother Dudley had entered the same college before him in 1598 at the age of fifteen and was much praised for 'his rare learning, joined with piety … accompanied with a pleasing carriage towards every man; which were the chief reasons that caused all good men to love him'. While Hugh Holland was educated at Trinity College, Cambridge, he may have received part of his learning from Balliol College, Oxford, but without taking a degree, for a scholar of the same name matriculated there in 1582, aged twenty-four. After his travels, 'he retired to Oxford, [spending] some years there as a sojourner for the sake of the public library' and was lodged in Balliol College.

Coryat's Crudities is not the only work produced by Coryate which illuminates the composition of a community which had strong associations with Oxford and which overlapped with figures attached to the creation of the First Folio. A number of these individuals are evoked in an illuminating later work, published in 1616, called *Thomas Coryat, Traveller for the English Wits*, which further details Coryate's travels, containing numerous letters he sent back to England from India in 1615. In one of these epistles he addresses a drinking group he refers to jocularly as the 'Worshipful Fraternity of Sireniacal Gentlemen' who met on the first Friday of every month at the Mermaid Tavern. He does not identify all of the members of this club but, in an addendum to the main letter dated Wednesday 8 November 1615, sends his hearty and 'dutiful respect[s]' to his good friends, including Ben Jonson, Hugh Holland, Inigo Jones, John Donne, John Hoskins of the Middle Temple (who became friendly with Donne while at Oxford University and who was a supporter, as we have seen, of Jonson) and the antiquary Sir Robert Cotton, among others. Jonson and Cotton were, at the time, both based in Blackfriars, just a stone's throw from the King's Men's indoor playhouse. The work had a further connection to two members of the First Folio syndicate, for it was printed as part of a collaboration between William Jaggard and Henry Fetherston, and in the letter Coryate mentions Edward Blount among 'Stationers in Paul's Churchyard' with whom he was 'especially' friendly. Blount himself knew of, and greatly admired, Cotton's own writings, which he recommended to Sir William Trumbull as 'worthy your view'.

The Mermaid Tavern was located on Bread Street in St Mildred's parish, within easy access of the stairs to the Thames. It would have stood at the intersection of present-day Cannon Street and Bread Street, the latter's Renaissance counterpart being the very street on which John Donne and John Milton were born. Milton would go on to write a poem in memory of Shakespeare in the Second Folio of 1632 and his father, John Milton senior, was recorded as a trustee of the Blackfriars Theatre in 1620.

The Mermaid Tavern has become the stuff of legend. It was the nineteenth-century editor and critic William Gifford who first placed Shakespeare as one of its fraternity, which 'combined more talent and genius, perhaps, than ever met together before or since', identifying Francis Beaumont, John Fletcher, Sir Robert Cotton and John Donne as frequenters. He was building on John Aubrey's account of this collective's inception, in the process capturing the imagination of later poets and artists who have fantasised about Shakespeare's raucous drinking bouts among that charmed circle of wits. Critics have since drawn attention to the fact that there is little evidence that Shakespeare identified with this group. He does not appear in any of Coryate's published accounts of the 'Sireniacal Gentlemen'.

But should we look again at this community? Others who have been associated with the Mermaid Tavern include William Strachey, investor in the Virginia Company, who probably supplied Shakespeare with a source for *The Tempest* and had been a sharer in the Blackfriars Theatre; notorious gossip and friend of Edward Blount, John Chamberlain; and William Trumbull, the king's ambassador in Brussels, for whom Blount acted as an agent and book supplier. Ben Jonson referred to the 'Bread Street's Mermaid' in his poems and plays, including *Bartholomew Fair* in which he satirises the 'pretenders to wit', the 'Mermaid men', who frequented it. In his verse epistle to Jonson, Francis Beaumont writes 'What things have we seen/Done at the Mermaid! Heard words that have been/So nimble, and so full of subtle flame'. In Coryate's own *Traveller for the English Wits* the Mermaid Tavern emerges as a convivial space where he and his fellow 'Sirenaicks' convened, setting the world to rights while swigging 'the purest quintessence of the Spanish, French, and Rhenish grape, which the Mermaid yieldeth'. It is possible that Coryate was thinking of his tavern friends when lauding those mentioned in his letter published therein for 'being the lovers of virtue, and literature', suggesting that the Mermaid group was a hub for intellectual exchange, literary appreciation and the cultivation of connoisseurship.

That it was a kind of drinking society, of which Coryate was a part, is perhaps evidenced by a Latin manuscript, surviving in the hand of John Chamberlain, which details a 'philosophical feast' of September 1611 at the Mitre Tavern on Fleet Street; the same street in which Henry Condell and the Jaggards owned impressive properties, and in which John Smethwick's shop was located. The list of attendees includes Thomas Coryate, Hugh Holland, Inigo Jones, John Donne, Sir Henry Goodere and John Hoskins among others. Of a total of fourteen members of this philosophical gathering, including Coryate himself, eight would be mentioned among his special friends in his account of the 'Sireniacal Gentlemen' included in his *Traveller for the English Wits*. There is therefore a considerable overlap between those Coryate identifies as his private friends and those who may have formed some kind of intellectual society, albeit potentially a loose one. At least eight of those who attended the Mitre Tavern party were attached to the Inns of Court, which makes sense, given that the Mitre was located on a road from which these legal institutions radiated. The physical proximity of the Mitre to this legal 'set' and to William Jaggard's properties may explain why the latter was selected as the printer for Coryate's second travel book.

Coryate's published texts can only help us identify some of his closest friends, alongside a wider, much less intimate, circle of admirers and eulogisers. They do not in fact confirm all the members of this Mermaid club and it is not certain that this 'Fraternity' persisted as a cohesive group for a significant length of time. The records tell us only that Coryate and some of his intimates met for drinking, dinner and discussion between 1611 and 1615, and may have thought of themselves as a kind of club. But friendships tend to endure longer than organised gatherings and Coryate's circle overlaps, in intriguing ways, with Shakespeare and with Oxford. Indeed, the Mitre gathering was referred to as a 'Convivium Philosophicum', overseen by a mysterious figure identified only through a Latinate pseudonym: 'Radulphus Colphabius', listed as being 'of Brasenose College, Oxford'. In other words, the presiding deity over the feast was attached to Oxford University.

The plot thickens when we note that among the long roll-call of poets who contributed commendatory verses to *Coryat's Crudities* is John Jackson. He turns out to be, intriguingly, one of the men Shakespeare engaged as a trustee for his purchase of the Blackfriars Gatehouse in 1613, along with John Heminges and one William Johnson. More interesting still is the fact that the latter was none other than the proprietor of the Mermaid Tavern, described in the document recording the purchase of the property, which Shakespeare and the trustees signed, as a 'Citizen and Vintner of London'. This indicates that Shakespeare not only knew the landlord of the Mermaid but also placed a certain degree of trust in him.

The Shakespeare connections do not end there. The parade of flatterers cavorting across the pages of *Coryat's Crudities* also included a William Baker, whose own laudatory verse states that Coryate's account will create in his readers the 'itch of travel', imagining a world in which the English 'straight grew travellers, and forsook our main,/To frolic on the gravely shelves of Spain'. The interest in Spain is apt here, for it might not surprise us to see Baker's poem in a collection alongside those of Hugh Holland and Leonard Digges's brother Dudley, given that we have a fascinating note from Leonard Digges himself, penned on a flyleaf at the beginning of a copy of a book now housed in Balliol College, Oxford, which proves they were closely acquainted. This is a document we have encountered before: a note prompted by the publication of the third edition of Lope de Vega's *Rimas* in Madrid in 1613. The full missive reads:

> Will Baker: Knowing that Mr Mabbe was to send you this book of sonnets, which with Spaniards here is accounted their Lope de Vega as in England we should of our Will Shakespeare; I could not but insert thus much to you, that if you like him not, you must never never read Spanish poet, Leo: Digges.

Our Will Shakespeare. Does this phrase merely suggest Shakespeare's status as a kind of national poet? Or is this a more personal statement, one which indicates that Digges, Mabbe and Baker consider Shakespeare to be a friend, together forming a close-knit community of author-scholars? It is obvious that, just three years before Shakespeare's death, all three were well acquainted with his work and thought highly of it. Digges expected Baker instantly to grasp the quality of Lope de Vega's sonnets through his knowledge and appreciation of Shakespeare's.

Digges had probably written this short missive from Spain, in the company of Mabbe, while in the entourage of Sir John Digby. There is a further Shakespeare connection here, for Digby hailed from the playwright's native Warwickshire and was the uncle of George Digby, who also accompanied John on his ambassadorial mission to Spain. George was described by Warwickshire land magnate Sir John Huband as 'my well beloved cousin' and made an executor of his estate in 1593, in the process granting to George half his lease for the Stratford Tithes. The other half was bequeathed to his brother Ralph Huband, who then sold his lease to Shakespeare in 1605. It is perhaps noteworthy that around the time Digges wrote his letter to Baker, Shakespeare seems to have become more interested in Spanish literature. His now-lost play *Cardenio*, fragments of which may have survived through the play *Double Falsehood* staged under the directorship of Lewis Theobald in 1727, was influenced by Cervantes' *Don Quixote* (popularised in England by Blount), and is thought to have been written in collaboration with John Fletcher and performed in 1613.

This might suggest the influence on Shakespeare of an Oxford clique of Hispanophiles. William Baker was born in Devonshire and, like the Digges brothers, entered University College, Oxford, matriculating within weeks of Leonard Digges, in July 1603, receiving his BA in 1607 and his MA in 1609. He may have been the William Baker who lived in Bread Street, in the immediate vicinity of the Mermaid Tavern, who died suddenly in 1617, with only enough time to hastily dictate his will. James Mabbe entered Magdalen College, Oxford, in the winter of 1586–7 at sixteen years of age. He became a 'perpetual Fellow' of the college, taking a Master of Arts in 1598, eventually becoming a university proctor, bursar and senior dean of arts. He taught there and remained closely connected with Oxford for most of his life.

Shakespeare may, therefore, have already been affiliated with an Oxford-based community, which included some of the very men who would memorialise him in the First Folio, several years before his death. These connections may have overlapped with the Mermaid Tavern crowd, with which Shakespeare had some direct links and which comprised members of the circle of Coryate and Jonson. There is another location where the playwright may have nurtured ties with Oxford scholars: the magnificent library of Sir Robert Cotton. This stood a stone's throw from the Blackfriars Theatre and was a magnet for the literati of the day. Jonson may have gravitated towards Cotton because he was a known Catholic, for the two became firm friends. Cotton lauded Jonson with Latin poems in *Volpone*, along with Donne, Beaumont, Fletcher and Dudley Digges, who wrote a dedicatory verse praising the 'art and wit' expressed in Jonson's characters, which made him worthy of the poet's 'laurel'. This play, in which Heminges and Condell both acted, was dedicated by Jonson to 'the most noble and most equal sisters, the two famous universities [Oxford and Cambridge], for their love and acceptance shown', but it was Jonson's association with Oxford University that would prove most enduring. He frequently borrowed books from Cotton's library while researching his plays and in one instance requested a tome to help him with the writing of *Sejanus*, in which Shakespeare had acted. Numerous members of Coryate's friendship group were also users of the library, including Hugh Holland, John Donne, Inigo Jones, probably members of the Digges family, and others who had been present at the feasts associated with the 'Convivium Philosophicum' in Fleet Street.

Ben Jonson had been involved with Sir Robert Cotton in an ambitious plan to create a Royal Academy, first proposed by the antiquary Edmund Bolton, whose projected members would also include Inigo Jones, Hugh Holland, Dudley Digges and Endymion Porter, whose sister, Margaret Porter, Bolton had married around 1606. Porter may in fact have had some acquaintance with personalities associated with Shakespeare. In 1595 his cousin Russell Porter was baptised by Thomas Russell, Leonard Digges's stepfather and the overseer of the playwright's will, and so Porter was a likely intimate of the Russell and Digges families. There is no reason to believe that the bibliophile Shakespeare, who shared a patron with Cotton in the form of George Carey, Lord Hunsdon (who was the Chamberlain's Men's patron from 1596 to 1603), did not visit Sir Robert's library. It was in the vicinity of the Blackfriars Theatre when work started on the construction of the playhouse in 1596. It remained there at least until around 1614, covering the entire period from the King's Men's reclamation of the Blackfriars Theatre in 1608 to Shakespeare's retirement. Shakespeare, like Jonson, would have needed a constant supply of books while writing his plays, and Cotton's library was the closest to one of the King's Men's main theatres.

Shakespeare himself may have come to know the Digges family not just through the Digges brothers' stepfather, but through their

geographical placement close to John Heminges and Henry
Condell in St Mary's, Aldermanbury. The playwright, as we have
seen, moved into nearby Silver Street in the early 1600s and kept
up his associations with the district until at least 1612. Heminges
and Condell served as churchwardens in the very church in which
Thomas Digges, Esquire, father to the Digges brothers, was a
parishioner and whose impressive home was located on Philip
Lane, adjacent to St Mary's. Thomas was a notable mathematician,
astrologer and cosmographer, whose treatise on the latest technologies of warfare had been printed by Shakespeare's former
Stratford neighbour Richard Field in 1579 and whose works, as we
have noted, have been identified as sources for Shakespeare's plays.
Circumstantial evidence of the dramatist's early familiarity with
the Diggeses comes from one Shakespeare sleuth's theory that he
may have seen the engraved portrait of Tycho Brahe, the Danish
proto-scientist, alchemist and astronomer, at Thomas Digges's
home some time after 1590, when Brahe had sent it to him. One
such portrait contains two names that have a talismanic power
today, thanks to Shakespeare: 'Rosenkrans' and 'Guldensteren'.
Had Shakespeare seen the portrait at the Diggeses' home in Philip
Lane, perhaps during a visit to Heminges or Condell, and incorporated these names into *Hamlet*?

Shakespeare's London and Stratford affiliations merge through
the Digges family in other ways. Leonard Digges was just twelve
years old when his father Thomas died on 24 August 1595 and was
buried in St Mary's Church. Thomas's will stipulates that he left
his wife Anne the house in Philip Lane, an estate in Kent and a
considerable annuity 'so long as she shall remain unmarried'.
Despite this, as Russell later testified, 'albeit she exceeded [me] in
age twenty years or near thereabouts ... [I] was drawn to become a
suitor in the way of marriage unto her.' The problems surrounding
the clauses in Thomas's will were evaded with the aid of John
Davies of Quinton, near Stratford-upon-Avon, who supported

Russell in the ensuing legalities. Davies cherished a mutual friend with Shakespeare in the form of John Combe. On 28 January 1613, John mentioned Shakespeare and Davies in his will, alongside Shakespeare's lawyer, Francis Collins (who drafted Shakespeare's own will), bequeathing 'to Master William Shakespeare five pounds and to my Landlord John Davies 40 shillings, Item: I give and bequeath unto Francis Collins the Elder of the borough of Warwick ten pounds'. John Combe's nephew, William Combe the younger, joined Leonard Digges at University College, Oxford, the very same week that the latter matriculated, making them fellow students.

Here we also find a closer Mabbe-Digges connection to intimates of Shakespeare via Oxford. Davies was very close to both James Mabbe and Leonard Digges, for he was a fellow of Magdalen College, as was Mabbe, to whom he left a fabulous silver bowl in his will. To Leonard Digges, whom he called 'my faithful good friend', he left 'the fellow of that bowl', a near-identical copy, inscribed with his initials. These friendly relations were maintained between Davies and Digges till at least close to the latter's death in 1635. A wonderfully lively letter of 1632 from Digges to a friend at Oxford University places Davies within his circle of intimate friends, along with William Combe junior. Digges was staying with Davies in Quinton and was 'called out of the parlor where I was writing' by his host and beckoned 'into the hall to drink' with a guest who had come to the house, where they passed the time convivially. 'I could write you mad relations of the town of Stratford, where I was last week,' he says, referring to Combe by the affectionate nickname 'Pilpit' and advising his friend that 'if you come at any time, know him by the name of Captain Combe, for he is Captain of Stratford Foot Trained Band' who, adds Digges wickedly, one should 'adore [as] the Golden Calf, for they say in Stratford that he cannot have less than £20,000 in his purse'. This was not the only missive Digges penned that day. He wrote another which he attached to the letter, adding a postscript: 'I pray send the enclosed to Ned Blount.' The exchange testifies to an enduring bond between Leonard Digges, Edward Blount and two figures associated with Shakespeare's Stratford coterie: William Combe and John Davies.

Leonard Digges was also much admired, it seems, by John Heminges' own son William, who remembered him in an elegiac verse as 'The famous Digges'. Young William, who was possibly named as a tribute to Shakespeare, became a 'King's scholar' at the University of Oxford, his father potentially having become interested in Oxford as a prospect for him, and cultivating ties there for that purpose. John appears in 1620 in a list of seventy individuals who contributed ten shillings towards the maintenance of the Clock of St Martin's, Carfax, in central Oxford. He is the only charitable individual not listed as a parishioner but as 'Mr Heminges of London'. There are suggestions that these affiliations were long-standing and had brought Digges into a more direct contact with Shakespeare's writing and potentially with the playwright himself. Blount published Digges's translation of a Latin work as *The Rape of Proserpine* in 1617, which was probably influenced by Shakespeare's popular *The Rape of Lucrece*. The strongest evidence that Leonard Digges knew the dramatist in a personal capacity comes from a touching commemorative poem he attached to the 1640 edition of Shakespeare's poems. This is considerably longer and more detailed than his offering in the 1623 First Folio and enshrines Digges's deep admiration and the cherishing of 'the glad remembrance I must love/Of never-dying Shakespeare'. The dramatist, he writes, proves the adage that 'Poets are born not made'. This seems deliberately to counter Ben Jonson's comment in his First Folio poem, in which he declares 'a good Poet's made, as well as born', before addressing Shakespeare directly, 'And such wert thou'. This is not the only hint that some ill-feeling had developed between Jonson and Digges, who draws on his experience of having seen and appreciated Shakespeare's plays to paint an unflattering picture of his rival playwright's dramatic works:

> So have I seen, when Caesar would appear,
> And on the stage at half-sword parley were,
> Brutus and Cassius: oh how the audience,
> Were ravished, with what wonder they went thence,
> When some new day they would not brook a line,
> Of tedious (though well laboured) Catiline's;
> Sejanus too was irksome, they prized more
> Honest Iago, or the jealous Moor.
> And though the Fox and Subtle Alchemist,
> Long intermitted could not quite be missed ...
> Yet these sometimes, even at a friend's desire
> Acted, have scarce defrayed the sea-coal fire
> And door-keepers: when let but Falstaff come,
> Hal, Poins, the rest you scarce shall have a room
> All is so pestered: let but Beatrice
> And Benedick be seen, lo in a trice
> The Cockpit, Galleries, Boxes, all are full
> To hear Malvolio, that cross-gartered gull.

Digges recalls the action and the audiences' warm responses to some of Shakespeare's most popular plays: *Julius Caesar*, *Othello*, the *Henry IV* plays, *Much Ado About Nothing* and *Twelfth Night*. What surprises here is his savage critique of Jonson's works. *Sejanus*, *Catiline*, *Volpone* and *The Alchemist* are not acclaimed plays and the profit derived from performances is scarce enough to pay for the heating of a playhouse or a doorkeeper's wages. In short they are 'tedious', 'irksome' and if left unperformed 'could not quite be missed'. Shakespeare's plays, on the other hand, will pack out every playhouse where they are showing, down to the very last seat in the last box. While Jonson and Digges were still close friends at the time of the First Folio's printing, they clearly had some kind of falling out before Jonson's death in 1637. What Digges's literary appraisal tells us is that he nurtured a 'love' of his 'glad remembrance' for a Shakespeare who, for him, was 'never-dying'.

But what do these intertwined lives tell us? They indicate that the decision to include poets primarily associated with Oxford University in the preliminaries to the First Folio, and under the patronage of Oxford University's chancellor, Sir William Herbert, and its high steward, Sir Philip Herbert, is likely to have originated with Shakespeare himself, rooted in his own intellectual and literary networks; networks that connected Stratford and London via Oxford. What contributes to the Folio's intricate beauty are the intertwined personalities that radiate from it like the roots and branches of a living tree. That Shakespeare's own life, as we have seen, was interleaved with those who memorialised him in that important volume, may suggest that the Folio syndicate or the King's Men chose them because they were the dramatist's friends. If this is so, there is something of Shakespeare's own will in his book.

There is one more textual piece of evidence to consider: a potentially 'lost' Shakespeare sonnet which, if genuinely composed by him, would indicate that the dramatist collaborated on a published text with at least two backers of the First Folio during his lifetime.

'Big with false greatness'

The Enigma of Cygnus and a Lost Shakespeare Sonnet?

In 1605 two of the poets who would later commemorate Shakespeare in the First Folio were brought together in print. The prefatorial material to Ben Jonson's *Sejanus* contains a sonnet in praise of its author by Hugh Holland. Adding his own pro-Jonsonian verse to these preliminaries was William Strachey. But another poem, on the same page and directly beneath the ditty written by Holland, has received rather less attention for its potential association with Shakespeare's Book. This is a sonnet whose author preferred to remain incognito, only signing with the pseudonym 'Cygnus'.

Scholars believe this sonnet was also probably penned by Holland because his own work, *Pancharis*, issued in 1603, included a long flattering poem by Jonson in which the playwright referred to him as a 'Black swan' and a 'sweet singer', a 'Cygnus' who, once 'high flying', was translated 'among the stars … and there [en]shrined'. This is the mythical Cygnus, who was first transformed into a swan and then into the constellation Cygnus. Case closed. The 'Cygnus' sonnet is by Holland. But is it really that simple? When I first read this *Sejanus* poem, certain of its elements reminded me of Shakespeare's own style. It is addressed 'To the deserving Author' and proceeds thus:

> When I respect thy argument, I see
> An image of those times: but when I view
> The wit, the workmanship, so rich, so true,
> The times themselves do seem retrieved to me.
> And as Sejanus, in thy tragedy,
> Falleth from Caesar's grace; even so the crew
> Of common playwrights, whom opinion blew
> Big with false greatness, are disgraced by thee.
> Thus, in one Tragedy, thou makest twain:
> And, since fair works of Justice fit the part
> Of tragic writers, Muses do ordain
> That all Tragedians, Masters of their Art,
> Who shall hereafter follow on this tract,
> In writing well, thy tragedy shall act.
>   CYGNUS.

That this could be an undiscovered Shakespeare sonnet led me to contact the Renaissance theatre scholar Martin Wiggins, chief compiler of the monumental multi-volume *British Drama 1533–1642: A Catalogue*. I asked him if, to his knowledge, anyone had ever attributed the poem to Shakespeare before. He answered that, yes, someone had: he himself. He drew my attention to volume 5 of his *Catalogue* in which he had noted: '"Cygnus" (perhaps a pseudonym for Hugh Holland ... or perhaps the Swan of Avon)'. The fact that we had both independently come to the conclusion that the sonnet was 'perhaps' by Shakespeare made me look again, in more detail, at the mysterious verse by 'Cygnus'. Who is the 'Swan of Avon' whom Wiggins mentions? It is Shakespeare, for this is how Jonson referred to him in his long poem in honour of the playwright in the First Folio, addressing him ecstatically in this manner:

Sweet Swan of Avon! What a sight it were
   To see thee in our waters yet appear,
And make those flights upon the banks of Thames,
   That so did take Eliza, and our James!
But stay, I see thee in the hemisphere
   Advanced, and made a constellation there!
Shine forth, thou Star of Poets, and with rage,
   Or influence, chide, or cheer the drooping stage;
Which, since thy flight from hence, hath mourned like night,
   And despair's day, but for thy volume's light.

These are the last words Jonson produces under his own name in the First Folio, and so the affecting conceit is placed as his climactic portrait of the playwright. The Cygnus of myth was transformed into a swan as he wept by the River Eridanus. Here it is the world that mourns Shakespeare's 'flight' as the Swan of the River Avon, whose living presence shall never again grace England's stages close to the flowing waters of London.

The Cygnus sonnet may well be by Hugh Holland. But why should Holland present two poems in the same text, one with a pseudonym and one without? The two sonnets have the same rhyme scheme, which one may feel seals the deal for both being by the same author. But stylistically they are very different. The one signed by Holland uses the more formal 'you' to address Jonson, while the sonnet by Cygnus uses the informal 'thy', the form favoured by Shakespeare in his *Sonnets*. The sonnet identified as being by Holland shows a fondness for using bracketed phrasing, which the Cygnus sonnet eschews. This is unlikely to be due to two compositors working on one small quarto-sized forme. It is more likely that the differences in punctuation and line grouping across the two poems show the habits of two different authors, the compositor working from two independent manuscripts. Of course, without detailed analysis this can only remain speculation.

For his worthy Friend, the Author.

IN that, this Booke doth deigne SEIANV'S name,
Him vnto more, then *Cæsars* Loue, it brings:
For, where he could not with Ambition's wings,
One Quill doth heaue him to the height of *Fame*.
Yee great-Ones though, (whose ends may be the same,)
Know, that (how euer we do flatter *Kings*)
Their Fauours (like themselues) are fading things,
With no lesse Enuie had, then lost with Shame.
Nor make your selues lesse honest then you are,
To make our Author wiser then he is:
Ne of such Crimes accuse him, which I dare
By all his *Muses* sweare, be none of his.
The Men are not, some Faults may be these Times:
He acts those Men, and they did act these Crimes.

HVGH HOLLAND.

To the deseruing Author.

WHen I respect thy argument, I see
An Image of those *Times*: but when I view
The wit, the workemanship, so rich, so true,
The *Times* themselues do seeme retriu'd to me.
And as *Seianus*, in thy *Tragedie*,
Falleth from *Cæsars* grace; euen so the Crew
Of common *Play-wrights*, whom Opinion blew
Big with false greatnesse, are disgrac'd by thee.
Thus, in one *Tragedie*, thou makest twaine:
And, since faire workes of Iustice fit the part
Of *Tragick* writers, *Muses* doe ordaine
That all *Tragedians*, Maisters of their Arte,
Who shall hereafter follow on this tract,
In writing well, thy *Tragedie* shall acte.

CYGNVS.

A 2

Sonnets by Hugh Holland and the mysterious Cygnus in Ben Jonson's *Sejanus His Fall* (London: Printed by G. Elld, for Thomas Thorpe, 1605), sig. A2. Could Cygnus really be William Shakespeare and this a 'lost' Shakespeare sonnet?

The sonnets, however, 'feel' as if they were written by two different people, expressing two different kinds of relation to Jonson.

If the Cygnus sonnet is by Holland, would it not have appeared odd to him that Jonson, who had so publicly praised him as Cygnus, the 'Black swan', would be using the same myth to refer to Shakespeare in the Folio, a book to which Holland himself was a contributor? This would have been less peculiar if Jonson, Holland and Shakespeare had shared a private joke, that Jonson had referred to both authors as swans, perhaps even with a recognition of difference which reflected something of their respective temperaments or complexions. We cannot know, of course, if Holland was of a darker complexion than Shakespeare. But the idea that both, as notable poets, shared the 'sweet' attributes of the swan (Jonson uses the word 'sweet' to refer to both), which is known in myth to produce the most beautiful music when dying, makes the possibility that Jonson would recognise both as equally deserving of that flattering appellation seem less far-fetched.

Shakespeare had acted in Jonson's *Sejanus*, alongside Richard Burbage, John Heminges, Henry Condell and several other King's Men actors. The Cygnus sonnet, as we would expect, is theatrical in nature, indicating that 'the crew/Of common playwrights, whom opinion blew/Big with false greatness, are disgraced by thee [Jonson]'. In other words, this is a tragedy for tragedians whose talents, meagre by comparison, have been undermined by Jonson's greatness, making a double tragedy out of Jonson's play: 'Thus, in one Tragedy, thou makest twain [that is, two]'. Had this been written by a playwright, its comically self-deprecating nature – particularly its suggestion that other playwrights project only a 'false greatness' – would have been more impactful. Similarly, the sonnet's culminating couplet would be devastatingly funny if this Cygnus had in fact been an actor in this very play. The shamed 'Tragedians', Cygnus argues, 'hereafter' will have to up their game, and 'In writing well, thy tragedy shall act'. This serves as a punchline for the sonnet's comic thrust, concealing a clever dual meaning which indicates both that other playwrights will re-*enact* Jonson's great tragedy by trying to emulate it (but failing, reproduce the 'fall' of Sejanus) and that a tragedian might also 'act' the play, with the implication that he will perform it better having learned from Jonson's immense gifts as a superior playwright. Shakespeare by this point had acquired a reputation as a tragedian of note, having written *Romeo and Juliet*, *Hamlet*, *Othello* and *King Lear* by the end of 1605. Indeed, as we have seen, the poet William Basse referred to Shakespeare as a 'rare Tragedian'. One might also detect in Cygnus's line 'Big with false greatness' strains of Shakespeare's own Sonnet 97, which personifies Time: 'And yet this time removed was summer's time,/The teeming autumn big with rich increase'. Here the expansiveness of 'big ... greatness' and 'big ... increase' has a similar amplificatory effect in both sonnets. But does the Cygnus sonnet stylistically remind us of Shakespeare in other ways?

Shakespeare appears to have been rather fond of the 'twain-in-one' motif. Cygnus's line 'Thus, in one tragedy, thou makest twain', is redolent of numerous sonnets composed by the playwright, including Sonnet 36 in which the sonneteer addresses the youth in these terms: 'Let me confess that we two must be twain/Although our undivided loves are one ... /In our two loves there is but one respect'. The same motif is elaborated in Sonnet 39:

Even for this let us divided live,
    And our dear love lose name of single one,
That by this separation I may give
    That due to thee which thou deserv'st alone.
O absence, what a torment wouldst thou prove
    Were it not thy sour leisure gave sweet leave
To entertain the time with thoughts of love,
    Which time and thoughts so sweetly doth deceive,

And that thou teachest how to make one twain
By praising him here who doth hence remain!

Here the 'twain-in-one' motif recurs with two references to 'time',
mirroring the Cygnus sonnet in which the 'times' are also twice
evoked. In Sonnet 42 the 'twain' conceit returns when the poet
muses on the loss of his love to a rival, lamenting how 'Both find
each other, and I lose both twain', before finding hope in the
thought that 'here's the joy: my friend and I are one ... Then she
loves but me alone'. Most captivating is Shakespeare's use of the
'twain-in-one' image in the narrative poem *The Phoenix and the
Turtle*, published in 1601, in which we are told that the birds 'loved
as love in twain/Had the essence but in one,/Two distincts, division none'. Shakespeare here draws on a paradox that interweaves
tragedy and celebration, much as the Cygnus sonneteer does, singing of 'How true a twain/Seemeth this concordant one; ... As
chorus to their tragic scene'.

There is another feature of the Cygnus sonnet that is something
of a recurring trope in Shakespeare's *Sonnets*: the connection
between the concepts 'argument' and 'muse'. The Cygnus sonnet
begins with the poet reflecting on Jonson's 'argument', one might
say plot or summary, of the play – its dramatisation of the hubristic
falls experienced by powerful individuals in past 'times' – and
wittily explains how the 'Muses do ordain' a similar fall from grace
for all 'tragedians' who will try, but fail, to live up to Jonson's own
greatness. Shakespeare makes this connection between 'argument'
and 'muse' explicitly in no fewer than four sonnets and potentially
in a more subtle way in two more. In Sonnet 38 he writes 'How
can my muse want subject to invent/While thou dost breathe, that
pour'st into my verse/Thine own sweet argument'. Sonnet 79 also
links the poet's 'sick muse' to the 'lovely argument' of his 'sweet
love', while in Sonnet 100 Shakespeare evokes the muse no fewer
than three times, and asks her to 'Sing to the ear that doth thy lays

esteem/And gives thy pen both skill and argument', referring to Time, its passing, spoils and decay, three times. In Sonnet 103 the connection is made again: 'Alack, what poverty my muse brings forth/That, having such a scope to show her pride,/The argument all bare is of more worth/Than when it hath my added praise beside!' In Sonnet 76 Shakespeare states of the beloved subject that 'you and love are still my argument', and while he does not refer to the muse he evokes 'invention', which he consistently associates with the muse in three sonnets we have identified here, as well as in two others, including Sonnet 105, in which 'invention' is again linked directly with a 'muse', through a brilliant variation on the 'twain-in-one' motif:

'Fair, kind, and true' is all my argument,
  'Fair, kind, and true' varying to other words,
And in this change is my invention spent,
  Three themes in one, which wondrous scope affords.
    'Fair, kind, and true,' have often lived alone,
    Which three till now never kept seat in one.

The 'twain-in-one' trope becomes here a 'three-in-one' conceit, amplifying one of Shakespeare's favourite motifs. The 'argument' in literature of the period denotes a statement at the beginning of a work that clarifies its theme. It is perhaps unsurprising that Shakespeare should link this with the operation of a muse, who first gives a poet inspiration to write. But the frequency of Shakespeare's association between the muse's prompting of invention and an 'argument' is notable, given the appearance of this word cluster in the Cygnus sonnet. The more one reads this enigmatic poem, the more 'Shakespearean' it appears.

Jonson's *Sejanus* was initially acquired by Edward Blount in 1604, who then transferred these rights to Thomas Thorpe in August 1605. Just four years later Thorpe would issue Shakespeare's

Sonnets. If the poem is by Shakespeare, therefore, it would mean that Thorpe had published a Shakespeare sonnet *before* he issued the larger collection of *Sonnets*. What is notable is that the Cygnus sonnet appears in a work that has a close association with three personalities behind the First Folio (Blount, Jonson and Holland) and two further figures connected with Shakespeare's works (Thorpe and Strachey). As a 'Shakespeare' sonnet then, its placement in a work bearing the traces of these personalities lends further weight to the idea that the playwright's own wishes – or at least what Heminges and Condell or members of the Folio syndicate *believed* to be his wishes – were known and taken into account when Shakespeare's Book was put together. It also points to stronger personal associations between Holland, Strachey, Thorpe and Shakespeare than have previously been established.

If Shakespeare did write the Cygnus sonnet but wanted to remain hidden from public view, placing it beneath a poem by Holland, with a pre-agreed rhyme scheme that turned them into companion pieces, would have led readers familiar with the relationship between Holland and Jonson to believe Cygnus was the poet dubbed the 'Black Swan' rather than Shakespeare. Had the earlier Jonsonian quip not survived in Holland's *Pancharis*, one wonders how many of us today would have more readily connected the Cygnus of the *Sejanus* preliminaries to Shakespeare. Interestingly, the Cygnus sonnet was removed when Jonson re-attached some of the commendatory poems which appeared in quarto versions of his plays to his folio of *Works* in 1616. The sonnet signed explicitly by Holland was, on the other hand, not only retained but given pride of place near the very beginning of his grand corpus of works. Why, if these poems were by the same hand, was the Cygnus sonnet not included when three poems by Francis Beaumont, for example, were incorporated into that folio's preliminaries? Whether or not the Cygnus poem is by Shakespeare, it represents a community of like-minded poets and scholars, gath-

ered around Ben Jonson, who were united in praising a play in
which the Sweet Swan of Avon had acted, testifying to the latter's
connection to at least some of those who memorialised him in the
Folio.

But how deep do the roots of the First Folio's tree go? Do they
stretch back to William Shakespeare in a more direct way? Is there
any evidence at all that he began to plan his own edition of
collected plays during his lifetime? To explore this question, we
will look at one final mystery which has long captivated
Shakespeare biographers and which might offer us some tantalising clues: the identity of Shakespeare's London lodger.

'Baseless fabric'?

Shakespeare's Lodger and the First Folio

As William Shakespeare approached his death a man called John Robinson was by his side. He appears in the list of witnesses who signed the final version of the playwright's last will and testament, which itself mentions a man of that name in relation to 'that messuage or tenement with the appurtenances wherein one John Robinson dwelleth, situate, lying and being in the Blackfriars in London'. This property was part of the Blackfriars Gatehouse, located just paces to the east of the Blackfriars Theatre, which the playwright had purchased in 1613. It is not certain if this is the same individual who witnessed the dramatist's will, who some believe was a neighbour in Stratford-upon-Avon. But who was Shakespeare's London lodger?

Pinning down the ever-elusive Robinson would tell us much about Shakespeare's state of mind in his final years. Why, in March 1613, did the playwright purchase rooms in the Gatehouse so close to the theatre? Most of his other investments had been in his native Warwickshire and he appears to have divested himself of his shares in the Globe Theatre following its burning down in the very year in which he embarked on this new property venture. He must also have sold his interest in the Blackfriars Theatre because he did not re-assign this to his heirs in his will. It has been suggested that the acquisition of the Gatehouse was connected with the First Folio; that Shakespeare secured it because he needed a base close to the Blackfriars Theatre, providing ready access to the King's Men's archives so that he could prepare his own edition of collected plays, his own First Folio. Even before the conflagration at the open-air Globe, it is likely that those papers were stashed at the indoor theatre, which was a more secure site, located in a wealthier and safer district. The fact that many of Shakespeare's authorial papers and performance scripts appear to have survived could indicate that these important documents – the company's bread and butter – were not held at the Globe.

What compounds the mystery is that Shakespeare was surrounded by John Robinsons. A man of that name signed Lady Elizabeth Russell's petition to remove the players from the Blackfriars Theatre in 1596. He was probably a 'cordwainer', someone who worked with cordwain or cordovan leather and who is likely therefore to have been a prosperous shoemaker. In this John Robinson's favour as a candidate is that by 1639 Shakespeare's tenant would be succeeded immediately by a John Dicks, also a 'cordwainer'. Could Dicks have been part of Robinson's extended family network, or an acquaintance from the shoemaking community? It does somewhat strain belief, however, that Shakespeare would have provided accommodation for an anti-theatricalist who backed a local crusade to ban the players from operating the company's costly new playhouse. When the dramatist was living in St Helen's Bishopsgate in the late 1590s, he was located practically next door to the wealthy and influential alderman John Robinson, whose mansion was no more than a hundred feet north-east of his own lodgings. Robinson died in 1600 but his eldest son, also named John, survived him. Would someone as wealthy and influential as this John Robinson junior have leased rooms that were almost certainly more modest than he was used to? In 1599 a 'Robinson', mentioned without a first name, was identified as a steward to 'Sir John Foskewe' living in Blackfriars, possibly the uncle of the 'John Fortescue, gent.' who was a previous owner of the Blackfriars Gatehouse; but the steward was dead by 1613 and there is no firm proof that a son named John was the most recent occupier of Shakespeare's tenement, though this has been suggested by some. The steward was living in a property 'over against Sir John's door', but this cannot be firmly identified as the Gatehouse. In any case, there was an intervening owner following Fortescue's vacating of the premises, Henry Walker (who had no known connection to a Robinson), from whom Shakespeare purchased the Gatehouse.

Some have speculated that John Robinson may have been Shakespeare's personal servant, or even his dresser. If the dramatist, however, had purchased a tenement in Blackfriars with a view to undertaking the ambitious project of a collected edition of his works, one would expect his lodger to be someone who could help with that endeavour. The most useful would have been a scrivener – a professional scribe whose job was to provide fair copies of documents – or someone working in the publishing industry, such as a stationer, bookseller or printer. Finding such a candidate would lend at least some credence to the notion that the Blackfriars Gatehouse was, in some way, connected to early plans for a First Folio. There is indeed a scrivener named John Robinson, who in 1660 was living on Chancery Lane, still the hub of London's institutions of law, indicating that the bulk of his work was legal in nature. Yet no other information ties this Robinson to Shakespeare or anyone known to him, or even to Blackfriars. He therefore seems an unlikely candidate for Shakespeare's tenant.

There is an eye-catching entry in one of the loan books of the Stationers' Company; a palpably tantalising record of a loan made out to one John Robinson. Describing himself as a 'Citizen and Stationer', he appeared before the then Master of the Stationers'

John Robinson's loan request of 1637 in both Latin and English, which is preserved in the archives of the Company of Stationers. William Aspley was one of the Wardens who granted the loan, with one Robert Kilborne (presumably John Robinson's friend, kinsman or neighbour), a blacksmith who lived not far from William Shakespeare's Blackfriars Gatehouse, indicated as guarantor.

Company, Edmund Weaver, and two Wardens, one of whom was William Aspley, on 11 August 1637. Weaver and Aspley had been confirmed in their elevated company offices in July of that year, and we know Weaver was also close to both Edward Blount and John Smethwick, describing the latter as one of his 'loving friends'. Robinson requested the sum of twelve pounds, placing two friends as surety for twenty-four pounds against the loan, one of whom was Robert Kilborne, a Blacksmith living in Thames Street in the parish of Saint Magnus All Hallows. Thames Street is just south of, and runs parallel to, Carter Lane, with the Blackfriars Gatehouse standing between these two streets.

John Robinson, a stationer. Could he be Shakespeare's lodger? If so, could he have been part of Shakespeare's plan to secure his own legacy in print? Where might this stray branch of the great tree that is the First Folio lead?

John Robinson took his 'freedom' of the Stationers' Company on 6 May 1613. This meant that he would have been looking to set up as a professional stationer just around the time that Shakespeare was finalising his purchase of the Blackfriars Gatehouse property. While trainee stationers were serving their apprenticeships, their masters were usually obliged to provide them with lodging. Once freed, they had to find their own accommodation. But where did this Robinson put down roots? It turns out, just minutes from the Blackfriars Gatehouse, in a shop in Paternoster Row identified by the sign of the Fleur de Luce and Crown (not to be confused with the Fleur-de-lis and Crown which had once operated from St Paul's Cross Churchyard). This stood nearly behind the businesses of Blount and Aspley, on the other side of the St Paul's precinct wall, connected through Paul's Gate in the north-eastern corner of St Paul's Cross Churchyard. To get to the Fleur de Luce and Crown from the Blackfriars Gatehouse, John Robinson would need only to step out of his door, traverse Carter Lane and walk

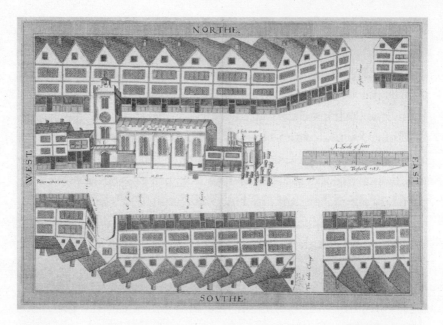

Drawing by Ralph Treswell showing St Paul's Gate, Paternoster Row, the Old Change and West-cheap (that is, Cheapside) in London in 1585. John Robinson, the stationer, partnered with William Tymme whose shop, the Fleur de Luce and Crown, stood in Paternoster Row, at the end of the street closest to Cheapside, just across from the north-eastern corner of St Paul's Cross Churchyard.

north up Old Change, which led directly into the intersection of Paternoster Row and Cheapside. Alternatively, he could cut through the churchyard, either through Paul's Chain or St Augustine's Gate, cross the eastern edge of the cathedral and walk through Paul's Gate. If Robinson had been looking for a new residence after attaining his freedom with the Stationers' Company, he could not have done much better than the Blackfriars Gatehouse.

The identification of this John Robinson as Shakespeare's lodger is strengthened by the fact that, unlike the other contenders, he has numerous connections to the playwright, and in particular to those responsible for disseminating his works in print. When this Robinson started working in Paternoster Row, some time after 1613, he joined forces with a more established publisher, one

William Tymme or Time, who had already been operating that shop. By 1601 Tymme was working with Shakespeare's first publisher, the Stratford-born Richard Field, selected by him as the printer for a work entitled *Saint George for England, Allegorically Described*. Perhaps they shared a passion for allegorical works at this time, for that very year Field was teaming up with Blount to produce another work, presented on its title page as 'Allegorically shadowing the truth of love': Robert Chester's *Love's Martyr*, a poetical compilation that included Shakespeare's *The Phoenix and the Turtle*. The printing press from which that text was issued, belonging to Field, stood just to the west of the Blackfriars Gatehouse, at the westernmost end of Carter Lane.

John Robinson's earliest recorded book was entered in the Stationers' Register jointly with Tymme on 28 April 1615 and called *The Mirror of Majesty*. On the very same day the printer Nicholas Okes logged two books at Stationers' Hall. It was to Okes that Robinson and Tymme turned when they needed a printer for their first collaborative book project, which was published that year with a dedication 'To the noble and right virtuous gentleman Sir Henry Carey ... heir apparent to the right honourable the Lord Hunsdon'. This is yet another connection between Robinson and Shakespeare, for Henry Carey was the son of the Chamberlain's Men's former patron Sir George Carey, Lord Hunsdon, himself the son of another Sir Henry Carey, one-time Lord Chamberlain, who had been the patron of the company named in his honour from 1594.

John Robinson's association with Tymme and Okes brought him into a circle with a particular interest in Shakespeare. Okes had been apprenticed under William King but received his freedom in 1607 under Richard Field, which may account for Okes's interest in the playwright's works, having been involved with editions of *The Rape of Lucrece*, *King Lear* and *Othello*. In 1613, the year in which Robinson became free of the Stationers' Company,

THE
MIRROVR OF
MAIESTIE.

Wherein the Mother-Church inviteth
her Damsels to Contemplate the
Harbourleſſe Gheſt, yet waiting at the doore
of mans heart for entertainment.

Set forth in fiue Sermons:

1 The Blameleſſe Separatiſt.
2 Sweete Contemplation.
3 Salomons Royaltie.
4 Chriſts Coronation.
5 The Saints Dignitie.

Preached in Aſcenſion weeke, by W. Hvll
Doctor in Divinitie.

prat.

NVMB. 16. 24.
Get yee vp from the Tabernacle of Corah, Dathan *and* Abiram.
MATH. 5. 8.
Bleſſed are the pure in heart : they ſhall ſee God.
PSAL. 21. 3.
Thou diddeſt ſet a Crowne of pure gold on his head.
REVE. 5. 10.
He hath made vs Kings and Prieſts to our God, and we ſhall reigne vpon earth.

Ἐν διδῷ τις ... ἰχύει πόνοε :   } G.Nazian.
Καὶ μὴ διδῷς ... ἀδει ἰχύει πόνοε.   } Senten.

Si praſit gratia, nil officit impius liuor :
Si deſit gratia, nil proficit improbus labor.

LONDON,
Printed by Nicholas Okes, for William Timme and Iohn Robinſon, and are to
bee ſold at their ſhop in Pater-noſter-row. 1 6 1 5.

Title page of *The Mirror of Majesty* (London: Printed by Nicholas Okes, for
William Tymme and John Robinson, 1615). This is the earliest known printed
work by John Robinson the stationer. Could this be a book published by
William Shakespeare's London lodger, John Robinson?

Okes printed a take on *Venus and Adonis* called *The scourge of Venus: or, The wanton lady with the rare birth of Adonis*, which was clearly an attempt to cash in on the perennial popularity of Shakespeare's risqué poem. Robinson's connection with stationers who published the dramatist's output may have stretched to his kinship ties, in particular to other publisher-printers by the name of Robinson. Some of these were almost certainly related to each other and possibly even part of a familial publishing network, one of whom developed a particularly close relationship with the King's Men, nurturing folio-production interests which promoted the playing company's work.

The earliest in this group is the stationer Thomas Robinson, active from 1568 to 1589, but possibly apprenticed to a Mistress Toy in 1559. Although he died without children, among his beneficiaries were his brother William Robinson and numerous figures connected with the publishing industry, four of whom are of particular interest: James Roberts, Augustine Laughton, George Bishop and Richard Watkins. Roberts we have met in the story of the First Folio. He initially held the rights to six plays from the Lord Chamberlain's/King's Men, including *The Merchant of Venice*, *Hamlet*, *Troilus and Cressida* and *As You Like It*, and his business would be taken over by William Jaggard. Augustine Laughton was a bookseller, freed of the Stationers' Company in September 1564 and active between 1567 and 1590. He was based for a time at the shop known by the sign of the Grasshopper in St Paul's Cross Churchyard, before moving to Maiden Lane, near Wood Street, just north-east of Tymme's and Robinson's Fleur de Luce and Crown. Laughton trained Nicholas Colman, who had teamed up with a Robert Robinson as the printer for the publication of a ballad in 1586. This is a first clue of a possible link between Thomas and Robert Robinson. Another connection is established through Thomas's friend the bookseller George Bishop, who had trained William Aspley and used a printer's device depicting a 'lost sheep', which passed into the possession of Robert Robinson.

This Robert Robinson was a printer based in Fetter Lane, in Holborn, a road radiating from Fleet Street. He started registering books from September 1586, printing *The Tragical History of Romeus and Juliet*, a core source text for Shakespeare's *Romeo and Juliet*, the following year. The dramatist's own play has an intriguing connection with Robert Robinson, for Robinson's apprentice John Danter later became notorious for his involvement with the publication of *Romeo and Juliet* in 1597. This text acquired a reputation among early scholars as a 'bad quarto', with some claiming it was a pirated edition. Three years before, Danter had printed *Titus Andronicus* for the publishing duo Edward White and Thomas Millington, who sold it from the sign of the Gun in St Paul's Cross Churchyard. These Shakespeare connections ran deep, for Robert's widow would go on to marry Richard Braddock, a printer and bookseller from around 1609, who produced two editions of *Venus and Adonis*, as well as *A Midsummer Night's Dream* and *A Yorkshire Tragedy*, the latter with its false attribution to Shakespeare.

Thomas Robinson's friend Richard Watkins was 'ordain[ed] the sole and only executor', and one of the main beneficiaries, of his will, indicating that they had some kind of close kinship. Robert Robinson collaborated on at least one work with Watkins, and almost all the latter's publications were co-financed with James Roberts. Watkins's shop was the premises that came to be known as the Golden Lion in St Paul's Cross Churchyard, but which may have originally been known by the sign of Love and Death. It was leased to him in 1581 and would remain in the family's hands until 1672 when it was transferred, tellingly, to a stationer named Jonathan Robinson. Watkins's shop, located 'toward the east upon the gate that leadeth out of the churchyard … into cheap[side] and toward the north upon the wall of the said churchyard', was probably the closest bookselling business within the walls of St Paul's precinct to John Robinson's own shop. In other words, Watkins, a friend and collaborator of both Thomas and Robert Robinson, was operating his business just paces away from John Robinson during the latter's tenure of the Fleur de Luce and Crown.

These intertwined Shakespeare interests point to a kinship between Thomas Robinson and Robert Robinson, who may have been Thomas's nephew or other close relation. Yet there is another Robinson, even more closely connected to the King's Men, who operated from St Paul's Cross Churchyard. Humphrey Robinson is a stationer and bookseller we have met before: the co-publisher with Humphrey Moseley of the Beaumont and Fletcher folio of collected plays in 1647, which indicated in its prefatorial material that it looked to Shakespeare's First Folio as a model. Humphrey took up his freedom with the Stationers' Company while the Folio was being printed, and became 'one of the largest and most important book-sellers in this period'. He and Moseley issued numerous works from the King's Men's repertory, particularly plays performed at the Blackfriars Theatre, establishing a firm relationship with the playing company.

The records indicate that Robert Robinson was related to Humphrey in some way; probably a family connection which meant that, ultimately, some of the legacy belonging to the former, particularly the rights to works owned by him, ended up under Humphrey's control. Based at the sign of the Three Pigeons in St Paul's Cross Churchyard from at least around 1627, Humphrey operated a business four doors to the west of the premises of Thomas Robinson's executor, Richard Watkins. Humphrey's friendship group included intimates of Henry Walley and Thomas Walkley (who, as we have seen, both held the rights to Shakespeare plays), as well as of Ralph Mabbe and Edmund Weaver, the latter having granted John Robinson his loan.

The kinship between Thomas Robinson and Robert Robinson, and between the latter and Humphrey Robinson, is on firmer ground, however, than a familial tie between John Robinson and these aforementioned Robinsons. What links John to the others is an engagement with Shakespeare publishing by a limited group of stationers. It is interesting to note that Robert had collaborated with Richard Field more than once between 1593 and 1595, precisely the period in which Field was working on Shakespeare's narrative poems, and not long before Field teamed up with John's business partner William Tymme. Furthermore, Robert had two apprentices, brothers George and Lionel Snowden, the former apprenticed between 1590 and 1597, the latter taking up a seven-year apprenticeship in the year his brother was freed. In 1608 they both sold their printing business to Nicholas Okes, the very same with whom John collaborated on one of his earliest publications. Another detail from John's trace in the archives catches the eye: among the list of those stationers taking up their freedom alongside him in 1613 is Isaac Jaggard himself.

If all this hints at a connection between John Robinson, stationer, and the other Robinsons in our detective story, particularly Robert, then it also indicates that John was part of a network that included some of the pioneers of Shakespeare printing. A curious addendum to the John Robinson trail is that this name appears again on a list of those freed in 1617, alongside another name which makes the heart skip a beat to read: a 'John Shakespeere' took up his freedom that very same month. This must be the John Shakespeare of Warwickshire who began his seven-year apprenticeship with William Jaggard in 1610. It is not known whether this is the same John Robinson we have been tracking, a relative, or simply an unrelated namesake, nor whether he received his training in tandem with a kinsman of William Shakespeare.

If our John Robinson, stationer, is Shakespeare's lodger, and the playwright had intended to involve him in a collected edition of his plays, perhaps this did not materialise because John did not become a successful publisher. He has all but disappeared from history and, among the minuscule number of hard-to-find references in the public record, he is glimpsed in some financial difficulty. While he would have appeared, as a freshly freed stationer, to have been a promising prospect, with some impressive contacts, he may have fallen short of the qualities required for such an ambitious project. That Humphrey Robinson achieved the reputation and magnificence his namesake lacked and then went on to co-finance a folio attached to the King's Men's repertory may suggest that members of the King's Men had a long acquaintance with what was in fact a Robinson family publishing dynasty, stretching back to the time when they were the Chamberlain's Men. It adds a poignant note to these speculations that Humphrey Robinson's nephew was named Hamlet.

It cannot be proved that John Robinson, stationer, is the man to whom Shakespeare rented his Blackfriars property. But he does give us a new candidate for the dramatist's mysterious tenant which bears further investigation, and which offers the enticing possibility that Shakespeare had been planning on overseeing his legacy in print in one resplendent volume, just as his friend and rival Ben Jonson had done. It provides us with an explanation for his investment in the Blackfriars Gatehouse just as he was relinquishing his shares in the company's playhouses. This provocative idea brings us closer than we ever have been to sensing the hand of William Shakespeare – his very touch – on the making of his own book.

Epilogue

1623 and Beyond

*From Shakespeare's Book
to the World's Book*

I'll break my staff,
Bury it certain fathoms in the earth,
And deeper than did ever plummet sound
I'll drown my book.

William Shakespeare, *The Tempest*

On 5 December 1623 Edward Dering became the earliest recorded purchaser of William Shakespeare's First Folio, after securing two copies of the playwright's collected works. He paid two pounds, suggesting that he was willing to part with an additional five shillings per book to have each one enveloped in sumptuous calf skin binding. Perhaps he had been inspired to make this acquisition after seeing a play that day, since his surviving account book records a payment of one shilling and six pence for a visit to a playhouse. As the days that winter were chilly and frequently rainy, it is possible he found his entertainment at the indoor Blackfriars Theatre. If so, his Folios may have been purchased directly from Edward Blount or William Aspley, just paces to the north of that venue in nearby St Paul's Cross Churchyard.

Simply seeing plays performed in the flesh was not enough for Dering. He was prepared to sacrifice a costly twenty shillings per book to own a piece of the 'Sweet Swan of Avon'. The scale of this avid play-lover's investment can be put into perspective when compared to his purchase, just three days before, of eighteen play-books in smaller individual quarto editions for a total of ten shillings. A few days prior to that, he bought thirty individual play-books for the same price as one of the Folios. While out shopping he had been on the lookout for suitably impressive gifts with which to ingratiate himself with James I's influential favourites. Like most ambitious courtiers, he had to take any opportunity to augment his powerbase at court. On the same day, therefore, he bought a magnificent case of knives for Sir Thomas Wotton for twelve shillings, a grand gesture that was still eight shillings cheaper than the First Folios he had bagged. He may have felt he was getting Ben Jonson's folio of collected works for a bargain-basement price when he snapped it up for nine shillings at the same time as his Shakespeare tomes. By this time, with Jonson's folio having been issued nearly eight years before, Shakespeare was clearly hotter property. Something of a budding deviser of plays himself, Dering would no doubt have relished the prospect of using his First Folios to mount amateur productions in his estate, Surrenden Manor in Kent, providing him with further opportunities to mix with powerful members of the nobility who could help him rise at court.

When the First Folio went on sale it was a luxury commodity, within the reach of only those privileged few who, like Dering, moved in the upper echelons of society, who had inherited a reasonable degree of wealth, or who were ensconced in well-paying professions. This is reflected in its other known early purchasers, some of whom appear to have been tapped into networks known to the book's makers and the King's Men. The Folio now at Stonyhurst College in Lancashire was, in all likelihood, purchased by Thomas, 2nd Baron Arundell of Wardour, in 1623, whose uncle on his mother's side was Shakespeare's one-time patron, Henry Wriothesley, 3rd Earl of Southampton, to whom the narrative poems *Venus and Adonis* and *The Rape of Lucrece* had been dedicated. Another intriguing Folio, now residing in Glasgow University Library, was annotated by someone who appears to have had an acquaintance with members of the King's Men. Though the annotator indicated that he knew Richard Burbage 'by report' and was aware of the actor John Lowine only as an 'eyewitness', he had written the word 'know' beside the names of two other actors in the troupe, Robert Benfield and Joseph Taylor, suggesting that he may have had a more direct and personal familiarity with them. The earliest owner of this Folio was probably Henry Cary, 1st Viscount Falkland, though it is signed by his son Lorenzo. The latter or, as has been speculated, his brother Lucius, may have been responsible for the annotations, recording impressions of plays he had seen and the actors he knew in the 1620s and 1630s. Henry's wife, Elizabeth Cary, was a notable poet and playwright who authored *The Tragedy of Mariam* in 1613, which has the distinct honour of being the first original play by a woman in the English language, making her a pioneer of female writing in the period. The Carys were very close to Ben Jonson, who wrote verses in their honour, providing them with another connection to the creators of Shakespeare's Book.

A Folio under private ownership conceals a purchase history which may link it with one of the volume's financiers. This could have been acquired by Thomas Johnson I, a well-to-do merchant tailor who lived on Fleet Street, just paces from the Jaggards' tenements and John Smethwick's shop in St Dunstan's in the West. In fact, Johnson served on the vestry of that very church with Smethwick, so is likely to have purchased the book from him. It is possible that a Folio bought by John Egerton, 1st Earl of Bridgewater, was also secured from the same area, which was close

The Workes of William Shakespeare,

containing all his Comedies, Histories, and
Tragedies: Truely set forth, according to their first
ORIGINALL.

The Names of the Principall Actors
in all these Playes.

William Shakespeare.

Richard Burbadge.

John Hemmings.

Augustine Phillips.

William Kempt.

Thomas Poope.

George Bryan.

Henry Condell.

William Slye.

Richard Cowly.

John Lowine.

Samuell Crosse.

Alexander Cooke.

Samuel Gilburne.

Robert Armin.

William Ostler.

Nathan Field.

John Underwood.

Nicholas Tooley.

William Ecclestone.

Joseph Taylor.

Robert Benfield.

Robert Goughe.

Richard Robinson.

Iohn Shancke.

Iohn Rice.

A First Folio owned by Glasgow University Library was probably purchased not long after it was printed by Henry Cary, 1st Viscount Falkland. It contains annotations, possibly by one of his sons, beside the 'Names of the Principal Actors', indicating that the annotator had an acquaintance with some of the actors, while others were only known through hearsay or 'by report'.

to the hub of the legal profession. Since he was trained as a lawyer, we might imagine he eagerly picked up the tome from one of the shops radiating from Fleet Street, close to the Inns of Court, possibly even Smethwick's. There may be a link here to another Folio purchaser, for it was Bridgewater's elevation to Lord Lieutenant of Wales which provided the occasion for the poet John Milton to compose the masque *Comus* in honour of his patron. Milton's father, we may recall, had been a trustee of the Blackfriars Theatre, and the poet would provide a commendatory verse in the Second Folio of 1632, in which he referred to the playwright as 'my Shakespeare' and the 'Dear son of Memory'. While these words have a personal ring to them, Milton was only seven years old when Shakespeare died. He was however, by his own admission, a lover of the theatre, stating in 1626 when still just seventeen: 'When I am weary of this [study], the retinue of the intricate theater welcomes, and the garrulous stage calls to its applause'. He carefully annotated his own First Folio (now in the Free Library of Philadelphia), outlining admired words and phrases and incorporating handwritten passages from quarto editions of the plays not included in the 1623 publication; the personal and personalised copy of an author who would become a giant of English letters and literary culture.

The appearance of a volume in folio solely devoted to commercial plays was a landmark moment in the history of printing. The translation of Shakespeare's words into a high-status object, purchased by so many wealthy and influential early readers, lapped them in an aura of prestige and could only have helped elevate the craft of playwriting in the process. John Heminges and Henry Condell must have looked upon the project to create a single volume of Shakespeare plays in folio with some satisfaction, having succeeded, with their fellow collaborators in that endeavour, not only in completing a challenging and financially risky venture, but in commemorating their one-time colleague in so extravagant a

Luc. Thankes gentle Romanes, may I gouerne so,
To heale Romes harmes, and wipe away her woe,
But gentle people, giue me ayme a-while,
For Nature puts me to a heauy taske :
Stand all aloofe, but Vnckle draw you neere,
To shed obsequious teares vpon this Trunke :
Oh take this warme kisse on thy pale cold lips,
These sorrowfull drops vpon thy bloud-slaine face,
The last true Duties of thy Noble Sonne.

Mar. Teare for teare, and louing kisse for kisse,
Thy Brother *Marcus* tenders on thy Lips :
O were the summe of these that I should pay
Countlesse, and infinit, yet would I pay them.

Luc. Come hither Boy, come, come, and learne of vs
To melt in showres : thy Grandsire lou'd thee well :
Many a time he danc'd thee on his knee :
Sung thee asleepe, his Louing Brest, thy Pillow :
Many a matter hath he told to thee,
Meete, and agreeing with thine Infancie :
In that respect then, like a louing Childe,
Shed yet some small drops from thy tender Spring,
Because kinde Nature doth require it so:
Friends, should associate Friends, in Greefe and Wo.
Bid him farwell, commit him to the Graue,
Do him that kindnesse, and take leaue of him.

Boy. O Grandsire, Grandsire : euen with all my heart
Would I were Dead, so you did Liue againe.
O Lord, I cannot speake to him for weeping,
My teares will choake me, if I ope my mouth.

Romans. You sad *Andronici*, haue done with woes,
Giue sentence on this execrable Wretch,
That hath beene breeder of these dire euents.

Luc. Set him brest deepe in earth, and famish him :
There let him stand, and raue, and cry for foode :
If any one releeues, or pitties him,
For the offence, he dyes. This is our doome :
Some stay, to see him fast'ned in the earth.

Aron. O why should wrath be mute, & Fury dumbe?
I am no Baby I, that with base Prayers
I should repent the Euils I haue done.
Ten thousand worse, then euer yet I did,
Would I performe if I might haue my will :
If one good Deed in all my life I did,
I do repent it from my very Soule.

Lucius. Some louing Friends conuey the Emp.hence,
And giue him buriall in his Fathers graue.
My Father, and *Lauinia*, shall forthwith
Be closed in our Housholds Monument :
As for that heynous Tyger *Tamora*,
No Funerall Rite, nor man in mournfull Weeds,
No mournfull Bell shall ring her Buriall :
But throw her foorth to Beasts and Birds of prey :
Her life was Beast-like, and deuoid of pitty,
And being so, shall haue like want of pitty.
See Iustice done on *Aaron* that damn'd Moore,
From whom, our heauy happes had their beginning :
Then afterwards, to Order well the State,
That like Euents, may ne're it Ruinate.   *Exeunt omnes.*

FINIS.

The prologue to Iuliet and Romeo

(LOUE,
Tow housholds both alike in dignitie,
(In faire Verona where wee lay o[u] scene)
From ancient grudge, breake to new mutinie
where ciuil blood makes ciuil hands uncleane:
from forth the fatall loynes of these tow foes,
A paire of starre-crost louers take their life:
whose misaduentur'd piteous ouerthrow
doth with their death burie their parents strife,

the fearfull passage of their death-markt
and the continuance of their parents rage:
Which but their childrens death naught could remoue,
Is now the tow howres traffique of our stage.
The weh if you wth patient eares attend,
what heere shall misse o[u] toyle shall striue to mend.

finis

fashion, entirely unaware that a product created for the eyes of the few would become the secular book of the world. Neither theatre manager lived to see the publication of the Second Folio in 1632, in which both William Aspley and John Smethwick became investors. Condell was buried in the parish church of St Mary's, Aldermanbury, on 29 December 1627, the very same year in which Isaac Jaggard died. Heminges was entombed on 12 October 1630, having requested to be 'near unto my loving wife Rebecca Heminges who lieth there interred and under the same stone which lieth in part over her there'. Condell's wife, Elizabeth, was buried in the same church in October 1635. Edward Blount perished penniless and indebted by 1632, while William Aspley died just months after reaching his goal of becoming a Master of the Stationers' Company in 1640. He was followed to his grave the following year by John Smethwick. While the core group of financiers were alive when the book was advertised at the Frankfurt Book Fair, and would have expected it to have been read in some parts of Europe, they could not have imagined just how far it would travel.

Not long after the last of the syndicate members was laid to rest, the First Folio began making its way across the globe. The first copy that can currently be identified as having left England was purchased by a Dutch diplomat named Constantine Huygens, a linguist and lover of English letters, who counted among his personal friends Ben Jonson and John Donne (whose poems he admired enough to undertake the labour of translating them into Dutch). He had been on ambassadorial missions to England from 1618 and sojourned there during the printing of the First Folio in 1622–3, little knowing that one day he would be the owner of that book. He purchased it in 1647, not in England but in the Hague, most probably from an English bookseller. Just as political pressures exerted their shaping influence on the First Folio's creation, they guided the book's cross-national adventures, for the individual who sold it to Huygens may have been an escapee from the English Civil War of the 1640s. Another Folio, discovered in what was once a Jesuit College in St Omer, was an early émigré that may have reached France by 1650. Plays were mounted by the student body of that institution, which would have included those crypto-Catholics escaping Protestant England to study in a setting more congenial to their faith, and this Folio could have provided them with a veritable cabinet of dramatic works from which to choose performance texts.

Around the same time, a Folio was making its way to Italy. It had been thought that one of Dering's Folios had ended up in the University Library of Padua, but it is more likely that this book had reached there, entirely appropriately for this opulent item, as a consequence of the commercial and diplomatic links between England and Venice, crossing the seas with ambassadors and merchants trading in the prized exotic goods that flowed through this bustling emporium city. It is possible that the Folio arrived not long after it had been used as a prompt book for performances in England in the 1640s. Its original owner was probably one of two Venetian consuls, both named John Hobson, the younger Hobson nephew to the elder. At his death Hobson junior left his entire book collection to the English students of Padua, with the intention of housing these precious volumes in a library that had been created there in 1649. The Folio subsequently found its way, with other books from Hobson's collection, to the monastic library of Santa Giustina. There, in that strange way fate has of operating almost poetically, it stood on a shelf beside one of the sources which had influenced Shakespeare, John Harington's translation of Ludovico Ariosto's *Orlando Furioso* of 1591, which provided the playwright with inspiration for *Much Ado About Nothing*. The majority of the other books with which it had been stored were the kind most helpful to merchants and diplomats, dealing with the arts of navigation, cosmography and the latest political developments. This Folio was relocated to Padua's University Library in 1840, and it seems fitting that it is the only first edition of Shakespeare's collected works outside of England to reside in a city in which one of the Folio plays is set, with Padua providing the scenic backdrop to *The Taming of the Shrew*.

In the intervening centuries, Shakespeare's Book voyaged further afield, with copies finding new homes in seven other European countries. The lion's share, however, would end up in the United States of America, 149 at the last count, thanks in no small part to the enormous collecting efforts of Folio-hunters Henry and Emily Folger. Folios can now be found from Ohio to Indiana, from New York to New Jersey, from Texas to Washington, with eighty-two kept at the Folger Shakespeare Library alone. The Folgers acquired one of the Folios which has a particularly important role in relation to the history of women's reading practices: the first securely identified as having an early female owner. In fact it was owned by no fewer than three women. With a provenance stretching back to around 1640, it was proudly inscribed by its earliest detectable female holder, who wrote therein: 'Mary Child is the true possessor of this book'. This is a bold statement in an age when women's educational prospects were limited and in which few females owned their own books. This Folio passed to an Elizabeth Brocket, who is likely to have owned it from around 1695 to at least 1712, remaining in the Brocket family for some time thereafter, and recorded as being in the possession of a 'Mrs Brocket' in the early 1900s. It was then purchased by Henry Folger in 1907. The book includes annotations that disclose an interest in women's moral conduct and it may have been Elizabeth Brocket who inscribed on its pages, among other poetical flourishes, the ditty: 'Wit, when wisdom is too weak to guide her,/Is like a headstrong horse that throws his rider.'

In 1913 Henry Folger purchased a Folio that has been linked to Shakespeare in interesting ways. Originally, it was probably

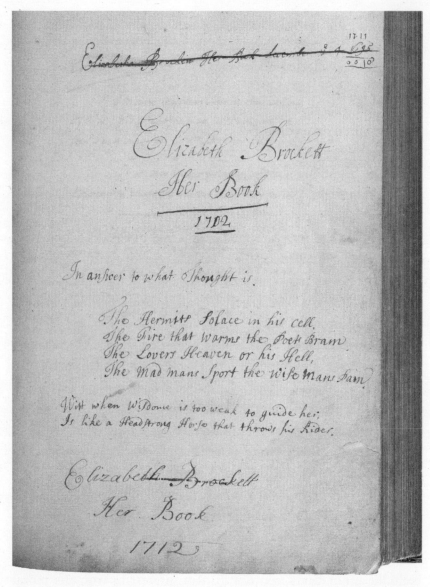

Elizabeth Brockett
Her Book
1702

In answer to what I thought is:

The Hermits Solace in his cell,
The Fire that warms the Poets Brain
The Lovers Heaven or his Hell,
The Mad mans Sport the wise mans Pain

Wit when Wisdome is too weak to guide her;
Is like a Headstrong Horse that throws his Rider.

Elizabeth Brockett
Her Book
1712

Folger Shakespeare Library First Folio 23. Purchased by Henry Folger in 1907, this is the earliest example of an extant Folio that can be securely traced to female owners. It had belonged to Mary Child from around 1640, and later passed to Elizabeth Brocket around 1695 (possibly directly transferred from Mary to Elizabeth after the former's death), who probably inscribed it with her signatures and fragments of poetry addressing female conduct and behaviour. The Folio was then in the possession of another 'Mrs Brocket', making at least three known female owners.

acquired by the Vaughan family of Trebarried in Wales not long after it was first printed, whose members traced their lineage back to Sir Roger Vaughan of Bredwardine. Roger, who is said to have been knighted by Henry V shortly before his death in the Battle of Agincourt, was the son-in-law of David Gam, who received an honourable name-check in Shakespeare's *Henry V* as the 'Davy Gam Esquire' who was among the titled men 'of name' to perish in the same battle. The family may have been particularly interested in purchasing the Folio that included this play in which their noble ancestor was commemorated. According to a long-standing tradition Shakespeare was once hosted at Trebarried and while in the area explored a cave called 'Fairy Glen' at Clydach Gorge, near Abergavenny, an excursion that inspired *A Midsummer Night's Dream*. A cave in that same gorge is still known as 'Shakespeare's Cave'.

The Folgers made another acquisition that year, one which stands as a poignant reminder of the sad history of Prince Charles, whose failed marriage negotiations with the Spanish Infanta Maria formed the dramatic backdrop to the creation of Shakespeare's Book. While he succeeded his father as King Charles I in 1625, and as the King's Men's patron, his execution in 1649 marked the blood-soaked crescendo to the English Civil War between the royalists and the parliamentarians, who wanted to remove the royal family and have England ruled as a republic. One such anti-royalist was Colonel John Hutchinson, whose family hailed from Owethorpe in Northamptonshire, and who is now famed for signing Charles I's death warrant. And so it was, that a Shakespeare lover and early owner of a First Folio helped end the life of the patron who supported the playing company whose historic labours gave birth to that most hallowed volume. A further touching note to this tragedy can be found in the Royal Collection at Windsor Castle where, alongside a finely preserved First Folio, can be found Charles's own copy of the Second Folio that he is said to have cherished while in prison. Apparently a comfort and a distraction during the long and tedious hours, this book bears his own annotations.

The Windsor Folio is just one of fifty that now remain in the United Kingdom. At least sixteen are housed in London, while the universities of Oxford and Cambridge boast four copies each. Dublin, Edinburgh, Leeds, Manchester, Yorkshire, Lancashire and Birmingham, among other locations, all have their own Folios, with the Shakespeare Centre, located in Shakespeare's birthplace of Stratford-upon-Avon, holding three. Japan is the next most plenteous in Folios, with fifteen in all, twelve of those kept in Tokyo's Meisei University. There are also Folios in Sydney, Auckland and Cape Town. The Folios in the latter two locations arrived there in the second half of the nineteenth century and stand as potent reminders of the sometimes insidious way in which the colonial enterprise can be disguised as philanthropy. These were once owned by Sir George Grey, an energetic coloniser, who had served as a governor of South Australia, New Zealand and Cape Colony in South Africa, as well as premier of New Zealand and high commissioner of South Africa. A traveller, explorer, pedagogue and diplomat, he supported the establishing of a library in Cape Colony, now Cape Town, in 1858, and created the Free Public Library in Auckland in 1880, with generous bequests of books to both fledgling institutions; including, eventually, a First Folio for each, as jewels at the centre of these libraries' rich intellectual treasure houses. Grey's intention was not simply to provide educational centres to which English and European colonisers could retreat to maintain some contact with their home cultures. He wanted to use these pedagogical hubs as part of an ambitious programme to establish English culture, literature and learning as the gold standard of human achievement, justifying a supposedly civilising mission to educate, in his own words, 'the savage' temperament of the indigenous peoples over which he governed. In his address following the inauguration of the Free Public Library in 1883, he declared triumphantly that 'the Anglo-Saxon language is to be our great medium of communication', insisting that a commitment to this endeavour would see New Zealand's 'population of so mixed a character … gradually merging into the use of that one familiar tongue … which is to dominate the world'. For Grey the library exemplified, in miniature, the task of educating 'people not civilized, but still barbarous' and a First Folio placed within such a temple to learning would be a shimmering talisman evidencing the superiority of the British Empire, for there book lovers would be able to 'read with the contemporaries of Shakespeare the first edition of his poems, and handle the volumes which undoubtedly the learned of England in that day handled and perused with delight'.

Other Folios are 'witnesses' to the similarly troubling or complex colonial histories with which they were bound. The Folio belonging to the University of Texas, Austin, has a provenance that can be traced back to seventeenth-century England, but it travelled with Sir Francis Alexander Newdigate, the governor of Tasmania and subsequently of Western Australia, in whose family it had long remained, till he sold it in 1920 at a then colossal £2,000; beyond even the budget of Henry Folger, who conceded defeat and allowed himself to be outbid. The Folio preserved in the State Library of New South Wales is a testament to the ways in which forms of educational and cultural colonialism were spurred on by the industrial age. It was donated in 1885 by Sir Richard Tangye and his brother George, pioneering engineers and philanthropists who expanded their manufacturing and hydraulics business from Birmingham in England to Australia, as part of their broader programme of supporting the arts and education. Richard was delighted to discover that next to his bequest, kept tightly sealed in a protective case, a facsimile was provided 'for students to examine'. A Folio in private hands in Colorado was probably acquired some

time in the first half of the nineteenth century by Sir Thomas
Munro who was involved with the colonisation of India as gover-
nor of Madras and was an investor in the East India Company.
Slightly after that, around 1860, another Folio, which is now in the
Huntington Library, is known to have been owned by Sir John
Baptist Joseph Dormer, 12th Baron of Dormer, of Grove Park in
Warwick, who had been an 'Inspector of Musketry for Madras and
Burmah'. In such instances the First Folio became a barometer of
the British colonial values that these men sought to impose on the
countries and the peoples with which they came into contact, and
over which they held sway. All too often in the recent history of
England's expansionist projects, where the empire ruled,
Shakespeare's works – through the Folio or some other medium –
were newly implanted, readily available to the colonisers' hands and
lips.

The First Folio's global infiltration has been a sometimes uneasy
and troubling one, interlaced with political agendas and imperial
ambitions that have not always been to the benefit of the countries
to which copies of that volume, and the so-called 'cultural capital'
of Shakespeare's words more broadly, have been transplanted. In
the fullness of time, the displaying of surviving Folios in museums
and public exhibitions, and their availability for study in libraries
and educational institutions (including the very same Folios that
were once in the possession of avid colonisers), facilitated the
embedding of the dramatist's plays and poems in school and
university curricula, and educated the public on the Folio's own
complex histories. No doubt the fact that this volume has left to
posterity the blueprints for the endless breathing reiteration of
Shakespeare's lines through speech, gesture and spectacle on stages,
and in film, television, the internet and digital media, has made the
playwright a towering presence in popular culture throughout the
planet. So many of those memorable characters who have, for four
centuries, been embodied by actors or read by generation after

generation of eager Bard lovers, becoming exemplars for humanity's moral dilemmas and part of the cultural fabric, would not exist without the First Folio. These plays are the mirrors in which we see ourselves.

When William Shakespeare played Prospero in *The Tempest* at the Globe, perhaps the last role he ever performed before retiring from acting, the character promised to 'drown my book', the source of his unearthly power. But Shakespeare's Book has cast a more lasting spell upon the wider globe, travelling far from its beginnings as a commodity that made so many of the dramatist's achievements available only to the privileged few. Today that book represents the co-ownership of Shakespeare by people everywhere, of all nationalities, localities, ethnicities, religions, genders, backgrounds, abilities, sexualities, classes and types of schooling. Shakespeare's Book made the world's Shakespeare; and more than that. The makers of the First Folio could little have imagined how, in preserving and cultivating that legacy in a manner that would create 'Shakespeare' as we have all come to know him today, they planted an ever-flourishing textual tree whose living leaves would be intertwined, in vital and legible ways, with the making of the modern world.

ACKNOWLEDGEMENTS

There are so many people without whom this book could never have come into being. Firstly I would like to thank my parents, Thalia and John, for their tireless support and belief in me, and my late brother George for everything he taught me. His life continues to be a gift to me, even years after his death. My family are the foundation for everything I do and no words will ever be enough to express my gratitude.

I am blessed to have incredibly supportive and kind friends and colleagues, past and present, at the Shakespeare Institute and University of Birmingham. Thank you (listed in no other order than alphabetical) Jessica Chiba, Matt Clulee, Juliet Creese, Sally Delbeke, Michael Dobson, Ewan Fernie, Victoria Flood, Ella Hawkins, Toria Johnson, John Jowett, Luke Kennard, Mark Richardson, Abigail Rokison-Woodall, Will Sharpe, Simon Smith, Robert Stagg, Tiffany Stern, Erin Sullivan, Karin Thomson, Kate Welch, Rebecca White and Martin Wiggins. I am especially grateful to Michael Dobson for his support of the project that became *Shakespeare's Book* from the earliest stages, to Michael Toolan, and to the awarding committee of the Birmingham Fellowships at the University of Birmingham, particularly Claire Preston who championed this project at its very inception. I am so fortunate to have begun this research with a Birmingham Fellowship, which nurtured the work and my career in more ways than I have room to outline here. The British Academy will also always have a place in my affections for supporting me as an early career researcher. I would like to extend a special thanks to Tom Lockwood and Karen Martin for their help and encouragement during a critical period in the writing of this book. Their generosity, positivity and practical problem-solving made a huge difference and I will be forever grateful to them.

I want to mention Martin Wiggins again here because he was the long-suffering sounding board for my theories, ideas and questions throughout the writing of this book. He gave up his time, shared his unpublished research, steered me in promising directions (and away from less fruitful paths) and mentored me in ways that fundamentally shaped this project. I have learned so much from his committed approach to research and his work ethic. I have also received phenomenal support over the years from René Weis and Helen Hackett, who have shaped my work and research interests since my University College London days and whose friendship has always been a guiding light. I am also grateful to all my former colleagues at UCL for giving me such a wonderful second home, and the best possible start to my career, while I was there.

I have gained inspiration and strength from other dear friends along the way. Again, in no order other than alphabetically, I am deeply indebted to Yasmin Arshad, Sally Bayley, Paul Edmondson, Keir and Lilly Elam, Helen Fry, Anita Garfoot, James Hamilton, Aaron Kent, Celia Lee, Rowan Mackenzie, Vicky McMahon, Shona McNeill, Kate McPherson, Kate Moncrief, Yewande Okuleye, Eleni Pilla, Susan Ronald, Katherine Scheil and Alison Weir. Susan Ronald and Alison Weir helped nurture my biographical writing from the beginning, and I am grateful for support from Tracy Borman and Kate Williams, particularly during the start of my commercial writing career where this made such a difference. Shona McNeill helped cultivate in me a love of literature, and still does, as did Carol Wells who, very sadly, passed away just before the publication of this book; both made studying Shakespeare a true delight and an adventure, and it is doubtful I would have entered into the field of Shakespeare scholarship without their influence. I hope I can continue sparking that flame in others which they lit in me. Recent projects I have been working on with (also alphabetically listed) Yasmin Arshad, Matt Clulee, Paul Edmondson, Aaron Kent, Rowan Mackenzie, Yewande Okuleye, Eleni Pilla and Katherine Scheil have also buoyed me up during the writing of *Shakespeare's Book*. Thank you all for your uplifting and positive energies!

I am ever obliged to my agents Julian Alexander of the Soho Agency (UK) and George Lucas of Inkwell Management (USA), as well as to Arabella Pike of William Collins and Claiborne Hancock of Pegasus, for believing in this project and for throwing their energy, commitment and enthusiasm behind it. Thanks to you all, and to your teams, for the tireless work you have put into making *Shakespeare's Book* a reality. This project could not have come together without the labours of so many involved in its physical manufacture. Again purely alphabetically, I would like to thank Martin Brown, Helen Ellis, Sam Harding, Graham Holmes, Iain Hunt and Mark Wells for going above and beyond the call of duty, working so diligently and self-sacrificingly, often during out-of-office hours, to get this book done, and with such cheerfulness, thoughtfulness and care. Thanks are also due (once more, alphabetically) to Jessica Case of Pegasus; Peter Foden, who supplied me with wonderful translations of Latin documents from the Stationers' Archives; Spencer Fuller at Faceout Studio (for the Pegasus version) and Ola Galewicz (for the William Collins version) who designed such stunning and attention-grabbing book covers for *Shakespeare's Book*; Lorentz Gullachsen, who took the cover author photograph, and who was such a joy to work with on the photoshoot; Dennis Levine, whose discussions with me about figures close to Shakespeare have been fascinating and are feeding into further projects; and Nicole Maher of Pegasus. I also want to add a further special thanks to Arabella Pike and Iain Hunt for their astute, precise and sensitive editing of *Shakespeare's Book*, which improved it immeasurably.

I would like to thank all my students – past, present and future – for the limitless inspiration they give me, and their commitment to, and love of, Shakespeare, literature and history, which reminds me daily how much I love researching these fields too!

All those mentioned in these acknowledgements, and those not included but who have influenced my path in life and this book, helped to cultivate what I hope will be a textual tree whose branches and leaves will bear fruit in ways that will be of some use to others. Thanks again to you all!

TABLES

First Folio Play	Last Known Rights Holder	Stationers' Register Entry
The Tempest*	King's Men	-
The Two Gentlemen of Verona*	King's Men	-
The Merry Wives of Windsor	Arthur Johnson	18 January 1602
Measure for Measure*	King's Men	-
The Comedy of Errors*	King's Men	-
Much Ado About Nothing	William Aspley (with Andrew Wise)	23 August 1600
Love's Labour's Lost	John Smethwick	19 November 1607
A Midsummer Night's Dream	Thomas Fisher (rights possibly claimed by Thomas Pavier)	8 October 1600
The Merchant of Venice	Lawrence Hayes	8 July 1619
As You Like It*	William Jaggard via James Roberts?	-
The Taming of the Shrew*	John Smethwick (rights possibly acquired through The Taming of a Shrew; not Shakespeare's play)	19 November 1607
All's Well That Ends Well*	King's Men	-
Twelfth Night, or What You Will*	King's Men	-
The Winter's Tale*	King's Men	-
The Life and Death of King John*	Thomas Dewe (Registered a play about the life of King John which was not Shakespeare's)?	-
The Life and Death of Richard the Second	Matthew Law	25 June 1603
The First Part of King Henry the Fourth	Matthew Law	25 June 1603
The Second Part of King Henry the Fourth	William Aspley (with Andrew Wise)	23 August 1600

First Folio Play	Last Known Rights Holder	Stationers' Register Entry
The Life of King Henry the Fifth	Thomas Pavier	14 August 1600
*The First Part of King Henry the Sixth**	King's Men	-
The Second Part of King Henry the Sixth	Thomas Pavier	19 April 1602
The Third Part of King Henry the Sixth	Thomas Pavier	19 April 1602
The Life and Death of Richard the Third	Matthew Law	25 June 1603
*The Life of King Henry the Eighth**	King's Men	-
*The Tragedy of Coriolanus**	King's Men	-
Titus Andronicus	Thomas Pavier	19 April 1602
Romeo and Juliet	John Smethwick	19 November 1607
*Timon of Athens**	King's Men	-
*The Life and Death of Julius Caesar**	King's Men	-
*The Tragedy of Macbeth**	King's Men	-
The Tragedy of Hamlet	John Smethwick	19 November 1607
King Lear	Nathaniel Butter (with John Busby)	26 November 1607
Othello, the Moor of Venice	Thomas Walkley	6 October 1621
*Antony and Cleopatra**	Edward Blount	20 May 1608
*Cymbeline, King of Britain**	King's Men	-
Troilus and Cressida	Henry Walley (with Richard Bonian)	28 January 1609

Table 1: William Shakespeare's First Folio plays and their most recent known rights holders before the publication of the Folio, with dates of entry in Stationers' Register. The plays are listed in the order presented in the First Folio's 'Catalogue', with *Troilus and Cressida* included last due to its later printing and exclusion from the 'Catalogue'. Play titles are based on the First Folio's titles with some modernisation and regularisation. Asterisks denote plays published in the First Folio for the first time. The issuing of so many Shakespeare plays for the first time in one volume was a potent marketing tool and selling point of the First Folio.

Rights Holders	Location of Business	First Folio Play
William Aspley	Parrot, St Paul's Cross Churchyard	*Much Ado About Nothing* *The Second Part of King Henry the Fourth*
Edward Blount	Black Bear, St Paul's Cross Churchyard	*Antony and Cleopatra*
Nathaniel Butter	Pied Bull, St Augustine's Gate, St Paul's Cross Churchyard	*King Lear*
Thomas Dewe	St Dunstan's Churchyard	His rights to another King John play giving him control of *The Life and Death of King John*(?)
Lawrence Hayes	Association with Green Dragon (occupied by father, Thomas Hayes), St Paul's Cross Churchyard	*The Merchant of Venice*
William Jaggard	Half-Eagle and Key, Barbican	*As You Like It*(?)
Arthur Johnson	White Horse, St Paul's Cross Churchyard	*The Merry Wives of Windsor*
Matthew Law	Fox, St Augustine's Gate, St Paul's Cross Churchyard	*The Life and Death of Richard the Second* *The Life and Death of Richard the Third* *The First Part of King Henry the Fourth*

Rights Holders	Location of Business	First Folio Play
Thomas Pavier	Ivy Lane	*The Life of King Henry the Fifth*
		The Second Part of King Henry the Sixth
		The Third Part of King Henry the Sixth
		Titus Andronicus
		A Midsummer Night's Dream(?)
John Smethwick	St Dunstan's Churchyard	*Love's Labour's Lost*
		The Taming of the Shrew (rights acquired through *The Taming of a Shrew*)
		The Tragedy of Hamlet
		Romeo and Juliet
Thomas Walkley	Eagle and Child, Britain's Burse, the Strand	*Othello, the Moor of Venice*
Henry Walley	Spread Eagle, St Paul's Cross Churchyard	*Troilus and Cressida*

Table 2: Known rights holders to William Shakespeare's plays, in alphabetical order by surname, and the works they owned, with locations of their shops/businesses or of businesses associated with them. Play titles are based on the First Folio's titles with some modernisation and regularisation. In order to publish the plays which the King's Men no longer controlled, the First Folio syndicate had to negotiate with the owners of the rights to those works and convince them to sell or lease their Shakespeare-related assets.

NOTES

Maps

The maps of St Paul's Cross Churchyard, its bookshops and St Paul's wider precinct are based on a collation of the following: the vital cartographical work of Peter W.M. Blayney, presented in his *The Bookshops in Paul's Cross Churchyard*, Occasional Papers of the Bibliographical Society, no. 5 (London: Bibliographical Society, 1990), as well as his *The First Folio of Shakespeare* (Washington D.C., Folger Shakespeare Library 1991), p. 27; the 'Map of Early Modern London' project overseen by Janelle Jenstad: 'The Agas Map. The Map of Early Modern London, Edition 7.0', https://mapoflondon.uvic. ca/agas.htm; supplemented with additional material from numerous other sources cited in *Shakespeare's Book* (including the Notes section), particularly the title pages of early published books, the Company of Stationers' Archives (CSA) and two useful reference works: H.G. Aldis et al., *A Dictionary of Printers and Booksellers in England, Scotland and Ireland, and of Foreign Printers of English Books, 1557–1640*, gen. ed. R.B. McKerrow (London: Bibliographical Society, 1910), and Henry R. Plomer, *A Dictionary of the Booksellers and Printers who were at work in England, Scotland and Ireland from 1641–1667* (London: Bibliographical Society, 1907). I have added to this, material from my own research into the Blackfriars district and its environs, particularly as presented in my book *Shakespeare and the Countess: The Battle that Gave Birth to the Globe* (London: Penguin, 2014). Also useful has been Julian Bowsher's *Shakespeare's London Theatreland: Archaeology, History and Drama* (London: Museum of Archaeology, 2012), pp. 118–19 and 203–209. The map of St Dunstan's in the West and Fleet Street has been reconstructed through Jenstad: 'The Agas Map. The Map of Early Modern London, Edition 7.0', https://mapoflondon.uvic.ca/agas.htm; helpful research in Ben Higgins' *Shakespeare's Syndicate: The First Folio, its Publishers, and the Early Modern Book Trade* (Oxford: Oxford University Press, 2022), pp. 170–210; Button v Whitfield, TNA C 2/JasI/B40/22, dated 1610; Indenture of Conveyance of Land to William Jaggard, LMA CLA/023/DW/01/294, item 14, dated 20 June 1618; David Kathman, 'Henry Condell and His London Relatives', *Shakespeare Quarterly*, vol. 63, no. 1 (Spring 2012), pp. 108–115;

and John Stow, *A Survey of London, Written in the Year 1598* (Stroud: Sutton Publishing, 2005), p. 334; the maps presented in *Shakespeare's Book* are not to scale, but intended as diagrammatic representations, providing a sense of the relative positions of key locations and buildings.

Epigraphs

All the epigraphs from William Shakespeare's plays, which head the various sections and 'acts' of *Shakespeare's Book*, are taken from: William Shakespeare, *The New Oxford Shakespeare: The Complete Works*, general editors, Gary Taylor, John Jowett, Terri Bourus and Gabriel Egan (Oxford: Oxford University Press, 2016).

The First Folio

All quotations from the First Folio's preliminary pages, as well as references to individual plays within it, throughout *Shakespeare's Book* are taken from *The Norton Facsimile: The First Folio of Shakespeare*, second edition, ed. Peter W.M. Blayney (New York and London: W.W. Norton and Company, 1996), unless otherwise stated. Other editions/Folios I have used, and collated with this, are *Mr. William Shakespeares Comedies, Histories, & Tragedies: A Facsimile of the First Folio, 1623*, ed. Doug Moston (New York and London: Routledge, 1998); *Mr. William Shakespeares Comedies, Histories, & Tragedies*, Folger Shakespeare Library First Folio 5, available via the Folger Shakespeare Library's 'Meet the Folger First Folios' online page: https://www.folger.edu/shakespeare/first-folio/meet-folger-folios; and *Mr. William Shakespeares Comedies, Histories, & Tragedies*, a copy of the First Folio once owned by the poet John Milton, accessible from the Free Library of Philadelphia: https://libwww.freelibrary.org/digital/feature/first-folio.

Prologue – The Covenant?: Shakespeare's 'Fellows' and the First Folio

p. 1, **selling at Christie's auction house** … Examples of articles detailing the sale of the First Folio include *Fine Books Magazine*, October 2020, https://www.finebooksmagazine.com/blog/shakespeare-first-folio-sells-just-under-10-million; BBC News, 14 October 2020, https://www.bbc.co.uk/news/entertainment-arts-54544737; and *Smithsonian Magazine*, 16 October 2020, https://www.smithsonianmag.com/smart-news/shakespeares-first-folio-sells-ten-million-dollars-180976074/. See also the announcement made by Christie's on its website, 14 October 2022: https://www.christies.com/about-us/press-archive/details?PressReleaseID=9826#:~:text=New%20York%20–%20William%20Shakespeare's%20Comedies%2C%20Histories%2C%20%26,October%202020%20and%20exceeded%20its%20estimate%20of%20%244%2C000%2C000-6%2C000%2C000. On the desirability of the First Folio see Andrea Mays, *The Millionaire and the Bard: Henry Folger's Obsessive Hunt for Shakespeare's First Folios* (New York: Simon and Schuster, 2015) and Eric Rasmussen, *The Shakespeare Thefts: In Search of the First Folios* (New York and London: Palgrave Macmillan, 2011).

p. 2, **one of the most significant conservation projects in history** … On the historical importance of the First Folio, both for the preservation of Shakespeare's plays and the shaping of his posthumous identity, see Chris Laoutaris, 'The Prefatorial Material [to the First Folio]', in *The Cambridge Companion to Shakespeare's First Folio*, ed. Emma Smith (Cambridge: Cambridge University Press, 2016), pp. 48–67; Emma Smith, *The Making of Shakespeare's First Folio* (Oxford: Bodleian Library, 2015), especially pp. 1–46; Emma Smith, *Shakespeare's First Folio: Four Centuries of an Iconic Book* (Oxford: Oxford University Press, 2016); Ben Higgins, *Shakespeare's Syndicate: The First Folio, its Publishers, and the Early Modern Book Trade* (Oxford: Oxford University Press, 2022), especially pp. 1–38; Gary Taylor, '*Comedies, Histories & Tragedies* (and Tragicomedies and Poems: Posthumous Shakespeare, 1623–1728)', *The New Oxford Shakespeare: Critical Reference Edition: The Complete Works*, general editors, Gary Taylor, John Jowett, Terri Bourus and Gabriel Egan (Oxford: Oxford University Press, 2017), pp. xvii–lxix; Paul Collins, *The Book of William: How Shakespeare's First Folio Conquered the World* (London: Bloomsbury, 2009); Peter W.M. Blayney, *The First Folio of Shakespeare* (Washington D.C.: Folger Shakespeare Library, 1991); Owen Williams and Caryn Lazzuri, eds, *Foliomania! Stories Behind Shakespeare's Most Important Book* (Washington D.C.: Folger Shakespeare Library, 2011); John Jowett, *Shakespeare and Text* (Oxford: Oxford University Press, 2007), especially pp. 69–92; and Sonia Massai, *Shakespeare and the Rise of the Editor* (Cambridge: Cambridge University Press, 2007), especially pp. 136–79. Of importance in the establishing of the First Folio as worthy of serious study are: R. Crompton Rhodes, *Shakespeare's First Folio: A Study* (Oxford: Blackwell, 1923); W.W. Greg, *The Shakespeare First Folio* (Oxford: Clarendon Press, 1955); Alfred W. Pollard, *Shakespeare Folios and Quartos: A Study in the Bibliography of Shakespeare's Plays 1594–1685* (New York: Cooper Square Publishers, 1970); and Charlton Hinman, *The Printing and Proof-Reading of the First Folio of Shakespeare*, 2 vols (Oxford: Clarendon Press, 1963).

p. 4, **Those plays not included in the First Folio have acquired canonical status more slowly** … For more on the canonicity of Shakespeare and his rise as a 'national poet' see Michael Dobson, *The Making of the National Poet: Shakespeare, Adaptation and Authorship, 1660–1769* (Oxford: Oxford University Press, 1994); Smith, *The Making of Shakespeare's First Folio*, pp. 10–15; and Emma Depledge, *Shakespeare's Rise to Cultural Prominence: Politics, Print and Alteration, 1642–1700* (Cambridge: Cambridge University Press, 2018).

p. 4, **this has not been to the benefit of all cultures, all classes and all ethnicities** … For examples of recent important work on the complex colonial histories of Shakespeare see Ania Loomba, *Shakespeare, Race, and Colonialism* (Oxford: Oxford University Press, 2002); Ania Loomba and Martin Orkin, eds, *Post-Colonial Shakespeares* (New York and London: Routledge, 1998); Joyce Green MacDonald, ed., *Race, Ethnicity, and Power* *in the Renaissance* (Madison and Teaneck: Fairleigh Dickenson University Press, 1997); Coen Heijes, *Shakespeare, Blackface and Race: Different Perspectives* (Cambridge: Cambridge University Press, 2020); Walter S.H. Lim, *The Arts of Empire: The Poetics of Colonialism from Ralegh to Milton* (Newark: University of Delaware Press, 1998); Ian Smith, *Black Shakespeare: Reading and Misreading Race* (Cambridge: Cambridge University Press, 2022); Geraldo U. de Sousa, *Shakespeare's Cross-Cultural Encounters* (Houndmills: Palgrave, 1999); Ayanna Thompson, ed., *Colorblind Shakespeare: New Perspectives on Race and Performance* (New York and London: Routledge, 2006); Ayanna Thompson, *Passing Strange: Shakespeare, Race, and Contemporary America* (Oxford: Oxford University Press, 2011); Ayanna Thompson, *The Cambridge Companion to Shakespeare and Race* (Cambridge: Cambridge University Press, 2021); Trevor Boffone and Carla Della Gatta, *Shakespeare and Latinidad* (Edinburgh: Edinburgh University Press, 2021); Ruben Espinosa, *Shakespeare on the Shades of Racism* (New York and London: Routledge, 2021); Farah Karim-Cooper, 'Shakespeare Through Decolonization', *English* (London), vol. 70, no. 271 (2022), pp. 319–24; Farah Karim-Cooper and Eoin Price, eds, special issue of *Shakespeare* journal on 'Shakespeare, Race and Nation', vol. 17 (2021), pp. 1–153; and Farah Karim-Cooper, *The Great White Bard: Shakespeare, Race and the Future of His Legacy* (London: Oneworld, 2023). A fascinating account of Shakespeare-related artefacts exchanged as gifts, as part of England's diplomatic relations with other countries, can be found in Helen Hopkins, 'Gifts of the World'?: Creating and Contextualising the Shakespeare Birthplace Trust's International Collections, unpublished doctoral thesis (Birmingham: Birmingham City University, 2022).

p. 4, **Around 235 complete or partially preserved copies of the First Folio are known to have survived** … The existing Folios are (apart from a couple of recent discoveries) itemised in *The Shakespeare First Folios: A Descriptive Catalogue*, eds Eric Rasmussen and Anthony James West (Houndmills: Palgrave, 2012), especially pp. xi–xii and pp. 866–72, the latter pages including lists of First Folios in different countries and repositories around the world.

p. 5, **a number of Folios, including those now in Texas, Australia, New Zealand and South Africa** … For these Folios see a longer account in the Epilogue; Rasmussen and West, eds, *The Shakespeare First Folios*, pp. 746–49, 772–73, 847–50; and Smith, *Shakespeare's First Folio*, pp. 95–107.

p. 5, **after Nelson Mandela was arrested for his activist resistance to apartheid** … For more on what came to be known as the 'Robben Island Bible', see Devaksha Moodley, 'Interview: Introducing Sonny – The Story of "The Robben Island Bible"', *Shakespeare in Southern Africa*, vol. 30, no. 1 (2017), pp. 107–12; David Schalkwyk, *Hamlet's Dreams: The Robben Island Shakespeare* (London: Arden, 2013); Matthew Hahn, *The Robben Island Shakespeare* (London: Bloomsbury, 2018); and Rowan Mackenzie, *Creating Space for Shakespeare: Working with Marginalized Communities* (London: Arden Bloomsbury, 2023), pp. 129–32.

p. 6, **William Shakespeare made a hasty addition to his will** … Shakespeare's Last Will and Testament, the final version of which was signed on 25 March 1616, is TNA PROB 1/4. All quotations from Shakespeare's will refer to this document. A transcript of the will appears in *Stratford-upon-Avon Wills: 1348–1701*, vol. 1, eds Stephanie Appleton and Mairi Macdonald (Stratford-upon-Avon: Dugdale Society, 2020), pp. 315–18.

p. 6, **a new series of bequests that were more personal in nature** … For a description of the personal nature of Shakespeare's final bequests, with a new interpretation of some of these, see Lena Cowen Orlin, *The Private Life of William Shakespeare* (Oxford: Oxford University Press, 2021), pp. 142–95.

p. 7, **the Globe on London's Bankside and the Blackfriars Theatre in the well-to-do district of Blackfriars** … The histories of the Theatre, Globe and Blackfriars playhouses, along with the changing patronage of the playing company to which Shakespeare belonged, are dealt with in detail in Laoutaris, *Shakespeare and the Countess*.

p. 8, **Sizes of surviving First Folios vary considerably** … Estimated sizes are derived from a range of Folios recorded in Rasmussen and West, eds, *The Shakespeare First Folios*.

p. 12, **an acrimonious legal suit with his own daughter, Thomasina, in 1615** … The suit is recorded in TNA KB 27/1454/1, rotulus 692, ff. 1v–2v. See also Shakespeare Documented, https://shakespearedocumented.folger.edu/resource/document/ostler-v-heminges.

p. 12, **'old stuttering Heminges'** … From a ballad recorded in *Gentleman's Magazine*, no. 86 (1816), p. 114 [quoted as my own edited version]. The ballad also records that 'The reprobates, though drunk on Monday,/Prayed for the fool and Henry Condye [Condell]'. In addition, Heminges' 'swollen eyes' are compared to a 'drunken Fleming's'. Does this chain of imagery convey a popular view that Heminges and Condell were fond of drink, or was this association made because both owned drinking establishments (Heminges' near the Globe Theatre and Condell's on Fleet Street)?

pp. 12–13, **Heminges' last recorded acting role would come in 1617** … **Condell's final known acting role would be in 1619** … The dates of Heminges' and Condell's last acting roles are based on important unpublished research by Martin Wiggins. I am grateful to him for sharing his knowledge of the Chamberlain's/King's Men personnel with me. Throughout *Shakespeare's Book* the dates of all actors' entries into the Chamberlain's/King's Men, and the years in which they took up shares in the company, are based on unpublished communications with Martin Wiggins, cross-referenced against Andrew Gurr's *The Shakespeare Company: 1594–1642* (Cambridge: Cambridge University Press, 2004 [2011 edition]), especially pp. 217–46, but resolving on Wiggins' dating where there are discrepancies or differences of opinion.

p. 13, **reissued the King's Men's licence** … Transcribed in Irwin Smith, *Shakespeare's Blackfriars Playhouse: Its History and Its Design* (London: Peter Owen), pp. 495–96.

p. 13, 'great living, wealth and power' with 'mighty and great friends' ...
From the bill of complaint of John Witter against John Heminges and
Henry Condell, 20 April 1619, TNA REQ 4/1/2/1.

p. 14, his first works probably being *Titus Andronicus*, *The Comedy of Errors*
and the *Henry VI* plays ... Which plays Shakespeare wrote first is a hotly
contested subject among Shakespeare scholars. Useful guides to the dating
of plays include the multi-volume *British Drama, 1533–1642: A Catalogue*,
ed. Martin Wiggins, in association with Catherine Richardson (Oxford:
Oxford University Press, from 2012), and *The Oxford Companion to
Shakespeare*, eds Michael Dobson and Stanley Wells, revised by Will
Sharpe and Erin Sullivan (Oxford: Oxford University Press, 2015).

p. 14, The First Folio's plays each originated in one or more of these varied
kinds of source text ... Useful guides to the source texts of the First Folio
include Gabriel Egan, 'The Provenance of the Folio Texts', in Smith, ed.,
The Cambridge Companion to Shakespeare's First Folio, pp. 68–85, and
Massai, *Shakespeare and the Rise of the Editor*, pp. 136–79.

p. 15, 'To the memory of John Heminge and Henry Condell, Fellow actors
...' Transcribed from the memorial. There are also transcripts, along with
details of Heminges' and Condell's burial site, in Charles Connell, *They
Gave Us Shakespeare: John Heminge and Henry Condell* (Boston and London:
Oriel Press, 1982), pp. 1–8, and Edwin Nungezer, *A Dictionary of Actors and
of Other Persons Associated with the Public Representation of Plays in England
before 1642* (New Haven: Yale University Press, 1929), p. 101.

p. 16, an age when playwrights did not always own the rights to their own
plays ... Some playwrights appear to have controlled the rights to their
own plays, and this is a hotly debated subject among scholars: see Andrew
Gurr, 'Did Shakespeare Own His Own Playbooks?', *Review of English
Studies*, New Series, vol. 60, no. 244 (April 2009), pp. 206–29, and E.A.J.
Honigmann, 'How Happy was Shakespeare with the Printed Versions of
his Plays?', *Modern Language Review*, vol. 105, no. 4 (October 2010),
pp. 937–51.

p. 16, Before a book could be published, stationer-publishers were obliged to
seek a 'licence' or 'allowance' ... A particularly useful account of the
function and purpose of the Stationers' Register is Tiffany Stern, 'Plays in
the Stationers' Registers in the time of Shakespeare', *Literary Print Culture:
The Stationers' Company Archive* (Marlborough: Adam Matthew, 2017):
http://www.literaryprintculture.amdigital.co.uk.bham-ezproxy.idm.oclc.
org/Essays/TiffanyStern.

Chapter 1 – England's 'Delightful Proteus': The Death of Richard Burbage

p. 21, a will dictated in haste from his deathbed ... Richard Burbage's will is
TNA PROB 1/32. It is also transcribed in E.A.J. Honigmann and Susan
Brock, eds, *Playhouse Wills, 1558–1642* (Manchester: Manchester
University Press, 1993 [2015 edition]), pp. 113–14. Those present at
Richard Burbage's bedside during his final hours are gleaned from this will.

p. 22, **Establishing the Theatre, serving as a permanent and fixed base for an acting troupe in London** … The location of the Theatre in Shoreditch, the proximity of the Burbage brothers, and Richard Burbage's early career are derived from the following: Julian Bowsher, *Shakespeare's London Theatreland: Archaeology, History and Drama* (London: Museum of Archaeology, 2012), pp. 55–62; John H. Astington, 'His Theatre Friends: The Burbages', in *The Shakespeare Circle: An Alternative Biography*, eds Paul Edmondson and Stanley Wells (Cambridge: Cambridge University Press, 2015), pp. 248–60, especially p. 257; Edwin Nungezer, *A Dictionary of Actors and of Other Persons Associated with the Public Representation of Plays in England before 1642* (New Haven: Yale University Press, 1929), p. 69; Mary Edmond, 'Yeomen, Citizens, Gentlemen, and Players: The Burbages and their Connections', in *Elizabethan Theater: Essays in Honor of S. Schoenbaum*, eds R.B. Parker and S.P. Zitner (Newark: University of Delaware Press, 1996), pp. 30–49; and the ODNB entry for 'Richard Burbage' by Mary Edmond. Richard Burbage was baptised on 7 July 1568 at St Stephen's Church, Coleman Street, London.

p. 22, **'beat him with a broom staff, calling him "murdering knave"'** … Richard Burbage's brawl is quoted from Nungezer, *A Dictionary of Actors*, pp. 67–68.

p. 22, **Ralph Crane was a scrivener** … Richard Burbage's will is identified as being in Crane's hand in Honigmann and Brock, eds, *Playhouse Wills*, pp. 113–14. For Crane's work for the King's Men see Martin Wiggins, ed., in association with Catherine Richardson, *British Drama, 1533–1642: A Catalogue, Vol. 7: 1617–1623* (Oxford: Oxford University Press, 2016), pp. 194–99, and Nungezer, *A Dictionary of Actors*, pp. 106–107. See also Paul Werstine, 'Ralph Crane and Edward Knight: professional scribe and King's Men's bookkeeper', in *Shakespeare and Textual Studies*, eds Margaret Jane Kidnie and Sonia Massai (Cambridge: Cambridge University Press, 2015), pp. 27–38, especially pp. 36–37.

p. 23, **Tooley had special reason to feel close to the Burbages** … On Nicholas Tooley see Nungezer, *A Dictionary of Actors*, pp. 374–76, and Edmond, 'Yeomen, Citizens, Gentlemen, and Players …', pp. 30–49. David Kathman described Edmond's identification of Nicholas Tooley as the son of the merchant William Tooley as 'good' but not 'ironclad'; see his 'John Rice and the Boys of the Jacobean King's Men', *Shakespeare Survey*, vol. 68 (2015), pp. 247–66, especially p. 252. Tooley's bequests in his will are itemised in Honigmann and Brock, eds, *Playhouse Wills*, pp. 124–28. Tooley had probably graduated from his apprenticeship with the Chamberlain's Men around 1601, becoming a sharer in the King's Men around 1610–11 (Dating based on Martin Wiggins' unpublished research, which he kindly shared with me). See also Andrew Gurr, *The Shakespeare Company 1594–1642* (Cambridge: Cambridge University Press, 2004 [2011 edition]), p. 244. On 14 January 1584 Susan Tooley, Nicholas's mother, married Thomas Gore at St Stephen's Church, Walbrook. The Gores had links with the theatre through the Davenant family, who would count among their descendants the playwright and theatre manager Sir William Davenant, later rumoured to have been Shakespeare's illegitimate son; see Edmond, 'Yeomen, Citizens, Gentlemen, and Players ...', pp. 37–38.

p. 23, **Richard Robinson, whose name appears twenty-fourth on the Folio's roll-call of actors** ... For Richard Robinson see Nungezer, *A Dictionary of Actors*, pp. 300–303; Edmond, 'Yeomen, Citizens, Gentlemen, and Players ...', p. 42; Honigmann and Brock, eds, *Playhouse Wills*, p. 128; Kathman, 'John Rice and the Boys of the Jacobean King's Men', p. 259. Robinson graduated from his apprenticeship around 1613 and took up his shares in the King's Men's playing company that very year (Dating based on Martin Wiggins' unpublished research, which he kindly shared with me). See also Gurr, *The Shakespeare Company*, pp. 238–39.

p. 23, **'very pretty fellow' and an 'ingenious youth'** ... Ben Jonson, *The Devil Is an Ass, a comedy acted in the year 1616, by His Majesty's servants* (London: 1641), Act 3, Scene 6, p. 29.

p. 24, **'essential to a play'** ... Abraham Cowley, *Love's Riddle: A Pastoral Comedy* (London: Printed by John Dawson for Henry Seile, 1638), sig. A3v.

p. 24, **Richard Cowley, who had lived on Holywell Street** ... Cowley's death and will are itemised in Honigmann and Brock, eds, *Playhouse Wills*, pp. 112–13. For his career see Nungezer, *A Dictionary of Actors*, pp. 105–106; Gurr, *The Shakespeare Company*, p. 225. In 1605 both Heminges and Burbage had acted as overseers for the will of another senior actor in the company, Augustine Phillips, who joined the Chamberlain's Men at its inception in 1594 after some time with Lord Strange's Men, and was one of the original sharers in the Globe venture. Left twenty shillings in gold by Phillips in his will, Cowley had been a senior member of the King's Men and was listed in 1601, when the company was the Chamberlain's Men, as joint-payee for three performances at court in the presence of Queen Elizabeth I, his name appearing after John Heminges'. Augustine Phillips' will is transcribed in Honigmann and Brock, eds, *Playhouse Wills*, pp. 72–75, and his career outlined in Nungezer, *A Dictionary of Actors*, pp. 280–82, and Gurr, *The Shakespeare Company*, p. 225. For Cowley's listing as joint-payee see *Dramatic Records in the Declared Accounts of the Treasurer of the Chamber 1558–1642, Malone Society Collections*, vol. 6 (Oxford: Oxford University Press for The Malone Society, 1961–2), p. 31. See also E.K. Chambers, *William Shakespeare: A Study of Facts and Problems*, vol. I (Oxford: Clarendon Press, 1931 [1951 edition]), pp. 79–82.

p. 24, **Cowley must have been very close to this theatrical family, since two of his children were named as tributes to the Burbage brothers** ... Nungezer, *A Dictionary of Actors*, pp. 105–106.

p. 25, **'undiscovered country, from whose bourn/No traveller returns'** ... William Shakespeare, *Hamlet*, ed. G.R. Hibbard (Oxford: Oxford University Press, 1994), 3.1.80–81.

p. 25, **James Burbage had been an out-of-pocket joiner turned theatrical impresario** ... For more on the context of the building of the Theatre see

Chris Laoutaris, *Shakespeare and the Countess: The Battle that Gave Birth to the Globe* (London: Penguin, 2014), especially pp. 112 and 316–17; C.C. Stopes, *Burbage and Shakespeare's Stage* (London: De la More Press, 1913), pp. 19–53; and Astington, 'His Theatre Friends: The Burbages', pp. 250–51. For the Red Lion theatre in Newington Butts and Shoreditch Theatre see Bowsher, *Shakespeare's London Theatreland*, pp. 49–62 and 213–14.

p. 26, **Where the Burbages led, others would soon follow. The very next year the Curtain playhouse was completed** … The building of the Curtain Theatre and the description of the surrounding Shoreditch area are reconstructed from: Bowsher, *Shakespeare's London Theatreland*, pp. 62–67 and 215–18; John Stow, *A Survey of London, Written in the Year 1598* (Stroud: Sutton Publishing, 2005), pp. 96–97, 105 and 356–97; Stopes, *Burbage and Shakespeare's Stage*, p. 19; Catharine Arnold, *Globe: Life in Shakespeare's London* (London and New York: Simon and Schuster, 2015), p. 62; Astington, 'His Theatre Friends: The Burbages', pp. 248–60, especially pp. 250–51. I would like to thank Christopher Whatmore for drawing my attention to the portion of Stow's *Survey* that distinguishes between the earlier and later phases of the parish's fortunes. There is a wonderful description of the building of the Theatre, James Burbage's career and the Shoreditch area in Geoffrey Marsh, *Living with Shakespeare: Saint Helen's Parish, London, 1593–1598* (Edinburgh: Edinburgh University Press, 2021), pp. 83–129.

p. 27, **When Richard Burbage came of age as an actor** … For the outline of Richard Burbage's early career see Mary Edmond, 'Yeomen, Citizens, Gentlemen, and Players …', pp. 30–49; ODNB entry for 'Richard Burbage' by Mary Edmond; Nungezer, *A Dictionary of Actors*, pp. 67–69; and Gurr, *The Shakespeare Company*, pp. 222–23.

pp. 27–28, **Most likely the son of a George Heminges, John was baptised on 25 November 1566** … On John Heminges' career see the ODNB entry for 'John Heminges' by Mary Edmond; Nungezer, *A Dictionary of Actors*, pp. 179–86; Gurr, *The Shakespeare Company*, p. 230; and Paul Edmondson, 'His Editors: John Heminges and Henry Condell', in *The Shakespeare Circle*, eds Edmondson and Wells, pp. 315–28. I am also grateful to Martin Wiggins for imparting his knowledge of Heminges' career in unpublished correspondence. It is possible that Heminges had initially joined the Queen's Men (before entering Strange's Men), for his wife, Rebecca, was the widow of William Knell, a member of that company who was murdered by an acting colleague named John Towne; see Edmondson, 'His Editors John Heminges and Henry Condell', p. 316.

p. 28, **Condell was ten years Heminges' junior and hailed from East Anglia** … Henry Condell's career and property investments are derived from David Kathman, 'Henry Condell and His London Relatives', *Shakespeare Quarterly*, vol. 63, no. 1 (Spring 2012), pp. 108–15; the ODNB entry for 'Henry Condell' by Mary Edmond; Nungezer, *A Dictionary of Actors*, pp. 98–101; Gurr, *The Shakespeare Company*, p. 225; and Edmondson, 'His

Editors John Heminges and Henry Condell', pp. 315–28. I am also grateful to Martin Wiggins for imparting his knowledge of Condell's career in unpublished correspondence.

p. 29, **Just two years into the Chamberlain's Men's operation, the company faced a crisis** … For the full story of the loss of the Shoreditch Theatre, the banning of the men from the Blackfriars Theatre and the way in which this led directly to the building of the Globe Theatre, see Laoutaris, *Shakespeare and the Countess*. The petition to prevent the players from occupying the Blackfriars Theatre, headed by Lady Elizabeth Russell, is TNA SP 12/260, f. 176, dated November 1596.

p. 30, **He was 'posthumous born, a month after his father's decease' and 'brought up poorly'** … Quoted from 'Ben Jonson's Conversations with William Drummond of Hawthornden', in *Ben Jonson, The Complete Poems*, ed. George Parfitt (Harmondsworth: Penguin, 1975 [1996 edition]), p. 465. Jonson's early life, parentage and schooling are also recounted in Ian Donaldson, *Ben Jonson: A Life* (Oxford: Oxford University Press, 2011), pp. 65–79, and in the ODNB entry for 'Ben Jonson', also by Ian Donaldson.

p. 30, **Philip Henslowe, meanwhile, had embarked on something of an aggressive head-hunting mission to entice Jonson** … Ben Jonson's association with Philip Henslowe can be traced through *Henslowe's Diary*, ed. R.A. Foakes (Cambridge: Cambridge University Press, 2002), pp. 52, 73, 85, 96, 123, 124, 182, 203, 238 and 285.

p. 30, **'a great lover and praiser of himself …'** The description of Ben Jonson's personality is referenced in 'Ben Jonson's Conversations with William Drummond …', pp. 462 and 479.

pp. 30–31, **Jonson entered into a feud with Gabriel Spencer** … On Jonson's murder of Spencer see Stopes, *Burbage and Shakespeare's Stage*, pp. 72–73 and 177–83; Arnold, *Globe*, pp. 163–69; and 'Ben Jonson's Conversations with William Drummond …', p. 467. It has been suggested that the feud was initially sparked by Spencer's defection from the Pembroke's Men's playing company at the Swan Theatre (to which he and Jonson had been attached) to the rival company, the Lord Admiral's Men at the Rose playhouse. Jonson and Spencer had shared a cell in the Marshalsea Prison, where they were incarcerated following the ill-judged decision to mount the satirical play *The Isle of Dogs*, which premiered in July 1597 (a play in which they had both acted and which Jonson had co-authored with Thomas Nashe). By 8 October a warrant for their release was ratified by the Privy Council, and within three days Spencer had made his move to Pembroke's Men. See Donaldson, *Ben Jonson*, pp. 109–13; TNA, Privy Council Register for the Reign of Elizabeth I, PC 2/22, pp. 345–46, 15 August 1597; and TNA, Privy Council Register for the Reign of Elizabeth I, PC 2/23, p. 13, dated 8 October 1597.

p. 31, **Shakespeare, Burbage, Heminges, Condell and Phillips among its 'principal comedians'** … Identified in *The Works of Benjamin Jonson* (London: Printed by William Stansby for Richard Meighen, 1616), p. 72.

p. 31, 'it is for me hard and heavy ... I have lost one of my company ...'
Quoted from *Henslowe's Diary*, p. 286.

p. 31, **Jonson escaped the death penalty** ... Jonson confessed to the crime but
sought to take advantage of a legal loophole called 'benefit of clergy'.
Dating back to the twelfth century, this enabled members of the church
ministry to be tried under canon law, allowing them to evade the secular
courts. It later became a means of avoiding the death sentence on a first
conviction for anyone able to demonstrate their learnedness by reading
Psalm 51, also known colloquially as 'the neck verse', in Latin. Jonson did
this 'like a clerk' and escaped with little more than a branded thumb,
designed to leave an indelible record in the flesh of the exploitation of this
legal get-out clause so that it could not be used twice. See Donaldson, *Ben
Jonson*, pp. 135–37. Duels were illegal, but nevertheless fashionable among
the rakish swaggering Elizabethan wits, for whom honour could be
defended with the tip of a rapier. On duelling see J.A. Sharpe, *Crime in
Early Modern England* (New York: Longman, 1984 [1999 edition]),
pp. 138–39.

p. 31, **'his religion by trust, of a priest who visited him in prison'** ... Ben
Jonson's conversion to Catholicism and his return to the Protestant Church
are described in 'Ben Jonson's Conversations with William Drummond ...',
p. 467.

pp. 31–34, **the Burbages and the players took the momentous decision to
dismantle the beams of the Theatre** ... For the creation of the Globe
Theatre and the new share structure this prompted, see Laoutaris,
Shakespeare and the Countess, especially pp. 307–38, and James Shapiro,
1599: A Year in the Life of William Shakespeare (London: Faber and Faber,
2005).

p. 34, **formal licence granted on 19 May** ... Transcribed in Irwin Smith,
Shakespeare's Blackfriars Playhouse: Its History and Its Design (London: Peter
Owen), p. 487.

p. 34, **reacquire the Blackfriars Theatre in 1608** ... On the history of the
Blackfriars Theatre see Laoutaris, *Shakespeare and the Countess*. See also
Andrew Gurr, *The Shakespearean Stage: 1574–1642* (Cambridge: Cambridge
University Press, 1992 [1997 edition]), pp. 156–64. For the early history of
the child actors (relating to what was the first Blackfriars Theatre, opened
before James Burbage created the second Blackfriars playhouse) see
Charles William Wallace, *The Children of the Chapel at Blackfriars: 1597–
1603* (New York: AMS Press, 1970 [based on the 1908 first edition]) and
Charles William Wallace, *The Evolution of the English Drama Up to
Shakespeare, with a History of the First Blackfriars Theatre* (Berlin: Georg
Reimer, 1912). On staging practices within the Blackfriars Theatre see
Andrew Gurr and Farah Karim-Cooper, eds, *Moving Shakespeare Indoors:
Performance and Repertoire in the Jacobean Playhouse* (Cambridge:
Cambridge University Press, 2014) and Will Tosh, *Playing Indoors: Staging
Early Modern Drama in the Sam Wanamaker Playhouse* (London: Arden
Shakespeare, 2018).

p. 34, **the 'best actor' in his play** *Bartholomew Fair* ... Ben Jonson, *Bartholomew Fair*, in *Ben Jonson: Five Plays*, ed. G.A. Wilkes (Oxford: Oxford University Press, 1988), 5.3.69–71.

p. 34, **'Master Burbage has been about and about with me ...'** *Christmas, His Masque, As it was Presented at Court, 1616*, in *The Works of Benjamin Jonson* (London: Printed [by John Beale, James Dawson, Bernard Alsop and Thomas Fawcet] for Richard Meighen [and Thomas Walkley], 1641), p. 4.

p. 35, **'declaimed bitterly against him, and so carried herself ...'** TNA SP 14/92, f. 132v.

p. 35, **'Whatsoever is commendable in the grave Orator ...'** *Sir Thomas Overbury his wife with new elegies upon his (now known) untimely death: whereunto are annexed, new news and characters* (London: Printed by Edward Griffin for Laurence L'Isle, 1616 [original edition 1614]), sigs M2–M3.

p. 35, **His home had certainly contained wonders enough to catch a thief's eye** ... The list of items stolen from Richard Burbage's home can be found in Sessions roll for 19 February 1615, 538/80, 83, 229, 230, 234; G.D.R. 2/44d; *County of Middlesex. Calendar to the Sessions Records: New Series, Volume 2, 1614–15*, ed. William Le Hardy (London: Middlesex Sessions Records. Clerk of the Peace, 1936), p. 62.

p. 35, **acquired over £300 worth of land** ... TNA SP 14/107, f. 61v, letter from John Chamberlain to Dudley Carleton, dated 19 March 1619.

p. 36, **Before his death Shakespeare had, like Heminges and Condell, acquired 'gentleman' status** ... On Shakespeare's acquisition of status, land and property see Robert Bearman, *Shakespeare's Money: How Much Did He Make and What Did This Mean?* (Oxford: Oxford University Press, 2016) and Robert Bearman, *Shakespeare in the Stratford Records* (Stroud: A. Sutton, 1994). Heminges did not acquire a coat of arms to back up his 'gentleman' status till 1629, so he had probably used his wealth and his wife's familial background to underpin his claim to such a status before that date; see Edmondson, 'His Editors John Heminges and Henry Condell', p. 318.

p. 36, **Heminges had built a splendid 'fair house' ... Condell also made some smart decisions** ... For Heminges' and Condell's property investments see their wills in Honigmann and Brock, eds, *Playhouse Wills*, pp. 164–69 and 156–60 respectively; Kathman, 'Henry Condell and His London Relatives', pp. 108–15; and Edmondson, 'His Editors John Heminges and Henry Condell', pp. 315–28. Heminges' 'fair house' near the Globe Theatre is also mentioned in the testimony of John Witter in his legal suit against Heminges and Condell, TNA REQ 4/1/2/3, dated 10 May 1619.

p. 36, **to which was attached a popular local tavern named the Queen's Head** ... I am making the assumption that Condell acquired most or all of the property eventually, or at least had the controlling interest in it, because Kathman (in 'Henry Condell and His London Relatives') has traced Condell's acquisition of shares or parts of the property belonging to his kinfolk and because Condell left it as a legacy in his will, without indicating that his ownership was only of part-shares. The Queen's Head

Tavern was located in St Bride's parish, which was just to the east of John Smethwick's shop. See also Condell's will in Honigmann and Brock, eds, *Playhouse Wills*, pp. 156–60 (p. 157). Kathman states that the tavern was located on the 'south side of Fleet Street between the gates of the Inner and Middle Temple' (Kathman, 'Henry Condell and His London Relatives', p. 114). The source cited by Kathman, from which this information is derived, seems to confirm that 'the Queen's Head, [stands] betwixt the Temple gates': *Letters and Papers, Foreign and Domestic, of the reign of Henry VIII*, vol. 11, ed. James Gairdner (London: Her Majesty's Stationery Office, 1888), p. 556. However, St Bride's parish is located further to the east of Temple Bar down Fleet Street. Since the record that seems to identify the tavern's location dates from 1536, and the other documents pertaining to Condell's property locate it in the neighbouring St Bride's parish, I theorise that the earlier record refers to a different tavern which was no longer extant by Condell's time. For the location of St Bride's parish see John Stow, *A Survey of London, Written in the Year 1598* (Stroud: Sutton Publishing, 2005), p. 334.

p. 36, **Heminges and Condell were connected by their acquisition of property in St Mary's, Aldermanbury** ... Heminges' and Condell's careers in St Mary's, Aldermanbury, London are outlined in their ODNB entries by Mary Edmond, and Edmondson, 'His Editors John Heminges and Henry Condell', pp. 315–28. The latter study notes an early account that describes Heminges as someone who was 'always held in good repute and estimation among his neighbours' and who, along with Condell, had been recorded as 'feofees' (that is, trustees) of parish land, indicating their standing in St Mary's, Aldermanbury (p. 315).

p. 37, **Shakespeare may have witnessed much of the drama of his fellow actors' lives** ... The best account of Shakespeare's time in Silver Street remains Charles Nicholl's *The Lodger: Shakespeare on Silver Street* (London: Allen Lane, 2007). The description of the street with its 'diverse fair houses', and its closeness to St Mary's Aldermanbury, is based on Stow, *A Survey of London*, pp. 252–55 and 259, checked against the 'Agas Map', which can be conveniently searched through the 'Map of Early Modern London' project overseen by Janelle Jenstad: 'The Agas Map. The Map of Early Modern London, Edition 7.0', https://mapoflondon.uvic.ca/agas.htm. See also Bowsher, *Shakespeare's London Theatreland*, pp. 202–205.

pp. 37–38, **Shakespeare probably moved to Silver Street from the parish of St Helen's Bishopsgate** ... The best account of Shakespeare's residency in St Helen's, Bishopsgate is Marsh, *Living with Shakespeare*. For the presence of other actors in the Shoreditch area see Gurr, *The Shakespeare Company*, p. 220; Astington, 'His Theatre Friends: The Burbages', pp. 252–53; Charles Nicholl, *The Reckoning: The Murder of Christopher Marlowe* (Chicago: Chicago University Press, 1995), pp. 178–79; Bowsher, *Shakespeare's London Theatreland*, p. 216.

p. 38, **in the cast list for Jonson's *Every Man in His Humour*** ... Jonson, *The Works of Benjamin Jonson*, p. 72.

p. 38, **Beeston had been apprenticed to Augustine Phillips who had left him the generous sum of 'thirty shillings in gold'** ... Honigmann and Brock, eds, *Playhouse Wills*, pp. 72–75.

p. 38, **though he 'lived in Shoreditch', he explained, 'he was not a company keeper'** ... Aubrey's interview is recorded in E.K. Chambers, *William Shakespeare: A Study of Facts and Problems*, vol. 2, p. 252.

pp. 38–39, **Upon a time when Burbage played Richard 3rd** ... The Diary of John Manningham, BL Harley MS 5353.

p. 39, **for the Accession Day tilt of March 1613** ... For the Shoreditch connection to the Manners family and Shakespeare and Burbage's impresa see Astington, 'His Theatre Friends: The Burbages', p. 251, and Chambers, *William Shakespeare: A Study of Facts and Problems*, vol. 2, p. 153. Burbage's fame as a painter is potentially alluded to in *Sir Thomas Overbury his wife with new elegies* ..., sigs M2–M3, and in John Davies, *Microcosmos: The discovery of the little world, with the government thereof* (Oxford: Printed by Joseph Barnes for John Barnes, 1603), sig. F4.

p. 40, **'My Lord Southampton and Lord Rutland come not to the court ...'** *Report on the Manuscripts of Lord de L'Isle and Dudley Preserved at Penshurst Place*, vol. 2., ed. C.L. Kingsford (London: Historical Manuscripts Commission, 1934), p. 401.

p. 40, **Lodged eternally in the same sacred space was the ill-fated Gabriel Spencer, as well as Burbage's fellow actor in the King's Men William Sly** ... See the wills of William Sly and Augustine Phillips, Honigmann and Brock, eds, *Playhouse Wills*, pp. 80–81 and 72–75 respectively. On St Leonard's, the 'actors' church', see Bowsher, *Shakespeare's London Theatreland*, p. 218.

p. 41, **'in London is not one eye dry ... But where's the grief should follow good Queen Anne?'** ... Quoted in Stopes, *Burbage and Shakespeare's Stage*, pp. 117–18.

p. 41, **'two such actors, as no age must ever look to see the like'** ... Richard Baker, *A Chronicle of the Kings of England* (London: Printed for Daniel Frere, 1643), p. 120.

p. 41, **'the best actors of our time'** ... Richard Baker, *Theatrum redivivum, or The Theatre Vindicated* (London: Printed by T.R. for Francis Eglesfield, 1662), p. 34.

pp. 41–42, **'a visible eclipse of playing'** ... **'Exit Burbage'** ... Quoted in Stopes, *Burbage and Shakespeare's Stage*, pp. 116–17.

p. 42, **'sent each passion to his heart' to 'languish in a scene of love, then look/Pallid for fear'** ... Thomas Bancroft, *Time's Out of Tune* (London: W. Godbid, 1658), p. 44. For the view that Bancroft may have seen Burbage perform, see Bart Van Es, *Shakespeare in Company* (Oxford: Oxford University Press, 2013), p. 241.

p. 42, **'a delightful Proteus, so wholly transforming himself into his part ...'** Richard Flecknoe, *Love's Kingdom a Pastoral Tragi-Comedy ... with a short Treatise of the English Stage* (London: Printed by R. Wood for Richard Flecknoe, 1664), sig. G6v.

p. 42, 'the soul of the stage' ... Richard Flecknoe, *Euterpe Revived* (London: [for Richard Flecknoe?], 1675), p. 78.

p. 42, **'Oft have I seen him leap into the grave ...'** John Fletcher's elegy for Richard Burbage, BL Stowe MS 962, ff. 62v–63.

p. 43, **the original sharers at the inception of the Chamberlain's Men in 1594** ... I am grateful to Martin Wiggins for discussing the First Folio's list of actors with me and for providing me with his own unpublished research on the dates of the actors' entries into the Chamberlain's/King's Men. Wiggins' research indicates that the early sharers in the Chamberlain's Men are presented in the Folio's list of actors largely in a cohesive sequence and given prominence at the head of the list, while the remaining actors are itemised neither strictly in the order in which they entered the company as apprentices, nor when they took up roles as professional actors, nor when they acquired their shares; though the list is broadly chronological. This register seems, as Wiggins has conjectured, to preserve an impression – a literal imprint – of the place of these actors in the minds of those who compiled it. This might indicate that this roll-call of personalities invests its earliest members with an emotional as well as professional seniority and that it represents, for those who conjured these men to their minds while devising this list, a reminiscence that looks back to the heyday of a company set on a path to its destined greatness by its first actor-sharers, its supremely talented playwright William Shakespeare and its show-stopping star Richard Burbage. This adds further evidence to the likelihood that this list was compiled by Heminges and Condell, and provides some insight into the emotive resonances that accompanied the process.

Chapter 2 – 'The loss of my old acquaintance': The First Folio's Patrons and the Courtiers' War

p. 46, **'queen's funeral is put off till the 29th of the next month ...'** TNA SP 14/107, f. 61v, letter from John Chamberlain to Dudley Carleton, 19 March 1619. For Chamberlain's location near St Paul's see his ODNB entry by P.J. Finkelpearl.

p. 46, **The next day Carleton heard that Anne's funeral would cost £24,000** ... TNA SP 14/107, f. 63, letter from Abraham Williams to Dudley Carleton, dated 20 March 1619.

pp. 46–47, **'perhaps longer, unless they can find out money faster ...'** TNA SP 14/107, f. 82, letter from John Chamberlain to Dudley Carleton, dated 27 March 1619.

p. 47, **There was talk of melting down her golden plate and an inventory was made of her jewels 'and other movables'** ... TNA SP 14/108, ff. 101–102, letter from John Chamberlain to Dudley Carleton, dated 24 April 1619. The number of carts required to move the queen's jewels was itemised in TNA SP 14/109, ff. 74–74v, letter from John Chamberlain to Dudley Carleton, dated 14 May 2019.

p. 47, **'still deferred'**, since there was 'no money to put the king and prince's servants in mourning [attire], as intended' ... TNA SP 14/108, ff. 125–125v, letter from Thomas Locke to Dudley Carleton, dated 30 April 1619. The quotations pertaining to this letter are taken from the Calendar of State Papers: *Calendar of State Papers, Domestic Series, of the reign of James I, 1603–1625, preserved in the State Paper Department of her Majesty's Public Record Office*, vol. 3 [1619–1623], ed. Mary Anne Everett Green (London: Longman et al., 1858), p. 41. The manuscript itself records 'the time [is] as bad as ever for many, for want whereof the King's and Prince's servants shall have no blacks', referring to mourning 'blacks' or attire.

p. 47, **so 'weak and faint'** … TNA SP 14/107, f. 82, letter from John Chamberlain to Dudley Carleton, dated 27 March 1619.

p. 47, **'during the king's sickness … carried their heads high'** … TNA, SP 14/108, ff. 71–71v, letter from John Chamberlain to Dudley Carleton, dated 17 April 1619.

pp. 47–49, **William's birth is recorded as being on 8 April 1580** … The outlines of the lives of William and Philip Herbert, their family backgrounds, and their career trajectories (presented in the subsequent three paragraphs) are derived from Michael G. Brennan, *Literary Patronage in the English Renaissance: The Pembroke Family* (New York and London: Routledge, 1988), especially, pp. 51–54, 137–39, 152–59 and 167–71; Brian O'Farrell, *Shakespeare's Patron: William Herbert, Third Earl of Pembroke 1580–1630, Politics, Patronage and Power* (London: Continuum, 2011), pp. 39–42, 59–71, 91–93; E.K. Chambers, 'The Elizabethan Lords Chamberlain', *The Malone Society Collections*, Part 1 (1907), pp. 31–42; and the ODNB entries for 'William Herbert' (by Victor Stater), 'Philip Herbert' (by David L. Smith) and 'Mary [née Sidney] Herbert' (by Margaret Patterson Hannay). For more on Mary Sidney Herbert, see Margaret P. Hannay, *Philip's Phoenix: Mary Sidney, Countess of Pembroke* (Oxford: Oxford University Press, 1990).

pp. 48–49, **'his pains and expenses of himself and the rest of his Company'** … *Dramatic Records in the Declared Accounts of the Treasurer of the Chamber 1558–1642, Malone Society Collections*, vol. 6 (Oxford: Oxford University Press for The Malone Society, 1961–2), p. 38.

pp. 49–50, **It was originally Sir William Herbert who had backed the out-of-pocket would-be courtier George Villiers** … On the rise of George Villiers, his career trajectory and his rivalry with Sir William Herbert, see Brennan, *Literary Patronage*, pp. 4, 135–37 and 167–74; O'Farrell, *Shakespeare's Patron*, pp. 65–75; and the ODNB entry for 'George Villiers' by Roger Lockyer.

pp. 50–51, **the Keepership of Denmark House on the Strand and an annual stipend** … Villiers' stipend was a 'gift' of revenues deriving from 'land of the king's'. TNA SP 14/109, ff. 74–74v, letter from John Chamberlain to Dudley Carleton, dated 14 May 2019.

p. 51, **'[The] prince and Buckingham grow very friendly'** … The quote is from the summation of their relationship in the *Calendar of State Papers, Domestic Series, of the reign of James I, 1603–1625*, vol. 3 [1619–1623], ed.

Green, p. 45. The manuscript letter indicates that 'there is great demonstration of love between them, and the prince putteth upon the marquess all his business of importance': TNA SP 14/109, ff. 77–77v, letter from Nathaniel Brent to Dudley Carleton, dated 15 May 1619.

p. 51, **All this while, the Earl of Pembroke, himself suffering ailing health** … On Pembroke's ailing health see O'Farrell, *Shakespeare's Patron*, p. 121.

p. 51, **'in his gift' as Lord Chamberlain, and he felt Villiers' attempt to grant it 'to a follower of his'** … The record of this dispute is in TNA SP 14/110, ff. 86–86v, letter from John Chamberlain to Dudley Carleton, dated 11 September 1619.

pp. 51–52, **If a rumour circulating in 1617** … The context for the attempts made to divest Sir William Herbert from his office of Lord Chamberlain itemised here, and the quotations presented in this paragraph, are found in TNA SP 14/105, ff. 95–96, letter from Thomas Wynn to Dudley Carleton, dated 28 January 1619; Dick Taylor, 'The Earl of Montgomery and the Dedicatory Epistle of Shakespeare's First Folio', *Shakespeare Quarterly*, vol. 10, no. 1 (Winter 1959), pp. 121–23; O'Farrell, *Shakespeare's Patron*, p. 121 (and see also p. 73); and TNA SP 14/112, ff. 1–2, letter from John Chamberlain to Dudley Carleton, dated 1 January 1620.

p. 52, **'behalf of himself and the rest of his Fellows …'** *Dramatic Records in the Declared Accounts of the Treasurer of the Chamber*, p. 70.

pp. 52–53, **13 May as Anne was finally led to her burial** … The description of Queen Anne's burial is derived from TNA SP 14/109, ff. 74–74v, letter from John Chamberlain to Dudley Carleton, dated 14 May 1619 and TNA SP 14/109, ff. 77–77v, letter from Nathaniel Brent to Dudley Carleton, dated 15 May 1619.

p. 53, **one poor spectator was killed by a large stone** … TNA SP 14/109, ff. 77–77v, letter from Nathaniel Brent to Dudley Carleton, dated 15 May 1619.

p. 53, **'swarm' to 'a new play' as if 'all these/Came to see …** *Pericles'* … *Pimlico, or Run Redcap* (London: Printed [by Thomas Purfoot] for John Busbie, and George Loftis, 1609).

p. 53, **'pelted …/With apples, eggs, or stones'** … Robert Tailor, *The Hog hath Lost his Pearl, A Comedy* (London: Printed [by John Beale] for Richard Redmer, 1614), sigs A3–A3v.

p. 54, **'by the King's Majesty's Players excellently presented'** … George Wilkins, *The Painful Adventures of Pericles Prince of Tyre, Being the true history of the play of Pericles* (London: Printed by T. P[urfoot] for Nathaniel Butter, 1608), sig. A3.

p. 54, **The role itself has 570 lines, about 260 lines more than the next longest part in the play** … Lucy Munro, *Shakespeare in the Theatre: The King's Men* (London: Arden, 2020), p. 92. On the popularity of *Pericles* see also pp. 91–95 of the same text.

p. 54, **taken over by Joseph Taylor** … On Joseph Taylor's role between 1619 and 1620 see Munro, *Shakespeare in the Theatre*, pp. 83–86 and 95–96, and Gurr, *The Shakespeare Company*, p. 243.

p. 54, **20 May 1619, during a sumptuous feast and entertainments at court** … The description of, and quotations relating to, the court performance of *Pericles* are derived from TNA SP 14/109, ff. 100–101v, letter from Gerard Herbert to Dudley Carleton, dated 24 May 1619.

p. 54, **'even now all the company are at the play, which I being tender-hearted …'** BL Egerton MS 2592, f. 81, 20 May 1619; quoted in Munro, *Shakespeare in the Theatre*, p. 96.

p. 54, **shortlist of potential royal performances ahead of the Christmas season of 1619–20** … BL Cotton Tiberius MS E.X., reproduced in facsimile in *The King's Office of the Revels 1610–1622: Fragments of Documents in the Department of Manuscripts, British Museum*, transcribed by Frank Marcham (London: Frank Marcham, 1925), pp. 11–21. Lucy Munro has also suggested that the King's Men sought 'to pay tribute to Burbage in their selection of plays' during this court performance season in *Shakespeare in the Theatre*, p. 86.

p. 55, *Hamlet*, **the** *Henry IV* **plays,** *The Spanish Tragedy* **and** *Volpone* **were referred to frequently** … For examples see Stopes, *Burbage and Shakespeare's Stage*, pp. 116–23; Nungezer, *A Dictionary of Actors*, pp. 70–79; Es, *Shakespeare in Company*, pp. 233–42; and the relevant sections of *Shakespeare's Book*, particularly chapter 4.

p. 55, **alluded to in numerous letters and other documents of the period, with Falstaff having become something of a household name** … For some of these allusions see Laoutaris, *Shakespeare and the Countess*, pp. 231–32.

pp. 55–56, **John Davies of Hereford** … The poems in which Davies alludes to Shakespeare and Burbage are in *Microcosmos: The discovery of the little world, with the government thereof* (Oxford: Printed by Joseph Barnes for John Barnes, 1603), p. 215, and *Humour's Heaven on Earth; with The Civil Wars of Death and Fortune* (London: Printed by A[dam] I[slip], 1609), sig. H6v.

p. 56, **'In the characters Shakespeare wrote for him Richard Burbage attained his greatest glory. Men did not realise that Shakespeare was dead while Burbage lived'** … Stopes, *Burbage and Shakespeare's Stage*, pp. 115–16.

p. 56, **Heminges would lose his wife Rebecca in September of that year** … Rebecca Heminges died on 2 September 1619; see Edmond, 'Yeomen Citizens, Gentlemen, and Players …', p. 44, and John Heminges' will in Honigmann and Brock, eds, *Playhouse Wills*, p. 165.

Chapter 3 – The 'Pavier-Jaggard Quartos': A Shakespearean Printing Mystery

p. 57, **printer's device: an emblematic rose and gillyflower** … For details of this printer's device see Ronald B. McKerrow, *Printers' and Publishers' Devices in England and Scotland, 1485–1640* (London: Bibliographical Society, 1949), p. 110.

p. 58, **His father, fifty-two-year-old William, who has been losing his sight for the last seven years** … See the summary of Jaggard's treatment for his blindness in BL Sloane MS 640, and the ODNB entry for 'William Jaggard' by Stanley Wells.

p. 58, **What you have purchased would come to be known collectively as the 'Pavier Quartos', or more sensationally as the 'False Folio'** … The content of the 'Pavier Quartos' and the role of Thomas Heywood's *A Woman Killed with Kindness* are derived from Zachary Lesser, *Ghosts, Holes, Rips and Scrapes: Shakespeare in 1619, Bibliography in the Longue Durée* (Philadelphia: University of Pennsylvania Press, 2021), especially pp. 1–32, 52–69 and 137–41; Zachary Lesser and Peter Stallybrass, 'Shakespeare between Pamphlet and Book, 1608–1619', in *Shakespeare and Textual Studies*, eds Margaret Jane Kidnie and Sonia Massai (Cambridge: Cambridge University Press, 2015), pp. 105–33; and R. Carter Hailey, 'The Shakespearian Pavier Quartos Revisited', *Studies in Bibliography*, vol. 57, no. 1 (2005), pp. 151–95.

p. 58, **referred to here as the 'Pavier-Jaggard Quartos'** … The recent uncovering of the prominent role William Jaggard (or the Jaggard press collectively, inclusive of his son Isaac) played in the 'False Folio' has led some bibliographers and book historians to refer to these plays as the 'Jaggard Quartos'. This includes James Marino, *Owning William Shakespeare: The King's Men and their Intellectual Property* (Philadelphia: University of Pennsylvania Press, 2011), especially pp. 110–15; Lesser and Stallybrass, 'Shakespeare between Pamphlet and Book …', pp. 105–33; Lesser in *Ghosts, Holes, Rips and Scrapes* …; and Ben Higgins in *Shakespeare's Syndicate: The First Folio, its Publishers, and the Early Modern Book Trade* (Oxford: Oxford University Press, 2022), especially pp. 104–106. Amy Lidster refers to them as the 'Jaggard-Pavier Quartos', partly in acknowledgement of this, in *Publishing the History Plays in the Time of Shakespeare: Stationers Shaping a Genre* (Cambridge: Cambridge University Press, 2022), especially pp. 180–205. Independently, before being made aware of Lidster's research, I had taken the decision, quite consciously, to include both names in my labelling of these quartos, but instead have placed Pavier in the senior position because ownership of the plays in the 'Pavier-Jaggard Quartos' can more firmly be connected to him and because, where there were uncertainties over the rights to print some of the plays in this collection, the closest connections to the last known rights holders were strongest with Pavier. I do, however, also refer to Pavier and the Jaggards as a 'syndicate' because they worked together collaboratively on the project and recent research has indicated the Jaggards are likely to have had a guiding hand in it.

p. 59, **'notorious piratical publisher'** … David Bevington, ed., *The Complete Works of Shakespeare* (New York: Longman, 1980 [third edition]), p. 1669, quoted in Gerald D. Johnson, 'Thomas Pavier, Publisher, 1600–25', *Library*, vol. 14, no. 1 (March 1992), pp. 12–50 (p. 12).

p. 59, **In 1908 the bibliographer and early First Folio scholar W.W. Greg made a startling announcement … originally discovered by fellow bibliographer Alfred W. Pollard** … See W.W. Greg, 'On certain false dates in Shakespearean Quartos', *Library*, vol. 9, no. 34 (1908), pp. 113–31 (p. 128). For Alfred W. Pollard's discoveries see his 'A Literary Causeries:

Shakespeare in the Remainder Market', *The Academy* (2 June 1906), pp. 528–29. The detailed analysis of William Neidig, following on from these discoveries, also confirmed that the 'Pavier-Jaggard Quartos' were collectively printed in the same printing house; see William Neidig, 'The Shakespeare Quartos of 1619', *Modern Philology*, vol. 8, no. 2 (1910), pp. 145–63.

p. 61, **Born around 1570 to John Pavier, a yeoman hailing from Shropshire, Thomas originally trained as a draper** … Johnson, 'Thomas Pavier …', pp. 12–15.

p. 61, **'for printing certain books and ballads without a licence'** … Pavier's misdemeanours are recorded in *Records of the Court of the Stationers' Company 1602–1640*, ed. William A. Jackson (London: Bibliographical Society, 1957), pp. 4, 442, 445, 446, 450 and 464.

pp. 61–62, **In June 1598 Stafford issued a bill of complaint in an attempt to prosecute Cuthbert Burby and five others** … The account of this case is derived from Star Chamber records, Elizabeth I, NA S7/22, Stafford vs Burby and Dawson, Bill of Complaint, with a full transcript printed as 'Appendix D' in Cyril Bathurst Judge, *Elizabethan Book-Pirates* (Cambridge: Harvard University Press, 1934), pp. 166–67, 169 and 173–75; Johnson, 'Thomas Pavier …', pp. 13–15 and 19–21; and 'The copy of the order of the Star Chamber' in the case of Simon Stafford and William Barley against Cuthbert Burby et al., SCA Liber A, Ref. TSC/1/A/05, ff. 74–74v.

p. 61, **Burby was a bookseller who clearly had an interest in Shakespeare** … On Cuthbert Burby and his Shakespeare-related output see Marta Straznicky, ed., *Shakespeare's Stationers: Studies in Critical Bibliography* (Philadelphia: University of Pennsylvania Press, 2013), pp. 237–38.

p. 62, **The Stationers were far from impressed with Simon Stafford's legal action** … For the outcome of the case see 'The copy of the order of the Star Chamber' in the case of Simon Stafford and William Barley against Cuthbert Burby et al., SCA Liber A, Ref. TSC/1/A/05, ff. 74–74v.

pp. 62–63, **Despite this, Pavier would later become a successful publisher** … The account of Pavier's total output, his publishing trends and his shop, the Cat and Parrots, is derived from Johnson, 'Thomas Pavier …', pp. 12–15 and 25–35.

p. 63, **the perfect spot to sell political gossip and tales of wonders beyond imagining** … The examples of Pavier's publications are derived from the following samples: Gerrit de Veer, *The True and Perfect Description of Three Voyages so Strange and Wonderful … with the cruel bears, and other monsters of the sea* … (London: [By W. White] for Thomas Pavier, 1605); *Newes from Ostend of … [the] fierce siege made by the Archduke Albertus his forces …* (London: Printed by V. S[immes] for Thomas Pavier, 1601); *A Strange Report of Six most Notorious Witches who by their Devilish Practices Murdered above the number of four-hundred Small Children …* (London: Printed by W[illiam] W[hite] for Thomas Pavier, 1601); and *Woeful News from the West Parts of England, Being the Lamentable Burning of the Town of Teverton, in Devonshire* (London: Printed by T. S[nodham] for Thomas Pavier, 1612).

Pavier issued numerous other pamphlets and ballads recounting sensational murders, scandals and catastrophes.

p. 63, **the foresight to secure the rights to Thomas Kyd's tremendously popular** *The Spanish Tragedy* ... On Thomas Pavier's rights to *The Spanish Tragedy* and other plays (including those by Shakespeare and those he would claim erroneously were by the dramatist) see Straznicky, ed., *Shakespeare's Stationers*, pp. 276–79; Johnson, 'Thomas Pavier ...', pp. 26–28 and 33–35; and Stationers' Register, entries for 4 August 1600, 19 April 1602 and 2 May 1608, SCA Liber C, Ref. TSC/1/E/06/02, respectively ff. 62v, 80v and 167.

p. 63, **quickly rose up the ranks of the Stationers' Company** ... Pavier's career trajectory in the Stationers' Company is traced through Jackson, ed., *Records of the Court of the Stationers' Company*, pp. viii, 13, 29, 31, 110, 145, 147, 152, 154, and Johnson, 'Thomas Pavier ...', pp. 21–22.

pp. 63–64, **By this point Pavier had relocated his business to Ivy Lane** ... The account of Pavier's move and the description of the area around Ivy Lane are derived from John Stow, *A Survey of London, Written in the Year 1598* (Stroud: Sutton Publishing, 2005), p. 292, and Johnson, 'Thomas Pavier ...', p. 16.

p. 64, *The Passionate Pilgrim* **was Jaggard's first foray into Shakespeare publishing** ... The details of this text are derived from *The Passionate Pilgrim*, attributed to William Shakespeare (London: Printed for W. Jaggard, 1599); *The Passionate Pilgrim ... Whereunto is newly added two love-epistles* (London: Printed by William Jaggard, 1612); Thomas Heywood, *Troia Britanica: or, Great Britain's Troy* (London: Printed by William Jaggard, 1609). For more on *The Passionate Pilgrim* see Higgins, *Shakespeare's Syndicate*, pp. 100–104, in which he contextualises the publication and casts doubt on its illicit nature.

p. 65, **'misquotations, mistaking of syllables, misplacing half-lines ...'** The quotations are taken from Thomas Heywood, *An Apology for Actors* (London: Printed by Nicholas Okes, 1612), sig. G4–G4v.

pp. 65–66, **Between 1595 and 1622, ten editions, encompassing seven plays, have title pages that attribute non-Shakespeare works to the playwright** ... See Lukas Erne, *Shakespeare and the Book Trade* (Cambridge: Cambridge University Press, 2013), pp. 56–89, especially pp. 56–57; and Higgins, *Shakespeare's Syndicate*, p. 103.

p. 66, **Shakespeare's single most reprinted work during his lifetime, going through ten known editions to 1616** ... Straznicky, ed., *Shakespeare's Stationers*, pp. 198–216.

p. 66, **Apart from small fines ... anything other than a much-decorated publisher** ... For William Jaggard's fines see Jackson, ed., *Records of the Court of the Stationers' Company*, pp. 57 and 452. See Higgins, *Shakespeare's Syndicate*, pp. 87–90, for the ratio of printed to published output from the Jaggards' business (as Higgins notes, these estimates do not include all 'job-work', more ephemeral forms of printing and other activities, which are almost impossible to trace).

p. 66, 'every parish church and chapel' … Record of William Jaggard's request for the monopoly of the supply of the Ten Commandments, TNA SP 38/7, f. 141v.

p. 66, noted as 'not sealed' … TNA SO 3/2, p. 278; Higgins, *Shakespeare's Syndicate*, p. 88.

pp. 66–67, securing the desirable monopoly on the printing of playbills 'for the company of stage players' … William Jaggard's attempts to secure these rights can be traced through Jackson, ed., *Records of the Court of the Stationers' Company*, pp. 1, 2 and 6. An attempt made in 1602 to acquire the monopoly merely confirmed the legitimacy of James Roberts' claim 'in the right of his wife', because she had inherited these rights from her late husband John Charlewood.

pp. 67–68, They would not have been wrong to do so … William Jaggard's career trajectory, as outlined in this paragraph, is derived from Lesser, *Ghosts, Holes, Rips and Scrapes* …, pp. 19–20; Tiffany Stern, '"On each Wall/ And Corner Post": Playbills, Title-pages, and Advertising in Early Modern London', *English Literary Renaissance*, vol. 36, no. 1 (Winter 2006), pp. 57–89, especially pp. 61–63; Tiffany Stern, *Documents of Performance in Early Modern England* (Cambridge: Cambridge University Press, 2009), pp. 39–43; Higgins, *Shakespeare's Syndicate*, p. 87 (in which he suggests that Jaggard bought out Roberts, who may have died around 1618); Gabriel Egan, '"As it was, is, or will be played": Title-pages and the Theatre Industry to 1610', in *From Performance to Print in Shakespeare's England*, eds Peter Holland and Stephen Orgel (Houndmills: Palgrave, 2006), pp. 92–110 (p. 96).

p. 68, The two had regularly worked together on publication projects … For some of these collaborations see Johnson, 'Thomas Pavier …', pp. 34–37; Ben Higgins, 'We have a constant will to publish': The Publishers of Shakespeare's First Folio, unpublished DPhil thesis (Oxford: University of Oxford, 2015), pp. 94–96; and Erne, *Shakespeare and the Book Trade*, p. 177.

p. 68, Both had served on the committee that governed the English Stock … For Jaggard's stints as 'auditor' on the English Stock committee see Jackson, ed., *Records of the Court of the Stationers' Company*, pp. 37 and 82, and for Pavier's see the same text, pp. 41, 42, 73, 98, 107, 164, 174. The shares in the Stock were valued hierarchically and included Assistants' shares, valued at £200; Livery shares, worth £100; and Yeomen's shares, worth £50. Jaggard had been petitioning for a Yeoman's share, while Pavier had applied for the more valuable Livery share, which led to his appointment as Stock-Keeper of the Livery. This paved the way for Pavier's 'election' to an Assistant's share in the Stock by February 1623. Jaggard succeeded in securing a more modest half-share of a 'yeoman's part' on 2 May 1609, and went on to pursue a Livery share in June 1620, finally claiming this more valuable share on 31 May 1621, the very same day that his brother John Jaggard was elected to the most coveted Assistant's share. For these developments see Jackson, ed., *Records of the Court of the Stationers' Company*, pp. viii, x, 13, 29, 31, 37, 123, 134–35, 145 and 154.

p. 68, **A petition by John Jaggard, William's brother, who was also a stationer, which sought to protect the Company of Stationers' exclusive printing rights** … 'The Humble Petition of John Jaggard, Bookseller and Stationer of London', SCA Memorandum Book: Liber A, Ref. TSC/1/A/05, f. 93.

p. 68, **as one of his 'very good friends'** … Will of William Jaggard, LMA/ Guildhall MS 9052/5, dated 28 March 1623. Jaggard left Pavier twenty shillings and made him overseer of his will. See Johnson, 'Thomas Pavier …', p. 36, and Higgins, *Shakespeare's Syndicate*, p. 106.

p. 69, **just one new edition appeared per year, excluding 1614 and 1618 when there were no editions at all** … Figures derived from Straznicky, ed., *Shakespeare's Stationers*, pp. 216–18.

p. 69, **This is a far cry from the state of play at the high point in Shakespeare's career** … The statistics highlighting Shakespeare publication as a percentage of the book market are derived from Erne, *Shakespeare and the Book Trade*, pp. 35–46. See also Chris Laoutaris. '"What's in a name?": Was William Shakespeare popular during his lifetime?', OUP Blog, Oxford University Press, 17 April 2016, https://blog.oup.com/2016/04/william-shakespeare-popular-early-modern-theatre/. The popularity of Shakespeare in print is a controversial subject. Just some of the works in this field include Peter W.M. Blayney, 'The Publication of Playbooks', in *A New History of Early English Drama*, eds John D. Cox and David Scott Kastan (New York: Columbia University Press, 1997), pp. 383–422; Alan B. Farmer and Zachary Lesser, 'The Popularity of Playbooks Revisited', *Shakespeare Quarterly*, vol. 56, no. 1 (2005), pp. 1–32; Peter W.M. Blayney, 'The Alleged Popularity of Playbooks', *Shakespeare Quarterly*, vol. 56, no. 1 (2005), pp. 33–50; Peter Berek, 'The Market for Playbooks and the Development of the Reading Public', *Philological Quarterly*, vol. 91, no. 2 (2012), pp. 151–84; and Alan B. Farmer, 'Shakespeare as Leading Playwright in Print, 1598–1608/09', in *Shakespeare and Textual Studies*, eds Margaret Jane Kidnie and Sonia Massai (Cambridge: Cambridge University Press, 2015), pp. 87–104.

p. 70, **Of far more interest to the buyers of playbooks** … The edition numbers have been calculated from the table of Shakespeare editions in Straznicky, ed., *Shakespeare's Stationers*, pp. 198–227.

p. 70, **'older, somewhat forgotten' works** … Lesser, *Ghosts, Holes, Rips and Scrapes* …, pp. 66–67.

p. 70, **a vogue for historical cycles and serials** … Tara L. Lyons, 'Serials, Spinoffs, and Histories: Selling "Shakespeare" in Collection before the Folio', *Philological Quarterly*, vol. 91, no. 2 (Spring 2012), pp. 185–220.

p. 70, **a 'pre-publicity stunt' for the First Folio** … Sonia Massai, *Shakespeare and the Rise of the Editor* (Cambridge: Cambridge University Press, 2007), pp. 106–35 (pp. 107 and 119).

Chapter 4 – 'Forged invention former times defaced': Negotiating and Printing the 'False Folio'

p. 71, **Who first suggested the bold scheme to create an edition of selected Shakespeare plays** … The sections of this chapter that reconstruct the order in which the individual plays of the 'Pavier-Jaggard Quartos' were printed, and the subsequent attempts to falsify the imprints on the plays' title pages, are derived from the extraordinarily painstaking and important research in Zachary Lesser, *Ghosts, Holes, Rips and Scrapes: Shakespeare in 1619, Bibliography in the Longue Durée* (Philadelphia: University of Pennsylvania Press, 2021); Zachary Lesser and Peter Stallybrass, 'Shakespeare between Pamphlet and Book, 1608–1619', in *Shakespeare and Textual Studies*, eds Margaret Jane Kidnie and Sonia Massai (Cambridge: Cambridge University Press, 2015), pp. 105–33; and R. Carter Hailey, 'The Shakespearian Pavier Quartos Revisited', *Studies in Bibliography*, vol. 57, no. 1 (2005), pp. 151–95. Significant interpretations of these events are also presented in Sonia Massai, *Shakespeare and the Rise of the Editor* (Cambridge: Cambridge University Press, 2007). The interpretation of the reasons behind the inclusion of individual plays, as attempts to incorporate works that reflected particularly memorable Burbage-Shakespeare collaborations (or second-best alternatives to such works), is my own and not presented in the above-listed works.

p. 71, **He would have found that he owned the rights to five works** … On Thomas Pavier's rights to plays included in the 'Pavier-Jaggard Quartos' see Marta Straznicky, ed., *Shakespeare's Stationers: Studies in Critical Bibliography* (Philadelphia: University of Pennsylvania Press, 2013), pp. 276–79; Gerald D. Johnson, 'Thomas Pavier, Publisher, 1600–25', *Library*, vol. 14, no. 1 (March 1992), pp. 12–50 (pp. 26–28 and 33–35); and Stationers' Register, entries for 4 August 1600, 19 April 1602 and 2 May 1608, SCA Liber C, Ref. TSC/1/E/06/02, respectively ff. 62v, 80v and 167.

p. 72, **Frequently recalled in elegiac responses to Burbage's death** … See the examples of elegies in C.C. Stopes, *Burbage and Shakespeare's Stage* (London: De la More Press, 1913), pp. 116–23, and Edwin Nungezer, *A Dictionary of Actors and of Other Persons Associated with the Public Representation of Plays in England before 1642* (New Haven: Yale University Press, 1929), pp. 70–79. One play in which Burbage's Richard III was alluded to was *The Second Part of the Return from Parnassus* (1602), in which a character named Dick Burbage auditions two students, one of whom he tells 'I like your face and the proportion of your body for Richard the 3rd', asking him to 'imitate me'; see Nungezer, *A Dictionary of Actors*, p. 71.

p. 72, **'he mistook a player for a King,/For when he would have said, King Richard died …'** Richard Corbet, *Certain Elegant Poems, Written by Dr. Corbet, Bishop of Norwich* (London: Printed by R. Cotes for Andrew Crooke, 1647), p. 12.

p. 72, **kept tightly in the clutches of the stationer Matthew Law** … Andrew Wise first entered *Richard III* in the Stationers' Register on 20 October 1597; see SCA Liber C, Ref. TSC/1/E/06/02, f. 25r. The rights were later passed to Matthew Law on 25 June 1603; see SCA Liber C, Ref. TSC/1/E/06/02, f. 98.

p. 72, **in publisher Edward Blount's possession since 1608** ... See Stationers' Register, entry for 20 May 1608, SCA Liber C, Ref. TSC/1/E/06/02, f. 167v.

p. 72, **entry in the register was an additional form of protection available to stationers** ... See Tiffany Stern, 'Plays in the Stationers' Registers in the time of Shakespeare', *Literary Print Culture: The Stationers' Company Archive* (Marlborough: Adam Matthew, 2017): http://www.literaryprintculture.amdigital.co.uk.bham-ezproxy.idm.oclc.org/Essays/TiffanyStern.

p. 73, **suggested that Pavier secured the licence to print the play from Gosson** ... See Johnson, 'Thomas Pavier ...', pp. 23–24, and Massai, *Shakespeare and the Rise of the Editor*, p. 113. For the connection between Gosson and Pavier through the 'Ballad Stock' see *Records of the Court of the Stationers' Company 1602–1640*, ed. William A. Jackson (London: Bibliographical Society, 1957), p. 171.

p. 73, **Stafford was still an active presence in the Stationers' Company till at least 9 March 1619** ... See Jackson, ed., *Records of the Court of the Stationers' Company*, pp. xiii–xiv, 53–54, 68.

p. 73, **'Master Pavier's right in Shakespeare's plays', in the Stationers' Register** ... Rights transferred to Edward Brewster and Robert Bird; see Stationers' Register, entry for 4 August 1626, SCA Liber D, Ref. TSC/1/E/06/03, ff. 126–128: 'Assigned ... all the estate, right, title and Interest which Master Thomas Pavier, her late husband, had in the Copies' of works he owned, including 'Master Pavier's right in Shakespeare's plays or any of them'.

p. 73, **work called Troubles in Bohemia, which they added to their printing schedule** ... This and the sequence of printing for the 'Pavier-Jaggard Quartos' follows Hailey's chronology in 'The Shakespearian Pavier Quartos Revisited', p. 178.

p. 74, **'I have seen the knave paint grief/In such a lively colour ...'** Thomas May, *The Heir, An Excellent Comedy* (London: Printed by B[ernard] A[lsop] for Thomas Jones, 1622), sig. B1.

p. 74, **as one Renaissance theatre scholar has confirmed, has 'all the hallmarks' of a prime Burbage part** ... Martin Wiggins in private correspondence with the author. I am grateful to Dr Wiggins for his advice and feedback regarding my interpretation of the plays' connections to Burbage roles.

p. 74, **'Not so New, as Lamentable and True'** ... *A Yorkshire Tragedy, Not so new as lamentable and true. Acted by his Majesty's Players at the Globe. Written by W. Shakespeare* (London: Printed by R[ichard] B[radock] for Thomas Pavier, 1608).

p. 74, **'the lamentable end of Don Horatio ...'** Thomas Kyd, *The Spanish Tragedy, containing the lamentable end of Don Horatio, and Bel-imperia: with the pitiful death of old Hieronimo* (London: Printed by Edward Allde, for

Edward White, 1592); Thomas Kyd, *The Spanish Tragedy: or, Hieronimo is mad again, containing the lamentable end of Don Horatio, and Belimperia; with the pitiful death of Hieronimo* (London: Printed by John White, for T. Langley, 1618).

p. 74, 'The Lamentable and True Tragedy' ... *The Lamentable and True Tragedy of M. Arden of Feversham [Faversham] in Kent, who was most wickedly murdered* (London: [By E. Allde] for Edward White, 1592).

p. 74, 'most lamentable Roman tragedy' ... William Shakespeare, *The Most Lamentable Roman Tragedy of Titus Andronicus* (London: Printed by John Danter, and are to be sold by Edward White and Thomas Millington, 1594).

p. 74, Edward White who had issued two editions of *The Spanish Tragedy*, two of *Arden of Faversham* and no fewer than three of *Titus Andronicus* ... Straznicky, ed., *Shakespeare's Stationers*, p. 298.

p. 74, secured the rights to both *The Spanish Tragedy* and *Titus Andronicus* in 1602 ... Stationers' Register, entry for 19 April 1602, SCA Liber C, Ref. TSC/1/E/06/02, f. 80v.

p. 75, recent extraordinary scholarship conducted on the paper stocks and watermarks ... Hailey, 'The Shakespearian Pavier Quartos Revisited', pp. 151–95.

p. 76, The carrier of this missive may have come from the Globe Theatre ... The location of the Stationers' Hall is based on Peter W.M. Blayney's identification of its position in Ave Maria Lane, in *The Bookshops in Paul's Cross Churchyard*, Occasional Papers of the Bibliographical Society, no. 5 (London: Bibliographical Society, 1990), figure 1, pp. 71 and 95–96, and the archives of the Stationers' Company, particularly its loans and bequests book, SCA Liber C2, Ref. TSC/1/G/01/02/01, which includes records, for example on ff. 17r and 110r, which describe the hall as standing in Paternoster Row in 1619 and 1622 respectively. I have cross-referenced this with my own mapping of the Blackfriars area which can be seen in Chris Laoutaris, *Shakespeare and the Countess: The Battle that Gave Birth to the Globe* (London: Penguin, 2014).

p. 76, 'complaint was heretofore presented to my dear brother ...' Philip Herbert's letter is printed in W.W. Greg, *The Shakespeare First Folio: Its Bibliographical and Textual History* (Oxford: Clarendon Press, 1955), pp. 24–25.

p. 77, 'It is thought fit and so ordered that no plays that his Majesty's Players do play ...' Jackson, ed., *Records of the Court of the Stationers' Company*, record for 3 May 1619, pp. 109–10.

p. 77, 'the Masters and Wardens of the Company of Printers and Stationers were advised ...' Greg, *The Shakespeare First Folio*, pp. 24–25.

p. 77, John Jaggard, William Jaggard's brother ... John Jaggard was appointed as an 'Assistant' to the Stationers' Company in 1612 and a Stock-Keeper in 1614. For his career and some of his appearances at the Court of Stationers see Jackson, ed., *Records of the Court of the Stationers' Company*, pp. 58, 64 and pp. 61–155. His 'freedom' is listed in W. Craig

Ferguson, *The Loan Book of the Stationers' Company, with a List of Transactions 1592–1692*, Occasional Papers of the Bibliographical Society, no. 4 (London: Bibliographical Society, 1989), p. 23.

p. 77, **he may have been informed by Pavier, who was there** ... Jackson, ed., *Records of the Court of the Stationers' Company*, record for 3 May 1619, pp. 109–10.

p. 78, **As recent scholarship has shown, the Jaggards had only used this device six times** ... For the use of the Half-Eagle and Key device on the Jaggards' trade-printed works see Ben Higgins, *Shakespeare's Syndicate: The First Folio, its Publishers, and the Early Modern Book Trade* (Oxford: Oxford University Press, 2022), pp. 92 and 108. The emblem is itemised in Ronald B. McKerrow, *Printers' and Publishers' Devices in England and Scotland, 1485–1640* (London: Bibliographical Society, 1949), pp. 49 and 142.

p. 80, **James Roberts had logged his rights to *The Merchant of Venice*** ... See Stationers' Register, entry for 22 July 1598, SCA Liber C, Ref. TSC/1/E/06/02, f. 39.

p. 80, **A bookseller and printer since 1593** ... For Roberts' career see Straznicky, ed., *Shakespeare's Stationers*, pp. 281–82.

p. 80, **including *Hamlet* ... and *Troilus and Cressida*** ... Stationers' Register, entries for 26 July 1602 and 7 February 1603, SCA Liber C, Ref. TSC/1/E/06/02, ff. 84 and 91 respectively. *Hamlet* was acquired by John Smethwick on 19 November 1607, SCA Liber C, Ref. TSC/1/E/06/02 f. 161.

p. 80, **Thomas Hayes, to whom publishing rights had been transferred** ... Stationers' Register, entry for 28 October 1600, SCA Liber C, Ref. TSC/1/E/06/02, f. 66.

p. 80, **he passed them to his son Lawrence Hayes in July 1619** ... Stationers' Register, entry for 8 July 1619, SCA Liber C, Ref. TSC/1/E/06/02, f. 303.

p. 80, *A Midsummer Night's Dream* **was originally published legitimately in 1600** ... Stationers' Register, entry for 8 October 1600, SCA Liber C, Ref. TSC/1/E/06/02, f. 65.

p. 80, **Many bibliographers believe that the rights to this play became 'derelict'** ... See, for example, Higgins, *Shakespeare's Syndicate*, p. 23, and Lesser, *Ghosts, Holes, Rips and Scrapes* ..., pp. 28–29. See also Massai, *Shakespeare and the Rise of the Editor*, pp. 112–14.

p. 80, **Fisher was a draper who had entered the Stationers' Company** ... Johnson, 'Thomas Pavier ...', p. 39.

p. 81, **recorded in the Stationers' Register in January 1602 by Arthur Johnson** ... Stationers' Register, entry for 18 January 1602, SCA Liber C, Ref. TSC/1/E/06/02, f. 78.

p. 81, **'a little bookseller's shop' identified by the sign of the Fleur-de-lis and Crown** ... Blayney, *The Bookshops in Paul's Cross Churchyard*, p. 68.

p. 81, **'no more young Hamlet, old Hieronimo ...'** John Fletcher, elegy for Richard Burbage, BL Stowe MS 962, f. 62v, c. 1619.

p. 81, **Nathaniel Butter, who had secured the rights to *King Lear*** ... Stationers' Register, entry for 26 November 1607, SCA Liber C, Ref.

TSC/1/E/06/02, f. 161v. The rights were secured in collaboration with John Busby.

p. 81, **His father, the bookseller Thomas Butter, had bequeathed to him the shop known by the sign of the Pied Bull** ... On Butter's career and collaborations see Higgins, *Shakespeare's Syndicate*, pp. 51–52; Ben Higgins, 'We have a constant will to publish': The Publishers of Shakespeare's First Folio, unpublished DPhil thesis (Oxford: University of Oxford, 2015), pp. 95–98; and Straznicky, ed., *Shakespeare's Stationers*, pp. 239–40.

p. 82, **This play was not a Burbage vehicle, according to recent scholarship** ... This scholarship has been conducted by Martin Wiggins and was communicated to me in private correspondence. In this correspondence Wiggins writes that the role of 'the Husband [in *A Yorkshire Tragedy*] has all the hallmarks of a Burbage role. *The London Prodigal* [which Butter's collaborator Thomas Pavier chose not to print as part of the "Pavier-Jaggard Quartos"] is a Condell-centred play ... so its non-inclusion might support your theory of a Burbage focus'.

p. 82, **According to calculations made by one theatre scholar** ... This work has been conducted by Bart van Es, *Shakespeare in Company* (Oxford: Oxford University Press, 2013), p. 237.

p. 82, **owned by Matthew Law, along with the popular** *Richard II* ... Stationers' Register, entry for 25 June 1603, SCA Liber C, Ref. TSC/1/E/06/02, f. 98.

p. 83, **Falstaff trod the boards by another name: that of Sir John Oldcastle** ... For the full history of the Oldcastle/Falstaff controversy and its contexts see Laoutaris, *Shakespeare and the Countess*, pp. 230–42 and 335–36. See also Gary Taylor, 'The Fortunes of Oldcastle', *Shakespeare Survey*, vol. 38 (1986), pp. 85–100.

p. 83, **It is no pampered glutton we present** ... Anthony Munday [and Michael Drayton, Richard Hathaway and Robert Wilson], *The first part of the True and Honourable History, of the Life of Sir John Oldcastle, the Good Lord Cobham* (London: Printed by V[alentine] S[immes] for Thomas Pavier, 1600), sig. A2.

p. 84, **the distinction between the original Oldcastle plays and the Admiral's Men's production may not have been instantly apparent** ... For a reading that confirms this possibility in relation to the 'conflicts between the players' and the publishers' notion of ownership of plays, see James J. Marino, *Owning William Shakespeare* (Philadelphia: University of Pennsylvania Press, 2011), pp. 107–42.

p. 85, **Recent stunning forensic work on the 'Pavier-Jaggard Quartos'** ... This is the work of Lesser, in his *Ghosts, Holes, Rips and Scrapes* ..., in which he reveals the extent of the potential deception.

p. 86, **It is commonly thought that Heminges and Condell heard about the 'Pavier-Jaggard' endeavour** ... This stems from W.W. Greg's interpretation in 'On certain false dates in Shakespearean Quartos', *Library*, vol. 9, no. 34 (1908), pp. 113–31; Greg's *The Shakespeare First Folio*, pp. 15–16; and E.K. Chambers, *William Shakespeare: A Study of Facts and Problems*, vol. 1

(Oxford: Clarendon Press, 1930), pp. 136–37. This theory has since been taken up as a popular explanation for the 1619 edict. Massai presents a fascinating alternative theory, arguing that Isaac Jaggard called a halt to the printing of the 'Pavier-Jaggard Quartos' because he conceived the idea of the First Folio and 'persuaded the King's Men to invoke the Lord Chamberlain's support' to protect the new venture; *Shakespeare and the Rise of the Editor*, p. 107. Marino emphatically states that the 1619 edict was 'retroactive', covering all King's Men plays, both unpublished and previously printed (*Owning William Shakespeare*, pp. 116–17), while Erne sees this as 'difficult to ascertain'; Lukas Erne, *Shakespeare and the Book Trade* (Cambridge: Cambridge University Press, 2013), p. 176. I follow Marino in interpreting this edict as covering both published and unprinted works, due in part to the fact that Sir William Herbert's letter makes an extraordinary claim: that members of the Stationers' Company had 'published and printed' King's Men plays 'procured' without licence. This, I believe, was a clever ploy on the part of the King's Men. It would invariably have meant any stationer or publisher wanting to print a play from the King's Men's repertory would have to *prove*, even if they had published the work before, that they held a legitimate 'copy' by presenting that evidence to Heminges and Condell. This would explain why Pavier and the Jaggards had no choice but to suspend the printing of their quartos, *despite* having already heavily invested in them and *despite* the fact that these were previously printed works. Neither the wording of the Lord Chamberlain's letter, nor that in the Stationers' own record of the edict, indicated that previously printed King's Men plays were exempt.

p. 86, **Indeed, that year saw the beginning of a series of King's Men plays by Francis Beaumont and John Fletcher** … The theory of the illicit printing of plays from the King's Men's repertory was presented by E.A.J. Honigmann in his *The Texts of Othello and Shakespearian Revision* (London and New York: Routledge, 1996); see especially pp. 22–29 (Honigmann suggested the 1619 edict, which banned the printing of King's Men's plays, was a response to this series of play thefts). Martin Wiggins kindly shared with me some of his own independent unpublished research on this. The theory of the 'thefts' has been challenged by Scott McMillin, *The First Quarto of Othello* (Cambridge: Cambridge University Press, 2001), especially pp. 15–17, 35–37 and 43–44, and Massai, *Shakespeare and the Rise of the Editor*, pp. 120 and 226, n. 32 (the latter highlighting the objections of other scholars to the theory). I am grateful to Martin Wiggins for discussing the publication of this sequence of plays and the significance of their reprintings with me.

Chapter 5 – 'Of great living, wealth and power': The King's Men's Public and Private Enemies

p. 88, **Located just south of Ludgate and south-west of St Paul's Cathedral** … The locations of Richard Field's printing press and Lady Elizabeth Russell's home, relative to the Blackfriars Theatre and St Anne's Church, as itemised in this chapter, were calculated by collating: Richard Field's lease agreement with William and George More, SHC LM 333/12, dated 22 September 1592; Gideon de Lawne's indenture, SHC LM 333/11, dated 20 September 1592; Lady Russell's letter to William More, SHC, Historical Correspondence 6729/6/98, dated 9 August c. 1580–81; Lewis de Mare's indenture, SHC LM 348/68, dated 3 September 1570; Paul Buck's indentures, SHC LM 348/216, dated 30 June 1591 and SHC LM 348/234, dated 31 January 1594; and William de Lawne's purchase agreement with William and George More, FSL, Lb.349, dated 31 October 1593. For more details of the area see Chris Laoutaris, *Shakespeare and the Countess: The Battle that Gave Birth to the Globe* (London: Penguin, 2014), in which the location of Field's press was revealed for the first time.

p. 89, **a petition of November 1596** … TNA SP 12/260, f. 176, November 1596.

p. 90, **The owner of the said playhouse doth, under the name of a private house** … The 'Petition of Precinct Officers to the Lord Mayor', 1619, is transcribed in Irwin Smith, *Shakespeare's Blackfriars Playhouse: Its History and Its Design* (London: Peter Owen, 1964), pp. 489–90.

p. 91, **'some remedy … that we may go to our houses in safety …'** The 'Petition of Precinct Inhabitants to the Lord Mayor', 1619, is transcribed in Smith, *Shakespeare's Blackfriars Playhouse*, pp. 491–92.

p. 91, **Field had, remarkably, acted against his own professional interests** … Field was assistant warden at St Anne's Church in 1592, before becoming a warden in 1598; see LMA, MS 9537, vol. 8, f. 77, 1592, and LMA, MS 9 537, vol. 9, f. 158. For more on the betrayal of Shakespeare and the playing company by Field and Hunsdon see Laoutaris, *Shakespeare and the Countess*.

p. 91, **acquired a new landlord, one William de Lawne** … See William de Lawne's purchase agreement with William and George More, FSL, Lb.349, dated 31 October 1593, and Laoutaris, *Shakespeare and the Countess*, pp. 127–130 and 274–76.

p. 91, **William's son, Paul Delane or De Laune** … For details about his career see Margaret Pelling and Frances White, 'DE LAUNE, Paul', in *Physicians and Irregular Medical Practitioners in London 1550–1640 Database* (London, 2004), British History Online: http://www.british-history.ac.uk/no-series/london-physicians/1550-1640/de-laune-paul.

p. 91, **'the said playhouse be suppressed …'** The 'Order by the Corporation of the City of London for the Suppression of the Blackfriars Playhouse', 16 January 1619, is transcribed in Smith, *Shakespeare's Blackfriars Playhouse*, pp. 493–94.

p. 92, **'at extreme rates' and with 'infinite cost and pains'** … See Laoutaris, *Shakespeare and the Countess*, p. 317.

p. 92, **'under our Great Seal of England'** … The 'License for the King's Players', 27 March 1619, is transcribed in Smith, *Shakespeare's Blackfriars Playhouse*, pp. 495–96.

p. 93, **In his will Phillips, an original sharer** … The will is transcribed in E.A.J. Honigmann and Susan Brock, eds, *Playhouse Wills, 1558–1642*

(Manchester: Manchester University Press, 1993 [2015 edition]), pp. 72–75.

p. 94, 'wrongfully and without any just title' ... Bill of complaint of John Witter against John Heminges and Henry Condell, dated 20 April 1619, TNA REQ 4/1/2/1.

p. 94, Heminges and Condell were ordered to appear in court ... Court appearance book, the case of John Witter against John Heminges and Henry Condell, TNA REQ 1/110, dated 23 April 1619.

p. 94, Heminges informed the court that he would undermine Witter's entire case ... Reply of John Heminges and Henry Condell in the case of John Witter against John Heminges and Henry Condell, TNA REQ 4/1/2/2, dated 28 April 1619.

p. 95, Witter returned his 'replication' or answer ... John Witter's replication in his suit against John Heminges and Henry Condell, TNA REQ 4/1/2/3, dated 10 May 1619.

p. 97, Heminges and Condell managed to track down witnesses to corroborate their case ... Witness book in the case of John Witter against John Heminges and Henry Condell, TNA REQ 1/200, dated c. 1620; the details about Woodford and Knasborough can be found in Shakespeare Documented: https://shakespearedocumented.folger.edu/resource/document/witter-v-heminges-and-condell-shareholdings-globe-witness-book. See also TNA REQ 1/29, p. 598 and TNA REQ 1/29, p. 613, which indicate the longevity of the case (https://shakespearedocumented.folger.edu/resource/document/witter-v-heminges-and-condell-shareholdings-globe-decree-and-order-books-first and https://shakespearedocumented.folger.edu/resource/document/witter-v-heminges-and-condell-shareholdings-globe-decree-and-order-books-second), as well as Smith, *Shakespeare's Blackfriars Playhouse*, p. 255.

p. 97, 'clearly and absolutely dismissed forever' ... Final decree in the case of John Witter against John Heminges and Henry Condell, TNA REQ 1/30, p. 761, dated c. 1620.

p. 97, 'built the Globe, with more sums of money taken up at interest ...' From the 'Sharers' Papers of 1635, transcribed in Smith, *Shakespeare's Blackfriars Playhouse*, p. 558.

p. 97, But was Witter responsible for more than just trying to seize a portion of the King's Men's shares in the Globe? ... The theory that John Witter had stolen the King's Men's manuscripts was suggested by E.A.J. Honigmann in his *The Texts of Othello and Shakespearian Revision* (London and New York: Routledge, 1996), p. 27; see the same text for the significance of these plays' reprintings, pp. 22–29. See also the discussion in Suzanne Gossett's introduction to Francis Beaumont and John Fletcher, *Philaster* (London: Arden, 2009), pp. 76–99. I am grateful to Martin Wiggins for discussing the possibility of these play thefts with me.

Chapter 6 – 'Care and pains': Hunting the King's Men's Lost
Shakespeare Plays

p. 102, **promised copies of the volume upon publication as a form of
remuneration** … See Ben Higgins, *Shakespeare's Syndicate: The First Folio,
its Publishers, and the Early Modern Book Trade* (Oxford: Oxford University
Press, 2022) p. 25.

p. 103, **the cost of producing each individual Folio is six shillings, eight
pence** … The costs and print run of the First Folio are derived from the
following: Peter W.M. Blayney, introduction to the second edition of *The
Norton Facsimile: The First Folio of Shakespeare* (New York and London:
W.W. Norton and Company, 1996), p. xxxiii; Eric Rasmussen, 'Publishing
the First Folio', *The Cambridge Companion to Shakespeare's First Folio*, ed.
Emma Smith (Cambridge: Cambridge University Press, 2016), pp. 18–29
(pp. 18 and 27); Higgins, *Shakespeare's Syndicate*, pp. 25–27; and Emma
Smith, *The Making of Shakespeare's First Folio* (Oxford: Bodleian Library,
2016), pp. 70–73. Estimates of today's equivalent prices and waged labour
calculations for this chapter were generated from https://www.
nationalarchives.gov.uk/currency-converter/.

p. 103, **Requiring around 229 sheets per book** … The costs of acquiring the
paper stocks for the First Folio have been derived from Carter Hailey's
calculations for two book projects in the Jaggards' printing house, with my
own adjustments to arrive at the cost for the First Folio alone: 'The Best
Crowne Paper', in *Foliomania! Stories Behind Shakespeare's Most Important
Book* (Washington D.C.: Folger Shakespeare Library, 2015), pp. 8–14
(p. 14).

p. 103, **'Some playbooks … are grown from Quarto to Folio'** … William
Prynne, *Histrio-Mastix: The players' scourge, or, actors' tragedy* (London:
Printed by E[dward] A[llde, Augustine Mathewes, Thomas Cotes] and
W[illiam] J[ones] for Michael Sparke, 1633); quoted in Hailey, 'The Best
Crowne Paper', p. 8. Prynne also writes that such Folios 'bear so good a
price and sale, that I cannot but with grief relate it' (quoted from the
original; early modern text, unpaginated).

p. 104, **a portion of pressworkers' wages paid for in kind, with copies of this
sumptuous volume** … Higgins, *Shakespeare's Syndicate*, p. 27.

p. 104, **commanded a fee of around six pence per work** … See examples in
the Stationers' Register, SCA Liber C, Ref. TSC/1/E/06/02.

p. 105, **with one survey of the process indicating that a standard charge** …
For this estimate see Higgins, *Shakespeare's Syndicate*, p. 25.

p. 105, **'Twere vain to mention the chargeableness …'** Humphrey Moseley's
epistle 'The Stationer to the Readers', *Comedies and tragedies written by
Francis Beaumont and John Fletcher* (London: Printed for Humphrey
Robinson and Humphrey Moseley, 1647), sigs A4–A4v.

p. 106, **The Jaggards were, in so many ways, ideal helmsmen** … The
biographical information about the Jaggards has been derived from:
Rasmussen, 'Publishing the First Folio', pp. 19–21; Marta Straznicky, ed.,
Shakespeare's Stationers: Studies in Cultural Bibliography (Philadelphia:

University of Pennsylvania Press, 2013), pp. 255–59; Higgins, *Shakespeare's Syndicate*, pp. 79–80; and the ODNB entry for 'William Jaggard' by Stanley Wells. The Jaggards' licence to operate two printing presses is indicated in *Records of the Court of the Stationers' Company 1602–1640*, ed. William A. Jackson (London: Bibliographical Society, 1957), pp. 75 (record for 9 May 1615) and 158 (record for 5 July 1623).

p. 108, **already experienced producers of folios** … The examples itemised are: Edward Topsell, *The History of Four-footed Beasts, Describing the true and lively figure of every beast* … (London: Printed by William Jaggard, 1607); Thomas Heywood, *Troia Britanica: or, Great Britain's Troy* (London: Printed by William Jaggard, 1609); Helkiah Crooke, *Mikrokosmographia, A description of the body of man* (Printed by William Jaggard, 1615).

p. 108, **an edition of the works of the cleric Edward Dering** … See Higgins, *Shakespeare's Syndicate*, p. 17. Jaggard owned the rights to a work included in this volume: *M[aster] Dering's Works, More at large than ever hath heretofore been printed in any one volume* (London: Printed by Edward Griffin for Edward Blount, 1614).

p. 109, **the price for fourteen plays, rather than for all sixteen listed in the register** … See Stationers' Register, SCA Liber D, Ref. TSC/1/E/06/03, f. 69. Peter W.M. Blayney noticed this anomaly and concluded that the syndicate only discovered the status of *Antony and Cleopatra* and *As You Like It* after they had paid for a search of the Stationers' archives, see: *The First Folio of Shakespeare* (Washington D.C., Folger Shakespeare Library 1991), pp. 18–21.

Chapter 7 – Bears, Parrots and Angels: St Paul's Cross Churchyard, London's Publishing Powerhouse

p. 111, **Around twenty-eight booksellers had set up shop within its boundary** … The size and make-up of St Paul's Cross Churchyard are rough estimates based on a collation of information from: Roze Hentschell, *St Paul's Cathedral Precinct in Early Modern Literature and Culture: Spatial Practices* (Oxford: Oxford University Press, 2020), pp. 119–20; the maps and calculations for a portion of the precinct in Peter W.M. Blayney, *The Bookshops in Paul's Cross Churchyard*, Occasional papers of the Bibliographical Society, no. 5 (London: Bibliographical Society, 1990); and the online Virtual Paul's Cross Project (NC State University), https://vpcross.chass.ncsu.edu/. The phrase 'St Paul's Cross Churchyard' or 'Paul's Cross Churchyard' refers specifically to the north-eastern corner of the wider St Paul's precinct, where the largest concentration of bookshops in the vicinity could be found. This is to be distinguished from the entire circumference of the churchyard and precinct grounds.

p. 112, **William Shakespeare's publisher and fellow Stratfordian Richard Field once operated a printing house** … The discovery of the precise location of Richard Field's printing press was first revealed in Chris Laoutaris, *Shakespeare and the Countess: The Battle that Gave Birth to the Globe* (London: Penguin, 2014), and was determined through the following documents: Richard Field's lease agreement with William and George More, SHC LM 333/12, dated 22 September 1592; Gideon de Lawne's indenture, SHC LM 333/11, dated 20 September 1592; Lady Russell's letter to William More, SHC, Historical Correspondence 6729/6/98, dated 9 August c. 1580–81; Lewis de Mare's indenture, SHC LM 348/68, dated 3 September 1570; Paul Buck's indentures, SHC LM 348/216, dated 30 June 1591 and SHC LM 348/234, dated 31 January 1594; and William de Lawne's purchase agreement with William and George More, FSL, Lb.349, dated 31 October 1593. The layout of the rest of St Paul's, as described in this paragraph, is based on the maps in Blayney, *The Bookshops in Paul's Cross Churchyard*, and Janelle Jenstad's project, 'The Agas Map. The Map of Early Modern London, Edition 7.0', https://mapoflondon.uvic.ca/agas.htm.

p. 113, **renovations to the crumbling cathedral, which James I authorised** … Hentschell, *St Paul's Cathedral Precinct* …, pp. 217–20.

p. 113, **But when they were done gazing in wonder** … The descriptions of St Paul's Cross Churchyard in this paragraph are derived from: Hentschell, *St Paul's Cathedral Precinct* …, pp. 221–22; the imaging and descriptions provided in the online Virtual Paul's Cross Project (NC State University), https://vpcross.chass.ncsu.edu/; and Tiffany Stern, "'On each Wall/And Corner Post": Playbills, Title-pages, and Advertising in Early Modern London', *English Literary Renaissance*, vol. 36, no. 1 (Winter 2006), pp. 57–89.

p. 113, **Overlooked by the cathedral's gargoyles** … The sounds and ambience of St Paul's Cross Churchyard have been reconstructed from the following: the online Virtual Paul's Cross Project (NC State University), which includes details of acoustic modelling for the St Paul's Cross area, https://vpcp.chass.ncsu.edu/; Blayney, *The Bookshops in Paul's Cross Churchyard*; Peter W.M. Blayney, *The First Folio of Shakespeare* (Washington D.C.: Folger Shakespeare Library, 1991), p. 27; Hentschell, *St Paul's Cathedral Precinct* …, pp. 104–43 and 217–22; and the research of Tiffany Stern on the bells of St Paul's Cathedral, as referenced in the 'Acoustic Model' produced for the Virtual Paul's Cross Project: https://vpcathedral.chass.ncsu.edu/?page_id=4218.

p. 115, **Around 145 feet north of Paul's Cross stood a line of bookshops** … The measurements and arrangements referenced in this paragraph are from: the online Virtual Paul's Cross Project (NC State University), https://vpcp.chass.ncsu.edu/; the maps and descriptions of bookshops in Blayney, *The Bookshops in Paul's Cross Churchyard*; Hentschell, *St Paul's Cathedral Precinct* …, pp. 119–21.

p. 115, **the bookshop identified by the sign of the Black Bear** … For Blount's tenure at the Black Bear, and the shop's location, see Blayney, *The Bookshops in Paul's Cross Churchyard*, pp. 26–27.

p. 115, **rights to *Antony and Cleopatra*, and had certainly once owned *Pericles*** … Stationers' Register, entry for 20 May 1608, SCA Liber C, Ref. TSC/1/E/06/02, f. 167v.

p. 115, **Blount, like other booksellers, acted as a courier** ... The account of Blount's activities is derived from the ODNB entry for 'Edward Blount' by Gary Taylor and Ben Higgins, *Shakespeare's Syndicate: The First Folio, its Publishers, and the Early Modern Book Trade* (Oxford: Oxford University Press, 2022), pp. 69–73, as well as the following surviving Blount letters: TNA SP 14/80, f. 136, dated 26 April 1615; TNA SP 14/80, f. 186, dated 23 June 1615; BL Additional MS 72361, ff. 68–69, dated 15 June 1621; BL Additional MS 72361, ff. 109–10, dated 6 July 1621; BL Additional MS 72364, ff. 125–26, dated 8 November 1622; BL Additional MS 72365, ff. 130–31, dated 9 May 1623; BL Additional MS 72365, ff. 116–17, dated 30 May 1623; BL Additional MS 78683, f. 73, dated 15 August 1631 (all of which are transcribed in Higgins, *Shakespeare's Syndicate*, pp. 224–36). In addition the following letters trace Blount's working life and contacts: (from John Chamberlain to Dudley Carleton) TNA SP 14/74, ff. 171–72v, dated 27 October 1613; TNA SP 14/75, ff. 52–53, dated 25 November 1613; TNA SP 14/81, ff. 117–18, dated 24 August 1615; TNA SP 14/88, ff. 227–28, dated 26 October 1616; TNA SP 14/103, ff. 40–41v, dated 14 October 1618; TNA SP 14/112, ff. 65–65v, dated 25 January 1620; (from John Chamberlain to Alice Carleton) TNA SP 14/77, ff. 107–107v, dated 30 June 1614; and (from John Chamberlain to Isaac Wake) TNA SP 14/78, ff. 59–60, dated 12 October 1614.

pp. 116–17, **Baptised in St Lawrence's Church, Pountney** ... Blount's background, publishing interests, career progression and biography, as presented in this chapter, are derived from: ODNB entry for 'Edward Blount' by Gary Taylor; *Shakespeare's Stationers: Studies in Cultural Bibliography* (Philadelphia: University of Pennsylvania Press, 2013), ed. Marta Straznicky, pp. 235–36; the manuscript book Call of the Livery, vol. 1, SCA TSC/1/C/01/06/01, f. 3; *Records of the Court of the Stationers' Company 1602–1640*, ed. William A. Jackson (London: Bibliographical Society, 1957), pp. 55, 128, 164 and 182; Leah Scragg, 'Edward Blount and the History of Lylian Criticism', *Review of English Studies*, vol. 46, no. 181 (February 1995), pp. 1–10; Leah Scragg, 'Edward Blount and the Prefatory Material to the First Folio of Shakespeare', *Bulletin of the John Rylands Library*, vol. 79, no. 1 (1997), pp. 117–26; Higgins, *Shakespeare's Syndicate*, pp. 19–20 and 68–76; John Jowett, *Shakespeare and Text* (Oxford: Oxford University Press, 2007), pp. 73–74; Lukas Erne, *Shakespeare and the Book Trade* (Cambridge: Cambridge University Press, 2013), pp. 157–59; and Chris Laoutaris, 'The Prefatorial Material [to the First Folio]', in *The Cambridge Companion to Shakespeare's First Folio*, ed. Emma Smith (Cambridge: Cambridge University Press, 2016), pp. 48–67 (pp. 54–55). The works issued by Blount referenced are: Michel de Montaigne, *The Essays or Moral, Politic and Military Discourses*, trans. John Florio (London: By Val[entine] Sim[me]s for Edward Blount, 1603); Michel de Montaigne, *Essays ... done into English*, trans. John Florio (London: Printed by Melch[ior] Bradwood for Edward Blount and William Barret, 1613); Samuel Daniel, *A Panegyricke Congratulatory* (London: Printed by

Valentine Simmes for Edward Blount, 1603); Lucan, *Pharsalia*, trans. Sir Arthur Gorges (London: Printed [by Nicholas Okes] for Edward Blount, 1614); William Alexander, *The Monarchic Tragedies* (London: By V[alentine] S[immes] [and G. Elde] for Edward Blount, 1604); William Alexander, *The Monarchic Tragedies … Newly enlarged …* (London: Printed by Valentine Simmes for Ed[ward] Blount, 1607); John Lyly, *Six Court Comedies* (London: Printed by William Stansby for Edward Blount, 1632); Robert Chester, *Love's Martyr: or, Rosalin's Complaint, Allegorically shadowing the truth of love, in the constant fate of the Phoenix and Turtle* [by William Shakespeare] (London: Imprinted [by Richard Field] for E[dward B[lount], 1601); and William Shakespeare, *Shakespeare's Sonnets* (London: By G. Eld for T[homas] T[horpe] and are to be sold by William Aspley, 1609).

p. 116, **'the most important publisher of the early seventeenth century'** … ODNB entry for 'Edward Blount' by Gary Taylor.

p. 117, **'his kind and true friend'** … Quoted in Eric Rasmussen, 'Publishing the First Folio', *The Cambridge Companion to Shakespeare's First Folio*, ed. Emma Smith (Cambridge: Cambridge University Press, 2016), pp. 18–29 (p. 21). See also BL Additional MS 72361, ff. 109–10, dated 6 July 1621.

p. 117, **'my particular duty … bind[s] me …'** Lorenzo Ducci, *Ars Aulica or The courtier's Art* (London: Printed by Melch[ior] Bradwood for Edward Blount, 1607), sigs A4–A4v. For more on Blount's closeness to the Herbert brothers see Sonia Massai, 'Edward Blount, the Herberts, and the First Folio', in Straznicky, ed., *Shakespeare's Stationers*, pp. 132–46, and Laoutaris, 'The Prefatorial Material [to the First Folio]', pp. 60–63 (for the theory that the First Folio taps into the Herbert brothers' interest in emblematic literature).

p. 117, **an act of 'public good'** … Gonzalo de Céspedes y Meneses, *Gerardo the Unfortunate Spaniard*, trans. Leonard Digges (London: Printed [by George Purslowe] for Ed[ward] Blount, 1622), sig. A2v.

p. 118, **Blount had known Mabbe for over a decade by this time** … Blount and Mabbe's friendship is attested to in BL Additional MS 72364, ff. 125–26, dated 8 November 1622; BL Additional MS 72365, ff. 116–17, dated 30 May 1623; Higgins, *Shakespeare's Syndicate*, pp. 70–76, 230 and 234; and in the ODNB entry for 'Edward Blount' by Gary Taylor.

p. 118, **James Mabbe, almost certainly the 'I.M.' or 'J.M.'** … For Mabbe's connections and other contenders for the 'I.M.' of the First Folio (including Jasper Mayne and John Marston), see Arthur W. Secord, 'I.M. of the First Folio Shakespeare and Other Mabbe Problems', *Journal of English and Germanic Philology*, vol. 47, no. 4 (October 1948), pp. 374–81; and Scragg, 'Edward Blount and the History of Lylian Criticism', pp. 1–10. For an analysis that identifies 'I.M.' as John Milton, father of the poet of the same name, see Gordon Campbell, 'Shakespeare and the Youth of Milton', *Milton Quarterly*, vol. 33, no. 4 (December 1999), pp. 95–105.

p. 118, **As the publisher of Thomas Shelton's translation of Cervantes' Don Quixote** … Miguel de Cervantes, *The history of the valorous and witty* *knight-errant, Don-Quixote,* part 1 (London: Printed by William Stansby, for Ed[ward] Blount and W[illiam] Barret, 1612); Miquel de Cervantes, *The second part of the history of the valorous and witty knight-errant, Don Quixote* (London: Printed [by Eliot's Court Press] for Edward Blount, 1620).

p. 118, **Blount's own epistle to the reader in** *The Rogue* … Mateo Alemán, *The Rogue, or, The life of Guzman de Alfarache,* trans. James Mabbe (London: Printed for Edward Blount, 1622), A4v–A5.

p. 118, **John Florio's** *Queen Anna's New World of Words* … **Mabbe's translation of a Spanish work entitled** *Christian Policy* … John Florio, *Queen Anna's New World of Words* (London: Printed by Melch[ior] Bradwood [and William Stansby], for Edw[ard] Blount and William Barret, 1611); Juan de Santa María, *Christian Policy, or, The Christian Commonwealth* (London: Printed by Thomas Harper, for Richard Collins, 1632). Blount died before he could publish the latter work.

p. 118, **his 'worthy Friend'** … Ben Jonson, *Sejanus His Fall* (London: Printed by G. Elld, for Thomas Thorpe, 1605), sig. A2.

pp. 118–19, **Holland, whose family hailed from Wales** … The biographical information about Holland is derived from: the ODNB entry for 'Hugh Holland' by Collin Burrow; William Camden, *Remains of a Greater Work, Concerning Britain* (London: Printed by G[eorge] E[ld] for Simon Waterson, 1605), p. 8; Anthony à Wood, *Athenae Oxonienses, an exact history of all the writers and bishops who have had their education in the most ancient and famous University of Oxford* (London: Printed for Tho[mas] Bennet, 1691), vol. 1, pp. 498–99.

p. 119, **led some to believe that Blount was responsible for gathering these scholarly poets together** … See Scragg, 'Edward Blount and the Prefatory Material to the First Folio of Shakespeare', pp. 117–26.

p. 119, **Ralph Mabbe had occupied between 1611 and 1613** … For Ralph Mabbe's bookshops in St Paul's Cross Churchyard see Blayney, *The Bookshops in Paul's Cross Churchyard,* pp. 23–24 and 28–29.

p. 120, **shop was identified by the sign of the Pied Bull** … Nathaniel Butter's shop is identified in the title pages of his published works. Examples include: William Shakespeare, *M[aster] William Shakespeare: His True Chronicle History of the Life and Death of King Lear* (London: Printed [by Nicholas Okes] for Nathaniel Butter, and are to be sold at his shop in Paul's Churchyard at the sign of the Pied Bull near St. Augustine's Gate, 1608) and Edward Hoby, *A Curry-Combe for a Cox-Combe* (London: Printed by William Stansby for Nathaniel Butter, and are to be sold at his shop near S[aint] Augustine's Gate at the sign of the Pied Bull, 1615).

p. 120, **three substantial loans from the Stationers' Company between 1619 and 1623** … For the list of his loans between 1619 and 1638 see loans and bequests book, entries for 6 September 1619, 21 May 1623, 20 March 1626 and 31 January 1638, SCA Liber C2, Ref. TSC/1/G/01/02/01, ff. 17, 110, 112v and 120v. I would like to thank Peter Foden for his precise translations of the Latin portions of the loan requests from SCA Liber C2.

Mabbe had mortgaged his shares three times between 1616 and 1622 (on 5 March 1616, 16 July 1617 and 6 May 1622), see Jackson, ed., *Records of the Court of the Stationers' Company*, pp. 82, 94 and 145 (taken together, this makes three large loans between 1619 and 1623).

p. 120, **Ralph may have been a kinsman or even the brother of the Folio's James Mabbe** ... See Secord, 'I.M. of the First Folio Shakespeare and Other Mabbe Problems', pp. 378–79.

p. 120, **where the dramatist's collected Sonnets would first be sold** ... William Shakespeare, *Shakespeare's Sonnets* (London: By G. Eld for T[homas] T[horpe] and are to be sold by William Aspley, 1609).

p. 120, **The shop directly next door to his, the Angel** ... For the location and occupancy of the Angel (and the neighbouring Parrot), see Blayney, *The Bookshops in Paul's Cross Churchyard*, pp. 23–25.

p. 120, **the first stationer to enter non-collaborative Shakespeare plays in the Stationers' Register in 1597-8** ... This is excluding *Titus Andronicus* (which is now believed to be a collaborative play), which was entered by John Danter on 6 February 1594, and *Edward III* (which Shakespeare may have contributed to but has been somewhat controversially included as part of his oeuvre in some modern Shakespeare collections; including *The New Oxford Shakespeare: The Complete Works*, general editors, Gary Taylor, John Jowett, Terri Bourus and Gabriel Egan (Oxford: Oxford University Press, 2016)), which was entered by Cuthbert Burby on 1 December 1595. See also Higgins, *Shakespeare's Syndicate*, pp. 130–35. Andrew Wise entered *Richard II*, *Richard III* and *Henry IV, Part 1*, on 29 August 1597, 20 October 1597 and 25 February 1598 respectively, see Stationers' Register, SCA Liber C, Ref. TSC/1/E/06/02, ff. 23, 25 and 31.

p. 120, **At the time Blount was based at the shop identified by the sign of the Bishop's Head** ... For the location and occupancy of the Bishop's Head, and its operation by William Ponsonby (to whom Edward Blount was apprenticed) during 1591–8, see Blayney, *The Bookshops in Paul's Cross Churchyard*, p. 17.

p. 120, **transferred to the stationer Matthew Law** ... The transfer took place on 25 June 1603; see Stationers' Register, SCA Liber C, Ref. TSC/1/E/06/02, f. 98.

p. 120, **Law's shop was known by the sign of the Fox** ... Matthew Law's shop is identified in the title pages of his published works: examples include Thomas Draxe, *An Alarum to the Last Judgement* (London: Printed by Nicholas Okes for Matthew Law, and are to be sold at the sign of the Fox in Paul's Churchyard, 1615) and Thomas Heywood, *A Pleasant Conceited Comedy, wherein is showed, how a man may choose a good wife from a bad* (London: Printed [by Thomas Purfoot] for Matthew Law, and are to be sold at his shop in Paul's Churchyard, near unto S[aint] Augustine's Gate, at the sign of the Fox, 1621).

p. 121, **Law had worked with Blount on James I's *Basilikon Doron*** ... James I, *Basilikon Doron. Or His Majesty's Instructions to his Dearest Son, Henry the Prince* (Edinburgh: Printed by Robert Waldegrave, Printer to the King's

Majesty, 1603). See Ben Higgins, 'We have a constant will to publish': The
Publishers of Shakespeare's First Folio, unpublished DPhil thesis (Oxford:
University of Oxford, 2015), p. 91.

p. 121, **These were** *Much Ado About Nothing* **and** *Henry IV, Part 2* ...
Stationers' Register, entry for 23 August 1600, SCA Liber C, Ref.
TSC/1/E/06/02, f. 163v.

p. 121, **Aspley clearly had a good instinct** ... For Aspley's publishing career
see Stationers' Register, entry for 4 September 1605 (for the *Eastward Ho!*
entry), SCA Liber C, Ref. TSC/1/E/06/02, f. 128v; Higgins, *Shakespeare's
Syndicate*, pp. 125–30; Rasmussen, 'Publishing the First Folio', p. 22;
Straznicky, ed., *Shakespeare's Stationers*, pp. 232–34; and the ODNB entry
for 'William Aspley' by James Travers.

p. 121, **'lusty strong poison'** ... 'Ben Jonson's Conversations with William
Drummond of Hawthornden', in *Ben Jonson, The Complete Poems*, ed.
George Parfitt (Harmondsworth: Penguin, 1975 [1996 edition]), p. 468.

p. 122, **Aspley had also worked with Nathaniel Butter** ... John Bond, *Auli
Persii Flacci Satyræ Sex* (London: Excudebat Felix Kingstonius impensis
Gulielmi Aspley, & Nathanielis Butterij, 1614), entered in the
Stationers' Register on 8 July 1613; see SCA Liber C, Ref. TSC/1/E/06/02,
f. 242.

p. 122, **Butter had used the Jaggards as his printers numerous times** ... For
example: Thomas Smith, *Sir Thomas Smith's Voyage* (London: [By W. White
and W. Jaggard] for Nathaniel Butter, 1605); *The Whole Works of Homer*
(London: Printed [by Richard Field and William Jaggard] for Nathaniel
Butter, 1616).

p. 122, **Aspley had been no less ambitious than Jaggard and Blount when it
came to his career in the Stationers' Company** ... For Aspley's career
progression in the Stationers' Company see SCA, Call of the Livery, vol. 1,
TSC/1/C/01/06/01, p. 4; Jackson, ed., *Records of the Court of the Stationers'
Company*, pp. 79, 153, 204–206, 207, 208, 217, 233, 242–49. In addition see
Higgins, *Shakespeare's Syndicate*, pp. 125–30; Rasmussen, 'Publishing the
First Folio', p. 22; Straznicky, ed., *Shakespeare's Stationers*, pp. 232–34; and
the ODNB entry for 'William Aspley' by James Travers.

p. 123, **Aspley may have consulted with William Jaggard** ... William
Jaggard, *A Catalogue of such English Books* (London: Printed by W[illiam]
Jaggard, 1618), sig. A2.

p. 123, **collaborated on numerous occasions on publishing projects** ... José
de Acosta, *The Natural and Moral History of the East and West Indies*
(London: Printed by Val[entine] Sims for Edward Blount and William
Aspley, 1604); Thommaso Buoni, *Problems of Beauty and all Human
Affections* (London: Printed by G. Eld, for Edward Blount and William
Aspley, 1606); Pierre Charron, *Of Wisdom* (London: Printed for Edward
Blount and Will[iam] Aspley, 1620); Richard Perceval, *A Dictionary in
Spanish and English* (London: By John Haviland for Edward Blount,
1623); and Richard Perceval, *A Dictionary in Spanish and English* (London:
By John Haviland for William Aspley, 1623). For Aspley's further interest

in Spain see *A Brief and True Declaration of the Sickness, Last Words, and Death of the King of Spain, Philip the Second* (London: By Edm[und] Bollifant, for William Aspley, 1599).

p. 123, **Recent research has indicated** ... Higgins, 'We have a constant will to publish' (unpublished DPhil thesis, University of Oxford), pp. 81 and 161–97, and Higgins, *Shakespeare's Syndicate*, pp. 142–67.

pp. 123–24, **When Aspley stood outside the door of the Parrot and looked directly ahead** ... On the Tiger's Head, the Spread Eagle, the White Horse, the Fleur-de-lis and Crown, and their occupiers, and on the nearby binderies, see Blayney, *The Bookshops in Paul's Cross Churchyard*, pp. 12–15 and 68–71, and Blayney, *The First Folio of Shakespeare*, p. 27.

p. 124, **rights to *Troilus and Cressida* ... the rights to *The Merry Wives of Windsor*** ... Stationers' Register, *Troilus and Cressida*, entry for 29 January 1609 (registered by Richard Bonian and Henry Walley), SCA Liber C, Ref. TSC/1/E/06/02, f. 178v; and *The Merry Wives of Windsor*, entry for 18 January 1602 (registered by Arthur Johnson, transferred from John Busby), SCA Liber C, Ref. TSC/1/E/06/02, f. 78.

p. 125, **pack up his shop and move to Dublin ... owned a share in a publication in 1611** ... Straznicky, ed., *Shakespeare's Stationers*, p. 260, and Higgins, 'We have a constant will to publish' (unpublished DPhil thesis, University of Oxford), pp. 79–80. The work they collaborated on was Josiah Sylvester, *Du Bartas his Divine Weeks and Works* (London: By Humfrey Lounes [and are to be sold by Arthur Johnson at the sign of the White Horse, near the great north door of Paul's Church, 1611]). One fact that might indicate that Pavier had entered into a legitimate agreement with Johnson over the rights to print *The Merry Wives of Windsor* in the 'Pavier-Jaggard Quartos' is that the latter also, like Pavier, had draper connections, having been apprenticed to the draper and bookseller William Young (Straznicky, ed., *Shakespeare's Stationers*, p. 260).

p. 125, **A year before, he and Blount had been jointly appointed as officers** ... Blount and Johnson's joint offices in the Stationers' Company and these debts are itemised in Jackson, ed., *Records of the Court of the Stationers' Company*, pp. 42 and 100.

Chapter 8 – Dials, Legs and Harts: In St Dunstan's Churchyard and Fleet Street

p. 127, **This was the heart of what was then, and still is, London's legal district** ... Incredibly useful for reconstructing the St Dunstan's area have been: Janelle Jenstad's project, 'The Agas Map. The Map of Early Modern London, Edition 7.0', https://mapoflondon.uvic.ca/agas.htm; Ben Higgins, 'We have a constant will to publish': The Publishers of Shakespeare's First Folio, unpublished DPhil thesis (Oxford: University of Oxford, 2015), pp. 198–208; and John Stow, *A Survey of London, Written in the Year 1598* (Stroud: Sutton Publishing, 2005), pp. 330–31.

p. 128, **carried a kind of residual memory of the dramatist's presence** ... For a detailed history of Shakespeare publication in the area see Ben Higgins,

Shakespeare's Syndicate: The First Folio, its Publishers, and the Early Modern Book Trade (Oxford: Oxford University Press, 2022), pp. 170–210.

p. 129, **by Smethwick, and acquired by him as part of a job lot** … Nicholas Ling had registered *The Taming of a Shrew*, *Romeo and Juliet* and *Love's Labour's Lost* on 22 January 1607, see the Stationers' Register, SCA Liber C, Ref. TSC/1/E/06/02, f. 147. He would also have acquired *Hamlet* from James Roberts (who had secured the rights on 26 July 1602; SCA Liber C, Ref. TSC/1/E/06/02, f. 84). John Smethwick had these plays, 'which did belong to Nicholas Ling', including *Hamlet*, transferred to him on 19 November 1607; see SCA Liber C, Ref. TSC/1/E/06/02, f. 161.

p. 129, **shop identified by the sign of the Crane** … See Peter W.M. Blayney, *The Bookshops in Paul's Cross Churchyard*, Occasional Papers of the Bibliographical Society, no. 5 (London: Bibliographical Society, 1990), pp. 27–28.

p. 129, **works of Michael Drayton** … *Works* of Ben Jonson … *Poems: by Michael Drayton Esquire* (London: Printed by W[illiam] Stansby for John Smethwick, and are to be sold at his shop in Saint Dunstan's Churchyard in Fleet Street, under the Dial, 1619); *The Works of Benjamin Jonson* (London: Printed by William Stansby for Richard Meighen, 1616).

pp. 129–30, **Smethwick's closest connections at this time were with the Jaggards** … John Smethwick's early life and career, including his working association with John Jaggard, are derived from: Eric Rasmussen, 'Publishing the First Folio', *The Cambridge Companion to Shakespeare's First Folio*, ed. Emma Smith (Cambridge: Cambridge University Press, 2016), pp. 18–29 (p. 22); Marta Straznicky, ed., *Shakespeare's Stationers: Studies in Critical Bibliography* (Philadelphia: University of Pennsylvania Press, 2013), pp. 291–93; Higgins, *Shakespeare's Syndicate*, pp. 17, 170–72 and 203; and Higgins, 'We have a constant will to publish' (unpublished DPhil thesis, University of Oxford), pp. 85–87 and 211–12. Smethwick was granted a Livery share in the English Stock on 22 December 1614 and elected a Stock-Keeper of the Livery on 1 March 1617. He was elected as one of the chief Assistants to the Masters and Wardens in 1629, claiming a profitable Assistant's share in the English Stock in 1631 and was elected Warden in 1635; see *Records of the Court of the Stationers' Company 1602–1640*, ed. William A. Jackson (London: Bibliographical Society, 1957), pp. 70, 91, 211, 233 and 269.

p. 130, **That the Jaggards were primarily responsible for the introduction of Smethwick to the First Folio syndicate** … As with the idea that Edward Blount brought William Aspley into the Folio syndicate, outlined in chapter 7 of *Shakespeare's Book*, this is my own theory based on the evidence I have collected.

p. 130, **shop in St Dunstan's known by the sign of the Hand and Star** … John Jaggard's shop was just to the west of John Smethwick's, as it was described on the title pages of his published works as being close to Temple Bar: Francis Bacon, *Essays. Religious meditations. Places of Persuasion and Dissuasion* (London: for John Jaggard dwelling in Fleet Street at the Hand

and Star, near Temple Bar, 1612), and Richard Hawkins, *The Observations of Sir Richard Hawkins, Knight, in his Voyage into the South Sea* (London: Printed by J[ohn] D[awson] for John Jaggard, and are to be sold at his shop at the Hand and Star in Fleet Street, near the Temple Gate, 1622).

p. 131, **a complex of tenements, houses and shops, identified by the sign of the Leg** ... The description of William Jaggard's tenements, the account of the legal feud they occasioned, and the quotations referenced are taken from the case of Button v Whitfield, TNA C 2/JasI/B40/22, dated 1610, and Indenture of Conveyance of Land to William Jaggard, LMA CLA/023/DW/01/294, item 14, dated 20 June 1618.

p. 132, *The Troublesome Reign* **was also printed in 1622 by stationer Thomas Dewe** ... *The first and second part of the Troublesome Reign of John, King of England ... Written by W. Shakespeare* (London: Printed by Aug[ustine] Mathewes for Thomas Dewe, and are to be sold at his shop in St Dunstan's Churchyard in Fleet Street, 1622).

p. 132, **Dewe had selected William as the printer for a work** ... Daniel Tuvill, *Christian Purposes and Resolutions* (London: Printed [by William Jaggard] for Thomas Dewe, and are to be sold at his shop in S[aint] Dunstan's Churchyard in Fleet Street, 1622); see Higgins, 'We have a constant will to publish' (unpublished DPhil thesis, University of Oxford), p. 105.

p. 132, **the sign of the White Hart, which stood in Fleet Street** ... The name and location of Fisher's shop are identified in the title pages to his works, including William Shakespeare's *A Midsummer Night's Dream* ([By Richard Bradock] for Thomas Fisher, and are to be sold at his shop, at the sign of the White Hart, in Fleet Street, 1600).

p. 133, **A prolific collaborator, he had worked on projects with John Smethwick and William Aspley** ... For Thomas Pavier's collaborations see Higgins, 'We have a constant will to publish' (unpublished DPhil thesis, University of Oxford), pp. 94–95, 97 and 106, and Gerald D. Johnson, 'Thomas Pavier, Publisher, 1600–25', *Library*, vol. 14, no. 1 (March 1992), pp. 12–50.

p. 134, **owned by Lawrence Hayes, who had inherited the play from his father Thomas** ... See the Stationers' Register, entry for 28 October 1600, SCA Liber C, Ref. TSC/1/E/06/02, f. 66, and entry for 8 July 1619, SCA Liber C, Ref. TSC/1/E/06/02, f. 303.

p. 134, **the shop known by the sign of the Green Dragon** ... Blayney, *The Bookshops in Paul's Cross Churchyard*, pp. 31–33.

p. 134, **Roberts had entered his 'copy' of the play in the Stationers' Register** ... See Peter W.M. Blayney, *The First Folio of Shakespeare* (Washington D.C.: Folger Shakespeare Library, 1991), pp. 18–21. See also the Stationers' Register, entry for 8 November 1623 (the registration of sixteen Shakespeare plays by Edward Blount and Isaac Jaggard), SCA Liber D, Ref. TSC/1/E/06/03, f. 69.

p. 135, **Thomas Walkley, who held the rights to** *Othello* ... Stationers' Register, entry for 6 October 1621, SCA Liber D, Ref. TSC/1/E/06/03, f. 21.

p. 135, **owned the rights to a non-Shakespearean King's Men play** … This play is Francis Beaumont and John Fletcher's *A King and No King*, which Blount entered in the Stationers' Register on 7 August 1618, SCA Liber C, Ref. TSC/1/E/06/02, f. 293. It was published by Walkley as *A King and No King* (London: Printed [by John Beale] for Thomas Walkley, and are to be sold at his shop at the Eagle and Child in Britain's Burse, 1619).

Chapter 9 – 'Sister of a star': Staging the Spanish Match

pp. 137–41 and 145, **a series of performances of Jonson's *The Masque of the Gypsies Metamorphosed*** … All quotations from this masque are taken from Ben Jonson, *Masques of Difference: Four Court Masques by Ben Jonson*, ed. Kristen McDermott (Manchester: Manchester University Press, 2007). The details of the performance venues, the King's Men's involvement, and those in attendance, are from the introduction to McDermott's edition (pp. 6–7, 26–27 and 53–71), and Martin Wiggins, ed., in association with Catherine Richardson, *British Drama, 1533–1642: A Catalogue, Vol. 7: 1617–1623* (Oxford: Oxford University Press, 2016), pp. 342–50.

p. 138, **By 1621 the marquess's influence with James I rivalled that of Sir William Herbert** … On George Villiers' career path in court see Michael G. Brennan, *Literary Patronage in the English Renaissance: The Pembroke Family* (New York and London: Routledge, 1988), pp. 167–70; Brian O'Farrell, *Shakespeare's Patron: William Herbert, Third Earl of Pembroke 1580–1630, Politics, Patronage and Power* (London: Continuum, 2011), pp. 65–67, 73 and 114–15; McDermott, ed., *Masques of Difference*, pp. 55–57; and the ODNB entry for 'George Villiers' by Roger Lockyer.

p. 138, **gypsies were, in the statutes of the period as well as in the popular imagination, connected with masterlessness, vagrancy and theft** … Examples of the popular association between gypsies, thieves and masterlessness can be found in *The Catholic Triumph* … (London: Printed for the Company of Stationers, 1610), p. 123; N.B., *The Court and Country, or A brief discourse dialogue-wise set down between a courtier and a country-man* … (London: G. Eld for John Wright, 1618), sig. B2; John Melton, *Astrologaster, or, The figure-caster* … (London: Barnard Alsop for Edward Blackmore, 1620), pp. 48 and 51.

p. 139, **'the bed's head could not be found between your Master and his Dog'** … Quoted in McDermott, ed., *Masques of Difference*, p. 56.

pp. 140–41, **'The king was so pleased and taken with his entertainment at the Lord Marquess's …'** TNA SP 14/122, ff. 124–124v, letter from John Chamberlain to Dudley Carleton, dated 18 August 1621.

p. 141, **Porter was a poet and Buckingham's confidant** … Endymion Porter's background and affiliations are recorded in Glyn Redworth, *The Prince and the Infanta: The Cultural Politics of the Spanish Match* (New Haven and London: Yale University Press, 2003), p. 43, and Leslie Hotson, *I, William Shakespeare do appoint Thomas Russell, Esquire* (London: Jonathan Cape, 1937), pp. 52 and 238. Redworth also mentions that Porter was 'related to Buckingham' and had served as a page in Olivares' household (p. 43).

p. 141, **Charles was only twenty-one years of age in 1621 and still impressionable** … The character of the prince and the emotional impact of his friendship with Villiers are derived from Redworth, *The Prince and the Infanta*, pp. 39–40; and the ODNB entry for 'Charles I' by Mark A. Kishlansky and John Morrill.

p. 142, **The cataclysmic events which concerned parts of the Bohemian estates** … For the contexts of the wars in the Palatinate see Brennan, *Literary Patronage in the English Renaissance*, p. 156; Redworth, *The Prince and the Infanta*, pp. 19–26 and 65–71; the ODNB entry for 'Princess Elizabeth [Elizabeth Stuart]' by Ronald G. Asch; and Simonds D'Ewes, *The Autobiography and Correspondence of Sir Simonds D'Ewes*, vol. 1, ed. James Orchard Halliwell (London: Richard Bentley, 1845), pp. 171–85.

p. 142, **'there is now no place left for deliberation, nor for mediation of peace …'** TNA SP 14/110, ff. 86–86v, letter from John Chamberlain to Dudley Carleton, dated 11 September 1619.

p. 143, **His mother, Mary Sidney Herbert, had created textual memorials** … See the ODNB entry for 'Mary [née Sidney] Herbert' by Margaret Patterson Hannay; Margaret P. Hannay, *Philip's Phoenix: Mary Sidney, Countess of Pembroke* (Oxford: Oxford University Press, 1990); and Mary Ellen Lamb, 'The Countess of Pembroke's Patronage', *English Literary Renaissance*, vol. 12, no. 2 (March 1982), pp. 162–79.

p. 143, **'I believe the king will be very unwilling to be engaged in a war …'** TNA SP 14/110, f. 126, letter from William Herbert to Dudley Carleton, dated 24 September 1619.

pp. 143–44, **That year his powerbase was expanding in the west of England** … See the ODNB entry for 'William Herbert' by Victor Stater, and Brennan, *Literary Patronage in the English Renaissance*, p. 171.

p. 144, **'chief object' was 'leaving to parliament the dissolution of the treaty with Spain'** … Quoted in O'Farrell, *Shakespeare's Patron*, p. 123.

p. 144, **'promised, with the people's assistance and consent, to aid the king of Bohemia …'** *The Autobiography and Correspondence of Sir Simonds D'Ewes*, vol. 1, p. 171.

p. 145, **'I made not choice of an old beaten soldier for my admiral …'** *The Autobiography and Correspondence of Sir Simonds D'Ewes*, vol. 1, p. 171.

p. 145, **After the prince 'should once have two or three children by the Spanish lady'** … *The Autobiography and Correspondence of Sir Simonds D'Ewes*, vol. 1, pp. 182–83.

pp. 145–46, **William Herbert, one of the most prolific patrons of arts in the period** … The best account of Herbert's patronage activities is O'Farrell, *Shakespeare's Patron*, which includes a useful appendix of works he patronised on pp. 198–201. See also the ODNB entry for 'William Herbert' by Victor Stater. On Herbert's patronage of Ben Jonson, see Ian Donaldson, *Ben Jonson: A Life* (Oxford: Oxford University Press, 2011), pp. 79, 104, 266–69, 284–85, 330 and 350, and Brennan, *Literary Patronage in the English Renaissance*, p. 147.

p. 146, '[n]either am I or my cause so much unknown to your lordship' …
Quoted in O'Farrell, *Shakespeare's Patron*, p. 82; see also Donaldson, *Ben Jonson*, p. 429.

pp. 146–47, 'Licence … to build an Amphitheatre' to one John Cotton …
TNA SP 14/116, f. 171, James I to the Earls of Pembroke and Arundel and others, dated 29 September 1620.

p. 147, the king being so taken with it that there was talk of knighting him
… Wiggins, ed., *British Drama*, vol. 7, p. 345.

p. 147, Jonson was granted the 'reversion' of the Mastership of the Revels …
See Richard Dutton, 'Patronage, Politics, and the Master of the Revels, 1622–1640: The Case of Sir John Astley', *English Literary Renaissance*, vol. 20, no. 2 (March 1990), pp. 287–319 (p. 298). See also TNA SP 14/123, ff. 87–87v, letter from John Chamberlain to Dudley Carleton, dated 27 October 1621, in which the former writes that Ben Jonson 'hath his pension from 100 marks increased to 200 [pounds] per annum, besides the reversion of the Mastership of the Revels' (f. 87v).

pp. 147–48, Two further attempts were made in 1621 to convince him to exchange the post for other offices … See TNA SP 14/123, ff. 41–42, letter from John Chamberlain to Dudley Carleton, dated 13 October 1621; and Dick Taylor, 'The Earl of Montgomery and the Dedicatory Epistle of Shakespeare's First Folio', *Shakespeare Quarterly*, vol. 10, no. 1 (Winter 1959), pp. 121–23 (pp. 122–23).

p. 148, 'the Bohemian cause [was] utterly overthrown …' *The Autobiography and Correspondence of Sir Simonds D'Ewes*, vol. 1, p. 172.

p. 148, 'subtle contrivements' and 'wicked instruments' … *The Autobiography and Correspondence of Sir Simonds D'Ewes*, vol. 1, pp. 182–83.

p. 148, Gondomar had arrived in England enveloped in a gilded cloud of splendour … Redworth, *The Prince and the Infanta*, p. 17.

pp. 148–49, In Dover he had been met by a caravan of royal coaches … The description of Gondomar's arrival and the quotations are from TNA SP 14/113, ff. 45–45v, letter from John Chamberlain to Dudley Carleton, dated 11 March 1620.

p. 149, Dr John Everard 'was sent to the Gatehouse for glancing … at the Spanish match …' TNA SP 14/120, ff. 20–20v, letter from John Chamberlain to Dudley Carleton, dated 10 March 1621.

p. 149, 'What is this Dr Ever-out? his name shall be Dr Never-out' … E.A.J. Honigmann, *The Texts of Othello and Shakespearian Revision* (London and New York: Routledge, 1996), p. 156.

p. 149, 'such a dislike betwixt the king and Lower House' … Thomas Scott, *Vox Populi. Or News from Spain, translated according to the Spanish copy* (London: Imprinted, 1620); quoted from Louis B. Wright, 'Propaganda against James I's "Appeasement" of Spain', *Huntington Library Quarterly*, vol. 6, no. 1 (February 1943), pp. 149–72 (p. 156, with the identification of Scott as author made on pp. 150–51).

pp. 149–50, Gondomar 'foams with wrath in every direction …' Quoted in Wright, 'Propaganda against James I's "Appeasement" of Spain', p. 152.

p. 150, **a royal proclamation was issued for the suppressing of apprentices** … James I, *By the King. A proclamation for suppressing insolent abuses committed by base people against persons of quality, as well strangers as others, in the streets of the city and suburbs of London* (London: By Bonham Norton and John Bill, printers to the King's most Excellent Majesty, 1621).

p. 150, **'abuse offered to the Spanish ambassador and his litter as he passed through the streets'** … TNA SP 14/120, ff. 111–112, letter from John Chamberlain to Dudley Carleton, dated 7 April 1621. See also TNA SP 14/120, ff. 145–146v, letter from John Chamberlain to Dudley Carleton, dated 18 April 1621, which confirms the king's 'proclamation to restrain [ap]prentices and other base people'.

p. 150, **'a general sadness in all men's faces …'** *The Autobiography and Correspondence of Sir Simonds D'Ewes*, vol. 1, pp. 182–83.

p. 150, **It was even rumoured that the Bishop of London, John King** … See ODNB entry for 'John King, Bishop of London' by P.E. McCullough.

pp. 150–52, **sent news of the 'scandal raised of that Bishop'** … The quotations from Edward Blount's letter refer to BL Additional MS 72361, ff. 68–69, letter from Edward Blount to Sir William Trumbull. This is also fully transcribed, with very useful commentary, in Ben Higgins, *Shakespeare's Syndicate: The First Folio, its Publishers, and the Early Modern Book Trade* (Oxford: Oxford University Press, 2022), pp. 226–28.

pp. 150–51, **unfortunate fate of a Catholic monk and controversialist** … This was Thomas Preston, alias Roland Preston, alias Roger Widdrington, who wrote a treatise defending his position on the oath of allegiance, describing a refusal to adhere to it as 'heretical': Thomas Preston, *A New-Year's Gift for English Catholics, or A brief and clear explication of the new Oath of Allegiance* (London: W. Stansby, 1620), p. 44.

p. 151, **'That he altered his Religion before his death, and died Catholic is most certain'** … This quotation is taken from George Fisher, *The Bishop of London his Legacy. Or certain motives of D[r] King, late Bishop of London, for his change of religion, and dying in the Catholic, and Roman Church* (Saint-Omer: English College Press, 1623), sig. A3.

p. 151, **John Bill, who had only recently, on 2 October 1620, been raised into the governing ranks** … Bill and Blount were both jointly sworn in as Officers of the English Stock on 1 March 1610 and both made Stock-Keepers of the Latin Stock on 1 March 1624; see Jackson, ed., *Records of the Court of the Stationers' Company*, pp. 42, 131 and 164.

p. 151, **Sir Robert Dallington, whose works Blount had twice published** … See Higgins, *Shakespeare's Syndicate*, p. 228. See also BL Additional MS 72365, ff. 116–17, letter from Edward Blount to Sir William Trumbull, dated 30 May 1623. These books included one for which Blount selected Richard Field as printer: *A Survey of the great dukes state of Tuscany, In the year of our Lord 1596* (London: Printed [by George Eld] for Edward Blount, 1605), and *Aphorisms Civil and Military* (London: Imprinted [by R. Field] for Edward Blount, 1613).

p. 152, 'though their [the Catholics'] redoubted wrestlers, in grappling with our Divines ...' Dedicatory epistle to the Archbishop of Canterbury, from Daniel Featley, *The Romish Fisher caught and held in his own net. Or, A true relation of the Protestant conference and popish difference* ... (London: Printed by H[umphrey] L[ownes and William Stansby] for Robert Milbourne, and are to be sold at the Great South Door of Paul's, 1624). For a further account see Edward Weston, *The repair of honour, falsely impeached by Featl[e]y, a minister* (Saint-Omer: [by the English College Press], 1624).

p. 152, **Robert Milbourne, who had made Blount's own shop his centre of operations in 1617–18** ... Blayney, *The Bookshops in Paul's Cross Churchyard*, pp. 26 and 28; and the title pages of Milbourne's books, for example Featley, *The Romish Fisher*, which states that the book was 'sold at the Great South Door of Paul's'.

p. 152, **Blount who had once acquired the rights to** *Pericles* ... Stationers' Register, entry for 20 May 1608, SCA Liber C, Ref. TSC/1/E/06/02, f. 167v.

p. 152, **Philip Massinger's** *The Woman's Plot* **before the king at Whitehall** ... Wiggins, ed., *British Drama*, vol. 7, p. 336.

p. 153, **Heminges and the players a retrospective payment of sixty pounds** ... *Dramatic Records in the Declared Accounts of the Treasurer of the Chamber 1558–1642*, *Malone Society Collections*, vol. 6 (Oxford: Oxford University Press for The Malone Society, 1961–2), p. 76.

p. 153, **The text of** *The Woman is Too Hard for Him*, **staged three weeks later** ... Wiggins, ed., *British Drama*, vol. 7, p. 340.

p. 153, **'called together all his clergy about this town, and told them he had express commandment ...'** TNA SP 14/112, f. 65v, letter from John Chamberlain to Dudley Carleton, dated 25 January 1620.

p. 153, **'Our pulpits ring continually of the insolence and impudence of women ...'** TNA SP 14/112, f. 130, letter from John Chamberlain to Dudley Carleton, dated 12 February 1620.

p. 153, *A Caveat or Warning for all sorts of men* ... *A Caveat or Warning for all sorts of men both young and old to avoid the company of lewd and wicked women, to the tune of Virginia* (London: For H.G., 1620).

pp. 153–54, **'masculine-feminines' who were 'most monstrous'** ... *Hic Mulier: or, The Man-Woman: being a medicine to cure the coltish disease of the staggers in the masculine-feminines of our times* (London: Printed [at Eliot's Court Press] for I. T[rundle], 1620), sigs A3–A4v, B2 and C1v.

p. 154, **'there is a report in the town that the Earl of Pembroke's staff ...'** TNA SP 14/123, ff. 138–138v, letter from Matthew Nicholas to Edward Nicholas, dated 5 November 1621.

p. 154, **the suggestive titles of plays they performed since James I's proclamation** ... See Wiggins, ed., *British Drama*, vol. 7, pp. 299–303, 332–36, 340 and 360–64.

p. 155, **On 21 November, any fears he may have had in this regard proved well-founded** ... The contextual account of this session of Parliament is derived from Redworth, *The Prince and the Infanta*, pp. 30–38, and O'Farrell, *Shakespeare's Patron*, pp. 113–20.

pp. 155–56, **On 3 December, James laid down the law, stating that 'some fiery and popular spirits'** ... John Rushworth, *Historical Collections of Private Passages of State* (London: Printed by Tho[mas] Newcomb for George Thomason, 1659), pp. 43–44.

p. 156, **'liberties, franchises, privileges, and jurisdictions of Parliament are the ancient ...'** J.R. Tanner, *English Constitutional Conflicts of the Seventeenth Century 1603–1689* (Cambridge: Cambridge University Press, 1928 [1937 edition]), pp. 47–49.

p. 156, **in a fit of blind rage, tore the Protestation out of the House of Commons' journal** ... For James I's enraged response see Redworth, *The Prince and the Infanta*, p. 37.

p. 156, **'were derived from the grace and permission of our ancestors'** ... TNA SP 14/124, ff. 97–97v, letter from James I to Secretary Calvert, dated 16 December 1621 (with copy in ff. 98–98v); see also the copy in TNA SP 14/124, ff. 172–172v, dated 22 December 1621.

Chapter 10 – 'The author's genius': Inside the Half-Eagle and Key

pp. 161–85, **Had you walked into the printing shop of William and Isaac Jaggard at the sign of the Half-Eagle and Key** ... The description of the interior workings of the seventeenth-century printing house, and the account of the practical processes of casting off, typesetting, inking, printing, paper-drying and collating, as described in this chapter, are based on: Joseph Moxon's *Mechanick Exercises: or, The doctrine of handy-works*, vol. 2 (London: Printed for Joseph Moxon, 1683), pp. 9–366; Paul Werstine, 'The Type of the Shakespeare First Folio', in *Foliomania! Stories Behind Shakespeare's Most Important Book*, eds Owen Williams and Caryn Lazzuri (Washington D.C.: Folger Shakespeare Library, 2011), pp. 15–20; Peter W.M. Blayney, *The First Folio of Shakespeare* (Washington D.C.: Folger Shakespeare Library, 1991), pp. 4, 9–18; Emma Smith, *The Making of Shakespeare's First Folio* (Oxford: Bodleian Library, 2015), pp. 139–59; the introductions to *The Norton Facsimile: The First Folio of Shakespeare*, second edition, ed. Peter W.M. Blayney (New York and London: W.W. Norton and Company, 1996), especially pp. xv–xxii (from Charlton Hinman's introduction) and pp. xxix–xxxvii (from Peter W.M. Blayney's introduction); and sections dealing with individual plays mentioned in this chapter in Charlton Hinman's two-volume magnum opus *The Printing and Proof-Reading of the First Folio of Shakespeare* (Oxford: Clarendon Press, 1963).

p. 169, **'A good compositor is ambitious as well to make the meaning of his author intelligent ...'** Moxon, *Mechanick Exercises*, pp. 220–25.

p. 171, **At some point before the casting-off process began, the professional scribe Ralph Crane was employed** ... For Crane's background, influence, work for the King's Men, and the Shakespeare plays he may have worked on see: T.H. Howard-Hill, 'Shakespeare's Earliest Editor, Ralph Crane', *Shakespeare Survey*, vol. 44 (1991), pp. 113–29; Paul Werstine, 'Ralph Crane and Edward Knight: professional scribe and King's Men's bookkeeper', in

Shakespeare and Textual Studies, eds Margaret Jane Kidnie and Sonia Massai (Cambridge: Cambridge University Press, 2015), pp. 27–38; and E.A.J. Honigmann, *The Texts of Othello and Shakespearian Revision* (London and New York: Routledge, 1996), pp. 71–77, 94–95, 100–102, 116–18, 127–28, 137, 140–45 and 165–68.

p. 171, **'some employment hath my useful pen ...'** Ralph Crane, *The Works of Mercy, both Corporal and Spiritual* (London: Printed by G. Eld and M. Flesher, 1621), sig. A6.

pp. 171–72, **Crane's influence can be traced through some of his working practices** ... For this see, in particular, Werstine, 'Ralph Crane and Edward Knight ...', pp. 28–30.

p. 175, **When setting his transcripts, however, the compositors did not always slavishly follow his texts** ... See Paul Werstine, 'Scribe or Compositor: Ralph Crane, Compositors D and F, and the First Four Plays in the Shakespeare First Folio', *Papers of the Bibliographical Society of America*, vol. 95, no. 3 (September 2001), pp. 315–39; Vernon Guy Dickson, 'What I Will: Mediating Subject; Or, Ralph Crane and the Folio's *Tempest*', *Papers of the Bibliographical Society of America*, vol. 97, no. 1 (March 2003), pp. 43–56.

p. 175, **As Moxon states, such texts represented 'bad, heavy, hard work'** ... Moxon, *Mechanick Exercises*, p. 211.

p. 176, **across their total of 898 pages of printed text** ... This figure is from B.D.R. Higgins, 'Printing the First Folio', in Emma Smith, ed., *The Cambridge Companion to Shakespeare's First Folio* (Cambridge: Cambridge University Press, 2016), pp. 30–47 (p. 39).

pp. 176–77, **Which texts formed the basis of the Folio's plays are hotly contested** ... For examples, and some of the debates surrounding identification of the source texts behind these plays, see Gary Taylor and John Jowett, *Shakespeare Reshaped, 1606–1623* (Oxford: Oxford University Press, 1993), especially pp. 51–106; Gabriel Egan, 'The Provenance of the Folio Texts', in Smith, ed., *The Cambridge Companion to Shakespeare's First Folio*, pp. 85–86; William Shakespeare, *Henry V*, ed. Gary Taylor (Oxford: Oxford University Press, 1994), editor's introduction, pp. 12–26; William Shakespeare, *Coriolanus*, ed. Peter Holland (London: Arden, 2013), editor's 'Textual analysis' of the play, pp. 449–63; William Shakespeare, *Antony and Cleopatra*, ed. John Wilders (London: Arden, 1995), editor's introduction, pp. 75–84; William Shakespeare, *Julius Caesar*, ed. Arthur Humphreys (Oxford: Oxford University Press, 1998), editor's introduction, pp. 72–83 (especially p. 75 for a consideration of the Folio text's origins in a prompt book); William Shakespeare, *Julius Caesar*, ed. David Daniell (London: Arden, 1998), editor's introduction, pp. 121–29 (Daniell believes it is more likely the Folio's text of the play was from Shakespeare's 'author's manuscript', rather than a prompt book, p. 127); William Shakespeare, *Much Ado About Nothing*, ed. Sheldon P. Zitner (Oxford: Oxford University Press, 1998), editor's introduction, pp. 86–87; William Shakespeare, *A Midsummer Night's Dream*, ed. Peter Holland (Oxford: Oxford University

Press, 1995), editor's introduction, pp. 115–17; William Shakespeare, *Richard II*, eds Anthony B. Dawson and Paul Yachnin (Oxford: Oxford University Press, 2011), editors' introduction, pp. 9–16 and 119–20; William Shakespeare, *King Richard II*, ed. Charles R. Forker (London: Arden, 2005), editor's introduction, pp. 1–23, 165–69, and Appendix 1, pp. 506–41, which challenges some aspects of the idea that the fifth quarto edition of the play was used to correct errors in the third quarto edition.

p. 177, *Romeo and Juliet* and *Love's Labour's Lost* **may have been edited by John Smethwick or an annotating reader** ... For this theory see Sonia Massai, *Shakespeare and the Rise of the Editor* (Cambridge: Cambridge University Press, 2007), pp. 158–79.

p. 177, **'valued the progressive improvement'** ... Massai, *Shakespeare and the Rise of the Editor*, p. 179.

p. 177, **'sometimes mis-led by doubt and difficulty of the copy'** ... Desiderius Erasmus, *Seven Dialogues, Very pleasant and Delightful for all Persons*, trans. William Burton (London: Printed for John Smithwick, and are to be sold at his shop in Saint Dunstan's Churchyard in Fleet Street, 1624), sig. A2v; also quoted by Massai, *Shakespeare and the Rise of the Editor*, p. 173.

p. 178, **'jestingly or profanely speak or use the Holy Name of God, or of Christ Jesus ...'** quoted from Egan, 'The Provenance of the Folio Texts', p. 81, along with the examples of the profanities used by Falstaff and Hamlet and the censorship applied to them (pp. 81–82). For more on the censorship of Falstaff's profanities see also William Shakespeare, *Henry IV, Part One*, ed. David Bevington (Oxford: Oxford University Press, 1998), editor's introduction, pp. 94–95.

p. 178, **The Folio version of *Othello*, for instance, has had over fifty profanities removed** ... For details of these changes see William Shakespeare, *Othello*, ed. E.A.J. Honigmann (Surrey: Arden, 1997), editor's Appendix 2, p. 352.

pp. 179–80, **from 1619 the King's Men's bookkeeper was Edward Knight** ... For Knight's potential interventions in the King's Men's plays and his entry to the company see Werstine, 'Ralph Crane and Edward Knight ...', pp. 36–38, and Paul Werstine, *Early Modern Playhouse Manuscripts and the Editing of Shakespeare* (Cambridge: Cambridge University Press, 2012), especially pp. 107–99 (which provides a detailed account of the role of bookkeepers in the Renaissance playhouse).

p. 180, **Enter the inkers, tasked with coating the type with an even layer of ink** ... For the inking process see Moxon, *Mechanick Exercises*, pp. 306–19.

p. 180, **surviving Folios' pages still preserve the inky fingerprints of the Jaggards' pressworkers** ... For a tantalising example of this see Smith, *The Making of Shakespeare's First Folio*, plate 15.

p. 181, **The tympan was then lifted back on its hinge and the paper peeled off and hung on lines or wooden frames to dry** ... For the parts of the process outlined here see Moxon, *Mechanick Exercises*, pp. 345–56.

p. 181, **Some estimates for the quantity of 'impressions' or printed sheets these pressworkers could produce** ... For this figure (derived from

Mechanick Exercises) and the likelihood that it was 'an optimistic maximum', see Higgins, 'Printing the First Folio', p. 39. It is the amount which Charlton Hinman suggested in *The Printing and Proof-Reading of the First Folio of Shakespeare*, 2 vols (Oxford: Clarendon Press, 1963), vol. 1, p. 244.

pp. 182–83, **The process of paper-making meant that each side of a Folio sheet would have created a different sensation** ... The description of the paper-making process and its resulting impact on the texture of paper is derived from Carter Hailey, 'The Best Crowne Paper', in *Foliomania! Stories Behind Shakespeare's Most Important Book* (Washington D.C.: Folger Shakespeare Library, 2015), pp. 8–14, especially pp. 9–12.

p. 184, **It is thanks to painstaking work by the bibliographer Charlton Hinman** ... See Werstine, 'The Type of the Shakespeare First Folio', pp. 15–16, and Hinman's own astounding labours in his two-volume *The Printing and Proof-Reading of the First Folio of Shakespeare*.

p. 184, **Over time dedicated bibliographers and scholars, along with experts on paper stocks and their watermarks, added to Hinman's findings** ... These include Peter W.M. Blayney, Carter Hailey, Trevor H. Howard-Hill, John S. O'Connor, Gary Taylor, Paul Werstine and others. Throughout *Shakespeare's Book*, the chronology of the printing of the plays in the First Folio has been arrived at by collating the work of these scholars and considering them carefully against Charlton Hinman's own findings.

Chapter 11 – 'Our Will Shakespeare': Comedies, Pilgrims and Spain's Golden Age

pp. 186–90, **The printing of the First Folio probably began early in 1622** ... Throughout this chapter the chronology of the printing of the First Folio's comedies is based on the incredibly intricate work conducted by Charlton Hinman in his weighty bibliographical tomes, *The Printing and Proof-Reading of the First Folio of Shakespeare*, 2 vols (Oxford: Clarendon Press, 1963), vol. 1, pp. 334–65, and vol. 2, pp. 519–24, and the relevant close analyses of each of the plays' individual 'quires', particularly in vol. 2, pp. 341–464. Some of Hinman's chronology, including his account of the specific 'compositors' who worked on the Folio's 'formes', has been adjusted and corrected by taking into consideration the more recent research presented in the following works: T.H. Howard-Hill, 'The Compositors of Shakespeare's Folio Comedies', *Studies in Bibliography*, vol. 26 (1973), pp. 61–106; Paul Werstine, 'Cases and Compositors in the Shakespeare First Folio Comedies', *Studies in Bibliography*, vol. 35 (1982), pp. 206–34; Paul Werstine, 'Scribe or Compositor: Ralph Crane, Compositors D and F, and the First Four Plays in the Shakespeare First Folio', *Papers of the Bibliographical Society of America*, vol. 95, no. 3 (September 2001), pp. 315–39; Vernon Guy Dickson, 'What I Will: Mediating Subject; Or, Ralph Crane and the Folio's *Tempest*', *Papers of the Bibliographical Society of America*, vol. 97, no. 1 (March 2003), pp. 43–56; S.W. Reid, 'B and 'J': Two Compositors in Two Plays of the Shakespeare First Folio', *Library*, vol. 7, no. 2 (1985), pp. 12–136; Carter Hailey, 'The Best Crowne Paper', in

Foliomania! Stories Behind Shakespeare's Most Important Book (Washington D.C.: Folger Shakespeare Library, 2015), pp. 8–14 (especially p. 14); and the tremendously valuable collation of Hinman's findings, adjusted against more recent discoveries, tabulated by Peter W.M. Blayney in his introduction to *The Norton Facsimile: The First Folio of Shakespeare*, second edition (New York and London: W.W. Norton and Company, 1996), especially pp. xxxv–xxxvii.

p. 187, **John Shakespeare, 'son of a Warwickshire butcher'** … It was Hinman who theorised that this John Shakespeare could be 'Compositor B'; Hinman, *The Printing and Proof-Reading of the First Folio of Shakespeare*, vol. 2, p. 513.

p. 187, **Throughout Compositor B appears to have undertaken the lion's share of the typesetting** … There are 441 two-page 'formes' in the whole First Folio, with around 168 set by Compositor B; see Blayney, ed., *The Norton Facsimile: The First Folio of Shakespeare*, p. xxxiii.

pp. 187–88, **If we were to take two photographs of the scene unfolding around the compositors' cases** … This reconstruction is based on Werstine, 'Cases and Compositors in the Shakespeare First Folio Comedies', pp. 229–34, and Blayney, ed., *The Norton Facsimile: The First Folio of Shakespeare*, p. xxxv.

p. 188, **working with his habitual practice of spelling 'heere' instead of 'here' and 'griefe' for 'grief'** … The spelling preferences of the First Folio's 'compositors' are based largely on Hinman, *The Printing and Proof-Reading of the First Folio of Shakespeare*, vol. 1, pp. 180–226, but taking into account the cautionary notes relating to the problems with identifying spelling patterns in the Folio outlined in the following sources: Werstine, 'Scribe or Compositor: Ralph Crane …', pp. 315–39; Dickson, 'What I Will: Mediating Subject; Or, Ralph Crane …', pp. 43–56, Reid, 'B and 'J': Two Compositors in Two Plays of the Shakespeare First Folio', pp. 12–136; Jeffrey Masten, 'Spelling Shakespeare: Early Modern "Orthography" and the Secret Lives of Shakespeare's Compositors', in *Queer Philologies: Sex, Language, and Affect in Shakespeare's Time* (Philadelphia: University of Pennsylvania Press, 2016), pp. 49–71; and Pervez Rizvi, 'The Use of Spellings for Compositor Attribution in the First Folio', *Papers of the Bibliographical Society of America*, vol. 110, no. 1, pp. 1–53.

p. 188, **The Tempest's very first page was checked for errors and corrected at least four times** … See Emma Smith, *The Making of Shakespeare's First Folio* (Oxford: Bodleian Library, 2015), pp. 43–44.

p. 188, **Prospero was, in all likelihood, the last role Shakespeare acted before retiring** … This has long been something of an apocryphal story, but exciting new (unpublished) research by Martin Wiggins suggests this was indeed the case. I am grateful to Dr Wiggins for discussing this point with me.

pp. 188–89, **They may also have calculated that this play, with its evocation of the wonders of the New World** … For the interest in New World investing by the Herbert brothers, William Strachey and Dudley Digges, see Leslie Hotson, *I, William Shakespeare do appoint Thomas Russell, Esquire* (London: Jonathan Cape, 1937), pp. 218–36; Keith Linley, *The Tempest in Context: Sin, Repentance and Forgiveness* (London and New York: Anthem Press, 2015), pp. 189–93 and 217–20; Brian O'Farrell, *Shakespeare's Patron: William Herbert, Third Earl of Pembroke 1580–1630, Politics, Patronage and Power* (London: Continuum, 2011), pp. 153–58; and Andrew Hadfield, 'Shakespeare and the Digges Brothers', *Reformation*, vol. 25, no. 1 (2020), pp. 2–17 (for Dudley Digges as the potential conduit for the Strachey manuscript, especially p. 17). The Earl of Pembroke was a major investor in the Virginia Company (its second-largest investor in fact) but, as O'Farrell notes, 'by the early 1620s the plans of the adventurers and the thriving [Virginia] colony itself, were coming under increasing attack in England' (*Shakespeare's Patron*, p. 155). As such, placing *The Tempest* as the first play in the First Folio could have been seen as a way of supporting William Herbert's interests in that precarious venture in particular.

p. 188, **William Strachey, who had been the owner of a one-sixth share in the Blackfriars Theatre** ... See C.J. Sisson, *New Readings in Shakespeare* (Cambridge: Cambridge University Press, 1956), pp. 188–91, and Mark Eccles, 'Martin Peerson and the Blackfriars', *Shakespeare Survey*, vol. 11 (1958), pp. 100–106. In the latter text, Eccles records that Strachey claimed that he received profit from plays performed at the Blackfriars 'sometimes once, twice and thrice in a week' (p. 104). For Strachey's interest in the theatre see the ODNB entry for 'William Strachey' by Betty Wood. The legal case from which knowledge of Strachey's share in the theatre derives is TNA C24/327/22, Evans and Hawkins v Rastell, Kirkham and Kendall, dated 1606.

p. 189, **a 'sea-fire' that appeared as 'an apparition of a little round light, like a faint star'** ... From the letter of William Strachey, 15 July 1610, first printed in *Purchas his Pilgrimes* (1625), quoted from William Shakespeare, *The Tempest*, ed. Stephen Orgel (Oxford: Oxford University Press, 1987), pp. 211–13.

p. 189, **'flamed amazement' among the soon-to-be shipwrecked crew** ... See Shakespeare, *The Tempest*, ed. Orgel, 1.2.198.

p. 190, **Thomas Wilson's *Christian Dictionary*** ... The chronology for the printing of Wilson's text is derived from Hinman, *The Printing and Proof-Reading of the First Folio of Shakespeare*, vol. 1, pp. 122, 342–46, 363–64, and vol. 2, pp. 378–79 and 519; checked and modified against Werstine, 'Cases and Compositors in the Shakespeare First Folio Comedies'.

p. 190, **For example, damage to two pieces of type – those for the letters 'n' and 'd'** ... Hinman, *The Printing and Proof-Reading of the First Folio of Shakespeare*, vol. 1, p. 344–45.

pp. 190–91, **Philip Massinger's *The Duke of Milan* and Thomas Middleton's *More Dissemblers Besides Women*** ... On the King's Men's performance of these plays and their licensing see Martin Wiggins, ed., in association with Catherine Richardson, *British Drama, 1533–1642: A Catalogue, Vol. 7: 1617–1623* (Oxford: Oxford University Press, 2016), pp. 360–67.

p. 191, **On the first day of 1622 the court celebrated the new year at Whitehall Palace with John Fletcher's** *The Pilgrim* … For the setting, performance and sources of the play see Wiggins, ed., *British Drama*, vol. 7, pp. 743–77.

p. 191, **allow the work to be received with 'courtesy in the Court of Great Britain'** … Miquel de Cervantes, *The second part of the history of the valorous and witty knight-errant, Don Quixote* (London: Printed [by Eliot's Court Press] for Edward Blount, 1620), sigs A2–A2v.

p. 191, **William Dutton's English translation of a work by Félix Lope de Vega** … Félix Lope de Vega's *El Peregrino en su Patria*, translated by William Dutton as *The Pilgrim of Castile* (London: Printed by [E. Allde for] John Norton, 1621).

p. 191–92, **'Mr Mabbe was to send you this book of sonnets … our Will Shakespeare'** … Quoted from Paul Morgan, '"Our Will Shakespeare" and Lope de Vega: An Unrecorded Contemporary Document', *Shakespeare Survey*, vol. 16 (1963), pp. 118–20.

p. 192, **probably in Spain together when this was written, part of an embassy to Madrid in the entourage of Sir John Digby** … Suggested by Morgan, '"Our Will Shakespeare" and Lope de Vega …', p. 119.

pp. 192–93, **It is thought that Mabbe, born around 1571–2** … The biographical information about James Mabbe is derived from: Arthur W. Secord, 'I.M. of the First Folio Shakespeare and Other Mabbe Problems', *Journal of English and Germanic Philology*, vol. 47, no. 4 (October 1948), pp. 374–81; the ODNB entry for 'James Mabbe' by David Kathman; Anthony à Wood, *Athenae Oxonienses, an exact history of all the writers and bishops who have had their education in the most ancient and famous University of Oxford* (London: Printed for Tho[mas] Bennet, 1691), vol. 2, p. 14; will of John Mabb, 'Goldsmith of London', TNA PROB 11/65/10, dated 15 January 1583 (in which James Mabbe's uncle Edward is mentioned); and will of John Mabbe or Mabb, 'Goldsmith of London', TNA PROB 11/71/109, dated 19 August 1587. The latter will seems to be that of a relative but not of James Mabbe's father, given that James is not mentioned as one of his sons, though another Edward Mabb (a son) is mentioned.

p. 192, **William Jaggard was brother-in-law to one Elizabeth Mabb** … This is revealed in Edwin Eliott Willoughby, *A Printer of Shakespeare: The Books and Times of William Jaggard* (London: Philip Allan & Co, 1934), p. 55. Ben Higgins suggests this link makes it 'likely that William [Jaggard] was brother-in-law to James Mabbe', because two of James Mabbe's siblings were named Elizabeth and Edward; Ben Higgins, 'We have a constant will to publish': The Publishers of Shakespeare's First Folio, unpublished DPhil thesis (Oxford: University of Oxford, 2015), p. 130. As Higgins states, it cannot be proved that James Mabbe and the Edward known to the Jaggards were brothers, any more than it can be currently confirmed that Ralph (the stationer) and James Mabbe were brothers. On the relation of James Mabbe to Ralph Mabbe, as possibly being brothers, see Secord, 'I.M.

of the First Folio Shakespeare and Other Mabbe Problems', pp. 378–79. These close associations, however, make it more likely that there is a kinship between James, Elizabeth, Edward and Ralph Mabbe.

p. 192, **Edward Mabbe who is listed as guarantor for a loan from the Stationers' Company** ... SCA Liber C2, Ref. TSC/1/G/01/02/01, f. 110. I would like to thank Peter Foden for his translations of the Latin portions of the loan requests from SCA Liber C2.

p. 193, **'Howsoever therefore these rigid reprehenders will not stick ...'** Fernando de Rojas, *The Spanish Bawd, represented in Celestina*, trans. James Mabbe (London: Printed by J[ohn] B[eale], 1631), sig. A4.

p. 193, **Born in 1588, the latter's mother was Anne, daughter of Sir Warham St Leger** ... The biographical information about Leonard Digges is derived from: ODNB entry for 'Leonard Digges' by Elizabeth Haresnape; Wood, *Athenae Oxonienses*, vol. 1, pp. 520, 797 and 856; Louise Diehl Patterson, 'Leonard and Thomas Digges: Biographical Notes', *Isis*, vol. 42, no. 2 (June 1951), pp. 120–21; and Hadfield, 'Shakespeare and the Digges Brothers'.

p. 193, **celebrated works on warfare some believe were plundered by Shakespeare when he wrote *Henry V* and *Coriolanus*** ... Hotson, *I, William Shakespeare do appoint Thomas Russell, Esquire*, pp. 114–24; Hadfield, 'Shakespeare and the Digges Brothers', pp. 11–16; and Eric Rasmussen, 'Who Edited the Shakespeare First Folio?', *Cahiers Élisabéthains*, vol. 93, no. 1 (2017), pp. 70–76.

p. 193, **After their father's death in 1595, Anne married Thomas Russell** ... The best account of the connection between William Shakespeare, Thomas Russell and the Digges family remains Hotson, *I, William Shakespeare do appoint Thomas Russell, Esquire*; see especially pp. 13–52 and 124–40.

p. 194, **'left wholly out' part of the text 'as superstitiously smelling of Papistical miracles ...'** Gonzalo de Céspedes y Meneses, *Gerardo the Unfortunate Spaniard*, trans. Leonard Digges (London: Printed [by George Purslowe] for Ed[ward] Blount, 1622), sigs A3–A3v.

p. 194, **his elevation to Earl of Bristol by James I** ... See the ODNB entry for 'John Digby, First Earl of Bristol' by David L. Smith, and Glyn Redworth, *The Prince and the Infanta: The Cultural Politics of the Spanish Match* (New Haven and London: Yale University Press, 2003), pp. 45–48.

p. 194, **working to popularise Spanish letters and intellectual culture in England** ... On the Spanish interests and connections of Blount, Digges and Mabbes see Rasmussen, 'Who Edited the Shakespeare First Folio?', pp. 71–72; Secord, 'I.M. of the First Folio Shakespeare and Other Mabbe Problems', pp. 1–5; Hadfield, 'Shakespeare and the Digges Brothers', pp. 4–6; and Higgins, 'We have a constant will to publish' (unpublished DPhil thesis, University of Oxford), pp. 260–70.

pp. 194–95, **two dedicatory verses by an 'I.F.' or 'J.F.'** ... The preliminaries referred to in this paragraph are from Mateo Alemán, *The Rogue, or, The life of Guzman de Alfarache*, trans. James Mabbe (London: Printed for Edward Blount, 1622), sigs A3v–A5. On Fletcher's *The Pilgrim* see also Wiggins, ed., *British Drama*, pp. 374–77.

p. 195, **John Heminges received a retrospective payment of sixty pounds at the end of March 1622** ... *Dramatic Records in the Declared Accounts of the Treasurer of the Chamber 1558–1642, Malone Society Collections*, vol. 6 (Oxford: Oxford University Press for The Malone Society, 1961–2), p. 76.

p. 195, **'the Palatinate ... restored out of hand'** ... TNA SP 14/127, ff. 12–12v, letter from John Chamberlain to Dudley Carleton, dated 4 January 1622.

pp. 195–96, **Ben Jonson's *The Masque of Augurs* was performed at Whitehall on 6 January** ... The description of the masque, its staging and costumes is from Wiggins, ed., *British Drama*, vol. 7, pp. 383–89, and the quotations from the masque are from Ben Jonson, *The Masque of Augurs, With the Several Antimasques. Presented on Twelfth Night* (London: S.N., 1621), sigs B3–B4.

p. 196, **the prince took off his own cloak and wrapped it around the Marquess of Buckingham's shoulders** ... Wiggins, ed., *British Drama*, vol. 7, p. 386.

p. 197, **Sir Simonds D'Ewes observed that a formal proclamation declaring the 'abortive dissolving of Parliament'** ... Simonds D'Ewes, *The Autobiography and Correspondence of Sir Simonds D'Ewes*, vol. 1, ed. James Orchard Halliwell (London: Richard Bentley, 1845), pp. 212–14.

p. 197, **William Herbert, the Earl of Pembroke, who had strenuously 'interceded with the king'** ... The quotations in this paragraph are taken from letters to and from the Rev. Joseph Mead, dated 10, 11 and 22 January 1622, recorded in *The Court and Times of James the First*, ed. Thomas Birch, vol. 2 (London: Henry Colman, 1848), pp. 281–82 and 287.

p. 197, **Charles began to learn Spanish, taking his first lesson on 19 January** ... Redworth, *The Prince and the Infanta*, p. 51.

p. 198, **'[I]t only rests now that, as we have put the ball to your foot ...'** Quoted from Redworth, *The Prince and the Infanta*, p. 47. The account of the Privy Council meeting is from the same text, p. 43.

p. 198, **'how unkindly he took it, that they should busy themselves and intermeddle so much in his marriage'** ... TNA SP 14/124, ff. 92–92v, letter from John Chamberlain to Dudley Carleton, dated 15 December 1621.

p. 198, **'the times are dangerous, and the world grows tender and jealous of free speech'** ... TNA SP 14/127, ff. 139–140, letter from John Chamberlain to Dudley Carleton, dated 16 February 1622.

p. 199, **a grand farewell to Ambassador Gondomar, who had been recalled to Madrid by King Philip IV** ... The attempts to re-stage the performance and the occasion of its reprising in May are recorded in Wiggins, ed., *British Drama*, vol. 7, pp. 383–89.

p. 199, **'I have never treated with another prince's ambassador with greater love'** ... This is from the Biblioteca Nacional, Madrid, MS 2394–xv, ff. 293–94 (Latin), ff. 294–95 (Spanish), dated 21 February 1622, translated in Redworth, *The Prince and the Infanta*, p. 41.

p. 199, **'priests and recusants [are] all at liberty ...'** BL Additional MS 150, ff. 353–56v, undated, quoted in Redworth, *The Prince and the Infanta*, p. 42.

Chapter 12 – 'Like an old Fencer upon the stage': William Jaggard's War and the Bard's Comeback

pp. 200–203, **In the Jaggards' printing house in April 1622** … Throughout this chapter the order of the continuing printing of the First Folio's comedies, the identification of the 'compositors' who worked on each play, and the Jaggards' other printing tasks and publications are based on a collation of the following works (in particular adjusting Charlton Hinman's findings against the discoveries of more recent scholarship): Charlton Hinman, *The Printing and Proof-Reading of the First Folio of Shakespeare*, 2 vols (Oxford: Clarendon Press, 1963), vol. 1, pp. 334–64, and vol. 2, pp. 519–24; T.H. Howard-Hill, 'The Compositors of Shakespeare's Folio Comedies', *Studies in Bibliography*, vol. 26 (1973), pp. 61–106; Paul Werstine, 'Cases and Compositors in the Shakespeare First Folio Comedies', *Studies in Bibliography*, vol. 35 (1982), pp. 206–34 (particularly p. 233); Paul Werstine, 'Scribe or Compositor: Ralph Crane, Compositors D and F, and the First Four Plays in the Shakespeare First Folio', *Papers of the Bibliographical Society of America*, vol. 95, no. 3 (September 2001), pp. 315–39; Carter Hailey, 'The Best Crowne Paper', in *Foliomania! Stories Behind Shakespeare's Most Important Book* (Washington D.C.: Folger Shakespeare Library, 2015), pp. 8–14 (especially p. 14); Edwin Eliott Willoughby, 'An Interruption in the Printing of the First Folio', *Library*, no. 9 (December 1928), pp. 262–65; Peter W.M. Blayney, introduction to *The Norton Facsimile: The First Folio of Shakespeare*, second edition (New York and London: W.W. Norton and Company, 1996), pp. xxxv–xxxvii.

p. 201, **They published William Burton's *The Description of Leicestershire*** … William Burton, *The Description of Leicestershire, containing matters of antiquity, history, armoury, and genealogy* (London: Printed [by William Jaggard] for John White, 1622), last page of the unpaginated epistle 'To the Reader'. Hinman includes André Favyn's *The Theatre of Honour and Knighthood* (London: Printed by William Jaggard, 1623) as a project that the Jaggards were also working on in this period (see *The Printing and Proof-Reading of the First Folio of Shakespeare*, vol. 1, pp. 364–51), but this has been challenged by Hailey, whose work on the paper stocks has revealed a different chronology for the printing of this book, which I follow in *Shakespeare's Book*; see 'The Best Crowne Paper', p. 14.

p. 203, **'discover and reform many things heretofore grossly mistaken, and abused by ignorant persons …'** Ralph Brooke, *A Catalogue and Succession of the Kings* (London: Printed by William Jaggard, 1619), sigs A3–A4v.

p. 204, **its many 'mistakings' were 'committed by the printer, whilst my sickness absented me from the press, at the first publication'** … Ralph Brooke, *A Catalogue and Succession of the Kings … Collected by Ralph Brooke, Esquire, Yorke Herald, and by him enlarged, with amendment of divers faults, committed by the printer, in the time of the author's sickness* (London: Printed by William Stansby, 1622), 'To the Honourable and judicious reader', sigs A2–A2v. For Brooke's somewhat difficult character see the ODNB entry for 'Ralph Brooke' by Wyeman H. Herendeen.

p. 204, **He had spent years cultivating a public persona as a careful, precise and learned printer** ... The best account of William Jaggard's career and the prestige he had acquired is Ben Higgins, *Shakespeare's Syndicate: The First Folio, its Publishers, and the Early Modern Book Trade* (Oxford: Oxford University Press, 2022), pp. 79–121.

pp. 204–206, **realised his own 'weakness' and 'unfitness to undertake a work of that strength'** ... All the quotations from this work are from William Jaggard's own unpaginated epistle from 'The Printer' in Augustine Vincent, *A Discovery of Errors in the first edition of the Catalogue of Nobility, published by Raphe Brooke, Yorke Herald, 1619* (London: Printed by William Jaggard, 1622).

p. 207, **This play, originally composed by Shakespeare around 1605, was probably revived in 1622** ... For discussions about the critical history of *All's Well That Ends Well* and the source text for the First Folio, see Michael Dobson and Stanley Wells, eds, *The Oxford Companion to Shakespeare*, revised by Will Sharpe and Erin Sullivan (Oxford: Oxford University Press, 2015), pp. 224–26, and the introduction to William Shakespeare, *All's Well That Ends Well*, ed. Susan Snyder (Oxford: Oxford University Press, 1993), pp. 52–65. On the theory that the play was written as a collaboration between Shakespeare and Thomas Middleton see Laurie Maguire and Emma Smith, 'Many Hands – A New Shakespeare Collaboration', *Times Literary Supplement*, 19 April 2012. I would like to thank Martin Wiggins for discussing this play and its revival with me.

p. 207, **No fledgling editions of his plays had been issued after the quarto version of *Troilus and Cressida*** ... Derived from the list of Shakespeare publications in Appendix A of Marta Straznicky, ed., *Shakespeare's Stationers: Studies in Critical Bibliography* (Philadelphia: University of Pennsylvania Press, 2013), pp. 198–227. See also Scott McMillin, *The First Quarto of Othello* (Cambridge: Cambridge University Press, 2001), p. 1.

p. 208, **Thomas Walkley, a bookseller and stationer from 1618, who had entered the play in the Stationers' Register** ... On Thomas Walkley's professional career see Straznicky, ed., *Shakespeare's Stationers*, pp. 296–97. On Walkley's ownership of the play see the Stationers' Register, entry for 6 October 1621, SCA Liber D, Ref. TSC/1/E/06/03, f. 21.

p. 208, **'the Author [Shakespeare] being dead, I thought good to take the piece of work upon me'** ... William Shakespeare, *The Tragedy of Othello, the Moore of Venice* (London: Printed by N[icholas] O[kes] for Thomas Walkley, and are to be sold at his shop, at the Eagle and Child, in Britain's Burse, 1622), 'The Stationer to the Reader', sig. A2.

pp. 208–10, **Walkley and Okes were among the stationer-printers involved in the publication of that peculiar group of King's Men plays** ... On the theory that these plays were stolen see E.A.J. Honigmann in his *The Texts of Othello and Shakespearian Revision* (London and New York: Routledge, 1996), pp. 22–29. On challenges to this theory see McMillin, *The First Quarto of Othello*, pp. 15–17, 35–37 and 43–44, and Sonia Massai,

Shakespeare and the Rise of the Editor (Cambridge: Cambridge University Press, 2007), pp. 120 and 226, n. 32.

p. 210, **Both had been accused of piratical practices, and Okes may have been alluded to by Ben Jonson as a 'ragged rascal'** ... On the reputations of Walkley and Okes see W.W. Greg, *The Shakespeare First Folio* (Oxford: Clarendon Press, 1955), p. 367; Honigmann, *The Texts of Othello*, pp. 22–23 and 28–31. The reference to Okes as a 'ragged rascal' is from Ben Jonson's *Time Vindicated* (1623) and is quoted in Straznicky, ed., *Shakespeare's Stationers*, p. 274.

p. 210, **'were stolen from the author' by the stationer and 'impertinently imprinted ...'** George Wither, *Fair-Virtue* (London: Printed [by Augustine Mathewes] for John Grismand, 1622), from 'The Stationer's Postscript', sig. P8, which mentions that 'three or four songs in this poem' were 'stolen'. See also L. Kirschbaum, 'Walkley's supposed piracy of Wither's *Workes* in 1620', *Library*, vol. 19, no. 3 (1938), pp. 339–46.

p. 210, *Bellona's Embrion* **by Sir Michael Everard** ... The account of the feud occasioned by this publication and the quotations referenced are from Honigmann, *The Texts of Othello*, pp. 152–56. The Walkley v Everard case is TNA C 3/390/88. Honigmann's text has useful transcriptions, with some conjectural reconstructions where the manuscript has been severely damaged.

p. 210, **Walkley was certainly present at a riot involving two hundred apprentices** ... TNA SP 16/486, f. 234, Examination of Thomas Walkley, dated 30 December 1641.

p. 210, **uttering 'indecent speeches' against a nobleman** ... TNA SP 16/438, f. 10, Petition of Thomas Walkley to Secretary Windebank, c. 1639–40.

p. 210, **arrest on charges of having distributed 'scandalous declarations'** ... TNA SP 25/63/2, f. 170, Writ to apprehend Thomas Walkley, Stationer, dated 1 December 1649. See also TNA SP 25/62, f. 11 and TNA SP 18/6, f. 1, both dated 1649.

p. 211, **Matthew Law reissued fresh quarto versions of** *Richard III* **and** *Henry IV, Part 1* ... On these reprintings see Massai, *Shakespeare and the Rise of the Editor*, pp. 119–20.

p. 211, **Dewe was working with William Jaggard on another project** ... Daniel Tuvill, *Christian Purposes and Resolutions* (London: Printed [by William Jaggard] for Thomas Dewe, and are to be sold at his shop in S[aint] Dunstan's Churchyard in Fleet Street, 1622); see Ben Higgins, 'We have a constant will to publish': The Publishers of Shakespeare's First Folio, unpublished DPhil thesis (Oxford: University of Oxford, 2015), p. 105.

p. 211, *The Prophetess*, **a play ... that bears the ghostly traces of Shakespeare's** *Julius Caesar* ... The play was licensed for performance on 14 May 1622 by Sir John Astley or his deputy, Sir Francis Markham; see Martin Wiggins, ed., in association with Catherine Richardson, *British Drama, 1533–1642: A Catalogue, Vol. 7: 1617–1623* (Oxford: Oxford University Press, 2016), pp. 402–406.

p. 212, **paid six shillings 'for not playing in the Hall'** … Recorded in 'The borough of Stratford-upon-Avon: Shakespearean festivals and theatres', in *A History of the County of Warwick*, vol. 3, ed. Philip Styles (London, 1945), pp. 244–47, which can be accessed through British History Online: http://www.british-history.ac.uk/vch/warks/vol3/pp244-247.

p. 213, **'Scholars have never given any consideration to the possibility that the Bard's wife might have been involved in the Folio project'** … Germaine Greer, *Shakespeare's Wife* (London: Bloomsbury, 2007), pp. 345–46 (see also pp. 352–56 for Greer's consideration of Anne Shakespeare's potential involvement in the preparation of the First Folio). See also Edgar Fripp, *Shakespeare, Man and Artist*, vol. 2 (Oxford: Oxford University Press, 1938), p. 852, for an earlier articulation of the theory that Heminges and Condell were in Stratford looking for Shakespeare's papers.

p. 213, **premiering another play by them entitled** *The Sea Voyage* … The play was licensed for performance on 22 June 1622 by Sir John Astley or his deputy, Sir Francis Markham; see Wiggins, ed., *British Drama*, vol. 7, pp. 415–18.

Chapter 13 – Calves, Cows and Cyphers: Edward Blount's Secrets and the Comedies' Completion

p. 215, **In the summer of 1622 a stifling heat wave began to set in over London** … The description of the heat wave and feast are from TNA, SP 14/132, ff. 226–27, letter from John Chamberlain to Dudley Carleton, dated 10 August 1622.

pp. 215–16, **'not henceforward to be troubled for … praying of mass …'** … Dr John Everard was once more committed to the Marshalsea Prison … TNA, SP 14/132, ff. 226–27, letter from John Chamberlain to Dudley Carleton, dated 10 August 1622.

p. 216, **'a Spanish sheep, brought into England in Edward the First's time, which infected most of the sheep of England …'** Simonds D'Ewes, *The Autobiography and Correspondence of Sir Simonds D'Ewes*, vol. 1, ed. James Orchard Halliwell (London: Richard Bentley, 1845), pp. 219–20; and TNA SP 14/132, f. 228, letter from Thomas Locke to Dudley Carleton, dated 10 August 1622.

p. 216, **George Villiers' mother, Mary, Countess of Buckingham, had** 'relapsed into Popery' … 'on condition that the king carry a good respect to the Roman Catholics …' TNA SP 14/133, ff. 32–33v, letter from John Chamberlain to Dudley Carleton, dated 25 September 1622.

pp. 216–17, **This play, which tapped topically into anxieties about the competition between siblings over lineage** … The plot, description and sources of *The Spanish Curate* are presented in Martin Wiggins, ed., in association with Catherine Richardson, *British Drama, 1533–1642: A Catalogue, Vol. 7: 1617–1623* (Oxford: Oxford University Press, 2016), pp. 430–35.

p. 217, **Digges presented himself as their 'devoted servant' and stated that he had undertaken the translation 'to do a public good …'** Gonzalo de

Céspedes y Meneses, *Gerardo the Unfortunate Spaniard*, trans. Leonard
Digges (London: Printed [by George Purslowe] for Ed[ward] Blount,
1622), sigs A2–A2v.

p. 217, **Digges, whose translation had also been a source for Thomas
Middleton and William Rowley's play *The Changeling* ...** The sources and
popularity of the play are itemised in Wiggins, ed., *British Drama*, vol. 7,
pp. 398–401. *The Changeling*, as Wiggins notes, was licensed for
performance on 7 May 1622.

p. 217, **Astley, however, had taken some exception to the work and 'refused
to allow [a licence] at first' ...** The context and details of the controversy
surrounding Osmond, the Great Turk are from: Wiggins, ed., *British
Drama*, vol. 7, pp. 422–25, and Richard Dutton, 'Patronage, Politics, and
the Master of the Revels, 1622–1640: The Case of Sir John Astley', *English
Literary Renaissance*, vol. 20, no. 2 (March 1990), pp. 287–319 (p. 301).

pp. 217–18, **commanding them to restrain the 'abuses, daily committed by
divers and sundry companies of Stage Players' ...** William Herbert, *The
Copy of a Warrant signed by the Right Honourable, the Earl of Pembroke*
(London: Lord Chamberlain's Office, 1622).

p. 218, **a scheme to push Herbert out of his office of Lord Chamberlain,
installing one of Villiers' own intimates in his stead ...** Dick Taylor, 'The
Earl of Montgomery and the Dedicatory Epistle of Shakespeare's First
Folio', *Shakespeare Quarterly*, vol. 10, no. 1 (Winter 1959), pp. 121–23
(p. 123).

pp. 218–20, **'I must needs come in with a Postscript too and tell that your
son is well and a great proficient in the Spanish tongue ...'** All the
quotations from this letter are from BL Additional MS 72364, ff. 125–26,
letter from Edward Blount to William Trumbull, dated 8 November 1622.
There is a full transcript of the letter in Ben Higgins, *Shakespeare's
Syndicate: The First Folio, its Publishers, and the Early Modern Book Trade*
(Oxford: Oxford University Press, 2022), pp. 230–32. Higgins' commentary
on this letter has been incredibly helpful in enabling me to arrive at my
own interpretation of its potential political context.

p. 219, **Thorpe, who had been acting as an agent between Trumbull and
Blount since at least July of the previous year ...** Indicated in a letter of 6
July 1621 from Edward Blount to William Trumbull, BL Additional MS
72361, ff. 109–10; fully transcribed in Higgins, *Shakespeare's Syndicate*,
p. 229, with useful commentary.

p. 219, **referring to 'Ned' Blount as 'his kind, and true friend' ...** in Lucan,
Lucan's First Booke (alternative title: *Pharsalia*), trans. Christopher Marlowe
(London: Printed by P. Short, for Walter Burre [and Thomas Thorpe?],
1600), dedicatory epistle from Thomas Thorpe to Edward Blount, sigs A2–
A2v.

p. 219, **part of a syndicate which funded the translation and printing of
Dutch works on matters of religion ...** *A proclamation given by the discrete
lords and states, against the slanders laid upon the evangelical and reformed
religion* (London: by G[eorge] E[ld] for Th[omas] Th[orpe] and Richard

Chambers, sold at the Sign of the Black Bear in Paul's Churchyard [at the shop of Edward Blount], 1618).

p. 220, 'bind[ing] up their wounds ... so maimed and deformed, as they at the first were' ... Francis Beaumont and John Fletcher, *Philaster, Or, love lies a bleeding* (London: Printed [by Nicholas Okes] for Thomas Walkley, and are to be sold at his shop, at the sign of the Eagle and Childe, in Britain's Burse, 1622), sigs A2–A2v.

p. 221, '619 (the King of Spain's) well intentions to gratify 653 (his Majesty [King James I])' ... TNA SP 77/15, ff. 367–70, letter from William Trumbull to Secretary Calvert, dated 2/12 November 1622. The portions transcribed in brackets are presented as superscript additions in the original manuscript.

p. 221, 'unless his Majesty would be pleased to take away the persecution of Catholics ... neither would the Pope dispense ...' TNA SP 94/25, ff. 312–315v, letter from John Digby to Secretary Calvert, dated 4 December 1622. For Digby's further missives to Calvert regarding the Spanish Match and agreements over the Palatinate see TNA SP 94/25, f. 257, dated 21 October 1622; TNA SP 94/25, f. 290, dated 2 November 1622; TNA SP 94/25, ff. 295v–296, dated 14 November 1622; TNA SP 94/25, ff. 301–301v, dated 26 November 1622; and TNA SP 94/25, ff. 306–306v, dated 28 November 1622. See also Digby's letter to Diego de la Fuente, TNA SP 94/25, ff. 220–230v, dated 12/22 September, and Glyn Redworth, *The Prince and the Infanta: The Cultural Politics of the Spanish Match* (New Haven and London: Yale University Press, 2003), p. 48.

pp. 222–25, production of Shakespeare's plays got back on an uneven and somewhat unsteady track from around October 1622 ... The chronology for the printing of the remainder of the comedies and the start of the histories, the identification of the compositors who worked on these, and the other presswork the Jaggards were overseeing at the time are derived from: Charlton Hinman, *The Printing and Proof-Reading of the First Folio of Shakespeare*, 2 vols (Oxford: Clarendon Press, 1963), vol. 1, pp. 334–65, and vol. 2, pp. 519–24, as well as relevant analyses of individual plays within these two volumes; T.H. Howard-Hill, 'The Compositors of Shakespeare's Folio Comedies', *Studies in Bibliography*, vol. 26 (1973), pp. 61–106; Paul Werstine, 'Cases and Compositors in the Shakespeare First Folio Comedies', *Studies in Bibliography*, vol. 35 (1982), pp. 206–34; Carter Hailey, 'The Best Crowne Paper', in *Foliomania! Stories Behind Shakespeare's Most Important Book* (Washington D.C.: Folger Shakespeare Library, 2015), pp. 8–14 (especially p. 14); and Peter W.M. Blayney, introduction to *The Norton Facsimile: The First Folio of Shakespeare*, second edition (New York and London: W.W. Norton and Company, 1996), pp. xxxv–xxxvii.

p. 222, 'Plays, written by M[aster] William Shakespeare, all in one volume, printed by Isaac Jaggard, in fol[io]' ... The English Frankfurt *Mess Katalog* entries are printed in W.W. Greg, *The Shakespeare First Folio: Its Bibliographical and Textural History* (Oxford: Clarendon Press, 1955), pp. 3–4.

p. 222, **Before the Folio, Isaac had been explicitly identified on the title pages of only three works** ... Blayney, introduction to *The Norton Facsimile: The First Folio of Shakespeare*, p. xxviii.

p. 223, **André Favyn's *The Theatre of Honour and Knighthood*** ... For the chronology of the printing of this work see Hayley's revision to Hinman's dating in 'The Best Crowne Paper', p. 14.

p. 224, **reported 'missing' in 1623, but a record of a search of the company archives between 1619 and 1620 indicated that the play was still where it should have been** ... Martin Wiggins, ed., in association with Catherine Richardson, *British Drama 1533–1642: A Catalogue, Vol. 6: 1609–1616* (Oxford: Oxford University Press, 2015), p. 118. The search for the King's Men's archives and identification of the play as among the company papers is from Dr Wiggins' unpublished research which he kindly shared with me.

p. 225, ***The Spanish Curate* again at Whitehall Palace on 26 December ... and *The Pilgrim* on 29 December ... by royal command for which John Heminges would be paid ninety pounds** ... Wiggins, ed., *British Drama*, vol. 7, pp. 433 and 376–77 respectively; *Dramatic Records in the Declared Accounts of the Treasurer of the Chamber 1558–1642*, Malone Society Collections, vol. 6 (Oxford: Oxford University Press for The Malone Society, 1961–2), p. 77.

p. 225, **domestic recital in his estate in Surrenden, Kent, before the end of February 1623** ... Details of Dering's domestic production are in Wiggins, ed., *British Drama*, vol. 7, p. 433, and Edward Dering, 'Book of Expenses', 1617–1628, transcribed by Laetitia Yeandlep, p. 146, with the whole account book available from the Kent Archaeological Society: https://kentarchaeology.org.uk/publications/member-publications/sir-edward-dering-1st-bart-surrenden-dering-and-his-booke-expences.

p. 225, **In fact his accounts bear testimony to the fact that he became the proud owner of two volumes** ... Dering, 'Book of Expenses', transcribed by Laetitia Yeandlep, p. 181.

Chapter 14 – A 'hazardous experiment': Playing Lovers and Printing Histories

pp. 229–30, **Perhaps it was their exaggerated beards that gave them away** ... See TNA SP 14/138, ff. 100–101, letter from John Chamberlain to Dudley Carleton, dated 22 February 1623; TNA SP 14/140, ff. 21–22, letter from John Chamberlain to Dudley Carleton, dated 21 March 1623; and Glyn Redworth, *The Prince and the Infanta: The Cultural Politics of the Spanish Match* (New Haven and London: Yale University Press, 2003), p. 78, from which this episode and the quotations presented in the first two paragraphs of this chapter are derived.

p. 230, **who reported it on 22 February, 'in every man's mouth'** ... TNA SP 14/138, ff. 100–101, 22 February 1623, letter from John Chamberlain to Dudley Carleton, 22 February 1623.

p. 230, **'very merry and jocund', and he allowed himself to believe 'the match is fully concluded on their parts'** ... TNA SP 14/137, ff. 6–7, letter from John Chamberlain to Dudley Carleton, 4 January 1623.

pp. 230–31, '[H]ere was nothing to write of but dancing and feasting' … TNA SP 14/137, ff. 52–53v, letter from John Chamberlain to Dudley Carleton, dated 25 January 1623.

p. 231, 'came unlooked for' … 'somewhat like fiddlers' … TNA SP 14/137, ff. 52–53v, letter from John Chamberlain to Dudley Carleton, dated 25 January 1623.

p. 231, 'Between us it shall be no strife:/For now 'tis Love, gives Time his life' … All the quotations from the masque are taken from Ben Jonson, *Time Vindicated to himself, and to his Honours* (London: S.N., 1623), sigs B3 and B6.

p. 231, It had taken six days to prepare the masque, and extensive rehearsals in the palace's Great Hall had been attended by the Spanish ambassador … Martin Wiggins, ed., in association with Catherine Richardson, *British Drama, 1533–1642: A Catalogue, Vol. 7: 1617–1623* (Oxford: Oxford University Press, 2016), pp. 455–58.

p. 231, 'for assisting and helping to sing a mass at the Spanish ambassador's on Christmas Day' … TNA SP 14/137, ff. 52–53v, letter from John Chamberlain to Dudley Carleton, dated 25 January 1623.

p. 231, The court began to buzz with news that the Infanta would arrive in May … TNA SP 14/137, ff. 6–7, letter from John Chamberlain to Dudley Carleton, 4 January 1623.

p. 232, 'how gallant and how brave a thing it would be … to fetch home his mistress' … 'whose nature was inclined to adventures' … Edward, Earl of Clarendon, *The History of the Rebellion and the Civil Wars in England*, vol. 1, part 1 (Oxford: Clarendon, 1807), pp. 17–19.

p. 232, There was even talk of dispatching Buckingham with a great English fleet of ten ships to escort the couple home … TNA SP 14/137, ff. 6–7, letter from John Chamberlain to Dudley Carleton, 4 January 1623; see also TNA SP 14/143, ff. 30–31, letter from John Chamberlain to Dudley Carleton, dated 19 April 1623.

p. 232, 'the cause why he imparted it not to them was that secrecy was the life of the business' … TNA SP 14/138, ff. 100–101, letter from John Chamberlain to Dudley Carleton, dated 22 February 1623.

p. 232, how he wept and pleaded with him not to go; and how Charles prevailed by entreating him on bended knees … Edward, Earl of Clarendon, *The History of the Rebellion and the Civil Wars*, vol. 1, part 1, pp. 18–19. See also Redworth, *The Prince and the Infanta*, pp. 74–75.

p. 232, Within days of their departure, even as the 'very weary' travellers made their way from Boulogne to Paris … TNA SP 14/139, ff. 86–86v, letter from John Chamberlain to Dudley Carleton, dated 8 March 1623.

p. 233, 'a monster among decisions … remote from all imagination … to say nothing of reason' … Quoted in Redworth, *The Prince and the Infanta*, p. 76.

p. 233, 'had his lesson' beforehand … 'desired God to be merciful unto him now that he was going into the House of Rimmon' … TNA SP 14/139, ff. 86–86v, letter from John Chamberlain to Dudley Carleton, dated 8 March 1623.

p. 233, **Serial silence-breaker Dr John Everard could not resist adding his voice to the chorus of objection** ... TNA SP 14/140, ff. 21–22, letter from John Chamberlain to Dudley Carleton, dated 21 March 1623.

p. 233, **'sing him down with a psalm before he had half done'** ... **'Many of our churchmen are hardly held in, and their tongues itch to be talking'** ... TNA SP 14/140, ff. 21–22, letter from John Chamberlain to Dudley Carleton, dated 21 March 1623.

p. 234, **the latest libels against it that began appearing with increasing frequency across the city** ... See TNA SP 14/137, ff. 52–53v, letter from John Chamberlain to Dudley Carleton, dated 25 January 1623, in which Chamberlain writes: 'now, touching libels, the report goes there be many abroad' (f. 52).

p. 234, **André Favyn's** *The Theatre of Honour and Knighthood*, **which had been ongoing since the commencement of the history plays** ... See the chronology for the printing of this play in the Jaggards' printing house in Carter Hailey, 'The Best Crowne Paper', in *Foliomania! Stories Behind Shakespeare's Most Important Book* (Washington D.C.: Folger Shakespeare Library, 2015), pp. 8–14 (p. 14), which revises the chronology in Charlton Hinman, *The Printing and Proof-Reading of the First Folio of Shakespeare*, 2 vols (Oxford: Clarendon Press, 1963).

p. 234, **Some of these libels were authored by Thomas Scott** ... This includes the libel *News From Parnassus* (1622). On Scott's libels and their political contexts see Louis B. Wright, 'Propaganda against James I's "Appeasement" of Spain', *Huntington Library Quarterly*, vol. 6, no. 1 (February 1943), pp. 149–72.

p. 234, **The decision to present the history plays in chronological sequence** ... For a detailed study of the printing of history plays in the period, including in the First Folio, see Amy Lidster, *Publishing the History Plays in the Time of Shakespeare: Stationers Shaping a Genre* (Cambridge: Cambridge University Press, 2022).

pp. 234–42, **towards the end of the previous year,** *King John* **and just over half of** *Richard II* **had been typeset and printed before the final comedy,** *The Winter's Tale*, **was largely completed** ... The chronology for the printing of the histories and tragedies referenced in this chapter, along with the identification of the compositors who worked on these, are derived from: Charlton Hinman, *The Printing and Proof-Reading of the First Folio of Shakespeare*, 2 vols (Oxford: Clarendon Press, 1963), vol. 1, pp. 351–65, and vol. 2, pp. 8–127 and 522–29, as well as relevant analyses of individual plays within these two volumes; Hailey, 'The Best Crowne Paper', p. 14; S.W. Reid, 'B and J': Two Compositors in Two Plays of the Shakespeare First Folio', *Library*, vol. 7, no. 2 (1985), pp. 12–136; and Peter W.M. Blayney, introduction to *The Norton Facsimile: The First Folio of Shakespeare*, second edition (New York and London: W.W. Norton and Company, 1996), pp. xxxv–xxxvii.

p. 235, **The** *Henry VI* **plays had been written between 1590 and 1592** ... For guides to the dating of William Shakespeare's plays two vital resources are:

British Drama, 1533–1642: A Catalogue, ed. Martin Wiggins, in association with Catherine Richardson (Oxford: Oxford University Press, from 2012), and *The Oxford Companion to Shakespeare*, eds Michael Dobson and Stanley Wells, revised by Will Sharpe and Erin Sullivan (Oxford: Oxford University Press, 2015). The title-page labelling and pitching for the plays referred to in this chapter are derived from the useful Appendix A, itemising editions of Shakespeare's plays in chronological order, in Marta Straznicky, ed., *Shakespeare's Stationers: Studies in Critical Bibliography* (Philadelphia: University of Pennsylvania Press, 2013), pp. 198–227.

p. 236, **The Jaggard print shop had issued grandiose works before that identified themselves as 'Catalogues'** ... Ralph Brooke, *A Catalogue and Succession of the Kings* (London: Printed by William Jaggard, 1619); William Jaggard, *A Catalogue of such English Books* (London: Printed by W[illiam] Jaggard, 1618); Thomas Milles, *A Catalogue of the Kings of Scotland* (London: [By W. Jaggard], 1610). Those works that incorporated the internal structuring device of a catalogue included Edward Topsell's *The History of Four-footed Beasts, Describing the true and lively figure of every beast* ... (London: Printed by William Jaggard, 1607); Augustine Vincent's *A Discovery of Errors in the first edition of the Catalogue of Nobility, published by Raphe Brooke, Yorke Herald, 1619* (London: Printed by William Jaggard, 1622); and *The History of Justine* (London: Printed by William Jaggard, dwelling in Barbican, 1606). See also Lidster, *Publishing the History Plays in the Time of Shakespeare*, pp. 186 and 205–16, and Ben Higgins, *Shakespeare's Syndicate: The First Folio, its Publishers, and the Early Modern Book Trade* (Oxford: Oxford University Press, 2022), pp. 112–13.

p. 237, **before the Court of Stationers on 2 December 1622, having failed to pay back money they had jointly borrowed 'to pay their debts to the English stock'** ... *Records of the Court of the Stationers' Company 1602–1640*, ed. William A. Jackson (London: Bibliographical Society, 1957), pp. 251–52.

p. 237, **Between October 1619 and October 1624, Law had also been fined four times by the court** ... Jackson, ed., *Records of the Court of the Stationers' Company*, pp. 463–64, 469 and 472.

p. 237, **he was 'indebted to the English Stock £120', which he had to pay at interest with his own shares as surety** ... Jackson, ed., *Records of the Court of the Stationers' Company*, p. 146. For Blount's other debts and loans see pp. 100, 105–106, 180, 190 and 217 of the same text.

p. 238, **This may all have been allowed – or endured – in exchange for the rights to print the plays** ... For differing theories surrounding the publication of these plays, including *Romeo and Juliet* (and the dating of the 1623 quarto edition), see R. Carter Hailey, 'The Dating Game: New Evidence for the Dates of Q4 "Romeo and Juliet" and Q4 "Hamlet"', *Shakespeare Quarterly*, vol. 58, no. 3 (2007), pp. 367–87; E.A.J. Honigmann, *The Texts of Othello and Shakespearian Revision* (London and New York: Routledge, 1996), pp. 22–29; Sonia Massai, *Shakespeare and the Rise of the Editor* (Cambridge: Cambridge University Press, 2007), pp.120–21; and Higgins, *Shakespeare's Syndicate*, pp. 24–25.

p. 240, **Folio-enshrined plays such as** *Titus Andronicus,* **the** *Henry VI* **plays,** *Macbeth* **and** *All's Well That Ends Well* ... For useful guides to the authorship of these plays see the relevant portions of Wiggins, ed., *British Drama, 1533–1642: A Catalogue,* and Dobson and Wells, eds, *The Oxford Companion to Shakespeare.*

p. 241, **two and a half to three months at most, from January till the middle or end of March 1623** ... I have widened the parameters of this printing schedule slightly from Hinman's estimation in *The Printing and Proof-Reading of the First Folio of Shakespeare,* vol. 1, pp. 358–59, to account for challenges to assumptions relating to some of the single-compositor stints made by later bibliographers, including: T.H. Howard-Hill, 'The Compositors of Shakespeare's Folio Comedies', *Studies in Bibliography,* vol. 26 (1973), pp. 61–106; Paul Werstine, 'Cases and Compositors in the Shakespeare First Folio Comedies', *Studies in Bibliography,* vol. 35 (1982), pp. 206–34; and Blayney, introduction to *The Norton Facsimile: The First Folio of Shakespeare,* especially pp. xxxv–xxxvii.

p. 241, **the re-pitching of some of these plays in a manner that mirrored editorial decisions made in relation to the rebranding of the histories** ... The title-page labelling and pitching for the relevant tragedies referred to here is derived from Appendix A of Straznicky, ed., *Shakespeare's Stationers,* pp. 198–227. See also G.P.V. Akrigg, 'The Arrangement of the Tragedies in the First Folio', *Shakespeare Quarterly,* vol. 7, no. 4 (Autumn 1956), pp. 443–45.

p. 241, **Aristotle in his treatise on Poetics, of 'elevated' individuals and their families, the 'magnitude'** ... Aristotle, *Poetics,* trans. Stephen Halliwell, Loeb Classical Library (Cambridge, Massachusetts: Harvard University Press, 1999), pp. 29–57.

p. 241, **'plays be neither right Tragedies, nor right Comedies: mingling Kings and Clowns ...'** Philip Sidney, *An Apology for Poetry* (London: Printed [by James Roberts] for Henry Olney, 1595), sig. A2.

p. 242, **William Painter was mooted as a candidate for the reversion after Jonson** ... Grant of 29 July 1622, *Calendar of State Papers, Domestic Series, of the Reign of James I, 1619–1623, preserved in the State Paper Department of her Majesty's Public Record Office,* vol. 3, ed. Mary Anne Everett Green (London: Longman et al., 1858), p. 432.

p. 242, **'a grant in reversion of the place of Master of the Revels to Master Thorrowgoode', one of his own clients** ... TNA SP 14/214, f. 5, record of a letter from Secretary Conway to William Herbert, dated 28 February 1623.

p. 242, **'to his Majesty's judgement, what the world may think when they shall find his Majesty hath denied me, for a place in mine own gift'** ... TNA SP 14/139, f. 26, letter from William to Secretary Conway, dated 2 March 1623. For the role of the Revels office see Philip J. Finkelpearl, '"The Comedians' Liberty": Censorship of the Jacobean Stage Reconsidered', *English Literary Renaissance,* vol. 16, no. 1 (December 1986), pp. 123–38, and N.W. Bawcutt, 'New Entries from the Office-Book of Sir Henry

Herbert', *English Literary Renaissance*, vol. 26, no. 1 (January 1996), pp. 155–66.

p. 242, **his 'Bill' was rejected by the king** ... TNA SP 14/214, f. 10, record of a letter from Secretary Conway to William Herbert, dated 21 March 1623.

p. 243, **as has been suggested, Painter was a client of the Marquess of Buckingham** ... Brian O'Farrell, *Shakespeare's Patron: William Herbert, Third Earl of Pembroke 1580–1630, Politics, Patronage and Power* (London: Continuum, 2011), p. 106.

p. 243, **emboldened by an obscenely generous pension of £2,000 per annum** ... TNA SP 14/134, ff. 134–35, letter from John Chamberlain to Dudley Carleton, dated 21 December 1622.

p. 243, **To Pembroke's dismay, Carlisle and Villiers were becoming closer, both serving as joint godparents ... the Privy Seal once more offered to Herbert** ... TNA SP 14/137, ff. 6–7, letter from John Chamberlain to Dudley Carleton, dated 4 January 1623. See also Dick Taylor, 'The Earl of Montgomery and the Dedicatory Epistle of Shakespeare's First Folio', *Shakespeare Quarterly*, vol. 10, no. 1 (Winter 1959), pp. 121–23 (p. 123).

p. 243, **'proceeded so far as to cross language, and some say further'** ... TNA SP 14/146 ff. 103–104, letter from John Chamberlain to Dudley Carleton, dated 14 June 1623.

Chapter 15 – 'Pursue the stars': An Apprentice, a Widow's Funeral and other Tragedies

p. 244, **'Nothing could have happened more strange and unexpected unto me' ... 'forget for a while their Spanish gravity'** ... TNA SP 94/26, f. 81, letter from John Digby to Dudley Carleton, dated 10/20 March 1623. See also Glyn Redworth, *The Prince and the Infanta: The Cultural Politics of the Spanish Match* (New Haven and London: Yale University Press, 2003), pp. 81–84.

p. 244, **which included Endymion Porter who reported that they had been 'the braveliest received that ever men were'** ... TNA SP 14/139, ff. 105–105v, letter from Endymion Porter to Olive Porter, dated 10 March 1623.

p. 245, **'nunc dimittis' ... as if he had 'attained the top of his desire'** ... TNA SP 14/142, ff. 88–89, letter from John Chamberlain to Dudley Carleton, dated 5 April 1623.

p. 245, **'[T]he prince hath taken such a liking to his mistress, that now he loves her as much for her beauty' ... 'for there was never seen a fairer creature'** ... TNA SP 14/139, ff. 105–105v, letter from Endymion Porter to Olive Porter, dated 10 March 1623.

p. 245, **Within days, news reached England that the Marquess of Buckingham was to be made a duke** ... TNA SP 14/140, ff. 21–22, letter from John Chamberlain to Dudley Carleton, dated 21 March 1623. See also TNA SP 14/145, ff. 16–17, letter from John Chamberlain to Dudley Carleton, dated 17 May 1623.

p. 245, **'vast and unnecessary expense at a time when the king's wants pressed him much'** ... Simonds D'Ewes, *The Autobiography and*

Correspondence of Sir Simonds D'Ewes, vol. 1, ed. James Orchard Halliwell (London: Richard Bentley, 1845), p. 226.

p. 245, 'this marriage one way or other is like to cost the king and realm as much as she brings' ... 'fall away as fast as withered leaves in autumn' ... TNA SP 14/142, ff. 88–89, letter from John Chamberlain to Dudley Carleton, dated 5 April 1623; TNA SP 14/143, ff. 30–31, letter from John Chamberlain to Dudley Carleton, dated 19 April 1623.

pp. 245–46, Unaware that Digby had already agreed, on behalf of James and Charles, a measure of freedom ... 'toleration in religion' and access to England's key ports for the king of Spain's naval fleet ... TNA SP 14/144, ff. 15–16, letter from John Chamberlain to Dudley Carleton, dated 2 May 1623; TNA SP 14/145, ff. 16–17, letter from John Chamberlain to Dudley Carleton, dated 17 May 1623.

p. 246, By early May James I was suffering another bout of ill health ... preparations for her arrival were 'so carried as if we were to receive some goddess' ... TNA SP 14/144, ff. 15–16v, letter from John Chamberlain to Dudley Carleton, dated 3 May 1623; TNA SP 14/145, ff. 102–103, letter from John Chamberlain to Dudley Carleton, dated 30 May 1623. For further information about the preparations and William Herbert's role in them see TNA SP 14/214, f. 22, memorandum from Secretary Conway to the Earl Marshal and Lord Chamberlain [William Herbert], dated 14 May 1623; TNA SP 14/214, f. 25, memorandum from Secretary Conway to the Lord Chamberlain [William Herbert], dated 27 May 1623.

pp. 246–47, On the evening of 29 May Edward Blount was enjoying a drink with the Spanish scholar and translator James Mabbe ... The account of this meeting and the quotations incorporated into it are from BL Additional MS 72365, ff. 116–117, letter from Edward Blount to William Trumbull, dated 30 May 1623. There is a full transcription in Ben Higgins, *Shakespeare's Syndicate: The First Folio, its Publishers, and the Early Modern Book Trade* (Oxford: Oxford University Press, 2022), p. 234. Higgins' annotative commentary on this letter has been tremendously helpful for elucidating the identities of 'Doctor Fox' and Robert Dallington, and the sources of the books mentioned in the letter. The focus on the Spanish political context and the significance of Ralph Mabbe's relation to James Mabbe and Edward Blount are my own interpretations of the letter.

p. 247, employed on a sensitive mission, 'but upon what errand ... I know not' ... TNA SP 14/142, ff. 88–89, letter from John Chamberlain to Dudley Carleton, dated 5 April 1623.

p. 247, Trumbull had been sending encrypted messages about the highly clandestine conditions for the Spanish Match ... For example, see TNA SP 77/15, ff. 367–70, letter from William Trumbull to Secretary Calvert, dated 2/12 November 1622.

p. 247, Nathaniel Butter, a former collaborator with the stationer Ralph Mabbe ... Evidenced through: *Duellum siue singulare certamen* ... (London: Excudebat G. Eld. impensis Nath[aniel] Butter, & R[alph] Mab[be], 1611)

and Daniel Dyke, *The Mystery of Self-Deceiving* (London: Printed by
Edward Griffin for Ralph Mab[be], and Nathaniell Butter, 1616).

p. 247, **The Catholic Moderator, a topical book by Henry Constable** ... *The
Catholic Moderator: or A Moderate examination of the doctrine of the
Protestants* (London: Printed [at Eliot's Court Press] for Nathaniel Butter,
1623).

p. 247, **'comparison of the Roman manner of wars with this of our time'** ...
From the title page of *The History of Xenophon*, trans. John Bingham
(London: Printed by John Haviland for Ra[l]phe Mabb[e], 1623).

p. 248, **who for five years operated shops steps away from the premises of
Blount and Aspley** ... These were the Angel and the Greyhound. Ralph
Mabbe's bookshops in St Paul's Cross Churchyard are identified in:
Thomas Taylor, *Japhet's First Public Persuasion* (Cambridge: Printed by
Cantrell Legge, printer to the University of Cambridge, and are to be sold
by Raph Mab[be] at the sign of the Angel in Paul's Churchyard, 1612);
Abraham Gibson, *The Land's Mourning for Vain Swearing* (London: Printed
by T.S. for Ralph Mab[be], and are to be sold in Paul's Churchyard, at the
sign of the Angel, 1613); and Thomas Adams, *The Devil's Banket [Banquet]
Described in Six Sermons* (London: Printed by Thomas Snodham for John
Budge [or Ralph Mab[be]], and are to be sold in Paul's Churchyard, at the
sign of the Greyhound, 1614). The Greyhound had been operated by John
Harrison between 1582 and 1592, the publisher of Shakespeare's narrative
poems *Venus and Adonis* and *The Rape of Lucrece*, with Richard Field as
initial financier and rights holder of the former work and the printer of
both; see Peter W.M. Blayney, presented in his *The Bookshops in Paul's Cross
Churchyard*, Occasional Papers of the Bibliographical Society, no. 5
(London: Bibliographical Society, 1990), pp. 28–29, and Appendix A of
Marta Straznicky, ed., *Shakespeare's Stationers: Studies in Critical Bibliography*
(Philadelphia: University of Pennsylvania Press, 2013), pp. 198–227.

p. 248, **Ralph's later logging of the rights to the play *The Spanish Bawd*, as
well as a series of texts by Cervantes** ... See Edward Arber, ed., *A Transcript
of the Registers of the Company of Stationers of London, 1554–1640 A.D.*
(London: Stationers' Company, 1875–94), vol. 4, pp. 195 and 419;
Fernando de Rojas, *The Spanish Bawd, represented in Celestina*, trans. James
Mabbe (London: Printed by J[ohn] B[eale], and are to be sold by Ralph
Mab[be], 1631); Miguel de Cervantes, *Exemplary Novels in Six Books*
(London: Printed by John Dawson, for R[alph] M[abbe], and are to be
sold by Laurence Blaicklocke: at his shop at the Sugar-loaf next [to]
Temple Bar in Fleet Street, 1640); and Arthur W. Secord, 'I.M. of the First
Folio Shakespeare and Other Mabbe Problems', *Journal of English and
Germanic Philology*, vol. 47, no. 4 (October 1948), pp. 374–81.

p. 248, **Sir William Herbert set out towards Southampton to oversee the
arrival of the Infanta** ... The details of these preparations are quoted from
TNA SP 14/146, ff. 103–103v, letter from John Chamberlain to Dudley
Carleton, dated 14 June 1623. Herbert would not have been pleased to
hear rumours suggesting that his rival, George Villiers, would soon be

made Lord High Constable of England, a defunct title that James had planned to resurrect especially for Villiers and which was, as Chamberlain reported, 'the greatest office known with us and hath been out of use many a day'.

p. 249, 'What is't to me,' he wrote, 'Whether the dispensation yet be sent ...' The poem quoted is 'An Epistle answering to One that Asked to be Sealed of the Tribe of Ben', from *Underwoods*, lines 31–42 and 63–66, in Ben Jonson, *The Complete Poems*, ed. George Parfitt (Harmondsworth: Penguin, 1975 [1996 edition]), pp. 191–93.

p. 249, commissioned to produce a new masque, *Neptune's Triumph for the Return of Albion* ... See Ian Donaldson, *Ben Jonson: A Life* (Oxford: Oxford University Press, 2011), p. 392.

pp. 249–56, Back in the Jaggards' printing house, work on the Folio's tragedies progressed hot on the heels of the histories ... The chronology for the printing of the tragedies and the compositors assigned to each play, presented in the remainder of this chapter, including the activities and specific tasks assigned to Compositor E, are derived from: Charlton Hinman, *The Printing and Proof-Reading of the First Folio of Shakespeare*, 2 vols (Oxford: Clarendon Press, 1963), vol. 1, pp. 24–25 and pp. 360–65, and vol. 2, pp. 128–340 and pp. 524–29, as well as relevant analyses of individual plays within these two volumes, and Charlton Hinman, 'New Light on the Proof-Reading for the First Folio of Shakespeare', *Studies in Bibliography*, vol. 3 (1950/51), pp. 145–53. These are compared to and corrected against Peter W.M. Blayney, introduction to *The Norton Facsimile: The First Folio of Shakespeare*, second edition (New York and London: W.W. Norton and Company, 1996), pp. xxxv–xxxvii, and T.H. Howard-Hill, 'New Light on Compositor E of the Shakespeare First Folio', *Library*, vol. 2, no. 2 (1980), pp. 156–78.

p. 249, a new apprentice, the so-called Compositor E. This is the only compositor we can name with some certainty: a John Leason ... For the identity of Compositor E see Hinman, *The Printing and Proof-Reading of the First Folio of Shakespeare*, vol. 2, pp. 512–13, and Howard-Hill, 'New Light on Compositor E ...', pp. 156–78.

p. 251, Leason made forty times as many errors as Compositor B ... For these statistics see Howard-Hill, 'New Light on Compositor E ...', p. 177.

p. 251, Whatever the cause, Walley called a halt to the printing of his play ... On Walley's intervention see Higgins, *Shakespeare's Syndicate*, p. 152, and Emma Smith, *The Making of Shakespeare's First Folio* (Oxford: Bodleian Library, 2015), pp. 142–43.

p. 254, The play had probably been co-authored with Thomas Middleton ... On the authorship of *Timon of Athens* see Martin Wiggins, ed., in association with Catherine Richardson, *British Drama, 1533–1642: A Catalogue, Vol. 5: 1603–1608* (Oxford: Oxford University Press, 2015), pp. 385–90, and *The Oxford Companion to Shakespeare*, eds Michael Dobson and Stanley Wells, revised by Will Sharpe and Erin Sullivan (Oxford: Oxford University Press, 2015), pp. 354–56.

p. 254, **Leason's lack of experience meant he made numerous errors that others in the pressroom had to root out and correct** ... Hinman, *The Printing and Proof-Reading of the First Folio of Shakespeare*, vol. 2, pp. 526–29, and Howard-Hill, 'New Light on Compositor E ...', pp. 173–78. See also Peter W.M. Blayney, *The First Folio of Shakespeare* (Washington D.C., Folger Shakespeare Library, 1991), pp. 14–16.

p. 254, **he omitted to add a decorative woodblock-printed tailpiece to it, an elaborate carving of a mythical satyr** ... Howard-Hill, 'New Light on Compositor E ...', p. 174.

p. 255, **John Jaggard junior, visited Stationers' Hall to request the transfer to himself of the fifty-pound loan his father** ... *Records of the Court of the Stationers' Company 1602–1640*, ed. William A. Jackson (London: Bibliographical Society, 1957), p. 160. For the original loan see SCA Liber C2, Ref. TSC/1/G/01/02/01, f. 110. I would like to thank Peter Foden for his translations of the Latin portions of the loan requests from SCA Liber C2.

p. 255, **only recently received his freedom of the Stationers' Company in 1620** ... His 'freedom' is itemised in W. Craig Ferguson, *The Loan Book of The Stationers' Company, with a List of Transactions 1592–1692*, Occasional Papers of the Bibliographical Society, no. 4 (London: Bibliographical Society, 1989), p. 23, and registered as having been taken up on 4 July 1620 in Edward Arber, ed., *A Transcript of the Registers of the Company of Stationers of London, 1554–1640 A.D.* (London: Stationers' Company, 1875–94), vol. 3, p. 320.

p. 255, **After John senior's passing, John junior and Edward Mabbe became joint guarantors for Elizabeth's other sons** ... See Ben Higgins, 'We have a constant will to publish': The Publishers of Shakespeare's First Folio, unpublished DPhil thesis (Oxford: University of Oxford, 2015), p. 130, and Higgins' *Shakespeare's Syndicate*, p. 17. Higgins believes the reference to 'John Jaggard' is 'a clerk's slip for "William Jaggard"' because John is identified in that record as 'stationer', without his having been one. I am assuming that the co-guarantor in this instance was John Jaggard junior (and that the clerk had logged the correct name) because he does appear to have been a stationer at this time. John Jaggard senior must have been alive on 12 October 1622 when he took out the loan that was later transferred to his son the following year (SCA Liber C2, Ref. TSC/1/G/01/02/01, f. 110; Jackson, ed., *Records of the Court of the Stationers' Company*, p. 160; Ferguson, *The Loan Book of The Stationers' Company*, p. 23; Arber, ed., *A Transcript of the Registers of the Company of Stationers*, vol. 3, p. 320).

p. 255, **a sum for the same amount paid to Ralph Mabbe 'Citizen and Stationer of London'** ... SCA Liber C2, Ref. TSC/1/G/01/02/01, f. 110.

p. 256, **It has been argued that at this point Leason's interventions proved too taxing and costly for the Folio's devisers** ... See Hinman, *The Printing and Proof-Reading of the First Folio of Shakespeare*, vol. 2, pp. 528–29.

p. 256, **This has been challenged by more recent scholarship which maintains that the rest of the typesetting of Shakespeare's Book was a two-hander** ...

See Howard-Hill, 'New Light on Compositor E ...', pp. 156–78, and Blayney, introduction to *The Norton Facsimile: The First Folio of Shakespeare*, p. xxxvii.

p. 256, **The Jaggards also had some pressing 'job work' at this time, including a 'Heralds' Visitation Summons'** ... See Hinman, *The Printing and Proof-Reading of the First Folio of Shakespeare*, vol. 1, pp. 24–25.

p. 257, **She was interred two days later in a freshly renovated chancel, close to her husband** ... See Edgar Fripp, *Shakespeare's Stratford* (Oxford: Oxford University Press, 1928), pp. 72–74, and Germaine Greer, *Shakespeare's Wife* (London: Bloomsbury, 2007), pp. 340–41.

p. 257, **elides the importance of her labours as the manager of a large and productive household** ... On Anne's role, responsibilities and life see Greer, *Shakespeare's Wife*; Lena Cowen Orlin, 'Anne by Indirection', *Shakespeare Quarterly*, vol. 65, no. 4 (2014), pp. 421–54; and Katherine Scheil, *Imagining Shakespeare's Wife: The Afterlife of Anne Hathaway* (Cambridge: Cambridge University Press, 2018).

p. 257, **You, mother, gave me milk and life with your breasts** ... This is my own translation of Anne Hathaway Shakespeare's epitaph in Holy Trinity Church, Stratford-upon-Avon. I have taken some liberties with the translation to emphasise aspects of the Latin original's poetical inflections.

p. 257, **Some scholars have challenged John Heminges' descent from George Heminges of Droitwich** ... On these challenges see Greer, *Shakespeare's Wife*, pp. 20 and 350–51.

p. 257, **the troupe mounted *The Winter's Tale* during the first winter season at court after Anne's death** ... *Dramatic Records in the Declared Accounts of the Treasurer of the Chamber 1558–1642*, *Malone Society Collections*, vol. 6 (Oxford: Oxford University Press for The Malone Society, 1961–2), pp. 77–78.

p. 258, **It is possible that Anne's death had caused the King's Men to report the prompt book of the play as missing ... On 19 August, it was relicensed** ... See Martin Wiggins, ed., in association with Catherine Richardson, *British Drama 1533–1642: A Catalogue, Vol. 6: 1609–1616* (Oxford: Oxford University Press, 2015), p. 118.

p. 258, **'It pleased the King at my Lord Chamberlain's motion to send for me unto his bedchamber'** ... Quoted in N.W. Bawcutt, 'Craven Ord Transcripts of Sir Henry Herbert's Office-Book in the Folger Shakespeare Library', *English Literary Renaissance*, vol. 14, no. 1 (December 1984), pp. 83–93 (p. 90).

p. 258, **While repeated attempts had been made ... to remove Sir William Herbert from his Lord Chamberlainship ... Ben Jonson could become Master of the Revels** ... For the contexts behind attempts made to remove William Herbert from the Lord Chamberlain's office and of the reversion of the Mastership of the Revels to Ben Jonson see TNA SP 14/105, ff. 95–96, letter from Thomas Wynn to Dudley Carleton, dated 28 January 1619; TNA SP 14/112, ff. 1–2, letter from John Chamberlain to Dudley Carleton, dated 1 January 1620; TNA SP 14/123, ff. 41–42, letter from

John Chamberlain to Dudley Carleton, dated 13 October 1621; TNA SP 14/123, ff. 87–87v, letter from John Chamberlain to Dudley Carleton, dated 27 October 1621; Dick Taylor, 'The Earl of Montgomery and the Dedicatory Epistle of Shakespeare's First Folio', *Shakespeare Quarterly*, vol. 10, no. 1 (Winter 1959), pp. 121–23; Brian O'Farrell, *Shakespeare's Patron: William Herbert, Third Earl of Pembroke 1580–1630, Politics, Patronage and Power* (London: Continuum, 2011), pp. 73, 82–83 and 121; Richard Dutton, 'Patronage, Politics, and the Master of the Revels, 1622–1640: The Case of Sir John Astley', *English Literary Renaissance*, vol. 20, no. 2 (March 1990), pp. 287–319 (especially p. 298); and Chris Laoutaris, 'The Prefatorial Material [to the First Folio]', in *The Cambridge Companion to Shakespeare's First Folio*, ed. Emma Smith (Cambridge: Cambridge University Press, 2016), pp. 48–67.

Chapter 16 – 'The Graver had a strife': Portraying Shakespeare Through National Crisis
p. 260, **the Lady Elizabeth's Men were playing** *The Spanish Gypsy* ... See Martin Wiggins, ed., in association with Catherine Richardson, *British Drama, 1533–1642: A Catalogue, Vol. 7: 1617–1623* (Oxford: Oxford University Press, 2016), pp. 482–86.
p. 260, **The King's Men, not to be outdone, may have been playing** *A Very Woman* ... Wiggins, ed., *British Drama*, vol. 7, pp. 474–77; the date of the performance is, however, a 'best guess'.
pp. 260–61, **'much delighted in bear baiting'** ... **'was the best sport of all'** ... TNA SP 14/148, ff. 99–100, letter from John Chamberlain to Dudley Carleton, dated 12 July 1623.
p. 261, **That July a caravan of camels and an elephant were seen parading through the city** ... **deaths of a man and two women who were 'struck dead' by lightning** ... TNA SP 14/148, ff. 99–100, letter from John Chamberlain to Dudley Carleton, dated 12 July 1623.
p. 261, **'the Spanish delays are like to wear out his patience as well as ours'** ... TNA SP 14/147, ff. 98–99, letter from John Chamberlain to Dudley Carleton, dated 28 June 1623. See also TNA SP 14/149, ff. 64–64v, letter from John Chamberlain to Dudley Carleton, dated 26 July 1623.
p. 261, **revelled in the image of a despairing prince who 'wishes to be at home'** ... TNA SP 14/148, ff. 99–100, letter from John Chamberlain to Dudley Carleton, dated 12 July 1623.
p. 261, **'the prince concluded the business himself with the king, so that it is now finished'** ... TNA SP 14/148, ff. 155–155v, letter from Endymion Porter to Olive Porter, dated 17 July 1623.
p. 262, **'the match was to be published'** ... **'great applause and rejoicing'** ... TNA SP 14/149, ff. 64–64v, letter from John Chamberlain to Dudley Carleton, dated 26 July 1623.
p. 262, **The Earl of Pembroke did not attend, sending his brother Philip** ... Brian O'Farrell, *Shakespeare's Patron: William Herbert, Third Earl of Pembroke 1580–1630, Politics, Patronage and Power* (London: Continuum,

2011), p. 122, and Michael G. Brennan, *Literary Patronage in the English Renaissance: The Pembroke Family* (New York and London: Routledge, 1988), pp. 172–73.

p. 262, **the king was moving forward with a more 'public toleration' of Catholics** ... TNA SP 14/151, ff. 119–119v, letter from John Chamberlain to Dudley Carleton, dated 30 August 1623.

p. 262, **They began preparing another strongly Spanish-inspired play, *The Maid of the Mill*** ... For this play, its licensing and performance dates see Wiggins, ed., *British Drama*, vol. 7, pp. 491–96.

p. 262, **'not settled in the king's good opinion, as he was against the Spanish Match ...'** Quoted in O'Farrell, *Shakespeare's Patron*, p. 122, with my additional interpolations in square brackets.

p. 262, **'my zeal to her service and love to her'** ... **'Nothing under heaven can be so dangerous unto her'** ... TNA SP 14/152, f. 124, letter from William Herbert to Dudley Carleton, no date but possibly September 1623.

p. 263, **Meanwhile, after a break in the printing of the First Folio, Compositor B, probably with the help of his apprentice Leason** ... The chronology for the printing of the final tragedies and the involvement of Compositor E are derived from: Charlton Hinman, *The Printing and Proof-Reading of the First Folio of Shakespeare*, 2 vols (Oxford: Clarendon Press, 1963), vol. 1, pp. 24–25 and pp. 360–65, and vol. 2, pp. 128–340 and pp. 524–29, as well as relevant analyses of individual plays within these two volumes, and Charlton Hinman, 'New Light on the Proof-Reading for the First Folio of Shakespeare', *Studies in Bibliography*, vol. 3 (1950/51), pp. 145–53. These are compared to and corrected against Peter W.M. Blayney, introduction to *The Norton Facsimile: The First Folio of Shakespeare*, second edition (New York and London: W.W. Norton and Company, 1996), pp. xxxv–xxxvii, and T.H. Howard-Hill, 'New Light on Compositor E of the Shakespeare First Folio', *Library*, vol. 2, no. 2 (1980), pp. 156–78.

p. 263, **as one scholar aptly put it, the play exemplified 'conflict resolution through dynastic marriage'** ... Gary Taylor, 'Making Meaning Marketing Shakespeare 1623', in *From Performance to Print in Shakespeare's England*, eds Peter Holland and Stephen Orgel (Houndmills: Palgrave, 2006), pp. 55–72 (p. 68).

p. 264, **By 4 November he was dead ... and recorded as Isaac's 'late father deceased'** ... Higgins, *Shakespeare's Syndicate*, p. 79.

p. 265, **'Ex dono Willi Jaggard Typographi, an[no] 1623'** ... Folger Shakespeare Library, First Folio 1.

p. 265, **'Master William Shakespeare's Comedies, Histories, and Tragedies'** ... **'so many of the said Copies as are not formerly entered to other men'** ... SCA Liber D, Ref. TSC/1/E/06/03, f. 69.

p. 265, **Blount and Jaggard therefore paid seven shillings, the price for registering fourteen of the plays** ... See Peter W.M. Blayney, *The First Folio of Shakespeare* (Washington D.C., Folger Shakespeare Library, 1991), pp. 18–21.

p. 266, **Incorporating the portrait of an author on the title page of their book was a relatively new and bold thing to do** … William Jaggard, Richard Field and Nathaniel Butter had teamed up in the year of Shakespeare's death to print *The Whole Works of Homer*, translated by Geroge Chapman, whose portrait was presented within a medallion in classical style in the book. See *The Whole Works of Homer*, trans. George Chapman (London: Printed [by Richard Field and William Jaggard] for Nathaniel Butter, 1616). On the newness of author portraits on title pages and within early printed books see Erin C. Blake and Kathleen Lynch, 'Looke on his Picture, in his Booke: The Droeshout Portrait on the Title Page', in *Foliomania! Stories Behind Shakespeare's Most Important Book*, eds Owen Williams and Caryn Lazzuri (Washington D.C.: Folger Shakespeare Library, 2011), pp. 21–31.

pp. 266–67, **In order to produce the title page, two techniques and two different kinds of press were needed** … The account of the First Folio title page's printing is derived from Blake and Lynch, 'Looke on his Picture, in his Booke: The Droeshout Portrait on the Title Page', pp. 24–28.

p. 268, **He has been identified by some Shakespeare scholars as the mastermind behind the preliminaries** … See Ian Donaldson, *Ben Jonson: A Life* (Oxford: Oxford University Press, 2011), pp. 370–76, and Chris Laoutaris, 'The Prefatorial Material [to the First Folio]', in *The Cambridge Companion to Shakespeare's First Folio*, ed. Emma Smith (Cambridge: Cambridge University Press, 2016), pp. 48–67 (pp. 61–62).

p. 268, **Coincidentally or not, Jonson was at exactly this time engaged with the official processes of legal 'censure'** … Donaldson, *Ben Jonson*, p. 376.

p. 269, **wearing the attire of a gentleman, a doublet embellished with 'metal braid decoration' and 'flat band' collar** … J.L. Nevinson, 'Shakespeare's Dress in His Portraits', *Shakespeare Quarterly*, vol. 18, no. 2 (Spring 1967), pp. 101–106.

p. 269, **Some critics have complained that the portrait 'has little technical merit' and that its deviser had 'much to learn about engraving'** … W.W. Greg, *The Shakespeare First Folio* (Oxford: Clarendon Press, 1955), p. 451; Nevinson, 'Shakespeare's Dress in His Portraits', p. 104.

p. 270, **There are in fact two contenders** … For the debates surrounding the portrait see Mary Edmond, 'It was for Gentle Shakespeare Cut', *Shakespeare Quarterly*, vol. 42, no. 3 (Autumn 1991), pp. 339–44; Christiaan Schuckman, 'The Engraver of the First Folio Portrait of William Shakespeare', *Print Quarterly*, vol. 8, no. 1 (March 1991), pp. 40–43; and June Schlueter, 'Martin Droeshout Redivivus: Reassessing the Folio Engraving of Shakespeare', *Shakespeare Survey*, vol. 60 (2007), pp. 237–51.

p. 270, **born in Brussels and is identified in some records as having worked as a limner or painter** … 'Grant to Martin Droeshout, painter, of Brabant', 20 January 1608, in Mary Anne Everett Green, ed., *Calendar of State Papers, Domestic Series, of the Reign of James 1, 1603–1610*, vol. 1 (London: Longman et al., 1857), p. 397.

pp. 270–71, **A recent discovery of engravings and prints … 'the same crude hand of the engraver …'** Schuckman, 'The Engraver of the First Folio Portrait of William Shakespeare', pp. 40–3.

p. 271, **The elder Martin was a committed Protestant … The younger Martin, however, emigrated to Spain** … See Schlueter, 'Martin Droeshout Redivivus …', pp. 237–51.

p. 271, **'Martin Drussett [Droeshout] Limner, born in Brussels … hath lived here 30 years'** … Certificate of Strangers born beyond the seas, who dwell … in the ward of Aldersgate [Parish of St Katherine, Coleman], TNA SP 16/305, 11.ii, f. 20, dated 12 November 1635. The manuscript also records that this Martin Droeshout's wife is named Jane, that she was born in Antwerp and that the couple had six children, all born in England.

p. 273, **It is possible that the king's ill health, which had been evident during the printing** … I would like to thank Martin Wiggins for his suggestions and comments in relation to James I's ill health as a possible reason for the lack of explicit reference to the King's Men's playing company in the First Folio.

p. 274, **Prince Charles returned to England on 'a very foul and rainy day'** … TNA SP 14/153, ff. 54–55, letter from John Chamberlain to Dudley Carleton, dated 11 October 1623.

pp. 274–75, **'I have not heard of more demonstrations of public joy … 'in the very nick' of time** … TNA SP 14/153, ff. 54–55, letter from John Chamberlain to Dudley Carleton, dated 11 October 1623.

pp. 275–76, **'a tedious torture to millions of loving and well-wishing hearts'** … **'loving Salamanders swallowed those liquid fires most sweetly and affectionately'** … John Taylor, *Prince Charles his Welcome from Spain* (London: Printed by G.E. for John Wright, 1623).

p. 276, **'No more let Brittany [that is, Britain] lament with cares …'** William Hockham, *Prince Charles his Welcome to the Court* (London: By Edward Allde for John Wright, 1623).

p. 276, **there was a general sense among the people that Charles's return without the Infanta spelled the end of the affair** … TNA SP 14/153, ff. 54–55, letter from John Chamberlain to Dudley Carleton, dated 11 October 1623.

p. 277, **'not able to bear the weight' and collapsed 'with such violence'** … **'they may easily perceive how welcome they are to our people'** … TNA SP 14/154, ff. 20–21, letter from John Chamberlain to Dudley Carleton, dated 8 November 1623.

p. 278, **'[S]peech of the Spanish Match grows daily more cool'** … TNA SP 14/153, ff. 54–55, letter from John Chamberlain to Dudley Carleton, dated 11 October 1623.

p. 278, **'The English generally so detested the Spanish Match …'** Simonds D'Ewes, *The Autobiography and Correspondence of Sir Simonds D'Ewes*, vol. 1, ed. James Orchard Halliwell (London: Richard Bentley, 1845), p. 257.

p. 278, **'the king is resolved not to forsake his old friends the Hollanders'** … **'congratulation for the prince's return'** … TNA SP 14/154, ff. 68–68v, letter from John Chamberlain to Dudley Carleton, dated 21 November 1623. For details of the masque at York House and its impact see Wiggins, ed., *British Drama*, vol. 7, p. 509.

pp. 278–79, **escape from the deadly 'sirens' who 'wooed him, by the way'** … **'How near our general joy was to be lost'** … Ben Jonson, *Neptune's Triumph for the Return of Albion* (London: S.N., 1624). For the circumstances behind the rewriting of the masque see Ian Donaldson, *Ben Jonson: A Life* (Oxford: Oxford University Press, 2011), pp. 392–93, and Roger D. Sell, 'Political and Hedonic Re-contextualizations: Prince Charles's Spanish Journey in Beaumont, Jonson and Middleton', *The Ben Jonson Journal*, vol. 22, no. 2 (2015), pp. 163–87.

p. 279, **a comedy by Thomas Middleton entitled** *A Game at Chess* … On the contexts of and controversy surrounding this play see Siobhan Keenan, *Acting Companies and their Plays in Shakespeare's London* (London: Arden, 2014), pp. 183–93; Adrian Streete, 'Polemical Laughter in Thomas Middleton's *A Game at Chess* (1624)', *English Literary Renaissance*, vol. 50, no. 2 (2020), pp. 296–333; and Thomas Cogswell, 'Thomas Middleton and the Court, 1624: *A Game at Chess* in Context', *Huntington Library Quarterly*, vol. 47 (1984), pp. 273–88.

Chapter 17 – 'Thy Stratford Monument': The Grave, the Folio and Selling Shakespeare's 'Works'

p. 281, **As all the financiers of Shakespeare's Book were entitled to a share of the completed work** … See Ben Higgins' *Shakespeare's Syndicate: The First Folio, its Publishers, and the Early Modern Book Trade* (Oxford: Oxford University Press, 2022), pp. 26–27.

p. 282, **a book buyer named Thomas Longe would acquire a newly minted unbound copy … most expensive book of plays in English history up till that point** … On the cost of the First Folio and its wholesale price see Peter W.M. Blayney, *The First Folio of Shakespeare* (Washington D.C., Folger Shakespeare Library, 1991), pp. 25–28; Peter W.M. Blayney's introduction to *The Norton Facsimile: The First Folio of Shakespeare*, second edition (New York and London: W.W. Norton and Company, 1996); Higgins, *Shakespeare's Syndicate*, pp. 46–47; Eric Rasmussen, 'Publishing the First Folio', *The Cambridge Companion to Shakespeare's First Folio*, ed. Emma Smith (Cambridge: Cambridge University Press, 2016), pp. 18–29 (p. 18); and Jean-Christophe Mayer, 'Early Buyers and Readers', in *The Cambridge Companion to Shakespeare's First Folio*, ed. Emma Smith (Cambridge: Cambridge University Press, 2016), pp. 103–19 (pp. 104–105).

pp. 282–84, **Adding to the cost for the purchaser was the charge for binding** … The account of the cost of binding, the various types of cover, and the description of the binding process are derived from: Blayney, *The First Folio of Shakespeare*, pp. 29–32, and Frank Mowery, 'The Bindings of the Folger's First Folios', in *Foliomania! Stories Behind Shakespeare's Most Important Book*, eds Owen Williams and Caryn Lazzuri (Washington D.C.: Folger Shakespeare Library, 2011), pp. 32–39.

p. 284, 'if the book please you, come home to my shop, you shall have it bound' … Quoted in Emma Smith, *Shakespeare's First Folio: Four Centuries of an Iconic Book* (Oxford: Oxford University Press, 2016), p. 4.

p. 285, as recent research has revealed, he was locked in an expensive legal case over potential debts of £2,000 … For the revisionist account of Blount's finances, the contexts for the belief that the First Folio bankrupted him, and his payment from the poor relief fund, see Higgins, *Shakespeare's Syndicate*, pp. 56–61. My own independent research into Blount's debts confirms that he was in financial difficulties long before the Folio was printed, as presented elsewhere in *Shakespeare's Book*.

p. 285, they would have needed to shift over half their printed stock to break even … See Emma Smith, *The Making of Shakespeare's First Folio* (Oxford: Bodleian Library, 2015), p. 72.

p. 285, Robert Allot, who in 1630 … took over the publisher's shop, buying out his share of the Shakespeare plays … See Stationers' Register, entries for 16 November 1630 and 1 July 1637, SCA Liber D, Ref. TSC/1/E/06/03, ff. 209 and 361–362 respectively.

p. 286, 'it was acted by the King's Majesty's servants at the Globe' … William Shakespeare, *The History of Troilus and Cressida, As it was acted by the King's Majesty's Servants at the Globe* (London: Imprinted by G. Eld for R[ichard] Bonian and H[enry] Walley, and are to be sold at the Spread Eagle in Paul's Churchyard, over against the Great North Door, 1609).

p. 286, 'it was acted by the King's Majesty's servants at the Globe' … 'born in that sea that brought forth Venus' … William Shakespeare, *The Famous History of Troilus and Cressida, Excellently expressing the beginning of their loves* … (London: Imprinted by G. Eld for R[ichard] Bonian and H[enry] Walley, and are to be sold at the Spread Eagle in Paul's Churchyard, over against the Great North Door, 1609), epistle to the reader.

p. 286, an anomaly in Walley's registering of *Troilus and Cressida* … On this anomaly and the negotiations over the play, see Blayney, *The First Folio of Shakespeare*, p. 21.

p. 286, registered by James Roberts in February 1603 and listed as having been 'acted by my Lord Chamberlain's Men' … Stationers' Register, entry for 7 February 1603, SCA Liber C, Ref. TSC/1/E/06/02, f. 91v.

p. 286, Walley and Bonian's own logging of the rights in January 1609 … Stationers' Register, entry for 28 January 1609, SCA Liber C, Ref. TSC/1/E/06/02, f. 178v.

p. 287, With an agreement in hand, Isaac Jaggard's pressworkers leaped into action … For the printing of the play in Isaac Jaggard's printing shop see Blayney, introduction to *The Norton Facsimile: The First Folio of Shakespeare*, p. xxxvi.

p. 288, 'Master Shakespeare's works, printed for Edward Blount, in fol[io]' … 'Plays, written by M[aster] William Shakespeare, all in one volume, printed by Isaac Jaggard, in fol[io]' … The English Frankfurt *Mess Katalog* entries are printed in W.W. Greg, *The Shakespeare First Folio: Its Bibliographical and Textural History* (Oxford: Clarendon Press, 1955), pp. 3–4.

p. 288, **By 1624 'Plays' had become 'works'** … See my treatment of this change in marketing strategy in 'The Prefatorial Material [to the First Folio]', in *The Cambridge Companion to Shakespeare's First Folio*, ed. Emma Smith (Cambridge: Cambridge University Press, 2016), pp. 48–67; especially pp. 49–51. The same theme is later explored by Higgins in *Shakespeare's Syndicate*, pp. 41–46. For the significance of the term 'works' in relation to the First Folio see John Freehafer, 'Leonard Digges, Ben Jonson, and the Beginning of Shakespeare Idolatry', *Shakespeare Quarterly*, vol. 21, no. 1 (Winter 1970), pp. 63–75.

p. 289, **'the harm that the scandal will bring to the Library'** … **'disgrace of the Library'** … *Letters to Thomas James, first Keeper of the Bodleian Library*, ed. George Wilson Wheeler (Oxford: Clarendon Press, 1926), p. 222.

pp. 289–90, **Changes had since been afoot in the literary landscape** … This account of other 'Works' published is largely derived from Laoutaris, 'The Prefatorial Material [to the First Folio]', pp. 50–51. For further examples of grand 'Works' and their title pages see Erin C. Blake and Kathleen Lynch, 'Looke on his Picture, in his Booke: The Droeshout Portrait on the Title Page', in *Foliomania! Stories Behind Shakespeare's Most Important Book*, eds Owen Williams and Caryn Lazzuri (Washington D.C.: Folger Shakespeare Library, 2011), pp. 21–31.

p. 289, **'Pray tell me Ben, where doth the mystery lurk,/What others call a play you call a work?'** … George Herbert, *Wits Recreations* (London: Printed by R[ichard] H[odgkinson and Thomas Paine] for Humphry Blunden, 1640), Epigram 269, sig. G3v.

pp. 289–90, **'the very plays of a modern poet, are called in print his works'** … John Boys, *An Exposition of the Proper Psalms*, part 2 (London: 1617); quoted in Freehafer, 'Leonard Digges, Ben Jonson, and the Beginning of Shakespeare Idolatry', p. 67.

p. 290, **Boys' own *Works* were published by First Folio syndicate member William Aspley … taking its place as one of a number of weighty theological *Works* competing for business** … John Boys, *The works of John Boys, Doctor in Divinity and Dean of Canterbury* (London: Imprinted [by John Haviland] for William Aspley, 1622). Other such tracts, sold close to Blount's and Aspley's shops, include Gervase Babington, *The Works of the Right Reverend Father in God, Gervase Babington, late Bishop of Worcester* (London: Printed by G. Eld and M. Flesher [for H. Fetherstone], and are to be sold by John Parker at the Sign of the Three Pigeons in Paul's Churchyard, 1622); and William Cowper, *The Works of Mr William Cowper, late Bishop of Galloway* (London: Imprinted [by Thomas Snodham and Felix Kyngston] for John Budge, and are to be sold at his shop in Paul's Churchyard, at the sign of the Green Dragon, 1623). For more on Aspley's association with, and printing of the works of, John Boys see Higgins, *Shakespeare's Syndicate*, pp. 142–67.

p. 291, **his mother had married Thomas Russell, Esquire, of Alderminster on 26 August 1603** … Leslie Hotson, *I, William Shakespeare do appoint Thomas Russell, Esquire* (London: Jonathan Cape, 1937), p. 210.

pp. 292–93, **Renowned Spenser, lie a thought more nye … Honour hereafter to be laid by thee** … My modernised version of the poem as quoted in Brandon S. Centerwall, 'Who Wrote William Basse's "Elegy on Shakespeare"?: Rediscovering a Poem Lost from the Donne Cannon', *Shakespeare Survey*, vol. 59 (2006), pp. 267–84.

p. 293, **Not everyone believes the poem to which Jonson was responding was written by William Basse** … On the attribution to Donne see Centerwall, 'Who Wrote William Basse's "Elegy on Shakespeare"?', pp. 267–84.

p. 293, **It was in fact first published in a book of poems by John Donne** … John Donne, *Poems, by J.D. [John Donne], With Elegies on the Author's Death* (London: Printed by M[iles] F[lesher] for John Marriot, and are to be sold at his shop in St Dunstan's Churchyard in Fleet Street, 1633), p. 149. This book was sold paces from the shop of John Smethwick, in St Dunstan's Churchyard.

pp. 293–94, **Basse most likely lived in Thame in Oxfordshire** … For Basse's Oxford connections see William Basse, *Great Britain's Sunset, Bewailed with a Shower of Tears* (Oxford: Printed by Joseph Barnes, 1613), and the ODNB entry for 'William Basse' by David Kathman.

Chapter 18 – The 'Sireniacal' Fraternity: Shakespeare and Oxford

pp. 299–301, **Pioneering research by the Renaissance scholar Lena Cowen Orlin** … The quotations from Orlin's study, which include the quotations from John Aubrey presented in this chapter, and the information about the Davenant family, are from Lena Cowen Orlin, *The Private Life of William Shakespeare* (Oxford: Oxford University Press, 2021), pp. 196–252 (especially pp. 225–31 and 235–48). Interestingly, many of these Oxford monuments, Orlin reveals, present their subjects holding, reading from, or leaning on large folios. Orlin also affirms that the fact Shakespeare did not leave provision in his will for his own burial and monument lends further credence to her theory that he commissioned his own effigial bust during his lifetime. Orlin's research has provided me with a valuable basis on which to build my own theory that the First Folio's preliminary pages continue Shakespeare's own monumental programme in Holy Trinity Church specifically *through* an Oxford connection, one anchored in the playwright's own personal and professional networks, and that the choice of scholar-poets memorialising him in the Folio was guided by (what the makers of the Folio knew to be) Shakespeare's own vision (initially communicated through his Stratford memorial).

p. 301, **the dramatist need not have visited Oxford regularly, or even attended lectures and sermons there** … Orlin does, however, argue convincingly that 'Shakespeare is nearly certain to have taken in lectures and sermons in college chapels' attached to Oxford University,' *The Private Life of William Shakespeare*, p. 248.

pp. 301–302, **His closeness to the wealthy Combe family brought him into contact with William Combe junior** … On Shakespeare's connections to the Combes see Stanley Wells, 'A Close Family Connection: the Combes', in *The Shakespeare Circle: An Alternative Biography*, eds Paul Edmondson and Stanley Wells (Cambridge: Cambridge University Press, 2015), pp. 149–60; E.K. Chambers, *William Shakespeare: A Study of Facts and Problems*, vol. 2 (Oxford: Clarendon Press, 1930 [1951 edition]), pp. 127–41; and C.C. Stopes, *Shakespeare and his Warwickshire Contemporaries* (Stratford-upon-Avon: Shakespeare Head Press, 1907), pp. 219–25.

p. 302, **with John had sold to Shakespeare 107 acres of land in Old Stratford** … For this purchase (which was made on 1 May 1602) and other property and land acquisitions by Shakespeare in Warwickshire see Robert Bearman, *Shakespeare in the Stratford Records* (Stroud: Alan Sutton Publishing, 1994), pp. 37–43 and 49–59.

p. 302, **John, who developed a reputation as a notorious money-lender and, as one account put it, 'a covetous rich man'** … On John Combe's reputation and relation to Shakespeare see Chambers, *William Shakespeare: A Study of Facts and Problems*, vol. 2, pp. 137–41. The quotation 'a covetous rich man' is from a manuscript at the Bodleian Library in Oxford, recording Nicholas Burgh's thoughts about the epitaph in 1650; see Chambers, *William Shakespeare: A Study of Facts and Problems*, vol. 2, p. 246.

p. 302, **left Shakespeare five pounds in his will** … Will of John Combe, TNA PROB 10/325, ff. 3–7. The registered copy of the will is PROB 11/126, ff. 419–421v, dated 28 January 1613. In this will John Combe mentioned lands 'known by the name of Parson's Close alias Shakespeare's Close' in Bishops Hampton, though a connection to the playwright's family cannot be proved.

p. 302, **wittily presented the devil as laying claim to the damned soul of 'my John a Combe'** … see the epitaph variants in Chambers, *William Shakespeare: A Study of Facts and Problems*, vol. 2, pp. 140–41 and 246.

p. 302, **Shakespeare, for the latter left him an intensely personal gift in his will: his own sword** … TNA PROB 1/4, dated 25 March 1616.

p. 302, **though some scholars accord this honour to Edward Blount** … For the varying theories about this, and the influence of Ben Jonson and Edward Blount on the Folio's preliminaries see: (on the influence of Jonson) Ian Donaldson, *Ben Jonson: A Life* (Oxford: Oxford University Press, 2011), pp. 370–76, and Chris Laoutaris, 'The Prefatorial Material [to the First Folio]', in *The Cambridge Companion to Shakespeare's First Folio*, ed. Emma Smith (Cambridge: Cambridge University Press, 2016), pp. 48–67 (pp. 61–62); (on the influence of Blount) Leah Scragg, 'Edward Blount and the Prefatory Material to the First Folio of Shakespeare', *Bulletin of the John Rylands Library*, vol. 79, no. 1 (1997), pp. 117–26, and Sonia Massai, 'Edward Blount, the Herberts, and the First Folio', in Straznicky, ed., *Shakespeare's Stationers*, pp. 132–46.

p. 303, **His own proper industry and addiction to books** … Anthony à Wood, *Athenae Oxonienses, an exact history of all the writers and bishops who have had their education in the most ancient and famous University of Oxford* (London: Printed for Tho[mas] Bennet, 1691), vol. 1, p. 518.

p. 303, **Sir William Herbert, Earl of Pembroke, in his capacity as chancellor of Oxford University … Montgomery became high steward of Oxford University in 1615** … On the Herberts' connections with Oxford and the posts they held attached to it, see the ODNB entries for 'William Herbert' by Victor Stater and 'Philip Herbert' by David L. Smith.

p. 304, **'Shakespeare wanted [that is, lacked] art'** … 'Ben Jonson's Conversations with William Drummond of Hawthornden', in *Ben Jonson, The Complete Poems*, ed. George Parfitt (Harmondsworth: Penguin, 1975 [1996 edition]), p. 462.

p. 304, **'Inigo Lantern'… 'There was nothing obnoxious but the very name, and he [Jonson] hath changed that'** … This incident is reconstructed from the account and letter dated 17 July 1613 in *The Life and Letters of John Donne, Dean of St Paul's*, ed. Edmund Gosse, vol. 2 (Gloucester, Mass: Peter Smith, 1959), p. 16, and Donaldson, *Ben Jonson*, p. 334.

p. 306, **an embarrassingly copious quantity of dedicatory epistles** … See the preliminary pages to Thomas Coryate, *Coryat's Crudities, Hastily gobbled up in five months travels* … (London: Printed by W[illiam] S[tansby for the author], 1611).

p. 306, **'by help of a great memory … but more by far in the Greek tongue'** … Wood, *Athenae Oxonienses*, vol. 1, pp. 358–59. See also the ODNB entry for 'Thomas Coryate' by Michael Strachan.

p. 306, **John Donne also received some of his learning at the same university** … Wood, *Athenae Oxonienses*, vol. 1, pp. 474–75. See also the ODNB entry for 'John Donne' by David Colclough.

p. 306, **Both Leonard Digges and his brother Dudley had been attached to University College, Oxford** … The account of the Digges brothers' education is derived from Wood, *Athenae Oxonienses*, vol. 1, pp. 421, 520, 527, 583, 586, 797, 856 and 879, and Leslie Hotson, *I, William Shakespeare do appoint Thomas Russell, Esquire* (London: Jonathan Cape, 1937), pp. 209, 237–38, 242 and 250. See also the ODNB entries on 'Leonard Digges' by Sidney Lee, revised by Elizabeth Haresnape, and 'Sir Dudley Digges' by Sean Kelsey.

p. 306, **'he retired to Oxford, [spending] some years there as a sojourner for the sake of the public library'** … Wood, *Athenae Oxonienses*, vol. 1, pp. 498–99. See also the ODNB entry for 'Hugh Holland' by Colin Burrow.

p. 307, **'Worshipful Fraternity of Sireniacal Gentlemen'** … Thomas Coryate, *Thomas Coryate, Traveller for the English Wits* (London: Printed by W[illiam] Jaggard, and Henry Fetherston, 1616), p. 37.

p. 307, **Wednesday 8 November 1615, sends his hearty and 'dutiful respect[s]'** … The list of Coryate's friends and the locations of some of them are in the addendum in Coryate, *Thomas Coryate, Traveller for the English Wits*, pp. 43–47. Wood also counts Ben Jonson, Dudley Digges, Hugh Holland, John Hoskins, Inigo Jones, John Donne, Michael Drayton and the Shakespeare enthusiast John Davies of Hereford among Coryate's personal friends in *Athenae Oxonienses*, vol. 1, p. 359.

p. 307, **who became friendly with Donne while at Oxford University** ... See I.A. Shapiro, 'The Mermaid Club', *Modern Language Review*, vol. 45, no. 1 (January 1950), pp. 7–17 (p. 10).

p. 307, **Blount himself ... recommended to Sir William Trumbull as 'worthy your view'** ... See BL Additional MS 72365, ff. 130–31, letter from Edward Blount to Sir William Trumbull, dated 9 May 1623; with full transcript in Ben Higgins, *Shakespeare's Syndicate: The First Folio, its Publishers, and the Early Modern Book Trade* (Oxford: Oxford University Press, 2022), p. 233.

p. 307, **Bread Street ... the very street on which John Donne and John Milton were born** ... See the ODNB entries for 'John Donne' by David Colclough and 'John Milton' by Gordon Campbell.

p. 308, **his father, John Milton senior, was recorded as a trustee of the Blackfriars Theatre in 1620** ... Herbert Berry, 'The Miltons and the Blackfriars Playhouse', *Modern Philology*, vol. 89, no. 4 (May 1992), pp. 510–14. For more on the association between Shakespeare and Milton see Gordon Campbell, 'Shakespeare and the Youth of Milton', *Milton Quarterly*, vol. 33, no. 4 (1999), pp. 95–105; Gordon Campbell, 'Obelisks and Pyramids in Shakespeare, Milton and Alcalá', *Sederi*, vol. 9 (1998), pp. 217–32. For the contested history of the Folio's 'I.M.', who some scholars believe to be John Milton, see Arthur W. Secord, 'I.M. of the First Folio Shakespeare and Other Mabbe Problems', *Journal of English and Germanic Philology*, vol. 47, no. 4 (October 1948), pp. 374–81.

p. 308, **'combined more talent and genius, perhaps, than ever met together before or since'** ... Quoted in Shapiro, 'The Mermaid Club', p. 7.

p. 308, **He was building on John Aubrey's account ... Others who have been associated with the Mermaid Tavern** ... For the evolution of the fantasy of the 'Mermaid Club', and its frequenters, see the ODNB entry for 'Patrons of the Mermaid Tavern' by Michelle O'Callaghan; Shapiro, 'The Mermaid Club', pp. 7–17; and Leslie Hotson, *Shakespeare's Sonnets Dated* (London: Rupert Hart-Davis, 1949), pp. 77–78.

p. 308, **Ben Jonson referred to the 'Bread Street's Mermaid' ... 'pretenders to wit', the 'Mermaid men'** ... 'On the Famous Voyage', in *Ben Jonson, The Complete Poems*, ed. George Parfitt (Harmondsworth: Penguin, 1975 [1996 edition]), l. 37; *Bartholomew Fair*, in *Ben Jonson: Five Plays*, ed. G.A. Wilkes (Oxford: Oxford University Press, 1988), 1.1.29–30.

p. 308, **'What things have we seen/Done at the Mermaid! ...'** Quoted from Shapiro, 'The Mermaid Club', p. 15.

p. 308, **'the purest quintessence of the Spanish, French, and Rhenish grape, which the Mermaid yieldeth'** ... Coryate, *Thomas Coryate, Traveller for the English Wits*, p. 42.

p. 309, **'being the lovers of virtue, and literature'** ... Coryate, *Thomas Coryate, Traveller for the English Wits*, p. 43.

p. 309, **Latin manuscript, surviving in the hand of John Chamberlain, which details a 'philosophical feast'** ... TNA SP 14/66, f. 2, Description of a 'philosophical feast', dated 2 September 1611.

p. 309, **At least eight of those who attended the Mitre Tavern party were attached to the Inns of Court** ... For these legal connections see Shapiro, 'The Mermaid Club', pp. 7–17. Shapiro is rightly cautious about the idea that these gatherings constituted the basis for a cohesive 'club' with one consolidated identity.

p. 310. **'Convivium Philosophicum', overseen by ... 'Radulphus Colphabius'** ... TNA SP 14/66, f. 2, Description of a 'philosophical feast', dated 2 September 1611.

p. 310, **John Jackson ... one of the men Shakespeare engaged as a trustee ... along with John Heminges and one William Johnson** ... Hotson, *Shakespeare's Sonnets Dated*, pp. 76–88 and 125–40, and Hotson, *I, William Shakespeare do appoint Thomas Russell, Esquire*, pp. 181–83 and 217–19. See also 'Shakespeare Purchases the Blackfriars Gatehouse', article by Alan H. Nelson on Shakespeare Documented: https://shakespearedocumented. folger.edu/shakespeare-purchases-blackfriars-gatehouse#:~:text=In%20 March%201613%20"William%20Shakespeare,the%20sum%20of%20£140. The indenture for the purchase of the Blackfriars Gatehouse, signed by Shakespeare and the other trustees, is LMA CLC/522/MS03738, dated 10 March 1613. John Jackson also signed the later indenture of 10 February 1618, FSL MS Z.c.22(44). See also the vendor's (Henry Walker's) copy, FSL MS Z.c.22 (45), dated 10 March 1613. John Jackson's poem is in Coryate, *Coryat's Crudities*, sig. N1.

p. 310, **William Baker ... 'itch of travel' ... '... To frolic on the gravely shelves of Spain'** ... The poem is in Coryate, *Coryat's Crudities*, sig. K4v.

p. 310, **alongside those of Hugh Holland and Leonard Digges's brother Dudley** ... See Coryate, *Coryat's Crudities*, sigs F2 and G1–G1v (Holland) and sig. D3v (Digges).

p. 311, **Will Baker: Knowing that Mr Mabbe was to send you this book of sonnets** ... Quoted from Paul Morgan, '"Our Will Shakespeare" and Lope de Vega: An Unrecorded Contemporary Document', *Shakespeare Survey*, vol. 16 (1963), pp. 118–20.

p. 311, **Digby hailed from the playwright's native Warwickshire ... 'my well beloved cousin'** ... Hotson, *I, William Shakespeare do appoint Thomas Russell, Esquire*, pp. 238–39, and Robert Bearman, *Shakespeare in the Stratford Records* (Stroud: Alan Sutton, 1994), pp. 41–42.

p. 311–12, **His now-lost play *Cardenio*, fragments** ... On this play and Shakespeare's interest in Spain, in relation to the letter from Leonard Digges to William Baker, see Andrew Hadfield, 'Shakespeare and the Digges Brothers', *Reformation*, vol. 25, no. 1 (2020), pp. 2–17.

p. 312, **William Baker was born in Devonshire ... within weeks of Leonard Digges** ... The biography of William Baker is derived from Morgan, '"Our Will Shakespeare" and Lope de Vega ...', pp. 118–20. Baker's death date and address are derived from my own research into the will of a William Baker, TNA PROB 11/130/234, dated 20 August 1617. On Leonard Digges's education see Wood, *Athenae Oxonienses*, vol. 1, pp. 520, 797 and 856.

p. 312, **James Mabbe entered Magdalen College, Oxford in the winter of 1586–7** ... The educational history of Mabbe is from Wood, *Athenae Oxonienses*, vol. 2, p. 14, and the ODNB entry for 'James Mabbe' by David Kathman.

p. 312, **the magnificent library of Sir Robert Cotton** ... See Donaldson, *Ben Jonson*, pp. 358–60. For the royal connections of the library see Janet Backhouse, 'Sir Robert Cotton's Record of a Royal Bookshelf', *British Library Journal*, vol. 18, no. 1 (Spring 1992), pp. 44–51. See also Colin G.C. Tite, 'A Catalogue of Sir Robert Cotton's Printed Books?', *British Library Journal*, vol. 17, no. 1 (Spring 1991), pp. 1–11.

p. 312, **Cotton lauded Jonson with Latin poems in** *Volpone* ... 'art and wit' ... **worthy of the poet's 'laurel'** ... Ben Jonson, *Volpone, or The Fox* (London: Printed [by George Eld] for Thomas Thorpe, 1607), sig. A2v.

p. 313, **requested a tome to help him with the writing of** *Sejanus* ... Martin Wiggins, ed., *British Drama, 1533–1642: A Catalogue, Vol. 5: 1603–1608*, in association with Catherine Richardson (Oxford: Oxford University Press, 2015), p. 58. For Ben Jonson in the records of Cotton's library see Robert Cotton, *Early Records of Sir Robert Cotton's Library: Foundation, Cataloguing, Use*, ed. Colin G.C. Tite (London: British Library, 2003), pp. 31, 34–35, 93 and 128.

p. 313, **Numerous members of Coryate's friendship group were also users of the library** ... Cotton, *Early Records of Sir Robert Cotton's Library*, ed. Tite, pp. 56, 57, 68 and 96 (Holland); pp. 35 and 217 (Donne); pp. 67, 69, 176 and 192 (Jones). For evidence that members of the Digges family were known to Robert Cotton and may have used his library see p. 143 of the same text which records that a letter from Thomas Digges to Dudley Digges, dated 23 June 1585, and now BL Harleian MS 6993, f. 91, was once part of Sir Robert Cotton's archive.

p. 313, **plan to create a Royal Academy, first proposed by the antiquary Edmund Bolton** ... For details of this projected academy see Donaldson, *Ben Jonson*, pp. 365–67.

p. 313, **Porter, whose sister, Margaret Porter, Bolton had married** ... See ODNB entry for 'Edmund Mary Bolton' by D.R. Woolf and P.J. Osmond.

p. 313, **Russell Porter was baptised by Thomas Russell, Leonard Digges's stepfather** ... On this and other connections between the Porters, Thomas Russell and the Digges family see Hotson, *I, William Shakespeare do appoint Thomas Russell, Esquire*, pp. 238–9, 266–71.

p. 313, **It remained there at least until around 1614** ... See entry for 'Sir Robert Bruce Cotton (1571–1631), of Blackfriars, London', in *The History of Parliament: The House of Commons 1604–1629*, eds Andrew Thrush and John P. Ferris (Cambridge: Cambridge University Press, 2010), available from The History of Parliament Online: https://www.historyofparliamentonline. org/volume/1604-1629/member/cotton-sir-robert-1571-1631.

p. 314, **Thomas Digges Esquire** ... **was a parishioner and whose impressive home was located on Philip Lane** ... Hotson, *I, William Shakespeare do appoint Thomas Russell, Esquire*, pp. 112–18.

p. 314, **treatise on the latest technologies of warfare** … Thomas Digges, *An Arithmetical Warlike Treatise Named Stratioticos* (London: Imprinted by Richard Field, 1590; originally published 1579).

p. 314, **may have seen the engraved portrait of Tycho Brahe** … The theory is Hotson's, *I, William Shakespeare do appoint Thomas Russell, Esquire*, pp. 123–24. However, I have traced printed engravings of this image which indicates the possibility that Shakespeare may have acquired knowledge of the names 'Rosenkrans' and 'Guldensteren' without having seen the original portrait. One example is the engraving by Jacques de Gheyn II, preserved at the Museum of Fine Arts, Houston, dated c. 1590.

pp. 314–16, **Shakespeare's London and Stratford affiliations merge through the Digges family in other ways** … The account of Thomas Russell's legal problems, his marriage to Anne Digges, John Davies' association with Russell, and Davies' friendship with Mabbe and Digges (including Thomas Digges's will, Thomas Russell's testimony, John Davies' will and Leonard Digges's letter) are derived from Hotson, *I, William Shakespeare do appoint Thomas Russell, Esquire*, pp. 139–40, 208–11 and 246–58.

p. 315, **John mentioned Shakespeare and Davies in his will, alongside Shakespeare's lawyer** … Stephanie Appleton and Mairi Macdonald, eds, *Stratford-upon-Avon Wills 1348–1701, Volume 1: 1348–1647* (Stratford-upon-Avon: Dugdale Society), pp. 307–13 (pp. 311–12).

p. 315, **William Combe the younger, joined Leonard Digges at University College, Oxford** … Hotson, *I, William Shakespeare do appoint Thomas Russell, Esquire*, p. 250.

p. 316, **John Heminges' own son William, who remembered him in an elegiac verse as 'The famous Digges'** … **became a 'King's scholar' at the University of Oxford** … Hotson, *I, William Shakespeare do appoint Thomas Russell, Esquire*, pp. 241–42, and Germaine Greer, *Shakespeare's Wife* (London: Bloomsbury, 2007), p. 351.

p. 316, **John appears in 1620 in a list of seventy individuals who contributed ten shillings** … See the ODNB entry for 'John Heminges' by Mary Edmond.

p. 316, *The Rape of Proserpine* **in 1617, which was probably influenced by Shakespeare's popular** *The Rape of Lucrece* … Claudian, *The Rape of Proserpine*, trans. Leonard Digges (London: Printed by G[eorge] P[urslowe] for Edward Blount, and are to be sold at his shop in Paul's Churchyard at the sign of the [Black] Bear, 1617). On this potential influence see Andrew Hadfield, 'Shakespeare and the Digges Brothers', *Reformation*, vol. 25, no. 1 (2020), pp. 2–17.

pp. 316–17, **'the glad remembrance I must love/Of never-dying Shakespeare'** … This and the subsequent quotations from Leonard Digges's poem are from William Shakespeare, *Poems: Written by Wil[liam] Shakespeare, Gent.* (London: By Tho[mas] Cotes, and are to be sold by John Benson, dwelling in St. Dunstan's Churchyard, 1640), unpaginated preliminary pages.

Chapter 19 – 'Big with false greatness': The Enigma of Cygnus and a Lost Shakespeare Sonnet?

p. 319, **In 1605 two of the poets who would later commemorate Shakespeare in the First Folio were brought together in print** ... The preliminary pages in which these authors praised Ben Jonson in verse are in Ben Jonson, *Sejanus His Fall* (London: Printed by G. Elld, for Thomas Thorpe, 1605), sigs A2–A3.

p. 319, **'Black swan' and a 'sweet singer', a 'Cygnus' ... translated 'among the stars ... and there [en]shrined'** ... Hugh Holland, *Pancharis* (London: By V. S[immes] for Clement Knight, 1603), sigs A7v–A10. For the link between 'Cygnus' and Hugh Holland see Philip J. Ayres, ed., *Sejanus His Fall* (Manchester: Manchester University Press, 1990), pp. 64–65.

p. 320, **When I respect thy argument, I see** ... Jonson, *Sejanus His Fall*, sig. A2.

p. 320, **'"Cygnus" (perhaps a pseudonym for Hugh Holland ... or perhaps the Swan of Avon)'** ... Martin Wiggins, ed., *British Drama, 1533–1642: A Catalogue, Vol. 5: 1603–1608*, in association with Catherine Richardson (Oxford: Oxford University Press, 2015), p. 58.

p. 324, **William Basse referred to Shakespeare as a 'rare Tragedian'** ... From William Basse's (or John Donne's) elegy for William Shakespeare, quoted in Brandon S. Centerwall, 'Who Wrote William Basse's "Elegy on Shakespeare"?: Rediscovering a Poem Lost from the Donne Cannon', *Shakespeare Survey*, vol. 59 (2006), pp. 267–84.

pp. 324–26, **'And yet this time removed was summer's time,/The teeming autumn big with rich increase' ... But does the Cygnus sonnet stylistically remind us of Shakespeare in other ways?** ... All quotations from and references to Shakespeare's *Sonnets* are from William Shakespeare, *All the Sonnets of Shakespeare*, eds Paul Edmondson and Stanley Wells (Cambridge University Press, 2020).

p. 325, **'loved as love in twain/Had the essence but in one ...' ... '... As chorus to their tragic scene'** ... William Shakespeare, *The Phoenix and the Turtle* (lines 25–27 and 45–52 respectively), in *Shakespeare's Poems: Venus and Adonis, The rape of Lucrece and the Shorter Poems*, eds Katherine Duncan-Jones and H.R. Woudhuysen (London: Arden, 2007).

p. 325, **connection between 'argument' and 'muse' explicitly in no fewer than four sonnets and potentially in a more subtle way in two more** ... In addition to those referenced in this chapter see Sonnet 59, in Edmondson and Wells, eds, *All the Sonnets of Shakespeare*.

p. 326, **Jonson's *Sejanus* was initially acquired by Edward Blount in 1604** ... For the acquisition and transfer of the play see Wiggins, ed., *British Drama*, vol. 5, p. 58.

p. 327, **The sonnet signed explicitly by Holland was, on the other hand, not only retained ... three poems by Francis Beaumont** ... See the unpaginated preliminaries to Ben Jonson, *The Works of Benjamin Jonson* (London: Printed by William Stansby for Richard Meighen, 1616).

Chapter 20 – 'Baseless fabric'?: Shakespeare's Lodger and the First Folio

p. 329, 'that messuage or tenement with the appurtenances wherein one John Robinson dwelleth ...' Shakespeare's Last Will and Testament, TNA PROB 1/4, dated 25 March 1616.

p. 329, **Blackfriars Gatehouse ... which the playwright had purchased in 1613** ... The indenture for the purchase of the Blackfriars Gatehouse, signed by Shakespeare and the other trustees, is LMA CLC/522/ MS03738, dated 10 March 1613. The vendor's (Henry Walker's) copy is FSL MS Z.c.22 (45), dated 10 March 1613.

pp. 329–30, **he appears to have divested himself of his shares ... It has been suggested that the acquisition of the Gatehouse was connected with the First Folio** ... See E.A.J. Honigmann, 'How Happy was Shakespeare with the Printed Versions of his Plays?', *Modern Language Review*, vol. 105, no. 4 (October 2010), pp. 937–51 (pp. 944–45). Honigmann also makes the valid point that from the Blackfriars Gatehouse 'London's printers were also close at hand, in the vicinity of St Paul's churchyard and Fleet Street' (p. 944).

p. 330, **A man of that name signed Lady Elizabeth Russell's ... He was probably a 'cordwainer'** ... For the petition of the residents of the Blackfriars against the Blackfriars Theatre and its backers, headed by Lady Elizabeth Russell, see TNA SP 12/260, f. 176, dated November 1596. The petition is examined in detail in Chris Laoutaris, *Shakespeare and the Countess: The Battle that Gave Birth to the Globe* (London: Penguin, 2014), in which the identification of John Robinson (who signed the petition) as a 'cordwainer' is made: see pp. 123, 278–80 and 451.

p. 330, **by 1639 Shakespeare's tenant would be succeeded immediately by John Dicks, also a 'cordwainer'** ... See the will of John Dicks, TNA PROB 11/198/510, dated 18 December 1646.

p. 330, **located practically next door to the wealthy and influential alderman John Robinson** ... For the Robinsons connected with St Helen's Bishopsgate see Geoffrey Marsh, *Living with Shakespeare: Saint Helen's Parish, London, 1593–1598* (Edinburgh: Edinburgh University Press, 2021), especially pp. 188–89, 230–33, 418–21 and 440–41.

p. 331, **steward to 'Sir John Foskewe' living in Blackfriars ... 'over against Sir John's door'** ... The manuscript in which this 'Mr Robinson' is reported is CP 70/67, Fra. Duckett to Richard Brother, dated 31 May 1599.

p. 331, **but the steward was dead by 1613** ... E.K. Chambers, *William Shakespeare: A Study of Facts and Problems*, vol. 2 (Oxford: Clarendon Press, 1931 [1951 edition]), p. 169. This Robinson has been the cause of much speculation, with some scholars identifying him as a Catholic recusant whose association with Shakespeare lends credence to the theory that Shakespeare was a crypto-Catholic. See Richard Wilson, *Secret Shakespeare: Studies in Theatre, Religion and Resistance* (Manchester: Manchester University Press, 2004), pp. 121 and 259–60, and Ian Wilson, *Shakespeare, The Evidence: Unlocking the Mysteries of the Man and His Work* (London: Hodder Headline, 1993), pp. 396–97 and 412. These latter two studies

identify a 'John Robinson' as the 'steward' of Sir John Fortescue who was
the uncle of the 'John Fortescue, gent.' who had once owned the
Gatehouse. Sir John was Master of the Royal Wardrobe, whose home both
Wilsons place as being directly next door to the Gatehouse. However, Sir
John's home would have been in what was a separate parish, that of St
Andrew by the Wardrobe, and early maps show a path between that and
the parish of St Anne's, Blackfriars, which separates them (though this
does not preclude the possibility that the two properties were very close to
each other). I have therefore not been able to verify that a John Robinson
had lived in the Gatehouse before its occupation by Shakespeare's tenant of
that name. Ian Wilson also appears to conflate the John Robinson who
signed Lady Elizabeth Russell's petition with the 'Robinson' identified in
CP 70/67, Fra. Duckett to Richard Brother, dated 31 May 1599. As
revealed in Laoutaris, *Shakespeare and the Countess*, pp. 278–80, they are
likely to have been two different Robinsons, since the petitioner of 1596
was a 'cordwainer' not a 'steward'.

p. 331, **there was an intervening owner following Fortescue's vacating** ... See
the vendor's (Henry Walker's) copy of the indenture and bargain of sale for
the Blackfriars Gatehouse, FSL MS Z.c.22 (45), dated 10 March 1613.

p. 331, **John Robinson may have been Shakespeare's personal servant, or
even his dresser** ... Germaine Greer, *Shakespeare's Wife* (London:
Bloomsbury, 2007), pp. 346–47. Greer also notes that John Robinson 'may
have been related to the actor Richard Robinson who married Richard
Burbage's widow' (p. 347). Richard Robinson appears twenty-fourth out of
twenty-six 'Principal Actors' listed in the First Folio's preliminaries.

p. 331, **There is indeed a scrivener named John Robinson** ... For this John
Robinson's will see TNA PROB 11/297/214, dated 29 March 1660.

pp. 331–33, **record of a loan made out to one John Robinson. Describing
himself as a 'Citizen and Stationer'** ... SCA Liber C2, Ref.
TSC/1/G/01/02/01, f. 23, dated 11 August 1637. I would like to thank
Peter Foden for his translations of the Latin portions of the loan requests
from SCA Liber C2.

p. 333, **Weaver and Aspley had been confirmed in their elevated company
offices in July** ... William A. Jackson, ed., *Records of the Court of the
Stationers' Company 1602–1640* (London: Bibliographical Society, 1957),
pp. 298–99.

p. 333, **Weaver was also close to both Edward Blount and John Smethwick,
describing the latter as one of his 'loving friends'** ... See Ben Higgins, 'We
have a constant will to publish': The Publishers of Shakespeare's First Folio,
unpublished DPhil thesis (Oxford: University of Oxford, 2015), p. 87; Ben
Higgins, *Shakespeare's Syndicate: The First Folio, its Publishers, and the Early
Modern Book Trade* (Oxford: Oxford University Press, 2022), p. 203; and
Edmund [or Edmond] Weaver's will, TNA PROB 11/177/292, dated 12
June 1638.

p. 333, **Robert Kilborne, a Blacksmith living in Thames Street** ... SCA Liber
C2, Ref. TSC/1/G/01/02/01, f. 23, dated 11 August 1637.

p. 333, **John Robinson took his 'freedom' of the Stationers' Company** …
Edward Arber, ed., *A Transcript of the Registers of the Company of Stationers of London, 1554–1640 A.D.* (London: Stationers' Company, 1875–94), vol. 3, p. 319; H.G. Aldis et al., *A Dictionary of Printers and Booksellers in England, Scotland and Ireland, and of Foreign Printers of English Books, 1557–1640*, gen. ed. R.B. McKerrow (London: Bibliographical Society, 1910), p. 230.

p. 335, **William Tymme or Time, who had already been operating that shop** … Son of a Gloucestershire Yeoman named John Tymme of the parish of Kemberton, William was apprenticed to a Humfrey Bate for eight years from 25 December 1588. He was admitted as a Freeman of the Stationers' Company on 26 March 1596. See Arber, *A Transcript of the Registers of the Company of Stationers of London*, vol. 2, pp. 62 and 340, and Aldis et al., *A Dictionary of Printers and Booksellers in England*, pp. 270–71.

p. 335, **By 1601 Tymme was working with Shakespeare's first publisher, the Stratford-born Richard Field** … Gerard Malynes, *Saint George for England, Allegorically Described* (London: By Richard Field for William Tymme, stationer, and are to be sold at the sign of the Fleur de Luce and Crown in Paternoster Row, 1601).

p. 335, **'Allegorically shadowing the truth of love'** … Robert Chester, *Love's Martyr: or, Rosalin's Complaint, Allegorically shadowing the truth of love, in the constant fate of the Phoenix and Turtle* [by William Shakespeare] (London: Imprinted [by Richard Field] for E[dward B[lount], 1601).

p. 335, **John Robinson's earliest recorded book was entered in the Stationers' Register** … Stationers' Register, entry for 28 April 1615, SCA Liber C, Ref. TSC/1/E/06/02, f. 260v.

p. 335, **On the very same day the printer Nicholas Okes logged two books** … Stationers' Register, entry for 28 April 1615, SCA Liber C, Ref. TSC/1/E/06/02, f. 260v. These were '*Albumazar*, a comedy acted before his Majesty at Cambridge 10 March 1614 [i.e. 1615]' and 'a book called *The Great Assise*'.

p. 335, **'To the noble and right virtuous gentleman Sir Henry Carey …'** William Hull, *The Mirror of Majesty* (London: Printed by Nicholas Okes, for William Timme and John Robinson, and are to be sold at their shop in Paternoster Row, 1615), sig. A2.

p. 335, **Okes had been apprenticed under William King but received his freedom in 1607 under Richard Field** … For Okes's career and Shakespeare-related publications see *Shakespeare's Stationers: Studies in Cultural Bibliography*, ed. Marta Straznicky (Philadelphia: University of Pennsylvania Press, 2013), pp. 274–75, and Aldis et al., *A Dictionary of Printers and Booksellers in England*, p. 206.

p. 335, **Okes having been involved with editions of *The Rape of Lucrece*, *King Lear* and *Othello*** … M[aster] *William Shakespeare: His True Chronicle History of the Life and Death of King Lear* (London: Printed [by Nicholas Okes] for Nathaniel Butter, and are to be sold at his shop in Paul's Churchyard at the sign of the Pied Bull, near St. Au[gu]stin[e]'s Gate, 1608); *The Rape of Lucrece* (London: Printed by N[icholas] O[kes] for John

Harison, 1607); and *The Tragedy of Othello, the Moor of Venice* (London: Printed by N[icholas] O[kes] for Thomas Walkley, and are to be sold at his shop, at the Eagle and Child, in Britain's Burse, 1622). Okes, we may recall, also printed Thomas Heywood's *An Apology for Actors* (London: Printed by Nicholas Okes, 1612), in which Heywood defended Shakespeare.

p. 337, **Okes printed a take on *Venus and Adonis* ... H.A.,** *The Scourge of Venus: or, The wanton Lady with the rare birth of Adonis* (London: Printed by Nicholas Okes, dwelling near Holborn Bridge, 1613).

p. 337, **Thomas Robinson, active from 1568 to 1589** ... For Thomas Robinson's career see Aldis et al., *A Dictionary of Printers and Booksellers in England*, p. 231.

p. 337, **among his beneficiaries were his brother William Robinson and numerous figures connected with the publishing industry** ... Thomas Robinson's will is TNA PROB 11/74/263, dated 1 October 1589.

p. 337, **He initially held the rights to six plays** ... See the relevant sections of *Shakespeare's Book* and Straznicky, ed., *Shakespeare's Stationers*, pp. 281–82.

pp. 337–38, **Augustine Laughton was a bookseller ... a 'lost sheep', which passed into the possession of Robert Robinson** ... The account of Laughton's career and connections is derived from Aldis et al., *A Dictionary of Printers and Booksellers in England*, pp. 35–36, 74 and 168–69; Straznicky, ed., *Shakespeare's Stationers*, pp. 232–34; and Ronald B. McKerrow, *Printers' and Publishers' Devices in England and Scotland, 1485–1640* (London: Bibliographical Society, 1949), p. 78.

p. 338, **This Robert Robinson was a printer based in Fetter Lane** ... For Robert Robinson's career see Aldis et al., *A Dictionary of Printers and Booksellers in England*, pp. 230–31. The source for Shakespeare's *Romeo and Juliet* is Arthur Brooke, *The Tragical History of Romeus and Juliet* (London: Imprinted by R[obert] Robinson, 1587).

p. 338, **Danter later became notorious for his involvement with the publication of *Romeo and Juliet* ... acquired a reputation among early scholars as a 'bad quarto'** ... For Danter's career, reputation, Shakespeare publications, and association with *Romeo and Juliet*, see Straznicky, ed., *Shakespeare's Stationers*, pp. 247–48; W.W. Greg, *The Shakespeare First Folio* (Oxford: Clarendon Press, 1955), pp. 52, 63, 220 and 225–35; Alfred W. Pollard, *Shakespeare Folios and Quartos: A Study in the Bibliography of Shakespeare's Plays 1594–1685* (New York: Cooper Square Publishers, 1970), pp. 69–70; and Aldis et al., *A Dictionary of Printers and Booksellers in England*, pp. 83–84. The record showing that Danter received his freedom under Robert Robinson is Arber, *A Transcript of the Registers of the Company of Stationers of London*, vol. 2, p. 335.

p. 338, **Robert's widow would go on to marry Richard Braddock** ... For Braddock's career see Straznicky, ed., *Shakespeare's Stationers*, p. 236, and Aldis et al., *A Dictionary of Printers and Booksellers in England*, pp. 46–47.

p. 338, **Thomas Robinson's friend Richard Watkins was 'ordain[ed] the sole and only executor'** ... Thomas Robinson's will, TNA PROB 11/74/263, dated 1 October 1589.

p. 338, **Robert Robinson collaborated on at least one work with Watkins ...
co-financed with James Roberts** ... Andreas Bertholdus, *The Wonderful and
Strange Effect and Virtues of a new Terra Sigillata lately found out in Germany*
(London: Printed by Robert Robinson for Richard Watkins, 1587).
Examples of co-financed works include *An Almanac and Prognostication for
the Year 1582* (London: R[ichard] Watkins and J[ames] Roberts, 1582), and
The Principal Fairs of England and Wales (London: By Richard Watkins and
James Roberts, 1599). Watkins and Roberts most often worked together on
the publication of almanacs. The fact that Robert Robinson's most frequent
collaborations were with Thomas Man, a stationer who operated from a
shop called the Talbot, close to William Tymme and John Robinson's Fleur
de Luce and Crown in Paternoster Row, may suggest a further connection
between John Robinson and Robert Robinson. For example, Henry Smith,
Three Prayers (London: [By R[obert] Robinson] for Thomas Man, dwelling
in Paternoster Row at the sign of the Talbot, 1592). Another work shows a
potential collaboration between Richard Field (a one-time collaborator
with William Tymme), Robert Robinson and Thomas Man: Henry Smith,
The Sermons of Master Henry Smith (London: Printed by Richard Field [T.
Orwin, and R[obert] Robinson] for Thomas Man, dwelling in Paternoster
Row, at the sign of the Talbot, 1593).

p. 338, **Watkins's shop was the premises that came to be known as the
Golden Lion ... 'toward the east upon the gate that leadeth out of the
churchyard ...'** The shop's history is outlined in Peter W.M. Blayney, *The
Bookshops in Paul's Cross Churchyard*, Occasional Papers of the
Bibliographical Society, no. 5 (London: Bibliographical Society, 1990),
pp. 40–41.

p. 339, **Humphrey Robinson is a stationer and bookseller ... 'one of the
largest and most important book-sellers in this period'** ... Henry R.
Plomer, *A Dictionary of the Booksellers and Printers who were at work in
England, Scotland and Ireland from 1641–1667* (London: Bibliographical
Society, 1907), pp. 155–56.

p. 339, **He and Moseley issued numerous works from the King's Men's
repertory** ... Examples include James Shirley, *The Cardinal, A Tragedy, as it
was acted at the private house in Blackfriars* (London: Printed for Humphrey
Robinson at the Three Pigeons, and Humphrey Moseley at the Prince's
Arms in St Paul's Churchyard, 1652); James Shirley, *The Sisters, a Comedy,
as it was acted at the private house in Blackfriars* (London: Printed for
Humphrey Robinson at the Three Pigeons, and Humphrey Moseley at the
Prince's Arms in St Paul's Churchyard, 1652); John Fletcher, *The Wild-
Goose Chase, a Comedy as it hath been acted with singular applause at the
Blackfriars* (London: Printed for Humphrey Moseley, 1652); and Francis
Beaumont and John Fletcher, *Comedies and Tragedies written by Francis
Beaumont and John Fletcher* (London: Printed for Humphrey Robinson and
Humphrey Moseley, 1647).

p. 339, **The records indicate that Robert Robinson was related to Humphrey
in some way** ... Robert Robinson's shop in Fetter Lane ended up in the

hands of the printer John Beale, who was related to Humphrey Robinson via marriage, indicating that his wife was probably a member of the Robinson family. There is a chain of intimate connections between Robert Robinson and John Beale, for Richard Braddock, who had inherited the business from Robert after marrying his widow, passed it on to Thomas Haviland and William Hall in 1609. Beale had collaborated with both Haviland and Hall on numerous publication projects. At Beale's death, the rights to works he held under his control were transferred to Humphrey Robinson. This all increases the likelihood that there was a close family connection between Robert Robinson and Humphrey Robinson. See Plomer, *A Dictionary of the Booksellers and Printers who were at work in England*, pp. 17–18 and 155–56.

p. 339, **Based at the sign of the Three Pigeons in St Paul's Cross Churchyard** … For the location of his shop see Blayney, *The Bookshops in Paul's Cross Churchyard*, pp. 33–34.

p. 339, **Humphrey's friendship group included intimates of Henry Walley and Thomas Walkley** … These links can be traced through the wills of John Weaver and John Budge. The latter took up his freedom of the Stationers' Company on 21 January 1606 and occupied the Green Dragon in St Paul's Cross Churchyard between 1618 and 1625. His will, dated 26 December 1625, shows his close friendship with Edmund Weaver to whom he left money 'to buy him a ring' as a memorial to him. Collectively, these wills show close ties with Henry Walley, Thomas Walkley, Ralph Mabbe and Humphrey Robinson, and extending outwards from this, to a friendship group including Weaver's friends Edward Blount, William Aspley and John Smethwick. Many of these figures appear in the story of the First Folio's creation. See Edmund [or Edmond] Weaver's will, TNA PROB 11/177/292, dated 12 June 1638; John Budge's will, TNA PROB 11/147/606, dated 26 December 1625; Blayney, *The Bookshops in Paul's Cross Churchyard*, p. 32; and Aldis et al., *A Dictionary of Printers and Booksellers in England*, p. 54.

p. 340, **Robert had collaborated with Richard Field more than once between 1593 and 1595** … Matthieu Virel, *A Learned and Excellent Treatise containing all the Principal grounds of Christian Religion* (London: By Robert Robinson [and R[ichard] Field] for Robert Dexter, dwelling in Paul's Churchyard at the sign of the Brazen Serpent, 1595), and Henry Smith, *The Sermons of Master Henry Smith* (London: Printed by Richard Field [T. Orwin, and R[obert] Robinson] for Thomas Man, dwelling in Paternoster Row, at the sign of the Talbot, 1593).

p. 340, **Robert had two apprentices, brothers George and Lionel Snowden … sold their printing business to Nicholas Okes** … Aldis et al., *A Dictionary of Printers and Booksellers in England*, p. 251.

p. 340, **stationers taking up their freedom alongside him in 1613 is Isaac Jaggard himself** … Arber, ed., *A Transcript of the Registers of the Company of Stationers of London*, vol. 3, p. 319.

p. 340, **a 'John Shakespeere' took up his freedom that very same month** … Arber, ed., *A Transcript of the Registers of the Company of Stationers of*

London, vol. 3, p. 319. He is listed as having taken up his freedom on 22 May 1617. For the apprenticeship of John Shakespeare with William Jaggard see Charlton Hinman, *The Printing and Proof-Reading of the First Folio of Shakespeare* (Oxford: Clarendon Press, 1963), vol. 2, p. 513.

p. 341, **Humphrey Robinson's nephew was named Hamlet** ... Will of Humphrey Robinson, TNA PROB 11/334/357, dated 10 November 1670.

Epilogue: 1623 and Beyond

p. 343, **Edward Dering became the earliest recorded purchaser of William Shakespeare's First Folio** ... Edward Dering, 'Book of Expenses', 1617–1628, transcribed by Laetitia Yeandlep, p. 181, with the whole expenses book available from the Kent Archaeological Society: https://kentarchaeology.org.uk/publications/member-publications/sir-edward-dering-lst-bart-surrenden-dering-and-his-booke-expences. See also the account, and contexts for, Dering's purchase of the First Folio in Emma Smith, *Shakespeare's First Folio: Four Centuries of an Iconic Book* (Oxford: Oxford University Press, 2016), pp. 1–23.

p. 343, **a payment of one shilling and six pence for a visit to a playhouse** ... Dering, 'Book of Expenses', transcribed by Yeandlep, p. 181.

p. 344, **purchase, just three days before, of eighteen playbooks** ... **A few days prior to that, he bought thirty individual playbooks** ... Dering, 'Book of Expenses', transcribed by Yeandlep, pp. 179 and 178 respectively.

p. 344, **a magnificent case of knives for Sir Thomas Wotton** ... **Ben Jonson's folio of collected works for a bargain-basement price** ... Dering, 'Book of Expenses', transcribed by Yeandlep, pp. 180 and 181 respectively.

pp. 344–45, **The Folio now at Stonyhurst College in Lancashire** ... Thomas, **2nd Baron Arundell of Wardour** ... *The Shakespeare First Folios: A Descriptive Catalogue*, eds Eric Rasmussen and Anthony James West (Houndmills: Palgrave, 2012), pp. 144–45.

p. 345, **Another intriguing Folio, now residing in Glasgow University Library, was annotated** ... *The Shakespeare First Folios*, eds Rasmussen and West, pp. 38–39. See also Emma Smith, *The Making of Shakespeare's First Folio* (Oxford: Bodleian Library, 2015), pp. 161–63.

p. 345, **The Carys were very close to Ben Jonson** ... See Ian Donaldson, *Ben Jonson: A Life* (Oxford: Oxford University Press, 2011), pp. 410–11 and 425–26. See also the ODNB entry for 'Elizabeth Cary [née Tanfield], Viscountess Falkland' by Stephanie Hodgson-Wright.

p. 345, **acquired by Thomas Johnson I, a well-to-do merchant tailor who lived on Fleet Street** ... *The Shakespeare First Folios*, eds Rasmussen and West, pp. 180–81.

pp. 345–47, **a Folio bought by John Egerton, 1st Earl of Bridgewater** ... This Folio, also known as the 'Bridgewater Copy' is in the Huntington Library and is Call Number: 56421. See *The Shakespeare First Folios*, eds Rasmussen and West, pp. 240–41.

p. 347, **'my Shakespeare' and the 'Dear son of Memory'** ... *Mr William Shakespeares Comedies, Histories, and Tragedies, published according to the true* *original copies* (London: Printed by Thomas Cotes, for Robert Allot [John Smethwick, William Aspley, Richard Hawkins, and Richard Meighen], 1632). Milton's paean to Shakespeare was his first published work and would be added to the 1640 edition of Shakespeare's poems, issued by Thomas Cotes who was also the printer of the 1632 Second Shakespeare Folio. The fact that changes had been made to the poem between these editions may indicate that Milton was involved in this later publication, which includes a prominent dedicatory poem by Leonard Digges, the very same who contributed a commemorative verse to the 1623 Shakespeare First Folio. See *Poems: Written by Wil[liam] Shakespeare, Gent.* (London: By Tho[mas] Cotes, and are to be sold by John Benson, dwelling in St Dunstan's Churchyard, 1640). For John Milton's potential authorial changes to the 1632 Folio's dedicatory poem for the 1640 edition of the *Poems* see Gordon Campbell, 'Shakespeare and the Youth of Milton', *Milton Quarterly*, vol. 33, no. 4 (December 1999), pp. 95–105 (especially p. 101).

p. 347, '**When I am weary of this [study], the retinue of the intricate theater welcomes ...**' Quoted in Herbert Berry, 'The Miltons and the Blackfriars Playhouse', *Modern Philology*, vol. 89, no. 4 (May 1992), pp. 510–14 (p. 510).

p. 347, **He carefully annotated his own First Folio** ... The copy belongs to the Free Library of Philadelphia, and following initial research by Claire M.L. Bourne, the identification of the annotations as being in the hand of John Milton was made by Jason Scott-Warren. See Terry Teachout, 'Duly Noted: John Milton's Marginalia; John Milton's annotations of Shakespeare's First Folio are just the latest example of how fascinating marginalia can be', *Wall Street Journal*, New York, 25 September 2019. For Claire M.L. Bourne's early findings see 'Vide Supplementum: Early Modern Collation as Play-Reading in the First Folio', in *Early Modern English Marginalia*, ed. Kathy Acheson (London: Routledge, 2019), pp. 195–234. See also Jason Scott-Warren's blog, 'Milton's Shakespeare?' (9 September 2019): https://www.english.cam.ac.uk/cmt/?p=5751. Milton's First Folio can be viewed in its entirety through the Free Library of Philadelphia website: *Mr. William Shakespeares Comedies, Histories, & Tragedies*: https://libwww.freelibrary.org/digital/feature/first-folio.

p. 349, **Neither theatre manager lived to see the publication of the Second Folio ... He was followed to his grave the following year by John Smethwick** ... For the death dates or burials of the figures mentioned in this paragraph see Charles Connell, *They Gave Us Shakespeare: John Heminge and Henry Condell* (Boston and London: Oriel Press, 1982), pp. 14–15; the ODNB entries for 'John Heminges' and 'Henry Condell' by Mary Edmond, of 'Edward Blount' by Gary Taylor, and of 'William Aspley' by James Travers; and Ben Higgins, *Shakespeare's Syndicate: The First Folio, its Publishers, and the Early Modern Book Trade* (Oxford: Oxford University Press, 2022), pp. 129, 167, 208 and 211–15.

p. 349, '**near unto my loving wife Rebecca Heminges who lieth there ...**', E.A.J. Honigmann and Susan Brock, eds, *Playhouse Wills, 1558–1642*

(Manchester: Manchester University Press, 1993 [2015 edition]), pp. 164–69.

p. 349, **just months after reaching his goal of becoming a Master of the Stationers' Company** ... *Records of the Court of the Stationers' Company 1602–1640*, ed. William A. Jackson (London: Bibliographical Society, 1957), p. 325.

p. 349, **purchased by a Dutch diplomat named Constantine Huygens** ... The contexts and history of this Folio (Folger Shakespeare Library First Folio 75) are derived from Anthony James West, 'Constantijn Huygens Owned a Shakespeare First Folio', *Notes and Queries*, vol. 55, no. 2 (2008), pp. 221–222; Anthony James West, 'Constantijn Huygens's Shakespeare First Folio: The First to Go Abroad; Now at the Folger', *Notes and Queries*, vol. 60, no. 1 (2013), p. 49; Anthony James West, 'The First Shakespeare First Folio to Travel Abroad: Constantine Huygens's Copy', in *Foliomania! Stories Behind Shakespeare's Most Important Book*, eds Owen Williams and Caryn Lazzuri (Washington D.C., Folger Shakespeare Library, 2011), pp. 40–44; Smith, *Shakespeare's First Folio*, pp. 91–92; and *The Shakespeare First Folios*, eds Rasmussen and West, pp. 531–32.

p. 350, **Another Folio, discovered in what was once a Jesuit College in St Omer** ... For details of this Folio see Smith, *Shakespeare's First Folio*, pp. 55 and 243–44.

p. 350, **It had been thought that one of Dering's Folios had ended up in the University Library of Padua** ... I had the pleasure of examining this Folio myself at the University Library of Padua and am grateful to the academic and library staff who provided me with access to the volume and information about its history, as well as to Keir Elam for facilitating my research expedition in Italy. The account of this Folio here is derived from: documentation provided to me during my investigation of the book, particularly the account of Lavinia Prosdocimi's paper, 'The First Folio and the merchants of Venice: A collection of English books from the *natio anglica* in the Biblioteca Universitaria in Padova', which was delivered at the 'Shakespeare and Padova' conference in Padua, Italy, on 10 June 2016; Leslie F. Casson, 'Notes on a Shakespearean First Folio in Padua', *Modern Language Notes*, vol. 51, no. 7 (1936), pp. 417–23; *The Shakespeare First Folios*, eds Rasmussen and West, p. 794.

p. 351, **The lion's share, however, would end up in the United States of America, 149 at the last count** ... See the itemisation of Folios across the globe in *The Shakespeare First Folios*, eds Rasmussen and West, pp. 868–72.

p. 351, **the first securely identified as having an early female owner** ... This is Folger Shakespeare Library First Folio 23. The history and contexts of this Folio are derived from *The Shakespeare First Folios*, eds Rasmussen and West, pp. 345–46, and the Folger Shakespeare Library's 'Meet the Folger First Folios' online page: https://www.folger.edu/shakespeare/first-folio/meet-folger-folios, especially https://www.folger.edu/first-folio-number-23.

p. 353, **acquired by the Vaughan family of Trebarried in Wales** … This is Folger Shakespeare Library First Folio 52. Its history and contexts are derived from *The Shakespeare First Folios*, eds Rasmussen and West, pp. 454–55, and William Shakespeare, *Henry V*, ed. Gary Taylor (Oxford: Oxford University Press, 1994), 4.8.102–103.

p. 353, **Colonel John Hutchinson … a Shakespeare lover and early owner of a First Folio** … This is Folger Shakespeare Library First Folio 54. For the story behind this Folio see *The Shakespeare First Folios*, eds Rasmussen and West, pp. 462–63.

pp. 353–54, **Royal Collection at Windsor Castle where … Charles's own copy of the Second Folio** … This Folio is part of the Royal Collection, and is identified as *Mr. Shakespeares comedies, histories, and tragedies. Published according to the true originall copies* (1632), RCIN ref: 1080415.

p. 354, **The Windsor Folio is just one of fifty that now remain in the United Kingdom** … The statistics in this paragraph are derived from *The Shakespeare First Folios*, eds Rasmussen and West, pp. 868–72.

pp. 354–55, **These were once owned by Sir George Grey, an energetic coloniser** … The account of Grey's Folios and his involvement in the colonial endeavour is derived from *The Shakespeare First Folios*, eds Rasmussen and West (First Folio in Auckland Central City Library, New Zealand) p. 847, and (First Folio in South African Library, Cape Town), p. 849; and Smith, *Shakespeare's First Folio*, pp. 95–107, with quotations from the ODNB entry for 'Sir George Grey' by James Belich, and George Grey, *Address delivered by Sir George Grey, K.C.B., at the Theatre Royal, Auckland, June 5th, 1883* (Auckland: Wilsons & Horton, 1883), pp. 8–9 and 27.

p. 355, **travelled with Sir Francis Alexander Newdigate, the governor of Tasmania** … This Folio is in the Harry Ransom Humanities Research Center, University of Texas at Austin, Call Number: Pforzheimer 905; see *The Shakespeare First Folios*, eds Rasmussen and West, pp. 745–47.

p. 355, **It was donated in 1885 by Sir Richard Tangye and his brother George** … *The Shakespeare First Folios*, eds Rasmussen and West, pp. 772–73. See also Smith, *Shakespeare's First Folio*, pp. 118–19 and pp. 317–18.

p. 356, **A Folio in private hands in Colorado was probably acquired … by Sir Thomas Munro** … *The Shakespeare First Folios*, eds Rasmussen and West, pp. 245–46.

p. 356, **another Folio, which is now in the Huntington Library, is known to have been owned by Sir John Baptist Joseph Dormer** … Also known as 'The Halsey Copy', this Folio is Call Number: 56420. See *The Shakespeare First Folios*, eds Rasmussen and West, pp. 230–31.

p. 356, **'cultural capital' of Shakespeare's words more broadly, have been transplanted** … For considerations of 'cultural capital', class and the risks of excluding marginalised communities from Shakespeare's work, see Rowan Mackenzie, *Creating Space for Shakespeare: Working with Marginalized Communities* (London: Arden Bloomsbury, 2023), pp. 71 and

118; Rowan Mackenzie, 'Disturbing Shakespeare and Challenging the Preconceptions', *Shakespeare Studies*, vol. 47 (2019), pp. 49–60; and *Shakespeare Without Class: Misappropriations of Cultural Capital*, eds Donald Hedrick and Bryan Reynolds (New York: Palgrave, 2000). On Shakespeare's 'cultural capital' more broadly see Sofía Muñoz-Valdivieso, '"All the World's a Stage": William Shakespeare's Cultural Capital 400 Years after his Death', *Changing English*, vol. 24, no. 1 (2017), pp. 67–80, and *Shakespeare's Cultural Capital: His economic impact from the sixteenth to the twenty-first century*, eds Dominic Shellard and Siobhan Keenan (London: Palgrave Macmillan, 2016).

p. 357, **perhaps the last role he ever performed before retiring from acting** … Exciting new research by Martin Wiggins appears to confirm this is the case. I am incredibly grateful to Martin for his advice and feedback, and for the unpublished information he generously shared with me, during the writing of *Shakespeare's Book*.

p. 357, **the character promised to 'drown my book'** … William Shakespeare, *The Tempest*, ed. Stephen Orgel (Oxford: Oxford University Press, 1987), 5.1.57.

BIBLIOGRAPHY

Abbreviations

BBC – British Broadcasting Corporation
BL – British Library, London
CP – Cecil Papers, Hatfield House, Hertfordshire
FSL – Folger Shakespeare Library, Washington
LM – Loseley Manuscripts, Surrey History Centre
LMA – London Metropolitan Archives
MS/MSS – manuscript/manuscripts
ODNB – *Oxford Dictionary of National Biography*
SCA – Stationers' Company Archives, London
SHC – Surrey History Centre
SHC, HC – Surrey History Centre, Historical Correspondence
SP – State Papers, National Archives, Kew
TNA – The National Archives, Kew
TNA C – The National Archives, Kew, Records of the Court of Chancery
TNA PC – The National Archives, Kew, Acts/Minutes of the Privy Council
TNA PROB – The National Archives, Kew, Prerogative Court of Canterbury Wills
TNA REQ – The National Archives, Kew, Court of Requests Proceedings

Note: For early printed texts I have indicated the location of publication (that is, the shops from which specific books, pamphlets and other printed materials were sold) only where this information is relevant to the story of the First Folio's creation as outlined in *Shakespeare's Book*. The publication information for early printed books and other texts is derived from or checked against the Early English Books Online database.

Magazines, Newspapers, Media and Databases

BBC News, 14 October 2020, https://www.bbc.co.uk/news/entertainment-arts-54544737

Christie's website: Christie's, 14 October 2022: https://www.christies.com/about-us/press-archive/details?PressReleaseID=9826#:~:text=New%20York%20–%20William%20Shakespeare's%20Comedies%2C%20Histories%2C%20%26,October%202020%20and%20exceeded%20its%20estimate%20of%20%244%2C000%2C000-6%2C000%2C000

Cotton, Robert, 'Sir Robert Bruce Cotton (1571–1631), of Blackfriars, London', in *The History of Parliament: The House of Commons 1604–1629*, ed. Andrew Thrush and John P. Ferris (Cambridge: Cambridge University Press, 2010), available from The History of Parliament Online: https://www.historyofparliamentonline.org/volume/1604-1629/member/cotton-sir-robert-1571-1631

Dering, Edward, 'Book of Expenses', 1617–1628, transcribed by Laetitia Yeandlep, available from the Kent Archaeological Society: https://kentarchaeology.org.uk/publications/member-publications/sir-edward-dering-1st-bart-surrenden-dering-and-his-booke-expences

Early English Books Online (EEBO) Database

Fine Books Magazine, October 2020, https://www.finebooksmagazine.com/blog/shakespeare-first-folio-sells-just-under-10-million

Gentleman's Magazine, no. 86 (1816)

Jenstad, Janelle, ed., 'The Agas Map. The Map of Early Modern London, Edition 7.0': https://mapoflondon.uvic.ca/agas.htm

Laoutaris, Chris, '"What's in a name?": Was William Shakespeare popular during his lifetime?', OUP Blog, Oxford University Press, 17 April 2016, https://blog.oup.com/2016/04/william-shakespeare-popular-early-modern-theatre/

Maguire, Laurie, and Emma Smith, 'Many Hands – A New Shakespeare Collaboration', *Times Literary Supplement*, 19 April 2012

Nelson, Alan H., 'Shakespeare purchases the Blackfriars Gatehouse', Shakespeare Documented: https://shakespearedocumented.folger.edu/shakespeare-purchases-blackfriars-gatehouse#:~:text=In%20March%201613%20"William%20Shakespeare,the%20sum%20of%20£140

Oxford Dictionary of National Biography (ODNB) Database

Pelling, Margaret and Frances White, *Physicians and Irregular Medical Practitioners in London 1550–1640 Database* (London, 2004), British History: http://www.british-history.ac.uk/no-series/london-physicians/1550-1640

Shakespeare Documented, https://shakespearedocumented.folger.edu/

Smithsonian Magazine, 16 October 2020, https://www.smithsonianmag.com/smart-news/shakespeares-first-folio-sells-ten-million-dollars-180976074/

Stern, Tiffany, 'Plays in the Stationers' Registers in the time of Shakespeare', *Literary Print Culture: The Stationers' Company Archive* (Marlborough: Adam Matthew, 2017): http://www.literaryprintculture.amdigital.co.uk.bham-ezproxy.idm.oclc.org/Essays/TiffanyStern

Styles, Philip, ed., 'The borough of Stratford-upon-Avon: Shakespearean festivals and theatres', in *A History of the County of Warwick*, vol. 3 (London, 1945), pp. 244–47; British History Online: http://www.british-history.ac.uk/vch/warks/vol3/pp244-247

Teachout, Terry, 'Duly Noted: John Milton's Marginalia; John Milton's annotations of Shakespeare's First Folio are just the latest example of how fascinating marginalia can be', *Wall Street Journal*, New York, 25 September 2019

Virtual Paul's Cross Project (NC State University): https://vpcross.chass.ncsu.edu/

Scott-Warren, Jason, blog, 'Milton's Shakespeare?' (9 September 2019): https://www.english.cam.ac.uk/cmt/?p=5751

Primary Manuscript Sources

Baker, William, Last Will and Testament, TNA PROB 11/130/234, dated 20 August 1617

Blackfriars Gatehouse, indenture signed by William Shakespeare, William Johnson, John Jackson and John Heminges, LMA CLC/522/MS03738, dated 10 March 1613

Blackfriars Gatehouse, Henry Walker's copy of the indenture, FSL MS Z.c.22 (45), dated 10 March 1613

Blackfriars Gatehouse, indenture signed by John Jackson, FSL MS Z.c.22(44), dated 10 February 1618

Blount, Edward, letter to Dudley Carleton, TNA SP 14/80, f. 136, dated 26 April 1615

Blount, Edward, letter to Dudley Carleton, TNA SP 14/80, f. 186, dated 23 June 1615

Blount, Edward, letter to William Trumbull, BL Additional MS 72361, ff. 68–69, dated 15 June 1621

Blount, Edward, letter to William Trumbull, BL Additional MS 72361, ff. 109–10, dated 6 July 1621

Blount, Edward, letter to William Trumbull, BL Additional MS 72364, ff. 125–26, dated 8 November 1622

Blount, Edward, letter to William Trumbull, BL Additional MS 72365, ff. 130–31, dated 9 May 1623

Blount, Edward, letter to William Trumbull, BL Additional MS 72365, ff. 116–17, dated 30 May 1623

Blount, Edward, letter to Christopher Browne, BL Additional MS 78683, f. 73, dated 15 August 1631

Brent, Nathaniel, letter to Dudley Carleton, TNA SP 14/109, ff. 77–77v, dated 15 May 1619

Buck, Paul, indentures, SHC LM 348/216, dated 30 June 1591 and SHC LM 348/234, dated 31 January 1594

Budge, John, Last Will and Testament, TNA PROB 11/147/606, dated 26 December 1625

Burbage, Richard, Last Will and Testament, TNA PROB 1/32, dated 12 March 1619

Call of the Livery, vol. 1, SCA TSC/1/C/01/06/01

Certificate of Strangers born beyond the seas, who dwell … in the ward of Aldersgate [Parish of St Katherine, Coleman], TNA SP 16/305, 11.ii, f. 20, dated 12 November 1635

Chamberlain, John, letters to Dudley Carleton and others, TNA SP 14/74, 77, 78, 81, 88, 92, 103, 107, 108, 109, 110, 112, 113, 120, 122, 123, 124, 127, 132, 133, 134, 137, 138, 139, 140, 142, 143, 144, 145, 146, 148, 149, 151, 152, 153, 154

Combe, John, Last Will and Testament, TNA PROB 10/325, ff. 3–7. The registered copy of the will is TNA PROB 11/126, ff. 419–421v, dated 28 January 1613

Conway, Secretary, memorandum to the Earl Marshal and Lord Chamberlain [William Herbert], TNA SP 14/214, f. 22, dated 14 May 1623

Conway, Secretary, memorandum to the Lord Chamberlain [William Herbert], TNA SP 14/214, f. 25, dated 27 May 1623

Conway, Secretary, record of a letter to William Herbert, TNA SP 14/214, f. 5, dated 28 February 1623

Conway, Secretary, record of a letter to William Herbert, TNA SP 14/214, f. 10, dated 21 March 1623

Description of a 'philosophical feast', TNA SP 14/66, f. 2, dated 2 September 1611

Dicks, John, Last Will and Testament, TNA PROB 11/198/510, dated 18 December 1646

Digby, John, letters, TNA SP 94/25 and 94/26

Duckett, Fra., letter to Richard Brother, CP 70/67, dated 31 May 1599

Field, Richard, lease agreement with William and George More, SHC LM 333/12, dated 22 September 1592

Field, Richard, records of St Anne's Church, recording his role as assistant warden in 1592, LMA, MS 9537, vol. 8, f. 77, 1592

Field, Richard, records of St Anne's Church, recording his role as warden in 1598, LMA, MS 9 537, vol. 9, f. 158

Fletcher, John, elegy for Richard Burbage, BL Stowe MS 962, ff. 62v–63, dated c. 1619

Heminges, John vs Thomasina Ostler, legal suit, TNA KB 27/1454/1, rotulus 692, ff. 1v–2v

Heminges, John, and Henry Condell, reply in the case of John Witter against John Heminges and Henry Condell, TNA REQ 4/1/2/2, 28 April 1619

Herbert, Gerard, TNA SP 14/109, ff. 100–101v, letter to Dudley Carleton, dated 24 May 1619

Herbert, William, TNA SP 14/110, f. 126, letter to Dudley Carleton, dated 24 September 1619

Herbert, William, TNA SP 14/139, f. 26, letter to Secretary Conway, dated 2 March 1623

Herbert, William, TNA SP 14/152, f. 124, letter to Dudley Carleton, no date but possibly September 1623

Jaggard, John, 'The Humble Petition of John Jaggard, Bookseller and Stationer of London', SCA Memorandum Book: Liber A, Ref. TSC/1/A/05, f. 93

Jaggard, William, case of Button v Whitfield, involving tenements Jaggard would acquire, TNA C 2/JasI/B40/22, dated 1610

Jaggard, William, Indenture of Conveyance of Land to William Jaggard, recording his tenements, LMA CLA/023/DW/01/294, item 14, dated 20 June 1618

Jaggard, William, Record of request for the monopoly of the supply of the Ten Commandments, TNA SP 38/7, f. 141v

James I, letter to the Earls of Pembroke and Arundel and others, TNA SP 14/116, f. 171, dated 29 September 1620

James I, letter to Secretary Calvert, TNA SP 14/124, ff. 97–97v, dated 16 December 1621 (with copy in ff. 98–98v)

James I, letter to Secretary Calvert, TNA SP 14/124, ff. 172–172v, dated 22 December 1621

Lawne, Gideon de, indenture, SHC LM 333/11, dated 20 September 1592

Lawne, William de, purchase agreement with William and George More, FSL, Lb.349, dated 31 October 1593

Lock, Thomas, TNA SP 14/108, ff. 125–125v, letter to Dudley Carleton, dated 30 April 1619

Lock, Thomas, TNA SP 14/132, f. 228, letter to Dudley Carleton, dated 10 August 1622

Mabb, John, 'Goldsmith of London', Last Will and Testament, TNA PROB 11/65/10, dated 15 January 1583

Mabbe or Mabb, John, 'Goldsmith of London', Last Will and Testament, TNA PROB 11/71/109, dated 19 August 1587

Manningham, John, Diary, BL Harley MS 5353

Mare, Lewis de, indenture, SHC LM 348/68, dated 3 September 1570

Nicholas, Matthew, TNA SP 14/123, ff. 138–138v, letter to Edward Nicholas, dated 5 November 1621

Petition of the residents of the Blackfriars against the Blackfriars Theatre and its backers, headed by Lady Elizabeth Russell, TNA SP 12/260, f. 176, dated November 1596

Porter, Endymion, letter to Olive Porter, TNA SP 14/139, ff. 105–105v, dated 10 March 1623

Porter, Endymion, letter to Olive Porter, TNA SP 14/148, ff. 155–155v, dated 17 July 1623

Privy Council Register for the Reign of Elizabeth I, TNA PC 2/22, pp. 345–46, dated 15 August 1597

Privy Council Register for the Reign of Elizabeth I, TNA PC 2/23, p. 13, dated 8 October 1597

Robinson, Humphrey, Last Will and Testament, TNA PROB 11/334/357, dated 10 November 1670

Robinson, John, record of loan, SCA Liber C2, Ref. TSC/1/G/01/02/01, f. 23, dated 11 August 1637

Robinson, John, Scrivener, Last Will and Testament, TNA PROB 11/297/214, dated 29 March 1660

Robinson, Thomas, Stationer, Last Will and Testament, TNA PROB 11/74/263, dated 1 October 1589

Russell, Elizabeth, letter to William More, SHC, HC 6729/6/98, dated 9 August c. 1580–81

Shakespeare, William, Last Will and Testament, TNA PROB 1/4, dated 25 March 1616

Stafford, Simon, and William Barley, Cuthbert Burby et al., 'The copy of the order of the Star Chamber', SCA Liber A, Ref. TSC/1/A/05, ff. 74–74v

Stationers' Company loans and bequests book, SCA Liber C2, Ref. TSC/1/G/01/02/01

Stationers' Register, SCA Liber C, Ref. TSC/1/E/06/02

Stationers' Register, SCA Liber D, Ref. TSC/1/E/06/03

Trumbull, William, letter to Secretary Calvert, TNA SP 77/15, ff. 367–70, dated 2/12 November 1622

Walkley, Thomas, Petition to Secretary Windebank, TNA SP 16/438, f. 10, dated c. 1639–40

Walkley, Thomas, Examination, TNA SP 16/486, f. 234, dated 30 December 1641

Walkley, Thomas, Writ to apprehend Thomas Walkley, Stationer, TNA SP 25/63/2, f. 170, dated 1 Dec 1649 (also TNA SP 25/62, f. 11 and TNA SP 18/6, f. 1, both dated 1649)

Weaver, Edmund [or Edmond], Last Will and Testament, TNA PROB 11/177/292, dated 12 June 1638

Williams, Abraham, TNA SP 14/107, f. 63, letter to Dudley Carleton, dated 20 March 1619

Witter, John, Bill of Complaint against John Heminges and Henry Condell, TNA REQ 4/1/2/1, dated 20 April 1619

Witter, John, Court appearance book in the case against John Heminges and Henry Condell, TNA REQ 1/110, dated 23 April 1619

Witter, John, Replication against John Heminges and Henry Condell, TNA REQ 4/1/2/3, dated 10 May 1619

Witter, John, Final decree in the case against John Heminges and Henry Condell, TNA REQ 1/30, dated c. 1620

Witter, John, Witness Book in the case against John Heminges and Henry Condell, TNA REQ 1/200, dated c. 1620

Wynn, Thomas, TNA SP 14/105, ff. 95–96, letter to Dudley Carleton, dated 28 January 1619

Primary Printed Sources

Acosta, José de, *The Natural and Moral History of the East and West Indies* (London: Printed by Val[entine] Sims for Edward Blount and William Aspley, 1604)

Adams, Thomas, *The Devil's Banket [Banquet] Described in Six Sermons* (London: Printed by Thomas Snodham for John Budge [or Ralph Mab[be]], and are to be sold in Paul's Churchyard, at the sign of the Greyhound, 1614)

Alemán, Mateo, *The Rogue, or, The life of Guzman de Alfarache*, trans. James Mabbe (London: Printed for Edward Blount, 1622)

Alexander, William, *The Monarchic Tragedies* (London: By V[alentine] S[immes] [and G. Elde] for Edward Blount, 1604)

Alexander, William, *The Monarchic Tragedies … Newly enlarged …* (London: Printed by Valentine Simmes for Ed[ward] Blount, 1607)

An Almanac and Prognostication for the Year 1582 (London: R[ichard] Watkins and J[ames] Roberts, 1582)

Appleton, Stephanie, and Mairi Macdonald, eds, *Stratford-upon-Avon Wills: 1348–1701*, 2 vols (Stratford-upon-Avon: Dugdale Society, 2020)

Arber, Edward, ed., *A Transcript of the Registers of the Company of Stationers of London, 1554–1640 A.D.* (London: Stationers' Company, 1875–94)

Aristotle, *Poetics*, trans. Stephen Halliwell, Loeb Classical Library (Cambridge, Massachusetts: Harvard University Press, 1999)

Babington, Gervase, *The Works of the Right Reverend Father in God, Gervase Babington, late Bishop of Worcester* (London: Printed by G. Eld and M. Flesher [for H. Fetherstone], and are to be sold by John Parker at the Sign of the Three Pigeons in Paul's Churchyard, 1622)

Bacon, Francis, *Essays. Religious meditations. Places of Persuasion and Dissuasion* (London: for John Jaggard dwelling in Fleet Street at the Hand and Star, near Temple Bar, 1612)

Baker, Richard, *A chronicle of the Kings of England* (London: Printed for Daniel Frere, 1643)

Baker, Richard, *Theatrum redivivum, or The Theatre Vindicated* (London: Printed by T.R. for Francis Eglesfield, 1662)

Bancroft, Thomas, *Time's Out of Tune* (London: W. Godbid, 1658)

Basse, William, *Great Britain's Sunset, Bewailed with a Shower of Tears* (Oxford: Printed by Joseph Barnes, 1613)

Beaumont, Francis, and John Fletcher, *Comedies and Tragedies written by Francis Beaumont and John Fletcher* (London: Printed for Humphrey Robinson and Humphrey Moseley, 1647)

Beaumont, Francis, and John Fletcher, *A King and No King* (London: Printed [by John Beale] for Thomas Walkley, and are to be sold at his shop at the Eagle and Child in Britain's Burse, 1619)

Beaumont, Francis, and John Fletcher, *Philaster, Or, love lies a bleeding* (London: Printed [by Nicholas Okes] for Thomas Walkley, and are to be sold at his shop, at the sign of the Eagle and Child, in Britain's Burse, 1622)

Beaumont, Francis, and John Fletcher, ed. Suzanne Gossett, *Philaster* (London: Arden, 2009)

Bertholdus, Andreas, *The Wonderful and Strange Effect and Virtues of a new Terra Sigillata lately found out in Germany* (London: Printed by Robert Robinson for Richard Watkins, 1587)

Bingham, John, trans., *The History of Xenophon* (London: Printed by John Haviland for Ra[l]phe Mabb[e], 1623)

Bond, John, *Auli Persii Flacci Satyræ Sex* (London: Excudebat Felix Kingstonius impensis Gulielmi Aspley, & Nathanielis Butterij, 1614)

Boys, John, *The works of John Boys, Doctor in Divinity and Dean of Canterbury* (London: Imprinted [by John Haviland] for William Aspley, 1622)

A Brief and True Declaration of the Sickness, Last Words, and Death of the King of Spain, Philip the Second (London: By Edm[und] Bollifant, for William Aspley, 1599)

Brooke, Arthur, *The Tragical History of Romeus and Juliet* (London: Imprinted by R[obert] Robinson, 1587)

Brooke, Ralph, *A Catalogue and Succession of the Kings* (London: Printed by William Jaggard, 1619)

Brooke, Ralph, *A Catalogue and Succession of the Kings ... Collected by Ralph Brooke, Esquire, Yorke Herald, and by him enlarged, with amendment of divers faults, committed by the printer, in the time of the author's sickness* (London: Printed by William Stansby, 1622)

Buoni, Thommaso, *Problems of Beauty and all Human Affections* (London: Printed by G. Eld, for Edward Blount and William Aspley, 1606)

Burton, William, *The Description of Leicestershire, containing matters of antiquity, history, armoury, and genealogy* (London: Printed [by William Jaggard] for John White, 1622)

Camden, William, *Remains of a Greater Work, Concerning Britain* (London: Printed by G[eorge] E[ld] for Simon Waterson, 1605)

The Catholic Triumph ... (London: Printed for the Company of Stationers, 1610)

A Caveat or Warning for all sorts of men both young and old to avoid the company of lewd and wicked women, to the tune of Virginia (London: For H.G., 1620)

Cervantes, Miguel de, *Exemplary Novels in Six Books* (London: Printed by John Dawson, for R[alph] M[abbe], and are to be sold by Laurence Blaicklocke: at his shop at the Sugar-loaf next [to] Temple Bar in Fleet Street, 1640)

Cervantes, Miguel de, *The history of the valorous and witty knight-errant, Don-Quixote*, part 1 (London: Printed by William Stansby, for Ed[ward] Blount and W[illiam] Barret, 1612)

Cervantes, Miquel de, *The second part of the history of the valorous and witty knight-errant, Don Quixote* (London: Printed [by Eliot's Court Press] for Edward Blount, 1620)

Céspedes y Meneses, Gonzalo de, *Gerardo the Unfortunate Spaniard*, trans. Leonard Digges (London: Printed [by George Purslowe] for Ed[ward] Blount, 1622)

Charron, Pierre, *Of Wisdom* (London: Printed for Edward Blount and Will[iam] Aspley, 1620)

Chester, Robert, *Love's Martyr: or, Rosalin's Complaint, Allegorically shadowing the truth of love, in the constant fate of the Phoenix and Turtle* [by William Shakespeare] (London: Imprinted [by Richard Field] for E[dward B[lount], 1601)

Claudian, *The Rape of Proserpine*, trans. Leonard Digges (London: Printed by G[eorge] P[urslowe] for Edward Blount, and are to be sold at his shop in Paul's Churchyard at the sign of the [Black] Bear, 1617)

Constable, Henry, trans., *The Catholic Moderator: or A Moderate examination of the doctrine of the Protestants* (London: Printed [at Eliot's Court Press] for Nathaniel Butter, 1623)

Corbet, Richard, *Certain Elegant Poems, Written by Dr Corbet, Bishop of Norwich* (London: Printed by R. Cotes for Andrew Crooke, 1647)

Coryate, Thomas, *Coryat's Crudities, Hastily gobbled up in five months travels* ... (London: Printed by W[illiam] S[tansby for the author], 1611)

Coryate, Thomas, *Thomas Coryate, Traveller for the English Wits* (London: Printed by W[illiam] Jaggard, and Henry Fetherston, 1616)

Cotton, Robert, *Early Records of Sir Robert Cotton's Library: Foundation, Cataloguing, Use*, ed. Colin G.C. Tite (London: British Library, 2003)

Cowley, Abraham, *Love's Riddle: A Pastoral Comedy* (London: Printed by John Dawson for Henry Seile, 1638)

Cowper, William, *The Works of Mr William Cowper, late Bishop of Galloway* (London: Imprinted [by Thomas Snodham and Felix Kyngston] for John Budge, and are to be sold at his shop in Paul's Churchyard, at the sign of the Green Dragon, 1623)

Crane, Ralph, *The Works of Mercy, both Corporal and Spiritual* (London: Printed by G. Eld and M. Flesher, 1621)

Crooke, Helkiah, *Mikrokosmographia, A description of the body of man* (Printed by William Jaggard, 1615)

Dallington, Robert, *Aphorisms Civil and Military* (London: Imprinted [by R. Field] for Edward Blount, 1613)

Dallington, Robert, *A Survey of the great dukes state of Tuscany, In the year of our Lord 1596* (London: Printed [by George Eld] for Edward Blount, 1605)

Daniel, Samuel, *A Panegyricke Congratulatory* (London: Printed by Valentine Simmes for Edward Blount, 1603)

Davies, John, *Humour's Heaven on Earth; with The Civil Wars of Death and Fortune* (London: Printed by A[dam] I[slip], 1609)

Davies, John, *Microcosmos: The discovery of the little world, with the government thereof* (Oxford: Printed by Joseph Barnes for John Barnes, 1603)

Dering, Edward, *M[aster] Dering's Works, More at large than ever hath heretofore been printed in any one volume* (London: Printed by Edward Griffin for Edward Blount, 1614)

D'Ewes, Simonds, *The Autobiography and Correspondence of Sir Simonds D'Ewes*, vol. 1, ed. James Orchard Halliwell (London: Richard Bentley, 1845)

Digges, Thomas, *An Arithmetical Warlike Treatise Named Stratioticos* (London: Imprinted by Richard Field, 1590; originally published 1579)

Donne, John, *The Life and Letters of John Donne, Dean of St Paul's*, ed. Edmund Gosse, vol. 2 (Gloucester, Mass: Peter Smith, 1959)

Donne, John, *Poems, by J.D. [John Donne], With Elegies on the Author's Death* (London: Printed by M[iles] F[lesher] for John Marriot, and are to be sold at his shop in St Dunstan's Churchyard in Fleet Street, 1633)

Dramatic Records in the Declared Accounts of the Treasurer of the Chamber 1558–1642, Malone Society Collections, vol. 6 (Oxford: Oxford University Press for The Malone Society, 1961–2)

Draxe, Thomas, *An Alarum to the Last Judgement* (London: Printed by Nicholas Okes for Matthew Law, and are to be sold at the sign of the Fox in Paul's Churchyard, 1615)

Drayton, Michael, *Poems: by Michael Drayton Esquire* (London: Printed by W[illiam] Stansby for John Smethwick, and are to be sold at his shop in Saint Dunstan's Churchyard in Fleet Street, under the Dial, 1619)

Drummond, William, 'Ben Jonson's Conversations with William Drummond of Hawthornden', in *Ben Jonson, The Complete Poems*, ed. George Parfitt (Harmondsworth: Penguin, 1975 [1996 edition])

Ducci, Lorenzo, *Ars Aulica or The courtier's Art* (London: Printed by Melch[ior] Bradwood for Edward Blount, 1607)

Duellum siue singulare certamen ... (London: Excudebat G. Eld. impensis Nath[aniel] Butter, & R[alph] Mab[be], 1611)

Dyke, Daniel, *The Mystery of Self-Deceiving* (London: Printed by Edward Griffin for Ralph Mab[be], and Nathaniell Butter, 1616)

Edward, Earl of Clarendon, *The History of the Rebellion and the Civil Wars in England*, vol. 1, part 1 (Oxford: Clarendon, 1807)

Erasmus, Desiderius, *Seven Dialogues, Very pleasant and Delightful for all Persons*, trans. William Burton (London: Printed for John Smithwick, and are to be sold at his shop in Saint Dunstan's Churchyard in Fleet Street, 1624)

Favyn, André, *The Theatre of Honour and Knighthood* (London: Printed by William Jaggard, 1623)

Featley, Daniel, *The Romish Fisher caught and held in his own net. Or, A true relation of the Protestant conference and popish difference* ... (London: Printed by H[umphrey] L[ownes and William Stansby] for Robert Milbourne, and are to be sold at the Great South Door of Paul's, 1624)

The first and second part of the Troublesome Reign of John, King of England ... Written by W. Shakespeare (London: Printed by Aug[ustine] Mathewes for Thomas Dewe, and are to be sold at his shop in St Dunstan's Churchyard in Fleet Street, 1622)

Fisher, George, *The Bishop of London his Legacy. Or certain motives of D[r] King, late Bishop of London, for his change of religion, and dying in the Catholic, and Roman Church* (Saint-Omer: English College Press, 1623)

Flecknoe, Richard, *Euterpe Revived* (London: [for Richard Flecknoe?], 1675)

Flecknoe, Richard, *Love's Kingdom a Pastoral Tragi-Comedy ... with a short Treatise of the English Stage* (London: Printed by R. Wood for Richard Flecknoe, 1664)

Fletcher, John, *The Wild-Goose Chase, a Comedy as it hath been acted with singular applause at the Blackfriars* (London: Printed for Humphrey Moseley, 1652)

Florio, John, *Queen Anna's New World of Words* (London: Printed by Melch[ior] Bradwood [and William Stansby], for Edw[ard] Blount and William Barret, 1611)

Gairdner, James, ed., *Letters and Papers, Foreign and Domestic, of the reign of Henry VIII*, vol. 11 (London: Her Majesty's Stationery Office, 1888)

Gibson, Abraham, *The Land's Mourning for Vain Swearing* (London: Printed by T.S. for Ralph Mab[be], and are to be sold in Paul's Churchyard, at the sign of the Angel, 1613)

Green, Mary Anne Everett, ed., *Calendar of State Papers, Domestic Series, of the Reign of James 1, 1603–1610*, vol. 1 (London: Longman et al., 1857)

Green, Mary Anne Everett, ed., *Calendar of State Papers, Domestic Series, of the Reign of James I, 1619–1623, preserved in the State Paper Department of her Majesty's Public Record Office*, vol. 3 (London: Longman et al., 1858)

Grey, George, *Address delivered by Sir George Grey, K.C.B., at the Theatre Royal, Auckland, June 5th, 1883* (Auckland: Wilsons & Horton, 1883)

H.A., *The Scourge of Venus: or, The wanton Lady with the rare birth of Adonis* (London: Printed by Nicholas Okes, dwelling near Holborn Bridge, 1613)

Hardy, William Le, ed., *County of Middlesex. Calendar to the Sessions Records: New Series, Volume 2, 1614–15* (London: Middlesex Sessions Records. Clerk of the Peace, 1936)

Hawkins, Richard, *The Observations of Sir Richard Hawkins, Knight, in his Voyage into the South Sea* (London: Printed by J[ohn] D[awson] for John Jaggard, and are to be sold at his shop at the Hand and Star in Fleet Street, near the Temple Gate, 1622)

Henslowe, Philip, *Henslowe's Diary*, ed. R.A. Foakes (Cambridge: Cambridge University Press, 2002)

Herbert, George, *Wits Recreations* (London: Printed by R[ichard] H[odgkinson and Thomas Paine] for Humphry Blunden, 1640)

Herbert, William, *The Copy of a Warrant signed by the Right Honourable, the Earl of Pembroke* (London: The Lord Chamberlain's Office, 1622)

Heywood, Thomas, *An Apology for Actors* (London: Printed by Nicholas Okes, 1612)

Heywood, Thomas, *A Pleasant Conceited Comedy, wherein is showed, how a man may choose a good wife from a bad* (London: Printed [by Thomas Purfoot] for Matthew Law, and are to be sold at his shop in Paul's Churchyard, near unto S[aint] Augustine's Gate, at the sign of the Fox, 1621)

Heywood, Thomas, *Troia Britanica: or, Great Britain's Troy* (London: Printed by William Jaggard, 1609)

Hic Mulier: or, The Man-Woman: being a medicine to cure the coltish disease of the staggers in the masculine-feminines of our times (London: Printed [at Eliot's Court Press] for I. T[rundle], 1620)

The History of Justine (London: Printed by William Jaggard, dwelling in Barbican, 1606)

Hoby, Edward, *A Curry-Combe for a Cox-Combe* (London: Printed by William Stansby for Nathaniel Butter, and are to be sold at his shop near S[aint] Augustine's Gate at the sign of the Pied Bull, 1615)

Hockham, William, *Prince Charles his Welcome to the Court* (London: By Edward Allde for John Wright, 1623)

Holland, Hugh, *Pancharis* (London: By V. S[immes] for Clement Knight, 1603)

Honigmann, E.A.J., and Susan Brock, eds, *Playhouse Wills, 1558–1642* (Manchester: Manchester University Press, 1993 [2015 edition])

Hull, William, *The Mirror of Majesty* (London: Printed by Nicholas Okes, for William Timme and John Robinson, and are to be sold at their shop in Paternoster Row, 1615)

Jackson, William A., ed., *Records of the Court of the Stationers' Company 1602–1640* (London: Bibliographical Society, 1957)

Jaggard, William, *A Catalogue of such English Books* (London: Printed by W[illiam] Jaggard, 1618)

James I, *Basilikon Doron. Or His Majesty's Instructions to his Dearest Son, Henry the Prince* (Edinburgh: Printed by Robert Waldegrave, Printer to the King's Majesty, 1603)

James I, *By the King. A proclamation for suppressing insolent abuses committed by base people against persons of quality, as well strangers as others, in the streets of the city and suburbs of London* (London: By Bonham Norton and John Bill, printers to the King's most Excellent Majesty, 1621)

James, Thomas, *Letters to Thomas James, first Keeper of the Bodleian Library*, ed. George Wilson Wheeler (Oxford: Clarendon Press, 1926)

Jonson, Ben, *Bartholomew Fair*, in *Ben Jonson: Five Plays*, ed. G.A. Wilkes (Oxford: Oxford University Press, 1988)

Jonson, Ben, *Ben Jonson, The Complete Poems*, ed. George Parfitt (Harmondsworth: Penguin, 1975 [1996 edition])

Jonson, Ben, *Christmas, His Masque, As it was Presented at Court, 1616*, in *The Works of Benjamin Jonson* (London: Printed [by John Beale, James Dawson, Bernard Alsop and Thomas Fawcet] for Richard Meighen [and Thomas Walkley], 1641)

Jonson, Ben, *The Devil is an Ass, a comedy acted in the year 1616, by His Majesty's servants* (London: 1641)

Jonson, Ben, *The Masque of Augurs, With the Several Antimasques. Presented on Twelfth Night* (London: S.N., 1621)

Jonson, Ben, *Masques of Difference: Four Court Masques by Ben Jonson*, ed. Kristen McDermott (Manchester: Manchester University Press, 2007)

Jonson, Ben, *Neptune's Triumph for the Return of Albion* (London: S.N., 1624)

Jonson, Ben, *Sejanus His Fall* (London: Printed by G. Elld, for Thomas Thorpe, 1605)

Jonson, Ben, *Sejanus His Fall*, ed. Philip J. Ayres (Manchester: Manchester University Press, 1990)

Jonson, Ben, *Volpone, or The Fox* (London: Printed [by George Eld] for Thomas Thorpe, 1607)

Jonson, Ben, *The Works of Benjamin Jonson* (London: Printed by William Stansby for Richard Meighen, 1616)

Kingsford, C.L., ed., *Report on the Manuscripts of Lord de L'Isle and Dudley Preserved at Penshurst Place*, vol. 2 (London: Historical Manuscripts Commission, 1934)

Kyd, Thomas, *The Spanish Tragedy, containing the lamentable end of Don Horatio, and Bel-imperia: with the pitiful death of old Hieronimo* (London: Printed by Edward Allde, for Edward White, 1592)

Kyd, Thomas, *The Spanish Tragedy: or, Hieronimo is mad again, containing the lamentable end of Don Horatio, and Belimperia; with the pitiful death of Hieronimo* (London: Printed by John White, for T Langley, 1618)

The Lamentable and True Tragedy of M. Arden of Feversham [Faversham] in Kent, who was most wickedly murdered (London: [By E. Allde] for Edward White, 1592)

Lope de Vega, Félix, *[El Peregrino en su Patria] The Pilgrim of Castile* (London: Printed by [E. Allde for] John Norton, 1621)

Lucan, *Lucan's First Booke* (alternative title: *Pharsalia*), trans. Christopher Marlowe (London: Printed by P. Short, for Walter Burre [and Thomas Thorpe?], 1600)

Lucan, *Pharsalia*, trans. Sir Arthur Gorges (London: Printed [by Nicholas Okes] for Edward Blount, 1614)

Lyly, John, *Six Court Comedies* (London: Printed by William Stansby for Edward Blount, 1632)

Malynes, Gerard, *Saint George for England, Allegorically Described* (London: By Richard Field for William Tymme, stationer, and are to be sold at the sign of the Fleur de Luce and Crown in Paternoster Row, 1601)

Marcham, Frank (transcribed by), *The King's Office of the Revels 1610–1622: Fragments of Documents in the Department of Manuscripts, British Museum* (London: Frank Marcham, 1925)

May, Thomas, *The Heir, An Excellent Comedy* (London: Printed by B[ernard] A[lsop] for Thomas Jones, 1622)

Melton, John, *Astrologaster, or, The figure-caster ...* (London: Barnard Alsop for Edward Blackmore, 1620)

Milles, Thomas, *A Catalogue of the Kings of Scotland* (London: [By W. Jaggard], 1610)

Montaigne, Michel de, *Essays ... done into English*, trans. John Florio (London: Printed by Melch[ior] Bradwood for Edward Blount and William Barret, 1613)

Montaigne, Michel de, *The Essays or Moral, Politic and Military Discourses*, trans. John Florio (London: By Val[entine] Sim[me]s for Edward Blount, 1603)

Munday, Anthony [and Michael Drayton, Richard Hathaway, and Robert Wilson], *The first part of the True and Honourable History, of the Life of Sir John Oldcastle, the Good Lord Cobham* (London: Printed by V[alentine] S[immes] for Thomas Pavier, 1600)

N.B., *The Court and Country, or A brief discourse dialogue-wise set down between a courtier and a country-man ...* (London: G. Eld for John Wright, 1618)

Newes from Ostend of ... [the] fierce siege made by the Archduke Albertus his forces ... (London: Printed by V. S[immes] for Thomas Pavier, 1601)

The Passionate Pilgrim, attributed to William Shakespeare (London: Printed for W. Jaggard, 1599)

The Passionate Pilgrim ... Whereunto is newly added two love-epistles (London: Printed by William Jaggard, 1612)

Perceval, Richard, *A Dictionary in Spanish and English* (London: By John
    Haviland for Edward Blount, 1623)
Pimlico, or Run Redcap (London: Printed [by Thomas Purfoot] for John
    Busbie, and George Loftis, 1609)
Preston, Thomas, *A New-Year's Gift for English Catholics, or A brief and clear
    explication of the new Oath of Allegiance* (London: W. Stansby, 1620)
The Principal Fairs of England and Wales (London: By Richard Watkins and
    James Roberts, 1599)
*A proclamation given by the discrete lords and states, against the slanders laid upon
    the evangelical and reformed religion* (London: by G[eorge] E[ld] for
    Th[omas] Th[orpe] and Richard Chambers, sold at the Sign of the Black
    Bear in Paul's Churchyard, 1618)
Prynne, William, *Histrio-Mastix: The players' scourge, or, actors' tragedy*
    (London: Printed by E[dward] A[llde, Augustine Mathewes, Thomas
    Cotes] and W[illiam] J[ones] for Michael Sparke, 1633)
Rojas, Fernando de, *The Spanish Bawd, represented in Celestina*, trans. James
    Mabbe (London: Printed by J[ohn] B[eale], and are to be sold by Ralph
    Mab[be], 1631)
Rushworth, John, *Historical Collections of Private Passages of State* (London:
    Printed by Tho[mas] Newcomb for George Thomason, 1659)
Santa María, Juan de, *Christian Policy, or, The Christian Commonwealth*
    (London: Printed by Thomas Harper, for Richard Collins, 1632)
Scott, Thomas, *Vox Populi. Or News from Spain, translated according to the
    Spanish copy* (London: Imprinted, 1620)
Shakespeare, William, *All the Sonnets of Shakespeare*, Paul Edmondson and
    Stanley Wells (Cambridge: Cambridge University Press, 2020)
Shakespeare, William, *All's Well That Ends Well*, ed. Susan Snyder (Oxford:
    Oxford University Press, 1993)
Shakespeare, William, *Antony and Cleopatra*, ed. John Wilders (London:
    Arden, 1995)
Shakespeare, William, *Coriolanus*, ed. Peter Holland (London: Arden,
    2013)
Shakespeare, William, *The Famous History of Troilus and Cressida, Excellently
    expressing the beginning of their loves ...* (London: Imprinted by G. Eld for
    R[ichard] Bonian and H[enry] Walley, and are to be sold at the Spread
    Eagle in Paul's Churchyard, over against the Great North Door, 1609)
Shakespeare, William, *Hamlet*, ed. G.R. Hibbard (Oxford: Oxford University
    Press, 1994)
Shakespeare, William, *Henry IV, Part One*, ed. David Bevington (Oxford:
    Oxford University Press, 1998)
Shakespeare, William, *Henry V*, ed. Gary Taylor (Oxford: Oxford University
    Press, 1994)
Shakespeare, William, *The History of Troilus and Cressida, As it was acted by the
    King's Majesty's Servants at the Globe* (London: Imprinted by G. Eld for
    R[ichard] Bonian and H[enry] Walley, and are to be sold at the Spread
    Eagle in Paul's Churchyard, over against the Great North Door, 1609)

Shakespeare, William, *Julius Caesar*, ed. Arthur Humphreys (Oxford: Oxford University Press, 1998)

Shakespeare, William, *Julius Caesar*, ed. David Daniell (London: Arden, 1998)

Shakespeare, William, *King Richard II*, ed. Charles R. Forker (London: Arden, 2005)

Shakespeare, William, *M[aster] William Shakespeare: His True Chronicle History of the Life and Death of King Lear* (London: Printed [by Nicholas Okes] for Nathaniel Butter, and are to be sold at his shop in Paul's Churchyard at the sign of the Pied Bull near St. Augustine's Gate, 1608)

Shakespeare, William, *A Midsummer Night's Dream* ([By Richard Bradock] for Thomas Fisher, and are to be sold at his shop, at the sign of the White Hart, in Fleet Street, 1600)

Shakespeare, William, *A Midsummer Night's Dream*, ed. Peter Holland (Oxford: Oxford University Press, 1995)

Shakespeare, William, *The Most Lamentable Roman Tragedy of Titus Andronicus* (London: Printed by John Danter, and are to be sold by Edward White and Thomas Millington, 1594)

Shakespeare, William, *Mr. William Shakespeares Comedies, Histories, & Tragedies*, Folger Shakespeare Library First Folio 5, available via the Folger Shakespeare Library's 'Meet the Folger First Folios' online page: https://www.folger.edu/shakespeare/first-folio/meet-folger-folios

Shakespeare, William, *Mr. William Shakespeares Comedies, Histories, & Tragedies*, a copy of the First Folio once owned by the poet John Milton, accessible from the Free Library of Philadelphia: https://libwww.freelibrary.org/digital/feature/first-folio

Shakespeare, William, *Mr. William Shakespeares Comedies, Histories, & Tragedies: A Facsimile of the First Folio, 1623*, ed. Doug Moston (New York and London: Routledge, 1998)

Shakespeare, William, *Mr William Shakespeares Comedies, Histories, and Tragedies, published according to the true original copies* (London: Printed by Thomas Cotes, for Robert Allot [John Smethwick, William Aspley, Richard Hawkins, and Richard Meighen], 1632)

Shakespeare, William, *Much Ado About Nothing*, ed. Sheldon P. Zitner (Oxford: Oxford University Press, 1998)

Shakespeare, William, *The New Oxford Shakespeare: The Complete Works*, general editors, Gary Taylor, John Jowett, Terri Bourus and Gabriel Egan (Oxford: Oxford University Press, 2016)

Shakespeare, William, *The Norton Facsimile: The First Folio of Shakespeare*, second edition, ed. Peter W.M. Blayney (New York and London: W.W. Norton and Company, 1996)

Shakespeare, William, *Othello*, ed. E.A.J. Honigmann (Surrey: Arden, 1997)

Shakespeare, William, *Poems: Written by Wil[liam] Shakespeare, Gent.* (London: By Tho[mas] Cotes, and are to be sold by John Benson, dwelling in St. Dunstan's Churchyard, 1640)

Shakespeare, William, *The Rape of Lucrece* (London: Printed by N[icholas] O[kes] for John Harison, 1607)

Shakespeare, William, *Richard II*, eds Anthony B. Dawson and Paul Yachnin (Oxford: Oxford University Press, 2011)

Shakespeare, William, *Shakespeare's Poems: Venus and Adonis, The rape of Lucrece and the Shorter Poems*, eds Katherine Duncan-Jones and H.R. Woudhuysen (London: Arden, 2007)

Shakespeare, William, *Shakespeare's Sonnets* (London: By G. Eld for T[homas] T[horpe] and are to be sold by William Aspley, 1609)

Shakespeare, William, *The Tempest*, ed. Stephen Orgel (Oxford: Oxford University Press, 1987)

Shakespeare, William, *The Tragedy of Othello, the Moore of Venice* (London: Printed by N[icholas] O[kes] for Thomas Walkley, and are to be sold at his shop, at the Eagle and Child, in Britain's Burse, 1622)

Shirley, James, *The Cardinal, A Tragedy, as it was acted at the private house in Blackfriars* (London: Printed for Humphrey Robinson at the Three Pigeons, and Humphrey Moseley at the Prince's Arms in St. Paul's Churchyard, 1652)

Shirley, James, *The Sisters, a Comedy, as it was acted at the private house in Blackfriars* (London: Printed for Humphrey Robinson at the Three Pigeons, and Humphrey Moseley at the Prince's Arms in St. Paul's Churchyard, 1652)

Sidney, Philip, *An Apology for Poetry* (London: Printed [by James Roberts] for Henry Olney, 1595)

Sir Thomas Overbury his wife with new elegies upon his (now known) untimely death: whereunto are annexed, new news and characters (London: Printed by Edward Griffin for Laurence L'Isle, 1616 [original edition 1614])

Smith, Henry, *Three Prayers* (London: [By R[obert] Robinson] for Thomas Man, dwelling in Paternoster Row at the sign of the Talbot, 1592)

Smith, Henry, *The Sermons of Master Henry Smith* (London: Printed by Richard Field [T. Orwin, and R[obert] Robinson] for Thomas Man, dwelling in Paternoster Row, at the sign of the Talbot, 1593)

Smith, Thomas, *Sir Thomas Smith's Voyage* (London: [By W. White and W. Jaggard] for Nathaniel Butter, 1605)

Stow, John, *A Survey of London, Written in the Year 1598* (Stroud: Sutton Publishing, 2005)

A Strange Report of Six most Notorious Witches who by their Devilish Practices Murdered above the number of four-hundred Small Children … (London: Printed by W[illiam] W[hite] for Thomas Pavier, 1601)

Sylvester, Josiah, *Du Bartas his Divine Weeks and Works* (London: By Humfrey Lounes [and are to be sold by Arthur Johnson at the sign of the White Horse, near the great north door of Paul's Church], 1611)

Tailor, Robert, *The Hog hath Lost his Pearl, A Comedy* (London: Printed [by John Beale] for Richard Redmer, 1614)

Tanner, J.R., *English Constitutional Conflicts of the Seventeenth Century 1603–1689* (Cambridge: Cambridge University Press, 1928 [1937 edition])

Taylor, John, *Prince Charles his Welcome from Spain* (London: Printed by G.E. for John Wright, 1623)

Taylor, Thomas, *Japhet's First Public Persuasion* (Cambridge: Printed by Cantrell Legge, printer to the University of Cambridge, and are to be sold by Raph Mab[be] at the sign of the Angel in Paul's Churchyard, 1612)

Topsell, Edward, *The History of Four-footed Beasts, Describing the true and lively figure of every beast* ... (London: Printed by William Jaggard, 1607)

Tuvill, Daniel, *Christian Purposes and Resolutions* (London: Printed [by William Jaggard] for Thomas Dewe, and are to be sold at his shop in S[aint] Dunstan's Churchyard in Fleet Street, 1622)

Veer, Gerrit de, *The True and Perfect Description of Three Voyages so Strange and Wonderful ... with the cruel bears, and other monsters of the sea* ... (London: [By W. White] for Thomas Pavier, 1605)

Vincent, Augustine, *A Discovery of Errors in the first edition of the Catalogue of Nobility, published by Raphe Brooke, Yorke Herald, 1619* (London: Printed by William Jaggard, 1622)

Virel, Matthieu, *A Learned and Excellent Treatise containing all the Principal grounds of Christian Religion* (London: By Robert Robinson [and R[ichard] Field] for Robert Dexter, dwelling in Paul's Churchyard at the sign of the Brazen Serpent, 1595)

Weston, Edward, *The repair of honour, falsely impeached by Featl[e]y, a minister* (Saint-Omer: [by the English College Press], 1624)

The Whole Works of Homer, trans. George Chapman (London: Printed [by Richard Field and William Jaggard] for Nathaniel Butter, 1616)

Wilkins, George, *The Painful Adventures of Pericles Prince of Tyre, Being the true history of the play of Pericles* (London: Printed by T. P[urfoot] for Nathaniel Butter, 1608)

Wither, George, *Fair-Virtue* (London: Printed [by Augustine Mathewes] for John Grismand, 1622)

Woeful News from the West Parts of England, Being the Lamentable Burning of the Town of Teverton, in Devonshire (London: Printed by T. S[nodham] for Thomas Pavier, 1612)

Wood, Anthony à, *Athenae Oxonienses, an exact history of all the writers and bishops who have had their education in the most ancient and famous University of Oxford*, 2 vols (London: Printed for Tho[mas] Bennet, 1691)

A Yorkshire Tragedy, Not so new as lamentable and true. Acted by his Majesty's Players at the Globe. Written by W. Shakespeare (London: Printed by R[ichard] B[radock] for Thomas Pavier, 1608)

Secondary Sources

Akrigg, G.P.V., 'The Arrangement of the Tragedies in the First Folio', *Shakespeare Quarterly*, vol. 7, no. 4 (Autumn 1956), pp. 443–45

Aldis, H.G., et al., *A Dictionary of Printers and Booksellers in England, Scotland and Ireland, and of Foreign Printers of English Books, 1557–1640*, gen. ed. R.B. McKerrow (London: Bibliographical Society, 1910)

Arnold, Catharine, *Globe: Life in Shakespeare's London* (London and New York: Simon and Schuster, 2015)

Astington, John H., 'His Theatre Friends: The Burbages', in *The Shakespeare Circle: An Alternative Biography*, eds Paul Edmondson and Stanley Wells (Cambridge: Cambridge University Press, 2015), pp. 248–60

Backhouse, Janet, 'Sir Robert Cotton's Record of a Royal Bookshelf', *British Library Journal*, vol. 18, no. 1 (Spring 1992), pp. 44–51

Bawcutt, N.W., 'Craven Ord Transcripts of Sir Henry Herbert's Office-Book in the Folger Shakespeare Library', *English Literary Renaissance*, vol. 14, no. 1 (December 1984), pp. 83–93

Bawcutt, N.W., 'New Entries from the Office-Book of Sir Henry Herbert', *English Literary Renaissance*, vol. 26, no. 1 (January 1996), pp. 155–66

Bearman, Robert, *Shakespeare in the Stratford Records* (Stroud: Alan Sutton, 1994)

Bearman, Robert, *Shakespeare's Money: How much did he make and what did this mean?* (Oxford: Oxford University Press, 2016)

Berek, Peter, 'The Market for Playbooks and the Development of the Reading Public', *Philological Quarterly*, vol. 91, no. 2 (2012), pp. 151–84

Berry, Herbert, 'The Miltons and the Blackfriars Playhouse', *Modern Philology*, vol. 89, no. 4 (May 1992), pp. 510–14

Blake, Erin C., and Kathleen Lynch, 'Looke on his Picture, in his Booke: The Droeshout Portrait on the Title Page', in *Foliomania! Stories Behind Shakespeare's Most Important Book*, eds Owen Williams and Caryn Lazzuri (Washington D.C., Folger Shakespeare Library, 2011), pp. 21–31

Blayney, Peter W.M., 'The Alleged Popularity of Playbooks', *Shakespeare Quarterly*, vol. 56, no. 1 (2005), pp. 33–50

Blayney, Peter W.M., *The Bookshops in Paul's Cross Churchyard*, Occasional Papers of the Bibliographical Society, no. 5 (London: Bibliographical Society, 1990)

Blayney, Peter W.M., *The First Folio of Shakespeare* (Washington D.C., Folger Shakespeare Library 1991)

Blayney, Peter W.M., 'The Publication of Playbooks', in *A New History of Early English Drama*, eds John D. Cox and David Scott Kastan (New York: Columbia University Press, 1997), pp. 383–422

Boffone, Trevor, and Carla Della Gatta, *Shakespeare and Latinidad* (Edinburgh: Edinburgh University Press, 2021)

Bourne, Claire M.L., 'Vide Supplementum: Early Modern Collation as Play-Reading in the First Folio', in *Early Modern English Marginalia*, ed. Kathy Acheson (London: Routledge, 2019), pp. 195–234

Bowsher, Julian, *Shakespeare's London Theatreland: Archaeology, History and Drama* (London: Museum of Archaeology, 2012)

Brennan, Michael G., *Literary Patronage in the English Renaissance: The Pembroke Family* (New York and London: Routledge, 1988)

Campbell, Gordon, 'Obelisks and Pyramids in Shakespeare, Milton and Alcalá', *Sederi*, vol. 9 (1998), pp. 217–32

Campbell, Gordon, 'Shakespeare and the Youth of Milton', *Milton Quarterly*, vol. 33, no. 4 (December 1999), pp. 95–105

Casson, Leslie F., 'Notes on a Shakespearean First Folio in Padua', *Modern Language Notes*, vol. 51, no. 7 (1936), pp. 417–23

Centerwall, Brandon S., 'Who Wrote William Basse's "Elegy on Shakespeare"?: Rediscovering a Poem Lost from the Donne Cannon', *Shakespeare Survey*, vol. 59 (2006), pp. 267–84

Chambers, E.K., 'The Elizabethan Lords Chamberlain', *The Malone Society Collections*, Part 1 (1907), pp. 31–42

Chambers, E.K., *William Shakespeare: A Study of Facts and Problems*, 2 vols (Oxford: Clarendon Press, 1931 [1951 editions])

Cogswell, Thomas, 'Thomas Middleton and the Court, 1624: *A Game at Chess* in Context', *Huntington Library Quarterly*, vol. 47 (1984), pp. 273–88

Collins, Paul, *The Book of William: How Shakespeare's First Folio Conquered the World* (London: Bloomsbury, 2009)

Connell, Charles, *They Gave Us Shakespeare: John Heminge and Henry Condell* (Boston and London: Oriel Press, 1982)

Depledge, Emma, *Shakespeare's Rise to Cultural Prominence: Politics, Print and Alteration, 1642–1700* (Cambridge: Cambridge University Press, 2018)

Dickson, Vernon Guy, 'What I Will: Mediating Subject; Or, Ralph Crane and the Folio's *Tempest*', *Papers of the Bibliographical Society of America*, vol. 97, no. 1 (March 2003), pp. 43–56

Dobson, Michael, *The Making of the National Poet: Shakespeare, Adaptation and Authorship, 1660–1769* (Oxford: Oxford University Press, 1994)

Dobson, Michael, and Stanley Wells, eds, *The Oxford Companion to Shakespeare*, revised by Will Sharpe and Erin Sullivan (Oxford: Oxford University Press, 2015)

Donaldson, Ian, *Ben Jonson: A Life* (Oxford: Oxford University Press, 2011)

Dutton, Richard, 'Patronage, Politics, and the Master of the Revels, 1622–1640: The Case of Sir John Astley', *English Literary Renaissance*, vol. 20, no. 2 (March 1990), pp. 287–319

Eccles, Mark, 'Martin Peerson and the Blackfriars', *Shakespeare Survey*, vol. 11 (1958), pp. 100–106

Edmond, Mary, 'It was for Gentle Shakespeare Cut', *Shakespeare Quarterly*, vol. 42, no. 3 (Autumn 1991), pp. 339–44

Edmond, Mary, 'Yeomen, Citizens, Gentlemen, and Players: The Burbages and their Connections', in *Elizabethan Theater: Essays in Honor of S. Schoenbaum*, eds R.B. Parker and S.P. Zitner (Newark: University of Delaware Press, 1996), pp. 30–49

Edmondson, Paul, 'His editors John Heminges and Henry Condell', in *The Shakespeare Circle: An Alternative Biography*, eds Paul Edmondson and Stanley Wells (Cambridge: Cambridge University Press, 2015), pp. 315–28

Egan, Gabriel, '"As it was, is, or will be played": Title-pages and the Theatre Industry to 1610', in *From Performance to Print in Shakespeare's England*, eds Peter Holland and Stephen Orgel (Houndmills: Palgrave, 2006), pp. 92–110

Egan, Gabriel, 'The Provenance of the Folio Texts', in Emma Smith, ed., *The Cambridge Companion to Shakespeare's First Folio* (Cambridge: Cambridge University Press, 2016), pp. 68–85

Erne, Lukas, *Shakespeare and the Book Trade* (Cambridge: Cambridge University Press, 2013)

Es, Bart Van, *Shakespeare in Company* (Oxford: Oxford University Press, 2013)

Espinosa, Ruben, *Shakespeare on the Shades of Racism* (New York and London: Routledge, 2021)

Farmer, Alan B., and Zachary Lesser, 'The Popularity of Playbooks Revisited', *Shakespeare Quarterly*, vol. 56, no. 1 (2005), pp. 1–32

Farmer, Alan B., 'Shakespeare as leading playwright in print, 1598–1608/09', in *Shakespeare and Textual Studies*, eds Margaret Jane Kidnie and Sonia Massai (Cambridge: Cambridge University Press, 2015), pp. 87–104

Ferguson, W. Craig, *The Loan Book of The Stationers' Company, with a List of Transactions 1592–1692*, Occasional Papers of the Bibliographical Society, no. 4 (London: Bibliographical Society, 1989)

Finkelpearl, Philip J., '"The Comedians' Liberty": Censorship of the Jacobean Stage Reconsidered', *English Literary Renaissance*, vol. 16, no. 1 (December 1986), pp. 123–38

Freehafer, John, 'Leonard Digges, Ben Jonson, and the Beginning of Shakespeare Idolatry', *Shakespeare Quarterly*, vol. 21, no. 1 (Winter 1970), pp. 63–75

Fripp, Edgar, *Shakespeare, Man and Artist*, vol. 2 (Oxford: Oxford University Press, 1938)

Fripp, Edgar, *Shakespeare's Stratford* (Oxford: Oxford University Press, 1928)

Greer, Germaine, *Shakespeare's Wife* (London: Bloomsbury, 2007)

Greg, W.W., 'On certain false dates in Shakespearean Quartos', *Library*, vol. 9, no. 34 (1908), pp. 113–31

Greg, W.W., *The Shakespeare First Folio* (Oxford: Clarendon Press, 1955)

Gurr, Andrew, *The Shakespearean Stage: 1574–1642* (Cambridge: Cambridge University Press, 1992 [1997 edition])

Gurr, Andrew, *The Shakespeare Company: 1594–1642* (Cambridge: Cambridge University Press, 2004 [2011 edition])

Gurr, Andrew, 'Did Shakespeare Own His Own Playbooks?', *Review of English Studies*, New Series, vol. 60, no. 244 (April 2009), pp. 206–29

Gurr, Andrew, and Farah Karim-Cooper, eds, *Moving Shakespeare Indoors: Performance and Repertoire in the Jacobean Playhouse* (Cambridge: Cambridge University Press, 2014)

Hadfield, Andrew, 'Shakespeare and the Digges Brothers', *Reformation*, vol. 25, no. 1 (2020), pp. 2–17

Hahn, Matthew, *The Robben Island Shakespeare* (London: Bloomsbury, 2018)

Hailey, Carter, 'The Best Crowne Paper', in *Foliomania! Stories Behind Shakespeare's Most Important Book* (Washington D.C.: Folger Shakespeare Library, 2015), pp. 8–14

Hailey, R. Carter, 'The Dating Game: New Evidence for the Dates of Q4 "Romeo and Juliet" and Q4 "Hamlet"', *Shakespeare Quarterly*, vol. 58, no. 3 (2007), pp. 367–87

Hailey, R. Carter, 'The Shakespearian Pavier Quartos Revisited', *Studies in Bibliography*, vol. 57, no. 1 (2005) pp. 151–95

Hannay, Margaret P., *Philip's Phoenix: Mary Sidney, Countess of Pembroke* (Oxford: Oxford University Press, 1990)

Hedrick, Donald, and Bryan Reynolds, eds, *Shakespeare Without Class: Misappropriations of Cultural Capital* (New York: Palgrave, 2000)

Heijes, Coen, *Shakespeare, Blackface and Race: Different Perspectives* (Cambridge: Cambridge University Press, 2020)

Hentschell, Roze, *St Paul's Cathedral Precinct in Early Modern Literature and Culture: Spatial Practices* (Oxford: Oxford University Press, 2020)

Higgins, B.D.R., 'Printing the First Folio', in Emma Smith, ed, *The Cambridge Companion to Shakespeare's First Folio* (Cambridge: Cambridge University Press, 2016), pp. 30–47

Higgins, Ben, *Shakespeare's Syndicate: The First Folio, its Publishers, and the Early Modern Book Trade* (Oxford: Oxford University Press, 2022)

Higgins, Ben, 'We have a constant will to publish': The Publishers of Shakespeare's First Folio, unpublished DPhil thesis (Oxford: University of Oxford, 2015)

Hinman, Charlton, 'New Light on the Proof-Reading for the First Folio of Shakespeare', *Studies in Bibliography*, vol. 3 (1950/51), pp. 145–53

Hinman, Charlton, *The Printing and Proof-Reading of the First Folio of Shakespeare*, 2 vols (Oxford: Clarendon Press, 1963)

Honigmann, E.A.J., 'How Happy was Shakespeare with the Printed Versions of his Plays?', *Modern Language Review*, vol. 105, no. 4 (October 2010), pp. 937–51

Honigmann, E.A.J., *The Texts of Othello and Shakespearian Revision* (London and New York: Routledge, 1996)

Hopkins, Helen, 'Gifts of the World'?: Creating and Contextualising the Shakespeare Birthplace Trust's International Collections, unpublished doctoral thesis (Birmingham: Birmingham City University, 2022)

Hotson, Leslie, *I, William Shakespeare do appoint Thomas Russell, Esquire* (London: Jonathan Cape, 1937)

Hotson, Leslie, *Shakespeare's Sonnets Dated* (London: Rupert Hart-Davis, 1949)

Howard-Hill, T.E., 'The Compositors of Shakespeare's Folio Comedies', *Studies in Bibliography*, vol. 26 (1973), pp. 61–106

Howard-Hill, T.E., 'New Light on Compositor E of the Shakespeare First Folio', *Library*, vol. 2, no. 2 (1980), pp. 156–78

Howard-Hill, T.E., 'Shakespeare's Earliest Editor, Ralph Crane', *Shakespeare Survey*, vol. 44 (1991), pp. 113–29

Johnson, Gerald D., 'Thomas Pavier, Publisher, 1600–25', *Library*, vol. 14, no. 1 (March 1992), pp. 12–50

Jowett, John, *Shakespeare and Text* (Oxford: Oxford University Press, 2007)

Judge, Cyril Bathurst, *Elizabethan Book-Pirates* (Cambridge: Harvard University Press, 1934)

Karim-Cooper, Farah, 'Shakespeare Through Decolonization', *English* (London), vol. 70, no. 271, (2022), pp. 319–24

Karim-Cooper, Farah, *The Great White Bard: Shakespeare, Race and the Future of His Legacy* (London: Oneworld, 2023)

Karim-Cooper, Farah, and Eoin Price, eds, 'Shakespeare, Race and Nation', *Shakespeare*, vol. 17 (2021), pp. 1–153

Kathman, David, 'John Rice and the Boys of the Jacobean King's Men', *Shakespeare Survey*, vol. 68 (2015), pp. 247–66

Keenan, Siobhan, *Acting Companies and their Plays in Shakespeare's London* (London: Arden, 2014)

Kirschbaum, L., 'Walkley's supposed piracy of Wither's *Workes* in 1620', *Library*, vol. 19, no. 3 (1938), pp. 339–46

Lamb, Mary Ellen, 'The Countess of Pembroke's Patronage', *English Literary Renaissance*, vol. 12, no. 2 (March 1982), pp. 162–79

Laoutaris, Chris, 'The Prefatorial Material [to the First Folio]', in *The Cambridge Companion to Shakespeare's First Folio*, ed. Emma Smith (Cambridge: Cambridge University Press, 2016), pp. 48–67

Laoutaris, Chris, *Shakespeare and the Countess: The Battle that Gave Birth to the Globe* (London: Penguin, 2014)

Lesser, Zachary, *Ghosts, Holes, Rips and Scrapes: Shakespeare in 1619, Bibliography in the Longue Durée* (Philadelphia: University of Pennsylvania Press, 2021)

Lesser, Zachary, and Peter Stallybrass, 'Shakespeare between pamphlet and book, 1608–1619', in *Shakespeare and Textual Studies*, eds Margaret Jane Kidnie and Sonia Massai (Cambridge: Cambridge University Press, 2021), pp. 105–133

Lidster, Amy, *Publishing the History Plays in the Time of Shakespeare: Stationers Shaping a Genre* (Cambridge: Cambridge University Press, 2022)

Lim, Walter S.H., *The Arts of Empire: The Poetics of Colonialism from Ralegh to Milton* (Newark: University of Delaware Press, 1998)

Linley, Keith, *The Tempest in Context: Sin, Repentance and Forgiveness* (London and New York: Anthem Press, 2015)

Loomba, Ania, *Shakespeare, Race, and Colonialism* (Oxford: Oxford University Press, 2002)

Loomba, Ania, and Martin Orkin, eds, *Post-Colonial Shakespeares* (New York and London: Routledge, 1998)

Lyons, Tara L., 'Serials, Spinoffs, and Histories: Selling "Shakespeare" in Collection before the Folio', *Philological Quarterly*, vol. 91, no. 2 (Spring 2012), pp. 185–220

MacDonald, Joyce Green, ed., *Race, Ethnicity, and Power in the Renaissance* (Madison and Teaneck: Fairleigh Dickenson University Press, 1997)

Mackenzie, Rowan, *Creating Space for Shakespeare: Working with Marginalized Communities* (London: Arden Bloomsbury, 2023)

Mackenzie, Rowan, 'Disturbing Shakespeare and Challenging the Preconceptions', *Shakespeare Studies*, vol. 47 (2019), pp. 49–60

Marino, James, *Owning William Shakespeare: The King's Men and their Intellectual Property* (Philadelphia: University of Pennsylvania Press, 2011)

Marsh, Geoffrey, *Living with Shakespeare: Saint Helen's Parish, London, 1593–1598* (Edinburgh: Edinburgh University Press, 2021)

Massai, Sonia, 'Edward Blount, the Herberts, and the First Folio', in *Shakespeare's Stationers: Studies in Cultural Bibliography*, ed. Marta Straznicky (Philadelphia: University of Pennsylvania Press, 2013), pp. 132–46

Massai, Sonia, *Shakespeare and the Rise of the Editor* (Cambridge: Cambridge University Press, 2007)

Masten, Jeffrey, 'Spelling Shakespeare: Early Modern "Orthography" and the Secret Lives of Shakespeare's Compositors', in *Queer Philologies: Sex, Language, and Affect in Shakespeare's Time* (Philadelphia: University of Pennsylvania Press, 2016), pp. 49–71

Mayer, Jean-Christophe, 'Early Buyers and Readers', in *The Cambridge Companion to Shakespeare's First Folio*, ed. Emma Smith (Cambridge: Cambridge University Press, 2016), pp. 103–19

Mays, Andrea, *The Millionaire and the Bard: Henry Folger's Obsessive Hunt for Shakespeare's First Folios* (New York: Simon and Schuster, 2015)

McKerrow, Ronald B., *Printers' and Publishers' Devices in England and Scotland, 1485–1640* (London: Bibliographical Society, 1949)

McMillin, Scott, *The First Quarto of Othello* (Cambridge: Cambridge University Press, 2001)

Moodley, Devaksha, 'Interview: Introducing Sonny – The Story of "The Robben Island Bible"', *Shakespeare in Southern Africa*, vol. 30, no. 1 (2017), pp. 107–112

Morgan, Paul, '"Our Will Shakespeare" and Lope de Vega: An Unrecorded Contemporary Document', *Shakespeare Survey*, vol. 16 (1963), pp. 118–20

Mowery, Frank, 'The Bindings of the Folger's First Folios', in *Foliomania! Stories Behind Shakespeare's Most Important Book*, eds Owen Williams and Caryn Lazzuri (Washington D.C., Folger Shakespeare Library, 2011), pp. 32–39

Muñoz-Valdivieso, Sofía, '"All the World's a Stage": William Shakespeare's Cultural Capital 400 Years after his Death', *Changing English*, vol. 24, no. 1 (2017), pp. 67–80

Neidig, William, 'The Shakespeare Quartos of 1619', *Modern Philology*, vol. 8, no. 2 (1910), pp. 145–63

Nevinson, J.L., 'Shakespeare's Dress in His Portraits', *Shakespeare Quarterly*, vol. 18, no. 2 (Spring 1967), pp. 101–106

Nicholl, Charles, *The Lodger: Shakespeare on Silver Street* (London: Allen Lane, 2007)

Nicholl, Charles, *The Reckoning: The Murder of Christopher Marlowe* (Chicago: Chicago University Press, 1995)

Nungezer, Edwin, *A Dictionary of Actors and of Other Persons Associated with the Public Representation of Plays in England before 1642* (New Haven: Yale University Press, 1929)

O'Farrell, Brian, *Shakespeare's Patron: William Herbert, Third Earl of Pembroke 1580–1630, Politics, Patronage and Power* (London: Continuum, 2011)

Orlin, Lena Cowen, 'Anne by Indirection', *Shakespeare Quarterly*, vol. 65, no. 4 (2014), pp. 421–54

Orlin, Lena Cowen, *The Private Life of William Shakespeare* (Oxford: Oxford University Press, 2021)

Patterson, Louise Diehl, 'Leonard and Thomas Digges: Biographical Notes', *Isis*, vol. 42, no. 2 (June 1951), pp. 120–21

Plomer, Henry R., *A Dictionary of the Booksellers and Printers who were at work in England, Scotland and Ireland from 1641–1667* (London: Bibliographical Society, 1907)

Pollard, Alfred W., 'A Literary Causeries: Shakespeare in the Remainder Market', *The Academy* (2 June 1906), pp. 528–29

Pollard, Alfred W., *Shakespeare Folios and Quartos: A Study in the Bibliography of Shakespeare's Plays 1594–1685* (New York: Cooper Square Publishers, 1970)

Prosdocimi, Lavinia, 'The First Folio and the merchants of Venice: A collection of English books from the *natio anglica* in the Biblioteca Universitaria in Padova', an account of a paper delivered at the 'Shakespeare and Padova' conference in Padua, Italy, on 10 June 2016

Rasmussen, Eric, 'Publishing the First Folio', *The Cambridge Companion to Shakespeare's First Folio*, ed. Emma Smith (Cambridge: Cambridge University Press, 2016), pp. 18–29

Rasmussen, Eric, *The Shakespeare Thefts: In Search of the First Folios* (New York and London: Palgrave Macmillan, 2011)

Rasmussen, Eric, 'Who edited the Shakespeare First Folio?', *Cahiers Élisabéthains*, vol. 93, no. 1 (2017), pp. 70–76

Rasmussen, Eric, and Anthony James West, eds, *The Shakespeare First Folios: A Descriptive Catalogue* (Houndmills: Palgrave, 2012)

Redworth, Glyn, *The Prince and the Infanta: The Cultural Politics of the Spanish Match* (New Haven and London: Yale University Press, 2003)

Reid, S.W., 'B and 'J': Two Compositors in Two Plays of the Shakespeare First Folio', *Library*, vol. 7, no. 2 (1985), pp. 12–136

Rhodes, R. Crompton, *Shakespeare's First Folio: A Study* (Oxford: Blackwell, 1923)

Rizvi, Pervez, 'The Use of Spellings for Compositor Attribution in the First Folio', *Papers of the Bibliographical Society of America*, vol. 110, no. 1, pp. 1–53

Schalkwyk, David, *Hamlet's Dreams: The Robben Island Shakespeare* (London: Arden, 2013)

Scheil, Katherine, *Imagining Shakespeare's Wife: The Afterlife of Anne Hathaway* (Cambridge: Cambridge University Press, 2018)

Schlueter, June, 'Martin Droeshout Redivivus: Reassessing the Folio Engraving of Shakespeare', *Shakespeare Survey*, vol. 60 (2007), pp. 237–51

Scragg, Leah, 'Edward Blount and the History of Lylian Criticism', *Review of English Studies*, vol. 46, no. 181 (February 1995), pp. 1–10

Scragg, Leah, 'Edward Blount and the Prefatory Material to the First Folio of Shakespeare', *Bulletin of the John Rylands Library*, vol. 79, no. 1 (1997), pp. 117–26

Secord, Arthur W., 'I.M. of the First Folio Shakespeare and Other Mabbe Problems', *Journal of English and Germanic Philology*, vol. 47, no. 4 (October 1948), pp. 374–81

Sell, Roger D., 'Political and Hedonic Re-contextualizations: Prince Charles's Spanish Journey in Beaumont, Jonson, and Middleton', *Ben Jonson Journal*, vol. 22, no. 2 (2015), pp. 163–87

Shapiro. I.A., 'The Mermaid Club', *Modern Language Review*, vol. 45, no. 1 (January 1950), pp. 7–17

Shapiro, James, *1599: A Year in the Life of William Shakespeare* (London: Faber and Faber, 2005)

Sharpe, J.A., *Crime in Early Modern England* (New York: Longman, 1984 [1999 edition])

Shellard, Dominic, and Siobhan Keenan, eds, *Shakespeare's Cultural Capital: His economic impact from the sixteenth to the twenty-first century* (London: Palgrave Macmillan, 2016)

Shuckman, Christiaan, 'The Engraver of the First Folio Portrait of William Shakespeare', *Print Quarterly*, vol. 8, no. 1 (March 1991), pp. 40–43

Sisson, C.J., *New readings in Shakespeare* (Cambridge: Cambridge University Press, 1956)

Smith, Emma, ed., *The Cambridge Companion to Shakespeare's First Folio* (Cambridge: Cambridge University Press, 2016)

Smith, Emma, *The Making of Shakespeare's First Folio* (Oxford: Bodleian Library, 2015)

Smith, Emma, *Shakespeare's First Folio: Four Centuries of an Iconic Book* (Oxford: Oxford University Press, 2016)

Smith, Ian, *Black Shakespeare: Reading and Misreading Race* (Cambridge: Cambridge University Press, 2022)

Smith, Irwin, *Shakespeare's Blackfriars Playhouse: Its History and Its Design* (London: Peter Owen)

Sousa, Geraldo U. de, *Shakespeare's Cross-Cultural Encounters* (Houndmills: Palgrave, 1999)

Stern, Tiffany, *Documents of Performance in Early Modern England* (Cambridge: Cambridge University Press, 2009)

Stern, Tiffany, '"On each Wall/And Corner Post": Playbills, Title-pages, and Advertising in Early Modern London', *English Literary Renaissance*, vol. 36, no. 1 (Winter 2006), pp. 57–89

Stopes, C.C., *Burbage and Shakespeare's Stage* (London: De la More Press, 1913)

Stopes, C.C., *Shakespeare and his Warwickshire Contemporaries* (Stratford-upon-Avon: Shakespeare Head Press, 1907)

Straznicky, Marta, ed., *Shakespeare's Stationers: Studies in Critical Bibliography* (Philadelphia: University of Pennsylvania Press, 2013)

Streete, Adrian, 'Polemical Laughter in Thomas Middleton's *A Game at Chess* (1624)', *English Literary Renaissance*, vol. 50, no. 2 (2020), pp. 296–333

Taylor, Dick, 'The Earl of Montgomery and the Dedicatory Epistle of Shakespeare's First Folio', *Shakespeare Quarterly*, vol. 10, no. 1 (Winter 1959), pp. 121–23

Taylor, Gary, '*Comedies, Histories & Tragedies* (and Tragicomedies and Poems: Posthumous Shakespeare, 1623–1728)', *The New Oxford Shakespeare: Critical Reference Edition: The Complete Works*, general editors, Gary Taylor, John Jowett, Terri Bourus and Gabriel Egan (Oxford: Oxford University Press, 2017)

Taylor, Gary, 'The Fortunes of Oldcastle', *Shakespeare Survey*, vol. 38 (1986), pp. 85–100

Taylor, Gary, 'Making Meaning Marketing Shakespeare 1623', in *From Performance to Print in Shakespeare's England*, eds Peter Holland and Stephen Orgel (Houndmills: Palgrave, 2006), pp. 55–72

Taylor, Gary, and John Jowett, *Shakespeare Reshaped, 1606–1623* (Oxford: Oxford University Press, 1993)

Thompson, Ayanna, ed., *Colorblind Shakespeare: New Perspectives on Race and Performance* (New York and London: Routledge, 2006)

Thompson, Ayanna, *The Cambridge Companion to Shakespeare and Race* (Cambridge: Cambridge University Press, 2021)

Thompson, Ayanna, *Passing Strange: Shakespeare, Race, and Contemporary America* (Oxford: Oxford University Press, 2011)

Tite, Colin G.C., 'A Catalogue of Sir Robert Cotton's Printed Books?', *British Library Journal*, vol. 17, no. 1 (Spring 1991), pp. 1–11

Tosh, Will, *Playing Indoors: Staging Early Modern Drama in the Sam Wanamaker Playhouse* (London: Arden Shakespeare, 2018)

Wallace, Charles William, *The Children of the Chapel at Blackfriars: 1597– 1603* (New York: AMS Press, 1970 [based on the 1908 first edition])

Wallace, Charles William, *The Evolution of the English Drama Up to Shakespeare, with a History of the First Blackfriars Theatre* (Berlin: Georg Reimer, 1912)

Wells, Stanley, 'A close family connection: the Combes', in *The Shakespeare Circle: An Alternative Biography*, eds Paul Edmondson and Stanley Wells (Cambridge: Cambridge University Press, 2015), pp. 149–60

Werstine, Paul, 'Cases and Compositors in the Shakespeare First Folio Comedies', *Studies in Bibliography*, vol. 35 (1982), pp. 206–34

Werstine, Paul, *Early Modern Playhouse Manuscripts and the Editing of Shakespeare* (Cambridge: Cambridge University Press, 2012)

Werstine, Paul, 'Ralph Crane and Edward Knight: professional scribe and King's Men's bookkeeper', in *Shakespeare and Textual Studies*, eds Margaret Jane Kidnie and Sonia Massai (Cambridge: Cambridge University Press, 2015), pp. 27–38

Werstine, Paul, 'Scribe or Compositor: Ralph Crane, Compositors D and F, and the First Four Plays in the Shakespeare First Folio', *Papers of the Bibliographical Society of America*, vol. 95, no. 3 (September 2001), pp. 315–39

Werstine, Paul, 'The Type of the Shakespeare First Folio', in *Foliomania! Stories Behind Shakespeare's Most Important Book*, eds Owen Williams and Caryn Lazzuri (Washington D.C., Folger Shakespeare Library, 2011), pp. 15–20

West, Anthony James, 'Constantijn Huygens Owned a Shakespeare First Folio', *Notes and Queries*, vol. 55, no. 2 (2008), pp. 221–22

West, Anthony James, 'Constantijn Huygens's Shakespeare First Folio: The First to Go Abroad; Now at the Folger', *Notes and Queries*, vol. 60, no. 1 (2013), p. 49

West, Anthony James, 'The First Shakespeare First Folio to Travel Abroad: Constantine Huygens's Copy', in *Foliomania! Stories Behind Shakespeare's Most Important Book*, eds Owen Williams and Caryn Lazzuri (Washington D.C., Folger Shakespeare Library, 2011), pp. 40–44

Wiggins, Martin, ed., *British Drama, 1533–1642: A Catalogue*, in association with Catherine Richardson (Oxford: Oxford University Press, from 2012)

Wiggins, Martin, ed., *British Drama, 1533–1642: A Catalogue, Vol. 5: 1603–1608*, in association with Catherine Richardson (Oxford: Oxford University Press, 2015)

Wiggins, Martin, ed., *British Drama, 1533–1642: A Catalogue, Vol. 7: 1617–1623*, in association with Catherine Richardson (Oxford: Oxford University Press, 2016)

Williams, Owen, and Caryn Lazzuri, eds, *Foliomania! Stories Behind Shakespeare's Most Important Book* (Washington D.C., Folger Shakespeare Library, 2011)

Willoughby, Edwin Eliott, 'An Interruption in the Printing of the First Folio', *Library*, no. 9 (December 1928), pp. 262–65

Willoughby, Edwin Eliott, *A Printer of Shakespeare: The Books and Times of William Jaggard* (London: Philip Allan & Co, 1934)

Wilson, Ian, *Shakespeare, The Evidence: Unlocking the Mysteries of the Man and his Work* (London: Hodder Headline, 1993)

Wilson, Richard, *Secret Shakespeare: Studies in Theatre, Religion and Resistance* (Manchester: Manchester University Press, 2004)

Wright, Louis B., 'Propaganda against James I's "Appeasement" of Spain', *Huntington Library Quarterly*, vol. 6, no. 1 (February 1943), pp. 149–72

INDEX

87, 106, 122, 134–5; members holding rights to WS plays, 87, 108, 115, 117, 121–2, 125–6, 129–35, 152, 238, 248, 256, 265; members of, 15–16, 106–8; negotiations over rights/licences, 17, 102–5, 109–10, 120–1, 124–6, 131–6, 207–11, 236–8, 251–4, 281, 285–7; production costs, 103–6, 282; registering of plays at Stationers' Hall, 108–9, 265, 277–8; and resurgence of WS play-printing (1622), 207–11, 214, 237–8; sale and marketing of the First Folio, 281–2, 287–90, 291
Fisher, George (alias Musket), 151–2
Fisher, Thomas, 80–1, 132, 133
Flecknoe, Richard, 42
Fleet Street, London, 28, 36, 77, 110, 127–8, *128*, 130–1, 135, 275–6; appeal of the WS brand in, 128–9, 132; Mitre Tavern, 309, 310, 313
Fletcher, John, 42, 81, 98, 105, 194–5, 208–10, 308, 312; as co-author of *Henry VIII*, 235, 240; as probable co-author of *Cardenio*, 312; *Comedies and Tragedies* (with Beaumont, folio), 105, 285, 339; *Demetrius and Enanthe*, 171; *The Maid of the Mill* (with Rowley), 262; *Philaster* (with Beaumont), 55, 86, 219–20; *The Pilgrim*, 191, 194–5, 225; *The Prophetess* (with Massinger), 211–12; *The Sea Voyage* (with Massinger), 213–14; *The Spanish Curate* (with Massinger), 216–17, 225
Florio, John, 116, 118
Folger, Henry and Emily, 184, 351–3, *352*, 355
Folger Shakespeare Library, Washington, 265, 351
Ford, John, 260
foreign policy of James I, 137, 139, 142, 154, 195, 197, 199, 243, 249, 262, 280, 295

Fortescue, John, 331
Foxe, John, *Acts and Monuments*, 235
France, 154, 197, 350
Frankfurt Book Fair, 222, 225, 287–8, 289, 291, 349
Frederick V, Elector Palatine ('The Winter King'), 142, 144, 148, 149, 155, 198
Free Library of Philadelphia, 347

Gam, David, 353
gambling, 27
Gascoigne, George, *Whole Works*, 289
Gaspar de Guzmán, Don, 271
Gheeraerts the Younger, Marcus, 146
Gifford, William, 308
Glasgow University Library, 345
Globe Theatre: built from beams of dismantled Shoreditch Theatre, 31–2; burning down of (1613), 12, 93–4, 96, 329, 330; Heminges' house in grounds of, 36, 96; opening of (1599), 32; share-holdings in, 6–7, 33–4, 43, 93–8, 329, 341; and uncertainty over Blackfriars, 92
Goad, Thomas, 151, 152
Goldsmiths' Company, 192
Gondomar, Diego Sarmiento de Acuña, 1st Count of, 148–50, 155, 197–8, 199, 244–5
Goodere, Sir Henry, 304, 309
Gosson, Henry, 73, 117
Gouge, William, 90
Greer, Germaine, 213
Greg, W.W., 59
Grey, Sir George, 354–5
Grocers' Company, 25, 28
Guzmán y Pimentel, Gaspar de, 3rd Count of Olivares, 141

Half-Eagle and Key, Barbican (William Jaggard's printing shop): Isaac Jaggard inherits (1623), 264, 265, 281; Jaggard takes over from Roberts at (1606), 67, 78, 130;